# Sociology of Medicine

# SOCIOLOGY OF MEDICINE

**Second Edition**

Rodney M. Coe

**McGraw-Hill Book Company**

New York   St. Louis   San Francisco   Auckland   Bogotá   Düsseldorf
Johannesburg   London   Madrid   Mexico   Montreal   New Delhi
Panama   Paris   São Paulo   Singapore   Sydney   Tokyo   Toronto

To Elaine

**SOCIOLOGY OF MEDICINE**

3 4 5 6 7 8 9 0    DODO    7 8 3 2 1 0 9

This book was set in Times Roman by University Graphics, Inc.
The editors were Lyle Linder, Donald W. Burden, and Barry Benjamin;
the cover was designed by Pencils Portfolio, Inc.;
the production supervisor was Milton J. Heiberg.
R. R. Donnelley & Sons Company was printer and binder.


Library of Congress Cataloging in Publication Data

Coe, Rodney M
    Sociology of medicine.

    Includes bibliographical references and index.
    1.  Social medicine.  I.  Title.  [DNLM:  1.  Eco-
nomics, Medical.  2.  Social medicine.  WA30 C672s]
RA418.C66    1978      301.5      77-16200
ISBN 0-07-011560-5

# Contents

# 1

## DISEASE AND THE SICK PERSON

# 2

## HEALTH PRACTICES AND PRACTITIONERS

# 3

## HEALTH INSTITUTIONS: THE HOSPITAL

# 4

## THE COST AND ORGANIZATION

# Preface to the Second Edition

Rapid changes in the fields of sociology and medicine in the past decade have prompted the desire to take a second look at their interaction to see what further contribution medicine might make to sociology and vice versa. Like its predecessor, this second edition has as its central objective an analysis of the field of medicine and medical care from a sociological perspective. The focus was, and is, on the development and clarification of sociological concepts in a medical context. The second edition extends the analysis to materials not available for the previous edition. For example, the discussion of the epidemiology of chronic diseases is extended to smoking behavior and illnesses related to socioenvironmental stress. Advances in theories of human response to illness are presented and evaluated. New organizational forms for delivery of health care such as neighborhood health centers and health maintenance organizations (HMOs) are discussed and implications of national programs for financing health care are explored.

Rapid change is expected to continue; thus this edition makes some effort to anticipate a number of sociological consequences of changes like national health insurance, increased centralization of authority, and decline in professional autonomy. In so doing, we are attempting to make a sociological contribution to medicine.

Not unexpectedly, revision of a previously published manuscript is a sizable task involving the assistance of many people. In this case, colleagues have helped clarify both the concepts and my ability to communicate them. The reviewers, Henry Brehm, Columbia, Maryland; Kimball Marshall, University of South Alabama; Richard L. Meile, The University of Nebraska-Lincoln; Peter K. New, University of Toronto; and Michael Rainey, Southern Illinois University, have been most helpful in pointing out where clear communication has not been made and where errors and omissions have occurred. Encouragement from the McGraw-Hill editorial staff has been yet another support as has been the patient help of the secretaries. Finally, but certainly not least, the students both in sociology and in medicine have contributed, sometimes unknowingly, through their responses to the ideas presented in this book. I am indebted to all of you.

*Rodney M. Coe*

# Preface to the First Edition

This book—like many books designed primarily for classroom use—actually began a few years ago with a more or less vague notion that an up-to-date, comprehensive presentation of a sociological interpretation of the field of medicine did not exist—at least not in one volume. The reference materials I had used as texts in courses on the sociology of medicine were widely scattered in the literature, too narrow in scope, or somewhat out of date. Thus, I was motivated to "sit down and write a textbook." My naïveté concerning the preparation of a textbook has been thoroughly dispelled by the many false starts and innumerable delays and interruptions. Nonetheless, the task is finished and the varied materials enclosed within the covers of this volume are, I hope, still timely and comprehensive.

As with many other books, the final form of this one is different from that which was originally envisioned. The basic purpose of this book, however, has remained unchanged since the first few ideas were set down on paper: to provide a sociological perspective and interpretation for the many facets of medicine and medical behavior. Essentially, the focus is on social interaction—between two people, the patient and the doctor; between groups of people in an organizational context, like the hospital or the medical school; and among laymen in the community. In addition, the sociological perspective is applied to medical practice as an occupation and to some economic and organizational aspects of medical care in a modern society.

In this volume, then, I have tried to be broad in scope—to touch all the bases, as it were—yet to give some depth to those aspects which ought to be particularly important. Thus, it is likely that some readers will agree with the perspective, some will be disappointed, but all should find something of value and interest, especially the students for whom the book was written in the first place.

The preparation of a manuscript like this involves a great many more people than appear on the title page. I would like to take this opportunity to thank the many colleagues and friends who read and commented on various parts of the manuscript and the students who reacted to the presentation of these ideas and thereby contributed to their clarification.

More than just an anonymous thank you is due to Albert F. Wessen for his invaluable assistance in the development of this book. In addition to detailed editorial and critical substantive comments for several drafts of some chapters, he has been the stimulus for many of the ideas found in this volume. Even more, he has given me permission to use some materials which he actually wrote or which closely parallel unpublished materials he had written originally. Examples of the former are the initial pages in Chapter 4 concerning the distinction between disease and illness; the description of Azande medicine in Chapter 5; and the first few pages of Chapter 10. Some materials found in Chapters 1 and 9 are based on themes which he had suggested. Obviously, I have been greatly influenced by his ideas and his approach to the field. Much of what is valuable in this book is a credit to him. I, alone, am responsible for any errors of commission or omission.

Finally, I must acknowledge the support of the Medical Care Research Center, jointly supported by Washington University, Saint Louis University School of Medicine, the Jewish Hospital of Saint Louis, and the Saint Louis County Health Department under the terms of a U.S. Public Health Service grant HS-00109 (formerly CH-00024). The Center has provided an opportunity to explore many of these ideas through research and with invaluable secretaries, Irene Levy and Freda Sofian, who labored faithfully through the many revisions of the manuscript.

*Rodney M. Coe*

# Chapter 1

# The Field of Medical Sociology

*. . . if medicine is the science of the healthy as well as of the ill human being (which is what it ought to be), what other science is better suited to propose laws as the basis of the social structure, in order to make effective those which are inherent in man himself? Once medicine is established as anthropology, and once the interests of the privileged no longer determine the course of public events, the physiologists and the practitioner will be counted among the elder statesmen who support the social structure. Medicine is a social science in its very bone and marrow.*

Rudolf Virchow
*Scientific Methods and Therapeutic Standpoints,* 1849

Disease is a universal phenomenon and therefore affects all people everywhere, but not always to the same degree or in the same way. The study of how diseases affect human groups and the ways in which groups react to disease provides an important substantive area for the application of sociological knowledge and research techniques. At least four dimensions of analysis may be mentioned at once. In the first place, diseases are neither uniform nor random in their occurrence; rather they are usually observed to be more or less common among various social groupings. The study of these differential distributions of illness in terms of our knowledge of the social structure and the differing life-styles it imposes on people frequently provides clues about the nature and causes of disease. Second, people tend to view the event of disease from the perspectives of their particular culture, and, based in part on these perspectives, they tend to respond to the disease in predictable ways. Third, people develop an array of institutions to treat systematically the diseases which appear in their group. These institutions may be relatively simple, such as the role of a medicine man, or they may be very complex, such as the modern university medical center. Fourth, we may suggest that the treatment of disease involves more than the mere application of medical knowledge through medical institutions. In our society, the institutions which purvey medical care are supported by many other organizations, such as voluntary health agencies, public health departments, pharmaceutical companies, and health insurance firms, which have emerged to provide physicians with necessities for effective therapy. All these medical institutions are further related to, and partly controlled by, other social institutions. Thus governmental agencies license physicians and hospitals, regulate pharmaceutical firms and other supporting institutions, and act to foster the availability of medical care to the population; educational institutions take responsibility for selecting and training health professionals; and religious organizations often sponsor or control hospitals and other health centers. Similarly, in simpler societies, the force of religious ritual and the presence of both kinsmen and neighbors usually combine to support the "medical" efforts of healers.

For all these reasons, social science, and particularly sociology, has much to contribute to the field of medicine. The distribution of diseases in society, the cultural perspectives on disease (and on ways of staying healthy), the roles, attitudes, and values emerging from the social organization of treatment centers, and the relationships of treatment and support facilities are all subjects well within the purview of sociology. At the same time, research by sociologists in the area of medicine provides many opportunities to make contributions to the field of general sociology. In addition, such information may well be valuable for lay persons and professionals alike. Because of the inevitability of illness and the pervasiveness of medical institutions, it is likely that many times during life the lay person will encounter medical agencies. Medical sociology can provide information concerning the purpose, scope, and organization of the elements of medicine which will affect the lay person. Concomitantly, medical training imbues in the practitioner a unique way of viewing disease and the patient. Medical sociology again can provide the practitioner with information about the perspectives of others.

Thus, more and more sociologists have recently turned to medical areas in which to study sociology. Consequently, there has been established within the field of general sociology a specialty area of medical sociology. As a scientific discipline grows in scope and knowledge and in the number of scholars attracted to its principles, special areas of interest and competence develop. This has repeatedly occurred in the physical sciences of physics, chemistry, and biology. It is no less true of the social sciences of psychology, sociology, economics, anthropology, and political science. The development of special areas in a discipline, however, is often fraught with difficulties concerning the relationship of the special area to the general discipline of which it is a part. At the root of such problems is the apparent conflict between "basic" versus "applied" orientation in science. Some members of a discipline see their mission as the development of knowledge through formulation and testing of theoretical propositions. They care little whether they study a particular population or social setting. Solving practical problems is not their aim; they are interested in developing scientific laws of universal validity. For them, the acquisition of knowledge *qua* knowledge is justification enough for devoting a lifetime of study to it. Others, on the contrary, see the development of *useful* knowledge as their major task; although they appreciate the importance of universal laws, they wish to devote their efforts to their application in particular situations. Fortunately for the development of science, this conflict is not absolute. Universal scientific laws cannot usually be discerned or verified without taking account of the specific context of real-life situations, and when this is done, general principles often suggest practical applications. Similarly, studying a practical problem is apt to raise—and sometimes to clarify—theoretical issues of which a scientist might not otherwise have been aware.[1]

Specialists within a discipline also must confront the issue of whether their research activities will be directed toward studying various aspects of the special area from the perspective of the broader discipline or whether they will be primarily designed to solve problems peculiar to the substantive, special area. In the area of medicine, this is the distinction made between the sociology *of* medicine and sociology *in* medicine.[2] The former refers to the use of medical settings and health and illness to study such sociological phenomena as organizational structure, role relationships, attitudes and values of persons involved in medicine—in a word, to study

[1]See, for example, Robert S. Lynd, *Knowledge for What?* Princeton, N.J.: Princeton University Press, 1939. See also Alvin W. Gouldner and S. M. Miller (eds.), *Applied Sociology,* New York: Free Press, 1965.

[2]Robert Straus, "The Nature and Status of Medical Sociology," *American Sociological Review,* 22 (April, 1957), 200–204.

medicine as a system of behavior. The latter refers to studies specifically designed either to help solve a problem in medical science or to provide knowledge about a practical problem in medical practice, the allocation of health resources, or the operation of health facilities. In the main, most medical sociologists probably try to achieve a balance between the two extremes, that is, to accumulate knowledge which will both contribute to sociology and solve practical problems in medicine.[3] As the title indicates, this volume is oriented toward the contributions in the development of general sociology that can be made by studying sociological factors in a medical context. We shall thus attempt a sociological interpretation of medicine and medical institutions. It will become abundantly clear, however, that much of the material discussed should be of use to nonsociologists in the health fields.

## THE CONVERGENCE OF SOCIOLOGY AND MEDICINE

Medical sociology as a special area of study is relatively new. Although a few sociologists had for years used medical settings in which to study some general sociological phenomena,[4] it was not until 1960 that the Section on Medical Sociology was established as a part of the American Sociological Association. An explanation of this rather recent formalization of a specialty in sociology is of interest in view of the fact that it represents more a reawakening than an emergence of mutual interests of sociology and medicine. It would appear that there has been an independent, but parallel, growth of the two fields since the turn of the twentieth century, prior to which, at least on the part of medicine, there had been recognition of social factors in disease and illness. In fact, for as long as medicine has existed, physicians have realized that there is an intimate connection between disease and the social environment, a perception that has made itself felt in both theory and practice. Yet until very recently, the social scientist who surveyed medical literature would be struck by the limited sociological approach and the paucity of data evidenced. Even today, many physicians frequently fail to understand what sociologists can study that is of medical relevance, although a century has passed since Virchow declared that "medicine is a social science." His dictum is still more a historical curiosity than an accepted medical postulate, particularly in the United States where social medicine—an application of special knowledge and skills by scien-

[3]Howard E. Freeman, Sol Levine, and Leo G. Reeder, "Present Status of Medical Sociology," in Howard E. Freeman, Sol Levine, and Leo G. Reeder (eds.), *Handbook of Medical Sociology,* 2d ed., Englewood Cliffs, N.J.: Prentice-Hall, 1972, pp. 511–522.
[4]See, for example, Bernard J. Stern, *American Medical Practice in the Perspective of a Century,* New York: Commonwealth Fund, 1945.

tists of various disciplines to problems of a sociomedical nature—did not develop as fully as in Europe in the nineteenth century.[5]

Sociology and the social sciences have, for their part, been slow to accept medicine as an area for study. Until about thirty years ago, it was a rare ethnographic study that included systematic information on medical beliefs and customs, to say nothing of the level of disease among the studied population.[6] The sociologists, too, largely ignored medicine before World War II, except for some development of interest in social aspects of psychiatry occasioned by the diffusion of psychoanalysis.[7] Nor did the policy sciences find the relation of medicine to economics or government of more than passing interest until after 1929. Even in psychology, interest in abnormal and clinical psychology did not become intense until about the same period.

Beginning with the decade of the thirties, however, and especially since World War II, there has been growing interest in the interrelationships between medicine and sociology as well as the other social sciences. Increasingly, "comprehensive medicine" and "social psychiatry" have become acceptable programmatic goals among physicians. Medical schools are currently indulging in intensive self-study concerning the improvement of instruction in these topics.[8] And at the present time, there are over 1,300

[5]George Rosen, "The Evolution of Social Medicine," in Freeman, Levine, and Reeder, *op. cit.*, pp. 30–60. By the same author see "Health, History and the Social Sciences," *Social Science and Medicine,* 7 (April, 1973), 233–248.

[6]See, for example, Steven Polgar, "Health and Human Behavior: Areas of Interest Common to the Social and Medical Sciences," *Current Anthropology,* 3(April, 1962), 159–205; Virginia L. Olesen, "Convergences and Divergences: Anthropology and Sociology in Health Care," *Social Science and Medicine,* 9 (August-September, 1975), 421–425. In the same issue, see George M. Foster, "Medical Anthropology: Some Contrasts with Medical Sociology," pp. 427–432.

[7]H. Warren Dunham, "Social Psychiatry," *American Sociological Review,* 13 (April, 1948), 183–197. See also Ernest W. Burgess, "The Influence of Sigmund Freud on Sociology in the United States," *American Journal of Sociology,* 45 (November, 1939), 356–374.

[8]The following suggests what various thinkers in medicine believe the social sciences can contribute to their interests: Hugh Leavell, "Contributions of the Social Sciences to the Solution of Health Problems," *New England Journal of Medicine,* 247 (Dec. 4, 1952), 885–897; Cecil G. Sheps and E. H. Taylor, *Needed Research in Health and Medical Care: A Biosocial Approach,* Chapel Hill: University of North Carolina Press, 1954; George Reader and Mary E. W. Goss, "The Sociology of Medicine," in Robert K. Merton, Leonard Broom, and L. S. Cottrell, Jr. (eds.), *Sociology Today,* New York: Basic Books, 1959, pp. 229–426. Patricia L. Kendall and George R. Reader, "Contributions of Sociology to Medicine," in Freeman et al., *op. cit.*, pp. 1–29. Teaching of behavioral science factors in the medical curricula has been discussed at length. See, for example, the final report of a survey of curricula in United States and Canadian medical schools conducted by the Medical Sociology Section of the American Sociological Association, in Donald A. Kennedy, Evan G. Pattishall, and C. Richard Fletcher, *Teaching Behavioral Sciences in Schools of Medicine,* vol. 1, summary report, Rockville, Md.: National Center for Health Services Research and Development, 1972. Similar points are made in Peter K. New and J. Thomas May, "Teaching Activities of Social Scientists in Medical and Public Health Schools," *Social Science and Medicine,* 2 (December, 1968), 447–460; Peter K. New and Herbert Bynder, "Issues and

sociologists in addition to anthropologists and social psychologists at work in major research projects in the medical field. In addition, eighty-six departments now offer graduate courses in medical sociology.[9]

Enough has been said to make it clear that until the middle of the nineteenth century at least, medicine recognized the importance of the social dimension, both in theory and in practice. However, just as sociology began to emerge as a science, there was a sharp shift in the emphasis of medical thought. For its part, the new discipline of sociology showed very little interest in those aspects of social life related to medicine. Thus, before examining in some detail a number of specific areas in which sociology and medicine have come to have common interests, it may be helpful to consider the factors which contributed to their mutual reticence.

## Sociology

The establishment of sociology as a specific discipline has taken place within the last century, but it has intellectual roots that reach far back into antiquity. They range from classical Greek philosophy to twentieth-century pragmatism, from the search for knowledge for its own sake to schemes to reshape the world to eliminate its evils.[10] Out of all this, sociology has developed as a scientific discipline and has seen the emergence of several sociological specialties.[11]

In part, it was this quest to become a science that led sociologists to slight medicine in their study of human culture. Despite a heavy emphasis on objectivity, sociology was strongly motivated during its formative years by Comtian visions of a "positive society" governed according to scientific norms. Because medicine, of all the institutions of Western society, seemed committed to the battle to achieve a scientific basis, sociologists sought more crucial fronts in which to push their quest. Thus many sociologists felt committed to an assault on the obvious social problems of the time, such as

---

Problems in the Teaching of Social Science in Health Professional Schools," *Social Science and Medicine,* 4 (December, 1970), 595–607; Evan G. Pattishall, "Concepts in the Teaching of Behavioral Sciences," *Social Science and Medicine,* 4 (July, 1970), 157–161; H. David Banta, "Medical Education, Abraham Flexner—A Reappraisal," *Social Science and Medicine,* 5 (December, 1971), 655–661; Brian L. Hillcoat, "Paradigms in Medicine: Consequences for Medical Education," *Journal of Medical Education,* 50 (January, 1975), 66–69; Mary W. Herman, "Developing Objectives for a Core Program on Social Aspects of Medicine," *Journal of Medical Education,* 50 (April, 1975), 389–391; and Rodney M. Coe, "Teaching Behavioral Sciences in Schools of Medicine: Observation on Some Latin-American Schools," *Social Science and Medicine,* 9 (April-May, 1975), 221–225.

[9]American Sociological Association, *Guide to Graduate Departments of Sociology,* Washington, D.C., 1976.

[10]See Harry Elmer Barnes and Howard Becker, *Social Thought from Lore to Science,* 3 vols., London: Constable, 1938. See also Don Martindale, *The Nature and Types of Sociological Theory,* Boston: Houghton Mifflin, 1960; Alvin W. Gouldner, *Enter Plato: Classical Greece and the Origin of Social Theory,* New York: Basic Books, 1965.

[11]See Merton, Broom, and Cottrell, *op. cit.*

the poverty and anomie arising from the Industrial Revolution. Others, less committed to practical problems, were concerned to explain the basis for order and morality in society or to demonstrate the scientific laws which accounted for the evolution of human societies. Indeed, before the First World War, sociologists drew their scientific inspiration largely from the biological *Weltanschauung* which also enveloped medicine. Moreover, the emphasis of scientific medicine was on the individual—and upon events internal to the organism—at a time when sociology proclaimed its unique interest in both the superindividual and the superorganic. The heritage of the nineteenth century, then, was such as to emphasize operational cleavages between medicine and the social sciences.

## Medicine

The information that we have about the practice of medicine in nonliterate cultures indicates that there is a general recognition both of social factors in the etiology of illness and of the importance of interpersonal relationships in therapy.[12] Much of whatever effectiveness this "nonscientific" medicine has probably rests on this fact.[13] Primitive medical practice, oriented as it usually is toward a religiomoral ideology, deals explicitly with anxieties and guilt associated with social living. With its emphasis on suggestive therapy, it tends to give free play to the effects of interpersonal relations in the therapeutic process. And, articulated as it normally is with the social structure, it tends to mobilize the solidary resources of the community to give aid and comfort to the sick person (see Chapter 5).

Something of the same perception governed much of ancient medicine. The Hippocratic corpus both pays explicit attention to the social environment as an etiological factor in disease and deals specifically with the doctor-patient relationship as a therapeutic tool.[14] Indeed, these classical Greek writings provide an orientation toward the sociology of medicine which is still suggestive. Throughout the Middle Ages and the Renaissance,

[12]See, for example, Jerome D. Frank, *Persuasion and Healing,* New York: Schocken, 1963; Donald T. Atkinson, *Magic, Myth and Medicine,* London: Routledge & Kegan Paul, 1962; Erwin H. Ackerknecht, "Psychotherapy, Primitive Medicine and Primitive Culture," *Bulletin of the History of Medicine,* 14 (June, 1943), 30–67; Ari Kiēv, *Curanderismo,* New York: Free Press, 1968; Ari Kiēv, *Magic, Faith and Healing,* New York: Free Press, 1964.

[13]There is also a large "rational" element in all "primitive" medicine, especially in its stock of herbal remedies. See Erwin H. Ackerknecht, "Natural Diseases and Rational Treatment in Primitive Medicine," *Bulletin of the History of Medicine,* 19 (May, 1946), 467–497.

[14]Hippocrates, "On Airs, Waters, and Places." For example, "These things one ought to consider most attentively . . . the mode in which the inhabitants live, and what are their pursuits, whether they are fond of drinking and eating to excess, and given to indolence, or are fond of exercise and labor, and not given to excess in eating and drinking." Quoted from Francis Adams, *The Genuine Works of Hippocrates,* Baltimore: Williams & Wilkins, 1939, p. 19. On the doctor-patient relationship, see the Hippocratic Oath, in Logan Clendening, *Source Book of Medical History,* New York: Dover, 1960.

whenever medicine transcended blind traditionalism, it retained an awareness of social etiology—witness the development of quarantines. Great Renaissance physicians and surgeons, such as Paré or Paracelsus, often exhibited greater perception of the patient's psychological situation than of his physiological processes.[15] In the seventeenth century, too, physicians like Sydenham emphasized observation of the natural history of disease in individuals *and* groups as prerequisite to medical understanding (see Chapter 6).

During the past century and a half, while medicine has become scientific in the modern sense of the word, it has never really lost the social insights of previous generations. However, for the first time a conscious distinction has been made between the "science" and the "art" of medicine and, except within modern psychiatry, *formal* instruction and academic interest alike have centered almost wholly on science. Because medical science has been defined almost entirely in biological terms, this distinction has pushed interest in the social aspects of medicine to the periphery of medical consciousness. With the development of the germ theory of disease and the concurrent progress in physiological medicine— the "medicine of the internal environment"—it seemed that the theory of pathology had been reduced to analysis of the response of the organism to deleterious physical and chemical stimuli. The tremendous successes in the management of disease which this theory won reinforced the tendency to think of medicine as exclusively a biological science. Even its social organization was conceived as ideally determined by criteria of efficiency in implementing technical, diagnostic, therapeutic, and preventive operations.

Moreover, scientific advance in medicine during the nineteenth century was difficult to achieve, largely because of social obstacles from within and without the profession.[16] So bitter was the battle against traditionalism and obscurantism that it seemed to many physicians that medical history had no lessons to teach other than to warn against past errors. And it is true that the valid social insights of primitive and ancient medicine are mixed with—often submerged in—biological ignorance and error. In keeping with the positivistic temper of the times, therefore, in the late nineteenth and early twentieth centuries medicine tended both to break with the past and to place its essential hopes upon the laboratory. As Merton has noted, this attitude has become the "great tradition" of modern medicine.[17]

[15]On this point, see any standard history of medicine. An especially clear statement of this position is found in Kenneth Walker, *The Story of Medicine,* London: Hutchinson, 1954.

[16]Bernard J. Stern, *Social Factors in Medical Progress;* Richard H. Shryock, *The Development of Modern Medicine,* New York: Knopf, 1947, especially chaps. 3, 6, and 13.

[17]Robert K. Merton, "Some Preliminaries to a Study of Medical Education," in R. K. Merton, George G. Reader, and Patricia L. Kendall (eds.), *The Student Physician,* Cambridge, Mass.: Harvard University Press, 1957, pp. 6–7.

Thus, in many respects, it would seem that sociology and medicine more or less ignored each other during their respective periods of development as scientific disciplines. Paradoxically, although the respective quests of sociology and medicine for scientific development tended to lead them in separate directions prior to the mid-twentieth century, the fruits of these efforts have led in recent years to converging interests among the disciplines. As we shall see, the changes brought about by sociological and especially medical discoveries have created a favorable situation for productive collaborative efforts.

## FACTORS EFFECTING CONVERGENCE

### Change in Morbidity

Underlying much of contemporary medical thought is a basic change in morbidity experience. As Chapter 2 will indicate, the past century has seen what has been called "the conquest of epidemic disease." Not only was the American death rate nearly halved between 1900 and 1960, but the contribution of the infectious diseases to this mortality declined from 40 to 6 percent in terms of "cause of death."[18] Just as this has made for an aging population, it has made for a relatively heavier burden of chronic disease at all age levels. It was only when physicians no longer found their days filled with acute cases of infectious disease that they could confront less urgent problems, such as metabolic and degenerative disorders, neuroses, psychosomatic complaints, or rehabilitation of the handicapped. Indeed, only as acute illness began to be controlled did many patients survive to feel the full and prolonged effects of chronic disease.[19]

Moreover, much of the burden of chronic physical handicap is the result of infectious disease, the lethal potential of which has been successfully contained. For example, much deafness is clearly the result of the aftereffects of infectious diseases such as otitis media, and among the possible aftereffects of streptococcal infections is rheumatic heart disease. One of the problems of contemporary medicine, however, is that even after effective preventive measures against infectious disease have been developed, all groups in the population are not at once eager to take advantage of them.[20] Thus, potential conquests of disease seem threatened by the recal-

---

[18]U.S. Bureau of the Census, *Statistical Abstract of the United States, 1974*, Washington, D.C.: Government Printing Office, 1974, p. 62.

[19]Albert F. Wessen, "Some Sociological Characteristics of Long-term Care," part 2, *Gerontologist*, 4 (June, 1964), 7–14. See also Ernest M. Gruenberg, "The Failure of Success," *Health and Society*, 55 (Winter, 1977), 3–24.

[20]Leila C. Deasy, "Social-economic Status and Participation in the Poliomyelitis Vaccine Trial," *American Sociological Review*, 21 (April, 1956), 185–190.

citrance of people to accept scientific advances. As the healing arts have become increasingly successful in controlling so many age-old threats to human life, those interested in public health have become increasingly impatient of the burden of preventable illness.

These changes in the pattern of disease have forced medicine to broaden its perspectives. This has been true with respect to both *epidemiology* (the study of factors related to the distribution of disease in a population) and therapy. Most chronic diseases have not yielded to the search for a single cause which could be attacked by the direct, traditional methods of public health; neither purification of drinking water nor "swat the fly" campaigns, for example, give hope of lowering the incidence of a disease like cancer. On the contrary, chronic illnesses in general appear to be the resultant of many causes. They often seem to be, as it were, the precipitate of a lifetime of psychological and/or biological attrition or trauma. The logic of epidemiologic study has therefore shifted. Instead of a search for a connection between cases of a disease and a specific cause, it is broadened into an attempt to find common denominators in the life-experience of afflicted persons which will differentiate their histories from those not affected by the disease under study.[21] Moreover, because of these considerations, preventive measures must be general—cast in such terms as motivating people to live more "healthfully." The epidemiology of chronic illness thus involves the study of the habits and social experience of human beings, and its control is in large part a problem in social motivation.[22]

The management of chronic illness is by definition a long-term matter (see Chapter 3). This means that therapeutic intervention will involve frequent and sustained alterations in patients' normal patterns of living. Their role modifications will involve continuing adjustments on the part of individuals and groups with whom patients are in contact, most particularly their families. Both the typically slow progress made by chronic patients and the demands placed upon them by their regimen highlight the motivational problem in treatment. And in terms of both time and money, care of the chronically ill is exceedingly costly. For these reasons social factors tend to become especially prominent in the management of long-term illness.[23] As priorities for research have placed increasing emphasis on

---

[21]Raymond Illsley, "Promotion to Observer Status," *Social Science and Medicine,* 9 (February, 1975), 63–67. One observer, however, believes the focus for behavioral change should be on health organizations rather than individual motivation. See Leon S. Robertson, "Behavioral Research and Strategies in Public Health: A Demur," *Social Science and Medicine,* 9 (March, 1975), 165–170.

[22]This is, of course, also true of the control of infectious disease. See Benjamin Paul (ed.), *Health, Culture, and Community,* New York: Russell Sage, 1955, for case material on this point.

[23]Two influential medical statements bearing on these points are George Canby Robinson, *The Patient as a Person,* New York: Commonwealth Fund, 1939; and Henry E. Richardson, *Patients Have Families,* New York: Commonwealth Fund, 1945. From a sociological perspective, see Albert F. Wessen, "Annual Administrative Review: Long-term Care,"

chronic disease (including mental illness), it is not surprising that medical science has more and more transcended the realm of the biological. In its exploration of social factors, modern medicine has discovered that the behavioral sciences have major implications for its future development. It is especially in the fields of public health and preventive medicine, psychiatry, and administrative medicine that these are to be seen.

## The Impact of Preventive Medicine and Public Health

One fundamental change is found in the development and reorientation of preventive medicine and public health. Although European thought has stressed the importance of "social medicine" for more than a century, until the past thirty-five years, public health in America was largely restricted to the environmental control of the communicable diseases.[24] Without discounting the important social implications of communicable disease control, recent developments in public health would seem to have the following important implications for social science:

1  The basis of *epidemiology* has been broadened from the study of the distribution of communicable diseases among the population to the study of the ecology (distribution in the population) of any disease or physical handicap.[25] At the same time, epidemiologic interest has come to center not merely upon the identification of the causes of disease, but upon their differential effects on different populations and in different environments. Out of all this has come the formulation that behind the "intimate" cause of disease (disease agent) stands the "ultimate" cause—factors of the social and physical environment providing the *linkages* between agent and host. Therefore, epidemiologists have increasingly found their theoretical interests converging upon those of demography and community studies.

2  As indicated above, increasing interest in control of the *chronic diseases* has also led to increased emphasis upon the concept of *multiple causation* in disease. That is, physicians have been forced to consider factors other than exclusively biological ones in treating their patients. Such matters as past history, personal habits, family relationships, and type of housing also may influence the outcome of treatment. This approach

---

*Hospitals,* 38 (April, 1964), 101–104; and Rodney M. Coe and Harry M. Rosen (eds.), "Symposium on Research in Long-term Care," part 2, *Gerontologist,* 4 (June, 1964), 1–58. More recent perspectives on the issues are found in Sylvia Sherwood (ed.), *Long-Term Care: A Handbook for Researchers, Planners and Providers,* New York: Spectrum Publications, 1975.

[24]George Rosen, "The Evolution of Social Medicine," in Freeman, Levine, and Reeder, *op. cit.,* pp. 30–60.

[25]Sidney L. Kark, *Epidemiology and Community Medicine,* New York: Appleton-Century-Crofts, 1974. Jacques M. May, *The Ecology of Human Disease,* New York: MD Publications, 1958, p. 2. See also Hugh R. Leavell and E. Gurney Clark, "An Epidemiologic Approach to Preventive Medicine," in *Preventive Medicine for the Doctor in His Community: An Epidemiologic Approach,* New York: McGraw-Hill, 1958, pp. 40–78.

may be seen not only in such technical procedures as "multiphasic screening," but also in an increased interest in the contribution of all aspects of the patients' experience to their health status.[26] Multiple causation also implies the notion that prevention of disease involves not merely a few environmental controls, but long-range efforts to protect individuals from the prenatal period to the grave. Because its effects are seen most often in older persons, chronic illness has tended to focus interest upon the *geriatric* age group. Nonetheless, major program efforts have been directed toward younger age groups, for example, well-baby clinics, immunization clinics, and school health programs.

   **3**   As the task of preventive medicine is increasingly seen to involve the long-range participation of every citizen, increased emphasis is placed upon *health education*.[27] The problems of public health seem, from this perspective, to depend upon the motivation of people to do those things which are conducive to health. This involves not only the use of mass media as teaching devices, but the determination of health attitudes among population groups. Of special importance is the matter of resistance to health practices and its relationship to subcultural differences among the population.[28]

   **4**   Both on national and on international levels, attention of public health officials has turned toward the problem of *providing adequate medical care facilities and programs* for communities.[29] At the international level, the problem is not merely the organization and financing of programs in underdeveloped areas with inadequate resources, but one of integrating them with the local culture and social structure. In this country, there is the problem of enlisting community support for health action

---

   [26]Leavell and Clark, *op. cit.* pp. 207–259. On the problem of chronic illness, the fullest discussion is Commission on Chronic Illness, *Chronic Illness in the United States,* 4 vols., Cambridge, Mass.: Harvard University Press, 1956–1957. On multiphasic screening, see Lester Breslow, "Multiphasic Screening Examination: An Extension of the Mass Screening Technique," *American Journal of Public Health,* 40 (March, 1950), 274–278; and by the same author, "Periodic Health Examinations and Multiple Screening," *American Journal of Public Health,* 49 (September, 1959), 1148–1156. See also Walter Boek, *An Analysis of the Multi-test Clinic of Richmond, Virginia,* New York: Health Information Foundation, 1951.
   [27]R. S. Patterson and B. J. Roberts, *Community Health Education in Action,* St. Louis: Mosby, 1951. See also any current issue of *Health Education Monographs* (published by the Society for Public Health Education, Inc.) for general articles, current bibliography, and dissertation abstracts on health education topics.
   [28]Lyle Saunders, *Cultural Difference and Medical Care,* New York: Russell Sage, 1954; and Earl L. Koos, *The Health of Regionville,* New York: Columbia University Press, 1954, provide basic orientation on this point. See also Edward A. Suchman, "Sociomedical Variations among Ethnic Groups," *American Journal of Sociology,* 70 (November, 1964), 319–331.
   [29]For general orientation see Association of Teachers of Preventive Medicine, Committee on Medical Care, *Readings in Medical Care,* Chapel Hill: University of North Carolina Press, 1958. More recently, see "Closing the Gaps in the Availability and Accessibility of Health Services," *Bulletin of the New York Academy of Medicine,* 41 (December, 1965), 1197–1401; and Ronald Anderson, Joanna Kravits, and Odin W. Anderson, *Equity in Health Services: Empirical Analyses in Social Policy,* Cambridge, Mass.: Ballinger, 1975; David Mechanic, *Public Expectations and Health Care,* New York: Wiley Interscience, 1972.

programs.[30] And always, there is the question of measurement of the need for medical care and of the quality and quantity of care available to communities and of finding means for overcoming indicated deficiencies.[31]

5   Attention is increasingly given to the necessity for *rehabilitation* of those who have suffered disability through illness or accident. It is apparent that this is as much a sociological as a medical problem, both with respect to the disabled individual (who faces difficult role adjustments as well as the need for physical therapies) and with respect to society. The literature indicates that physical handicap is as much the function of social stereotype as physical disability, and the practical problems of placement, to say nothing of stereotype correction, are of major magnitude.[32]

6   Beginning with the isolation and study of specific industrial toxins, *occupational medicine* has developed into a major public health specialty. The relationship of occupation to health is not only of epidemiologic significance, but from the viewpoint of industrial sociology a ripe field for the application of nonmedical knowledge about occupational life.[33]

7   Finally, and perhaps of greatest significance of all, is the development of *positive* rather than negative *conceptions of health*. Increasingly, public health sees the province of medicine as more than the study, prevention, and cure of disease; rather, it extends its area of interests to include promotion of elements contributing to "the good life" and motivating the public to live more healthfully. The World Health Organization, for

[30]Paul A. Miller, *Community Health Action,* East Lansing: Michigan State College Press, 1953. Solon T. Kimball and Marion Pearsall, *The Talladega Story: A Study in Community Process,* University: University of Alabama Press, 1954; Peter Marris and Martin Rein, *Dilemmas of Social Reform: Poverty and Community Action in the United States,* New York: Atherton, 1967; Health Task Force of the Urban Coalition, *Rx for Action,* Washington, D.C., 1969.

[31]See Association of Teachers of Preventive Medicine, *op. cit.,* pp. 76–115, for an orientation to the literature. See also J. H. F. Brotherston, "Medical Care Investigation in the Health Service," in *Toward a Measure of Medical Care,* New York: Oxford University Press, 1962. More recent methodology is discussed in National Academy of Sciences, *Contrasts in Health Care, A Strategy for Evaluating Health Services,* Washington, D.C.: 1973, and a survey article by Charles E. Lewis, "The State of the Art of Quality Assessment—1973," *Medical Care,* 12 (October, 1974), 799–806.

[32]On rehabilitation and its organization, see W. Scott Allen, *Rehabilitation: A Community Challenge,* New York: Wiley, 1958. The best single source of information on social aspects of problems of the handicapped is still Roger G. Barker, Beatrice A. Wright, and Mollie R. Gonick, *Adjustment to Physical Handicap and Illness: A Survey of the Social Psychology of Physique and Disability,* New York: Social Science Research Council, Bulletin 55, 1946. Also Beatrice A. Wright, *Physical Disability: A Psychological Approach,* New York: Harper & Row, 1960; and Herbert S. Rabinowitz and Spiro B. Mitsos, "Rehabilitation as Planned Social Change: A Conceptual Framework," *Journal of Health and Human Behavior,* 5 (Spring, 1964), 2–14; Marvin B. Sussman (ed.), *Sociology and Rehabilitation,* Washington, D.C.: American Sociological Association, 1966; F. J. Kottke, *Handbook of Rehabilitation Medicine and Rehabilitation,* New York: Saunders, 1965; Sidney Licht (ed.), *Rehabilitation in Medicine,* New Haven: Licht Publications, 1968.

[33]On industrial health, see Leavell and Clark, *op. cit.,* pp. 433–462; and Donald Hunter, *The Diseases of Occupations,* Boston: Little, Brown, 1969; International Labor Office, *Encyclopedia of Occupational Health and Safety,* New York: McGraw-Hill, 1971.

example, defines health as "a state of complete physical, mental, and social well-being, not merely the absence of disease and infirmity."[34] Such a definition indeed requires a conception of medicine as a social science.

These closely allied developments in the field of preventive medicine and public health may be summarized as efforts to find new techniques with which to cope with changed types of disease incidence in the community. As a discipline, public health arose in an era which had as its main health problem the control of epidemic diseases. Drawing upon the new bacteriological theories of disease, public health became a coherent field of practice by centering its attention upon techniques of ensuring sanitation and vermin control. It has long been established, however, that these techniques are fully effective only when appropriate sociological conditions have been met. The differing theoretical and practical problems which have arisen as the chronic diseases have taken the center of the stage have served further to enlarge the interest of public health workers in sociological problems.[35] It should be emphasized, however, that—in contrast with the case of social psychiatry—this social interest has been largely pragmatic and has never been fully integrated into a comprehensive social theory of public health, nor has it provided theoretical inspiration to social scientists.

### The Impact of Modern Psychiatry

We cannot describe here either the development of modern psychiatry or its distinguishing features.[36] Rather, our interest lies in the implications of this development for medicine generally. At least four factors should be noted here.

1  The recognition that psychological mechanisms are responsible for apparently neurological symptoms, first worked out for the hysterias by Freud, rendered an exclusively biological theory of disease untenable. Experimental verification by Cannon and others of the effect of emotions on physiological processes made it necessary to conceive of physiology in other than purely mechanistic terms. Thus, through psychosomatic medicine, psychophysiological as well as biochemical considerations became

---

[34]From the Constitution of the World Health Organization. Quoted in Leavell and Clark, *op. cit.,* p. 13. See also the discussion in John D. Jago, "Hal-Old Word, New Task: Reflections on the Words 'Health' and 'Medical,'" *Social Science and Medicine,* 9 (January, 1975), 1–6.

[35]David Mechanic, "Sociology and Public Health: Perspective for Application," *American Journal of Public Health,* 62 (February, 1972), 146–151.

[36]A brief historical analysis of modern psychiatry which emphasizes its impact upon modern medical thought is to be found in Alexander Leighton, John A. Clausen, and Robert N. Wilson, *Explorations in Social Psychiatry,* New York: Basic Books, 1957, especially chap. 5. See also John G. Howells (ed.), *Modern Perspectives in Psychiatry,* New York: Brunner-Mazel, 1975.

important in the theory of internal medicine.[37] Moreover, further research emphasized that bodily reactions to the environment are the result not only of specific stimuli, but also of the cumulative effect of threats and pressures upon the individual. The term *stress* came to be applied to these environmental pressures, and it soon became apparent that among human beings, stress was most significantly located in their social environment. And their reaction to stress is seen as both conscious and unconscious; it is manifested not only in symptoms but in a total way of life.[38]

2   The whole generic approach of psychoanalytic theory led to a formulation of the hypothesis that mental illnesses have distinctively *social etiologies* and are essentially behavioral phenomena. Practically, this meant that, in both epidemiology and history taking, physicians have been forced to direct their attention to the social environment of the individual as well as to the search for exposure to noxious agents in the physical environment.[39]

3   At the practice level, a major significance of dynamic psychiatry lies in its rediscovery of the therapeutic nature of the *doctor-patient relationship*. Both doctrinal rigidities and theoretical ignorance have thus far prevented adequate scientific understanding of this relationship, but a number of approaches give promise of reducing this bastion of the art of medicine to scientific analysis.[40]

[37]W. B. Cannon's original research is summarized in his *Bodily Changes in Pain, Hunger, Fear and Rage,* New York: Appleton, 1920. The psychodynamic approach to psychosomatic medicine is summarized by Franz Alexander and Thomas M. Szasz, "The Psychosomatic Approach in Medicine," in F. Alexander and Helen Ross (eds.), *Dynamic Psychiatry,* Chicago: University of Chicago Press, 1952, pp. 369–400. The standard handbook of the psychosomatic literature is Flanders Dunbar (ed.), *Emotions and Bodily Changes,* New York: Columbia University Press, 1954. More recent developments are discussed in S. J. Lachman, *Psychosomatic Disorders: A Behavioristic Interpretation,* New York: Wiley, 1972; and R. D. Laing and A. Esterson, *Sanity, Madness and the Family,* Baltimore: Penguin, 1973.

[38]Gordon E. Moss, *Illness, Immunity and Social Interaction: The Dynamics of Biosocial Resonation,* New York: Wiley, 1973; Sol Levine and Norman A. Scotch (eds.), *Social Stress,* Chicago: Aldine, 1970. See also Stanley H. King, "Social Psychological Factors in Illness," in Freeman, Levine, and Reeder, *op. cit.,* pp. 129–147. From the medical side, Hans Selye developed a general theory of stress and the organism's adaptation to it. See his *The Stress of Life,* New York: McGraw-Hill, 1956. Important research further developing this perspective is summarized in H. G. Wolff, *Stress and Disease,* Springfield, Ill.: Charles C Thomas, 1953.

[39]This concept is stated with special emphasis by Harry Stack Sullivan. See his *Conceptions of Modern Psychiatry,* William Alanson White Psychiatric Foundation, 1940; and his *Interpersonal Theory of Psychiatry,* New York: Norton, 1951. See also Michael Balint, *The Doctor, His Patient and the Illness,* New York: International Universities Press, 1957.

[40]A good brief statement of psychiatric thinking about this matter written for a general medical audience is Avery D. Weisman, "The Doctor-patient Relationship: Its Role in Therapy," *American Practitioner and Digest of Treatment,* 1 (1950), 1144ff. The psychoanalytic concept of the therapeutic relationship is discussed at great length by Karl Menninger, *Theory of Psychoanalytic Technique,* New York: Basic Books, 1958; and by Henry L. Lennard and Arnold Bernstein, *The Anatomy of Psychotherapy,* New York: Columbia University Press, 1960. See the more sociological analysis of the therapeutic role in Talcott Parsons, *The Social System,* New York: Free Press, 1951, especially chap. 10.

**4** Corollary to the perception of the importance of the doctor-patient relationship in therapy is the recognition of the possibility of applying the entire environment of the patient to therapeutic purposes. In this concept of *milieu therapy* the entire social structure of medical practice becomes itself an instrument of therapy.[41]

It should be emphasized that these four contributions are not solely the discovery of psychiatry, nor do they exhaust its relevance for general medicine. Nonetheless, it is probably true that the assimilation of these notions into medical thinking—still imperfect—has largely been spearheaded by modern psychiatry.

**The Impact of Administrative Medicine**

Concern with the organization of medicine represents a fourth trend which has heightened the interest of the medical profession in social science. This concern stems from several sources. For at least forty years, the profession has been subject to constant criticism by those who feel that the traditional individualistic, fee-for-service organization of medical care is not competent to achieve adequate health standards for Americans.[42] This criticism has produced many plans for the reorganization of medical practice, ranging all the way from group-practice clinics and voluntary health insurance to socialized medicine; each plan has produced in its day a considerable polemic literature.

Moreover, there has been an increasing feeling among some physicians that the trend toward specialization, set off by scientific medicine, has reached the point of diminishing returns. Feeling that functional specialization results in "fractionation" of patient care, in unnecessarily impersonal

---

[41]See David Mc. K. Rioch and Alfred H. Stanton, "Milieu Therapy," *Psychiatry,* 16 (February, 1953), 65–72. The possibilities of milieu therapy in the mental hospital forms a central theme of Milton Greenblatt, Richard H. York, and Esther Lucille Brown (eds.), *From Custodial to Therapeutic Patient Care in Mental Hospitals,* New York: Russell Sage, 1955. A classical description of milieu therapy in a mental hospital setting is Maxwell Jones, *The Therapeutic Community,* New York: Basic Books, 1953.

[42]For a thorough discussion of the strengths and weaknesses of medical care organization in the United States, see Michael M. Davis, *Medical Care for Tomorrow,* New York: Harper & Row, 1955. Attention to the problems of medical care was focused nationally by the report of the Committee on Costs of Medical Care, *Medical Care for the American People,* Chicago: University of Chicago Press, 1932. Other critiques and polemics include: Hugh Cabot, *The Doctor's Bill,* New York: Columbia University Press, 1935; Hugh Cabot, *The Patient's Dilemma,* New York: Reynal & Hitchcock, 1940; Carl Malmberg, *140 Million Patients,* New York: Reynal & Hitchcock, 1947; Richard Carter, *The Doctor Business,* New York: Doubleday, 1958; Selig Greenberg, *The Troubled Calling: Crisis in the Medical Establishment,* New York: Macmillan, 1965; Health PAC, *The American Health Empire,* New York: Vintage Books, 1970; Abraham Ribicoff, *The American Medical Machine,* New York: Saturday Review Press, 1972, or Edward M. Kennedy, *In Critical Condition, The Crisis in America's Health Care,* New York: Simon and Schuster, 1972; and Vicente Navarro, "From Public Health to Health of the Public," *American Journal of Public Health,* 64 (June, 1974), 538–542.

doctor-patient relations, and in the kind of ignorance of the patient as a person which breeds unsatisfactory care, these critics have often asked for a renaissance of general medicine.[43] This attempt to stimulate interest in general medicine is spurred also by concern about the distribution of physicians, which slights rural areas in favor of urban regions. At the same time, the trend toward specialization has undoubtedly raised standards of technical medical care, and the problem becomes one not of fighting progress, but of combining the best of the family physicians's role with the technical virtuosity of the specialist.

Finally, the long-established interest in improving technical standards of hospitals is beginning to be coupled with concern for the human aspects of these institutions.[44] This may be seen in increased concern for the adjustment of the patient to the hospital environment and in a rising interest in the hospital's role in ambulatory and home care. At another level, the very high turnover rates and endemic personnel shortages to which hospitals are subject have caused administrators to consider whether there might be structural defects in hospital organization which drive personnel away. These concerns are heightened by the continuing rapid increase in the complexity of hospital services and organization, a phenomenon which is manifest most obviously to the public in the skyrocketing costs of medical care. The constant tension between medical staffs and hospital administration also has caused some to wonder if a more tranquil organization is possible. But it is perhaps the situation of nursing which has caused most concern in hospitals, and to which most research interest has thus far been directed. In their concern to combine improved service with enhanced status, nurses have actively recruited the help of social scientists.[45]

[43]Rosemary Stevens, *American Medicine and the Public Interest,* New Haven: Yale University Press 1971. Earlier statements are: Stern, *American Medical Practice in the Perspective of a Century,* pp. 45–62; and George Rosen, *The Specialization of Medicine,* New York: Froben Press, 1944. Typical of a large literature on the status of general practice are: J. S. Collings and Dean M. Clark, "General Practice Today and Tomorrow," *New England Journal of Medicine,* 248 (Jan. 29, 1953), 193–196; W. D. Hildebrand, "The Future of General Practice," *GP,* 11 (May, 1955), 133–141; J. H. Means, "Role of the Generalist in Modern Medicine," *American Practitioner and Digest of Treatment,* 5 (March, 1954), 169–174; E. Richard Weinerman, "Research into the Organization of Medical Practice," Health Service Research Papers, National Institute of Health, 1966.

[44]A well-known social science study stemming from this interest is Temple Burling, Edith M. Lentz, and Robert N. Wilson, *The Give and Take in Hospitals,* New York: Putnam, 1956. See also George G. Reader and Mary E. W. Goss "Medical Sociology with Particular Reference to the Study of Hospitals," *Transactions of the Fourth World Congress on Sociology,* 2 (1959), 139–152; and Basil Georgopoulos and Floyd C. Mann, *The Community General Hospital,* New York: Macmillan, 1962; and William R. Rosengren and Mark Lefton, *Hospitals and Patients,* New York: Atherton, 1969.

[45]Everett C. Hughes, Helen MacGill Hughes, and Irwin Deutscher, *20,000 Nurses Tell Their Story,* Philadelphia: Lippincott, 1958; Leonard Reissman and John H. Rohrer, *Change and Dilemma in the Nursing Profession,* New York: Putnam, 1957; Fred Davis (ed.), *The Nursing Profession,* New York: Wiley, 1966.

All these concerns are focused upon the improvement of patient care. It is not surprising, too, that the professional schools have been greatly influenced by these trends. Numbering among their faculties many of the creative minds in the health professions, these schools have been centers for the development and dissemination of new insights. They also have felt compelled to reevaluate their curricula in the light of trends such as those mentioned above.[46] This reevaluation is leading to attempts to measure the effectiveness of professional education and to the study of the sociology of medical education.[47] New and experimental programs are, as a result, being developed to foster and implement trends of social interest in medicine (see Chapter 7).[48]

Concern for improved health care is a pervasive cultural value in the contemporary Western world. The public has expressed an increasing interest in improving medical care. This has been manifest not only in terms of the many articles on medical care to be found in the public press, but in numerous action programs. One need only mention the interest of labor unions in the development of health programs, the interest of communities in establishing better neighborhood health services, and the participation of governmental agencies in paying for care under Medicare and Medicaid as well as in stimulating the development of new facilities with Hill-Burton funds for hospital construction. These interests, of course, entail the allocation of scarce resources for which improved medical programs are only one of many claimants. This competition has inevitably led to scrutiny of the present medical care system in search of possible economies. In the hospital field, for example, interest in operational research as a means of achieving better use and delivery of services has burgeoned. And it has become apparent that the medical care system as a whole is uneven and often contains unnecessarily duplicative facilities. This, of course, has led to an interest in rationalizing the system through planning. Thus, we witnessed the development of state and local comprehensive health agen-

[46]J. S. Millis, *The Graduate Education of Physicians: Report of the Citizens Commission on Graduate Medical Education,* Chicago: American Medical Association, 1966. See also Ralph B. Freidin, Arthur J. Barsky, David Levine, and Sherman B. Williams, "Medical Education and Physician Behavior: Preparing Physicians for New Roles," *Journal of Medical Education,* 47 (March, 1972), 163–168.

[47]Merton, Reader, and Kendall, *op. cit.;* Helen Hofer Gee and Robert J. Glaser, "The Ecology of the Medical Student," *Journal of Medical Education,* 33 (October, 1958), part 2; Samuel W. Bloom, "The Sociology of Medical Education: Some Comments on the State of a Field," *Milbank Memorial Fund Quarterly,* 43 (April, 1965), 143–184.

[48]Some of these are summed up by John A. D. Cooper, "New Directions in Programs of Medical Education," in Gee and Glaser, *op. cit.,* 189–215. See also Thomas E. Bryant and Raymond Cotton, "Issues in Health Care: A New Course for Beginning Medical Students," *Journal of Medical Education,* 47 (March, 1972), 216–218; George G. Reader and Mary E. W. Goss, (eds.), *Comprehensive Medical Care and Teaching,* Ithaca, N.Y.: Cornell University Press, 1967.

cies, whose task it was to coordinate the operations of existing health resources and review proposals for new facilities. By 1976, these programs had given way to health systems agencies which had not only a similar mission, but more power (through grant funds) to effect coordination of scarce resources. Such efforts have obvious sociological implications for the study of social change and its impact on different forms of social organization.[49]

Quite naturally, there is a defensive element in all these organizational concerns of medicine. Neither the medical nor the nursing profession wishes to give less than the best possible service, yet each covets professional independence and freedom of action. At the same time, the professions feel that criticism is frequently not justified by the facts and is often motivated by special interests or unsound ideologies.[50] These feelings can result in doctrinaire rigidity on the part of the professions and in suspicion of any outside scrutiny of professional problems. They also, happily, can result in a willingness to study the possibilities of professional and institutional reorganization upon the basis of sound research findings.[51] Those health service administrators who take the latter view have awakened to the potentialities of the work of the sociologist as organizational analyst.

Changing theories and changing conditions thus have aroused a new interest within medical circles in the possibility of making the old dogma that "medicine is a social science" become a fact. This interest, which has received its clearest theoretical expression in psychiatry and most practical expression in the emergence of community medicine, has been assimilated to varying degrees among the several branches of medicine, but it has never been unified. For example, one who appreciates the need for new social tactics in dealing with changed community health problems may well be hostile to psychiatric thinking. Those whose therapeutic efforts are focused on individual patients may have little interest in coping with the diffuse effects of neighborhood environments. Likewise, the three sources of a social approach on medicine outlined above lead to quite different focuses of sociological interest. Psychiatric attention has been focused largely upon cultural, interpersonal, and psychological factors in the etiology of mental illness and upon the study of the therapeutic relationship. Public health

[49]Herbert H. Hyman, *Health Planning: A Systematic Approach,* Germantown, Md.: Aspen Publications, 1975. See also Ruth Roemer, Charles Kramer, and Jeanne E. Frink, *Planning Urban Health Services: From Jungle to System,* New York: Springer, 1975.

[50]See, for example, William J. Goode, "Encroachment, Charlatanism and the Emerging Professions," *American Sociological Review,* 25 (December, 1960), 902–914; and Stephen P. Strickland, *Politics, Science and Dread Disease,* Cambridge: Harvard University Press, 1972.

[51]See, for example, the paradigm in Albert F. Wessen, "The Apparatus of Rehabilitation: An Organizational Analysis," in Sussman, *op. cit.,* pp. 160–164; E. Evelyn Flook and Paul V. Sanazaro, (eds.), *Health Services Research and R & D in Perspective,* Ann Arbor: University of Michigan Health Administration Press, 1973.

interest, on the other hand, has emphasized the development and organization of facilities for better medical practice and the study of ecological
factors in disease causation. Administrative concern about the status of
medicine and the effectiveness of service has largely centered upon operational problems of medical care organization and medical economics.
Taken together, however, these interests have stimulated research on a
wide range of sociologically relevant topics.[52]

Needless to say, the social sciences could not effectively have coped
with so wide a set of interests a generation ago. Academic parochialisms
had to give way to a broad conception of behavioral science. Special
mention should be accorded to the work of Talcott Parsons, which not only
attempted to integrate the fields of sociology, psychology, and anthropology under the umbrella of a "general theory of action," but also specifically
demonstrated the relevance of medical phenomena to this general theory.
But Parsons' work is representative of more general movements which
have conceived the variables accounting for individual behavior, social
relationships, and cultural patterns as mutually dependent.[53] The significance of such a broad conception of the behavioral sciences for the
sociology of medicine is apparent in at least two respects.

First, the perception of the interdependence of individual behavior and
social and cultural systems complements the awareness in medicine of the
interaction between psychological and physiological mechanisms.[54] Thus,
at a theoretical level, the contribution of sociology to the understanding of
medical behavior depends upon an integrated view of science. Otherwise,
although sociologists might study the evolution of medical institutions and
their relationship to other aspects of the social structure, their work would

[52]Milton I. Roemer and Ray H. Elling, "Sociological Research on Medical Care,"
*Journal of Health and Human Behavior,* 4 (Spring, 1963), 49–68. See also Odin W. Anderson,
"Social Research in Medical Care," *Monthly Labor Review,* 84 (March, 1961), 239–241. A
more recent accounting is given in Ozzie G. Simmons and Emil Berkanovic, "Social Research
in Health and Medicine," in Freeman, Levine, and Reeder, *op. cit.,* pp. 523–584.

[53]For Parsons' work, see Talcott Parsons, Edward A. Shils, et al., *Toward a General
Theory of Action,* Cambridge, Mass.: Harvard University Press, 1951; Talcott Parsons, *The
Social System,* New York: Free Press, 1951; T. Parsons, "Some Theoretical Considerations
Bearing on the Field of Medical Sociology," in his *Social Structure and Personality,* New
York: Free Press, 1964, pp. 325–359. On the convergence of the behavioral sciences, see John
Gillin et al., *For a Science of Social Man,* New York: Macmillan, 1954.

[54]The integrative effects are stressed in Douglas Hooper, "Some Necessary Assumptions of Social/Behavioral Science in Relation to Medicine," *Social Science and Medicine,* 4
(July, 1970), 153–156, and Sidney M. Stahl, Clarence E. Grim, Kathy Donald, and Helen Jo
Neikirk, "A Model for the Social Sciences and Medicine: The Case for Hypertension," *Social
Science and Medicine,* 9 (January, 1975), 31–38. The political as well as social importance of
biological phenomena are noted in Stephen J. Kunetz, "Some Notes on Physiologic Conditions as Social Problems," *Social Science and Medicine,* 8 (April, 1974), 207–211.

be of peripheral interest to physicians who could rightly claim that such studies had little significance for their understanding of sick human beings.

Second, medical behavior clearly involves the selection and implementation of specific roles and cultural norms by persons who see themselves as sick and by at least some of their fellows. Their behavior—and concomitant modifications of other roles and norms—is conditioned by a complex set of feelings. These anxieties, pains, and hopes are themselves either engendered by or closely related to specific bodily changes. If these statements are true, it is apparent that the study of medical behavior constitutes a strategic setting for the development of social science knowledge. The field of medicine affords almost a unique opportunity to study the range of behavioral science theory.[55]

But general theoretical perspectives alone could not prepare sociologists for the convergence of disciplines here being chronicled. So long as theory and empirical research were largely divorced, the researches of sociologists could all too frequently be characterized as mindless fact gathering—a situation ruthlessly criticized outside the field.[56] Here, the contributions of sociologists such as Robert K. Merton were crucial. Merton insisted on a conscious interaction between theory and research and emphasized the necessity of developing a "middle-range" theory if this was to be accomplished.[57] In science, the payoff comes neither from the acquisition of facts alone nor from the elaboration of logical theories which cannot be tested empirically. It comes rather from the explanation of a set of facts by a generalization which can be shown to hold good in all comparable situations. Sociologists, therefore, had to demonstrate their willingness to eschew grand theories—or at least to draw from them implications which could be checked against a delimited, yet relevant, body of data—before they were ready to develop a scientific sociology. But this depended upon the perfection of a host of methodological skills and upon the acquisition of a great deal of systematic data.

We can only enumerate a few of the principal innovations which were of importance. On the methodological side, they include refinements in interviewing, participant-observation techniques, survey design and analy-

[55]This has been especially recognized in the research programs sponsored by the National Institute of Mental Health. See R. H. Williams, "The Strategy of Sociomedical Research," in Freeman, Levine, and Reeder, *op. cit.,* pp. 459–483. Examples of textbooks employing this perspective are: Theodore Millon, *Medical Behavioral Science,* Philadelphia: Saunders, 1975; and Stephen E. Gray and Hollis N. Matson, *Health Now,* New York: Macmillan, 1976.

[56]See, for example, the barb of the great reformer of medical education, Abraham Flexner, in his *Universities: American, English, German,* New York: Oxford University Press, 1930, *passim.*

[57]Robert K. Merton, *Social Theory and Social Structure,* New York: Free Press, 1957.

sis, the development of scales of measurement, content analysis, and work on the application of principles of experimental design to social situations.[58] In a word, the advances which enabled sociologists to make empirical studies of social settings (particularly of small groups and organizations) with increased precision and skill made their effective entry into the medical area possible. Moreover, the heritage of empirical studies of community structure, social stratification, family behavior, and bureaucratic and professional organizations provided a necessary basis for the study of medical sociology. Although this base was notably thin in 1930, by 1950 it had achieved enough solidity that students of medical behavior had a substantive base adequate for developing their special studies. For example, the study of the effects of social class on mental illness undertaken by Hollingshead and others depended heavily upon the groundwork laid by the extensive community studies of social stratification made in previous years.[59]

To sum up, our thesis is that medical sociology became an attractive option for sociologists only when the discipline had developed some semblance of maturity in substantive, theoretical, and methodological terms. There was little demand for it until sociologists had demonstrated that they could make contributions to medical science. This created research opportunities and some respect for their status on the part of physicians and others. It also enabled sociologists to recognize not only an opportunity for service to the practicing professions, but the possibility that these tasks would facilitate the advance of their discipline itself.[60] The extensive

[58]For a recent statement of the use of these skills, see Jack Elinson, "Methods of Socio-medical Research," in Freeman, Levine, and Reeder, op. cit., pp. 483–500. See also the series on methodology published annually and sponsored by the American Sociological Association, for example, David R. Heise (ed.), Sociological Methodology, 1975, San Francisco: Jossey-Bass, 1974. Special techniques are illustrated in Donald Light, "The Sociological Calendar: An Analytic Tool for Fieldwork Applied to Medical and Psychiatric Training," American Journal of Sociology, 80 (March, 1975), 1145–1164.

[59]See A. B. Hollingshead and F. C. Redlich, Social Class and Mental Illness, New York: Wiley, 1958. This research depended on such studies as Robert S. Lynd and Helen M. Lynd, Middletown, New York: Harcourt, Brace & World, 1929; Robert S. Lynd and Helen M. Lynd, Middletown in Transition, New York: Harcourt, Brace & World, 1937; John Dollard, Caste and Class in a Southern Town, New York: Harper & Row, 1937; W. Lloyd Warner and Paul S. Lunt, The Social Life of a Modern Community, New Haven, Conn.: Yale University Press, 1941; Allison Davis, Burleigh B. Gardner, and Mary R. Gardner, The Deep South, Chicago: University of Chicago Press, 1941; W. Lloyd Warner et al., Democracy in Jonesville, New York: Harper & Row, 1949; W. Lloyd Warner et al., Social Class in America, Chicago: Science Research, 1949; and especially A. B. Hollingshead, Elmtown's Youth, New York: Wiley, 1949.

[60]Manfred Pflanz, "Relations between Social Scientists, Physicians and Medical Organizations in Health Research," Social Science and Medicine, 9 (January, 1975), 7–13; Anthony M. M. Payne, "Integration of Medical and Social Sciences As a Basis for Innovation," Cuadernos Medico-Sociales, 8 (December, 1967), 5–11 (in Spanish); Leonard S. Cottrell and Eleanor B. Sheldon, "Problems of Collaboration between Social Scientsts and the Practicing

bibliographies of the burgeoning literature of medical sociology attest to how much has already been done.[61] And the changing problematics of the fields of medicine discussed above have obviously tremendously facilitated the emergence of medical sociology. It is a field that can rightly be called the result of changing disciplines.

## ROLE OF THE MEDICAL SOCIOLOGIST

In the wake of these developments in psychiatry, public health, administrative medicine, and, indirectly, academic medicine, a host of opportunities for the development of sociologists has arisen. By far the majority of sociologists in the medical field are engaged in research activities, although an increasing number are becoming involved in teaching medical students specialized courses in social epidemiology, public health practice, or hospital administration. Not a few sociologists have accepted administrative roles in medical centers in conjunction either with various research programs or with appointments to medical, nursing, dental, or public health faculties. Some have accepted full-time positions in public health departments or in hospitals as well.[62]

Despite the increasingly rapid, if not dramatic, rise in the number of sociologists engaged in one or more roles in the area of medicine, there remain many unresolved problems. Some of these are only temporary and will eventually be overcome. For example, a sociologist who holds a full-time appointment in a school of medicine is not infrequently the only sociologist and, perhaps, the only social scientist on the staff. In these circumstances, he or she tends to be more or less isolated from colleagues in other academic settings and especially liable to being ignored by medical colleagues, who may or may not be sensitive to what the sociologist's contribution to the general program can be. Then, too, sociologists are often appointed in departments of psychiatry which may be oriented

---

Professions," *Annals of the Academy of Political and Social Science,* 346 (March, 1963), 126–137. See also Ozzie G. Simmons and James A. Davis, "Inter-disciplinary Collaboration in Mental Illness Research," *American Journal of Sociology,* 63 (November, 1957), 297–303; and Mary E. W. Goss, "Collaboration between Sociologist and Physician," *Social Problems,* 4 (July, 1956), 82–89; Donald Young, "Sociology and the Practicing Professions," *American Sociological Review,* 20 (October, 1955), 641–648.

[61]Ozzie G. Simmons and Emil Berkanovic, "Social Research in Health and Medicine: A Bibliography," in Freeman, Levine, and Reeder, *op. cit.,* pp. 523–584. In addition, over one thousand research projects in progress were reported in a survey by the Health Information Foundation. See *An Inventory of Social and Economic Research in Health,* 10th ed., New York: Health Information Foundation, 1965. Marion Pearsall, *Medical Behavioral Science: A Selected Bibliography of Cultural Anthropology, Social Psychology and Sociology in Medicine,* Lexington: University of Kentucky Press, 1963.

[62]Straus, *op. cit.*

toward theories which postulate intrapsychic causes of behavior, thereby creating a value conflict for the sociologist who is committed to theories of social causes of behavior. It may be reasonably anticipated, however, that problems of this sort can be resolved with time and the increase in colleagues engaged in similar endeavors. In addition, sociologists and other behavioral scientists (including physicians) from different institutions have developed a professional association as a mechanism for better communication among members engaged in teaching and research in medical settings. The Association for Behavioral Science and Medical Education (ABSAME) holds meetings twice each year to exchange ideas and techniques for teaching and research (and to reduce the sense of occupational isolation).

More serious are the problems engendered in attempting to apply general sociological theories to the medical field.[63] Since medical sociology is an applied field, it is incumbent upon sociologists to demonstrate their value by solving problems which result in a product with a clear practical utility for their "client"—in this case, the medical professions. Moreover, the sociologist is more or less constrained to use concepts which have some meaning to nonsociological colleagues. Part of the problem, of course, lies in translating concepts which may be useful in pursuing the value of science into similarly meaningful applied concepts. This is not an easy task, to say the least.

These difficulties pertain mostly to sociologists whose major commitment is to some medical institution, i.e., hospital, medical center, school of medicine, or public health department. For sociologists whose interest is in medical sociology, but who operate out of a department of sociology, the pursuit of knowledge in the sociology of medicine may be more acceptable. In fact, their major task is to develop studies in which medical sociology will be able to make some contribution to general sociology. Because they work primarily in terms of interests which are basic to their discipline and which may have little theoretical applied interest, they may have problems in obtaining access to medical settings. Experience has suggested that the development of interdisciplinary research centers provides a way of helping solve not only this problem but that of the isolation of sociologists in practice settings. For example, organizations such as the Medical Care Research Center in St. Louis were developed in the early 1960s with the principal objective of making it possible for members of various social science and medical and nursing disciplines to devote their talents to cooperative research on topics in health and medical care. By 1966–1967, the focus had shifted to more specifically applied and evaluative research

[63]Alvin W. Gouldner, "Theoretical Requirements of the Applied Social Sciences," *American Sociological Review*, 22 (February, 1957), 92–102.

efforts, but again with an interdisciplinary and collaborative effort on the parts of social and medical scientists. In 1976, this emphasis on research on health services delivery was reinforced with the creation of several new centers (and continuation of some previously established ones) in the United States. Despite the shift in emphasis, the opportunities remain great for sociologists to make a contribution to both sociology and medicine. The problems remain also, but they are not unique to medical sociology nor are they unresolvable. The progress made thus far holds promise of even more fruitful collaboration in the future.

## PLAN OF THE BOOK

As we have noted in the beginning of the present chapter, this text represents an effort to discuss some significant areas in the sociology *of* medicine. The discussion bears on a sociological interpretation of various aspects of the field of medicine. Even so, some important areas have been more or less neglected. For example, except for occasional comparisons, we have not included material on mental health or mental illness. Individuals tend to perceive problems engendered by mental diseases as having somewhat special characteristics, and the organizations developed to treat mental illnesses pose special problems for sociological analyses. In addition, it would require a volume larger than the present one to discuss mental health and mental illness properly, and a number of good books are already available.[64] Other areas, such as roles of unorthodox practitioners, have been only briefly treated, mostly to serve as an example of broader sociological phenomena.

The material included in the text is divided into four major areas. The first concerns the nature of health, illness, and disease and the patient's response to them. Chapter 2, for example, is concerned with how much

[64]See, for example, the series published by Basic Books, New York: Leighton, Clausen, and Wilson, *op. cit.;* Marie Jahoda, *Current Concepts of Positive Mental Health,* 1958; Gerald Gurin, Joseph Verhoff, and Sheila Feld, *Americans View Their Mental Health,* 1960; Joint Commission on Mental Illness and Health, *Action for Mental Health,* 1961. See also Frank, *op. cit.;* Milton Greenblatt, Daniel J. Levinson, and Richard Williams (eds.), *The Patient and the Mental Hospital,* New York: Free Press, 1957; Leo F. Srole, Thomas S. Langer, Stanley T. Michael, Marvin K. Opler, and Thomas A. C. Rennie, *Mental Health in the Metropolis: The Midtown Manhattan Study,* vol. 1, New York: McGraw-Hill, 1962; Thomas S. Langner and Stanley T. Michael, *Life Stress and Mental Health: The Midtown Manhattan Study,* vol. 2, New York: Free Press, 1963; Thomas J. Scheff, *Being Mentally Ill,* Chicago: Aldine, 1966; Jerome K. Meyers and Lee L. Bean, *A Decade Later: A Follow-up of Social Class and Mental Illness,* New York: Wiley, 1968; Bruce P. Dohrenwend and Barbara S. Dohrenwend, *Social Status and Psychological Disorder,* New York, Wiley, 1969; David Mechanic, *Mental Health and Social Policy,* Englewood Cliffs, N.J.: Prentice-Hall, 1969; R. Perrucci, *Circle of Madness: On Being Insane and Institutionalized in America,* Englewood Cliffs, N.J.: Prentice-Hall, 1975; and Thomas J. Scheff, *Labeling Madness,* Englewood Cliffs, N.J.: Prentice-Hall, 1975.

disease exists, how one goes about measuring it, and how variations in the rates of different diseases are related to social characteristics. The following chapter is an effort to describe three sociological classes of diseases, each with its own medical characteristics and sociological implications. This section is concluded with a chapter which describes a sociological theory explaining why people differ in their perception of and response to various diseases and illnesses. Thus, the first two chapters of Part One provide a basic orientation for the phenomenon of disease—its characteristics and scope—as it affects *human populations*. The strategies employed by various health agencies to ward off the effects of disease are a direct outgrowth of the knowledge of disease. The last chapter, however, is more concerned about the *individual* and his or her perception of and reaction to disease and the description of social factors which affect behavior.

Part Two focuses on various health practices and health practitioners. The chapter on primitive medicine describes how and why different cultures provide different meanings for the event of illness. It concludes that despite widely divergent understanding of the meaning of disease, there are remarkable continuities which make clear the universal character of medical behavior. Chapter 6 is a brief outline of factors contributing to the emergence and development of Western medicine. It also provides the groundwork for the following chapter, which discusses the importance of professional status and how medicine maintains that status through socialization of the medical student. Here are described the mechanisms by which not only knowledge and skills are taught, but also attitudes, values, and a general perspective on the rest of the world are inculcated. Finally, in this section, the paradigm of professional behavior is related to the growth and activities of other health professions, along with some unorthodox practitioners, which enables us to examine the degree to which they have become professionalized.

The third section is devoted entirely to the hospital as modern society's single most important health organization. Chapter 9 traces the development of the hospital from its origin as a shelter for the poor to its modern role as a multipurpose community center for medical care, education, and research. Chapter 10 relates some research findings on the social organization of the hospital, what kinds of problems arise from occupational and status stratification and the subsequent channelization of communication, and how these problems are solved. Finally, the impact of hospitalization on the patient is considered, combining the social-structural features of the hospital and the social-psychological meaning of illness.

Part Four contains a discussion of three additional factors in medical sociology—the complex nature of medical organization, the cost of financing of medical care, and the "politics" of health care. In Chapter 12, the pros and cons of various forms of private medical practice are noted. But there is more to medical practice than the doctor and the patient. Indeed, there are several supporting organizations without which the modern physician could not practice modern medicine. Included among these are public health agencies, voluntary health agencies, health insurance companies, pharmaceutical companies, and health and hospital-equipment supply groups. A discussion of each of these supporting groups is included.

Concern for the ways in which medical practice is organized is continued in Chapter 13. Here the sheer magnitude of expenditures is noted and the trends discussed. Reasons for increasing health care costs are highlighted, along with an examination of ways in which the public attempts to cope with the economic problems of illness, e.g., health insurance. Finally, there is a discussion of the adequacy of medical care in which the National Health Service of Great Britain is contrasted with the organization of medical services in the United States. This discussion is extended into the final chapter on the politics of health care and sociological aspects of planning, resource allocation, and evaluation.

## SUMMARY

Current trends in the development of both medical practice and sociology suggest an approaching convergence—a recognition of the importance of, and the ability to support, each other. Technically, this mutual awareness is really a "reconvergence," inasmuch as, until the late nineteenth century, a concern for the social dimensions of medicine had always been manifest. For several reasons, both medicine and sociology developed more or less separately from about 1890 until after World War II. Several factors are operating now, however, to bring about a reconvergence. Among these are (1) the change in morbidity experience which has forced medicine to look at chronic diseases, especially their social-psychological components; (2) the development of social psychiatry emphasizing the social causes of mental illness; (3) the changing nature of public health services; (4) the emergence of variegated forms of medical care organization with the community general hospital as the locus of health care for the community; and (5) the development of a mature sociology which was both theoretically and methodologically ready to expand its concerns.

## SUGGESTED READINGS

Freeman, Howard E., Sol Levine, and Leo G. Reeder (eds.), *Handbook of Medical Sociology*, 2d ed., Englewood Cliffs, N.J.: Prentice-Hall, 1972.
Jaco, E. Gartly (ed.), *Patients, Physicians and Illness*, 2d ed., New York: Free Press, 1972.

Somers, Anne R., *Health Care in Transition: Directions for the Future,* Chicago: Hospital Research and Educational Trust, 1971.

Susser, M. W., and W. Watson, *Sociology in Medicine,* 2d ed., New York: Oxford University Press, 1971.

Twaddle, Andrew C., and Richard M. Hessler, *A Sociology of Health,* St. Louis: Mosby, 1977.

Part One

# Disease and the Sick Person

Chapter 2

# Measuring Disease in
# Human Groups

*Medical statistics will be our standard of measurement: we will weigh life for life
and see where the dead lie thicker, among the workers or among the privileged.*

Rudolf Virchow (1821–1902)

From the perspective of the sociologist, the field of medicine has much to
offer in terms of opportunities for studying human behavior. In this regard,
the present chapter and the next one are devoted to consideration of the
relationships between disease and human groups. In many ways, the study
of disease in human groups is analogous to the study of disease in the
individual. In the latter, an attempt is made to understand the course of the
disease process in the human victim through its biochemical, physiological,
and anatomical effects. What parts of the body are affected by disease?
What is the effect on the structure and functioning of the human organism?
How does the body defend itself? Similarly, study of the relationships
between disease and human groups may entertain very similar questions.
How much disease is there and where is it found in a human population?

How does disease affect the structure and functioning of human groups? How do groups organize to defend themselves against disease?

Answers to these and related questions are important for both the development of theory and the application of sociological knowledge. In the first place, the study of social processes in a group context must take into account environmental influences[1] of which disease is certainly one. The variety of attitudes, values, beliefs, and practices found among different groups is reflected in their response to the presence of disease (among other things). For example, attitudes toward and beliefs about pain affect the use of medical care facilities and services. Changing attitudes toward old people in a society may be related to increased longevity of a population because of shifts in the causes of death.

Second, in a more practical vein, answers to these questions give some insight into what kinds of diseases we have to deal with and how large the problem is. Knowledge about the scope of diseases and how they are distributed in the population helps determine the burden of disease as it is related to subgroups in the population. That is, some diseases are found mostly among impoverished groups, others among the wealthy. Some diseases find victims without regard to social class. Similarly, some diseases are most likely to occur in children, others in middle-aged persons, still others in old people. Some diseases are most common among men, others in women. Knowledge of this kind points to target groups which could benefit most from action programs as well as identifying areas needing further research. For example, if it is known that a certain disease most often afflicts a particular sex or particular age group or social class, then preventive or restorative efforts can be focused on that group.[2] Similarly, if the appearance of considerable numbers of cases of some disease cannot adequately be explained, research efforts on such a problem could be intensified.

An example of such an event is the increasing number of new cases of venereal disease that have been reported. From the end of World War II in 1945–1946 until 1957, reported new cases of venereal diseases had been declining each year, but since 1957 they have been increasing. From 1957 to

[1]Paul M. Insel and Rudolph H. Moos (eds.), *Health and the Social Environment,* Lexington, Mass.: Heath, 1974.

[2]An eighteen-year prospective study of a small community produced data allowing investigators to identify persons most likely to develop specific diseases or experience incidents of illness. See Thomas R. Dawber, William B. Kannel, and Philip A. Wolf, "An Evaluation of the Epidemiology of Atherothrombotic Brain Infarction," *Health and Society,* 53 (Fall, 1975), 405–488. A general reference to the Framingham project is T. Gordon, P. Sorlie, and W. B. Kannel, *An Epidemiological Investigation of Cardiovascular Disease, Coronary Heart Disease, Atherothrombotic Brain Infarction, Intermittent Claudication. A Multivariate Analysis of Some Factors Related to Their Incidence: The Framingham Study 16 Year Follow-up,* Washington, D.C., Government Printing Office, 1971.

1973 the rate of increase doubled while the number of new cases almost tripled, involving nearly a million cases.[3] The increase in cases of gonorrhea among teen-agers was particularly noticeable. Is this because known remedies are no longer adequate or because teen-agers are more promiscuous now than in previous generations? Or could it be due to more accurate reporting of cases or to the relaxation of effort to provide health education with regard to venereal diseases because they were no longer thought to be a serious problem? Perhaps, it is a combination of several of these factors. In any event, the U.S. Public Health Service is attempting to encourage renewed interest in research on this problem. However, without the knowledge that the number of reported cases is increasing, recognition that there is a problem may have been delayed or never have taken place.

To understand more fully the meaning of disease for human groups, which is presented in detail in Chapter 3, some ways of measuring disease in the community are presented in this chapter. The immediate concern is to describe the principal ways in which data are collected that are most often used in sociological analysis.

## STUDYING THE SCOPE OF DISEASE

The study of the distribution of diseases in a defined population is called epidemiology or, as Webster defines it, "medical science treating of epidemics." Although Webster's definition is historically correct, i.e., early epidemiologic studies were focused on contagious diseases during epidemic outbreaks, the contemporary definition of epidemiology is much broader. Maxcy's definition, for example, is "The field of science dealing with the relationships of the various factors which determine the frequencies and distributions of an infectious process, a disease, or a physiological state in a human community."[4] This definition does not restrict epidemiology to epidemic diseases, but treats chronic diseases and other disabilities as well. Moreover, this approach is not limited to physical health, but has been found to be useful for studying mental illness, suicide, accidents, and other phenomena.[5]

The epidemiologist, then, studies the occurrence and distribution of diseases in a population through the collection of a variety of data from

[3]U.S. Department of Health, Education, and Welfare, *VD Fact Sheet,* HEW Publication No. 74-8195, 1973.

[4]Kenneth F. Maxcy, *Dorland's Illustrated Medical Dictionary,* 24th ed., Philadelphia: Saunders, 1965.

[5]Robert E. L. Faris and H. Warren Dunham, *Mental Disorders in Urban Areas,* Chicago: University of Chicago Press, 1939. See also Ronald W. Maris, *Social Forces in Urban Suicide,* Homewood, Ill.: Dorsey Press, 1969, and Albert P. Iskrant and Paul V. Joliet, *Accidents and Homicide,* Cambridge: Harvard University Press, 1968.

different sources and by constructing logical chains of inference to explain the multiple factors in disease causation.[6] Although interest in the study of diseases in given populations has been present since the early days of medicine,[7] its importance today has been increased by advanced technology and by methods based on scientific principles.[8] Despite marked advances in medical science, however, there is much that remains unknown, especially in regard to chronic, noncommunicable diseases. In addition, many of the diseases most common today are not caused by a single, readily identifiable agent, but seem rather to be the product of the interaction of several factors. In searching for answers to questions about the causes of diseases, it has been found that often we must look beyond a specific individual with a disease to the occurrence and distribution of the disease in a larger group, perhaps even a whole national population—hence the importance of the epidemiologist. That is to say, clues to causes of diseases have been found through observation of the habits, interaction patterns, and customs of particular groups. More than that, answers to community problems of disease have been found through observations of the behavior of the population. Over the years, this kind of approach has led to the discovery that many diseases show predictable increases or decreases in extent which can be attributed to identifiable factors.[9]

### Some Basic Concepts

In conducting his research, the epidemiologist employs some basic concepts as tools for examining the distribution of diseases in a population. Frequently encountered terms would include mortality, morbidity, life expectancy, incidence, and prevalence. *Mortality,* of course, refers to deaths. One is interested not only in the number of deaths from certain diseases in a given population but also in the shifting trends in causes of death. For example, fifty to sixty years ago a leading cause of death was tuberculosis, which annually accounted for 154 deaths per 100,000 persons in the population. Today, this disease accounts for only about 2 deaths per 100,000 population. On the other hand, cancers or malignant neoplasms now are responsible for 160 deaths per 100,000 population, whereas fifty years ago only 76 per 100,000 died because of cancer.[10]

[6]Brian MacMahon and Thomas F. Pugh, *Epidemiology: Principles and Methods,* Boston: Little, Brown, 1970.

[7]Hippocrates, "On Airs, Waters and Places," in Ralph H. Major, *A History of Medicine,* vol. 1, Springfield, Ill.: Charles C Thomas, 1954.

[8]For example, see Abraham M. Lilienfeld, *Foundations of Epidemiology,* New York: Appleton-Century-Crofts, 1976.

[9]MacMahon and Pugh, *op. cit.,* p. 4.

[10]U.S. Bureau of the Census, *Statistical Abstract of the United States, 1964,* Washington, D.C.: Government Printing Office, 1964, and 96th ed., 1975.

The reporting of deaths is probably, by most standards, very adequate or comprehensive, at least in industrialized societies, because a licensed physician must certify as to the cause of every death. It is estimated that, for the United States, between 95 and 97 percent of the deaths are duly certified and reported in the vital statistics.[11] The problem of accuracy of determining the cause of death is another matter, however. If a physician has not been attending a person while alive, there may be some difficulty in diagnosing the precise cause of death. Fifty years ago, many deaths were attributed to old age, consumption, fever, and other ill-defined causes. Improved diagnostic techniques, increased medical knowledge, and greater frequency of visits to the doctor's office have improved the accuracy a good deal. However, in the case of an older person, it is still often difficult to determine if the cause of death was some degenerative disease or an acute episode of a communicable disease or something else. For example, a person who has cancer may succumb to a respiratory infection or a heart attack. Often in these cases, the primary cause of death is difficult to determine.

A much more difficult task is to measure *morbidity,* or the amount of disease in a population. Morbidity is more difficult to measure because although there are objective criteria for death, some people do not always recognize that they have a disease. As we shall see later, the subjective definition of being sick varies considerably from one person to another. Even if one feels sick, treatment may consist of home remedies, or, for some other reason, one's illness may not be brought to the attention of medical authorities. For a variety of reasons, a doctor who examines a patient may decide not to report or even record the results of the examination. Moreover, the law does not require the reporting of all cases of all diseases. To be sure, certain communicable diseases are reportable, such as tuberculosis and poliomyelitis as well as certain childhood diseases like measles, mumps, chicken pox, and some others. Diseases like cancer or cardiovascular diseases are sometimes reported, but information about morbidity does not generally come from routinely submitted reports.

The lack of uniform standards for reporting diseases is only one kind of methodological problem related to the study of morbidity. Another, perhaps more serious, problem is that the study of morbidity from records—whether hospital case records or the records from the offices of private physicians or public health agencies—is limited to the study of *treated* cases of diseases. That is, only the records of patients who have been seen by a health official would be available. There would be no way of determin-

---

[11]Hugh H. Wolfenden, *Population Statistics and Their Compilation,* Chicago: University of Chicago Press, 1954, p. 63.

ing from the records how many cases of disease existed at the time of the study, which had not come to the attention of officials. Obviously, this could lead to underreporting of some diseases. The example of venereal disease, noted above, is a case in point. No one knows exactly how many cases of syphilis are extant today because not every case is brought to the attention of a physician and, furthermore, not every physician agrees that syphilis *ought* to be reported to public health agencies, even though many states require it. Thus, if one studied the records of an official agency, only a portion of the actual number of cases would be included.

Of the two, mortality data are usually much more complete than morbidity data. Not infrequently, mortality data are used to estimate morbidity, but this procedure also involves some important problems. In the first place, not all diseases are fatal, but they may nonetheless be sociologically important because they result in impairment. Thus, nonfatal chronic diseases such as arthritis would tend to be underreported. Similarly, a number of communicable diseases can be combated effectively by medical science; therefore, the number of cases could rise to serious proportions but not be included in mortality statistics because of the intervention of effective therapy. Moreover, mortality data are affected by age; that is, older people die at a faster rate than younger people. Thus, the use of accurate and readily available mortality data for estimating morbidity presents some difficult problems. As we shall see later in this chapter, health surveys of morbidity provide an approach to the study of *true* rather than *treated* morbidity.

Another important concept is *life expectancy,* the average number of years at a given age that a person with characteristics such as sex and race can be expected to live. Here again, one can compare different segments of a population or different populations for variations which yield important information. Anticipating the discussion later in this chapter, it is known that women have a longer life expectancy than men, that whites outlive nonwhites, that with each passing year, the life expectancy of infants born that year increases. For example, Figure 2-1 shows how average length of life has risen since 1900 in the United States and the differential in life expectancy by race and sex.

Two other concepts employed by the epidemiologist are the incidence and prevalence of disease. *Incidence* is the number of new cases which occurs during a given period of time, and *prevalence* is the number of cases that exists at any given point in time. To take a hypothetical example, one can say that on June 30 of a given year, the prevalence of disease X, that is, the number of cases known to exist on that date, in the United States, was 100. Between July 1 and July 31, 10 more cases were reported; i.e., the incidence for July was 10, and the prevalence of disease X in the United

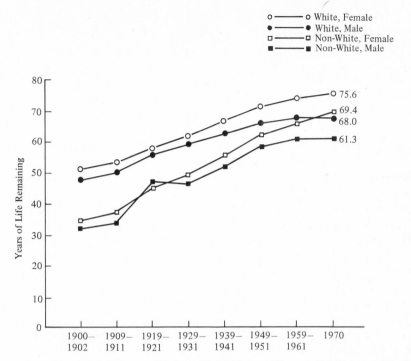

○━━━○ White, Female
●━━━● White, Male
□━━━□ Non-White, Female
■━━━■ Non-White, Male

**Figure 2-1**  Average length of life in the United States. *(Source: U.S. Bureau of the Census, Historical Statistics of the United States, Washington, D.C.: Government Printing Office, 1961, p. 29, and Statistical Abstract of the United States, 1975, p. 59.)*

States on August 1 was 110 (assuming that none of the extant cases recovered or died).

It is important that these two concepts do not become confused, because they are very different for different diseases.[12] For example, the incidence of measles in a community for the last two weeks will approximate the prevalence of that disease. But the incidence of measles in a twelve-month period will be much greater than the prevalence rate because the length of time a person is sick with the disease is about two weeks; thus most of the cases contracted during the year would have recovered by the end of the year. On the other hand, a different relationship exists for chronic, long-term illnesses such as cancer. The case reported in the incidence during one period may still be reported in a prevalence study

[12]John E. Dunn, "The Use of Incidence and Prevalence in the Study of Disease Development in a Population," *American Journal of Public Health,* 52 (July, 1962), 1107–1118; and also in this issue, Sidney Cobb, "A Method for the Epidemiologic Study of a Remittent Disease," 1119–1125.

many months later. The choice of which concept should be used, that is, incidence or prevalence, depends upon the use of the data. If one is interested in studying the spread of a disease, it would be important to know how many persons have contracted the disease since its outbreak. In other words, an incidence study would be appropriate in this case. However, if one wanted to determine what needs a community has in terms of the number of physicians required, amount of drugs and pharmaceuticals, how many hospital beds, etc., one would do a prevalence study.

An analysis of the number of deaths or cases of disease could be misleading, especially if one is examining trends or comparing different populations, because of differences in population size and in the age and sex composition of the population being studied. For this reason, these concepts are usually measured in terms of *rates* to permit comparison of different populations and of variations over time. It should be noted, though, that there are several kinds of rates, each of which permits analysis at different levels.

The simplest rate is called a *crude* (mortality, morbidity) *rate,* which is the number of persons for some unit of the population, usually 1,000 or 100,000, who have the characteristics being measured for some unit of time. In the case of the crude mortality rate, it is the number of persons who die from all causes during a specified period of time. This rate for the United States, for example, is the number of persons who died during a calendar year divided by the estimated population at the midpoint of that year and multiplied by 1,000. In 1972, the crude death rate for the United States was 9.4, computed as follows:

$$\text{Crude death rate} = \frac{1,961,950 \text{ deaths}}{208,837,000 \text{ persons}} \times 1,000 = 9.4$$

However, this rate is useful only for gross comparisons because it obscures the fact that certain age, sex, ethnic, occupational, and other socially identifiable categories have differing rate of sickness and death.

If the only available information on mortality in the United States was the rate of 9.4 deaths per 1,000 population, just calculated in the example above, we would not be able to determine that older people have a higher death rate than young people or that infants have a higher mortality rate than children over one year old or that nonwhites have a higher death rate than whites. In order to make such observations, *age-specific rates* or other "characteristic-specific" rates are computed. In the case of age-specific rates, the number of deaths of persons in a given age category (usually five-year categories) is divided by the number of persons in that age group alive at midyear. For example, in 1972 in the United States

71,250 children under age five died from all causes. The estimated number of children in this age group on June 30, 1972, was 17,242,000. The age-specific death rate *for this age group* would be 4.1 per 1,000 computed as follows:

$$\text{Age-specific death rate} = \frac{71{,}250 \text{ deaths}}{17{,}242{,}00 \text{ children}} \times 1{,}000 = 4.1$$

Age-specific rates permit the investigator to evaluate differences in mortality rates within the same population. The wide variation in death rates is illustrated in the selected age-specific mortality rates per 1,000 population in the United States in 1972:

| | |
|---|---|
| Children under 5 years | 4.1 |
| Children 5 to 14 years | 0.4 |
| Adults 45 to 64 years | 11.3 |
| Adults 75 years and over | 96.2 |

compared with a crude mortality rate of 9.4 for the entire population.[13] Similarly, higher mortality rates for certain diseases are found in the lower socioeconomic classes and, as a corollary, among certain ethnic groups.[14] The information could not be determined, however, from the crude death rates alone.

There is a third type of rate, called the *standardized rate,* in which age-specific rates are adjusted for different proportions of persons in age groupings in different populations to be compared. Suppose, for example, that it was desired to compare the mortality rates of the United States and Chile for 1972. The crude death rate for the United States that year was 9.4 per 1,000 and Chile's was also 9.4 per 1,000.[15] Thus it might be inferred that the health status of the two populations was about the same. But the crude rate would not be an accurate measure, since the age distributions of the populations of the two countries are not the same. Consequently, the standardized rate would be used. It is computed by making the proportion of persons in each age category the same by using a population of one of the countries of some earlier era as the base line. This standard population is then multiplied by the age-specific rates for each sex which exist in each country, the product of which is the number of deaths which would have occurred if each age category was the size of the chosen standard. The

[13]United Nations, *Demographic Yearbook, 1973,* New York: United Nations, 1974.
[14]See, for example, John Kosa, Aaron Antonovsky, and Irving K. Zola (eds.), *Poverty and Health, A Sociological Analysis,* Cambridge: Harvard University Press, 1969.
[15]United Nations, *Demographic Yearbook,* 1973.

number of deaths in each age group is then summed, and a rate per thousand is computed in the usual manner.[16] These calculations are shown in Table 2-1. By controlling for differences in age and sex distributions in the two populations, one can get a more accurate measurement of the difference in mortality rates in the two countries. In this case, the standardized mortality rates clearly favor the United States over Chile. However, had the comparisons between these two countries been made on the basis of the crude death rates, a very different but distorted picture would have emerged. It should also be noted that in the example the largest differences between the two countries are in the rates for children under the age of five years, the rates in other age and sex categories being more comparable. These differences provide further evidence that the population of the United States enjoys a favorable position with respect to mortality because the lower death rates for young children are a reflection of lower infant and neonatal mortality rates. Infant mortality refers to deaths of infants under one year of age. Neonatal mortality refers to deaths in the first twenty-eight days after birth. These rates are usually higher than for any age group except the aged and often are the single most sensitive indicator of the health standards in a population.

## EPIDEMIOLOGIC METHODS

Before considering in detail the steps in epidemiologic investigation, it may be instructive to examine a classic example. In 1855, there occurred in London a terrible outbreak of cholera which had caused over 500 deaths in less than ten days. At the time, Sir John Snow attempted to determine the source of the epidemic in an effort to stop it. In poring over the lists of deceased and afflicted individuals while looking for common factors, he noted that the epidemic was most severe in a particular part of London and that although cases of cholera had been reported in several areas, the majority of them had occurred in the neighborhood of Broad Street. Upon interviewing members of the families of the deceased, Snow was able to isolate a single common factor, namely, the Broad Street pump, from which victims had drunk in every case. Corroborating evidence was obtained from the observation that in the local workhouse, also in the Broad Street area, only a few inmates had contracted cholera and that in every case they had contracted it before being admitted to the workhouse. Snow hypothesized (and found) that the workhouse drew water from a separate well. Similar findings were made in other establishments. The payoff for Snow's careful investigation occurred when, finally convinced

[16]George W. Barclay, *Techniques of Population Analysis,* New York: Wiley, 1958, pp. 161–166.

Table 2-1  Standardized Mortality Rates, United States and Chile (1972)

| Age group | Standardized population United States, 1960 (in thousands) | | United States, 1972 | | | | Chile, 1972 | | | |
|---|---|---|---|---|---|---|---|---|---|---|
| | | | Age-specific death rates per 1,000 | | Number of deaths expected | | Age-specific death rates per 1,000 | | Number of deaths expected | |
| | Males | Females | Males | Females | Males | Females | Males | Females | Males | Females |
| Under 5 | 10,330 | 9,991 | 4.6 | 3.6 | 47,518 | 35,968 | 21.4 | 18.9 | 221,062 | 188,830 |
| 5–14 | 18,028 | 17,346 | 0.5 | 0.3 | 9,014 | 5,204 | 1.0 | 0.7 | 18,028 | 12,142 |
| 15–44 | 34,841 | 36,079 | 2.4 | 1.2 | 83,618 | 43,295 | 4.2 | 2.1 | 146,332 | 75,766 |
| 45–64 | 17,629 | 18,429 | 15.1 | 7.5 | 266,198 | 138,418 | 19.4 | 11.4 | 342,003 | 210,091 |
| Over 65 | 7,503 | 9,057 | 72.4 | 49.5 | 543,217 | 448,322 | 79.4 | 66.6 | 595,738 | 603,196 |
| Total all ages | 88,331 | 90,992 | — | — | 940,565 | 671,007 | — | — | 1,323,163 | 1,090,025 |
| Total all ages, both sexes | 179,323 | | Crude rate = 9.4 | | 1,611,572 | | Crude rate = 9.4 | | 2,413,188 | |
| Standardized rates | | | $\dfrac{1,611,572}{179,323,000} \times 1,000 = 8.99$ | | | | $\dfrac{2,413,188}{179,323,000} \times 1,000 = 13.46$ | | | |

Source: Adapted from United Nations, Demographic Yearbook, 1973, New York: United Nations, 1974.

that impure water from the Broad Street pump was the cause of the cholera, Snow appealed to the authorities to have the pump closed. As a consequence, there was an immediate decline in the number of new cases of cholera. What makes this investigation unusual is the fact that the cholera bacillus was not discovered by Robert Koch until some twenty-eight years after Snow's investigation. Thus, even though Snow did not know the precise cause of cholera, by following a logical sequence of steps he was able to isolate and identify the source of the infection and to prescribe ways of combating it.[17]

To understand more fully the stages of epidemiologic research illustrated in Snow's investigation, it may be helpful to point out the major elements about which information is collected in contemporary investigations, namely, disease agents, the environment, and the human host. *Disease agents* include (1) biologic agents, such as insects, fungi, bacteria, and viruses; (2) nutrient agents, such as fats and carbohydrates; (3) chemical agents, such as gases, dust, and solid particles in the air; and (4) physical agents, such as radiation, temperature, and humidity. The *environment* includes (1) the physical environment, such as weather factors, climate, and geography; (2) the biologic environment, involving the presence or absence of known disease agents cited above; and (3) the social and economic environment of socioeconomic status, type of occupation, location of home, etc. Finally, the *human host* is a consideration of demographic factors such as age, sex, and race as well as physical condition or constitution, habits and customs, and styles of life. The epidemiologist must take all these factors into consideration in any investigation. In Figure 2-2, which diagrammatically depicts the relationship of these elements, clinical investigators would concentrate their efforts on the relationship between the disease agent and the human host. Preventive medicine, on the other hand, focuses its activities mainly on removing or changing aspects of the environment which are deleterious to human health, such as by sanitation or by manipulating the human host in such a way as to prevent harmful aspects of the environment from taking effect, e.g., by immunization programs. Environmental medicine studies the environmental conditions which permit the disease agent to survive in it.[18]

In making an investigation, then, the epidemiologist attempts to answer several questions with respect to some disease. For example, he or she would want to know the *source* of infection, the *means* by which the disease was transmitted to a particular case under study, some characteristics of infected *cases* and the *persons* to whom the infection may have been

[17]John Snow, *On the Mode of Communication of Cholera,* London: Churchill, 1855, reported in MacMahon and Pugh, *op. cit.,* pp. 7–10. See also Berton Roueché, *Curiosities of Medicine,* Boston: Little, Brown, 1958.
    [18]Hugh R. Leavell and E. Gurney Clark (eds.), *Preventive Medicine for the Doctor in His Community: An Epidemiologic Approach,* New York: McGraw-Hill, 1958, pp. 51ff.

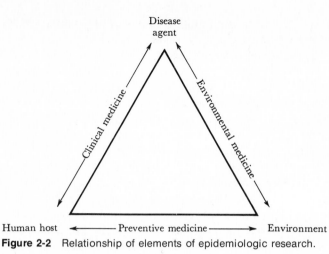

**Figure 2-2** Relationship of elements of epidemiologic research.

passed on, and what *preventive action* can be taken to stop the spread of the disease.[19] However, the broadened definition of epidemiology means that other phenomena besides contagious diseases may be studied using the same methods.[20]

In other words, the investigator looks at characteristics of the disease agent, the host(s), and the environment. Nowadays, the predominance of noninfectious diseases has led the epidemiologist to change the basic questions somewhat, but the method of obtaining the answers remains about the same. In general, the procedure is in three stages: descriptive, analytical, and experimental epidemiology.[21] In the *descriptive* stage, answers to general questions about location, time, and population involved are sought, often through surveys, with the intention of formulating a hypothesis about the observations made in the survey. These hypotheses are then subjected to further examination in the *analytic* process in which more data are collected bearing on the variables in the hypothesis under study. Finally, these results are subjected to *experimentation* under rigorously controlled conditions. At the present time, however, most experimentation is limited to animal subjects, with inferences for human populations.

Throughout all three stages of epidemiologic research, the focus of observation is on a group. It may be on a total population, or on all the cases of a disease reported to a health department, or it may be on a group thought to be "high risk," that is, people who do not yet exhibit symptoms,

[19]Philip E. Sartwell (ed.), *Maxcy-Rosenau Preventive Medicine and Public Health,* 10th ed., New York: Appleton-Century-Crofts, 1973.
[20]Sidney L. Kark, *Epidemiology and Community Medicine,* New York: Appleton-Century-Crofts, 1974.
[21]Sartwell, *op. cit.,* chap. 1.

but who have certain characteristics found to be associated with a specific disease. For example, heavy smokers are thought to be at high risk with respect to the development of lung cancer. In effect, the epidemiologist studies the natural history of a disease in a group, and a clinician is interested in the natural course of a disease in an individual patient.

An example of epidemiologic research has been described by Roueché in *Eleven Blue Men*.[22] In the title story, he described the case of eleven skid row derelicts who were brought to a community hospital, sick and in a cyanotic condition (that is, the skin of their extremities had turned blue). At first, the diagnosis was carbon monoxide poisoning, but further investigation led the epidemiologist to discard this hypothesis because some clinical symptoms of gas poisoning were absent. Instead, the cause was thought to be food poisoning. This hypothesis was later supported when it was found that the victims had in common the fact that they had eaten breakfast at the same restaurant on the same day. Two important questions remained: what food or drink specifically could have caused the poisoning, and why did only these eleven men become ill when literally hundreds of old men had eaten in the same restaurant? Through interviews with the victims, the investigator finally isolated oatmeal as the vector (carrier) of the poisoning, and a careless cook was the cause. It was found through laboratory analysis that the cook had used what he thought was salt or sodium chloride, but which turned out to be sodium nitrite, a mild poison. The answer to the second question—why only eleven cases when hundreds had eaten the oatmeal—took longer to discover. The hypothesis was formulated that perhaps the same error had been made in filling the saltshakers on the individual tables. Investigation showed that of all the saltshakers, only one contained sodium nitrite, the one on the table at which all eleven men had sat. The riddle was finally solved when it was remembered that some people—especially alcoholics—use salt instead of sugar on oatmeal to replace the salt deficiency in their blood. As it turned out, the amount of sodium nitrite in the oatmeal was not sufficient to be toxic, but when "salt" was added the amount became toxic; hence only the eleven men who sat at that particular table and put "salt" on their oatmeal became ill.

The improved quality of recent epidemiologic studies is shown in the case of cigarette smoking and the development of lung cancer and other diseases. Early descriptive studies, reported in 1964 by the Office of the Surgeon General, revealed that (1) the incidence of lung cancer was rising, (2) the majority of lung cancer patients have a history of smoking, and (3) more males than females developed the disease.[23] Analytic studies were then developed to test the hypothesis from early studies that cigarette

[22]Berton Roueché, *Eleven Blue Men*, Boston: Little, Brown, 1947.
[23]Report of the Advisory Committee to the Surgeon General of the Public Health Service, *Smoking and Health*, U.S. Public Health Service Publication 1103, Washington, D.C.: Government Printing Office, 1964.

smoking was causally linked to lung cancer. In the 1967 report by the Surgeon General, the earlier trends had been confirmed and more clearly specified. Deaths from lung cancer were rising rapidly. Males who smoked less than one pack per day had a mortality ratio from lung cancer 10 times greater than nonsmokers. For heavy smokers (more than one pack per day), the ratio was 30 times greater. Mortality rates for female smokers also had risen although they remained lower than rates for males.[24]

Not only were rates of mortality and morbidity from lung cancer correlated with cigarette smoking, but associations were also established between the latter and general mortality rates and a host of other diseases: cardiovascular diseases, chronic pulmonary diseases, and cancer at other sites, especially the mouth, larynx, and esophagus.[25] The 1973 Surgeon General's report summarized research that further specified the greater risks of developing these diseases by smokers. Data were presented from several studies which led to the following conclusions about cigarette smoking:

**1**  It is a major risk factor in development of coronary heart disease and peripheral vascular diseases.

**2**  It is associated with increased prevalence of respiratory symptoms, decreased pulmonary function and pulmonary emphysema.

**3**  It is the major cause of lung cancer and increases the risk of cancer at other sites.

**4**  It is associated with "problem" pregnancies (low birth weight, stillbirth, spontaneous abortion, and infant mortality).

**5**  It is associated with greater mortality from peptic ulcer disease.[26]

The 1973 report also provided information on experimental studies to test further the causal relationships between smoking and disease that had been demonstrated in the analytic studies. Because of the high risk, experimental production of cancer, pulmonary and coronary disease, and problem pregnancies has been limited to laboratory animals. These studies, however, do support conclusions drawn from the analytic epidemiologic investigations.[27]

[24]Daniel Horn, "Health Consequences of Smoking," in Edgar F. Borgatta and Robert R. Evans (eds.), *Smoking, Health and Behavior,* Chicago: Aldine, 1968, pp. 52–80.

[25]*Ibid.,* pp. 69–78.

[26]U.S. Department of Health, Education, and Welfare, *The Health Consequences of Smoking,* Washington, D.C.: Government Printing Office, 1973.

[27]Some typical examples would be O. Auerback, E. C. Hammond, D. Kirman, and L. Garfinkel, "Effects of Cigarette Smoking on Dogs, II: Pulmonary Neoplasms," *Archives of Environmental Health,* 21 (December, 1970), 754–768; R. Rylander, "Lung Clearance of Particles and Bacteria: Effects of Cigarette Smoke Exposure," *Archives of Environmental Health,* 23 (November, 1971), 321–326; B. Bhagat, A. Ruehl, P. Rao, M. W. Rana, and M. J. Hughes, "Effect of Cigarette Smoke on the Cardiovascular System in Dogs," *Proceedings of the Society for Experimental Biology and Medicine,* 137 (July, 1971), 969–972.

Epidemiologic methods have also been applied to health problems even more complex than those involving cancer and smoking behavior. These relate to the current interest in the relationships of human behavior and social and environmental stress to the onset of physical and mental disorders.[28] As we noted in Chapter 1, the search for causal factors in chronic diseases has shifted from single factors (biologic agents) that were typical for communicable diseases to multiple factors that include both biologic agents in the environment and socially derived "stress" factors. Although many methodological issues of definition of stress, of sampling populations and research design to permit inferences of causation remain unresolved, several investigations have provided suggestive, if not always consistent, data. For example, Dohrenwend reviewed much of the current literature linking cultural and psychological factors with the development of symptoms of mental illnesses.[29] Some factors identified were life events[30] and conditions of personal influence.[31] Stressful life events were also associated with the development of physical illness,[32] especially chronic conditions.[33] A more sociological perspective has attempted to link characteristics of the individual (host) with the social environment (behavior) and physical environment (pollutants),[34] with population density,[35] and with social mobility.[36] A broader, anthropological view cited the ramifications of social change in non-Western societies as associated with development of various diseases.[37]

[28]Sol Levine and Norman A. Scotch (eds.), *Social Stress,* Chicago: Aldine, 1970.

[29]Bruce P. Dohrenwend, "Socio-cultural and Social-psychological Factors in the Genesis of Mental Disorders," *Journal of Health and Social Behavior,* 16 (December, 1975), 365–392. This issue contains four other review articles on stress and disease.

[30]Barbara S. Dohrenwend and Bruce P. Dohrenwend (eds.), *Stressful Life Events: Their Nature and Effects,* New York: Wiley, 1974. See also Jerome K. Myers, Jacob J. Lindenthal, and Max Pepper, "Life Events, Social Integration and Psychiatric Symptomatology," *Journal of Health and Social Behavior,* 16 (December, 1975), 421–429.

[31]Curt Mettlin and Joseph Woelfel, "Interpersonal Influence and Symptoms of Stress," *Journal of Health and Social Behavior,* 15 (December, 1974), 311–319.

[32]T. Theorell, E. Lind, and B. Floderus, "The Relationship of Disturbing Life Changes and Emotions to the Early Development of Myocardial Infarction and Other Serious Illnesses," *International Journal of Epidemiology,* 4 (December, 1975), 281–295.

[33]Ernest M. Gruenberg, Danielle Turns, Steven P. Segal, and Murray Solomon, "Social Breakdown Syndrome: Environmental and Host Factors Associated with Chronicity," *American Journal of Public Health,* 62 (January, 1972), 91–94.

[34]Saxon Graham, "The Sociological Approach to Epidemiology," *American Journal of Public Health,* 64 (November, 1974), 1046–1049.

[35]Douglas L. Carnahan, Avery M. Guest, and Omer R. Galle, "Congestion, Concentration and Behavior: Research in the Study of Urban Population Density," *Sociological Quarterly,* 15 (Autumn, 1974), 488–506.

[36]Patrick M. Horan and Bradford H. Gray, "Status Inconsistency, Mobility and Coronary Heart Disease," *Journal of Health and Social Behavior,* 15 (December, 1974), 300–310.

[37]Solomon H. Katz and Anthony F. C. Wallace, "An Anthropological Perspective on Behavior and Disease," *American Journal of Public Health,* 64 (November, 1974), 1050–1052. See also Joseph Eyer, "Hypertension as a Disease of Modern Society," *International Journal of Health Services,* 5 (Fall, 1975), 539–558.

These results of empirical investigations often are contradictory and seem seldom to be interrelated in any theoretically comprehensible way. In part this is due to development of theoretical explanations largely along disciplinary lines. Bahnson, for example, has summarized much of the psychological perspective linking symptoms of mental and physical diseases with disturbances in psychological processes.[38] Somatic symptoms can result when organ systems are selected cognitively and symbolically for expression of unresolved conflict and when organ systems are related to emotions in which secondary physiological effects produce strain on selected tissues, thereby contributing to later symptom formation. Thus, a situation that results in anger may lead, over time, to hypertension (elevated blood pressure) and to gastric hyperacidity (overproduction of acids in the digestive tract). Another example of work reviewed associated the development of diseases like cancer with alterations in immunological processes (natural protection) where the intervening psychological process was depression over "object loss" such as death of a spouse.

A sociological perspective follows the model of epidemiologic investigation, but focuses on diseases in relation to concepts such as social roles described in terms of age and sex, marital status, social class, and place of residence. These are associated with social stress induced by status inconsistency, perceived deprivation, rapid change in cultural standards, loss of family ties, etc.[39] A more ecologically based social theory views physical and mental diseases as the end result of an "ecological chain" in which the physical and social environments provide a setting influencing the outcomes of interaction of behavior patterns and characteristics of the host.[40] Thus, the physical environment might involve degree of pollution; the social environment takes into consideration attributes of social class, occupation, and housing location; behavior patterns include factors such as smoking, diet, work habits as they influence the host in terms of genetic makeup, physiological functioning, attributes of status, and role. The vectors (carriers) are identified in terms of tars and nicotine, alcohol, and calories, but also in terms of social stress and coping behavior.

As we noted above, no unidisciplinary theoretical framework could account for the wide variety of findings linking onset of symptoms with stressful situations. Some writers have rejected adopting any single theory because conceptual limitations do not permit understanding of the whole process which they claim is larger than any of its constituent parts. Rather,

---

[38]Claus Bahne Bahnson, "Epistomological Perspectives of Physical Disease from the Psychodynamic Point of View," *American Journal of Public Health,* 64 (November, 1974), 1034–1040.

[39]Leonard S. Syme, "Behavioral Factors Associated with the Etiology of Physical Disease: A Social Epidemiological Approach," *American Journal of Public Health,* 64 (November, 1974), 1043–1045.

[40]Graham, *op. cit.*

they urge adoption of a "multiplex variable" which takes into account the combined effects of several variables whose sum is larger than any of the parts and whose parts are not in fixed relationship to one another.[41] A similar view was promoted by Cassel, who argued that the effort to link stress with *specific* diseases has misled researchers because psychological and socioenvironmental processes are unlikely to be directly pathogenic.[42] Rather, understanding of the processes will come from efforts to generalize findings from research to social situations broadly rather than trying to link stress with specific disease entities. For example, laboratory studies of crowding in rats have produced various diseases and maladaptive behaviors. Efforts to link crowding with specific diseases in human situations have been inconclusive, at best. The point is that diseases in human groups are not linked to crowding per se, but to its consequences, such as social disorganization, domination and subordination, presence of "social buffers," and generalized stress.[43]

## HEALTH SURVEYS

The foregoing examples illustrate the fact that there are several methods employed in the conduct of epidemiologic research. These methods, ranging from laboratory tests to epidemiologic field investigations, provide many answers for questions concerning sources and transmission routes of disease as well as numbers of new cases which are reported over a period of time. However, in addition to incidence of diseases, epidemiologists (and others) are interested in prevalence of diseases, how much exists in large populations, in discovering cases not yet reported, and in locating persons who are most likely to contract or develop a disease but have not yet developed any symptoms, i.e., "persons at risk." To answer these questions, household surveys of samples of the population are used, particularly to study the prevalence of morbid conditions.

To date, there have been four major surveys of the prevalence of morbidity in the United States. The first was in 1926 in Hagerstown, Maryland, conducted by the U.S. Public Health Service, in which some

---

[41]Eric J. Cassell and Michael D. Lebowitz, "Causality in the Environment and Health: The Utility of the Multiplex Variable," *Perspectives in Biology and Medicine,* 19 (Spring, 1976), 338–343.

[42]John Cassel, "Psychosocial Processes and 'Stress': Theoretical Formulation," *International Journal of Health Services,* 4 (Summer, 1974), 471–482.

[43]John Cassel, "An Epidemiological Perspective of Psychosocial Factors in Disease Etiology," *American Journal of Public Health,* 64 (November, 1974), 1040–1043. This broader approach has already led to recommendations for health education programs. See John W. Farguhar, Nathan Maccoby, Alfred L. McAlister, and Carl E. Thoreson, "Behavioral Science Applied to Cardiovascular Health: Progress and Research Needs in the Modification of Risk-Taking Habits in Adult Populations," *Health Education Monographs,* 4 (Spring, 1976), 45–67.

7,500 families were interviewed in an attempt to assess how much sickness had been present in the household for the past five years.[44] During the 1930s, the Eastern Health District of Baltimore Survey, conducted by Johns Hopkins University, was begun in an effort to collect similar data.[45] The third survey, and first on a national scale, was conducted between 1935 and 1937 by the U.S. Public Health Service.[46] This first National Health Survey investigated some 40,000 individuals in an effort to determine the amount and types of sickness, the frequency with which health professions had been utilized, the cost of care, and other information.

At the present time, the U.S. Public Health Service is carrying out a second National Health Survey which began in 1956 and continues today, in an effort to determine, on a sample basis, the extent of morbidity in the United States. The current survey is designed to meet several needs arising from the recognition of healthy people as a great natural resource. The information collected in these surveys is used by directors of health programs, social security, and vocational rehabilitation programs to assess the future requirements for their clients. Survey data are also used frequently in medical research to seek answers to questions about causation, incidence, and problems of acute and chronic ailments. More recently, these data have become important to social science research in assessing the extent of illness and disability in relation to sociological and psychological factors, economics, and political science.[47]

Specifically, the U.S. National Health Survey program has three major tasks. The first, of course, is a continuing collection of data on the amount and kind of illness and the frequency and type of medical care services received in relation to demographic and sociological variables such as age, sex, and place of residence. The second task is that of conducting a special survey, known as the health examination survey, which attempts to collect information that reveals undiagnosed illness and latent disease states in the

[44]Edgar Syndenstricker, "A Study of Illness in a General Population Group," *Public Health Reports,* 41 (September, 1926), 2069–2088. See also the following report, "Reporting of Notifiable Diseases in a Typical Small City," *Public Health Reports,* 41 (October, 1926), 2186–2191.

[45]Jean Downes and S. D. Collins, "A Study of Illness among Families in the Eastern Health District of Baltimore," *Milbank Memorial Fund Quarterly,* 18 (January, 1940), 5–26.

[46]George St. J. Perrott, Clark Tibbits, and R. H. Britten, "The National Health Survey: Scope and Method of the Nationwide Canvas of Sickness in Relation to Its Social and Economic Setting," *Public Health Reports,* 54 (September, 1939), 1663–1687.

[47]See, for example, David Mechanic, *Public Expectations and Health Care,* New York: Wiley, 1972; Lu Ann Aday and Ronald Anderson, *Access to Medical Care,* Ann Arbor, Mich.: Health Administration Press, 1975; Gordon E. Moss, *Illness, Immunity and Social Interaction: The Dynamics of Biosocial Resonation,* New York: Wiley, 1973; Seymour E. Harris, *The Economics of Health Care,* Berkeley, Calif.: McCutcheon Press, 1975; and Stephen P. Strickland, *Politics, Science and Dread Disease,* Cambridge, Mass.: Harvard University Press, 1972.

population as a whole. These data are particularly useful in estimating the response of the individual to various types of disease. Finally, the third major task is to work at continuous improvement of survey methodology, including increasing the representativeness of the sample and improving the interview schedules.[48]

In addition to these major surveys, there have been a number of more limited surveys of specific communities and of specific diseases in the population.[49] These have also contributed information which allows comparison of local and regional variations with the total population.[50] One must be cautious in interpreting morbidity data collected in surveys, however, because many of these studies are based in part on "treated" prevalence as opposed to "real" prevalence. That is, often the sources of data on the prevalence of some disease are populations of treated cases. For example, study of a sample of cancer patients taken from a hospital's tumor register would not reveal the amount of undiagnosed cancer in the community's population. Other surveys, such as the Health Examination Survey, attempt to estimate the real prevalence of a disease by finding cases of undiagnosed or untreated disease along with the treated cases in a representative sample of the whole population.

Despite the care taken to establish a representative sample of the population and to develop a questionnaire which would yield valid answers to perplexing problems about the amount of disease in the population, several criticisms have been made of the surveys. In the first place, according to one writer, these surveys are merely a collection of facts which will not affect, in any measurable way, the response of the community.[51] In fact, no action at all is implied from facts about illness. Of course,

[48]U.S. Department of Health, Education, and Welfare, *Health Statistics*, ser. A-1, Washington, D.C.: Government Printing Office, 1958, p. 7.
    [49]Earl L. Koos, *The Health of Regionville*, New York: Columbia University Press, 1954. See also Solon T. Kimball and Marion Pearsall, *The Talladega Story*, University: University of Alabama Press, 1954.
    [50]H. F. Dorn and S. J. Cutler, *Morbidity from Cancer in the United States*, Public Health Monograph 56, Washington, D.C.: Government Printing Office, 1959; W. Haenszel, S. C. Marcus, and E. G. Zimmerer, *Cancer Morbidity in Urban and Rural Iowa*, Public Health Monograph 37, Washington, D.C.: Government Printing Office, 1956; Johannes Ipsen, "Prevalence and Incidence of Multiple Sclerosis in Boston," *Archives of Neurology and Psychiatry*, 64 (November, 1950), 631–640. For surveys of mental illness, see Marvin K. Opler, "Epidemiological Studies of Mental Illness," in *Symposium of Preventive and Social Psychiatry*, Walter Reed Army Institute of Research, Washington, D.C., 1958, 111–145. From an international perspective, see Kerr L. White, Donald O. Anderson, Thomas W. Bice, Esko Kalimo, and Elizabeth Schach, "Health Care: An International Comparison of Perceived Morbidity, Health Services Resources and Use," *International Journal of Health Services*, 6 (Summer, 1976), 199–218.
    [51]Andrew C. Fleck, "A Public Administrator Looks at Chronic Illness Surveys," *Public Health Reports*, 77 (December, 1962), 1077–1080.

a collection of facts can provide the base line of information with which action programs can be planned, and this is one of the stated purposes of the survey data.[52] A second, more serious, problem is the over- or underreporting of certain disease categories or experiences with sickness. For example, the underreporting of hospitalization reaches serious proportions with length of time since discharge and varies inversely with length of stay. That is, a patient who had been discharged from a hospital for several months and who was in the hospital for only a short time is less likely to report that hospitalization occurred than a former patient who was discharged more recently or stayed in the hospital longer. Furthermore, underreporting increases when disease is seen by the respondent as being threatening, such as cancer and syphilis.[53] Finally, but not exhaustively, the criticism has been made that large discrepancies are found when interview data on illness are compared with clinical examinations.[54] However, as Woolsey et al. pointed out, surveys are not designed to replace clinical examinations, but are used for entirely different purposes, e.g., program planning and cost estimation.[55] Moreover, at least one recent study reported a high positive correlation between self-reports of illness and doctors' reports of illness in the same subject.[56]

Proponents of health surveys are quick to point out that, in addition to providing the basic knowledge on which programs can be established, survey data also yield much information about the interrelationship of health and demographic characteristics and can be used to collect special data, such as attitudinal information, which can be correlated with data on

[52]Theodore D. Woolsey, Philip S. Lawrence, and Eva Balamuth, "An Evaluation of Chronic Disease Prevalence Data from the Health Interview Survey," *American Journal of Public Health,* 52 (October, 1962), 1631–1637.

[53]Walt R. Simmons and E. Earl Bryant, "An Evaluation of Hospitalization Data from the Health Interview Survey," *American Journal of Public Health,* 52 (October, 1962), 1638–1647.

[54]Barkev F. Sanders, "Have Morbidity Surveys Been Oversold?" *American Journal of Public Health,* 52 (October, 1962), 1648–1659. More recent studies continue to cite the problem of discrepancy between information reported in interviews and clinic records. See John R. Moore, "Accuracy of Health Interview Surveys in Measuring Chronic Illness Prevalence," *Health Services Research,* 10 (Summer, 1975), 162–167; Leon Gordis, Milton Markowitz, and Abraham M. Lilienfeld, "The Inaccuracy in Using Interviews to Estimate Patient Reliability in Taking Medications at Home," *Medical Care,* 7 (January–February, 1969), 49–54; and John Kosa, Joel J. Alpert, and Robert J. Haggerty, "On the Reliability of Family Health Information—A Comparative Study of Mothers' Reports on Illness and Related Behavior," *Social Science and Medicine,* 1 (July, 1967), 165–181.

[55]Woolsey et. al., *op. cit.*

[56]George L. Maddox and Elizabeth B. Douglass, "Self-assessment of Health: A Longitudinal Study of Elderly Subjects," *Journal of Health and Social Behavior,* 14 (March, 1973), 87–93. See also H. J. Friedsam and Harry W. Martin, "A Comparison of Self and Physician's Health Ratings in an Older Population," *Journal of Health and Human Behavior,* 4 (Fall, 1963), 179–183.

health status and medical behavior.[57] Furthermore, data from household surveys have been useful in providing information on estimates of health care needs of a population[58] and for assessing outcomes of health services programs.[59]

## INTERPRETATION OF EPIDEMIOLOGIC DATA

Now that we have some idea of the methodology and concepts used in epidemiology, we can turn to sociological implications of some data. The purpose here is twofold. First, the presentation of these data gives some indication as to the extent of disease present in different populations and the direction of changes in trends. Second, and more important, these data will permit us to explore some relationships between sociological factors and disease in human populations.

### Sex, Age, and Disease

Although it may be common knowledge that patterns of disease vary with sex and age, it is probably not so well known how the pattern varies or the extent to which it varies. Look, for example, at the data for the United States presented in Table 2-2. Several features stand out clearly. First of all, there has been a consistent decline in the death rates for both sexes and races since 1900. Second, it is noted that the greatest improvement has been made for both sexes in the nonwhite category. Third, and more germane to the topic here, is the observation that, within racial groups,

[57]See, for example, Robert L. Berg (ed.), *Health Status Indexes*, Chicago: Hospital Research and Educational Trust, 1973; also Thomas S. Langner, Joanne C. Gerster, and Jeanne Eisenberg, "Approaches to Measurement and Definition in the Epidemiology of Behavior Disorders: Ethnic Background and Child Behavior," *International Journal of Health Services*, 4 (Summer, 1974), 483–501.

[58]Richard M. Scheffler and Joseph Lipscomb, "Alternative Estimations of Population Health Status: An Empirical Example," *Inquiry*, 11 (September, 1974), 220–228. See also Esko Kalimo and Kai Sievers, "The Need for Medical Care: Estimation on the Basis of Interview Data," *Medical Care*, 6 (January–February, 1968), 1–17. More recently, see Sidney Katz and Akpom C. Amechi, "A Measure of Primary Sociobiological Functions," *International Journal of Health Services*, 6 (Summer, 1976), 493–507, and, in the same issue, Athilia Siegmann, "A Classification of Sociomedical Health Indicators: Perspectives for Health Administrators and Health Planners," pp. 521–538.

[59]Cf., for example, the use of the "Sickness Impact Profile." Betty S. Gilson, John S. Gilson, Marilyn Bergner, Ruth Bobbitt, Shirley Kressel, William Pollard, and Michael Vesselago, "Development of an Outcome Measure of Health Care," *American Journal of Public Health*, 65 (December, 1975), 1304–1310. Related reports by this research team include "The Sickness Impact Profile: Validation of a Health Status Measure," *Medical Care*, 14 (January, 1976), 57–67; "The Sickness Impact Profile: Reliability of a Health Status Measure," *Medical Care*, 14 (February, 1976), 146–155; and "The Sickness Impact Profile: Conceptual Formulation and Methodology for the Development of a Health Status Measure," *International Journal of Health Services*, 6 (Summer, 1976), 393–415. See also Willime Carr and Samuel Wolfe, "Unmet Needs As Sociomedical Indicators," *International Journal of Health Services*, 6 (Summer, 1976), 417–430.

**Table 2-2   Mortality Rates per 1,000 Population by Sex and Race,
United States, 1900–1973**

| Year | Total | White | | Nonwhite | |
|------|-------|-------|--------|----------|--------|
| | | Male | Female | Male | Female |
| 1900 | 17.2 | 17.7 | 16.3 | 25.7 | 24.4 |
| 1910 | 14.7 | 15.4 | 13.6 | 22.3 | 21.0 |
| 1920 | 13.0 | 13.0 | 12.1 | 17.8 | 17.5 |
| 1930 | 11.3 | 11.7 | 9.8 | 17.4 | 15.3 |
| 1940 | 10.8 | 11.6 | 9.2 | 15.1 | 12.6 |
| 1950 | 9.6 | 10.9 | 8.0 | 12.5 | 9.9 |
| 1960 | 9.5 | 10.9 | 8.0 | 11.4 | 8.6 |
| 1970 | 9.5 | 10.9 | 8.1 | 11.2 | 7.8 |
| 1973 | 9.4 | 10.7 | 8.2 | 10.8 | 7.6 |

*Source:* U.S. Bureau of the Census, *Statistical Abstract of the United States, 1962,* Washington, D.C.: Government Printing Office, 1962, table 67, p. 63; U.S. Bureau of the Census, *Statistical Abstract of the United States, 1975,* Washington, D.C.: Government Printing Office, 1975, p. 61.

males have consistently higher mortality rates than females. Since 1950, females of either race have had lower mortality rates than males. When one looks at morbidity data, however, the picture is very different. From the data shown in Table 2-3, it can be seen that with respect to acute conditions, females are affected more often than males, except for injuries. Similarly, the percentage of persons (1969) with one or more chronic conditions was 47.3 percent for females and 43.4 percent for males.[60] Moreover, it should be pointed out that in 1973, the number of days lost by restricted activity was 18.1 for females and 14.7 for males.[61]

The explanation of the sex differentiation in mortality and morbidity rates is partly biological and partly sociological. For example, it can be

**Table 2-3   Number of Acute Conditions per 100 Persons, by Sex,
United States, 1974**

| Condition group | Total | Male | Female |
|-----------------|-------|------|--------|
| Infectious and parasitic diseases | 19.5 | 18.1 | 20.9 |
| Respiratory conditions | 94.4 | 92.2 | 96.5 |
| Digestive system conditions | 7.8 | 6.0 | 9.5 |
| Injuries | 30.4 | 36.0 | 25.2 |
| All other acute conditions | 23.5 | 19.2 | 27.5 |

*Source:* Adapted from National Center for Health Statistics, *Current Estimates from the Health Interview Survey,* U.S., 1974, ser. 10, no. 100, Washington, D.C.: Government Printing Office, 1975, p. 7.

[60]National Center for Health Statistics, *Health Characteristics by Color,* ser. 10, no. 56, Washington, D.C.: Government Printing Office, 1969, p. 5.
[61]*Statistical Abstract of the United States, 1975,* table 133, p. 85.

shown that in any given year, more males than females are born; that is, the sex ratio at birth favors males. Yet at any given stage of life it can be seen that there is always an excess of females; that is, death rates are higher for males than females in every age category. One explanation is that females are physiologically stronger than males.[62] But one can also account for the lower female mortality rate in later years because in our culture, despite the women's liberation movement, females are defined as the weaker sex and they more often take precautionary measures to protect their health. Moreover, social role definitions in our society prescribe certain activities for males which, more often than for females, expose them to dangerous environmental conditions such as mining and heavy labor. This, too, may affect the mortality and morbidity rates. Similarly, cultural definitions with respect to competition, or more generally, the conduct of relationships with others in the workaday world, are thought to increase the chances for males to develop certain diseases and disabilities more frequently than females.[63] For example, for diseases with a primarily biological cause, such as diabetes or arthritis, the morbidity rate for females exceeds that of males. In the case of arthritis it is nearly double, 80.7 per 1,000 for females and 46.1 per 1,000 for males. In part, this may reflect the greater number of females than males in the older age groups, where these diseases are most common. For diseases or injuries thought to be associated with social stress, such as ulcers, or physical exertion, such as hernias, the rates for males are greater than for females. For ulcers, the rates (1973) were 22.0 per 1,000 for males and 12.6 for females.[64] The 1973 rates for hernias were 20.9 and 12.6 per 1,000 for males and females, respectively. For still other diseases or conditions in which biological and sociological influences cannot readily be distinguished, the rates are more nearly the same. For instance, the prevalence of asthma is 31.7 and 28.8 per 1,000 per males and females, respectively; for dental conditions, 1.6 and 1.8 per 1,000; for visual impairments, 50.8 per 1,000 for males and 44.2 per 1,000 for females.[65]

[62]Ashley Montagu, *The Natural Superiority of Women,* New York: Macmillan, 1954.

[63]Jean Downes and Margaret Keller, "The Risk of Disability for Persons with Chronic Disease," *Milbank Memorial Fund Quarterly,* 30 (October, 1952), 311–340. A more recent report emphasizes the relationship between illness as a function of the number and character of role obligations. See Constance A. Nathanson, "Illness and the Feminine Role: A Theoretical Review," *Social Science and Medicine,* 9 (February, 1975), 57–62. Another report suggests that sex differentials may be an artifact of females' interview and illness behavior. See Lois M. Verbrugge, "Sex Differentials in Morbidity and Mortality in the United States," *Social Biology,* 23 (Winter, 1976), 275–296.

[64]It is interesting to speculate on the relationship between changes in rates of ulcers and the increased participation of women in the work force. In the past ten years, the rates have not changed for men, but they have increased by 64 percent for women.

[65]National Center for Health Statistics, *Prevalence of Selected Chronic Respiratory Conditions,* 1970, ser. 10, no. 84, Washington, D.C.: Government Printing Office, 1973; National Center for Health Statistics, *Prevalence of Chronic Digestive Conditions,* 1968, ser. 10, no. 83, Washington, D.C.: Government Printing Office, 1973.

With respect to different age groups, we find further differentiation of the extent and type of disease. The data presented in Table 2-4 clearly show the consistent decline in death rates since 1900 in almost all age groups, but especially in infants under one year of age. The great reduction in the infant mortality rate is an important factor in the increase and change in composition in the world's population. It can be further noted from Table 2-4 that in the United States, if a person survives the first year of life, he or she has a very good chance of growing old. Note, however, that after passing the puberty stage, the death rates begin to climb and increase rapidly with advancing years.

With respect to morbidity, there is a further interesting age differentiation. Among younger age groups, the rates for acute ailments, such as infectious and parasitic diseases and respiratory conditions, are higher than for older age groups. On the other hand, the rates for chronic conditions, such as heart disease, cancer, diabetes, and arthritis, increase with age. For example, in 1974 the rate per 100 persons of all infectious diseases was 47.4 for a population under 6 years old, but only 8.0 for those over age 45.[66] Persons with a heart condition, however, had a rate per 100 population of 2.5 for the 17- to 44-year age group, but 199.0 for those 65 and older.[67] Moreover, there is a consistency of trend rates between the extremes for acute and chronic conditions.

**Table 2-4    Death Rate per 1,000 Population by Age, United States, 1900–1973**

| | Year | | | | | | | | |
|---|---|---|---|---|---|---|---|---|---|
| Age group | 1900 | 1910 | 1920 | 1930 | 1940 | 1950 | 1960 | 1970 | 1973 |
| All ages | 17.2 | 14.7 | 14.2 | 11.3 | 10.8 | 9.6 | 9.5 | 9.5 | 9.4 |
| Under 1 | 162.4 | 151.8 | 92.3 | 69.0 | 54.9 | 33.0 | 28.8 | 21.3 | 18.0 |
| 1–4 | 19.8 | 14.0 | 9.9 | 5.6 | 2.9 | 1.4 | 1.1 | 0.9 | 0.8 |
| 5–14 | 3.9 | 2.9 | 2.6 | 1.7 | 1.0 | 0.6 | 0.5 | 0.4 | 0.4 |
| 15–24 | 5.9 | 4.5 | 4.9 | 3.3 | 2.0 | 1.3 | 1.0 | 1.3 | 1.3 |
| 25–34 | 8.2 | 6.5 | 6.8 | 4.7 | 3.1 | 1.8 | 1.4 | 1.6 | 1.5 |
| 35–44 | 10.2 | 9.0 | 8.1 | 6.8 | 5.2 | 3.6 | 3.0 | 3.1 | 3.0 |
| 45–54 | 15.0 | 13.7 | 12.2 | 12.2 | 10.6 | 8.5 | 7.3 | 7.4 | 7.1 |
| 55–64 | 27.2 | 26.2 | 23.6 | 24.0 | 22.2 | 19.0 | 17.0 | 16.4 | 16.4 |
| 65–74 | 56.4 | 55.6 | 52.5 | 51.4 | 48.4 | 41.0 | 41.2 | 37.2 | 35.9 |
| 75–84 | 123.3 | 122.2 | 118.9 | 112.7 | 112.0 | 93.3 | 87.0 | 83.4 | 83.4 |
| 85 and over | 260.9 | 250.3 | 248.3 | 228.0 | 235.7 | 202.0 | 209.6 | 166.7 | 180.2 |

*Source:* U.S. Bureau of the Census, *Statistical Abstract of the United States, 1962,* Washington, D.C.: Government Printing Office, 1962, table 67, p. 63; U.S. Bureau of the Census, *Statistical Abstract of the United States, 1975,* Washington, D.C.: Government Printing Office, 1975, p. 61.

[66]National Center for Health Statistics, *Current Estimates from the Health Interview Survey,* 1974, ser. 10, no. 100, Washington, D.C.: Government Printing Office, 1975.

[67]National Center for Health Statistics, *Health in the United States, 1975, A Chartbook,* Washington, D.C.: Government Printing Office, 1975, p. 58.

In the same way that disease varies by sex categories, it also is affected by age. That is, from a biological frame of reference we would expect a higher rate of morbidity from chronic diseases among older persons because chronic diseases are primarily due to the degeneration of body tissue and the inability of organs to function normally. Similarly, older persons may be more immune to communicable diseases because they have had greater exposure. Hence, among infants whose systems have not built up strong defenses, a higher rate of acute illnesses could be expected.

However, it should be pointed out that sociological factors also affect the differential age rates of morbidity. For example, the public has an entirely different attitude toward care of children than toward care of the aged. Although these attitudes are also related to other nonmedical factors, it should be noted that pediatrics, devoted to the control of childhood diseases, has been a recognized medical specialty for over fifty years. In contrast, the field of geriatrics, or the treatment of problems of old age, is only beginning and is not yet a formally recognized specialty.

The combined biological and sociological influences on morbidity and mortality have further important implications for current trends in population changes. It has already been shown (Tables 2-2 and 2-4) that the death rates for the United States population have declined markedly since 1900. This decline is a consequence of several important factors. Progress in medical science, e.g., the discovery of antibiotics, sulfanilamides, and other drugs, of new surgical procedures, and of improved diagnostic techniques, and, in general, the control of communicable diseases, has contributed greatly to the reduction of the death rate, especially infant mortality. In addition, improved public health measures, preventive medicine, health education, and a general rise in the standard of living have also played a part in this decrease. In fact, there is good evidence that these general measures of public health and rising living standards initiated the downward trends in morbidity and mortality from communicable diseases and that medical science only continued a trend already well established.[68] At the same time, the birth rate has declined slightly with some variation. The important point, however, is that the birth rate is slightly less than double the death rate, thus producing a net increase in the population (excluding consideration of immigration and emigration). The significance of these trends is most noticeable when changes in the age composition of the population are examined. In Table 2-5, it can be seen that the percentage of persons under age 15 has begun to decline (because of the falling birth rate) and that large increase in population in the 1950s and 1960s has moved into the 15 to 44 age group. It is important to note especially the continued

[68]John Powles, "On the Limitations of Modern Medicine," in Robert L. Kane (ed.), *The Challenges of Community Medicine*, New York: Springer, 1974, pp. 91–122.

## Table 2-5  Population of the United States, by Age, 1930–1974

| Year | Total thousands | Under 15 | 15–44 | 45–64 | 65+ |
|------|------|------|------|------|------|
| 1930 | 122,755 | 29.4 | 47.7 | 17.4 | 5.4 |
| 1940 | 131,669 | 25.0 | 48.3 | 19.8 | 6.9 |
| 1950 | 150,697 | 26.9 | 44.7 | 20.3 | 8.4 |
| 1960 | 179,323 | 31.1 | 39.5 | 20.1 | 9.2 |
| 1970 | 203,235 | 30.4 | 39.1 | 20.6 | 9.9 |
| 1974 | 211,390 | 27.8 | 41.4 | 20.5 | 10.3 |

*Source:* U.S. Bureau of the Census, *Statistical Abstract of the United States, 1962,* Washington, D.C.: Government Printing Office, 1962, table 18, p. 26; U.S. Bureau of the Census, *Statistical Abstract of the United States, 1975,* Washington, D.C.: Government Printing Office, 1975, p. 31.

increase in the percentage of population age 65 and over. The increase in the number of aged reflects the length of life and life expectancy for the population. A person born in 1920 could, on the average, expect to live for 54.1 years. A baby born in 1973, however, would be expected to live, again on the average, for 71.3 years.[69] In any case, with such shifts in the composition of the population, one would expect shifts in the way in which disease affects the population. The data in Table 2-6 support this contention. Although the rates for all accidental deaths have remained relatively stable, the rates of deaths from chronic diseases continue to rise with a

[69] *Statistical Abstract of the United States, 1975,* p. 59. In every case the life expectancy for females is slightly more than that for males. An interesting estimate of life expectancy of a child born A.D. 100–200 was from 15 to 25 years. See John D. Durand, "Mortality Estimates from Roman Tombstone Inscriptions," *American Journal of Sociology,* 65 (January, 1960), 365–374.

## Table 2-6  Death Rates Per 100,000 Persons from Selected Chronic and Acute Conditions, United States, 1950–1973

| | 1950 | 1960 | 1970 | 1973 |
|------|------|------|------|------|
| Chronic conditions | | | | |
| Ischemic heart disease | 285.1 | 321.8 | 328.1 | 326.0 |
| Cancers | 139.8 | 149.2 | 162.8 | 167.3 |
| Cirrhosis of the liver | 9.2 | 11.3 | 15.5 | 15.9 |
| Acute conditions | | | | |
| Diseases of early infancy | 40.5 | 37.4 | 21.3 | 14.5 |
| Influenza and pneumonia | 31.3 | 37.3 | 30.9 | 29.8 |
| Tuberculosis | 22.5 | 6.1 | 2.6 | 1.8 |
| Accidents | | | | |
| Motor vehicle | 23.1 | 21.3 | 26.9 | 26.5 |
| All other | 37.5 | 31.0 | 29.5 | 28.7 |

*Source:* Bureau of the Census, *Statistical Abstract of the United States, 1975,* Washington, D.C.: Government Printing Office, 1975, table 80, p. 64.

corresponding decline in mortality from acute diseases. In 1973, more than three-fourths of all deaths were due to chronic diseases. All these factors will certainly affect the community's (or nation's) needs in regard to health services. The different emphases in community needs become more pronounced when the population is relatively homogeneous in age, such as in a retirement village or a typical suburb with many small children.

### Geography and Disease

At various times in the development of medicine, the causes of disease have been attributed to many phenomena. Even today, when some diseases are known to be caused by parasites, viruses, and other bacteriological agents, the importance of environmental factors is still recognized. In this respect, the relative importance of geography and its relationship to disease is examined here. For many years it was felt that climate, location, soil, and other natural features were closely linked to the causation of disease. For example, certain diseases are prominent in tropical areas, but not elsewhere.[70] To be sure, geography is related to disease to the extent that the disease-causing agent can survive in a particular climate, e.g., the anopheles mosquito and malaria. On the other hand, one wonders if this is as important as other relationships. When the data on crude mortality and infant mortality, presented in Table 2-7, are examined, several features become readily apparent. First, crude death rates from all causes vary only modestly from a low of 7.6 per 1,000 to 11.7 per 1,000 in 1960 and from 6.6 to 11.9 per 1,000 in 1973. A much greater range is seen in infant mortality rates with a thirteenfold difference between the extremes shown here (India and the Netherlands). A second feature is the relative stability in crude death rates over the thirteen-year period shown. The changes reflecting both increases and decreases are slight for most countries. A third feature of Table 2-7, and more germane to the discussion here, is the fact that some countries which have roughly equivalent geographic position have similar rates, but others show wide variations in infant mortality rates (the more sensitive of the two rates shown in Table 2-7). On the other hand, some nations in completely dissimilar geographic positions have similar rates while others do not. For example, Canada and the United States share many geographic features and had rates in 1973 that differed by less than 1 death per 1,000 population. At the same time, however, it can be seen that the infant mortality rate in Portugal is more than twice the rate for neighboring Spain. Similarly, two countries as different in geographic features as the Netherlands and Japan have similar infant mortality rates.

----

[70]There are, of course, exceptions. For example, the first case of dysentery was discovered in the Arctic region of Russia, although it is caused by an organism which is favored by a tropical environment.

**Table 2-7    Crude Mortality Rates and Infant Mortality Rates for Selected Nations, 1960 and 1973**

| Nation | Crude mortality rate per 1,000 population | | Infant mortality rate per 1,000 live births | | Per capita income (U.S. dollars, 1972) |
|---|---|---|---|---|---|
| | 1960 | 1973 | 1960 | 1973 | |
| Canada | 7.8 | 7.4 | 27.3 | 16.8 | $4,231 |
| United States | 9.5 | 9.4 | 25.6 | 17.6 | 4,981 |
| Argentina | 8.1 | 9.5 | 59.1 | 59.6 | 1,171 |
| Chile | 11.2 | 8.5 | 127.3 | 70.9 | 515 |
| Mexico | 11.7 | 9.1 | 75.1 | 60.9 | 681 |
| Japan | 7.6 | 6.6 | 30.7 | 11.7 | 2,462 |
| Malaysia | 9.5 | 12.5 | 68.9 | * | 391 |
| India (registration area) | 11.1 | 9.7 | * | 139.0 | 88 |
| England | 11.5 | 11.9 | 16.6 | 18.1 | 2,503 |
| Sweden | 10.0 | 10.5 | 21.9 | 9.6 | 4,669 |
| Netherlands | 7.6 | 8.2 | 16.5 | 11.6 | 3,159 |
| Spain | 8.7 | 8.5 | 35.3 | 15.1 | 1,239 |
| Portugal | 10.4 | 11.1 | 77.5 | 44.4 | 763 |
| Italy | 9.7 | 9.9 | 43.8 | 25.7 | 1,987 |

*No data.

*Source:* United Nations, *Demographic Yearbook, 1961, 1973,* New York: United Nations, 1961, 1973; and United Nations, *Population and Vital Statistics Report,* 26 (July, 1974), 1–27.

Although it must be recognized that certain environmental conditions enable some disease-causing agents to flourish and others to die, it is apparent that some other factor or factors are influencing the relationship. One clue to another factor is that where advanced technology is available, the environment can be changed to protect human beings from certain diseases. This would suggest that the level of health is related to the stage of economic development of the country. Looking again at Table 2-7, we can see that there is a strong correlation between economic progress in terms of per capita income and low infant mortality rates. The rates are approximately the same for the United States, England, the Netherlands and Canada—countries all judged to be well advanced in economic development.[71] Similarly, countries with high mortality rates, for example, Chile, Mexico, Italy, and Portugal, are also in about the same economic stage with each other, but much behind countries with low mortality rates.

Further support for the explanation that level of health is related to the stage of economic development is found in data from "emerging" nations.

[71]W. W. Rostow, *The Stages of Economic Growth,* New York: Cambridge University Press, 1961. See also John Bryant, *Health and the Developing World,* Ithaca, N.Y.: Cornell University, 1969.

**Table 2-8    Selected Vital Statistics for South Africa, 1970**

| Racial group | Birth rate per 1,000 population | Crude death rate per 1,000 population | Infant mortality rate per 1,000 live births |
|---|---|---|---|
| White European | 23.6 | 9.2 | 21.6 |
| Asiatic | 33.8 | 7.0 | 36.4 |
| Colored (Negro) | 36.8 | 14.3 | 132.6 |

*Source:* United Nations, *Demographic Yearbook, 1973,* New York: United Nations, 1973, pp. 225, 256, 279.

If one looks, for example, at the vital statistics for South Africa, shown in Table 2-8, it can be seen that within the same geographical area there is a substantial difference between the rates of mortality and births. These data suggest that the white population enjoys a health situation not unlike that of many other industrialized nations, but the native population is still subject to diseases characteristic of peasant societies. Moreover, it has been pointed out that "the contrasting prevalence of disease in adjacent neigh-bourhoods can be explained only in terms of South Africa's history, and the development of her economic and social systems."[72] The history referred to in the above quotation suggests that extreme social differentiation has occurred because the benefits of rapid industrial expansion in South Africa have gone to the politically dominant white minority. The native population is segregated into urban areas, which rapidly become overcrowded and a source of disease. In addition, most of the native population remains at a subsistence level, without the benefit of good public health provisions. These factors, plus the high mobility of males in the population (that is, males leave the tribal areas to come to urban areas for work, then return to tribal areas). spread infectious diseases to the villages in the hinterland. Other social problems, such as crime, illegitimacy, and venereal infection, are very high in the native sections of urban areas.[73]

The health problems of South Africa are not limited to that country alone, but present a general pattern which can be found in almost every emerging nation, although the problem of segregation is not always present. In most underdeveloped countries, one finds high birth rates and high death rates, with a relatively young population. The prevailing causes of death are infectious diseases, since few live long enough to develop chronic diseases. When modern medicine and public health practices are applied to these situations, there is a rapid decline in the death rate, while the birth rate remains at a relatively high level, thus providing a maximum net gain in population. Gradually, as the nation becomes industrialized and urbanized,

[72]M. W. Susser and W. Watson, *Sociology in Medicine,* 2d ed., New York: Oxford University Press, 1971, p. 41.
[73]*Ibid.,* pp. 40–45.

there is a decline in the birth rate, but an increase in the number of young children because fewer of them die in childhood. As a consequence of these changes, the average life expectancy for the individual increases, and there is a concomitant shift in the predominant cause of death from acute infectious diseases to chronic degenerative diseases. This pattern has been described above for the United States. In Table 2-9 further data are presented on mortality rates from selected chronic and acute diseases for selected nations whose stages of economic growth are different. It is clear that underdeveloped nations have a great problem with infectious and parasitic diseases, causes of death which have been much reduced or eliminated in advanced countries. There are, however, some notable exceptions. One is Japan, a country which underwent a very rapid industrialization during and following World War II. Since then, there has been a dramatic decline in overall death rates for Japan. This is reflected in Table 2-9 which shows an inconsistent picture of cause of death. For some chronic-disease categories, Japan exceeds underdeveloped nations, but has not yet reached the proportions of advanced nations. Similarly, the acute-disease death rates are generally higher for Japan than advanced nations, but in some cases lower than those for underdeveloped countries. This confused picture probably represents the extreme differences between urban areas in Japan, which are very similar to urban areas in the United States, and rural areas in Japan, which have retained some of the traditional culture of the preindustrial period.

## Social Class and Disease

The argument that stage of economic development is an important category for examining the extent of disease on an international scale applies to intranational studies as well. That is, epidemiologic studies conducted in various countries reveal that socioeconomic status is clearly associated with certain kinds of disease. English studies, for example, indicate that mortality rates in general, but especially infant and neonatal mortality rates, increase from the highest to the lowest social class.[74] Morbidity rates for certain diseases, mostly infectious and parasitic diseases associated with poverty, follow the same pattern. For example, gastroenteritis among infants, bronchitis, pneumonia, and tuberculosis are major causes of deaths in classes IV and V (two lowest social classes), while the rates for these diseases are much lower in classes I and II. On the other hand, some diseases are more common among the wealthy classes, such as coronary heart disease, leukemia, and cirrhosis of the liver. For the most part, the differences in the rates can be ascribed to relatively healthy environment or lack of it and to the nature of occupation and style of life associated with the

[74]*Ibid.*, pp. 138ff.

**Table 2-9   Mortality Rates per 100,000 Population from Selected Causes for Selected Nations, All Ages, 1970–1972**

| | Ischemic heart disease | Hypertensive heart disease | Cerebrovascular disease | Malignant neoplasms | Diabetes mellitus | Avitaminoses | Syphilis | Typhoid | Dysentery | Enteritis | Tuberculosis |
|---|---|---|---|---|---|---|---|---|---|---|---|
| **Advanced nations** | | | | | | | | | | | |
| United States (1971) | 326.1 | 10.3 | 100.4 | 160.6 | 18.2 | 1.1 | 0.2 | 0.0 | 0.1 | 1.2 | 1.6 |
| England & Wales (1972) | 309.3 | 18.8 | 167.1 | 242.6 | 10.9 | 0.5 | 0.3 | 0.0 | 0.0 | 1.2 | 2.0 |
| Sweden (1971) | 365.3 | 8.5 | 111.6 | 215.6 | 11.9 | 0.1 | 0.1 | 0.0 | 0.0 | 0.7 | 3.0 |
| Israel (1972) | 201.0 | 6.6 | 92.8 | 117.2 | 9.6 | 0.5 | 0.1 | 0.0 | 0.1 | 5.6 | 1.0 |
| Japan (1972) | 36.7 | 16.5 | 166.7 | 120.4 | 7.5 | 0.5 | 0.4 | 0.0 | 0.0 | 3.7 | 11.3 |
| **Emerging nations** | | | | | | | | | | | |
| South Africa (1970) | | | | | | | | | | | |
| Asiatic | 97.1 | 32.7 | 73.8 | 38.4 | 18.5 | 1.9 | * | 0.0 | 1.0 | 40.9 | 8.8 |
| Colored | 60.9 | 32.3 | 95.0 | 86.6 | 7.1 | 12.7 | 0.9 | 0.4 | 1.5 | 305.1 | 49.2 |
| White | 229.3 | 19.0 | 102.7 | 137.0 | 8.6 | 0.5 | 0.2 | 0.0 | 0.2 | 6.5 | 2.4 |
| Angola (1971) | 1.5 | 2.0 | 8.2 | 6.5 | 0.6 | 3.6 | 0.1 | 1.2 | 1.7 | 41.4 | 6.5 |
| Costa Rica (1971) | 31.1 | 3.4 | 29.6 | 63.7 | 8.9 | 6.8 | 0.6 | 0.2 | 1.2 | 55.7 | 5.7 |
| Chile (1970) | 61.1 | 8.4 | 59.1 | 104.7 | 9.0 | 16.0 | 0.7 | 0.6 | 0.2 | 42.2 | 21.6 |
| Spain (1971) | 59.7 | 10.1 | 125.9 | 139.9 | 16.7 | 0.6 | 0.9 | 0.1 | 0.0 | 3.8 | 9.5 |

*No data.

Source: United Nations, *Statistical Yearbook, 1973*, New York: United Nations, 1973.

social-class position. This explains the high incidence of infectious and parasitic diseases among the lower social classes who live under conditions of poverty, filth, overcrowding, and general absence of public health measures of sanitation. Persons in the highest social class generally have more healthful living conditions and live longer. However, they have more sedentary occupations and different dietary patterns which increase the probability of the occurrence of heart disease.[75]

In the United States, one finds a very similar pattern. A study by Ellis, for example, showed the death rates from all causes for the white population in a Texas city varied from 6.17 per 100,000 in class I (highest class) to 9.91 per 100,000 in class V (lowest class).[76] In a further detailed analysis, death rates from tuberculosis, penumonia, some forms of cancer, heart disease, and other causes were always higher in the lowest class than in the highest class, although one of the intermediate classes often had lower death rates from heart disease, diabetes, nephritis, and vascular lesions.[77] Other studies reported that chronic-disease rates were greater in poor and very poor families than in comfortable and well-to-do families.[78] Given this distribution among the social classes, it might be expected that the burden of physical disabilities would also be greater in lower-class than in upper-class families. Some data supporting that expectation are shown in Table 2-10. Although there is some inconsistency in rates among the very highest-income families, the inverse association between family income as an indicator of socioeconomic status and prevalence of disabilities is very strong, with rates being about 3 times greater in the lowest-income families than in the highest-income families. Finally, it should be noted that despite various methodological problems of measurement and comparability, studies of mental diseases have also shown a remarkably consistent inverse relationship between social-class position and the prevalence of certain mental disorders such as schizophrenia and personality disorders.[79]

It should be clear from the discussion thus far that epidemiologic studies contribute significantly to knowledge about disease. These studies have shown consistently that environmental factors, especially social class,

---

[75]*Ibid.*, pp. 130–135.

[76]John M. Ellis, "Socio-economic Differentials in Mortality from Chronic Disease," in E. Gartly Jaco (ed.), *Patients, Physicians, and Illness,* New York: Free Press, 1958, pp. 30–37.

[77]*Ibid.*

[78]P. S. Lawrence, "Chronic Illness and Socio-economic Status," *Public Health Reports,* 63 (November, 1948), pp. 1507–1521. See also Aaron Antonovsky, "Social Class and the Major Cardiovascular Diseases," *Journal of Chronic Diseases,* 21 (February, 1968), 65–106. A more general discussion may be found in Aaron Antonovsky, "Social Class, Life Expectancy and Overall Mortality," in E. Gartly Jaco (ed.), *Patients, Physicians and Illness,* 2d ed., New York: Free Press, 1972, pp. 5–30, and in Kosa et al., *op. cit.*

[79]See the review by Dohrenwend, *op. cit.*

**Table 2-10   Family Income and Prevalence of Selected Impairments, United States, 1971**

| Family income | Prevalence of impairment* | | Speech defect | Paralysis |
| | Visual | Hearing | | |
| --- | --- | --- | --- | --- |
| Under $3,000 | 126.5 | 166.9 | 17.7 | 16.8 |
| 3,000–4,999 | 68.2 | 101.2 | 13.4 | 10.5 |
| 5,000–6,999 | 41.9 | 70.6 | 10.7 | 6.4 |
| 7,000–9,999 | 34.7 | 57.9 | 8.4 | 5.3 |
| 10,000–14,000 | 28.9 | 49.4 | 7.2 | 4.4 |
| 15,000 and over | 34.5 | 48.6 | 6.4 | 4.6 |

*Number of cases per 1,000 population.

Source: National Center for Health Statistics, Prevalence of Selected Impairments, U.S., 1971, ser. 10, no. 99, Washington, D.C.: Government Printing Office, 1975.

but also physical environment, exert a considerable effect on the scope of disease. First of all, differences in the environment produce differences in the potential of disease. One finds a higher incidence and prevalence of cases of acute infectious diseases in a slum environment than in a better environment. At the same time, safeguards against disease, such as good nutrition, medical care services, and knowledge about disease and illness, are less available. Second, poor environmental conditions lead to increased exposure to disease, partly because of overcrowding, but also because of the hazards of the types of work performed, e.g., heavy labor. Third, and a corollary of the second, is a lower level of resistance associated with continuous exposure to unhealthy conditions. A weakened condition from contracting one disease makes the individual more susceptible to other diseases, which further complicates the health problem. Finally, access to good medical facilities is also associated with environmental differences. Generally speaking, the poorer social groups seldom are able to consult specialists, such as pediatricians, internists, and ophthalmologists. In addition, the high cost of health services also limits the medical care received by these classes.

Perhaps a word of caution should be introduced here regarding the relationship between social class and the incidence and prevalence of diseases. Social class is itself a multidimensional concept (occupation, education, income, etc.), and over time, its component elements may change in relation to each other and in relation to morbidity. For example, rising incomes in working-class families may facilitate the spread of behavior such as dietary habits formerly associated only with upper-class families. Furthermore, the relationship between social class and certain diseases may not be consistent from one geographic area to another. Thus, it is not surprising that differences between social classes in the incidence of some diseases such as coronary heart disease or diabetes have been reported as reduced or even reversed.[80] The point is that social factors in disease require continued investigation so that the knowledge gained from epidemiologic studies can play an important part in constructing defenses against disease.

## SUMMARY

Epidemiology is a method of examining how much disease is present in a given population. The contemporary epidemiologist studies the relationship among the many factors which influence the frequency of occurrence and the distribution of diseases in human communities. These factors include (1) disease agents, such as bacteria, nutrient agents, gases, and radiation; (2) the environment, both physical (weather, geography) and social (place of residence, social class, etc.); and (3) characteristics of the human host, such as age, sex, race, occupation, style of life.

Much of the information concerning these factors is obtained through health surveys of populations or from representative samples of populations. Data are also obtained from experiments in the laboratory and in the field. Surveys, experiments, and other studies enable the epidemiologist to test hypotheses concerning the sources of disease in a population, the ways in which diseases are transmitted from one person or group to another, and, often, the efficacy of programs of prevention and treatment of disease.

In evaluating these data, the epidemiologist employs several basic concepts. Different rates are calculated—depending on their intended use and the nature of the data—to examine trends in mortality and morbidity. Moreover, it is important for the epidemiologist to know how much sickness is present at a given time (prevalence) and how many new cases occur during a specified period of time (incidence). Progress in the fight against disease can also be seen in a measure of life expectancy. For example, the average length of life in the United States has increased 85 percent in the more than one hundred years since 1850.

The interpretation of epidemiologic data shows quite clearly the relevance of sociological variables for the distribution of diseases in a population—for example, the explanation of variations by age and sociocultural factors. Similarly, it was shown that factors relating to social class and the stages of economic development of different nations were important in understanding the amount and distribution of diseases in their respective populations.

[80]Kark, *op. cit.*, pp. 114–116.

## SUGGESTED READINGS

Bryant, John, *Health and the Developing World,* Ithaca, N.Y.: Cornell University Press, 1969.

Dubos, René, *Mirage of Health,* New York: Harper and Row, 1959.

MacMahon, Brian, and Thomas F. Pugh, *Epidemiology: Principles and Methods,* Boston: Little, Brown, 1970.

Roueché, Berton, *Eleven Blue Men,* Boston: Little, Brown, 1947.

Sartwell, Philip E. (ed.), *Maxcy-Rosenau Preventive Medicine and Public Health,* 10th ed., New York: Appleton-Century-Crofts, 1973.

Susser, M. W., and W. Watson, *Sociology in Medicine,* 2d ed., New York: Oxford University Press, 1971, chap. 1.

Chapter 3

# Characteristics of Disease

*In the physician's search for the nature of disease. . . nothing has been so important as the advent of the* biographic *concept of disease. . . . We therefore must not focus our magnifying glass on a single facet of the patient, but we must look at the whole man as if through a reducing glass.*

Felix Marti-Ibañez, M.D.
"Disease as Biography," in *Centaur: Essays on the History of Medical Ideas,* 1958.

As long as medicine has been practiced as a special occupation, anyone interested in studying symptoms, causes, and consequences of disease has been faced with the problem of classification. Basically, classification is a process of sorting information into categories or "families" of data which will be useful to the investigator or practitioner. Needless to say, the same information can usually be classified in many different ways depending upon one's intent and theoretical framework.[1] When one is faced with a

[1]William J. Goode and Paul K. Hatt, *Methods in Social Research,* New York: McGraw-Hill, 1952, pp. 322ff.

very large amount of knowledge, such as that which has been accumulated in the field of medicine, a choice of categories becomes more complex. For example, with respect to any given disease, say arteriosclerotic heart disease, a pathologist would be most interested in the nature and source of injury to the body. On the other hand, a physiologist would be more concerned with the impact of the disease on the functions of the involved organs. A clinician might be most concerned with how the body functions under stress of disease, what symptoms are observed, and how the disease developed in the first place. These same characteristics could be studied from several other points of view as well, such as those of the epidemiologist, the public health physician, family members, employers, and so on. Thus, this one disease could be classified in many different ways to provide different kinds of information.

From a sociological frame of reference, one would be more interested in the impact of diseases on group life than in a particular disease entity. Diseases, like some other human enemies, constitute a threat to group unity and survival, whether the size of the group is a family or a society. Diseases can disrupt communication between group members, incapacitate leadership (or followership), reduce the ability of group members to carry out assigned or ascribed social roles and tasks, and alter the ways in which group members perceive and respond to one another. It is therefore important for the continued existence of a society that it enacts defenses against disease. It is from the standpoint of group defenses and their consequences that strategic characteristics of disease will be examined, and, as we shall see, these can involve many types of behaviors.[2] In a sense, describing diseases in terms of defense measures taken by human groups reflects the history and development of public health, particularly the attitudes of society toward the sick person.[3] That is, if we may anticipate somewhat the materials in this and later chapters, some groups deal with disease by isolation or destruction of the patient, some by attempting to treat the victim, and some by trying to prevent the disease from reaching healthy members of the group. Although these responses to disease may be viewed historically in terms of stages in the development of public health or cross-sectionally in terms of the various ways different cultures approach the problem of disease today—in either case the disease can have some impact on the structure and functioning of the group itself.

Ideally, any classificatory system would permit one to place relevant information into mutually exclusive categories. In practice, however, this is

[2]This approach was suggested in Bradley Buell et al., *Community Planning for Human Services,* New York: Columbia University Press, 1952.
[3]Felix Marti-Ibañez, *Centaur,* New York: MD Publications, 1958, pp. 357- 361. See also Kerr L. White, "Life and Death and Medicine," *Scientific American,* 229 (September, 1973), 3–13.

rarely the case. For the purposes of this discussion, characteristics of specific disease entities are not the main concern; rather the focus will be on broad categories of disease which permit examination of particular sociological characteristics of human behavior. The categories of disease chosen are (1) communicable diseases, (2) chronic diseases, and (3) mental diseases. Obviously, the use of such generic terms will result in some overlap, both of characteristics and of resulting behavior; nonetheless, significant sociological differences may be seen in each of the categories.

## COMMUNICABLE DISEASES

The present state of medical knowledge indicates that most communicable diseases are caused by a wide variety of microorganisms which become parasites on the human host, e.g., bacteria, viruses, fungi, worms, rickettsiae. In fact, much of the success story of medicine stems from the identification of specific causes of disease, beginning with the contributions made by the early pioneers in the late nineteenth and early twentieth centuries. Not only were scientists like Louis Pasteur, Robert Koch, and Paul Ehrlich able to identify the cause of many diseases, such as cholera, tuberculosis, and syphilis, but in many cases, e.g., cholera and smallpox, means were discovered for preventing the disease as well. Discoveries of this sort put public health practices on a scientific basis and paved the way for rapid successes on the part of the public health movement.[4]

It was discovered that the agents of some communicable diseases such as tuberculosis can be transmitted from individual to individual or group to group by "droplet infection"; that is, the disease germs are exhaled by an infected individual in droplets of moisture (or discharged in larger amounts of mucus or sputum, which then through evaporation may provide droplets in the atmosphere). These droplets may be inhaled by other uninfected individuals. Since droplets in the air usually soon evaporate, with lethal effects on many disease organisms, or become dispersed, droplet infection usually requires intimate contact between an infected person and the new host. Other diseases such as cholera are transmitted from one individual to another by ingestion of the disease-bearing organism into the alimentary canal of the new host, most often through drinking contaminated water or eating contaminated food. Another direct means of transmission involves physical contact between the carrier and the host, e.g., venereal disease. A fourth type, including malaria and plague, is transmitted by bites of insects

[4]George Rosen, *The History of Public Health,* New York: MD Publications, 1958. A recent report from the World Health Organization predicts that smallpox will soon be eradicated and become only of historical interest. See "Smallpox Eradication in 1975," *WHO Chronicle,* 30 (April, 1976), 152-157.

or other vectors which carry the causative agent. The consistent factor in transmission is contact, directly or indirectly, between the carrier and the new host.

There are other characteristics of communicable diseases besides etiological factors which have sociologically significant consequences. For example, most communicable diseases are self-limiting. When a healthy individual is infected with most communicable diseases, he is sick for a short period of time and then he either fully recovers or dies, although extensive complications may occur. For example, some communicable diseases such as streptococcal infections can often have sequelae which reflect permanent structural damage, (i.e., rheumatic heart disease). In communicable diseases, the disease cycle is a relatively short one, ranging from less than one day for some types of flu to about two weeks for chicken pox. In addition to this, there is typically an incubation period between the time infection actually occurs and the time symptoms occur. This is generally specific to the particular disease, and during this subclinical period, the existence of the disease in a patient is not apparent. In some patients, the infection may be contained by the body's defenses before symptoms actually become manifest. After the incubation period, when the individual's body has been sufficiently affected by the invading disease organism and by the automatic tissue responses to the invasion, he or she may feel sick and display clearly defined symptoms characteristic of that particular disease. Eventually, however, the body repairs itself (usually faster with medical intervention), or the infectious process continues to advance and the victim dies. There is a noteworthy exception to this characteristic. Some infectious diseases such as tuberculosis and syphilis are not self-limiting; that is, the effects do not pass off in a short period of time. Others such as poliomyelitis or rheumatic heart disease often leave severe physical disabilities. These diseases have the characteristic cycle of chronic diseases, which is discussed below.

Another important characteristic is that most communicable diseases are caused by a single disease agent or at least one that is dominant over all others. This means that prevention of and treatment for these diseases can be largely biological in nature, with little notice paid to the human host as a person. That is, attention can be focused on the disease agent itself and/or on the parts of the body affected, with a high degree of success. As we shall see, such is not the case for other categories of disease.

Still another characteristic is that there is always a possibility that these diseases could reach epidemic proportions. By definition, these diseases can be communicated, that is, spread from one human host to another (although the vector, or carrier, is not always human). Thus, communicable diseases represent a more serious threat in places where population density is greatest, i.e., in large cities and particularly among the impoverished classes, who not only are more crowded together, but live under conditions fostering the spread of certain communicable diseases and have few, if any, resources for medical care. The body reacts to the invasion of disease-bearing organisms by producing antibodies which often mitigate the impact of disease. The production of antibodies frequently produces a *natural immunity* to further attacks from that disease, and this is characteristic of many communicable diseases even though in some cases immunity may be only partial or temporary. This knowledge led to the discovery that the level of natural immunity, if any, could be increased in healthy persons and thus could prevent their contracting the disease at all. Thus the field of immunology was developed to promote the prevention of disease in human populations. This is especially important as it relates to the characteristic of *differential susceptibility*. Data presented below show that persons in certain age groups are more likely (susceptible) than others to contract communicable diseases and to suffer more severe consequences from such diseases. Consequently, pediatricians routinely administer DPT (diphtheria-pertussis-tetanus) injections to infants, who would be most adversely affected by these diseases. Similarly, inoculation against influenza is frequently recommended for aged people.

The characteristics of communicable diseases suggest strategies of direct intervention as a defense against them. In part, this is because a considerable store of knowledge of cause, mode of transmittal, and effective therapy has been developed. It means also that not only are these diseases treatable, but they are also preventable. Thus, one may talk about (1) *primary prevention* as all means taken to avoid the occurrence of disease in the first place, (2) *secondary prevention* as any treatment given to halt the progress of a disease and its side effects, and (3) *tertiary prevention* as means taken to restore to the highest possible level of functioning any organs or limbs disabled by disease, i.e., the process of rehabilitation.[5]

One of the main features of communicable diseases, then, is that they require contact between the disease agent or organism and the new host. The first line of defense, that is, primary prevention, would be to break the chain of transmission to prevent the carrier from reaching and infecting the new host. One obvious way is to isolate infected persons from contact with others. The techniques of isolation or quarantine used in Biblical times to segregate lepers and others from a population also played an important role in the fourteenth century when used by Italian seaport officials to prevent

[5]See Commission on Chronic Illness, *Prevention of Chronic Illness,* vol. I, Cambridge, Mass.: Harvard University Press, 1957, p. 16. For a more detailed description of the levels of prevention of communicable diseases, see Philip E. Sartwell (ed.), *Maxcy-Rosenau Preventive Medicine and Public Health,* 10th ed., New York: Appleton-Century-Crofts, 1976, pp. 59–459.

incoming ships from bringing the Black Death, or bubonic plague, to their cities. Thirty years ago, one could observe a quarantine sign posted on the door of a house in which someone had a communicable disease such as measles, mumps, or chicken pox. Tuberculosis sanatoria are traditionally located at the edge of town, and within the sanatorium, certain precautions of isolation are routinely observed.[6] It should be clear, however, that this means of defense will be effective only for those diseases spread by direct interpersonal contact or, to a lesser extent, through airborne infection.

Although most communicable diseases are self-limiting, one cannot depend entirely on the ability of the human body to heal itself through natural processes. Furthermore, breaking the chain of transmission through isolation is an effective defense only for individuals or at best for small groups. Consequently, one of the early ways developed to negate the effects of chain of transmission on a large-scale basis is through sanitation. This was first described as a means of primary prevention nearly 200 years ago by Johann Peter Frank and is now effectively employed by public health administrators.[7] It should be remembered that the growth, development, and transmission of many communicable disease agents, and hence the incidence of disease, are rooted in conditions of filth and squalor, impure water, and inadequate means of sewage disposal. The development of modern means of sanitation (some of which were employed at the time the Roman Empire was at its peak) has done much to reduce the breeding grounds and break the transmission routes of some types of disease agents.

Another means of breaking the chain of transmission on a large-scale basis is through immunization. As noted above, immunization is the process by which any natural immunity to the disease is strengthened through controlled introduction of attenuated or killed disease-causing agents to which the body reacts by building up specific resistance to those foreign bodies. One of the major achievements in modern medicine has been the development of vaccines for prevention of many communicable diseases which had previously accounted for most of the deaths which occurred, especially in infants.[8] For example, several consistent patterns emerge from the incidence of cases of some acute diseases shown in Table 3-1. It can be seen that for those diseases for which effective methods of primary prevention (including, but not limited to, immunization) have been devel-

[6]For an interesting account of how preventive measures in a tuberculosis sanatorium, such as wearing a mask and gown, are associated with social status, see Julius A. Roth, "Ritual and Magic in the Control of Contagion," *American Sociological Review,* 22 (June, 1957), 310-314.

[7]George Rosen, "The Evolution of Social Medicine," in Howard E. Freeman, Sol Levine, and Leo G. Reeder (eds.), *Handbook of Medical Sociology,* 2d ed., Englewood Cliffs, N.J.: Prentice-Hall, 1972, pp. 30-60.

[8]Paul de Kruif, *The Microbe Hunters,* New York: Harcourt, Brace & World, 1926.

**Table 3-1  Selected Reportable Diseases—Cases Reported,
United States, 1945–1973**

| Diseases | 1945 | 1950 | 1955 | 1960 | 1965 | 1970 | 1973 |
|---|---|---|---|---|---|---|---|
| Diphtheria | 18,675 | 5,796 | 1,984 | 918 | 164 | 435 | 228 |
| Dysentery (shigellosis) | 34,943 | 23,367 | 13,912 | 12,487 | 11,027 | 13,845 | 22,642 |
| Encephalitis, acute | 785 | 1,135 | 2,166 | 2,341 | 1,722 | 1,580 | — |
| Measles | 146,000 | 319,000 | 555,000 | 442,000 | 262,000 | 47,000 | 27,000 |
| Poliomyelitis, acute | 13,624 | 33,300 | 28,985 | 3,190 | 72 | 33 | 8 |
| Scarlet fever and streptococcal sore throat | 186,000 | 64,000 | 148,000 | 315,000 | 395,000 | 433,000 | — |
| Tuberculosis, all forms | 114,931 | 121,742 | 98,860 | 70,843 | 49,016* | 37,137* | 31,015* |
| Typhoid fever | 4,211 | 2,484 | 1,704 | 816 | 454 | 346 | 680 |
| Gonorrhea | 313,000 | 287,000 | 236,000 | 259,000 | 325,000 | 600,000 | 843,000 |
| Syphilis | — | 218,000 | 122,000 | 122,000 | 133,000 | 91,000 | 87,000 |
| Whooping cough (pertussis) | 133,792 | 120,718 | 67,786 | 14,809 | 6,799 | 4,249 | 1,759 |

*Newly reported cases only.

Source: U.S. Bureau of the Census, Statistical Abstract of the United States, 1975, Washington, D.C.: Government Printing Office, 1975, p. 87. Data for 1945 are from U.S. Bureau of the Census, Statistical Abstract of the United States, 1962, Washington, D.C.: Government Printing Office, 1962, p. 84.

oped, there has been a relatively consistent decline in the number of cases reported each year. This is the trend for diphtheria, tuberculosis, typhoid, whooping cough, and especially poliomyelitis. On the other hand, diseases such as dysentery and gonorrhea had shown a marked decline, but are increasing again. At least in the case of venereal disease, this increase reflects changes in methods of reporting cases and, perhaps, a shift in the patterns of sexual relationships, particularly among teen-agers, since most of the increase is among younger age groups.[9] Finally, other diseases for which no consistently effective vaccine has been developed, such as encephalitis and streptococcal infections, show a consistent increase. A part of this latter increase may also be attributed to better diagnostic methods and more complete reporting.

One of the more sociologically relevant issues here is that the advent of large-scale immunization has not been uniformly accepted, although it has resulted in a significant decrease in the incidence of those diseases for which they are available. It may be instructive here to single out the case of

[9]Department of Health, Education, and Welfare, VD Fact Sheet, Publication No. (CDC) 74-8195, Washington, D.C., 1973.

poliomyelitis because the first vaccine was developed (in 1954) long enough ago so that a large amount of social science research has been accomplished on the acceptance and utilization of immunization in various population groups.[10] Poliomyelitis, or infantile paralysis, is generally considered to be a disease of childhood, although it can be contracted by adults. It is not known for certain how the virus enters the new host, but in clinical cases of the disease, the virus works its way into the central nervous system and attacks the brain and spinal cord. Within a short time, certain muscles are paralyzed, and in serious cases, the victim is unable to swallow or continue respiration. Although no total cure for the more serious forms of polio has yet been found, many functions can be restored through rehabilitation, physical therapy, the use of the "iron lung," and sufficient bed rest.

The potential severity of the disease, the widespread fear of polio epidemics, its attack on children, who represent a highly valuable asset to any human group, and the relative effectiveness of the Salk and Sabin vaccines would suggest that when programs are presented to the public, there should be widespread participation. But such was apparently not always the case. For example, Glasser's study[11] showed that a large proportion of the target group, e.g., persons under forty years of age, were not protected by Salk vaccine. The reasons for nonparticipation were related to (1) social factors such as income and educational level; that is, the higher the social status, the more likely the person was to participate; (2) characteristic "response to illness," that is, a person who did not feel ill was less likely to participate; (3) lack of knowledge about poliomyelitis and prevention through inoculation. Another investigation revealed that although social class was an important variable in nonparticipation, mothers whose friends were unfavorable toward the use of vaccine tended not to participate either. This was especially true in the areas where the incidence of the disease had previously been low.[12] The incidence of poliomyelitis among lower-class families was found to be much higher in the city where

[10]A more recent development, of course, is the vaccine for measles. The impact of the vaccine shows in Table 3-1 in the sharp decline in the number of cases reported in 1970 and 1973.

[11]Melvin A. Glasser, "A Study of the Public's Acceptance of the Salk Vaccine Program," *American Journal of Public Health,* 48 (February, 1958), 141-145. See also Monroe G. Sirken, "National Participation Trends, 1955-1961, in the Poliomyelitis Vaccination Program," *Public Health Reports,* 77 (August, 1962), 661-670; and Leila C. Deasy, "Socio-economic Status and Participation in the Poliomyelitis Vaccine Trial," *American Sociological Review,* 21 (April, 1965), 185-191.

[12]Malcolm H. Merrill, Arthur C. Hollister, Steven F. Gibbens, and Ann W. Haynes, "Attitudes of Californians toward Poliomyelitis Vaccination," *American Journal of Public Health,* 48 (February, 1958), 146-152.

Salk vaccine had not been readily accepted than in the city where acceptance had been relatively good.[13] Finally, Winkelstein and Graham found
that nonparticipation in the field trials of poliomyelitis vaccine was highest
among (1) older age groups, (2) those who lived in the central city, (3) those
in the lower socioeconomic status, (4) parochial, compared with public,
school children, and (5) those who lived in an area in which the incidence of
poliomyelitis had been low.[14] These and other studies indicate that for
several sociologically relevant reasons—influence of friends, lack of
knowledge, attitudes reflecting social-class position, etc.—persons do not
participate on the scale desired by medical personnel charged with controlling and preventing diseases in the population. Moreover, it would appear
that the same problems exist for other diseases and other preventive
programs.[15]

Sanitation and immunization, then, represent a first line of defense for
human groups, by providing a means for reducing the danger of contact
between a disease agent and a noninfected host. However, this is not the
only means of defense available. Secondary prevention is provided by a
bewildering array of drugs that have been developed to arrest or destroy
disease germs already at work in the body. In the case of acute communicable disease, probably the most important discovery is that of antibiotics
such as penicillin, streptomycin, and aureomycin. Antibiotics work effectively to halt the progress of more than a hundred varieties of infection-
causing organisms; hence, they are an important weapon added to the
human group's arsenal against disease, even though many organisms
develop resistance to the effects of antibiotics.[16] One implication of these
developments is that secondary prevention contributes to primary prevention for the population at risk through the cure of affected carriers. That is,
infected persons may be cured through these drugs before they have had an
opportunity to spread the germs to noninfected hosts. A further contribution of antibiotics and other drugs is the prevention of harmful side effects
of disease. Some types of organisms may not be directly affected by the
drug employed, but secondary debilitating conditions arising as complications of the original infection may be prevented, thus enabling the body to
recover faster. Behind all these developments of sanitation, immunization,

[13]Tom D. Y. Chin and William M. Marine, "The Changing Patterns of Poliomyelitis
Observed in Two Urban Epidemics," *Public Health Reports,* 76 (July, 1961), 553-563.

[14]Warren Winkelstein and Saxon Graham, "Factors in Participation in the 1954 Poliomyelitis Vaccine Field Trials, Erie County, New York," *American Journal of Public Health,* 49
(November, 1959), 1454-1466.

[15]See Ray Elling, Ruth Whittemore, and Morris Green, "Patient Participation in a
Pediatrics Program," *Journal of Health and Human Behavior,* 1 (Fall, 1960), 183-191.

[16]Donald G. Cooley, *The Science Book of Modern Medicines,* New York: F. Watts,
1963, pp. 53-66.

pharmaceuticals, etc., is the continuous expansion of medical knowledge, which has provided the base line from which the most spectacular medical achievements have so far been made.

## CHRONIC DISEASES

In erecting defenses against chronic diseases, human groups are faced with very different, and in some ways more difficult, problems than are posed by communicable diseases. The causes of many chronic diseases are already known, e.g., tuberculosis and syphilis. For many others, however, like heart disease, cancer, and arthritis, medical knowledge of causes is yet incomplete. Many chronic diseases involve the degeneration of tissue and inefficient functioning of vital organs; that is to say, these are chiefly diseases of old age. Others, like rheumatic fever, are primarily found in younger age groups. It may be noted here again that advanced nations have a low death rate from acute infectious diseases, but a high death rate from chronic illnesses, and the reverse tends to be true for emerging nations. In the United States, the chief killers are cardiovascular diseases, with a rate per 100,000 persons (all age groups) in 1973 of 494.4.[17] The second major killer is cancer or malignant neoplasms, with the rate of 167.3, followed closely by strokes, vascular lesions of the central nervous system, with 102.1 deaths per 100,000 population. In fact, seven of the ten leading causes of death in the United States are of chronic nature and account for over 70 percent of the annual deaths.

The problems encountered by human groups in dealing with chronic diseases stem from two sources. First, medical knowledge, which serves so well in combating acute diseases, has proved inadequate with respect to the etiology and often the treatment of chronic diseases. Although research on these questions is in continuous process, complete answers have not yet been formulated. A substantial explanation of this incomplete knowledge may be traced to the fact that most chronic diseases are the result of *multiple causes* rather than a single disease agent, as in the case of many communicable diseases. As we shall presently see, these multiple causes may include any combination of things from side effects of acute ailments to the wearing down of tissues from sheer age, from traumatic damage to unhealthy living, e.g., smoking, excessive drinking.

Secondly, the strategies employed for communicable disease are not applicable to most chronic diseases. Of major importance is the fact that

---

[17]This rate and those which follow immediately are from U.S. Bureau of the Census, *Statistical Abstract of the United States, 1975,* Washington, D.C.: Government Printing Office, 1975, p. 64.

most chronic diseases are not communicable; hence the strategy of breaking the chain of transmission is not relevant. Moreover, the disease cycle is very different in that chronic diseases are not usually self-limiting. Often, by the time the individual feels sick, the deterioration of tissues or organ functioning has progressed considerably. Following an attack of a chronic ailment, the individual rarely fully recovers, although immediate symptoms can often be alleviated. However, the damage has been done, so that subsequent attacks may tend to be more severe, leading to further impairment and perhaps death. Hence, although it may seem redundant, the very chronicity of these diseases has important ramifications for problems encountered and for defense measures established by human groups. This is not to say that these factors are not important in other kinds of illnesses, but the social-psychological effects of acute illness are usually of short duration. Physical impairments are often long-term conditions which require new adjustments on the part of the impaired persons and their families.[18]

At this point, it seems appropriate to introduce the distinction between a physical impairment and a physical disability. Physical impairment is an *objective* medically demonstrable state or condition whereby the individual has lost the function of some organ or appendage; i.e., a blind person cannot see, a double amputee cannot walk without assistance. A physical disability, on the other hand, is a *subjective* state and the cumulative result of obstacles interposed between the individual and satisfacory adjustment.[19] For example, the blind person has an impairment in being unable to see, but the blindness is not a disability to reading if the person has learned Braille. Similarly, the loss of both legs becomes an impairment to walking only if the patient rejects prostheses, crutches, or other devices to assist in performing that function. This subtle, but important, distinction is the basis of a social-psychological analysis of physical impairment. The therapeutic task is to overcome the disabling aspects of an impairment, and this must take into consideration not only techniques of physical medicine, but motivation, self-concept, cultural factors in response to illness, and a host of other sociological and psychological variables.

Of all the various issues involved in the social psychology of adjustment to physical impairment, two seem to be most important: (1) social

---

[18]A personal accounting is given in Eric Hodgins, *Episode: A Report on the Accident inside My Skull,* New York: Atheneum, 1964.

[19]Roger G. Barker, Beatrice A. Wright, and Mollie R. Gonick, *Adjustment to Physical Handicap and Illness: A Survey of the Social Psychology of Physique and Disability,* New York: Social Science Research Council, Bulletin 55, 1946. See especially pp. 55-117, 228-264. A more recent review is in Gary L. Albrecht (ed.), *The Sociology of Physical Disability and Rehabilitation,* Pittsburgh: University of Pittsburgh Press, 1976.

devaluation of the disabled and (2) psychological insecurity.[20] Many writers have observed that the social position of impaired persons, especially if the impairment is visible, is very much like that of members of a minority group in that they are noticeably different from the majority, and this difference makes them inferior. At the same time, unlike members of a true minority group, the impaired persons often may have no similar group with which they can identify or from which they can draw support.[21] The observable differences between the impaired and the nonimpaired majority lead to social distance and stereotyping, which operate to the disadvantage of the impaired, especially vocationally. It has also been found that minority groups tend to accept the implicit judgment of the majority and, in the case of the impaired, that devaluation is increased because many of them had been members of the majority and held majority views.[22] Cutsforth, at least, went so far as to suggest that this situation makes all impaired persons maladjusted and leads to one of two responses, compensation or withdrawal.[23] Barker's research, however, would suggest that this is an oversimplified generalization. Barker did report that impaired persons more frequently exhibited maladjustive behavior but the kinds of maladjustive behavior were not peculiar to the impaired nor even to a particular kind of impairment.[24] Social devaluation, resulting in maladjustive behavior, stems from many sources, but especially from attitudes toward established social norms. Some reflect more recent values such as stress on physical beauty and achievement. Others have developed historically from religious beliefs such as impairment being punishment for sins or indicating a lack of grace (but there is also a belief that the impaired acquired moral virtue because of their impairment). Conflicting beliefs such as this result in ambivalent behavior toward the impaired, like extreme overprotection or outright rejection or inconsistent behavior in both extremes. This devaluation is also passed on through child-rearing practices, especially in homes which teach, however implicitly, discrimination and stress compliance with established standards of appearance and behavior.[25]

[20]See Roger G. Barker and Beatrice A. Wright, "Social Psychology of Adjustment to Physical Disability," in James F. Garrett (ed.), *Psychological Aspects of Physical Disability,* Office of Vocational Rehabilitation, Rehabilitation Service Series, no. 210, Washington, D.C.: Government Printing Office, 1958, pp. 18-32.

[21]J. V. Berreman, "Some Implications of Research in the Social Psychology of Physical Disability," *Journal of Social Issues,* 4 (Fall, 1948), 28–35.

[22]Lee Meyerson, "Physical Disability as a Social Psychological Problem," *Journal of Social Issues,* 4 (Fall, 1948), 2-10.

[23]Thomas D. Cutsforth, "Personality Crippling through Physical Disability," *Journal of Social Issues,* 4 (Fall, 1948), 62-67.

[24]Barker, Wright, and Gonick, *op. cit.;* Barker, "The Social Psychology of Physical Disability," *Journal of Social Issues,* 4 (Fall, 1948), 28–35.

[25]William Gellman, "Roots of Prejudice against the Handicapped," *Journal of Rehabilitation,* 25 (January-February, 1959), 4-6.

The impact of being in a social status which is devalued, of encountering prejudice and discrimination, and of experiencing characteristic responses to illness results in the second major aspect of physical impairment—insecurity, anxiety, and maladjustment. The acceptance of a devalued social role and an appraisal of themselves as inferior are a reflection of the attitudes of persons with whom the impaired persons come into contact. Moreover, partial or complete segregation from normal interaction means "a consistent loss of vital experiences [which] culminates in significant differences in perception and behavior between the handicapped and the nonhandicapped."[26] Another aspect of the response to impairment is the evaluation of one's physical self. In many cases, especially when the impairment is highly visible like facial disfigurement,[27] one feels shame, fear, and even disgust if these are the responses received from others. Similarly, the loss of an arm or leg has led to a feeling of "not being a whole person."[28] The former involves the development of a negative self-image— a negative evaluation of one's self derived from responses received from others. The loss of an arm or leg is associated with an incomplete body image—feelings of devaluation and unworthiness. All these factors, when present, tend to induce anxiety and insecurity in the impaired person, thus leading to a situation in which the impairment may very likely become a disability.

The first important implication of chronicity is the fact that chronic diseases often require treatment over a long period of time. In some cases, such as diabetes mellitus, treatment may be lifelong, although the effects of the disease can be controlled. In any case, treatment of chronic diseases is a long-term process and may be very expensive because of the frequent visits to physicians, purchase of drugs, and, perhaps, periodic hospitalization. The problem of expense for long-term medical care becomes compounded when it is recalled that chronic diseases are typically diseases of old age; hence the age group most susceptible to chronic ailments is the one often least likely to be able to pay for medical care required to treat them.

A second implication is that of family involvement. Although not unique to chronic diseases and subsequent disabilities, family involvement in these cases tends to be prolonged and more frequent. It has already been pointed out that the course of many chronic diseases can be stabilized to a point at which, although it may incapacitate a patient to some degree, it will not always require further hospitalization. If the ill person is the family

[26]*Ibid.*, p. 5. See also David N. Wiener, "Personality Characteristics of Selected Disability Groups," *Genetic Psychology Monographs,* 45 (May, 1952), 175-255.
[27]See Frances Cook McGregor, "Some Psycho-social Problems Associated with Facial Deformation," *American Sociological Review,* 16 (October, 1951), 629-638.
[28]Tamara Dembo, Gloria Ladieu-Leviton, and Beatrice A. Wright, "Acceptance of Loss: Amputations," in Garrett, *op. cit.*, pp. 80-96.

breadwinner, the problems of income maintenance presented by the need for a long-term convalescence are obvious. Family roles may also be disrupted if the ill person is the parent upon whom the family depends for running the household. However, it is more likely that the ill person will be an aging parent of one of the adults in the family. Some analysts of the contemporary family, such as Parsons and Fox, maintain that the presence of a sick older person in a typical nuclear family may create an almost intolerable strain on familial roles.[29] This strain is introduced by the fact that complementary familial roles are organized on the basis of adult parents and their children as the only members of the family; i.e., there is no room for sick and aging grandparents whose dependency on others would, theoretically at least, disrupt the carrying out of normal roles by other family members.

More recent evidence, however, suggests that emphasis on the nuclear family organization and the exclusion of aging parents of the adults may be unwarranted. Shanas[30] found that older persons who were living with children or others, but not as head of the household, accounted for only 17.4 percent of her sample of 1,405 persons aged sixty-five or older. More importantly, almost 90 percent of the aged persons in her sample who were faced with a hypothetical crisis, namely, a convalescence from surgery requiring nursing care, said they would turn for help to daughters, sons, and other relatives in that order.[31]

In any case, it is clear that treatment of a chronic disease is likely to be a long-term affair with little hope for cure, but, in many cases, a good chance for stabilization of the disease. This, however, is likely to require changes in the habits of the victim of the disease. For example, patients recovering from a heart attack have their activities sharply curtailed at least for a time; diabetic patients must watch their diet closely and take medication, usually for the rest of their lives; the hypertensive patient must also

[29]Talcott Parsons and Renee Fox, "Illness, Therapy and the Modern Urban Family," in E. Gartly Jaco (ed.), *Patients, Physicians and Illness,* New York: Free Press, 1958, pp. 234-245.

[30]See Ethel Shanas, *The Health of Older People,* Cambridge, Mass.: Harvard University Press, 1962.

[31]*Ibid.,* p. 121. In an international study, Shanas found that most older people in the European countries being studied also felt they could depend upon their families for support. See Ethel Shanas, Peter Townsend, Dorothy Wedderburn, Henning Friis, Paul Miløj, and Jan Stehouwer, *Old People in Three Industrial Societies,* New York: Atherton Press, 1968. See also similar conclusions drawn by Albert J. E. Wilson, "Effects of Health Problems on the Family Life of Older People," in Charles O. Crawford (ed.), *Health and the Family: A Medical-sociological Analysis,* New York: Macmillan, 1971, pp. 203–215. On the ability of families to cope with health problems, see Klaus J. Roghmann, Pamela Hecht, and Robert J. Haggerty, "Family Coping with Everyday Illness: Self Reports from a Household Survey," *Journal of Comparative Family Studies,* 4 (Spring, 1973), 49-62.

take medication, avoid tension-producing situations, and so on. More importantly, changes in behavior as a result of the disease are likely to be in the direction of increased dependency on others, a culturally devalued situation in the United States. It is at this point that the family is again implicated.[32] Many observers feel that medical treatment of chronic diseases (and other diseases as well) is not sufficient by itself, but requires the emotional support of members of the victim's family. If, as Parsons and Fox suggest, familial roles in the modern family are organized in a way that would limit the ability of the family to give this needed emotional support, then American society is facing a social problem of considerable magnitude, since the number of aged persons in the society is increasing along with increasing rates of chronic diseases.

These characteristics of chronic diseases—multiple causation, non-communicability (with a few exceptions), chronicity, lack of immunity— have led to the development of a very different strategy of defense. Even though medical knowledge about causes of specific chronic diseases is not yet fully developed, emphasis is still placed on prevention, although the potential for direct intervention is much less than for communicable diseases. The strategy for secondary prevention of chronic diseases is much like that for communicable diseases. In addition to periodic health examination and screening tests, emphasis is placed on provision of trained health personnel in the community and on educating the public. For example, the demonstrated statistical association between smoking tobacco and the incidence of lung cancer has resulted in a drive to reduce the amount of smoking in adults and also a campaign to encourage schoolchildren not to start smoking. The public is being taught to be more sensitive to "danger signals," or early symptoms, of cancer, heart disease, tuberculosis, and other diseases.[33]

The most effective technique developed thus far is early detection of the presence of the disease. This technique is based on the assumption that treatment of diseases detected in very early stages has a higher probability of successful outcome and may minimize permanent damage to the body. Programs have been developed for mass screening of the general population, both well and sick persons. Multiple screening and periodic physical examinations provide simple and quickly administered tests, such as x-rays

[32]See Henry B. Richardson, *Patients Have Families,* New York: Commonwealth Fund, 1945. A different perspective on the family as a "health maintenance" rather than an "illness coping" organization is found in Lois Pratt, *Family Structure and Effective Health Behavior: The Energized Family,* Boston: Houghton Mifflin, 1976.

[33]Commission on Chronic Illness, *op. cit.* See also Godfrey M. Hochbaum, *Public Participation in Medical Screening Programs: A Social Psychological Study,* U.S. Public Health Service Monograph 572, Washington, D.C.: Government Printing Office, 1958.

for tuberculosis and cancer; urine and/or blood tests to detect diseases such as diabetes, syphilis, and anemia; and cytological tests for cancer of certain sites, especially the cervix.[34] Of course, another aspect of prevention of chronic disease is the prevention and control of communicable diseases whose side effects often result in the chronic ailment.

As one of the strategies of defense, rehabilitation—or tertiary prevention—has emerged as an important aspect, particularly with reference to the chronic diseases, although it is certainly not limited to them. In fact, the concept of rehabilitation is an elusive one largely because of the broad interpretation often given to it. For example, it can mean anything from resocializing penitentiary inmates to urban renewal. Even if the concept is limited to medical care, it has at least three meanings.[35] In the first place, it is an *ideology* reflecting the cultural value of humanitarianism and referring to the belief that it is morally right to help one's neighbor. For physicians, it is not only morally right but a moral obligation to utilize their special knowledge to help others. Secondly, rehabilitation is a *method* which, since the Barden–La Follette Act of 1943, has come to mean total rehabilitation, or restoration, of not only physical and mental capabilities, but social, vocational, and economic potentials as well. Prior to 1943, the rehabilitation process was largely one of adjustment to an impairment and the reduced scope of activity imposed thereby. In other words, rehabilitation consisted of working around the impairment. The Barden–La Follette Act financed provisions for reducing the impairment to its lowest point first, then providing means for adjustment to the new situation. There is, of course, a very interesting parallel between the shifting meaning of rehabilitation and the emergence of comprehensive medicine. Finally, rehabilitation is also a *goal* or, as Rusk stated, "the third phase of medical care."[36] After diagnosis and treatment, the next step is to restore individuals to their former level of functioning or as close to it as possible. This goal is derived in part from the ideology but also from the recognition that an industrial economy cannot afford to have a large minority of its population in a nonproductive role.[37]

When employed by human groups as a second line of defense against

[34]Lester Breslow, "Prevention and Control of Chronic Disease: Periodic Health Examinations in Multiple Screening," *American Journal of Public Health,* 49 (September, 1959), 1148-1156.

[35]W. Scott Allan, *Rehabilitation: A Community Challenge,* New York: Wiley, 1958.

[36]Howard A. Rusk, "Rehabilitation," in *Readings in Medical Care,* Chapel Hill: University of North Carolina Press, 1958, p. 416. A fuller statement is in Howard A. Rusk (ed.), *Rehabilitation Medicine,* St. Louis: Mosby, 1971.

[37]Hubert W. Yount, "Rehabilitation in a Dynamic Economy," *Proceedings of the Conference on Rehabilitation Concepts,* Philadelphia: University of Pennsylvania, 1962, pp. 3-9.

disease and its consequences, the concept of rehabilitation encompasses all three meanings described above. The emphasis, however, is probably on rehabilitation as a method which reflects the state of medical knowledge (in some areas) and as a goal for restoring group members to a point where they can again contribute to the maintenance and development of the groups to which they belong.

One of the significant consequences of the characteristics of chronic disease is the change in the ways in which disease is treated.[38] Unlike many acute communicable diseases which can be treated effectively by one physician or perhaps one or two specialists, chronic diseases require medical care at various levels; i.e., other health personnel besides the physician become involved. As pointed out in Chapter 1, this situation served as a stimulus (although not the only one) for the development of the concept of "comprehensive medicine." According to one report, comprehensive medicine is the concept that "medical care of patients can be improved now by the utilization of psychodynamic knowledge and sociological knowledge, along with generally available biological skills."[39] Although there is not complete agreement as to what comprehensive medicine entails, two major points are generally accepted. First, it involves a team approach, with each member of the team having responsibility for the conduct of care in his or her area. This implies freedom for all the team members, regardless of their professional status, to operate autonomously according to their professional competence and to contribute effectively to the development of a sound comprehensive treatment plan. In practice, this has often proved difficult to achieve because of poor communication between team members, status differences, and professional jealousies. Ordinarily, the team consists of a physician, who is usually regarded as the team leader, a nurse, a social caseworker, and, perhaps, other health personnel as required, such as a physical therapist. Finally, the patient and the patient's family may become a part of the team.[40] In any case, the team has the potential for providing medical and social-psychological care in a variety of settings—the hospital, the clinic, and the home. This is advantageous because once a chronic disease is stabilized, patients do not always require intensive care as provided in the hospital, but may do nicely with

[38]T. P. Anderson, "An Alternative Frame of Reference for Rehabilitation: The Helping Process vs. The Medical Model," *Archives of Physical Medicine and Rehabilitation*, 56 (April, 1975), 101–104.

[39]William A. Steiger, Francis H. Hoffman, A. Victor Hansen, and H. Neibuhr, "A Definition of Comprehensive Medicine," *Journal of Health and Human Behavior*, 1 (Summer, 1960), 83–86.

[40]G. E. Goodell, "Rehabilitation: Family Involved in Patient's Care," *Hospitals*, 49 (Mar. 16, 1975), 96–98.

supervised care provided in an intermediate care institution or in the home, at a considerably reduced expense.[41]

The second feature of comprehensive medicine is the shift from viewing the patient as a case of disease to seeing him or her *as a person* who is sick.[42] This change has the obvious advantage of leaving open for exploration possible social-psychological causes or complications of observed physical symptoms. It also permits the team to take into consideration the needs and wishes of the patient and family in organizing the social situation in which medical care is administered. A more subtle consequence of the shift from disease-oriented treatment to patient-centered treatment is the support provided for the patient's self-concept. Other studies have indicated that the traditional disease orientation tends to undermine the patient's self-image through "fractionated care," lack of concern for the patient's feelings, etc., even though the patient's self-concept has been shown to be important in the recuperation from and adjustment to disease.[43]

Perhaps some of the characteristics of chronic diseases and methods of coping with them can be made more clear through the use of an example. For this purpose, we shall examine some aspects of cancer, which manifests many of the characteristics of chronic diseases. At the present time, the specific cause or causes of most cancers are unknown, but some organic and inorganic chemicals such as benzene, coal tar, certain petroleum products, asbestos, and nickel, some physical agents such as radiation from x-rays and solar radiation, and some viruses are among the etiological factors. These agents vary with different sites and types of the disease. In addition, several other agents are suspected causes or are demonstrated causes in laboratory animals, but not in humans. These include chloroform, DDT, cobalt, burns.[44] What is not yet known is *how* and under what conditions these agents cause the cancer which develops, since it is clear that they rarely automatically and quickly cause the disease.

In addition to these factors of physical environment, certain sociologically relevant factors have been found to be associated with the occurrence

[41]See David Littauer, I. Jerome Flance, and Albert F. Wessen, *Home Care,* American Hospital Association, Monograph Series, no. 9, Chicago: American Hospital Association, 1961.

[42]See Steiger, Hoffman, Hansen, and Niebuhr, *op. cit.,* p. 85.

[43]See, for example, Stanley H. King, "Psychosocial Factors Associated with Rheumatoid Arthritis," *Journal of Chronic Diseases,* 2 (September, 1955), 287-302; Henry D. Lederer, "How the Sick View Their World," *Journal of Social Issues,* 8 (Fall, 1952), 4-15. The importance of the self-image in recovery was demonstrated in Theodor J. Litman, "Self-conception and Physical Rehabilitation," in Arnold M. Rose, *Human Behavior and Social Processes,* Boston: Houghton Mifflin, 1962, pp. 550-574. Setting individual goals in adjustment to disability is discussed in R. B. Trieschmann, "Coping with Disability: A Sliding Scale of Goals," *Archives of Physical Medicine and Rehabilitation,* 55 (December, 1974), 556–560.

[44]Commission on Chronic Illness, *op. cit.,* pp. 131-132.

of cancer. For example, cancer of certain sites (lung, stomach, esophagus) has a higher incidence in lower classes, while breast cancer has a higher incidence in upper social classes.[45] Ethnic background is also associated with the development of cancer at different sites.[46] Although these findings do not directly aid in the determination of specific causes of cancer, they do point out certain target groups toward whom different tactics of primary and secondary prevention may be directed.[47] Thus, there are programs to deter young people from smoking, protect workers from exposure to certain chemicals or radiation, etc. Secondary prevention emphasizes education of the population and early treatment of detected cancerous or precancerous tissues. Effective control of cancer depends largely upon early detection through mass screening and physical examinations so that treatment measures may be more effective. Treatment of cancer at the present time relies mostly upon surgical removal of diseased tissue if the disease has not spread (metastasized) too far and upon radiation therapy which permits access to diseased tissues difficult to reach by surgery.

Such characteristics of cancer as the frequent failure of treatment, lingering illness and disability, the presence of pain, and finally death have important sociological and psychological ramifications. It should be remembered that treatment of cancer that is detected early has the highest probability of success. Yet many investigations reveal that people delay seeking advice and treatment for suspicious symptoms. Early studies emphasized utilitarian factors for this delay, such as "symptoms were not serious enough," "negligence," "ignorance," or "expense."[48] A more recent study by Goldsen[49] and her associates, however, indicated that some factors contributing to delay in seeking help—especially generalized fear and personal reticence to submit to examinations—are closely associated with the diagnosis of cancer. The predominant finding of this study is that persons who promptly seek treatment for cancer symptoms do so to the

[45]This relationship is thought to be related to the lower frequency of breastfeeding found in the upper classes. See Saxon Graham and Leo G. Reeder, "Social Factors in the Chronic Illnesses," in Freeman, Levine, and Reeder, *op. cit.,* pp. 63-107.

[46]William Haenzel, "Cancer Mortality among the Foreign Born in the United States," *Journal of the National Cancer Institute,* 26 (January, 1961), 37-132.

[47]Abraham M. Lilienfeld, "Prevention and Control of Chronic Disease: Cancer," *American Journal of Public Health,* 49 (September, 1959), 1135-1140. Further information may be found in David Schottenfeld, *Cancer Epidemiology and Prevention,* Springfield, Ill.: Charles C Thomas, 1975.

[48]C. F. Harms, J. A. Plant, and A. W. Oughterson, "Delay in the Treatment of Cancer," *Journal of the American Medical Association,* 121 (Jan. 30, 1943), 335-338; Jean Aitken-Swan and Ralston Paterson, "The Cancer Patient: Delay in Seeking Advice," *British Medical Journal,* 1 (Mar. 12, 1955), 623–627.

[49]Rose K. Goldsen, Paul R. Gerhardt, and Vincent H. Handy, "Some Factors Related to Patient Delay in Seeking Diagnosis for Cancer Symptoms," *Cancer,* 10 (January-February, 1957), 1-7.

extent that they promptly seek treatment for any symptoms. In other words, one's characteristic response to symptoms of illness of any kind operate for symptoms of cancer also.

The finding of nondifferentiation of response to symptoms of cancer and response to other symptoms has been challenged by Kutner and Gordon.[50] Their investigation of the medical histories of 808 randomly selected residents in a metropolitan area revealed: "Patterns of promptness and delay in seeking care for cancer appear to be dependent upon sociological, demographic and psychological factors differing in nature from those involved in responding to other symptoms."[51] Analysis of their data collected in interviews showed that there were no sex differences in seeking care for cancer and that although delay in seeking treatment for symptoms of diseases of any kind is greatest in the lower classes, delay is more pronounced for cancer. Similarly, amount of education is negatively related to delay in seeking care for general symptoms, but there is a very pronounced negative relationship between the amount of education and delay in seeking care for cancer. It was also found that specific knowledge of cancer symptoms was inversely related to delay in seeking treatment. A study by Levine provides further explanation of these variables.[52] He found that a nationwide sample of nearly 3,000 persons rated cancer as the disease they feared most. Fear of cancer was not seen as important as a cause of delay in seeking treatment in the early studies noted above. However, Levine's analysis showed that fear (or anxiety or apprehension) about cancer is inversely related to amount of education, but that those who are personally acquainted with the victim of cancer are more apprehensive, regardless of educational attainment. At the same time, respondents who felt that they "knew a lot" about cancer were more fearful than those who confessed ignorance. Although these findings may seem inconsistent, it is likely that educational attainment and knowledge about cancer are independently related to anxiety over cancer. The point is that delay in seeking advice or treatment for cancer, found to be highest in the lower classes, may be more a function of anxiety or fear than ignorance, concern over expense, or some other factor. The evidence on this point, like answers to other questions about cancer—and chronic diseases generally—must await further research.

[50]Bernard Kutner and Gerald Gordon, "Seeking Care for Cancer," *Journal of Health and Human Behavior,* 2 (Fall, 1961), 171-178.

[51]*Ibid.,* p. 178. A more recent study reported an increased knowledge about cancer and heightened optimism about the curability of cancer when detected early. Even so, delay in seeking care continued to vary with social class position, knowledge about cancer, attitude toward the examination process, and degree of anxiety. See Andrea Knopf, "Changes in Women's Opinions about Cancer," *Social Science and Medicine,* 10 (March–April, 1976), 191–195.

[52]Gene N. Levine, "Anxiety about Illness: Psychological and Social Bases," *Journal of Health and Human Behavior,* 3 (Spring, 1962), 30-34.

## MENTAL DISEASES

The third category of disease in this classificatory scheme concerns the mental diseases. Since the scope of such a topic is far too great for adequate exploration here, this discussion must be confined to some general characteristics and measures of defense.[53] The magnitude of the problem, however, can be indicated by the fact that there were over 656,000 persons hospitalized for mental illnesses in 1971, a rate per 100,000 population of 320.2. This figure, of course, does not include almost 5.5 million patients receiving outpatient and private treatment or those who have not yet come to the attention of the authorities. This figure, however, does represent a continuation of the decline in the rate of hospitalized mental patients from a high of 407.3 in 1945,[54] but, even so, mental illness is still the most costly disease burden placed upon the national economy.[55]

In some ways, even less is known about the causes of most mental illnesses than is known about communicable and chronic degenerative diseases. Initially, mental diseases are classified as having either an organic or a functional basis. Organic disorders are those diseases in which the cause can be attributed to some identifiable physiological malfunction, such as syphilitic paresis, pellagrous dementia, bacterial infection of the brain, senility.[56] On the other hand, nearly every other case of mental illness for which no organic cause can be found is classified as a "functional" disorder. It should be noted, however, that organic theories are still important in explaining some kinds of functional disorders. Many psychiatrists believe that some as yet undiscovered chemical or constitutional agent may be responsible for functional disorders, especially the psychoses.

One characteristic of some functional disorders is that the illness is manifested in physical symptoms. These are the *psychosomatic* diseases, a term which comes from the Greek *psyche* (mind) and *soma* (body) and which reflects the ancient concern for the mind-body dualism. More than

[53]Further discussions can be found in any of the following references: Robert Perrucci, *Circle of Madness: On Being Insane and Institutionalized in America,* Englewood Cliffs, N.J.: Prentice-Hall, 1975; David Mechanic, *Mental Health and Social Policy,* New York: Prentice-Hall, 1969; Thomas S. Szasz, *The Myth of Mental Illness,* New York: Harper, 1961; Joint Commission on Mental Illness and Health, *Action for Mental Health,* New York: Basic Books, 1961; Gerald Gurin, Joseph Verhoff, and Sheila Feld, *Americans View Their Mental Health,* New York: Basic Books, 1960; Marvin K. Opler, *Culture and Mental Health,* New York: Macmillan, 1959; Marie Jahoda, *Current Concepts of Positive Mental Health,* New York: Basic Books, 1958; Alexander Leighton, John A. Clausen, and Robert N. Wilson, *Explorations in Social Psychiatry,* New York: Basic Books, 1957; and John A. Clausen, *Sociology in the Field of Mental Health,* New York: Russell Sage, 1956.

[54]National Center for Health Statistics, *Inpatient Health Facilities As Reported from the 1971 MFI Survey,* ser. 14, no. 12, Washington, D.C.: Government Printing Office, 1974, pp. 33, 37.

[55]Raschi Fein, *The Economics of Mental Health,* New York: Basic Books, 1958.

[56]See John A. Clausen, "Sociology of Mental Disorder," in Freeman, Levine, and Reeder, *op. cit.,* pp. 169–188.

that, it reflects an age-old recognition that mental and physiological processes can be and often are interdependent. It was Aristotle in *De Anima*
who said: "Probably all the afflictions of the soul are associated with the
body—anger, gentleness, fear, pity, courage, and joy—as well as loving
and hating; for when they appear, the body is also affected."[57] The
importance of psychological factors in disease has long been recognized
and taken account of in prescribed treatments, from the time of Hippocrates until the last half of the nineteenth century. The rapid discovery of
causes and cures for specific diseases during that time shifted the orientation of physicians from psychological factors to the search for organic
etiologic agents for *all* diseases. This trend has been modified somewhat
through the efforts of Freud and others who began examining patients who
were ill, but for whose illness no organic etiologic agent could be found.[58]

The following case study described by Berlinger and Greenhill[59] will
serve to illustrate the basic features of psychosomatic illness. The patient
was a thirty-nine-year-old white female, married, with four teen-age children. Her symptomatology suggested a diagnosis of early ulcerative colitis,
but further laboratory tests and other diagnostic procedures did not reveal
any organic causes. The patient was then referred to a psychotherapist,
who elicited the following information from her. For twenty-five years the
patient had exhibited periodic symptoms of nervousness, abdominal
cramps, gynecological complaints, diarrhea, asthma, nausea and vomiting,
and bloody stools, as well as some other physical problems. In *every*
instance, the appearance of one or more of these symptoms coincided with
interpersonal conflicts or traumatic events in the patient's life experiences.
These events included conflict with her parents over her marriage to a man
they felt to be socially inferior and, later, the engagement of her daughter to
someone the patient felt to be socially inferior, the suicide of her father and
death of her mother and brother, an automobile accident involving the
patient's husband and son, and infidelity by her husband. Moreover, the
patient also revealed that in the two years prior to her referral to the
psychotherapist, she had consulted and obtained treatment from no less
than twelve different physicians, most of whom were unaware of the
others' treatment and each of whom described the patient as "cooperative,
but resistant to treatment."

The case briefly described above is more or less a classic example of
the appearance of physical symptoms without any identifiable organic
causes. Another interesting point, however, is that therapeutic measures

[57]Quoted in Gregory Zillboorg, "Psychosomatic Medicine: A Historical Perspective,"
*Psychosomatic Medicine*, 6 (January-February, 1941), 1-6.
[58]Cf., for example, S. J. Lachman, *Psychosomatic Disorder: A Behavioristic Interpretation*, New York: Wiley, 1972.
[59]Klaus W. Berlinger and Maurice H. Greenhill, "Levels of Communication in Ulcerative Colitis," *Psychosomatic Medicine*, 16 (March-April, 1954), 156-162.

employed by the patient's many physicians apparently were designed for treatment of organic symptoms and, therefore, proved to be ineffective. Although there is no explicit evidence that her physicians were unaware of, or at least unwilling to treat, the psychological aspects of her symptoms, this could be inferred from the fact that (1) she made frequent changes in physicians, indicating dissatisfaction with symptomatic treatment; (2) her long history of complaints did not become known until she was engaged in psychotherapy, which suggests poor medical-history-taking technique (or lack of interest) on the part of her earlier physicians; and (3) her earlier doctors referred to her as "cooperative, but resistant" and showed a reluctance to resume treatment of her.

By contrast, one of the most important sociological characteristics of mental illness is that it is manifested primarily in *social* behavior.[60] That is to say, whatever the specific etiologic agent, the suspicion (by lay people) and confirming diagnosis (by professionals) of mental illness are not usually entertained until the individual's behavior deviates from the established group standards beyond a point at which such behavior can be tolerated. This deviant behavior, of course, can take many forms, and the degree of toleration may vary widely from one group to another. That is, the behavior of a person may be defined by one group as "queer" but acceptable, and another group might define the same behavior as intolerable and requiring some kind of professional attention. The difference in these definitions is often dependent upon the kind of behavior exhibited. Violent, unpredictable behavior tends to be less tolerable than passive, introverted behavior. In addition, these differences are reflected in such factors as kinship, social class, living in a rural versus an urban area, attitude toward the medical profession, beliefs about mental illness.[61]

Like other chronic illnesses, mental illness is a long-term condition which greatly affects the family of the patient. Obviously, the incapacitation or, perhaps, hospitalization of one parent will alter the structure and functioning of the family.[62] In addition, however, mental illness carries with it a stigma which affects not only the afflicted person, but other family

[60]See Clausen, "Sociology of Mental Disorder," in Freeman, Levine, and Reeder, *op. cit.* More recently, see Thomas J. Scheff, *Labeling Madness,* Englewood Cliffs, N.J.: Prentice-Hall, 1975.

[61]August B. Hollingshead and Frederick C. Redlich, *Social Class and Mental Illness,* New York: Wiley, 1958. See also Morris Freilich and Peter Hirsch, "Mental Health Culture in Rural Missouri," Final Report, Missouri State Department of Health and the Medical Care Research Center, St. Louis, 1965.

[62]John A. Clausen and Marian Radke-Yarrow, "Introduction: Mental Illness and the Family," *Journal of Social Issues,* 11 (Fall, 1955), 3-5. For an interesting study of the impact of mental illness on the family in another culture, see Lloyd H. Rogler and August B. Hollingshead, *Trapped: Families and Schizophrenia,* New York: Wiley, 1965. This study showed that in Puerto Rico, when the wife was mentally ill, family cohesion deteriorated rapidly. When the husband was the patient, the wife reorganized her role to encompass her husband's, with the result that the family remained intact.

members as well and serves to compound the difficulties in social adjustment made by the family members.[63] Other evidence, however, suggests that the family may be an effective therapeutic force, at least under certain conditions.[64] One study, for example, indicated that patients who were discharged from the hospital to their own homes (with spouse and children) more often made a better work and social adjustment than did patients who were discharged to the home of their parents.[65] On the other hand, of those patients who made a poor adjustment, rehospitalization was higher for patients in the conjugal home than in the parental home. This would suggest that if the patient can perform at a satisfactory level and if the other family members hold somewhat liberal attitudes toward the patient and his or her mental illness, then the family may offer the most effective therapeutic setting for the patient's recovery. However, if the patient is unable to meet even the modified expectations of his or her former role in the family, the pressures to return the individual to the hospital are greater where dependency is more dysfunctional to the family, e.g., in the conjugal unit.[66]

The inability of practitioners to associate behaviors diagnosed as symptomatic of a mental illness with a clear-cut organic cause does not mean that no causative factors have been postulated for these disorders. On the contrary, there are several theories "explaining" the appearance of functional disorders, including psychosocial conflict, stress and social isolation, and inadequate socialization.

Probably the most popular conceptualization of the development of functional mental diseases is that developed by Sigmund Freud and his followers.[67] The central thesis of this approach is that human beings have within them certain drives which they attempt to gratify. Often, however, gratification must be delayed or perhaps denied altogther because such behavior conflicts with cultural standards of the group to which that individual belongs. Consequently, a series of defense mechanisms are developed with which the individual attempts to cope with the conflict.

---

[63]Marian Radke-Yarrow, John A. Clausen, and Paul R. Robbins, "The Social Meaning of Mental Illness," *Journal of Social Issues,* 11 (Fall, 1955), 33-48.

[64]Howard E. Freeman, "Attitudes of Mental Illness among Relatives of Former Patients," *American Sociological Review,* 26 (February, 1961), 59-67. See also John G. Howells, *Principles of Family Psychiatry,* New York: Brunner-Mazel, 1975.

[65]Howard E. Freeman and Ozzie G. Simmons, "Mental Patients in the Community: Family Settings and Performance Levels," *American Sociological Review,* 23 (April, 1958), 147-154.

[66]For a discussion on changing attitudes of the public toward mental illness, see Derek L. Phillips, "Public Identification and Acceptance of the Mentally Ill," *American Journal of Public Health,* 56 (May, 1966), 755–763. See also the review by J. Rabkin, "Public Attitudes toward Mental Illness: A Review of the Literature," *Schizophrenia Bulletin,* 10 (Fall, 1974), 9-33.

[67]Franz Alexander and Helen Ross (eds.), *Dynamic Psychiatry,* Chicago:University of Chicago Press, 1952.

Thus, the unexpressible urges may be repressed (driven into the unconscious), sublimated (expressed in a different, but socially acceptable way), and so on. Mental illness expressed as deviant behavior appears when the delicate balance between the biologically derived urges and the culturally derived mechanisms of control is disturbed. When the individual's behavior becomes intolerable to other people, the "machinery" for treatment of mental illness is begun.[68]

A different theoretical approach to the problem of identifying etiological factors has emerged from epidemiologic and ecological studies of mental illness. Much of the current research in this area has been stimulated by the ground-breaking efforts of Faris and Dunham.[69] More recent studies have shown the significant relation between human perception of and reaction to the environment and the number and kinds of illnesses experienced.[70] This, in turn, has led to the testing of specific hypotheses with respect to etiology, such as social isolation and stress.[71] Social isolation is seen as an interactional variable in which persons deprived of normal interaction with others may develop fantasies and hallucinations through lack of social stimulation. The evidence accumulated thus far, however, would suggest that social isolation per se is not the cause of the illness, but rather it is "a sign that the individual's interpersonal difficulties have become so great that he is no longer capable of functioning in interpersonal relationships."[72] On the other hand, there is also evidence that stressful interaction can result in mental illness. For example, one study showed that the discrepancy between occupational achievement and aspiration was significantly greater in psychopathologic subjects than in their "normal" controls.[73] Other investigators have measured the effects of stress on mental health status in terms of ordinary life events such as marriage, divorce, job change or loss, a death in the family, changing residence, and so on. An accumulation of these events, both positive and negative, has

[68]Erving Goffman, "The Moral Career of the Mental Patient," *Psychiatry*, 22 (May, 1959), 123-142.

[69]Robert E. L. Faris and H. Warren Dunham, *Mental Disorders in Urban Areas*, Chicago: University of Chicago Press, 1939.

[70]See L. E. Hinkle, "Ecological Observations on the Relation of Physical Illness, Mental Illness and Social Environment," *Psychosomatic Medicine*, 23 (July-August, 1961), 289-297; and August B. Hollingshead, "Some Issues in the Epidemiology of Schizophrenia," *American Sociological Review*, 26 (February, 1961), 5-13.

[71] John A. Clausen and Melvin L. Kohn, "The Ecological Approach to Social Psychiatry," *American Journal of Sociology*, 50 (September, 1954), 140-148. See also Norman Cameron, "The Paranoid Pseudo-community," *American Journal of Sociology*, 49 (July, 1943), 32-38.

[72]Melvin L. Kohn and John A. Clausen, "Social Isolation and Schizophrenia," *American Sociological Review*, 20 (June, 1955), 265-273. The quote is on page 273. See also Edwin M. Lemert, "Paranoia and the Dynamics of Exclusion," *Sociometry*, 25 (March, 1962), 3-20.

[73]Robert J. Kleiner and Seymour Parker, "Goal Striving, Social Status and Mental Disorder: A Research Review," *American Sociological Review*, 28 (April, 1963), 189-202.

been found to be associated with symptoms and behaviors of mental disorders.[74]

Finally, it should be noted that epidemiologic research has pointed to the significance of socialization practices in accounting for variations in types and incidence of mental illness in different social classes.[75] Research of this type shows that the incidence of mental illness, especially schizophrenia, is generally higher in the lower social classes, although specific socialization practices causing mental illness have not yet been precisely identified. These studies further indicate that the availability and quality of treatment of mental disorders are greater for upper classes than for lower classes.[76]

As might be expected, with such fragmentary empirical knowledge and so many different variables to account for, prevention, control, and treatment of mental diseases are not in a very advanced stage. Although preventive measures have, for the most part, been ineffective, attempts to control and minimize the severity of the illness have shown considerable promise. Various therapeutic measures have been utilized to shorten the duration and decrease the severity of the illness, such as psychotherapy, electroshock therapy, hydrotherapy, and drugs. Moreover, it has been suggested that emergency psychiatric services be provided as a part of expanded outpatient services.[77]

These various efforts became embodied in a broad-scale attack on mental illness in the development of programs of community psychiatry or

[74]Barbara Snell Dohrenwend and Burce P. Dohrenwend (eds.), *Stressful Life Events: Their Nature and Effects,* New York: Wiley, 1974. See also Jerome K. Myers, Jacob J. Lindenthal, and Max P. Pepper, "Life Events and Psychiatric Impairment," *Journal of Nervous and Mental Disease,* 152 (March, 1971), 149–157, and by the same authors, "Life Events, Social Integration and Psychiatric Symptomatology," *Journal of Health and Social Behavior,* 16 (December, 1975), 421-427.

[75]See, for example, Hollingshead and Redlich, *op. cit.;* Jerome K. Myers and Bertram H. Roberts, *Family and Class Dynamics in Schizophrenia,* New York: Wiley, 1959; and more recently, Leo Srole, Thomas S. Langner, Stanley T. Michael, Marvin K. Opler, and Thomas A. C. Rennie, *Mental Health in the Metropolis,* New York: McGraw-Hill, 1962, especially pp. 190-252. Some methodological advances in this kind of epidemiologic research are reported in Leo Srole, "Measurement and Classification in Socio-psychiatric Epidemiology: Midtown Manhattan Study (1954) and Midtown Manhattan Restudy (1974)," *Journal of Health and Social Behavior,* 16 (December, 1975), 347-364.

[76]*Ibid.;* Jerome K. Myers and Leslie Schaffer, "Social Stratification in Psychiatric Practice," *American Sociological Review,* 19 (June, 1954), 307-310; Bert Kaplan, Robert B. Reed, and Wyman Richardson, "A Comparison of the Incidence of Hospitalized and Non-hospitalized Cases of Psychoses in Two Communities," *American Sociological Review,* 21 (August, 1956), 472-479; Robert H. Hardt and Sherman J. Feinhandler, "Social Class and Mental Hospitalization Prognosis," *American Sociological Review,* 24 (December, 1959), 815-821.

[77]Warren T. Vaughn and Mark G. Field, "New Perspectives of Mental Patient Care," *American Journal of Public Health,* 53 (February, 1963), 237-242.

community mental health.[78] Under the terms of the community Mental Health Centers Act of 1963, programs were developed to (1) address mental health needs of whole populations in communities, (2) focus attention on biologic as well as social-psychological factors in causation, and (3) through collaborative efforts, make more effective use of all community resources in prevention, treatment, and rehabilitation.[79] These key objectives were based on principles of "proximity, immediacy and expectancy"; that is, care of a troubled individual takes place in a familiar community setting where normal social bonds can be maintained. Care takes place without delay and, whenever possible, on an ambulatory basis. Expectancy refers to a positive, advocacy view by the health care team.[80] Comprehensive services included inpatient as well as outpatient services, emergency care, health education, and community organization.

The long-term impact of the community mental health center movement is not yet clear. There have been short-run gains in creating opportunities for new allied health professionals, for extending individual and group services into the community, where they were more accessible to those in need, and in stimulating research on environmental sources of stress. The movement is not without its critics, however. Some have challenged the benefits of services offered in ambulatory clinics,[81] while others have questioned the very principles on which the movement was based.[82] A critical review of the movement, based on experiences in one center, pointed to many unresolved issues such as professional versus community control, inability to meet public expectations that have been raised by an effective health education program, the difficulty of coordinating the services of independent providers, and the irrelevance of medical education

[78]Herzl R. Spiro, "On beyond Mental Health Centers," *Archives of General Psychiatry,* 21 (December, 1969), 646–654. For a general reference, see Bruce Denner and Richard H. Price (eds.), *Community Mental Health: Action and Reaction,* New York: Holt, Rinehart and Winston, 1973, or Richard H. Williams and Lucy D. Ozarin (eds.), *Community Mental Health, An International Perspective,* San Francisco: Jossey-Bass, 1968.

[79]Ralph G. Herschowitz, "Community Mental Health," *Current Medical Dialog,* 39 (July, 1972), 726-731. On prevention, see Bernard Rubin, "Community Psychiatry in the Decade of the 70's," *ibid.,* pp. 742-746; and W. M. Bolman and J. C. Westman, "Prevention of Mental Disorder: An Overview of Current Programs," *American Journal of Psychiatry,* 123 (March, 1967), 1058-1068. On the role of private psychiatry, see Perry C. Talkington, "The Private Psychiatric Hospital: Current Involvement in Community Mental Health," *Journal of the National Association of Private Psychiatric Hospitals,* 2 (Summer, 1970), 9-18.

[80]Herschowitz, *op. cit.* See also the social science perspective in Donald C. Klein, "The Meaning of Community in a Preventive Mental Health Program," *American Journal of Public Health,* 59 (November, 1969), 2005–2012.

[81]A. Jacobson, "A Critical Look at the Community Psychiatric Clinic," *American Journal of Psychiatry,* 124 (October, 1967), 14-20.

[82]Lawrence S. Kubie, "Pitfalls of Community Psychiatry," *Archives of General Psychiatry,* 18 (March, 1968), 257-266.

for community mental health services.[83] These and other key issues will have to be resolved before a final judgment can be made about community mental health centers as a strategy of defense against mental diseases.

## SUMMARY

It is quite apparent that there are many ways of classifying diseases and that we have chosen only one which permits a discussion of their sociologically relevant characteristics and of defense measures employed by human groups. With some variations, it has been shown that the types of defense measures employed vary with the amount of accumulated knowledge with respect to diseases in the particular categories chosen. Perhaps it should be emphasized that even with acute communicable diseases, where the amount of scientifically demonstrated knowledge is greatest, these diseases continue to take a toll of human lives each year. In part, this reflects differences in stages of developments of different areas of the country, but it also reflects the failure of social action and programs in prevention. In this respect, we found that social-psychological factors in response to disease and illness were important in understanding why people do not take advantage of prevention programs, thus permitting preventable diseases to continue to flourish in a population.

Similarly, we noted that in defending themselves against diseases about which less information is known, people look to treatments which tend to become social in nature, with hopes for a biological breakthrough. That is, when the cause of and cure for a disease are known, the disease can be treated directly (and often quickly), with less need for consideration of social-psychological facets. When such knowledge is lacking, however, and when prolonged treatment is necessary, that treatment more often tends to involve others besides the patient, such as the family.

## SUGGESTED READINGS

Albrecht, Gary L. (ed.), *The Sociology of Physical Disability and Rehabilitation,* Pittsburgh: University of Pittsburgh Press, 1976.

Alexander, Franz, *Psychosomatic Medicine,* New York: Norton, 1950.

Barker, Roger S., Beatrice A. Wright, and Mollie R. Gonick, *Adjustment to Physical Handicap and Illness: A Survey of the Social Psychology of Physique and Disability,* New York: Social Science Research Council Bulletin 55, 1946.

Hollingshead, A. B., and F. C. Redlich, *Social Class and Mental Illness,* New York: Wiley, 1958.

Srole, Leo, Thomas S. Langner, S. T. Michael, and Marvin K. Opler, *Mental Health in the Metropolis,* rev. ed., New York: Harper and Row, 1975.

[83]Anthony F. Panzetta, *Community Mental Health: Myth and Reality,* Philadephia: Lea & Febiger, 1971.

# Chapter 4

# The Response to Illness

*There are many occasions when the disease requires no treatment, but the patient does. It is rare when the disease requires treatment, but the patient does not.*

Leandro M. Tocantis, M.D.
Jefferson Medical College, Philadelphia

The noted anthropologist Bronislaw Malinowski long ago observed that human behavior, and hence the institutions that organize it into meaningful patterned activities, arises in the first instance because of the biological needs of humans. He tried to develop a scientific theory of culture on this premise, explaining all the manifold activities of people as being either directly or indirectly related to their attempts to assure for themselves the basic needs which they, as organisms, require in order to survive and to thrive.[1] The whole area of medicine as an aspect of human behavior would seem directly to fit Malinowski's assertion that human institutions are

[1]Bronislaw Malinowski, *The Scientific Theory of Culture and Other Essays,* Chapel Hill: University of North Carolina Press, 1944.

based upon individual biological needs. What could be closer to an attempt
to fulfill people's biological needs for survival than their attempts to understand, prevent, and cure the diseases to which the human organism is
prone?

It is nonetheless true, as any doctor will attest, that a great deal of
medical activity on the part of both patients and professionals is at best only
indirectly related to people's need to protect themselves against the ravages
of physical illness. Physicians complain that 50 percent and more of the
patients who come to their waiting rooms "have nothing physically wrong
with them."[2] By this they mean that modern medicine cannot discern that
many of those who come to the examining room are the victims of any
known organic disease. These patients, however, have complaints which
from their point of view are just as real as are the complaints of those for
whom medicine can provide a diagnosis and, hopefully, a cure. Similarly, a
great deal of the activity of physicians and others whose occupations have
to do with the maintenance of the health of the public touches only
indirectly, if at all, upon actual attempts to deal with the phenomenon of
sickness, in terms of either diagnosing and treating it or attempting to
prevent it. Physicians in private practice, for example, are forced to pay a
great deal of attention to the mundane matters of supporting themselves
and the nurses, secretaries, and assistants who are their employees.
Patients must be billed and the bills must be collected. Supplies must be
ordered, paid for, and made ready for use. Records must be kept, not only
about patients' diseases, but about when they may be expected to see the
physician and about many other matters which are required by insurance
companies, other prepayment agents, health departments, or other governmental agencies. The same physicians may spend much of their time
training new employees in their offices and in lecturing to student nurses or
participating in the training of young physicians in hospitals. And some
physicians are frequently engaged in representing the interests of their
colleagues through the activities of organized medicine. All this professional activity, of course, is designed to make direct medical activity on the
part of professionals more efficient and more effective. But it is also
designed to achieve other ends, ranging from an individual's need to
support self and family to a conviction that medicine can be effectively
practiced only within the context of a certain kind of socioeconomic order,
or to the faith that physicians have a responsibility for the improvement of
community patterns of living, or to the belief that it is important for health

---

[2]See, for example, Allen C. Johnson, Hilda H. Kroeger, Isadore Altman, Dean A. Clark,
and Cecil G. Sheps, "The Office Practice of Internists: III. Characteristics of Patients,"
*Journal of the American Medical Association,* 193 (Sept. 13, 1965), 916–922. See also H. P.
Dreitzel (ed.), *The Social Organization of Health,* New York: Macmillan, 1971, p. viii.

professionals to be interested in and to participate in the development of basic science (even though this understanding may have no direct relationship to the problem of dealing with illness).

The fact that both patients and professionals do many things within the context of medical behavior which are not readily related to their need to prevent or cure disease is not unusual. It is a characteristic of human behavior that even though institutions may be developed to deal quite directly with obvious basic human needs, all of them tend to become involved to a greater or lesser degree in the attempt to serve other basic needs or, more usually, needs which can only be connected indirectly, at best, to the needs of people as organisms.[3] That this is true of an aspect of culture so obviously connected with the specific and tangible needs of people as organisms is fundamental evidence for an important principle of human behavior, namely, that all human activity stems from multiple motives and may, therefore, serve multiple functions. It also means, for purposes of our present analysis, that medicine and medical behavior must always be seen in the context of human interactions and cultural understandings as a whole and not merely as a set of activities which relate to specific biological needs of human beings.

## THE CONCEPTS OF DISEASE AND ILLNESS

Part of the reason why medicine cannot be confined to an attempt to alleviate and overcome specific biological needs stems from the nature of disease itself. It is true that modern medicine understands disease as being specifically related to changes in specific organs of the body caused by specific agents, which, if once allowed to affect the body, do so in predictable ways, but the situation almost never appears thus to people suffering from the disease or to their lay associates. For when individuals are sick, they feel that something is wrong with them *as whole individuals,* and their sickness is apt to permeate everything that they do and all the ways in which they perceive themselves.[4]

Disease, as we have pointed out, is a universal phenomenon, the scope of which can be shown to vary according to a host of factors, among them those of the social environment. But diseases are, according to the understanding of modern medicine, specific kinds of biological reactions to some kind of injury or change affecting the internal environment of the body.[5] As

[3]This was, of course, an important part of Malinowski's theory of culture itself. Malinowski, *op. cit.*

[4]Some evidence on this point is given in Irving Kenneth Zola, "Pathways to the Doctor—From Person to Patient," *Social Science and Medicine,* 7 (November, 1973), 677–689.

[5]See Wiley Forbus, *Reaction to Injury,* Baltimore: Williams & Wilkins, 1952.

such, they can be understood and dealt with only after they have somehow been brought to the attention of persons skilled in biological science. The usual way in which this happens stems from the fact that someone feels sick and, in an attempt to do something about this matter, consults a physician or someone else who can understand and deal with whatever disease is making him or her feel ill.

A basic distinction, then, which is fundamental for an understanding of medical behavior, is that between *disease* and *illness.* By *disease,* we mean an objective phenomenon characterized by altered functioning of the body as a biological organism. However apparent their manifestations, diseases are hidden processes which can only be understood as their observable signs are related to a body of knowledge about the way in which the human organism works. By *illness,* we mean a subjective phenomenon in which individuals perceive themselves as not feeling well and therefore may tend to modify their normal behavior. The distinction between these two concepts is important to sociology in that it permits analysis of behavior of sick persons and those around them as a consequence not only of differences in knowledge and perception, but also of structural properties of the interaction (roles and statuses). The special case of the interaction between doctor and patient, as we shall see later, lends itself to a sociological perspective on deviance and social control.[6]

### The Concept of Disease

Diagnosis of a disease is made by correlating the observable *signs* or *symptoms* of a disease with knowledge about the functioning of the human organism. Thus, understanding of disease depends upon observations of altered, abnormal states of the human organism. These signs may be objectively observed and even measurable, such as elevated body temperature or skin rash, or they may be subjective symptoms, such as a pain in the back.[7] They may involve an overt behavior which is not regularly expected of normal people, such as a limp or a cough, or a reported change in motivation, such as lack of appetite. They may involve an observed difference in the state of the body, such as a changed or abnormal coloration of the skin, or of various bodily excretions as, for example, a bloody stool. It should be emphasized that the concept of symptom usually implies a change in the status of an organism, a departure of some sort from the normal or expected situation.

[6]Andrew C. Twaddle, "Illness and Deviance," *Social Science and Medicine,* 7 (November, 1973), 751–762.

[7]Strictly speaking, a symptom is a subjective phenomenon which is apparent only to the individual perceiving it, and a sign is an objective manifestation observable by someone other than the patient and perhaps by the patient as well. See Cyril M. MacBryde, *Signs and Symptoms,* Philadelphia: Lippincott, 1964, p. 1.

Many of the signs of disease are not directly observable, and it has been one of the basic sources of the success of modern medicine to have found methods for taking "readings" of bodily function which allow skilled observers to pick up signs which they would ordinarily not be able to sense. The stethoscope—invented by Laennec in 1816—is a case in point. This simple acoustical device, acting to channel sounds of breathing and heart-beat to the ear made possible the description of numerous signs of respiratory and cardiac diseases. The function of the whole gamut of laboratory tests in modern medicine is basically to provide new ways in which the physician's power to observe the signs of disease can be enhanced.

It is characteristic of signs and symptoms that they are patterned and that their appearance can be related to other events. Thus, the rash which lay people call poison ivy and which medical people describe as "an inflammation . . . accompanied by erythema, swelling, vesicles, bullae and a serous discharge when the lesions rupture"[8] appears on the skin from a few hours to several days after it was brought into contact with *Rhus toxicodendron,* the poison ivy plant. And, barring infection or other complications, the rash ordinarily subsides in one to three weeks, usually producing considerable discomfort while it lasts. Thus, the physician who has learned to recognize the skin rash characteristic of poison ivy may infer something about the events which brought it about and also can predict what will happen with respect to the rash. All this is an example of the fact that signs and symptoms can be related to an ordered and predictable chain of events—that diseases have a natural history.[9] As Klemperer put it, disease is "life under altered conditions . . . disease is the experiment of nature; we see only the results, and we are ignorant of the conditions under which the experiment has been performed."[10] As scientific knowledge about these "experiments of nature" develops, the concepts of disease become more and more precise.

Signs and symptoms are always understood by medical science against the background of what is known about the way the human organism works. Thus, basic to the development of a "science" of medicine (as opposed to lore about the treatment of illness) is an understanding of the structure and functioning of the body—of anatomy and physiology. This knowledge is, of course, extremely complex and specialized, and it is not

[8]Oliver S. Ormsby and Hamilton Montgomery, *Diseases of the Skin,* 8th ed., Philadelphia: Lea & Febiger, 1954, p. 205. *The American Pocket Medical Dictionary* defines *inflammation* as "a morbid condition characterized by redness, pain, heat and swelling"; *erythema* as "redness of skin or rose rash of many varieties"; *vesicle* as "a small blister or bladder"; and *bulla* as a bleb (skin vesicle filled with fluid).

[9]See John Ryle, *The Natural History of Disease,* New York: Oxford University Press, 1948.

[10]Paul Klemperer, "Introduction" in W. A. D. Anderson, *Pathology,* 4th ed., St. Louis: Mosby, 1961, p. 18.

our purpose to discuss it in detail here. We might note, however, that medical science is developing at an accelerating rate and that, as a whole, this development has proceeded from the general to the specific, from gross to microscopic, and from a static to a dynamic, process-oriented understanding of human biology. Prerequisite to an understanding of how the body works is a clear grasp of how it is built; thus, it is not surprising that anatomical knowledge has been basic to medicine. This knowledge has progressively been extended to more and more microscopic levels—from knowledge of the principal organ systems to knowledge of the various tissues of the body and thence to knowledge of cellular and subcellular structures. As knowledge of normal bodily structure has been increased at a microscopic level, so also has knowledge of the structural results of disease (pathology) and of the biological environment. Indeed, the microscopic investigation of this environment by fields such as bacteriology and virology has been of critical importance in the contemporary understanding of disease.

Moreover, just as knowledge of bodily structure has increased at a microscopic level, so has that of function. After the early, great achievements of physiology, devoted to elucidating the way organ systems operate—preeminent among them Harvey's demonstration of the mechanism of the circulation of the blood—attention was increasingly paid to the behavior of cells. This kind of study inevitably emphasized the *chemical* reactions and transfers occurring within the body; hence biochemical processes came to be seen as fundamental, not only for the understanding of the normal functioning of the body, but for the understanding of the processes of disease as well.

Without pursuing further here the nature and direction of development of the medical sciences, it should be clear that the concept of disease utilizes knowledge about the structure and functioning of the human body at a number of levels—the organism itself, its organs, tissues, and cells. It emphasizes the relationship between the ongoing physical and biochemical processes taking place within the body and the events of the natural history which a patient's symptoms betoken. And it focuses particularly upon those correlations between signs and symptoms, associated regularities in the patient's environment, and relevant physiological processes which seem to explain (in biological terms) the patient's illness.

The physician's job as an applied medical scientist, therefore, may be seen as threefold. First, from observing the signs of the patient's physiological status, eliciting the symptoms the patient perceives, and uncovering the relevant facts about the patient's background and experience, the physician arrives at a diagnosis—a fitting of the facts of the patient's situation to the abstract pattern of conditions and events which we call a disease. Second, the physician "thinks physiologically," relating what is known of the patient and the disease to what can be inferred to be occurring inside the patient. And third, the physician evolves a plan of remedial action, which seeks to make use of his or her knowledge of physiology and pathology in such a way as to restore to normal functioning (as nearly as possible) the disordered cells, tissues, and organs. In this way the physician hopes to cure the patient.

From this cursory account of the concept of disease and the nature of medical science, it should be clear that the physician deals with much more—and also much less—than what can be observed about the sick person who may come to the consulting room. Indeed, it may be proper to say that, as medical scientist, he or she does not deal with the sick person at all, but with the physiological processes that occur within the organism, particularly as these are given relevance by the diagnosis that it is a "case" of a disease. In doing so, the physician brings to bear an immensely rich and complex heritage of scientific knowledge about the organism, utilizes a formidable scientific technology, and makes judgments involving discernment born of rich experience and skill.

## The Concept of Illness

Contrasted with disease, which is a concept of biology—more specifically, of pathology—illness is a phenomenon which is apparent to the *individual* in terms of an altered state of perception of self. He or she feels sick and, hence, may act in ways which are different from those which might normally be expected of him or her. Because it is commonly the case that some kind of physical disorder about which a medical scientist can think and act in terms of concepts of *disease* is associated with the feelings of *sickness,* these ideas are often thought of as virtually synonymous. Yet it is true that a disease can occur in individuals without any awareness of feelings of sickness and without anyone else knowing them to be other than in a "normal" state. Thus, a disease process may take place within individuals without recognizable symptoms ever being produced.[11] They

[11]Physicians refer to this as a disease which runs "a subclinical course," never obtruding upon the attention of the individual. Yet it is not uncommon to find evidence that the individual was exposed to a disease agent even though he or she was never aware of being sick and experienced no recognizable pattern of symptoms. For example, a substantial proportion of the adult population of the United States reacts positively to a tuberculin test. The majority of people, it is believed, have at some time been infected by the tuberculosis bacillus, which produced changes in the body sufficient to elicit a positive response to a specific biological test. In some of these people, this is the only observable evidence ever found of an encounter with this disease. In others, there may have been a slight illness, perhaps interpreted as a cold, which never became serious enough to warrant seeing a physician or, if one was consulted, for the physician to think of tuberculosis as a possible correlate of the signs of disease then visible. In still others—a small minority—a positive test may be a record of a past history of known tuberculosis or a currently active condition.

may, for example, complain of being unusually tired or of not having a good appetite, never thinking that this may be the result of a disease process underway within their bodies. Only later, when symptoms become more pronounced or more dramatic, may they understand that they are sick and consult medical advice. At this point, the physician may diagnose a disease such as cancer, for example, and indicate that the patients may have had the disease for some time. Many diseases, especially chronic ones, have this kind of insidious onset. The lack of clarity and pattern of the symptoms produced in the early stages of these diseases frequently makes it difficult for medical science to intervene before the pathological process has advanced to the point where significant damage has already occurred.

On the other hand, it is also possible that persons may feel sick—even so miserable that they are incapacitated—without any of the organic processes of disease being manifested. In this case, as we have pointed out in Chapter 3, physicians talk about illnesses that are psychosomatic in origin. These illnesses either represent the results of disease processes which are as yet not scientifically validated or must be interpreted as the result of something other than an organic pathological process.

Not only does the concept of illness differ from that of disease, but we must also distinguish between illness as a personal event and illness as a social phenomenon. Illness is a personal event to the extent that each of us attempts first to evaluate for himself or herself the meaning of any symptoms of which we become aware. Quite naturally, this evaluation would be conditioned by our knowledge of and experience with these symptoms. Thus, symptoms which we have had before and which always seem to go away by themselves are not likely to cause much concern. New symptoms, however, especially if they are accompanied by pain, may well motivate the individual to do something. The point is that as long as what we feel is not communicated to others or what we do is not observed by others, illness remains a personal event.

On the other hand, illness becomes a social phenomenon when it becomes visible to others and when this leads to modification of the social interaction patterns between the sick person and other people. The awareness by others that someone is ill usually occurs through one or both of two routes. First, it may be a result of direct observation of the sick person's actions. He or she may fail to fulfill normal role expectations or perform them inadequately. Although this may occur for many reasons, attention to this failure of performance may cause those around the sick person to realize that the inadequate behavior may be due to the fact of sickness. Their observation of his or her behavior may help to confirm this as they see that he or she looks sick; behaves in a biologically abnormal fashion, such as limping, breathing rapidly, or trembling; or exhibits altered external characteristics (is pale, flushed, has a rash, etc.). Secondly, their observation would be supplemented by the sick person's communicating his or her feelings to others. What is important to note here is that in different social situations, the opportunity to observe and be told about a person's sickness may vary considerably.[12] The more prolonged and intimate the social contact, the greater the chances for observation of and communication about the illness. This means, in general, that members of one's family and primary groups have a better chance to become aware of illness than do others. Similarly, those whose attention is directed to evaluating the performance of others are more apt to detect problems than are more casual observers. For this reason, mothers, spouses, employers, and work partners may in some cases be more prone to see changes in role performance possibly caused by illness than persons who are related to the individual in other ways.

What is the *sociological* significance of all this? In the first place, one may inquire how this pragmatic and empirical, yet notably abstract and selective way of thinking about and dealing with disease came about. What forces encouraged its development? Certainly, the scientific concept of disease is not intuitively apparent, but it is rooted in knowledge which itself is available only to those who are privy to what the Victorians called "the secrets of nature." It is but one way of thinking about illness, and, for that matter, it is the appropriate way only insofar as one's object is to alter and improve the *biological* state of the sick man. The procedures of medical science are not necessarily sources of *psychological* reassurance, and they may be completely irrelevant to what some might take to be a sick person's spiritual needs. The very evolution of scientific medicine—and its acceptance—involved the development of a value perspective and set of institutional arrangements which were uniquely developed in the Western tradition. It is this sociological structure which forms the principal subject matter of this volume.[13]

Second, it cannot be too strongly emphasized that scientific knowledge

[12]These observations have been made many times. See, for example, the review in Irving Kenneth Zola, "Studying the Decision to See a Doctor: Review, Critique, Corrective," in Z. Lipowski (ed.), *Advances in Psychosomatic Medicine,* Basel, Switzerland: Karger, 1972, pp. 216–236. See also D. R. Hannay and E. J. Maddox, "Symptom Prevalence and Referral Behaviour in Glasgow," *Social Science and Medicine,* 10 (March–April, 1976), 185–189.

[13]Because the physician, in dealing with the patient, is always involved in a person-to-person interaction, he or she behaves toward that patient in ways over and above this model of the pure role of the "medical scientist." Doctors not only deal with cases of disease, but treat sick people. However, the degree to which the physician's behavior as medical scientist versus the social and supportive aspects of the role meets the patient's expectations forms a part of the patient's evaluation of the "quality" of care received and of his or her satisfaction with the encounter. See Donald E. Larsen and Irving Rootman, "Physician Role Performance and Patient Satisfaction," *Social Science and Medicine,* 10 (January, 1976), 29–32.

of disease has developed and, to a large extent, has remained in the custody of a small, highly educated group of specialists.[14] Although increasingly the rudiments of a scientific concept of disease have become diffused to the lay majority, most people know so little about the scientific basis for medicine that they call antibiotics and similar pharmacologic agents "wonder drugs" and frequently regard their physicians as little short of miracle workers.[15] Perhaps the common lay attitude toward scientific medicine is not unlike our attitude toward the rest of science: we accept and take for granted the remarkable benefits of its technology, but only vaguely understand the scientific principles upon which it is based—and are dependent upon experts to translate these principles into practical results. For example, consider the average person's avid acceptance of and dependence upon the applied results of physical knowledge about electricity, the vague understanding of the theory of electric currents and their behavior, and the inability to make more than the most minor repairs to appliances without expert help.

This suggests several things about the differences between the lay person's and the scientific specialist's approach to medicine:

**1** Lay persons and specialists have widely divergent understandings about the events of illness. Although the lay person's understanding of diseases is, in our culture, certainly strongly dependent upon the scientific knowledge concerning diseases and is informed by its general perspectives, lay understanding is scientifically quite imperfect both in detail and in its broad outlines.[16]

**2** The person who has a disease not only understands it differently, but regards it from a different perspective than does a medical scientist. The person who has a disease is emotionally involved in a way that other people—and particularly specialists, who have an abstract scientific understanding and methodology as tools to confront an illness—can never be. In short, while the physician exercises objectivity in evaluating the meaning of

---

[14]In Chap. 5, we shall analyze some of the ways of thinking about and acting toward illness found in other cultures, which do not involve a scientific concept of disease. In Chap. 6, we shall try to sum up the salient features of the development of Western medicine. In Western societies, however, control of knowledge and its application is a basic element in a sociological analysis of the profession of medicine.

[15]See the analysis in Marshall H. Becker and Lois A. Maiman, "Sociobehavioral Determinants of Compliance with Health and Medical Care Recommendations," *Medical Care,* 13 (January, 1975), 10–24.

[16]Earl L. Koos, *The Health of Regionville,* New York: Columbia University Press, 1954. See also Lionel S. Lewis and Joseph Lopreato, "Arationality, Ignorance and Perceived Danger in Medical Practices," *American Sociological Review,* 27 (August, 1962), 508–514. More recently see Eric J. Cassell, "Disease as an 'IT': Concepts of Disease Revealed by Patients' Presentation of Symptoms," *Social Science and Medicine,* 10 (March–April, 1976), 143–146.

symptoms, the patient's perspective is a subjective one—the patient is the one who feels the pain. It is the patient's life that is affected by the illness.

   3  For the most part specialists see a case of disease in terms of knowledge they already possess—although even after they have been fully trained, physicians certainly learn from their patients; the lay people ordinarily find that their perspectives about disease change markedly as a result of their experience with it and particularly because of what they learn from the specialists whom they may consult about the disease.

   4  The basis for deciding what action to take with respect to a disease is often quite different for the patient than for the professional. Physicians have their detailed knowledge of pathology as a basis against which to evaluate what they are doing. Particularly, they are able to make a prognosis or an estimate of the probabilities of a particular patient's situation in view of what they can understand about the disease that the patient may have and about the patient's general physiological condition. Moreover, they have professional standards against which to judge their ability and effectiveness in diagnosis and treatment.

   Patients, on the other hand, must make their evaluation primarily in terms of their own direct experience. Do they feel better or do they not? At the same time, it must be said that most patients and most lay persons have a great deal of faith in their professional helpers and are willing to assume that even though they do not seem to feel better very fast, their doctors are doing the best that they can for them.[17] In the third place, then, the conditions for this *confidence* (on the part of patients) are an important problem for the sociological interpretation of medical behavior. Here we can only suggest that confidence is, in part, a function of the fact that the lay cultural perspective sees disease as a phenomenon which requires special understanding, and this allows lay people to be dependent upon the good offices of professionals who are legitimately trained for their office.[18] Thus, lay people tend to trust reputable physicians out of necessity, but this is subject to change, depending in part upon the outcomes of the interaction.[19]

   Physicians as scientists not only see the problem of a patient's sickness differently from their patients, but have a radically more sophisticated intellectual perspective from which to understand disease. This being so, one would expect that an important part of every physician's job must be in

   [17]Cf., James R. Sorenson, "Biomedical Innovation, Uncertainty and Doctor-Patient Interaction," *Journal of Health and Social Behavior,* 15 (December, 1974), 366–374.
   [18]The most extensive analysis of this unequal relationship between doctor and patient and of its consequences is Eliot Freidson, *Profession of Medicine,* New York: Dodd, Mead, 1970.
   Lawrence S. Linn, "Factors Associated with Patient Evaluation of Health Care," *Health and Society,* 53 (Fall, 1975), 531–548.

some way to communicate with patients—to be able to understand and to apply what the patients say to the scientific medical perspective and at the same time to be able to advise the patients on their condition, its causes, and its prognosis in language which the patients can understand. Unfortunately, this kind of communication is too seldom successful when it does occur.[20] In part, this may be due to the physician being uncertain about the diagnosis and not wishing either to raise falsely the patients' hopes or to make the patients unduly anxious about their situation. Thus, the physician may be deliberately vague in relating information to the patients. For their part, patients are often reluctant to press the doctor for definitive answers because then the patients would appear to be questioning the physician's expert judgment.

In the process involved in disclosing approaching death, Glaser and Strauss reported that

> . . . doctors typically do not give details of the illness, and the type of patient under consideration does not ask for them. Primarily, this is a problem of communication: the doctor finds it hard to explain the illness to a working class patient, while lack of familiarity with the technical terms, as well as a more general deference to the doctor, inhibits the patient's impulse to question him.[21]

As the quotation suggests, the lack of communication stems from the different attitudes and expectations which both the doctor and the patient bring to their mutual interaction. More often than not there will be a difference in their respective social, cultural, and educational backgrounds. Certainly, the physician's scientific training is likely to be more extensive than the patient's, and it is partly for this reason that doctors tend not to listen to what the patient says, but rather to depend upon what signs they can observe for themselves to make a diagnosis. Thus, when discussing their findings with the patient, they find it hard to relate them to what the patient has said, and there is a tendency to couch the information in technical language which the patient is unlikely to understand.[22] Moreover, in certain situations, physicians may feel that their reticence is justified because the patient does not really want to know the diagnosis.

[20]Eliot Freidson, *Professional Dominance,* New York: Atherton, 1970. See also Raymond S. Duff and August B. Hollingshead, *Sickness and Society,* New York: Harper and Row, 1968.

[21]Barney C. Glaser and Anselm Strauss, *Awareness of Dying,* Chicago: Aldine, 1965, p. 123.

[22]However, physicians tend to underestimate patients' ability to understand. See John B. McKinlay, "Who Is Really Ignorant—Physician or Patient?" *Journal of Health and Social Behavior,* 16 (March, 1975), 3–11.

The patient, on the other hand, may contribute to the lack of communication by not wishing to ask for an explanation because this might reveal ignorance. Moreover, the patient's reluctance may be due to a belief that to question the expert too closely would show a lack of *confidence* in the expertise of the doctor. A substantial part of the cooperation between doctor and patient depends upon this confidence because medical knowledge has increased so much and become so technical and because control over this knowledge and its use are limited to the profession of medicine.[23]

## ILLNESS AND THE SOCIAL SYSTEM: THE SICK ROLE

These critical observations of the nature of the doctor-patient relationship—institutional arrangements, differential perceptions, and unequal statuses—have provided a means for analysis of larger social processes, namely deviance and social control. A seminal contribution to our understanding of the processes and to stimulation of much research by others on the concepts was made by Talcott Parsons.[24] In developing a perspective on general social theory, he used the doctor-patient relationship to illustrate some principles of social systems that are still being discussed and investigated today.[25]

Parson's original formulation held that from the point of view of the groups to which the sick belong—their social systems, if you will—the inability of one or more members to fulfill competently and completely their normal obligations to the group may have serious ramifications. It may delay or even obviate goal achievement. It may require reassignment of role tasks to others who, temporarily at least, perform not only their own duties, but the sick person's as well. More generally, we may describe the group member's inability to meet the expectations of other members as a special case of deviant behavior. It is deviant in that group standards or norms for performance are violated, and it is a special case in that, ordinarily, sick people are unwilling victims of disease and through no fault of their own fail to perform as expected. Irrespective of responsibility for the condition, illness as a form of deviant behavior represents a problem in social control. That is, each group must develop ways to cope with illness and the sort of behavior exhibited by sick people.

In this regard, we may note the part played by sick people themselves. If they are not able (or not allowed) to play their normal roles, then some

[23]Freidson, *op. cit.*
[24]Talcott Parsons, *The Social System,* New York: Free Press, 1951, chap. 10.
[25]A recent review of twenty-five years of influence of Parsons' concept of sick role is in Alexander Segall, "The Sick Role Concept: Understanding Illness Behavior," *Journal of Health and Social Behavior,* 17 (June, 1976), 162–169.

other arrangements for them must be made in the social structure of the group; i.e., most groups recognize a "sick role." That the sick role is a social role may be seen in that it has certain rights and obligations as well as complementary roles. Since sick people are presumed not to be at fault for their condition, one of the rights accorded them is *to be excused from normal duties*. This, of course, is of crucial importance to the continued functioning of the group inasmuch as sick persons often not only do not perform their own tasks, but may also interfere with the performances of others. Groups often have alternative arrangements for carrying out necessary tasks, and the advent of illness in one of their members initiates the new role arrangements. This right has importance for individuals also in that they do not lose status by being temporary nonperformers, but rather their nonperformance is excused by the group. Moreover, sick persons are not expected to recover without help; that is, it is appropriate in this situation that they have a *claim upon others for assistance and care*. This assistance may be in the form of technical help and advice or it may be help in carrying out the activities of daily living or both. These two rights, then, are designed to relieve sick persons of normal duties which they could perform only with great effort, if at all, and to legitimate their demand for help. However, even temporary nonperformance of duties of group members may cause functional problems for the group. The more critical the duties are for group processes, the more likely it is that these tasks will temporarily be assigned to well members of the group. At the other extreme, less important duties may simply not be performed at all for the duration of the illness.

As we have noted above, the sick role is a social role, and, as such, it imposes certain obligations on sick people. These obligations are designed to bring the sick people back to a state of health as rapidly as possible and at the same time minimally limit the disruption of group processes from nonperformance of roles. The normal state of being well means that being ill is undesirable, and, therefore, one is obliged *to want to get well as quickly as possible*. Related to this is the obligation *to seek competent technical help and cooperate in the process of getting well*.

The first obligation serves to reduce the likelihood that patients may come to "enjoy" their state of being ill, that is, to receive some "secondary gain"[26] from being dependent upon others. Obtaining some gratification from being ill would tend to prolong the time during which the ill persons would not be contributing to the functioning of the groups to which they belong. The second obligation—to seek technical help—is an explicit recognition of the complex nature of modern medicine and the need for expert advice. As we have noted above, acceptance of expert advice is also

---

[26]Parsons, *op. cit.*

partly a matter of the patients' confidence in the physician. The obligation to cooperate with the doctor in getting well serves to reinforce acceptance of advice. These obligations, then, serve to direct the motivation and behavior of the sick person toward recovering from the illness and, subsequently, resuming normal roles in the most expeditious manner.

There is another element of the sick role which is important for group processes, namely, legitimation of being ill. It is not enough for people simply to announce that they are ill, but this definition must be acceptable to others in the group. What Suchman has termed as "provisional validation"[27] is a process in which others around sick people accept their statement that they feel ill, perhaps confirming it by their observations of more objective changes, resulting in group approval for the sick members' temporary relief from normal duties. However, if people accept the rights of the sick role, they must also accept the obligations, namely, to seek competent help in getting well. In the process, they receive official validation of the claim to the sick role. That is, through observation of objective signs, the doctor can officially validate the fact that the patients have a disease. This puts the physician in a position of being an agent of social control since without this validation, the people may be defined as malingerers and exposed to group sanctions. More generally, failure on the part of the sick persons either to exercise the rights or fulfill the obligations of the sick role may well elicit sanctions from the group. If sick people perform normal roles only inadequately, they may be forced by the group to vacate them because their inadequate performance is more disruptive than redistributing their tasks among well members or not having them done at all. Similarly, sick people who exercise their rights, but are not motivated to get well or, worse, who *enjoy* being sick—relieved from duties, dependent upon others—are also likely to be censured by the group. Just what sanctions would be employed, of course, depends a great deal on the type of group, the sanctions available to it, the people to be censured, etc. In general it could be said that illness is but one form of deviance with which a group must deal and that a group is likely to deal with it in a manner similar to other, equivalent forms of deviance.

The rights and obligations associated with the sick role imply the existence of complementary roles; i.e., roles played by others in regard to the behavior of the sick person. We have already noted the roles of other group members and the ways in which groups cope with the sick person. Similarly, at least in our society, the obligations of the sick role include the complementary role of the therapist, particularly the physician as the principal healer.

[27]Edward A. Suchman, "Stages of Illness and Medical Care," *Journal of Health and Human Behavior,* 6 (Fall, 1965), 114–128.

Early writers such as Henderson, and later Parsons, viewed the doctor-patient relationship as a special case of social relationships governed by sets of explicit norms concerning the behavior of both parties.[28] Their analyses tended to focus on how the specific attributes of the roles of doctor and patient complement each other and, therefore, contribute to the functioning of the relationship. Implicit in this analysis is the assumption that both doctor and patient know and understand what behavior is expected of both parties. Bloom has adopted a similar model, except that role attributes are shown to be influenced by other factors such as kinship and subcultural groups for the patient, professional colleagues and other reference groups for the physician, and by generalized sociocultural values for both.[29]

More recently, several questions have been raised about this perspective on the functioning of the doctor-patient relationship. First, few of the recent research investigations offer strong support for the broad conceptual model. Rather, most of these studies indicate a higher degree of variability in acceptance of rights and obligations of the sick role or of behavior predicted by the model.[30] Second, the "optimistic" view of functioning of the doctor-patient relationship has been challenged because it assumes the model of acute diseases inasmuch as treatment can be confined to one or two encounters and is often successful because of a specific therapeutic intervention. However, none of the role characteristics of this model seems to be satisfied for a *chronic* health problem.[31] When one looks at characteristics of chronic diseases, as we did in Chapter 3, there is much less reason to assume that both doctor and patient share expectations concerning their

[28]L. J. Henderson, "Physician and Patient as a Social System," *New England Journal of Medicine,* 18 (May, 1935), 819–823. Also Parsons, *op. cit.*

[29]Samuel Bloom, *The Doctor and His Patient,* New York: Russell Sage, 1963.

[30]Segall, *op. cit.* See also Andrew C. Twaddle, "Health Decisions and Sick Role Variations: An Exploration," *Journal of Health and Social Behavior,* 10 (June, 1969), 105–115; and Emil Berkanovic, "Lay Conceptions of the Sick Role," *Social Forces,* 51 (September, 1972), 53–64.

[31]Rodney M. Coe and Albert F. Wessen, "Social-psychological Factors Influencing the Use of Community Health Resources," *American Journal of Public Health,* 55 (July, 1965), 1024–1031. In a recent statement, Parsons has noted that the original formulation was not intended to be dependent upon a model of acute diseases. Talcott Parsons, "The Sick Role and the Role of the Physician Reconsidered," *Health and Society,* 53 (Summer, 1975), 257–278. In a special issue of *Social Science and Medicine,* Gallagher suggested some modifications of Parsons' concept to take account of chronicity, status differences, and the focus on the acute model of disease in medical organization. Gerson, however, argued that the use of the concept of deviance was misleading in this context and that interaction between doctor and patient and among health institutions was more understandable if conceptualized as a political process. See Eugene B. Gallagher, "Lines of Reconstruction and Extension of Parsonian Sociology of Illness," *Social Science and Medicine,* 10 (May, 1976), 207–218; and Elihu M. Gerson, "The Social Character of Illness: Deviance or Politics?" *ibid.,* pp. 219–224. An example of the political nature of the interaction was provided in David E. Hayes-Bautista, "Modifying the Treatment: Patient Compliance, Patient Control and Medical Care," *ibid.,* pp. 233–238.

respective behavior. Chronic diseases often require not just one but many modes of therapy and usually require long periods of treatment. Moreover, the success of the medical management of chronic diseases has been much less dramatic than for acute ailments.

Similarly, the general concept of the sick role seems not to fit psychiatric illnesses.[32] Not only do most psychiatric problems have the characteristics of chronic rather than acute diseases, but the question of personal responsibility for the illness often arises. Furthermore, the sick person has to face the potential burden of stigma and rejection not normally involved in recovery from physical illnesses. Even for physical illnesses, Freidson has shown how the general sick-role concept is only one of several types of responses to deviance depending upon degree of seriousness of the illness and degree of legitimacy.[33] Thus, Freidson's analysis and critique help explain the variation in functioning of the sick role as a mechanism of control on deviant behavior as reported in the literature.

Finally, it has been noted that the equilibrium model in which the sick role has been set is not the only theoretical perspective on the functioning of a social system. There is also the conflict model which views deviance as a positive and necessary element in social change.[34] From this perspective, the sick role would be seen as a conservative, *dysfunctional* role because it temporarily relieves the potential for conflict (and, therefore, change) by "excusing" deviant behavior and prevents addressing deeper issues of inequity in the social structure of the group.[35] Where a functional theorist would see the sick role as an effort to maintain stability of the system, the conflict theorist would see it as preventing "needed" social change. The roles of doctor and patient (representing medicine and society) can also be cast in Marxian concepts in analyzing the system of stratification and the potential for professional "exploitation" and "imperialism."[36] The recommendations for change as outcomes of the dialectic, however, do not differ much from those made by functionalist critics. At least for the United States, nationalization of the health system, centralized planning, etc., have been proposed by others as well. The conflict perspective seems only to be an alternative explanation, but not an advance in understanding of the sick role.

[32]Frank Petroni, "Correlates of the Psychiatric Sick Role," *Journal of Health and Social Behavior,* 13 (March, 1972), 47–54.

[33]Freidson, *op. cit.,* 237–240.

[34]Lewis A. Coser, *The Functions of Social Conflict,* Glencoe, Ill.: Free Press, 1956. See also Alvin W. Gouldner, *The Coming Crisis in Western Sociology,* New York: Basic Books, 1970.

[35]Howard B. Waitzkin and Barbara Waterman, *The Exploitation of Illness in Capitalist Society,* Indianapolis: Bobbs-Merrill, 1974.

[36]*ibid.*

## VARIATIONS IN RESPONSE TO ILLNESS

It cannot be too greatly stressed that what people do about illness is largely done as a result of the social interactions which develop around the emergence of this phenomenon. If illness is at all severe, it is almost impossible to prevent it from becoming visible and hence an occasion for social interaction. Even when it does not become visible to others, sick individuals can act about it in terms of what they have learned from being involved in other situations of sickness or from instruction about what to do in these cases. While the feelings which signalize the process of illness may be a private phenomenon, the behavior which is associated with an illness is, from the beginning, social in nature.

Mechanic and Volkart have provided a working definition of *illness behavior* as "the way in which symptoms are perceived, evaluated and acted upon by a person who recognizes some pain, discomfort or other signs of organic malfunction." They add that "two persons having much the same symptoms, clinically considered, may behave quite differently; one may become concerned and immediately seek medical aid while the other may ignore the symptoms and not consider seeking treatment at all."[37] Our purpose here is to describe the kinds of responses which are subsumed under the category of "illness behavior." Although these responses may be quite variable—indeed may involve incompatible alternatives—they are ordinarily guided by the understandings found in one's culture. It may further be suggested that the process of defining oneself as sick and determining what to do about it is an example of the more general process of "definition of the situation" according to generalized cultural understandings and alternatives.[38]

In the case of the sick person, these influencing factors may range from the effects of group structure and general cultural prescriptions and proscriptions to particular psychological motivations. For example, group pressures to conform and to perform according to the group's standards are

[37]David Mechanic and Edmund H. Volkart, "Stress, Illness Behavior and the Sick Role," *American Sociological Review,* 26 (February, 1961), 51–58. Also by the same authors, see "Illness Behavior and Medical Diagnosis," *Journal of Health and Human Behavior,* 1 (Summer, 1960), 86–94. Other authors differentiate "health" behavior and "sick-role" behavior. Thus, health behavior is any activity undertaken by a healthy person to prevent disease; illness behavior is any activity undertaken by sick people to define their state of ill health; and sick-role behavior is any activity by sick people to get well. See Stanislav V. Kasl and Sidney Cobb, "Health Behavior, Illness Behavior and Sick Role Behavior," *Archives of Environmental Health,* part I, 12 (February, 1966), 246–266 and part II, 12 (April, 1966), 531–541.

[38]Erving Goffman, *Presentation of Self in Everyday Life,* New York: Doubleday, 1959; Erving Goffman, *Encounters,* Indianapolis; Bobbs-Merrill, 1961; and Erving Goffman, *Behavior in Public Places,* New York: Free Press, 1963. The definition of the situation was W. I. Thomas's concept. See Edmund H. Volkart (ed.), *Social Behavior and Personality,* New York: Social Science Research Council, 1951.

exerted on every individual, sick or not. Thus, a person's family, business associates, and peers expect certain standards of performance of the individual (including taking good care of himself or herself). These pressures may lead one to deny feeling ill and to attempt to carry out roles in a normal fashion. They may, on the other hand, lead one to define seeking immediate care for perceived feelings of sickness as appropriate behavior. Concern for financial cost of care and for being absent from work (thus, being expendable) may also influence the sick person's decisions.

There are also culturally embedded anxieties which may alter the meaning of illness. Beliefs about disability, disfigurement, and death are all cultural components which may motivate patients to seek care or to delay (perhaps fatally) in seeking care. A case was reported in which a young couple deferred seeking treatment for their young daughter because the physician had advised them that the disease would necessitate the removal of one eye. The parents took their daughter to a chiropractor because they were told he could "cure" their daughter without disfiguring her. This practitioner's ministrations, however, left the spreading cancer unaffected and the young patient died.[39] Cultural differences also bear on the extent of one's knowledge about disease and sickness and beliefs about causation and cure. At the same time, there are certain cultural "blind spots" in recognizing illness. For example, venereal diseases carry with them an enormous social stigma, which often leads people to deny infection or to seek care in such a way that the knowledge of their condition is not made public. Public health officials often complain that otherwise cooperative physicians fail to report cases of venereal disease treated by them because of their patients' requests or because it violates the confidentiality of the doctor-patient relationship. Similar cultural attitudes are often associated with mental illness.

Bound up with group pressures and cultural factors are a host of psychological factors. Frequently, fear or anxiety accompanies the onset of undefined symptoms.[40] The degree of fear or anxiety seems to be inversely related to knowledge about the symptoms. It appears also to be directly related to unknown outcomes, e.g., fear of disability, and to personal knowledge of the suffering of a victim. Then, too, certain diseases such as cancer generate more fear than do diseases such as influenza or diabetes.[41] In addition to fear, however, there is another psychological factor called "secondary gain." As noted earlier, this refers to the possibility that illness may represent a welcome relief from arduous role performance and a way

[39]"Crackdown on Quackery," *Life,* 55 (Nov. 1, 1963), 72, 83.

[40]See Michael Balint, *The Doctor, His Patient and the Illness,* New York: International Universities Press, 1957.

[41]Gene N. Levine, "Anxiety about Illness: Psychological and Social Bases," *Journal of Health and Human Behavior,* 3 (Spring, 1962), 30–34.

of obtaining personal attention from others. On the other hand, being waited upon carries with it a connotation of dependency, a culturally unapproved state for adults. Thus, ambivalence from conflicting motivations may emerge as another psychological problem.

## STAGES OF ILLNESS BEHAVIOR

From whatever source and in whatever combination, these factors—social, cultural, and psychological—all play some part in influencing the way sick people define their situation and, hence, their decision-making process. Consequently, illness behavior for any given set of symptoms may vary widely. Perhaps one may be able to gain a better understanding of differences in patterns of illness behavior by viewing each episode of illness as involving a series of *stages* or phases. One early attempt to do this was made by Barker and his associates, who emphasized the psychosocial factors of sickness and rehabilitation.[42] They point out that when people become ill, they experience a "reduced scope of their world." This refers to reduced mobility, i.e., to being confined to bed in the sickroom or at least restricted to the home; to inability to play one's normal roles; and to reduced interaction with others. The sick person's world becomes not only smaller in terms of physical range, but less diversified and less demanding. Secondly, the sick person's concern for the meaning of illness tends to focus attention on bodily condition to the exclusion of other matters which may ordinarily be of interest. When people are sick, their attention and concern with their body and its natural processes tend to be heightened. The process of medical care, with its questions and its tests, tends to reinforce this preoccupation. Moreover, when one is anxious or in pain, it becomes difficult to concentrate on other exterior matters. Because one's own needs seem so important, one may tend to have less appreciation than usual for the situation of others; sick persons are notoriously imperious, demanding attention "right now." For all these reasons, people frequently think that sick people are apt to be egocentric. These factors, coupled with sick people's increased dependence upon others, place them in a sort of childlike status; hence, the sick are said to "regress." Finally, according to Barker, the sick people's interest in anything except themselves may wane; lost in their anxiety and pain, they become apathetic.

The convalescence stage is a period of testing. As sick people begin to regain strength and renew their interests in the outside world, they must, "like an adolescent," test their returning adult skills in an adult world.

[42]Roger G. Barker, Beatrice A. Wright, and Mollie R. Gonick, *Adjustment to Physical Handicap and Illness: A Survey of the Social Psychology of Physique and Disability,* New York: Social Science Research Council, Bulletin 55, 1946.

Often this involves their attempting, too soon, to get up or to go back to work. It may also involve ready expression of their frustrations and peevishness and their overt rebellion against the advice of their physician, nurse, or family. Finally, upon fully recovering, they resume their position in various groups to which they belong. It should be clear that this conceptualization of the stages of an illness is an ideal type, an attempt to describe a *typical* behavior sequence. Needless to say, these stages of illness do not always clearly manifest themselves in the behavior of every sick individual.

A similar analysis was made by Lederer, who emphasized primarily psychological reactions.[43] To Barker's stages of illness and convalescence, Lederer has added the period of becoming sick. This period involves the unpleasantness of painful sensations and the anxiety aroused by them, subsequent aggressive or passive behavior, the trauma associated with entering the treatment relationship, and further stimulation of anxiety from undergoing tests and, perhaps, hospitalization. Lederer described the period of "accepted illness" as involving many of the same factors discussed by Barker, i.e., constriction of interests, egocentrism, emotional dependency, and regression. After treatment has stopped or contained the physical problem, the third stage of convalescence is begun. During this period, the patient must face problems of return to normalcy, such as reestablishing adult independence, beginning to take part in normal activities, and regaining emotional maturity.

A more recent formulation by Suchman not only separates the illness experience into more stages, but, more importantly, describes them in terms of social and cultural as well as psychological factors.[44] The stages as described by Suchman include (1) symptom experience, (2) assumption of the sick role, (3) medical care contact, (4) dependent-patient role, and (5) recovery or rehabilitation. These stages are shown in Figure 4-1.

    **1** *Symptom experience stage.* The whole medical care process begins with the individual's *perception* that "something is wrong." This perception may include awareness of physical change, such as a pain, rash, or blurred vision; an *evaluation* of the change as to its degree of severity; and some kind of emotional *response* attached to the evaluation. Generally speaking, the responses may range from denial or a "flight into health" to acceptance in which the individual decides he or she is sick and enters the second stage or assumption of the sick role. Intermediate to the two extremes is delay, a situation in which the individual literally cannot make a decision, but awaits further development of symptoms or feels that assumption of the sick role is unnecessary. During this stage, the sick

    [43]Henry D. Lederer, "How the Sick View Their World," E. Gartly Jaco (ed.), *Patients, Physicians and Illness,* New York: Free Press, 1958, pp. 247–256.
    [44]Suchman, *op. cit.*

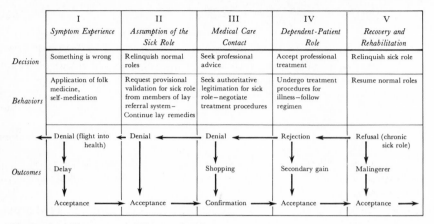

**Figure 4-1**  The stages of illness experience.

person may also attempt self-treatment by a variety of means to achieve relief from the symptoms.

   **2**  *Assumption of the sick role.* Assuming, however, that the symptoms persist and are severe, the individual will likely enter a second stage in which he or she decides to adopt the sick role and seeks to obtain "provisional validation" for that claim. In other words, the illness now becomes a social phenomenon because the sick person seeks agreement from significant others that he or she is sick and should be excused from regular duties. As one would expect, initial contacts are often made by the sick person first with others with whom he or she has close ties, usually a spouse or family, perhaps friends. Many individuals seek professional help at once, often upon the advice of family or friends. Others may continue self-treatment and try various remedies suggested by others concerned for the individual's health. Here patent medicines, home remedies, traditional "cures," etc., are likely to be employed. At some point, however, if the symptoms persist or are severe, a decision concerning further treatment must be made. One important element in this decision is whether the lay remedies have effected a change in the symptoms. Frequently, the period of self-treatment and seeking advice from other lay persons only delays eventual contact with a doctor—a period during which the damage from the disease may have reached serious proportions. The range of decisions here is similar to that of the first stage. At one extreme, others in the lay referral system[45] may reject the person's claim to the sick role. In this case, the

----

[45]Freidson defines a "lay referral system" as the sequence of events—during the symptom experience and sick-role stages—requiring the sick person to make a series of decisions about what to do about the symptoms. In the decision-making process, he or she is influenced by others—family and friends—who, like the sick person, are lay persons. This concept may be contrasted to the "professional referral system," which is a hierarchy of diagnostic authority in which decisions are based more or less objectively on the professional needs of a case. See Eliot Freidson, *Patients' Views of Medical Practice,* New York: Russell Sage, 1961, pp. 146–147.

individual is defined as well and, therefore, either must resume normal obligations or experience more symptoms. At the other extreme, the individual's family may concede that he or she is sick, and, thereby, the request to play the sick role is provisionally granted. The provisional aspect refers to the fact that in our society only a trained physician can tell if one *really* has a disease and what should be done about it. Thus, provisional validation of the sick role by the family leads one into the third stage—the medical care contact.

3  *Medical care contact stage.* At this point, the sick person leaves the lay care system and enters the professional care system (although it is possible to vacillate between them). Essentially, the individual is seeking authoritative validation for the claim to the sick role as well as treatment. In addition, however, he or she is seeking an explanation of symptoms, although the level of explanation may vary from simple assurance that the disease is not serious to a detailed physiological description of the cause, course, and likely outcome of the disease. The outcomes of this first encounter with a physician may also be arrayed on a continuum. On the one hand, the physician may judge the person to be well, i.e., withhold authoritative validation of the sick-role claim. The individual may then reject the physician's judgment. In either case, the relationship between the individual and the physician would likely be discontinued. The patient either resumes his or her normal roles or, as often occurs, goes to other physicians until the diagnosis wanted is achieved—a phenomenon known as "shopping." Alternatively, the sick person and the doctor may agree that the former is ill, thus providing legitimation for the sick-role claim and entry into the next stage.

4  *Dependent-patient role.* Upon reaching a decision to undergo treatment for the illness, the sick person becomes a patient. As many other analyses noted above have suggested, this stage is fraught with problems. It is here that the patient must wrestle with the discrepancy between childlike dependence upon the physician and the normal state of adult independence. This problem may well be superimposed upon others, concerning the meaning of the symptoms, the prognosis for recovery, the impact on the family, etc. The range of possible outcomes of treatment would include increasing resistance to the treatment regimen by the patient, i.e., the recalcitrant patient, in which the patient may break off the encounter and "go shopping." Some patients, however, may succumb to the temporary benefits of dependence and focus on the "secondary gain" rather than devote their efforts to getting well. In this case, the physician may well discourage continuing the relationship. Or, logically, the patient and physician may work together and commence a recovery of the normal physical state and a subsequent resumption of normal roles.

5  *Recovery and rehabilitation.* In some instances, for example, for some acute ailments, recovery may be rather abrupt—a fever may "break" or a pain subside—and the patient resumes normal activities. For other ailments, however, this stage may be somewhat longer and involve a more or less gradual recovery. As Barker and Lederer pointed out, the process of convalescence is not without its problems too. The patient must renounce

any pleasures attained from being dependent on others. He or she must often forgo some former activities, perhaps permanently, but at least temporarily until strength returns, and must often relearn many of the activities previously taken for granted. Patients who cannot effectively leave the sick role may take on the chronic sick role or be classed as malingerers. At the other extreme is the achievement of a cure. The patient once again joins the ranks of the well.

An effort to extend the scope of Suchman's stages of illness behavior and at the same time provide greater precision for predicting behavior has been made by Fabrega.[46] Not only is the number of stages extended to nine, but the focus is on decision making which takes into account judgments by the individual as to the degree of "danger" implied by symptoms, weighing costs against anticipated benefits, and choice of behavior based on previous experiences with illness. The model concentrates on information evaluated by the sick person along a temporal dimension of "logical time" (rather than metric time) and leads to a finite number of outcomes relating to earlier stages.[47] Like Suchman's model, this one starts with an identification and labeling of a problem as illness (Stage I) and an evaluation of the presumed danger or degree of disability (Stage II). What action to take includes selecting from a range of available treatment options, assessing the potential outcomes based on previous experiences, *and* making a judgment of expected benefits against potential costs (social as well as economic). These represent Stages III to VII. The patient then selects a treatment plan (Stage VIII) and evaluates the outcomes, which information becomes part of memory system for subsequent experiences (Stage IX), thus "feeding back" to Stage I.

Since this model follows decision-theory models, there is less concern than in Suchman's model with specific sociological variables such as sick role, provisional validation, dependent-patient role, etc., except insofar as these are elements in the decision-making process. However, the decision-theory model is designed to be applicable in cross-cultural research, where culturally defined roles are only part of the resources for decisions and not inherent in the stages themselves.[48]

A general taxonomy such as the stages of illness experience provides a useful framework for purposes of description, but it does not explain nor

---

[46]Horacio Fabrega, "Toward a Model of Illness Behavior," *Medical Care,* 6 (November–December, 1973), 470–484.

[47]*ibid.,* p. 472.

[48]For another critique of the limited applicability of Suchman's model, see Reed Geertsen, Melville R. Klauber, Robert L. Kane, Mark Rindflesh, and Robert Gray, "A Reexamination of Suchman's Views on Social Factors in Health Care Utilization," *Journal of Health and Social Behavior,* 16 (June, 1975), 226–237.

take account of all the variations that do, in fact, occur. It should be noted that although these stages are likely to occur in the order presented, they may not be uniform in duration. For example, the length of time for the first stage, that is, for a person to decide that he or she is sick, may vary considerably depending upon the degree of pain, the time at which symptoms are experienced, the particular interpretation of their meaning, etc.[49] Similarly, the time needed to obtain provisional validation from significant others may vary. Either of these stages may involve delay while waiting for results of self-treatment. Moreover, the time involved in finding and seeing the "right" doctor and certainly the time needed for treatment and to recover will vary from case to case.

We may also note that not every illness experience will involve all the stages. It is conceivable that a person living alone or one who experiences sharp, unrelenting pain or a disability may proceed directly from the symptom experience stage to the medical care contact stage.[50] It also frequently happens that at the time of the medical care contact, initial treatment is quickly effective and the patient fully recovers, thus effectively skipping the fourth stage of the dependent-patient role. In addition, we may note that entry into and exit from each stage involves decision making on the part of the sick person and other people. The sociological significance of this decision making lies not only in the behavioral consequences, but also in observing the combinations of factors which influence the decisions. Thus, in defining the situation in each of the various stages, the sick person must evaluate not only his or her position, but also what is appropriate to do about it in terms of resources, available alternatives, and an estimate of success in regaining a normal state of health.

We should take note of at least one other effort to develop a conceptual model of human behavior in response to illness or the threat of illness that is not dependent upon "stages." This is the *health belief model*[51] which, although developed independently, incorporates elements of the decision-making model and the social and psychological variables inherent in descriptive stages. As originally formulated in the 1950s, the health belief model was based on concepts derived from psychology and social psychology and was concerned only with explaining preventive health behavior, that is, behavior in the absence of symptoms of illness. This approach emerged, in part, because the team of investigators were mostly social

[49]Suchman, *op. cit.,* p. 119; Fabrega, *op. cit.,* p. 477.

[50]This was the case for Eric Hodgins as described in *Episode.* Within a hour of suffering a stroke, he was seen by a physician and admitted to a nearby hospital. See Eric Hodgins, *Episode: A Report on the Accident inside My Skull,* New York: Atheneum, 1964.

[51]Marshall H. Becker (ed.), "The Health Belief Model and Personal Health Behavior," *Health Education Monographs,* 2 (Winter, 1974), 326–473. This special issue is devoted to discussions of various aspects of the health belief model.

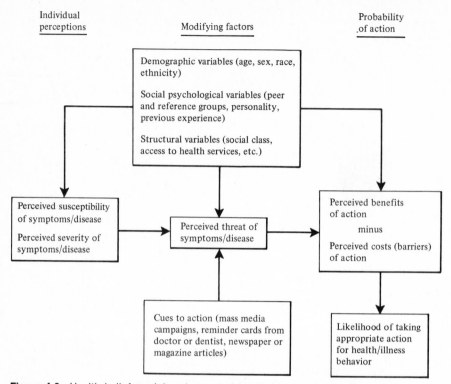

**Figure 4-2**  Health belief model and personal health behavior. *(Source: Adapted from Marshall H. Becker (ed.), "The Health Belief Model and Personal Health Behavior,"* Health Education Monographs, *2 (Winter, 1974), p. 334.)*

psychologists interested in perceptions, motivation, and cues to behavior, and because the Public Health Service for which they worked was specifically concerned with why the public did not respond as expected to programs of preventive medicine (such as screening for TB and cervical cancer, immunizations for polio, etc.). Since those early beginnings, the model has been expanded to include sociocultural and environmental variables in predicting illness behavior as well as health behavior.[52]

The elements of the health belief model are shown in Figure 4-2. It may be seen that the dependent variable—the probability that an individual would take appropriate action either to prevent illness or to recover health—depends upon individual perceptions of threat as these are influenced by a host of modifying factors. The perception of threat includes a

[52]Irwin M. Rosenstock, "Historical Origins of the Health Belief Model," in Becker, *ibid.*, 328–335. See also footnote 37 in this chapter for the definitions of health behavior, illness behavior, and sick-role behavior.

measure of susceptibility ("Can I be affected?") and of severity ("How much could I be affected?"). These perceptions vary by age and sex, social class, social and physical environments, exposure to media sources, and so on. In reaching a state of "readiness to act," the individual weighs the potential benefits against the social and economic costs of alternative courses of action. To the degree that benefits are superior to costs, the probability of appropriate behavior (health, illness, or sick role) increases. Considerable empirical support for the health belief model has accumulated which indicates its ability to predict behavior in response to illness (or the threat of illness) better than descriptive "stage" models or other decision-theory models. Nonetheless, much further investigation remains to be done. There are still methodological problems such as measurement of concepts of motivation and perception. The generalizability of this model to other cultures has not been adequately documented nor has there been sufficient prospective evaluation of behavior after the decision to act has been made and the patient role has been adopted.[53]

## SELECTED RESEARCH FINDINGS

That variations in health and illness behavior are an important phenomenon with significant sociological implications may be seen from the amount of research directed to it.[54] For example, a recent study reported that one of the strongest predictors of use of physician's services was perceived need for care (where need was defined as illness).[55] Campbell has reported that even though the tendency to attribute illness to others in the family varies by age (older to younger) and role (parents to children), the attribution (definition) of illness was a strong predictor of health-relevant behavior.[56] These results are consistent with those reported some years ago by Apple,[57] who noted that the kinds of health problems most often defined as illness were those which were recent in onset and which interfered with

[53]Becker, op. cit., pp. 415–417; see also Becker and Maiman, op. cit., for one review of studies of patients' compliance.

[54]There are several extensive bibliographies available. See, for example, Ozzie G. Simmons and Emil Berkanovic, "Social Research in Health and Medicine: A Bibliography," in Howard E. Freeman, Sol Levine, and Leo G. Reeder (eds.), Handbook of Medical Sociology, 2d ed., Englewood Cliffs, N.J.: Prentice-Hall, 1972, pp. 523–584.

[55]Thomas T. H. Wan and Scott J. Soifer, "Determinants of Physician Utilization: A Causal Analysis," Journal of Health and Social Behavior, 15 (June, 1974), 100–108.

[56]John D. Campbell, "Attribution of Illness: Another Double Standard," Journal of Health and Social Behavior, 16 (March, 1975), 114–126.

[57]Dorrian Apple, "How Laymen Define Illness," Journal of Health and Human Behavior, 1 (Fall, 1960), 219–225. See also Barbara Bauman, "Diversities in Conceptions of Health and Physical Fitness," Journal of Health and Human Behavior, 1 (Spring, 1961), 39–46; and, more recently, Julia Brown and May Rawlinson, "The Morale of Patients Following Open-heart Surgery," Journal of Health and Social Behavior, 17 (June, 1976), 135–145.

usual activities. Moreover, people accustomed to frequent health care were more sensitive to role disturbances than people who did not seek or receive health care so often. In general, most respondents felt that the time to seek care was when sickness was felt, not before.

From the standpoint of group structure, Suchman[58] has reported that many factors which have been singled out for study, such as extent of knowledge, degree of delay in seeking treatment, use of home remedies or patent medicines, are all related to the social organization of the group(s) to which the individual belongs. He found that "parochial" persons who were bound by close personal and ethnic ties to kinship groups also tended to be less knowledgeable about disease, more reluctant to seek professional care, and more likely to use home remedies for their illnesses. These characteristics distinguished the parochial from the "cosmopolitans," who tended to be less attached to extended kinship or ethnic groups, were generally more knowledgeable about disease, and were more likely to seek competent, professional care quickly.

In an earlier study, Koos[59] demonstrated the importance of social-class membership for illness behavior. Not only were patterns of utilization of medical care different—upper classes usually used orthodox physicians and went to them more often—but also extent of knowledge and beliefs about disease varied by class level. For example, lower-class respondents more or less ignored any but the most serious symptoms, partly for economic reasons, but partly because nonserious symptoms were not defined as illness; therefore help was not required. Similarly, upper-class respondents were more likely to have some scientific understanding about the causes of disease than were lower-class respondents, who more readily accepted lay explanations.

In the more than two decades since Koos's original study, the influence of social class on illness behavior has moderated somewhat, in part, because of rising affluence of lower classes, increased availability of health care programs, government sponsored health insurance, etc. A recent replication of the survey in Regionville noted diminished differences among social classes in perceptions of issues related to medical care.[60] Other

---

[58]Edward A. Suchman, "Sociomedical Variations among Ethnic Groups," *American Journal of Sociology,* 70 (November, 1964), 319–331. Some evidence supporting the influence of group structure (social class and social participation) for preventive health behavior is found in David Coburn and Clyde R. Pope, "Socio-economic Status and Preventive Health Behavior," *Journal of Health and Social Behavior,* 15 (June, 1974), 67–77.

[59]Koos, *op. cit.*

[60]Stephen J. Kunitz, Andrew A. Sorenson, and Suzanne B. Cashman, "Changing Health Care Opinions in Regionville," *Medical Care,* 13 (July, 1975), 549–561. Another study noted the disappearance of class differences in use both of prescribed and non-prescribed medications. See David L. Rabin and Patricia J. Bush, "Who's Using Medicines?" *Journal of Community Health,* 1 (Winter, 1975), 106–117.

surveys, however, have continued to find that social class (income and education) exercises pervasive effects on illness behavior[61] and health behavior.[62]

There is, of course, a considerable literature examining cultural differences in response to illness, patterns of providing care, and beliefs about and practices in medicine.[63] Saunders,[64] for example, has reported on the extent to which cultural background influences the medical beliefs and practices of Spanish Americans in the Southwestern United States. Although they can and often do draw on the tenets of scientific medicine as practiced in urban areas, more frequently their explanations of disease and prescriptions for treatment are drawn from medieval Spanish folklore, Mexican folk medicine, and even from the culture of American Indians. Thus, the beliefs and practices of these Spanish Americans tend to be a mixture of old and new, of modern science and ancient superstitions.

There are also ethnic, religious, educational, and other characteristics which influence medical behavior. Zborowski[65] reported a study which compared the responses to pain of a sample of Jewish, Italian, Irish, and "Old American" patients. From interviews and observation, Zborowski reported that Jewish and Italian patients overtly responded to pain in a similar fashion. They were very emotional and sensitive and had a tendency to exaggerate. However, their attitudes toward pain were very different. Italian patients tended to focus on the immediacy of the pain and were concerned about relief from hurt. Jewish patients, however, seemed more concerned about what the pain sensation meant in terms of the future—their eventual recovery, ability to perform family and occupational roles, etc. Moreover, "Old Americans" held attitudes toward pain that were similar to those of Jewish patients, but they were less emotional and less sensitive in their response to it. The former tended to endure stoically their pain when reassured as to its temporary nature. These patterns of response to pain were shown to have been learned, along with other cultural attitudes and values, during the socialization process.

Similar findings regarding perception of physical disabilities have also

[61]S. E. Berki and B. Kobashigawa, "Socioeconomic and Need Determinants of Ambulatory Care Use: Data Analysis of the 1970 Health Interview Survey Data," *Medical Care*, 14 May, 1976), 405–421.

[62]James L. Steele and William H. McBroom, "Conceptual and Empirical Dimensions of Health Behavior," *Journal of Health and Social Behavior*, 13 (December, 1972), 382–392.

[63]See, for example, Benjamin D. Paul (ed.), *Health, Culture and Community*, New York: Russell Sage, 1955.

[64]Lyle Saunders, *Cultural Differences and Medical Care*, New York: Russell Sage, 1954.

[65]Mark Zborowski, "Cultural Components of Response to Pain," in Jaco, *op cit.*, pp. 256–268. More recently, see his *People in Pain*, San Francisco: Jossey-Bass, 1969. See also Alexander Segall, "Sociocultural Variation in Sick Role Behavioural Expectations," *Social Science and Medicine*, 10 (January, 1976), 47–51.

been reported.[66] Children's preferences for pictures of normal children over physically disabled children reflect a general cultural value in our society, and differences were found between the choices of normal and mentally retarded or disturbed children and between the sexes; e.g., girls tended to emphasize social handicaps, but boys showed more concern for functional handicaps. More importantly, subcultural factors also provided differences in the preferences. Specifically, Jewish and Italian children, who are believed to have differing cultural beliefs about disfigurement, showed preferences in the predicted direction.

In addition to Levine's study of anxiety and illness reported above, another study has suggested also that perceived danger from a disease is an important factor in responding to it. (Levine had suggested that the more prevalent a disease the more fear there would be about it.) Lewis and Lopreato[67] showed that when respondents—in this case, mothers of sick children—had little knowledge about the disease afflicting their children, there was a tendency to engage in medically nonrational behavior—acts which from a scientific point of view were inappropriate to the desired ends. Similarly, the frequency of nonrational behavior was found to be directly related to the degree of perceived danger from disease. A more recent study of low-income mothers suggested that the greater the perceived danger of symptoms in their children, the more likely they were to seek professional care.[68] Anxiety about the meaning of symptoms and about the potential unpleasantries of treatment procedures tends to delay seeking professional care.[69]

Finally, it should be noted that environmental factors such as availability of health care resources will influence health and illness behavior in addition to the social and psychological factors. Thus, the concept of access to medical care covers a number of specific attributes such as distribution of services, travel time, operational procedures, waiting time, etc.[70] Characteristics associated with poverty areas in the community and

[66]Norman Goodman, Stephen A. Richardson, Sanford M. Dornbusch, and Albert H. Hastorf, "Variant Reactions to Physical Disabilities," *American Sociological Review*, 28 (June, 1963), 429–435. See also Stephen A. Richardson, Norman Goodman, Albert H. Hastorf, and Sanford M. Dornbusch, "Cultural Uniformity in Reaction to Physical Disabilities," *American Sociological Review*, 26 (April, 1961), 241–246.

[67]Lewis and Lopreato, *op. cit.* See also Balint, *op. cit.*

[68]John P. Kirscht, Marshall H. Becker, and John P. Eveland, "Psychological and Social Factors and Predictors of Medical Behavior," *Medical Care*, 14 (May 1976), 422–431.

[69]M. H. Banks, S. A. A. Beresford, D. C. Morrell, J. J. Waller, and C. J. Watkins, "Factors Influencing Demand for Primary Medical Care in Women Aged 20–44: A Preliminary Report," *International Journal of Epidemiology*, 14 (September, 1975), 189–195; Andrea Knopf, "Changes in Women's Opinions about Cancer," *Social Science and Medicine*, 10 (March–April, 1976), 191–195; and David S. Gochman, "The Organizing Role of Motivation in Health Beliefs and Intentions," *Journal of Health and Social Behavior*, 15 (May–June, 1972), 285–293.

[70]Lu Ann Aday and Ronald Anderson, *Access to Medical Care*, Ann Arbor, Mich.: Health Administration Press, 1975.

noneconomic barriers also limit the use of professional services despite acknowledged need.[71] Variations in the ability of hospitals to provide needed services[72] and even the physician's responses to patients have been found to influence patient behavior.[73]

From this cursory look at some research findings, two things are immediately apparent. First, a host of social, cultural, and psychological factors influence an individual's concern for health and response to illness. Of course, not every factor is present in every case of illness, nor, when present, are they always there in the same degree. Rather, it is the varying combinations of these factors which influence medical behavior. The second feature of this description is that much of the evidence is fragmentary; some of it is contradictory; some may even be spurious. Nonetheless, from the various research reports, one can begin to observe some characteristic patterns of medical behavior.

## SUMMARY

In this chapter we have discussed some basic analytic concepts which are important in understanding why people react to the onset of illness as they do and in accounting for the wide variation in their responses. First, it was pointed out that a distinction must be made between disease and illness. Disease was defined as a biological process which results in an altered physical state of the individual and which can be identified in objective terms by a series of scientific tests. Illness, on the other hand, was a subjective evaluation by the individual that something was wrong with him or her *as an individual* and usually first noted in terms of a reduced ability to perform social roles. The physician is more likely to view the episode in terms of disease, while the patient is more likely to be concerned about illness. These discrepant approaches to what is wrong with the sick individual are often at the heart of discord between the patient and the doctor.

We also discussed some strengths and weaknesses of the concept of the sick role—a social role involving the right to be excused from normal duties and to depend upon others for care during the period of illness. The sick role, however, also obligates the incumbent to perceive illness as undesirable, to recover as quickly as possible, and to seek out and cooper-

[71]Gerald Sparer and Louise M. Okader, "Chronic Conditions and Physician Use Patterns in Ten Urban Poverty Areas," *Medical Care,* 12 (July, 1974), 549–560, and Lu Ann Aday, "Economic and Non-economic Barriers to the Use of Needed Medical Services," *Medical Care,* 13 (June, 1975), 447–456.

[72]David Barton Smith and Arnold D. Kaluzuy, "Inequality in Health Care Programs: A Note on Some Structural Factors Affecting Health Care Behavior," *Medical Care,* 12 (October, 1974), 860–870.

[73]Barbara S. Hulka, Lawrence L. Kupper, John C. Cassel, and Robert A. Babinerr, "Practice Characteristics and Quality of Primary Medical Care: The Doctor-patient Relationship," *Medical Care,* 13 (October, 1975), 808–820.

ate with competent technical help. From the perspective of the group, the sick role provides a control on deviance by legitimating the temporary nonperformance of a sick member and minimizing the disruption in the role performance of other members of the group.

Finally several models of response to illness were identified. It was noted that the illness experience of any individual involved a decision-making process and, further, that at various stages the social, cultural, and psychological factors influencing the decisions could be identified.

## SUGGESTED READINGS

Balint, Michael, *The Doctor, His Patient and the Illness,* New York; International Universities Press, 1957.

Becker, Marshall H. (ed.), "The Health Belief Model and Personal Health Behavior," *Health Education Monographs,* 2 (Winter, 1974), 326–473.

Freidson, Eliot, *Patients' Views of Medical Practice,* New York: Russell Sage Foundation, 1961.

Koos, Earl L., *The Health of Regionville,* New York: Columbia University Press, 1954.

Mechanic, David, *Medical Sociology: A Selective View,* New York: Free Press, 1968.

Part Two

# Health Practices and Practitioners

Chapter 5

# Systems of Medical Beliefs
# and Practices

*Primitive medicine is primarily magico-religious, utilizing a few rational elements, while our (scientific) medicine is predominantly rational and specific, employing a few magic elements.*

Erwin D. Ackerknecht, 1946

In this age of rapid progress in medical technology, one might wonder why we pause here to consider "backward," or nonscientific, systems of medicine.[1] We do so for reasons which have both theoretical and practical importance. First, it is generally agreed that sickness and disease are a

[1]See, for example, Henry E. Sigerist, *A History of Medicine: I. Primitive and Archaic Medicine,* Fair Lawn, N.J.: Oxford University Press, 1951, pp. 105–216; Steven Polgar, "Health Action in Cross- cultural Perspective," in Howard E. Freeman, Sol Levine, and Leo G. Reeder (eds.), *Handbook of Medical Sociology,* Englewood Cliffs, N.J.: Prentice-Hall, 1963, pp. 397–422; Jerome D. Frank, *Persuasion and Healing,* New York: Schocken, 1963; Paul R. Benedict and Irving Jacks, "Mental Illness in Primitive Societies," *Psychiatry,* 17 (November, 1954), 377–390; Forrest E. Clements, "Primitive Concepts of Disease," *University of California Publications in American Archeology and Ethnology,* 32 (1932), 185–252.

universal threat to individual and group survival, and in Chapter 3 some ways in which modern groups meet this threat were pointed out. It is important for the development of a parsimonious theoretical framework for understanding medical behavior, however, that we also know how groups in other cultures meet this challenge, the attitudes and beliefs they hold, and the means they employ. As with all aspects of human behavior, the social scientist studying medicine must always keep in the foreground the question of whether specific behavior patterns are universal, reflecting the exigencies of the human situation, or whether they are the special product of the configuration of a specific culture. We may assume that problems people face and the psychological needs arising from these problems are everywhere at least similar despite differences in theories about and techniques for coping with them. Thus, studying non-Western societies provides an opportunity to observe human behavior with respect to a universal problem—that of illness—in the context of radically different cultural settings. The development of a conceptual scheme, of course, depends, in part, on the availability of accurate descriptions of different systems of medical care, their techniques and functions.

The development of such a conceptual framework, however, has at least two practical consequences. It provides us with a better understanding of our own system of medicine and medical practice, and it provides insights on the application of Western scientific medicine in nonindustrial societies.[2] For these reasons, then, this chapter is concerned with the attitudes and beliefs of different societies with respect to causes of disease and illness and with measures of therapy and prevention taken by individuals and groups in such societies.

Before looking at specific, detailed characteristics of nonscientific medical beliefs and practices, it may be helpful to point out, in a broad perspective, some features they hold in common with scientific medicine. First, medical culture patterns are not isolated, but rather are integrated into a complex network of beliefs and values that are a part of the culture of

[2]William Caudill, "Applied Anthropology in Medicine," in A. L. Kroeber (ed.), *Anthropology Today,* Chicago: University of Chicago Press, 1953, pp. 771–806; John Adair, Kurt Deuschle, and Walsh McDermott, "Patterns of Health and Disease among the Navahos," *Annals of the American Academy of Political and Social Science,* 311 (May, 1957), 80–94; John Cassel, "A Comprehensive Health Program among South African Zulus," in Benjamin D. Paul (ed.), *Health, Culture and Community,* New York: Russell Sage, 1955, pp. 15–42; McKim Marriott, "Western Medicine in a Village in Northern India," *ibid.,* pp. 239–268; Alice Joseph, "Physician and Patient: Some Aspects of Interpersonal Relationships between Physicians and Patients with Regard to the Relationship between White Physicians and Indian Patients," *Applied Anthropology,* 1 (August, 1942), 1–6; Erwin D. Ackerknecht, "Natural Diseases and Rational Treatment in Primitive Medicine," *Bulletin of the History of Medicine,* 19 (May, 1946), 467–497.

# Disability Certificate

Patient's Name _____

According to my diagnosis. this patient was physically unable to perform his or her job duties

from _____ to _____

Remarks _____

_____

_____

Signature _____

Date _____

Address _____

any society.[3] In modern industrialized nations, disease and illness are most often seen as natural phenomena and hence subject to investigation and study by scientific methods. Consequently, beliefs about causes of various diseases require scientific proof for substantiation. Thus, answers to questions of etiology are sought in the laboratory and in the field under controlled conditions. In most primitive societies, however, many if not most diseases are seen as manifestations of *supernatural* powers; thus causal explanations in these societies take on a magicoreligious tenor.[4]

Although this generalization will hold in most instances, it should be noted that the integration of medical beliefs with other aspects of the culture is not perfect in either modern or primitive societies. For example, the rate at which an innovation or new idea or practice diffuses will vary markedly both between modern and primitive societies and within them. This means, among other things, that the degree to which different segments of the population are even aware of the innovation, much less accept it, will vary. One consequence of variations in awareness of new ideas and techniques is that even in urban areas where sophisticated scientific medicine predominates, one can find situations in which unverified beliefs are the basis upon which people act. Thus, in the city one can find faith healers and quacks, patent medicines and home remedies, and lay explanations for the causes of common ailments alongside scientific methods of treating diseases. For example, the appearance of symptoms such as fever, sore throat, and frequent coughing are often attributed to the *behavior* of the victim—something he did or did not do—rather than to the appropriate *biological* cause such as a virus. Thus, the explanation that one "catches" a cold by not dressing properly or not taking vitamins regularly, etc., is commonly found even in areas where the best scientific medicine is available.

The tendency for simpler societies to provide supernatural explanations of illness is not surprising. When compared with industrial societies, they tend to be pervasively religious. In agriculture, politics, war, and the activities of daily living, as well as in medicine, members of primitive societies tend not to make the sharp distinctions so ingrained among us between natural and supernatural causes. In these societies, where science and technology are rather little developed, human control over the environment is relatively limited. The scope of the "aleatory element" is large. Human beings, needing explanations of the world, tend to ascribe what they cannot explain in terms of the regularities of the natural world to

[3]Stanley F. King, *Perceptions of Illness in Medical Practice,* New York: Russell Sage, 1962, pp. 91–92.
[4]Ackerknecht, *op. cit.*

cosmic forces (often personified) which they cannot see. As Malinowski has pointed out, these magical or religious explanations tend to supplant naturalistic and scientific ones precisely in those areas of life where events are most unpredictable and least amenable to control, where fate seems inexorable and the human will least able to achieve its ends.[5]

When one surveys the health situation of most primitive peoples—and of most historical and contemporary "underdeveloped" societies—one sees how extensive the domain of the aleatory element in medicine must be. Life expectancy is low and infant mortality high. Despite the best efforts of fond parents, children survive to adulthood only if they are "lucky." Death, with its attendant effect, lurks as the threatened outcome of illnesses of the young as well as the old. Epidemic diseases are common, terrifying both in the suddenness with which they can sweep through a community and in the apparent arbitrariness with which they strike their victims. Whether through the ravages of dietary deficiency or exposure to the stresses of an environment relatively uncushioned by technological skills, the resistance of many to disease is commonly attenuated.[6] In cultures whose world views assume the immanence of the spirit life, sensitivity—and suggestibility—to supernatural explanations of illness is only natural. When the emotionally satisfying closure which such explanations can achieve is considered, the wonder is that primitive medicine contains elements other than those which Westerners would classify as magical or religious. For until the advent of modern medical science, there were few really effective ways of controlling disease through natural means. As Sigerist pointed out,[7] until after the seventeenth century, the therapeutic powers of Western medicine and the prevalence of religiomagical viewpoints in Europe were such that a European peasant and an American Indian would have found many similarities among their medical beliefs.

Yet the medicines of primitive cultures include many treatments which are empirically successful and which modern Western medicine can explain in a rational, scientific way. The use of physical, dietary, and pharmacologic treatments is universal, and Western medicine owes many of the drugs which are important in modern treatments to the discovery by primitive peoples of the medicinal efficacy of various herbs or roots.

---

[5]On the "aleatory element," see William Graham Sumner and Albert G. Keller, *The Science of Society*, vol. 2, New Haven, Conn.: Yale University Press, 1927. And on the whole problem of the relationships of magic, science, and religion, see Bronislaw Malinowski, *Magic, Science and Religion and Other Essays,* Boston: Beacon Press, 1948.

[6]Health problems in underdeveloped nations are well documented in John Bryant, *Health and the Developing World,* Ithaca, N.Y.: Cornell University Press, 1969.

[7]Sigerist, *op. cit.,* p. 166.

Among modern drugs which have come to the West from the medicines of other cultures are quinine, opium, ephedrine, cascara sagrada, chaulmoogra, and digitalis.[8] Similarly, many primitive groups knew of the therapeutic value of applications of heat to affected parts or of the importance of massages. It should be stressed, however, that in using these kinds of treatments, primitives often did so for what, to modern scientific medicine, would be the wrong reasons. Thus, the use of empirically effective drugs might be undertaken not because it was known that the drug itself was effective but because it was a necessary part of a religious or magical ritual. Even this apparent confusion, however, points to another reason for the effectiveness of primitive medicine—its tendency to "treat the whole man," to deal concurrently with human psychological and physical needs. Thus it may be that a primitive's belief that a ritual will be of help is as important in the cure as the effect of the herbal remedy which we know to be pharmacologically active. As Sigerist put it,

> The very unity of primitive medicine, the fact that it never addresses itself to either body or mind but always to both, explains many of its results also in the somatic field. That a ceremonial in the course of which the patient comes into complete harmony with nature and the universe must have a strong psychotherapeutic value goes without saying.[9]

Second, in every society treatment of illness as well as any preventive measures follows more or less logically from beliefs about causation, although every society may have some isolated examples of practices based on tradition rather than current knowledge of etiology.[10] For example, scientific medicine, which characterizes most Western societies, is largely a rational application of scientific knowledge. Thus, a pure water supply prevents cholera, immunization prevents many communicable diseases, diseased tissue may be removed through surgery, and so on. Although the specific forms of treatment in primitive societies are radically different from procedures employed by the Western physician, they are just as logically related to etiological beliefs. If illness is thought to be caused by the patient's violation of tribal norms, thus offending ancestors or gods, appeasement may be made in ritualistic form or by some kind of social restitution. If the sickness is seen as a case of malevolent sorcery, counter-sorcery and other spells are employed. As mentioned above, such practices

[8]*Ibid.*, pp. 203–204.

[9]*Ibid.*, p. 201. See also the study reported in Horacio Fabrega and P. K. Manning, "An Integrated Theory of Disease: Ladino-Mestizo Views of Disease in the Chiapas Highlands," *Psychosomatic Medicine,* 35 (May–June, 1973), 223–299.

[10]Frank, *op. cit.*

are often effective, however irrational and superstitious they may seem to the Western observer.[11] This phenomenon will be discussed further below.

A third common characteristic is the chain of referral, or the sequence of actions and interaction concerning their illness which sick persons follow between the time they recognize that they are sick and the time they consult a recognized practitioner.[12] As was noted in our discussion of illness behavior in Chapter 4, when someone feels sick, the first step is usually self-diagnosis and self-treatment. If symptoms persist or get worse or if new ones develop which cannot be identified by the sick person, the advice of relatives or close friends is sought for a remedy. If advice is not forthcoming or if it is ineffective, the sick person engages a medical practitioner as a final step in the referral system. In our society there are, of course, many levels of practitioners from faith healers to the most specialized licensed physician, just as there may be many categories of relatives and friends seen before referral to a specialist. The point is, however, that most sick persons will attempt self-diagnosis and treatment before seeking advice from those immediately around them and friends will usually be called upon for advice before a recognized specialist.[13] A remarkably similar procedure is found in many simpler societies. Marriott, for example, described the practice of medicine in a village in northern India in which sick people, after exhausting their knowledge of herbs, drugs, and magical incantations, turned to their immediate family and other kinfolk for advice and comfort. Even when a local practitioner, or as a last resort a Western physician, was engaged, the family still was consulted on the treatment to be applied.[14] Although the specific beliefs and practices with respect to illness and disease vary widely—not only between primitive and scientific medicine, but also within each system—the recognition of some common patterns is important for the understanding of the influence of these beliefs and practices on human behavior.

## CHARACTERISTICS OF PRIMITIVE AND FOLK MEDICINE

One important implication of these common elements in scientific and nonscientific medicine is that there are only a few *basically different* explanations of the causes of disease despite the fact that human behavior in response to disease may vary almost endlessly.[15] To facilitate under-

[11]See, for example, a case described by Elspeth Huxley, "Science, Psychiatry—or Witchery?" *New York Times Magazine,* (May 31, 1959), 17–19.

[12]See Polgar, *op. cit.,* pp. 398–400.

[13]Eliot Freidson, *Patients' Views of Medical Practice,* New York: Russell Sage, 1963.

[14]Marriott, *op. cit.,* A similar point was made by Irwin Press, "The Urban Curandero," *American Anthropologist,* 73 (June, 1971), 741–756.

[15]Ackerknecht, *op. cit.*

| *Theoretical Orientation* | *Role of the Practitioner* | |
| --- | --- | --- |
| | *Undifferentiated* | *Differentiated* |
| *Nonscientific* | "Folk-primitive" | "Primitive specialist" |
| *Scientific* | "Folk-modern" | "Modern specialist" |

**Figure 5-1**  Systems of medical beliefs and practices.

standing of beliefs about disease causation and their relationship to systems of primitive and folk medical practice, a schematic diagram, shown in Figure 5-1, is provided. The two major dimensions are, first, the nature of beliefs about the cause of disease, dichotomized here as nonscientific and scientific, and secondly, the nature of the role of the practitioner, either undifferentiated, indicating that the medical practices being discussed do not involve the esoteric knowledge and skills of healer or differentiated, meaning that medical theories and practices are fully understood and are prescribed only by the occupants of a specialized role.

Basically, nonscientific medicine refers to those beliefs and practices founded in tradition and which are generally accepted uncritically by the people. That is, these practices are continued from one generation to another largely because "things have always been done this way" and because the people have faith in the effectiveness of the practices as well as the correctness of the beliefs. The fact that these beliefs and practices are often associated with the supernatural lends a moral credence or, more strongly, a moral imperative to their appropriateness. Scientific medicine, on the other hand, is a set of beliefs and practices requiring empirical evidence for verification and demands that one continuously seek ways to make practices more effective. It is naturalistic in its approach and positivistic in its methodology. By the same token, beliefs are critically examined and evidence sought to improve them.

The emergence of differentiated roles for healers in a society reflects the presence of knowledge which is not understood by or accessible to most members and of practices which individuals cannot do for themselves. They may not have access to ritual secrets nor have developed the skills necessary to perform the healer role. More importantly, it reflects an increased division of labor in the society, the added roles of healer and apprentices and, of course, a different definition of the patient's role. Moreover, there are other influences such as the goal of economic support of the differentiated roles of healers. This introduces a new dimension of motivation in performing the role of healer as well as consideration of relative status, for example, esteemed status among the Azande or low status among the Cheyenne. The point is that the presence of specialized roles for healers has pervasive influence on the social structure of a society.

For this discussion, the important aspect of this formulation is that folk medicine and primitive medicine reflect two separate dimensions of beliefs about the causes of diseases. *Primitive medicine* is basically a nonscientific medicine and may be a set of beliefs and practices shared by or engaged in by almost everyone in the society; it may also be the special province of a differentiated group of recognized healers. *Folk medicine,* on the other hand, is literally medicine of the people—a set of beliefs and behaviors shared and practiced by everyone—which may be based on theories either nonscientific or quasi-scientific in nature. It is to be sharply distinguished from the specialized and more or less codified medicine practiced by specialized healers. Thus, only in one case would both primitive and folk medicine be identical, namely, in those societies in which beliefs and practices were essentially traditional and were widely shared or practiced by everyone in the society and in which no stable specialized role patterns for shamans or other healers existed.

## PRIMITIVE MEDICINE

As we have just indicated, one of the distinguishing characteristics of primitive nonscientific medicine is the uncritical acceptance of traditional explanations and practices, especially those supported by reference to the supernatural and those involving the use of magic or sorcery.[16] It should be recalled, however, that the use of magic in primitive societies is not confined to illness and disease. On the contrary, magic, as a part of the network of the religious belief system, pervades nearly every aspect of village life. In describing the natives of the Trobriand Islands, Malinowski wrote: "Everything that vitally affects the native is accompanied by magic. All economic activities have their magic; love, welfare of babies, talents and crafts, beauty and agility—all can be fostered or frustrated by magic."[17] In this respect, magic functions to help primitives gain control over their environment. As part of their environment, the inhabitants have empirical knowledge based on observation and passed on by tradition. Another part of the environment, however, is "unknown and unknowable," filled with mystery and unanticipated events. It is in this area that

---

[16]A general discussion of magic in medical practice may be found in William H. R. Rivers, *Medicine, Magic and Religion,* London: Routledge & Kegan Paul, 1924; Donald T. Atkinson, *Magic, Myth and Medicine,* Greenwich, Conn.: Fawcett, 1962; Samuel Leff and Vera Leff, *From Witchcraft to World Health,* New York: Macmillan, 1958, pp. 14–19; John Middleton, (ed.), *Magic, Witchcraft and Curing,* Garden City, N.Y.: Natural History Press, 1967.

[17]Bronislaw Malinowski, *Argonauts of the Western Pacific,* New York: Dutton, 1961, p. 73.

magic is employed. For example, when a Trobriand native performs gardening chores, Malinowski argues that there is a recognizable division between

> the well-known set of conditions, the natural course of growth, as well as ordinary pests and dangers to be warded off by fencing and weeding . . . [and] the domain of the unaccountable and adverse influences, as well as the great unearned increment of fortunate coincidence. The first conditions are coped with by knowledge and work, the second by magic.[18]

Thus, magic serves to allay anxieties generated by the unknown. For instance, the use of magic in fishing in the Trobriand Islands depends upon whether one fishes in the lagoon which is protected and involves relatively little risk or in the open sea where tides, currents, winds, and other unknown dangers may lurk. In the first case, no magic practices are used; the second requires extensive magic ritual.[19]

In much the same way, magic is employed for illness and disease. Certainly, most natives would recognize some natural causes of illness, such as burns, heat, cold, overeating, falls. For these ailments, certain traditional, more or less objective therapeutic practices are employed. On the other hand, much of the illness and disease cannot be accounted for *except* by magic or other supernatural explanations.[20] Since magic is often believed to be the cause of illness, it is not surprising that it is also extensively employed in treatment. What is surprising, however, are the accounts of the effect of magic—patients who have been cursed die without any other apparent explanation, or, alternatively, the ritual removal of a curse revives a victim who is on the brink of death. Although explanations have been hypothesized in terms of relationships between physiological functioning and emotional states, some writers have stressed the role of group influences as reinforcement of beliefs by the victims that they are dying from a curse or that they will recover. Moreover, emotional shock due to the belief that one has been sorcerized is often sufficient to cause death.[21] By the same token, breaking a spell (also in proper ritualistic fashion) is believed to contribute directly to a rapid recovery.

[18]Malinowski, *Magic, Science, and Religion . . ., op. cit.*

[19]*Ibid.*, pp. 30–31. See also Allan Young, "Internalizing and Externalizing Medical Belief Systems: An Ethiopian Example," *Social Science and Medicine,* 10 (March–April, 1976), 147–156.

[20]Dorothy M. Spencer, "Disease, Religion and Society in the Fiji Islands," *Monographs of the American Ethnological Society,* 1941.

[21]See, for example, W. B. Cannon, "Voodoo Death," *American Anthropologist,* 44 (April–June, 1942), 169–181.

For example, among the Nakanai—a Melanesian society located on the north coast of New Britain Island—magic is extensively employed in the diagnosis of and therapy for illness. Sorcery is a frequently suspected cause of a person's illness or misfortune. Although a number of practices are available to counter the effects of sorcery,

> . . . by far the most important of these depends primarily on the participation of the patient himself. The suffering victim either remembers a wrong he has committed or a quarrel he has had and assumes that the other party in the situation must be avenging himself with sorcery, or more dramatically, he dreams of a man with whom he is in conflict and realizes that this individual is practicing sorcery on him. Having identified the sorcerer, the victim either goes or sends an intermediary to resolve the conflict, usually by a transfer of wealth—but sometimes by a simple admission of guilt and an apology. The perpetrator of the sorcery usually declares himself satisfied and promises to neutralize the magic, whereupon the patient recovers. . . . It is possible, however, that the practitioner may be so incensed that he will refuse the reconciliation which his victim seeks, and in such a case death or chronic illness is usually the result. Once again the psychosomatic mechanisms of anxiety, guilt, confession and suggestion can be seen operating, this time in a context of interpersonal conflict probably often first operating unconsciously, then realized, and finally resolved at the conscious, social level.[22]

There is a second point to be made here, however. The success of a treatment acts as a reinforcement for that behavior. That is, if the use of a certain ritual or charm is thought to be the cause of recovery, it is likely that the same technique will be tried again if the illness recurs. As noted above, moreover, many of the native practices are found to be empirically correct by Western medical standards. For example, if a native is bitten by a snake, the shaman might open the wound further and suck out the evil spirit which had entered. In this treatment, venom is also extricated from the wound, thus accomplishing what is essential in objective scientific terms for curing the patient.

Three propositions will summarize the reasons why the use of magic in primitive medicine is often effective. First, in all societies, most patients most of the time will recover whether they are treated or not; that is, the human body has a tremendous ability to heal itself. Second, because primitives have a strong belief in and sensitivity to supernatural powers, magical practices can have a great deal of psychotherapeutic value even if they do nothing more than make the patient more comfortable. Third, many

---

[22]Charles A. Valentine, "Health in a Changing Society: The West Nakanai of New Britain," unpublished manuscript, Washington University, St. Louis, 1967, pp. 65–66. See also Frank, *op. cit.*, pp. 39–41.

of the medical practices employed, although invested with superfluous supernatural beliefs and ritually carried out, are empirically correct by Western standards of medical practice. This is especially the case in the use of a wide variety of herbal concoctions by native healers which have been demonstrated by scientific investigation to be pharmacologically more or less effective.

As a final note on the efficacy of magic, it may be noted that there rarely is a disconfirming case. That is, the effects of magic are not empirically verifiable. Thus, if magic is employed in therapy either alone or in conjunction with other elements and the patient recovers, success can be attributed to the magic, thereby reinforcing the belief and the behavior. Although accompanied by an objectively correct therapeutic procedure which actually effects the cure, magic is given the credit for the cure. If magic is used without good results, the failure may be attributed not to magic *qua* magic, but to the improper performance of the ritual or to the "fact" that the illness-causing magic was more powerful. Nevertheless, the belief in magic remains. (It might be noted that often the same kind of reasoning can be applied to our own system of thought as well.[23])

The extensive use of magic in explaining illness implies that the causes of almost all diseases in primitive societies are known at least in theory, although problems of diagnosing the source of an evil spell often still remain. There are, of course, many instances of illness or injury, such as colds and minor burns, which are not important enough to warrant a causal explanation or for which the cause is correctly identified. But in serious cases, the cause of illness is usually attributed to the supernatural, either directly or through other humans acting as agents. It is a characteristic of primitive medicine that stress is placed on spiritual elements in explanations, but in Western medicine physical elements generally take precedence. In fact, one of the consequences of the development of Western scientific medicine has been to greatly reduce the importance of spiritual elements in assessing the causes of disease.[24]

We have noted that it is a characteristic of medical behavior that its practices follow more or less logically from its theories of disease causation. Further light on the pervasiveness of magical and religious methods may therefore be shed by a brief survey of the theories of primitive medicine. These theories, it should be noted, are applications of more basic beliefs about human nature and the nature of the cosmos in which human beings live. In general, the causes of illness (or death) in primitive societies

---

[23]See, for example, the analysis in Tina Carmeli, "Magical Elements in Orthodox Medicine: Diabetes as a Medical Thought System," London: Bedford College, February, 1976 (mimeo).

[24]See Frank, *op. cit.*, p. 37.

can be ascribed to soul loss, spirit intrusion, disease-object intrusion, or breach of taboo—or to some combination of these.[25]

*Soul loss* reflects a widespread belief in the body-spirit bifurcation, that the soul is the spiritual replica of the living person. It is believed that the separation of the soul from the body, whether by accident or intentionally, will cause illness and finally death.[26] Among the natives of Dobu, for example, it is thought that the soul leaves the body at night when the individual is sleeping and returns in the morning. Hence, it is dangerous to awaken the individual too suddenly for fear that the soul may not have time to return. The soul may also be lost through the evil magic of a sorcerer who may be seeking personal revenge or acting as the agent for a human enemy. Whatever the cause of the separation, there are several cases on record of the victims of the "loss of soul" becoming lethargic, slowly wasting away, and dying. Among the Murngin in northern Australia, for example, when the loss of a person's soul becomes general knowledge, death is hastened not only by the person's own belief in that fate, but also by kinfolk, who socially isolate the victim because they believe that an improperly buried soul will bring illness and death to others in the group.[27] In this regard, we might consider our own fate if family, friends, and other associates should suddenly cease to interact with us.[28]

The key to successful treatment of a case of soul loss is to cause the soul to return to the body. This can be done only through ritual magic compatible with the cultural beliefs of the group. For example, if the loss of soul is deemed accidental, certain rites, spells, or charms may be employed by the individual, as in Dobu, or in other cultures in conjunction with the

[25]For an early work describing the origin and distribution of these explanations, see Clements, *op. cit.* See also John M. Whiting and Irvin L. Child, *Child Training and Personality,* New Haven, Conn.: Yale University Press, 1953. Whiting and Child attempt to account for the presence of the basic types of explanation of illness in various societies by correlating these explanations with the character of child-rearing patterns in the society. Thus they see explanations of illness as reflecting projection and similar psychological mechanisms, which are commonly found in various social groups.

[26]A variant of this belief is illness or death caused by loss of some vital organ by witchcraft. Usually loss of the heart, liver, spleen, or genitals will cause the death of the victim unless the organ is (magically) replaced.

[27]W. Lloyd Warner, *A Black Civilization,* New York: Harper & Row, 1941, quoted in Frank, *op. cit.,* pp. 41–42.

[28]The high death rate of American soldiers in Chinese prisoner of war camps during the Korean war has been attributed, in part, to the extreme psychological isolation imposed upon the prisoners by clever Chinese tactics. See Albert D. Biderman, *March to Calumny,* New York: Macmillan, 1963. Social isolation could also be cited as a factor in the increased death rates among the elderly newly admitted to nursing homes and other long-term care institutions. Harold J. Wershow, "The Four Percent Fallacy: Some Further Evidence and Policy Implications," *The Gerontologist,* 16 (February, 1976), 52–55. See also the discussion of social isolation in Robert N. Butler and Myrna J. Lewis, *Aging and Mental Health,* Saint Louis: Mosby, 1973. More recently, see Robert N. Butler, *Why Survive: Being Old in America,* New York: Harper and Row, 1975.

village or tribal witch doctor. If the loss is attributed to the malefic actions of a sorcerer, then other magic ritual may be used, including divination, to determine the source of malefic action, and appeal (or appeasement) to this source for return of the soul or, perhaps, countersorcery to force the return of the soul. The particular cultural form taken is not so important as the recognition that soul loss is a widely accepted cause of disease among primitive peoples. King points out that vestiges of the belief in soul loss may also be exhibited by modern patients who show fear of or reluctance to undergo anesthesia before an operation because of the "unconscious secrets" they may disclose.[29]

Another common etiologic explanation is *spirit intrusion*. Common symptoms include many forms of aberrant behavior, such as excessive gesticulating, frenzied bodily movements, hallucinating as well as a general feeling of ill-being. The causes of becoming inhabited by an evil spirit can be many, but generally are due to improper appeasement of ancestors, failing to take proper precautions against evil spirits "known" to frequent certain places, or, again, as a result of witchcraft or sorcery. "Possession" by evil spirits is by no means limited to isolated primitive tribes; in fact, as late as the nineteenth century it was a common explanation for the behavior of the mentally ill in Western societies.

As one might suspect, the cure for such an affliction is to get the evil spirit to leave. The specific therapy employed depends upon the definition of why the spirit entered the body of the victim. If it is because he or she had not properly performed some ritual, penitence must accompany the ritual cleansing by the witch doctor or shaman. One might cite any of several Biblical passages which describe the casting out of spirits. For example, a man brought his son to Jesus and said:

> I have brought unto thee my son, which hath a dumb spirit; and wheresoever he taketh him, he teareth him; and he foameth, and gnasheth with his teeth, and pineth away. . . . If thou canst do any thing, have compassion on us, and help us.
>
> Jesus said unto him, If thou canst believe, all things *are* possible to him that believeth . . . [and Jesus] rebuked the foul spirit, saying unto him, *Thou* dumb and deaf spirit, I charge thee, come out of him, and enter no more into him.
>
> And *the spirit* cried, and rent him sore, and came out of him.[30]

Or if the victim is not at fault, that is, if the disease reflects sorcery on the part of another, different rituals are performed. Often these involve only more or less elaborate ceremonies composed of incantations, chants, oaths,

[29]King, *op. cit.,* pp. 103–104.
[30]Mark 9:17–26, King James Version.

etc. On the other hand, these spells may also involve bloodletting (to let the spirit out), induction of vomiting, or other means of symbolic release.[31] It is interesting to note that archeological expeditions have uncovered skulls, thought to be thousands of years old, which show evidence of trephining (cutting a small piece out of the skull). It is believed that trephining the skull was a therapeutic measure for permitting the possessing spirits to escape the body of the victim. It may incidentally also have relieved any pressure on the brain which could have been causing the unusual behavior.[32]

It should not be thought, however, that the intrusion of a spirit into a person is always thought by primitives to have undesirable results, such as illness. Possession is often thought to be the sign of the *favor* of the spirit world to an individual. Primitives in many societies thus may not only seek communication with the unseen world, but may offer themselves as the vehicle through which the transcendental powers may help humanity. In many groups—important among them the Ural-Altaic tribes of Siberia— the shamans obtain their powers through having had such close intercourse with the spirits that they possess the shamans. These powers are then used, among other things, to help cure the sick. But it should be noted also that shamans are often thought to have come to their power through sickness; they find their own cure precisely through using their "possession" for social ends. Thus one Yakut-Tungus shaman reported not only that his ability to shamanize came after a period of illness and hallucinations but also that when he did not exercise his "profession," he was likely to become ill himself.[33]

*Disease-object intrusion* is a third generally recognized cause of disease and illness. In one sense, this causal explanation is very similar to spirit intrusion in that the evil spirits may be at work in both cases. With disease-object intrusion, however, the evil spirits are invested in some physical object; that is, they are the essence of some object, such as a piece of wood, a rock, a feather, or other element. Moreover, the intrusion of the disease object is often the consequence of malefic behavior of a sorcerer. Dobuans, for example, practice disease-object intrusion. Benedict reports that to cause the death of his enemy, the Dobuan native

> . . . breathes the spell into the excreta of the victim or into a creeper which lays across the path of his enemy, biding nearby to see that the victim actually brushes against it. . . . When the victim has brushed against the creeper [the native] takes the creeper home with him and lets it wither in his hut. When he is ready for his enemy's death he burns it in his fire.[34]

[31]Whiting and Child, *op. cit.*
[32]Henry Cohen, "Evolution of the Concept of Disease," in Brandon Lush (ed.), *Concepts of Medicine,* New York: Pergamon Press, 1961, pp. 159–169.
[33]Sigerist, *op. cit.,* pp. 172ff.
[34]Ruth Benedict, *Patterns of Culture,* New York: Mentor Books, 1959, p. 136.

It is important, of course, that the victim be aware that a fatal spell has been cast upon him or her and that unless a "cure" is employed, death may follow. Fortunately, countersorcery, if properly applied, can be used to negate the magical effects of the first spell. Countersorcery, as has been noted many times, is a frequently employed therapy. There is, however, another commonly found therapeutic procedure, the symbolic removal of the object itself (hence, also the evil spirit or essence). In describing the tactics of Kwakiutl shamans, Benedict reported that

> Each shaman had a trick that differed slightly from those of his rivals [other shamans]. . . . Some shamans sucked out illness, some rubbed, some restored lost souls. A favourite device was to produce the illness from the body of the patient in the form of a small "worm." In order to be prepared for this demonstration, the shaman carried a roll of birds' down between his teeth and upper lip. When he was called upon to cure, he first rinsed his mouth with water. When he had thus proved that he had nothing in his mouth he danced and sucked and finally bit his cheeks so that his mouth was full of bloody saliva. He spat out the roll of down into a bowl with the blood he had supposedly sucked also from the seat of the illness. . . and exhibited it as evidence that he had removed the cause of pain and illness.[35]

This passage not only illustrates a typical treatment for illness caused by object intrusion, but it also implies that this treatment, like other magic treatments, is faked for the benefit of the patient. As Ackerknecht pointed out, however, the patient is also aware that the removal of some object from the body was faked, and it is the *symbolism* that is important, not the actual techniques used.[36]

The fourth and last class of causal explanations considered here is *breach of taboo*. All human groups establish standards by which they live. Many of these standards become a moral imperative and are buttressed by a religious sanction. In modern society, violation of such norms may result in excommunication from the church or may result in a fine or imprisonment if the particular behavior has also been secularly defined as a violation of established law. In primitive society, illness or death may well be the consequence of breaking a taboo. Even in modern society, examples are given of people becoming physically ill from violating a moral commandment—for instance, the oft-repeated tale of the orthodox Jew who becomes sick from eating pork.

Hsu demonstrates the tenacity of beliefs in diseases being caused by violation of taboos in his analysis of an outbreak of cholera in a Chinese

[35]Benedict, *op. cit.*, p. 187.
[36]Ackerknecht, *op. cit.* Cf., Asen Balikci, "Shamanistic Behavior among the Netsilik Eskimos," in Middleton, *op. cit.*, pp. 191–209.

village. According to the local interpretation, the wave of illness which ultimately killed some 200 inhabitants was caused by angered ancestors who had become disturbed by the immoral behavior of the town's population. It is noteworthy that these people had available to them Western-trained medical practitioners and reasonably modern facilities, such as a hospital. Yet they were largely unused because the Western explanation of the cause of the epidemic was less believable than the firmly entrenched explanation derived from the cult of ancestor worship and traditional morality.[37]

The logical treatment for illness caused by breach of taboo is atonement in some form. It may be by confession, repentance, restoration of material goods, payment for misdeeds, or appeal to the offended deities.[38] Hsu's report on the cholera epidemic showed that since natives believed the epidemic was caused by angered spirits offended by the immorality of the villagers, the main therapeutic efforts were prayer meetings and certain behaviors designed to please these gods. In addition, local folk remedies such as certain medicinal preparations and "fairy" water were used along with immunization programs by Western-trained doctors in the province. The main point is that while scientific procedures were used by Western doctors in combating the epidemic, traditional religious practices were seen by the natives as the most logical therapeutic effort.

It would be well to pause here and observe that although these classes of causal explanations and their associated therapies may appear quaint to us, they are in some ways analogous to our own etiologic beliefs. For example, illness from soul loss is attributed to the loss of a sustaining part of the body, which is somewhat like our belief that illness may be due to nutritional deficiency or to the absence of sustaining parts of the body. Similarly, modern germ theory holds that disease may occur when one ingests or otherwise comes into contact with disease-causing germs. It is thus broadly similar to the disease-object intrusion (or spirit intrusion), explanations which are characteristic of primitive societies. Moreover, the effects of breach of taboo or violation of traditional standards of behavior are analogous to the use made of the modern psychoanalytic concept of guilt in accounting for neurotic behavior and associated physical symptoms. One could, of course, carry these analogies too far. We mention them here only to emphasize that the practices of people in other cultures and in other times may not be so unusual when examined in the cultural fabric within which they occur.

[37]Francis L. K. Hsu, "A Cholera Epidemic in a Chinese Town," in Paul, *op. cit.,* pp. 135–154.
[38]Erwin D. Ackerknecht, "Medical Practices," in Julian H. Steward (ed.), *Handbook of South American Indians,* vol. 5, Washington, D.C.: Smithsonian Institution, Bureau of American Ethnology, 1949, pp. 621–643.

## ETHNOGRAPHIC EXAMPLES OF PRIMITIVE MEDICINE

To give a little more substance to this description of the elements of primitive medical beliefs and practices, some ethnographic materials are presented below. One of the major points of this chapter is that observed medical practices cannot be readily understood out of the context of other values, beliefs, and practices of the society.[39] Therefore, it is necessary to present some information on other aspects of the culture, its social organization, major social institutions, dominant values, etc. With this added information, the description of particular medical practices takes on meaning and permits a better comparison with other cultures as well.

### Azande Medicine

As we have noted above, some primitive societies have an elaborately developed system of practitioner roles. Among the Azande, for example, there is a sort of AWA (Azande Witchcraft Association) which is a closed group of witch doctors, each of whom has purchased knowledge of medicine from another witch doctor and has been initiated into the corporation, who collectively keep their special knowledge secret from nonmembers of the group. Since witchcraft is seen as a socially relevant cause in every case of Azande disease, illness, and misfortune, there is considerable need for consultation with witch doctors, who not only have knowledge of counter-magic, but can also predict future illnesses and misfortunes through the use of various oracles.

The Azande, an agricultural people who reside along the Congo-Nile divide in the Sudan and in the Congo (now Zaïre), provide opportunity to examine further both the relation of medical beliefs to the ethos of the culture as a whole and the characteristics of medical practitioners in a primitive society. Our data on the Azande will be drawn from one of the classics of anthropology, Professor E. E. Evans-Pritchard's *Witchcraft, Oracles and Magic among the Azande.*[40] Since Evans-Pritchard's data were collected on expeditions made to Zandeland between 1926 and 1930, the picture presented is of a people whose effective culture contact with the West was a generation old and who, despite evidences of many recent changes, adhered to a culture which had as yet largely escaped the disorganizing impact of modernity.

[39]Erwin D. Ackerknecht, "Primitive Medicine and Culture Patterns," *Bulletin of the History of Medicine,* 12 (November, 1942), 545–574.

[40]E. E. Evans-Pritchard, *Witchcraft, Oracles and Magic among the Azande,* Oxford, England: Clarendon Press, 1937. See also Evans-Pritchard's comparison of magic among the Azande and Malanowski's Melanesians; E. E. Evans-Pritchard, "The Morphology and Function of Magic: A Comparative Study of Trobriand and Zande Ritual and Spells," in Middleton, *op. cit.,* pp. 1–41.

As the title of Evans-Pritchard's study indicates, Azande culture is permeated by belief in supernatural forces. It is emphasized that witchcraft, oracles, and magic form a mutually reinforcing set of beliefs, inconsistent by Western standards, but in practice forming a satisfying and all-encompassing way of explaining life's vicissitudes. As is frequently the case among primitive groups, distinctions which seem to us to be fundamental axioms of logical thought are made only imperfectly. Yet given the Azande assumptions that the events of this world are conditioned by both empirical and transempirical causes and that no single generalization can explain any given event, their use of magic and oracles is quite understandable. Indeed, the genius of Professor Evans-Pritchard's book is that he succeeds in communicating the cultural matrix within which Azande witchcraft and medicine can make sense to us.

For the Azande, the causes of the events of this life involve *both* the kinds of explanation which we would call natural and those which we would call supernatural. Thus the man who injures his toe by stubbing it against a stump does so both because he physically kicked the stump (which may have been hidden along the jungle path) *and* because witchcraft influenced his foot in the fateful direction which it took. The Azande are not satisfied with explanations of *how* the foot was injured; they wish to explain *why* as well. Moreover, they see it as elementary to explain the bruise in terms of its general cause, the stubbed toe; to them it is of equal or greater importance to know why at this particular time this *particular* person would kick against this *particular* stump. Azande logic is not content with necessary and sufficient causes, but it is not blind to them either.

To the Azande, it is axiomatic that human misfortune is caused by *mangu,* or "witchcraft substance," a substance found in the body of certain persons (witches), the "psychic emanations" from which cause injury to men. Two characteristics of *mangu* are worth emphasis here: its presumed material existence and its ability to operate both in supra-empirical ways and at the behest of men. Azande believe that witches inherit *mangu,* boys from their fathers and girls from their mothers. They believe further that certain oracles, principally involving poisoning chickens, can detect witchcraft and that it is possible for a witch to recall his or her witchcraft. Moreover, other magical substances, *ngua,* or "medicines," can, properly directed, attain the same effect. The Azande believe *mangu* and *ngua* to be pervasive, causing, as it were, the forces of the natural world to operate in the particular ways in which they do. So pervasive is their belief in *mangu* that it is seen as the principal cause of human misfortune. Yet it must be emphasized that, contrary to Western ideas about witchcraft, it is not seen as diabolical and it is not something which, in the abstract at least, evokes great fright. It is simply a fact of life. As such, it is seen as a principal cause of illness.

Illness, however, can be treated both in terms of its symptoms and of its causes. And in fact, the Azande distinguish many diseases in terms of their symptoms. Thus they may name a disease after the affected part or after the sensations it produces, e.g., headache, dim-sightedness. They may also name diseases after something in nature to which they bear resemblance; thus a throat abscess is called *aduru,* after *duru,* a snail which is thought to spit out a white saliva. The Azande also explain some diseases in terms of what they believe to be their causes. Sometimes these causes may have some empirical foundation (e.g., insect bites); they may also be quite fanciful to Western ears, e.g., the belief that deep body ulcers (called "the sickness of the crocodile") can be caused by a man's having intercourse with a married woman whose husband "touched her back during sleep with the tooth of a crocodile, while asking this animal to punish any man who has relations with her." Still other diseases are named after their cure; for example, stiff neck is called "spear-shaft sickness" because the cure is "to move the neck from side to side between two intersecting spear-shafts." What is significant here is not only that Azande explain diseases in terms of something other than witchcraft but that they believe that there is a specific medicine for each disease. This medicine is usually a magical substance, *ngua,* typically a preparation of herbs. And not only do most lay persons know many medicines, but specialized knowledge of medicines exists among both witch doctors and others.

Yet the specific disease which a person may have may be caused by witchcraft or sorcery, and if it does not respond to its medicine in reasonable time or if it is unusually painful or serious in its manifestations, it will almost certainly be attributed to witchcraft.[41] To make matters still more complex, illness can also be caused by breach of taboo or some other crime and in this case must be dealt with by some restitutive activity. Enough has been said to indicate that Azande beliefs about medicine are complex and involve multiple alternatives of action. Sick Azande, therefore, face both the problem of diagnosing what is wrong and choosing what action to take about the illness. Often enough, they will need the help of their fellows or of specialists in the process.

Several aspects of Azande belief about witchcraft and medicine should be stressed, however, if the social context of Azande medical behavior is to be understood. First, both *mangu* and *ngua* are subject to human direction and control. Medicine involves the participation of human agents in its use; it must, as it were, be told what to do. Of importance here is the belief that medicines may lose their potency if their owner—and all Azande medicines are owned by someone—violates certain taboos or if they are used by a

---

[41]Sorcery or "black magic" constitutes the antisocial use of *ngua* for evil ends; it is thought usually to cause acute illness which kills quickly unless it can be overcome by an antidote. Of the two causes of disease, witchcraft seems by far the more important.

person without adequate compensation to their owner. In these ways, the use of medicine involves a number of social bonds. One must not only behave toward a medicine in a proper way, which often involves the collaboration of certain of one's fellows, but must motivate the medicine to work, as it were, by satisfying its owner. This means that the practice of medicine involves a body of reciprocal obligations, both economic and otherwise. Second, Azande interest in witchcraft is less in the phenomenon itself, or even in the fact that witches exist, than in determining the application of witchcraft in a particular case. When the source of witchcraft that may be directed against one is known, one may obtain relief by persuading the witch to remove the spell, by directing one's own medicine against it, or by the indirect means of frightening the witch into redirecting the witchcraft through fear of discovery. On the one hand, therefore, witchcraft provides a way of explaining misfortune in terms of known tensions in human relations and opens the possibility of coping with illness and other misfortunes through reconciling the strains in human relationships. On the other hand, the very uncertainty as to specific causes of illness and other misfortune inherent in the Azande belief in multiple causation and in the real difficulty in confirming the existence of witchcraft acts to reduce the possibility of vendettas against supposed witches. Rather, the belief that anyone (even oneself) may be a witch and that one may at any time be bewitched acts as a *general* control on social behavior.[42]

In dealing with their illnesses, as in the rest of their lives, the Azande base their actions not only on empirical knowledge and observation, but on the magical revelations available to them about what has happened or is likely to happen. The use of *oracles* is fundamental in Azande society. As in the case of medicine, people may use their own oracle, seek the aid of an acquaintance who may have a more powerful oracle, or seek the aid of a professional shaman. In the case of oracles, all these means are subject to confirmation by the oracles of the local princes, which alone can give legal basis for action. Every person may use simple oracles. Thus three sticks may be piled up outside one's hut overnight and according to whether or not they remain piled up the next morning, the Azande will know whether the question is answered affirmatively or negatively. Rubbing boards can be purchased which have magical powers to answer the same kinds of questions. The termite oracle can answer questions on the basis of whether a termite colony devours one or another of two different kinds of wood thrust into their anthill. Shamans, by virtue of their owning the *ngua* of their profession, can provide oracular data in the process of their dances. And of

---

[42]Scarlett Epstein, "A Sociological Analysis of Witch Beliefs in a Mysore Village," in Middleton, *op. cit.,* pp. 135–154.

greatest validity of all is thought to be the poison oracle, in which a poison *ngua,* properly questioned, is administered to a fowl; this oracle is usually administered twice, and if the answer to a question is first confirmed by the fowl's death and later by its survival (or vice versa), the Azande may know very well what he ought to do. The prince's poison oracle, as indicated above, is the ultimate oracular sanction known to the Azande.

As suggested above, there is a hierarchy of validity ascribed to the various Azande oracles—and to their medicines as well; some are more powerful than others. In general, those most obviously subject to human manipulation, such as an individual's rubbing board or a witch doctor's dancing, are thought to be less valid than the more impersonal wisdom of the poison oracle. But poison is rare and fowls expensive; hence simpler means are used first. And when witch doctors dance, even though their oracles may not be entirely valid, it is believed that their medicine may have other salutary results; because their dance is a public affair, while other uses of the oracles are at best semiprivate, the witch doctors' dances also can act simultaneously to allay the fears of a whole community.

Azande medicine, as thus far described, involves a complex of beliefs, any one of which may be thought to be operative in a given situation. These beliefs may include material or supernatural mechanisms or both simultaneously. They always entail the need for acquiring information—a diagnosis and a prognosis—to overcome uncertainty and to provide the basis for further action. This further action almost always involves both the use of specific substances or medicines and beliefs which frequently require cooperation from others—persuading an acquaintance to help in a poison oracle, buying a medicine or its use from its owner, making amends for misdeeds so that an individual will deprive the magic of its power, etc. Since any person may own a medicine, almost any Azande is a potential player in the sick person's efforts to overcome illness.

Yet there exist among the Azande special societies of witch doctors, who from time to time practice their special art to help others overcome their misfortunes or to help to protect them. Among the Azande, witch doctors are believed to have their power because they possess—and have consumed—certain powerful *ngua,* or medicines. These *ngua* are known only to members of the society, and the specialty group reinforces the power of their medicine among them from time to time both in meetings of their own in which they "cook" their medicines and by participating together in their séances. Membership in the association of witch doctors is gained through apprenticeship, in which an individual pays a mentor to reveal the *ngua* and teach their uses; it is confirmed by a rite of initiation.

Witch doctors usually act both as "leeches," that is, as experts in the prescription of specific medicines for various diseases, and as oracles to determine the source of the witchcraft that may be besetting a sick person.

Their utility depends in part on the fact that they possess both kinds of knowledge; but the Azande assume that any spectacular successes of witch doctors will depend upon their special magical powers, probably obtained because they themselves are witches. Witch doctors vehemently deny being witches, ascribing their powers to their *ngua*. It has already been noted that the validity of a witch doctor's revelations is often not highly regarded. The Azande society is, in a word, somewhat cynical about the usefulness of any given witch doctor. Yet there is no doubt that they believe that some witch doctors perform miracles some of the time, and there is also no doubt that both the witch doctors' knowledge of medicines and their ability to plausibly suggest the presence or absence of witchcraft in certain social situations are recognized by lay persons as useful and valid. There is also little doubt that witch doctors can exert powerful effects on their patients and on the community as well through the suggestive drama in which their practice is couched.

Azande witch doctors both "shoot" bones or other magical missiles into the bodies of bystanders during their dances and remove them from their victims. More importantly, they demonstrate their healing powers by magically removing disease-causing objects from sick patients. This is accomplished through sleight of hand, and the shamans (as well as, perhaps, some of the laity) know of this deception. Evans-Pritchard reports how shaken one of his servants was when, in the course of being initiated into the society of shamans, he learned the tricks of their trade. Yet

> . . . the Azande witch doctor, in spite of his extra knowledge is as deep a believer in magic as his slightly less-informed fellows. At first I used to think that to some extent he understood the folly of his divination and leechcraft, but after a while I began to realize how little he really understood. He knows that he cheats laymen but does not know how he is cheated by his own ignorance. Just as laymen express their skepticism in a mystical idiom, so witch doctors express their knowledge in mystical terms. They know that their extraction of objects from the bodies of their patients is a fake, but they believe that they cure them by the medicines they administer. They know that the objects they are supposed to shoot into people are hidden in their hands, yet they think that they somehow, nevertheless, injure their rivals by assailing them with psychical ammunition. Here, as everywhere, we are confronted with the same tangle of knowledge and error. It is especially evident in the manner of divination employed by witch doctors: they seem to reason so acutely, to weigh probabilities of enmity so evenly. Yet they believe as firmly in witchcraft as their clients and believe as steadfastly that the medicines they have eaten enable them to identify witches. They display an intellectual acuteness which might have expressed itself in skepticism and disillusionment were they not enclosed in the same network of thought, the same web of witchcraft, oracles, and magic, as are laymen. Within the limited situation of their professional practice

they are able to think differently from laymen, but their thought is limited by the same cultural conditions outside these special situations.[43]

Azande witch doctors, then, may be seen as experts in the beliefs of the societal folk medicine who, by virtue of their special training and their particular abilities, have become recognized as of potential use in time of trouble. They have organized themselves into a closed society of practitioners, entry into which is dependent both upon the novice's ability to pay for learning and upon the master's willingness to accept a pupil. And like all other professions, the societies of Azande shamans—even while full of individual rivalries—stand together in solidarity both as custodians of their secrets and as collaborators in their service to society. In the simple society of Zandeland, however, practice is not a full-time occupation. The witch doctors most of the time till their land just as do their neighbors. And because they are members of Azande society, they are sure to know enough of their fellows' thoughts and anxieties to make their slender knowledge have maximum use. However, the fact that lay persons are so acutely aware of the fallibility of their shamans indicates that in this society the laity are the arbiters of the conditions of the practitioner's calling. The Azande witch doctor's mandate is limited.

On the other hand, there are primitive societies in which the medical beliefs and practices have primarily a folk character. For example, Benedict has described the overwhelming preoccupation of the natives of Dobu with sorcery and witchcraft, magic spells, incantations, amulets, and charms. About disease charms she writes that they

> . . . have a malevolence all their own. Every man and woman in Tewara village owns from one to five. Each is specific for a particular disease, and the person who owns the incantation owns also the incantation for removing the same affliction. Some persons have a monopoly of certain diseases and hence are sole owners of the power to cause it and cure it. Whoever has elephantiasis or scrofula in a locality, therefore, knows at whose door to lay it. The charms make the owner powerful and are greatly coveted.[44]

The Cheyenne, moreover, exhibit a marked indifference to disease. Although they believe in supernatural causes of disease and employ certain ceremonial procedures against it, their main concern is that disease may cause a warrior's death before he has had a chance to die in battle, the ultimate goal of Cheyenne braves.[45] Among the Cheyenne, only minor

[43]Evans-Pritchard, *Witchcraft,* pp. 255–256.

[44]Benedict, *op. cit.,* p. 135.

[45]Ackerknecht, "Primitive Medicine and Culture Patterns." See also E. Adamson Hoebel, *The Cheyenne: Indians of the Great Plains,* New York: Holt, 1960.

differentiation of a practitioner role occurs in the form of a part-time shaman who is seen as playing a feminine role. That is, a nonwarrior male, who has developed a special knack for dealing with certain kinds of health problems, is often sought out for advice. However, this is not a valued role in the Cheyenne culture.

The foregoing account of Azande medicine and the brief comparisons made among the medicines of the Azande, Dobuans, and Cheyenne suggests that there is a great deal of variation in the ways in which medicine is institutionalized in primitive cultures. In all these cultures, a commonly held primitive folk medicine exists. All adult members of each society share a set of beliefs about the significance and causation of illness, although there may be some disagreement about the application of these theories. On this basis, sick persons and their kin make decisions about what should be done for specific illnesses and when the help of an outside practitioner must be sought. The societies vary not only with respect to the specifics of their theories and practices, but also in the way their practitioner roles are differentiated.

In these three societies—and among primitive peoples generally—differentiation in medical knowledge and competence does exist. Some persons, whether through their superior interest and skill in medical lore, their hereditary position, or their economic status, become expert in one or another medical problem and are thus consulted by their compatriots in time of need. When such expertise does not depend upon an independent body of knowledge which is the unique possession of a special society of healers, we have not yet reached the level of differentiation which separates folk and pracitioners' medicine. For example, among the Dobuans, possession of a powerful amulet thought to cure a specific disease *may* give its owner the monopoly of curing that illness, but this is an incidental result of possession of an amulet and is not associated with playing a practitioner's role. Similarly, in many societies, old women are thought to be particularly good at compounding and prescribing herbal remedies, but their knowledge is the product of their years and, perhaps, of their special interest, not of their having elected to become "healers." They are not formally set apart from their fellows as occupants of a specialized role. Quite different are the Azande witch doctors or the Siberian shamans, with their secret societies and their socially recognized special powers. To them are accorded both special knowledge and powers which ordinary people cannot achieve and a special role in society. They practice a kind of specialist medicine, and it is the essence of their role that their knowledge and skill are different from those of lay people and inaccessible to them.

The extent to which practitioner roles develop for healers in various primitive societies is subject to a great deal of variation. Sometimes, these roles are specifically defined, and distinctions are made among "surgeons," diviners, and sorcerers; at other times, they are ill-defined and diffuse.

Sigerist notes that shamans in primitive societies frequently deal not only with medical phenomena, but with such things as ensuring a successful harvest and victory in war.[46] Almost always, in simple societies, the emergence of a specialist shaman implies a concept of function which is much broader than our language and expectations would indicate. Similarly, the social status of practitioners varies from society to society, from the marginal status of the Cheyenne healer to the great power and prestige of the Azande or Australian aboriginal witch doctor.[47] In many primitive societies, there are several kinds of medical practitioners, as in our own. In many tribes, a distinction is made between herbalist-healers, expert in empirical remedies and simple ceremonies, and the shaman, whose knowledge of coping with the unknown is more extensive because of a mastery of magic and religious ceremony and whose power has been authenticated by a special "calling." Thus, in primitive societies as well as in our own, the transaction of medical behavior may involve many people, both lay and specialist. And the medical culture of the lay person is usually overlaid by an esoteric subculture of the practitioner.

## FOLK MEDICINE IN WESTERN SOCIETIES

As was noted above, folk medicine is literally medicine of the people. It is comprised of medical beliefs and practices which are, in principle, available to all the members of a society without reference to their incumbency in a differentiated role or achievement in specialized courses of training. Folk medicine, in other words, represents the uninstitutionalized aspects of the medical cultural pattern. Being more or less integrated with other cultural patterns, folk beliefs and practices tend to persist over time and remain in force long after their origins and justifications may have been forgotten.

How did they develop? To begin with, it has probably always been the case that people have tried, mostly through trial and error, to cure themselves when they felt sick. Thus, cures which someone reported as effective would tend to remain in practice; as with magic, it is difficult to disconfirm a cure (except under experimental conditions). Folk beliefs are part of the oral tradition, passed on from parents to children, from older generations to the young; they thus develop the potent sanction of tradition. Then, too, reliance on natural remedies developed from the close relationship of people to their land, especially in agrarian areas; consequently, in traditional societies, the common person's knowledge about medicinal plants and herbs is frequently extensive.

[46]Sigerist, *op. cit.,* pp. 166–179.
[47]For a sympathetic and extensive account of the role of medicine in one primitive society, see A. P. Elkin, *Aboriginal Men of High Degree,* Sydney, Australia: Australasian Publishing Company, 1946.

An example of a folk concept which prevails even today, especially in Latin American cultures, is the belief about hot and cold as causes of disease.[48] A healthy state is thought to exist when one maintains a balance between hot and cold forces. Disease and illness occur when these opposing phenomena become unbalanced. Certain objects such as food, liquid, or even states of nature are described as inherently hot or cold, depending upon cultural definitions. Thus, the general rule is that one should balance the intake of hot with something cold and vice versa. Similarly, one takes hot medicine for cold illnesses and so on. The balance concept also extends to body fluids, especially blood. To be healthy, one must maintain a proper balance not only between various fluids, but must also maintain them in the proper amounts and densities. The theory of balance of body fluids or humors was expounded in the Hippocratic writings nearly 2,500 years ago, thus illustrating the extraordinary persistence of these ideas. Although scientific medicine has long since discarded the humoral theories of Hippocrates, they survive in a corrupted form in contemporary folk medicine. Meanwhile, scientific medicine has evolved sophisticated balance theories, such as homeostasis, which, however, lead to practical conclusions far different from those of either Hippocrates or Latin folk medicine.

Folk medical beliefs usually contain many prescriptions for special potions and medicines. For example, a natural substance widely used by people in Vermont to prevent a variety of illnesses is honey. Observation of and faith in the instinct of bees is said to have led to the use of honey as a sedative for nervous conditions and as a cough syrup and to ward off bacterial infections. It has been pointed out that for whatever reasons honey is taken, it has certain properties which allow it to accomplish in some degree the goals for which it is used. For example, honey absorbs moisture, which is necessary for bacteria to grow, thereby inhibiting the growth of bacteria in the throat and reducing infections. Honey is also used in folk belief for preventing bed-wetting, inducing sleep, clearing stuffy noses, and even reducing pain from arthritis.[49] Folk practices such as these have continued to the present time, largely because they are still perceived as being effective.

These and similar folk beliefs are said to be empirical, and many may stem from observing what sick animals do by instinct. In curing themselves, it is said that sick animals will

. . . first seek solitude and absolute relaxation, then they rely on the complete remedies of Nature—the medicine in plants and pure air. . . . An animal with fever quickly hunts up an airy, shady place near water, there remaining quiet,

[48]Lyle Saunders, *Cultural Difference and Medical Care,* New York: Russell Sage, 1954, pp. 144–145.
[49]DeForrest C. Jarvis, *Folk Medicine,* New York: Holt, 1958.

eating nothing, but drinking often until its health is recovered. On the other hand, an animal bedeviled by rheumatism, finds a spot of hot sunlight and lies in it until the misery bakes out.[50]

Similarly, one can observe what kinds of plants or herbs animals seek out to cure sores, boils, snake bite, and other ailments which may befall them. Thus, in an age of an impersonal and highly technological scientific medicine, some persons find the simplicity and "naturalness" of traditional folk beliefs attractive. They may justify them—and in the case of nature food stores commercialize them—with a kind of Rousseauean appeal to "go back to nature."

In the area of folk obstetric and pediatric beliefs, Eaton has described the practices of the Hutterites, which reveal a curious mixture of understanding of cause-and-effect relationships and belief in supernatural causes.[51] For example, women are prepared for motherhood from early childhood by being given responsibility for care of younger siblings. As a result, when they marry or become pregnant, they already have a considerable repertory of practices to follow, many of which are scientifically sound. While they are expecting, they eat special diets of foods such as milk and eggs which are rich in protein, calcium, and other growth-promoting nutrients, and they refrain from certain chores such as heavy lifting which could cause miscarriage. At the same time, they are careful to think "pure" thoughts to avoid "marking" the fetus, and they believe that if a mother sees mice and rats, her child may have birthmarks. After the infant is born, certain other precautions are followed, such as wearing a red ribbon around the wrist to avoid the "evil eye."

Hutterite families do not generally seek pediatric care from physicians except for certain physical illnesses. This is partly because they feel they know more about child care than a physician does, but it also serves to reduce the impact of scientific practices and ideas on their own subcultural beliefs. One consequence is the occurrence of a few cases of preventable diseases, but "by American medical standards, infants are generally given good care."[52]

One of the conclusions which may be drawn from these examples is that, compared with practitioners' medicine, folk medical practices are often scarcely differentiated from values and behaviors in other areas of life, such as daily work, esthetics, or religious beliefs. For example, a norm of body cleanliness may be followed in order not to offend others and to

---

[50]*Ibid.*, p. 10.

[51]Joseph W. Eaton, "Folk Obstetrics and Pediatrics Meet the MD: A Case Study of Social Anthropology in Medicine," in E. Gartly Jaco (ed.), *Patients, Physicians and Illness*, New York: Free Press, 1958.

[52]*Ibid.*, p. 218.

allow a proper "presentation of self" as well as for recognized health reasons.[53] Furthermore, it may be noted here that in well-developed societies, folk beliefs and practices become less and less compatible with scientific medical beliefs and practices as the level of education declines and as groups become more isolated. Thus, esoteric folk practices seem to be more common among the lower classes and in communities more removed from urban areas.

These examples illustrate another characteristic of folk medicine; namely, its effect tends to be palliative, dealing with symptoms, not causes. The folk medicine of every culture consists of a vast collection of "recipes" concerning what to do for various ailments. These recipes may involve herbal concoctions, often of a very unpleasant variety; prescriptions concerning rest or activities; prayers, charms, or a combination of these. Quite often, these recipes are but loosely related to folk theories concerning disease; they are passed on from generation to generation because they are thought to work. In American society, it is probably true that many folk recipes have survived long after such special folk theories as were described above have been discarded.

Our folk medicine includes an enormous range of drugs, potions, balms, salves—both home remedies and patent medicines. Thus one takes aspirin for headaches and Geritol for "tired blood," soaks in Epsom salt to reduce swelling, and puts butter on burns and insect bites. The emphasis is on achieving observable effects; e.g., the use of aspirin to "cure" a headache is a means of relieving symptoms, but does nothing to the cause of the headache, such as a stress situation. For the most part, these remedies are empirically correct or at least do no further damage, although some cases of death have occurred from self-treatment, usually because the cause went untreated. The extent of self-treatment is indicated by the fact that in addition to over two billion dollars spent for prescription drugs, Americans spend an additional one billion dollars for self-medications. Many of these products have real value, but it is also known that "some 10 million Americans spend about $50 million a year for such products as Royal-Bee Jelly, alfalfa, and ground raw bones, guaranteed by some 50,000 food and drug salesmen who peddle such wares from door to door, to do anything from clearing complexions to curing cancer and restoring sexual potency."[54]

In addition to a large selection of drugs, one can also purchase a number of appliances such as sun lamps, vibrators which relax the body

---

[53]See, for example, the ethnographic spoof by Horace Miner, "The Body Ritual of the Nacirema," *American Anthropologist,* 58 (June, 1956), 503–507.

[54]Herman M. Somers and Anne R. Somers, *Doctors, Patients, and Health Insurance,* Washington, D.C.: Brookings Institution, 1961, p. 139.

and prevent "stress diseases," exercising machines, and heating pads; and certainly no home with children could do without a vaporizer. All these chemical and mechanical aids are used to support various procedures followed to maintain one's health. These procedures include diets, eating health foods, regular exercise, sleeping with wide-open windows, and taking cold showers, or alternatively, Turkish baths.

Modern folk medicine represents the operative beliefs and practices of lay persons with respect to their illnesses. It represents, in part, a set of traditional beliefs and remedies which have been passed down from generation to generation or which are diffused "across the back fence." But in a modern society where educational levels are relatively high and where contact with health professionals is frequent, the traditional and esoteric beliefs of the past cannot easily survive. Where such beliefs are viable, they are usually rationalized in terms of the lay person's conception of what is true of scientific medicine, deal with areas where professional medicine has little to offer (or is not apt to be consulted, e.g., minor illnesses such as colds), or survive in cultural enclaves relatively untouched by modern life.

Thus to find examples of folk medical practices which are notably different from those of modern medicine, one must today look to groups on the periphery of modern culture, such as Latin American peasants or unassimilated immigrants, or to rural areas isolated by poverty or—as in the case of the Hutterites—by deliberate choice. The folk medicine practiced among groups more closely related to the mainstream of modern life tends to be a more or less clear, if oversimplified and somewhat vulgarized, reflection of scientific medicine. Its approximation to professional norms is constantly fostered by articles on "health" in the popular press, by efforts of professional health educators in and out of the school system, and by strenuous efforts of doctors and other health professionals as they see their patients. For it is the adequacy of the folk medicine that we practice which will, in the first instance, determine the adequacy of our medical care. Our self-treatment and our decisions to consult a physician alike are based upon the folk medicine we know.

Even among lay persons of moderately sophisticated education, however, characteristic folk beliefs can be faintly discerned. One may believe that illnesses are the result of violating a norm. Thus, lay people may attribute their stomach upsets to overindulgence or to their perverse desire to eat something that they know "doesn't agree" with them. They may attribute their colds to their wearing clothing inappropriate to the weather. Parents frequently feel an overwhelming psychological need to find reasons why they are responsible, through some oversight, for their children's illnesses. People often accept uncritically their parents' beliefs about health and hygiene, in the absence of specific medical sanction. Thus, one may be sure that some foods, like strawberries, tend to cause rashes or that others, like crackers, are "binding" and still others, like apples or prunes, are a general preventive of illness because they foster regularity. Certainly, Americans tend to have their favorite patent medicines, which they may use for relief from specific symptoms and as preventives of sickness. But, except where folk medical beliefs fulfill an important function in an individual's psychic economy, they tend to be supplanted when it is learned that modern medicine "knows better." We may offer the general proposition, then, that modern folk medicine, unlike primitive folk medicine, tends to change as the lay population's appreciation of the conclusions of professional medicine is enhanced. Modern folk medicine will differ from these conclusions to the degree that varying groups are denied contact with scientific medicine, whether through lack of education, lack of contact with professionals, or because of special subcultural barriers. A recent study by Suchman suggests that even in urban areas if groups exhibit a high degree of solidarity based on ethnicity, kinship, or similar factors, certain folk beliefs and practices may be perpetuated.[55] Principally, there is a tendency for these groups to be skeptical of the effectiveness of physicians, to use home remedies or patent medicines to a great extent, and generally to underutilize available professional medical care resources. To summarize, modern folk medicine tends to be a "filtered-down" version of scientific specialized medicine. As such, it is always subject to some culture lag and to vulgarization. The degree of this distortion will, among other things, affect the saliency which lay persons accord to professional medicine.

## ETHNOGRAPHIC EXAMPLES OF FOLK MEDICINE

Some characteristics of folk medicine as practiced by a *peasant* group may be illustrated by the medical beliefs and practices of the people who live in the town of Magdalena, Guatemala, the population of which was 850 persons in 1950.[56] Magdalena is the administrative center for the *municipio* which lies about two-thirds of the way between Guatemala City and Antigua. The town lies high in the mountains (elevation about 7,000 feet) and is populated mostly by Indians. The inhabitants engage in agriculture; the major crop is corn. In addition, however, other vegetables and flowers are produced for sale in the nearby cities along with firewood and charcoal. Many of the natives also engage in handicraft, a major component of the national economy.

[55]Edward A. Suchman, "Sociomedical Variations among Ethnic Groups," *American Journal of Sociology,* 70 (November, 1964), 319–331.
[56]The following material is taken from Richard N. Adams, *Un Análisis de las creencias y prácticas médicas en un pueblo indígena de Guatemala,* Publicaciones Especiales del Instituto Indigenista Nacionale, no. 17, Editorial del Ministerio de Educación Publica, Guatemala, Centroamérica, 1962.

By and large, families are patrilineal and extended, and the predominant form of marriage is monogamy. Most Magdalenans are nominally Roman Catholic, although some elements of the original religions remain. These Indians live at a subsistence level, but their proximity to urban areas has influenced their way of life to the extent that little remains of many traditional practices still found among villagers farther into the hinterland. The preoccupation with earning a living, however, reduces their interest in and ability to participate in national affairs.

The Magdalenans were chosen as an illustration of a peasant people practicing folk medicine because vestiges of both primitive and scientific medical beliefs and practices are also present. For example, these natives have knowledge of many vital organs of the body, such as the heart, lungs, stomach, and kidneys. Yet at the same time, anything long and tubular, like arteries or intestines, is considered to be a vein. Moreover, they believe that during gestation, the fetus resides in the woman's stomach. Other anatomical parts, although more or less correctly located, are most often incorrectly described with respect to function.

An important belief which tends to give coherence to Magdalenan folk medicine concerns the central importance of the state of the blood in maintaining health. Adams reported that

> A great many disabilities are connected with blood in bad condition, lack of blood, or a weak body resulting from these two. Variations in status of one's blood may be quantitative or qualitative. Quantitative differences consist of total amount of blood present . . . the loss of any part will permanently weaken the body . . . there are also variations in blood quality correlated with the degree to which a person has become hot or cold.[57]

One can ascertain from Adams's comments an emphasis on balance. A healthy state requires the proper amount of blood (balanced with other fluids) and also depends on the state of equilibrium between hot and cold.

Another reference to balance can be seen in the explanation given by these Indians of the occurrence of disease and illness. Any case of sickness can be "understood" if one can identify the specific state of two factors, namely, the condition of the body and some environmental factor. All illnesses require both elements; that is, an imbalance of an *internal condition* of the body (e.g., too hot or too cold), which is influenced by some *external factor*. For example, if one becomes "overheated" from eating chili (inner condition) and then goes out into the cold night air (external factor), one is likely to get a stomach ache. Again, the normal condition of the body (believed to be warm) can be altered by the addition of a hot

[57]*Ibid.,* p. 15.

substance such as the local liquor, a consequence of which is an inflamed stomach or stomach ache.

Other patterns of causal explanation can also be observed. For example, Magdalenans believe that children have a "natural" weakness and that this inner condition makes them especially susceptible to harm from external factors. There is, of course, some empirical truth to this insofar as children, having not yet built up acquired immunities, are more susceptible to communicable diseases than are adults. They also are less able to bear the stresses of life at a subsistence level than are adults, whose physiological mechanisms are more tolerant of privation. Another common complaint is "strain" or "stretching of the veins" (hernia), which is thought to be caused by physical exertion in combination with another condition which has some magical or supernatural properties. A third pattern reflects the recognition of worms, which are endemic to the population. Although the presence of worms is somewhat uncomfortable, they usually do not result in serious medical consequences. Illness is thought to result, however, when the worms are "disturbed" and they begin to "rise," causing choking or vomiting. Again, there are some beliefs which are primarily supernatural in nature, in which illness is thought to be caused by "loss of soul" or *susto*. For example, it is believed that a sudden shock, such as being frightened by a snake, will "loosen" the soul, so that it may be captured by evil spirits which inhabit the mountains. Another remnant of primitive beliefs is that a native who fails to provide the proper number of novenas will be molested by the returning soul of a deceased family member.

In taking medicine for prevention as well as for cure, Magdalenans depend heavily on their knowledge of the natural resources around them. "The most generally used materials employed in curing are those which are readily available in Magdalena. These include a great variety of herbs and certain animal and other food products."[58] In addition, patent medicines such as Mejoral and Aspirol are used for coughs, head colds, headaches, toothaches, influenza, and the like. Dr. Ross's Pink Pills are available for "liver problems."

When Magdalenans become ill, they exhaust their own knowledge about potions and cures before seeking other help. Typically, they would go first to other members of their family before going to a specialist. The Magdalenans have access to at least five kinds of specialist, although not all would be helpful or useful in any given case. The most common is the "practical curer" or folk specialist, who is really only a person who has more knowledge in certain areas than the average Indian, such as in combating worms or "stretched veins." These practitioners, like another specialist, the amateur *curandero,* who knows some secret kinds of cures, usually render their services for religious reasons and therefore do not

---

[58] *Ibid.,* p. 47.

charge the patient.[59] A *comadrona* is primarily a midwife, but she can also effect certain kinds of cures, especially for children. There are also diviners or shamans, who specialize in recovering souls lost from shock or in placating disturbed ancestors. At the time this study was completed, however, no diviner lived in Magdalena, although there was one in a nearby village. Finally, Western-trained doctors are accessible to some degree; they are usually the last to be sought out and then only for certain physical illnesses.[60]

As indicated above, folk medicine tends to be well developed in areas which are isolated by distance, poverty, or other factors from the mainstream of the society. In the United States, such communities tend to be found in rural, depressed areas such as the Appalachian or Ozark highlands. As the following summary of research reported by Carl Withers will show, however, the traditional folk beliefs which are markedly deviant from the precepts of scientific medicine cannot be maintained even in a relatively isolated American farm community. Withers[61] reported on a small rural community on the edge of the Missouri Ozarks; this town (population 300) was at the time of the study (some thirty years ago) a poor community with limited economic opportunities, functioning on the margins of the developed agricultural and industrial economy of the Middle West.

Toward the end of the nineteenth century, the population believed in witches as having the power to bring misfortunes such as poor crops, illness, or death. They believed also in diviners, who, among other things, were thought to have special abilities in locating underground sources of water. At the time of the study, however, these beliefs had largely died out except among a few older people. However, there was apparently a resurgence of faith healing, especially among fundamentalist religious groups.

By and large, the medical folklore of this population at the time of the investigation was related to two themes: first, the use of home remedies for symptomatic treatment of self-diagnosed ailments, and second, a kind of pseudorational practice associated with orthodox medical practice and involving extensive use of patent medicines.

According to Withers, a very broad range of home remedies and patent medicines were used to combat symptoms or to prevent their appearance. These may have ranged from potions derived from flowers or the bark of a

[59]See the extensive analysis of the psychiatric role of the native healer in Ari Kiēv, *Curanderismo,* New York: Free Press, 1968.

[60]Adams, *op. cit.* In this regard the author suggests that Western doctors would receive greater acceptance if instead of ridiculing certain native beliefs, especially supernatural ones, they would describe their medical practices within the cultural framework of the Indians.

[61]Carl Withers, "The Folklore of a Small Town," *Transactions of the New York Academy of Sciences,* 8 (May, 1946), 234–251, reprinted in W. Richard Scott and Edmund A. Volkart (eds.), *Medical Care: Readings in the Sociology of Medical Institutions,* New York: Wiley, 1966, pp. 233–246.

tree to sulfur or even kerosene. Onions, calamus root, vinegar, witch hazel, whiskey, and similar strong-tasting and odoriferous products were frequently used in these remedies. They were particularly popular for combating coughs, sore throats, upset stomachs, constipation, etc., but also were used for warts, boils, and rheumatism. Patent medicine generally consisted of aspirin, petroleum jelly, salves, some antiseptics, liver pills, and the like. It is interesting to note that the citizens of this community distinguished between home remedies made from materials "we know," and patent medicines, prepared from materials that "city doctors" know.

The important point here is that knowledge about the preparation and use of these materials was widespread throughout the community. Everyone seemed to have a favorite recipe for a cure for specific ailments, and there was a great deal of exchanging of information and testimony about the efficacy of various concoctions. The use of these remedies was tied to some pseudoscientific beliefs about the causes of disease and a shared belief that doctors frequently were of little help to their patients. For example, cases of malaria and typhoid fever, prevalent in the past century, have largely disappeared. Yet much of the population still believes that their reduction is due to the fact that the climate has become much drier nowadays rather than to public health measures, even though they acknowledge that mosquitoes are somehow connected with malaria (and, some believe, typhoid fever, too). Similarly, there is some suggestion that "balance" of fluids was believed to be important for health. Thus, sulfur and molasses were taken each spring to "thin out the blood" which had "thickened" during the cold winter weather. Moreover, it was believed that "poisons" can build up in the system, so that periodically a "physic" should be taken to "keep regular."

Some illnesses and many injuries, however, were believed to require a doctor's attention. This was particularly true for sudden, severe illness or for chronic symptoms that did not respond to home remedies. People with injuries, such as deep cuts, gunshot wounds, broken bones and snakebites, were usually taken directly to a physician for treatment, including antitetanus injections. At the same time, immunization against smallpox and other communicable diseases was viewed with suspicion, in part because the theory was unacceptable to the populace. Withers also reported that the strong skepticism concerning "city doctors" and hospitals which had been seen as places where "more come out dead than alive" was beginning to wane. Although few infants were born in the nearby hospital, people were being more frequently admitted for surgery than before (and, to a minor extent at least, some status was derived from having survived a city operation).

Somewhat similar findings were later reported by Koos.[62] However, in

---

[62]Earl L. Koos, *The Health of Regionville,* New York: Columbia University Press, 1954.

this case the emphasis was not so much on isolation of the community, as in the cases of the Magdalenans and the Ozark people, but rather on social-class differences within a community. "Regionville" could not be considered isolated in view of the fact that transportation routes were good and mass communication media were available. Yet, as we shall see, folk beliefs and practices did exist and were most common among the lowest social class.[63]

The respondents of this study, a sample of 514 households in the upstate New York community of Regionville, were purported to be typical Americans. At least, this small community was selected by the researchers because of its "averageness," in size, proportion of persons in the various age categories, facilities, distribution of wealth, general level of health, etc. Regionville is a small business and manufacturing town, although most of its trade is with farmers who live in the surrounding area. In turn, it is dependent upon a larger metropolitan area some 60 miles away. The people of Regionville were a good deal more sophisticated in their medical beliefs and practices than the Missouri population described above, yet many similarities were found, especially among the lower classes. In general, Koos found that the definition of illness, beliefs about causation, attitudes toward medical care and medical practitioners, response to illness, and a host of related health phenomena were strongly related to social class. With respect to definitions of illness, Koos found that respondents in the highest class (class I) generally had the most knowledge of and were most responsive to various symptoms of disease and illness. Class III (lower-class) persons were more or less indifferent to symptoms of illness except those of a very serious nature. Moreover, it was found that class III respondents tended to rely on self-diagnosis and home remedies more than did class I respondents.

Whether treatment was sought for illness depended not only upon class position, but also on whether the illness was disabling or nondisabling. In either case, class I respondents more often sought professional treatment than did class III persons. It is interesting to note that, of the treated illnesses, 70 percent were treated to completion by a health professional, most often by a physician. In 10 percent of the cases, treatment was discontinued. In the remaining 20 percent, folk medical practices were employed (mostly by class III respondents). In this last group, home remedies were employed, such as a shot of whiskey for grippe, along with various patent medicines suggested by friends or relatives and the local druggist.[64]

[63]Since this early study, the importance of social class differences in beliefs and opinions has declined. See Stephen J. Kunitz, Andrew A. Sorenson, and Suzanne B. Cashman, "Changing Health Care Opinions in Regionville, 1946–1973," *Medical Care,* 13 (July, 1975), 549–561.

[64]Koos, *op. cit.,* p. 91.

Another reflection of differences in belief was indicated by the kinds of medicines kept on hand for self-prescription. Class I families most often had such products as antiseptics, cough medicine, and cold pills. Class III families generally relied on kidney and liver pills and "stomach" medicine, implying certain traditionally held beliefs about the functioning of organs, especially in regard to maintaining a "clean system" or a balance of fluids in the body. For example, Koos quotes one class III respondent who stated "I always take S____ compound every fall. It thickens my blood and gets me ready for cold weather."[65]

Moreover, class differences were found with respect to knowledge about and use of physicians and other health practitioners. Class I respondents generally went to physicians for treatment and scoffed at the ministrations of chiropractors. Class III respondents, however, felt very differently toward the latter. Although some patients went to chiropractors "because they charged less," not all the reasons for selecting them were economic in nature. Class III respondents were less likely to know that the amount of formal training and medical knowledge of physicians was different from that of chiropractors. Similarly, the latter was apparently more responsive to the patient's psychological needs; that is, they were "better listeners."

Wherever it is found, the medicine practiced by specialist practitioners involves relatively rare skills and knowledge which the general public does not possess. As such, it is particularly applicable to difficult problems. In all cultures, practitioners tend to be consulted when illness seems serious, protracted, disabling, or frightening. Those maladies which do not partake of these characteristics are usually dealt with by lay persons themselves in terms of their folk medicine. Two characteristics follow from this. First, practitioners' medicine, from the point of view of lay persons, has an esoteric quality; they cannot understand it fully. Second, if lay persons are to avail themselves of practitioners' medicine at all, they must not only feel a need for outside help but must find the advanced knowledge of specialists credible. They must have some confidence in their efficacy. Thus, although practitioners' medicine differs from folk medicine not only in the extensity of its information and the depth of skill involved, but also in its theories and viewpoints, this difference may not be so great that lay people find it not believable. This limitation on the degree to which it may differ from folk medical understanding will be particularly sharp when practitioners' medicine has only indifferent success in effecting cures.

Our argument may be stated in another way. As a body of knowledge is differentiated from the common property of most adult members of a society, it inevitably becomes esoteric. To the extent that it is associated

[65]*Ibid.*, p. 90.

with autonomous social groups and roles, it may tend to become less and less understandable to the laity. Differences which originally were of degree may become those of kind. But if these specialists' body of knowledge is to have any application to the affairs of common people, their lack of understanding of what it is and what it can do cannot be complete. In practice, this means that practitioners' knowledge and doctrine must be compatible with the fundamental themes and values of the common culture.

Thus, Azande adults may recognize their inability to deal with certain illnesses and realize their need of help by shamans. Although they may not have knowledge either of the grounds on which these practitioners make their diagnoses and prognoses or of the magical methods which they apply, the Azande do have certain expectations of what it is reasonable for the practitioners to do. Because both shamans and their clients subscribe to a world view which emphasizes magic and share a common structure of myths, the sick find it reasonable to expect that the shamans' sorcery can help them. And this expectation is bolstered both by the practitioners' performance and by the fact that they often apparently succeed in accomplishing their therapeutic goals. Similarly, Christian Science practitioners in our society may have knowledge of the doctrines of that faith which transcend those of their clients as well as a conviction of their efficacy to communicate. But their knowledge and assurances will mean little to people who do not share a belief in this religious group's claims. Likewise, physicians certainly have at their disposal both specific facts and ways of thinking which are almost incomprehensible to many lay people. Not only do they talk in a "foreign" jargon about diseases which the lay people may never have heard of, but they think physiologically, arriving at conclusions which are decidedly not those of commonsense folk knowledge. But lay confidence in physicians rests upon the belief that the latter act in terms of the scientific premises in which lay people have faith (even though their understanding of them is imperfect). It rests also on a belief that physicians share with lay people certain expectations about ethical norms that should govern the conduct of the patient-doctor relationship. And it rests upon the lay people's knowledge that scientific medicine is effective.

Hollingshead and Redlich[66] have shown that psychiatrists who subscribe to psychodynamic theories frequently have difficulty in keeping their lower-class patients in treatment (should they consider them as treatable at all). In large part, this is because these patients find their psychiatrists' advice and actions to be not credible. Believing their illness to be a physical disease and expecting their doctors to treat them by physical methods, by

---

[66]A. B. Hollingshead and F. C. Redlich, *Social Class and Mental Illness,* New York: Wiley, 1958, pp. 266–275.

prescribing pills, etc., the patients lose confidence when they apparently seem unable to arrive at a diagnosis and expects them to talk on and on about such apparent irrelevancies as their feelings about their parents, their childhood experiences, or their dreams. The point is that for this group in our society, psychodynamic theories are not only esoteric, but so different from folk medical beliefs and so apparently unrelated to their generalized expectation about what scientific medicine does that credibility is lost. Nor is the psychiatrists' problem eased by the inability magically to achieve quick cures!

Given the fact that there must be a certain correspondence between folk medicine and practitioners' medicine, what factors will enhance the development and autonomy of the latter? We shall suggest four. First, the general level of societal development must be such as to support specialized role differentiation. Practitioners' roles cannot develop extensively in the most primitive economies. Second, practitioners' medicine tends to develop in an autonomous direction where its body of knowledge develops *systematic* qualities, and when this systematic knowledge becomes the recognized criterion for practice. Obviously, this implies not only a mechanism for intensive socialization of practitioners but the opportunity for some specialists to reflect upon their knowledge, to codify and evaluate it. Such systemization ordinarily cannot go far without an extensive organization of healers, and it is tremendously facilitated by literacy.[67] Third, practitioners' medicine will not develop far where significant rewards—in terms of wealth, prestige, and power—cannot be achieved by healers. Such rewards depend both on the demonstrated effectiveness of their specialty and upon its relationship to the power structure of the society. Fourth, the autonomy of practitioners' medicine is enhanced to the degree that it receives a *mandate* from the society,[68] that is, that the specialists not only are allowed to demonstrate their special skills, but are permitted to "define what is proper conduct of others toward the matters concerned with [their] work."

In general, practitioners' medicine in primitive societies does not achieve a great deal of autonomy because these four conditions are met only to a small degree. But it might be suggested that the practitioners' medicine of the Azande is more developed and more autonomous than that of the Cheyenne because the Azande shamans have more of a mandate, can claim greater rewards for their work, and have the organization and accompanying intensive socialization which could lead to some systematization of

[67]See the comments by Max Weber on the importance of the priestly role in the rationalization and systematization of religious systems. Max Weber, *Sociology of Religion,* Ephraim Fischoff (tr.), Boston: Beacon Press, 1963.

[68]Everett C. Hughes, *Men and Their Work,* New York: Free Press, 1958, pp. 78ff.

their knowledge. Similarly, as the following chapters will show, modern scientific medicine has achieved autonomy and success as these four criteria have increasingly been satisfied. Competing forms of medical practice such as osteopathy or chiropractic have had less success insofar as their body of knowledge has been inadequate and their mandate insecure. On the other hand, they tend to find recognition from those groups in society who find scientific medicine ineffective or whose folk beliefs are compatible with their particular viewpoints.

Finally, we may conclude this discussion of the relationships between folk and practitioners' systems of medicine by comparing certain characteristics which appear to distinguish the one from the other. We have already indicated that practitioners' medicine tends to be systematic in character and to function with a relatively high degree of expertise. By contrast, folk medicine tends to be comprised of a mixture—even a jumble—of beliefs and practices which are rather uncritically diffused from one lay person to another and which are only imperfectly developed into a logical system. As we have stressed, although folk medicine is more or less adequate for ordinary times, its expertise is not sufficient to allow it to deal with serious or unusual illnesses. Folk medicine, moreover, is the medicine practiced by the sick person and by family and friends. What they do, therefore, is always conditioned by their affective involvement in the illness. As Chapter 4 indicated, the approach of the physician—and of practitioners' medicine—is characterized by its lack of involvement in the particulars of a specific illness, by its relative objectivity. For this reason, folk medicine tends to be a trial-and-error kind of medicine in which one practice or explanation follows another in an intense search for good results. By contrast, because it has a systematic theory and a relatively objective approach, the medicine of the specialist can be characterized by a degree of consistency and of therapeutic restraint. As compared with folk medicine, specialist medicine is a disciplined kind of behavior. There is, thus, much more indeterminacy in the practice of folk medicine than in that of the specialist-healer. Because they have little expertise and no systematic body of knowledge to guide them, lay people are less apt to behave consistently in their unaided attempts to deal with illness than is the practitioner.

## CULTURE AND ILLNESS BEHAVIOR

In the beginning of this chapter, it was noted that there were really only a few basically different types of beliefs about the nature of illness, but that the specific behaviors associated with the occurrence of disease or illness varied widely from one culture to another. Further, it was pointed out that medical beliefs and behaviors are like any other set of beliefs and behaviors, generally consistent with the prevailing cultural values of a particular society. These principles are at least implicit in the various ethnographic examples reported above. For instance, where the causal explanation was in terms of the supernatural, so also was the form of therapy heavily laden with supernatural practices. Where the explanation was in terms of balance of body fluids or temperature, the therapeutic effort was aimed at correcting a perceived imbalance. Similarly, in societies where much of available medical knowledge is widespread and generally held by most inhabitants, there also would one likely find folk medicine as a major source of medical care and a weak institutionalization of special practitioner roles; such societies usually function at a simple technological level and show little differentiation of their structures. The point is, of course, that much of the form and content of medical belief and practice systems is dictated by the culture of a particular group.

The potent force of cultural consistency in social change has been amply demonstrated in studies of the general process of innovation.[69] Most of these studies stress certain preconditions for change, e.g., the perception of need for change or dissatisfaction with existing artifacts or ideas. An innovation, when presented, is more readily adopted if (1) the presentation is made (or approved) by someone with status in a group, (2) the innovation is superior to that which it replaces, and (3) the meaning or use of the innovation is consistent with already existing cultural values.

These principles may be applied specifically to the introduction of Western medical beliefs and practices into non-Western (or better, nonindustrialized or underdeveloped) settings. In general, it may be suggested that where concepts and practices of Western medicine are incompatible with concepts and practices of the existing culture, the former will likely be rejected—unless, after a period of time, the Western medicine can be reinterpreted in terms consistent with the local culture. For example, Christian missionaries had tried to alter several practices of Nyansongan villagers—including eliminating witchcraft and sorcery—and had failed, mostly because the practice of witchcraft and belief in the power of magic permeated the cultural fabric of that society.[70] Similarly, Wellin has described an attempt to get women in a remote Peruvian village to boil drinking water.[71] In this case, a resident hygiene worker with the aid of a visiting physician had persuaded only eleven women out of 200 families to boil contaminated drinking water before it was consumed by their families

---

[69]H. G. Barnett, *Innovation: The Basis of Cultural Change,* New York: McGraw-Hill, 1953. See also Everett M. Rodgers, *Diffusion of Innovations,* New York: Free Press, 1962; and James S. Coleman, Elihu Katz, and Herbert Menzel, *Medical Innovation, A Diffusion Study,* Indianapolis: Bobbs-Merrill, 1966.

[70]Robert A. LeVine and Barbara B. LeVine, "Nyansongo: A Gusii Community in Kenya," in Beatrice B. Whiting (ed.), *Six Cultures: Studies of Child Rearing,* New York: Wiley, 1963, pp. 19–202.

[71]Edward Wellin, "Water Boiling in a Peruvian Town," in Paul, *op. cit.,* pp. 71–103.

(fifteen other women already were in the habit of boiling their water). The reasons given for rejecting the practice of boiling water before drinking varied from not having

> . . . available an after-breakfast interval which, by virtue of local circumstance and belief, was the only possible and appropriate time to boil water . . . [to] . . . allegiance to cultural values [which] precluded acceptance of new and competing health values.[72]

Even in societies which have had considerable contact with Western ideas of medicine, traditional ways are still practiced, although they may exist side by side with Western practices. For example, in northern India, infections are, as reported by Marriott, traditionally dealt with by

> . . . blowing, sweeping and the wearing of charms . . . magical exorcism has the special advantage that if the infection has been caused by spirit invasion, the spirit can simply be invited to depart without creating any further trouble. The same spirit is likely to become angered if direct medication is applied to his abode in the body. *Only if medication can be understood as cleansing a wound rather than as killing the infection, can it remain theoretically compatible with magical exorcism.* Thus, one priest of Kishan Garhi "vigorously cleaned" his son's dog-bite wound with potassium permanganate which I had given him; on alternate days, without conflict, he had it swept and blown by the magician.[73]

Gould has reported that in India when primitive (or "village") medicine and scientific medicine exist side by side, there is a tendency for a division of function to develop. In his study, natives employed scientific medicine for acute incapacitating illnesses such as headaches, rheumatism, and stomach trouble. Furthermore, Gould pointed out that choice of scientific over village medicine increases with social class, especially with the amount of formal education. As we have noted in the studies in the Ozarks and Regionville, similar behavior patterns have been observed in our own culture.[74]

[72]*Ibid.,* p. 102.

[73]Marriott, pp. 252–253. Italics supplied.

[74]Harold A. Gould, "The Implications of Technological Change for Folk and Scientific Medicine," *American Anthropologist,* 59 (June, 1957), 507–516. More recent evidence on India supports Gould's early findings both in terms of traditional healers employing some modern techniques and in terms of patients selecting traditional or modern practitioners depending upon the nature of the problem. See J. C. Bhatia, Dharam Vir, A. Timmappaya, and C. S. Chuittani, "Traditional Healers and Modern Medicine," *Social Science and Medicine,* 9 (January, 1975), 15–21, and Surinder M. Bhardwaj, "Attitude towards Different Systems of Medicine: A Survey of Four Villages in the Punjab–India," *Social Science and Medicine,* 9 (November–December, 1975), 603–612. Similar results in a different country were reported in Paul C. Y. Chen, "Medical Systems in Malaysia: Cultural Bases and Differential Use." *Social Science and Medicine,* 9 (March, 1975), 171–180. Some consequences of the wrong choice are described in Richard W. Lieban, "Traditional Medical Beliefs and the Choice of Practitioners in a Philippine City," *Social Science and Medicine,* 10 (June, 1976), 289–296.

From the reports of Marriott, Gould, and others,[75] it may be inferred that non-Western peoples learn to discriminate between Western and non-Western medicine for their particular illnesses. Moreover, it may also be seen that Western practices are more readily accepted to the degree that they can be interpreted in terms of the local culture. Another study, this time of folk medical practices among farmers in northern Mexico, suggests that the acceptance of sophisticated Western practice can be hastened by making allowances for certain local practices that are not viewed as injurious by Western standards. Kelly[76] has reported that popular (folk) medicine in the town of El Cuije receives official recognition along with that accorded Western medical practice.

> The *ejido* [rural community] pays its quota to the Servicios Medicos Rurales and the families of all *ejidatarios* may therefore avail themselves of the medical services provided by the national government. The ailing are taken in the *ejido* truck to Torreón, where they receive professional attention at the Ejido Hospital. However, once a week all those suffering from maladies attributed to sorcery are transported in the *ejido* truck to Matamoros, there to be treated by a local woman curer. Her fee is paid from *ejido* funds and the remedies she prescribes are similarly at public expense. . . . It is evident that the *ejido* officially recognizes witchcraft and considers treatment by a witch as legitimate a public expense as the medical attention provided by the government hospital.[77]

These investigations of the acceptance of Western medicine in non-Western societies also have some implications for understanding the medical behavior of some segments of our own social structure, particularly the lower class. As has been suggested already, American folk medicine is still a very important element in medical behavior inasmuch as it represents a stage of illness behavior as well as an alternative to seeking professional care in the context of legitimate medical care organizations. To the degree that the alternative of folk medicine is seen as compatible with other beliefs and also as efficacious as orthodox medicine, it will continue to be the chosen path. The differences between orthodox medicine and American folk medicine are less sharply drawn than those between orthodox medicine and the folk medicine of a different culture. Nonetheless, the same principles of innovation which have been and continue to be applied in introducing Western medicine into non-Western societies might well be applied also to subcultures in our own society.

[75]The volume cited above, *Health, Culture and Community,* edited by Paul, is essentially a series of studies of interaction between Western and non-Western medical ideas and practices.
[76]Isabel Kelly, *Folk Practices in North Mexico,* Austin: University of Texas Press, 1965.
[77]*Ibid.,* p. 22.

## SUMMARY

This chapter has examined the similarities of and differences between primitive and folk medicine. Primitive medicine was viewed as nonscientific medicine and, in large part, dependent upon supernatural explanations of disease and magic as an essential ingredient of therapy. Folk medicine was defined as medical beliefs and practices which were widely shared among a people as compared with that knowledge which was the property of practitioners in specialized roles. Both analytic types (and scientific medicine, too) have in common the fact that beliefs about the nature of disease and illness are woven into and are an integral part of the fabric of the particular culture of which they are a part. Second, treatment as well as any preventive measures is logically related to beliefs about causation. Third, sick people in many different cultures follow roughly the same behavior pattern in coping with illness, i.e., self-treatment, seeking advice from others, seeking help from a professional healer (or folk specialist). Finally, it was noted that the introduction of Western medical beliefs and practices in non-Western societies is a special case of innovation, which emphasizes the importance of culture as one determinant of observed medical behavior.

## SUGGESTED READINGS

Atkinson, Donald T., *Magic, Myth and Medicine,* New York: Fawcett, 1962.

Frank, Jerome D., *Persuasion and Healing,* New York: Schocken, 1963.

Kiev, Ari, *Magic, Faith and Healing,* New York: Free Press, 1964.

Middleton, John (ed.), *Magic, Witchcraft and Curing,* Garden City, N.Y.: Natural History Press, 1967.

Saunders, Lyle, *Cultural Difference and Medical Care,* New York: Russell Sage, 1954.

Sigerist, Henry E., *A History of Medicine: I. Primitive and Archaic Medicine,* New York: Oxford University Press, 1951, pp. 105–216.

# Chapter 6

# The Development of Western Medicine

*Medicine . . . learned from a monk how to use antimony, from a Jesuit how to cure agues, from a friar how to cut stone, from a soldier how to treat gout, from a sailor how to keep off scurvy, from a postmaster how to sound the Eustachian tube, from a dairy maid how to prevent small pox, and from an old market woman how to catch the itch-insect. It borrowed acupuncture and the moxa from the Japanese heathen, and was taught the use of lobelia by the American Savage.*

Oliver Wendell Holmes,
*Medical Essays,* 1883

It may seem unusual to begin a discussion of scientific medicine in industrialized societies by going back to ancient Greece, but we do so for a good reason. A great many changes and improvements have occurred in medicine in the past thirty-five years, let alone the past twenty-five hundred, but, as we shall see, there are some continuities of thought and practice, begun in those early days, which are still discernible today. Some of these continuities are found in the area of medical ethics, in the changing explanation of illness according to knowledge of the times, and in adaptation and innovation in the organization and practice of medicine. At the same time, a review of historical antecedents provides a necessary basis for understanding the changes occurring in contemporary medicine.

## ANCIENT GREECE AND THE ROMAN EMPIRE

Although some writers begin the history of Western medicine with the age of the classical Greeks, it should be pointed out that evidence of certain therapeutic practices such as cauterization and amputation dates back to 5000 B.C. and possibly back to Cro-Magnon man, some 20,000 years ago.[1] In addition, evidence of diseases of bones and organs has been found in remains that are reputed to be 500,000 years old.[2] Before 500 B.C. (and in some places afterward, too), there was a commonly held belief that illness was caused by evil spirits which entered the human body. Remedies were largely magicoreligious in nature, consisting of magic spells, incantations, and charms. In ancient Greece, during the fifth and fourth centuries B.C., however, there developed a school of medicine which was quite different from anything which had come before. For the first time as part of a broader intellectual revolution, human beings began to approach the practice of medicine from a dispassionate and more or less scientific point of view.

The most famous of all physicians, Hippocrates, lived during this time, and it is his writings, or at least writings attributed to him, that laid the foundation for modern medicine.[3] We can perhaps get a better idea of the nature of Hippocratic medicine by quoting a few lines from his writings.

> Old persons endure fasting most easily; next, adults; young persons not nearly so well; and most especially infants, and them such as are of a particularly lively spirit.

> Use purgative medicines sparingly in acute diseases, and at the commencement, and not without proper circumspection.

> In whatever disease sleep is laborious, it is a deadly symptom; but if sleep does good, it is not deadly.

> Persons who are naturally very fat are apt to die earlier than those who are slender.[4]

[1]Henry E. Sigerist, *A History of Medicine: Primitive and Archaic Medicine,* vol. I, New York. Oxford University Press, 1951.

[2]Ralph H. Major, *A History of Medicine,* vol. I, Springfield, Ill.: Charles C Thomas, 1954, pp. 4–5.

[3]Some scholars maintain that many of the Hippocratic writings are actually the work of Hippocrates's disciples. See, for example, Henry E. Sigerist, *A History of Medicine: Early Greek, Hindu and Persian,* vol. II, New York: Oxford University Press, 1961, pp. 260ff.

[4]Logan Clendening (ed.), *Source Book of Medical History,* New York: Dover, 1960, pp. 15–16.

In addition to *The Aphorisms,* Hippocrates wrote *Medical Geography; On Airs, Waters, and Places;* and *The Book of Prognostics,* in which he utilized a combination of theory and observation in predicting outcome of therapy for illness; he wrote on acute diseases, epidemics, head injuries, surgery, fractures, and many specific illnesses including epilepsy.[5] The basic postulates of the Hippocratic theory of illness lay in an equilibrium model of a humoral theory, in which he believed the body was invested with four humors: blood, phlegm, black bile, and yellow bile. As long as these humors were in balance, that is, in equilibrium, the body was healthy. Whenever any one of these was overrepresented or underrepresented in the body, the individual had contracted a disease. Symptoms of a disease were seen in the exuding of the humor which was out of balance, e.g., a runny nose. The approved therapy for disease relied heavily on the restorative powers of nature, augmented by various diets and infrequent use of certain drugs and potions. These and many other writings contained in the Hippocratic corpus are representative of the rational, cautious approach to medicine, based on detailed observations made at the bedside and in nature. Needless to say, many of the insights based on these early observations are still an accepted part of the body of contemporary medical knowledge.

The continuity of medical ethics, however, can probably best be seen in the Hippocratic oath, presumably sworn to by young aspirants who wished to study with Hippocrates.[6] In any event, this document is so important that it bears quoting in full.

> I swear by Apollo Physician, by Asclepius, by Health, by Panacea and by all the gods and goddesses, making them my witnesses, that I will carry out, according to my ability and judgment, this oath and this indenture. To hold my teacher in this art equal to my own parents; to make him partner in my livelihood; when he is in need of money to share mine with him; to consider his family as my own brothers, and to teach them this art, if they want to learn it, without fee or indenture; to impart precept, oral instruction, and all other instruction to my own sons, the sons of my teacher and to indentured pupils who have taken the physician's oath, but to nobody else. I will use treatment to help the sick according to my ability and judgment, but never with the view to injury and wrongdoing. Neither will I administer a poison to anybody when asked to do so, nor will I suggest such a course. Similarly I will not give a woman a pessary to cause abortion. But I will keep pure and holy both my life and my art. I will not use the knife, not even, verily, on sufferers from stone, but I will give place to such as are craftsmen therein. Into whatsoever houses I enter, I will enter to help the sick, and I will abstain from all intentional wrongdoing and harm, especially from abusing the bodies of man or woman,

[5]Major, vol. I, *op. cit.,* pp. 126ff.
[6]Sigerist, vol. II, *op. cit.,* p. 301.

bond or free. And whatsoever I shall see or hear in the course of my profession, as well as outside my profession in my intercourse with men, if it be what should not be published abroad, I will never divulge, holding such things to be holy secrets. Now if I carry out this oath, and break it not, may I gain forever reputation among all men for my life and for my art; but if I transgress it and foreswear myself, may the opposite befall me.[7]

This represents a substantial part of the basic medical ethics which has motivated the medical profession from ancient times to the present. Note the prohibitions in the body of the oath: not to give fatal drugs, not to perform abortions, not to practice surgery, to refrain from sexual contacts with patients, and not to divulge information obtained under professional confidence. Many of these precepts still function in medical ethics. Closer examination of the oath reveals something about the nature of classical Greek society and about the organization of the practice of medicine. For example, the Greek physician was admonished to refrain from sexual contacts with the bodies of women or of men whether freemen or slaves. Thus, Greek physicians were cautioned against using their position as a doctor to establish any sexual relationships with patients, including homosexual relations, which were socially approved in another context.[8] Further, human life, especially a healthy human life, was highly valued, and the physician was duly constrained not to use medical knowledge to take it by fatal drugs or potions or by abortion.

Similarly, we can note certain aspects of the organization of medical practice. First, there was an admonition not to engage in surgery, but to leave that to the practitioner of that craft. This reflects a division between the brotherhoods of medicine and surgery and suggests that here was an early specialization in medicine. The reason for this prohibition was probably that so little was known about the human body and about the uses of surgery that death of the patient frequently followed an incision. Since the Greek physician was not to use medical knowledge to take a life, it is no wonder that this was left to others (who were considered to practice an inferior craft).

Perhaps most interesting from a historical point of view is the first part of the oath. After appealing to the gods, we note the identification of the pupils with the master; they revere their master as their own parent; they become siblings to the master's children; they become obligated to the master's family as if it were their own. This reflects the fact that medicine was organized along familial lines except for persons duly apprenticed, who then became as one of the family. This would seem to imply that the practice of medicine was probably a profession in which the teacher had

[7]Clendening, *op. cit.*, pp. 14–15.
[8]Sigerist, vol. II, *op. cit.*, p. 219.

maximum control over the pupils. From this information, we get a picture of a group of physicians who maintained strict control over entry to the profession, who set up and enforced standards of practice and ethics by withholding recognition from violators of the oath, and who thus carried medicine on a highly prestigious and widely recognized plane. The profession, then, validated the right of approved physicians to practice medicine and imparted to them the sanction of its wisdom and prestige if, and only if, they maintained their ethical standards.

Some sources suggest that Greek medical practice was organized in many ways much like our own.[9] For example, there were private practitioners and public doctors. The private physicians catered mostly to the Greek aristocratic social classes, usually on an outpatient basis, but sometimes on an inpatient basis in the physician's clinic. Public doctors were found in almost every large town and were retained by the town partly for prestige and partly for serving those who were in need of medical care. However, both the private and the public physician tended to concentrate their services on the wealthy, and the poor and the slaves seldom received high-quality medical care.[10] For the last two groups, medical care was provided by the physician's assistant. Plato described this situation in *The Laws* where he wrote:

> There are doctors and there are doctor's servants, who are styled [called] doctors . . . whether slaves or freemen makes no difference; they acquire their knowledge by obeying and observing their masters . . . the slave doctors run about and cure the slaves or wait for them in dispensaries—practitioners of this sort never speak to their patients individually or let them know about their own individual complaints. The slave doctor prescribes what mere experience suggests, as if he had exact knowledge; and when he has given his order . . . he rushes off with equal assurance to some other servant who is ill; and so he relieves the master of the house of the care of his invalid slaves.[11]

Further evidence of the quality of medical treatment for the poor is indicated by this statement.

> When a carpenter is ill, he asks the physician for a rough and ready cure, an emetic, or a purge, or a cautery, or the knife—These are his remedies and if someone prescribes for him a course of dietetics, and tells him he must swathe and swaddle his head and all that sort of thing, he replies at once he has no time

[9]*Ibid.,* pp. 305–307.

[10]George Rosen, "The Evolution of Social Medicine," in Howard E. Freeman, Sol Levine, and Leo G. Reeder (eds.), *Handbook of Medical Sociology,* Englewood Cliffs, N.J.: Prentice-Hall, 1963, p. 18.

[11]Plato, *The Laws,* IV, Benjamin Jowett (tr.), Chicago: Britannica Great Books, 1952, vol. 7, pp. 684–685.

to be ill, and that he sees no good in a life that is spent in nursing his disease to the neglect of his customary employment.[12]

This suggests the existence of two kinds of medicine for two social groups: scientific medicine for the aristocracy and a condensed version of medicine given by the physician's assistant to the poor classes, including slaves.

In the centuries between Hippocrates and the Christian era, advances in medicine were made slowly but surely, through the recording of observations, following the example of Hippocratic physicians. However, probably the most important contributions to medical knowledge between the time of Hippocrates and before the fall of the Roman Empire were made by Aristotle. In addition to being one of the greatest philosophers produced by the Greeks, Aristotle was probably also their greatest scientist. His contributions to medicine came through his writings on comparative anatomy and embryology, even though he was frequently mistaken in his descriptions of physiological processes. Aristotelian thought also made an impact in the development of theory. Because of the nature of his philosophical background, Aristotle emphasized purpose for existence (or function) and first and ultimate causes. In this way he developed his "soul theory." Aristotle postulated that each human body contained three souls: a *vegetative soul,* which accounted for each human's ability to nourish itself; an *animal soul,* which, in common with all animals, gave humans a sensitivity for responding to their environment; and, finally, a *rational soul,* which gave humans the power of enlightenment.[13]

After the passing of Aristotle, the center of the intellectual world shifted to Alexandria, around 300 B.C. Here a new school of medicine developed which, founded on Aristotelian writings, made further contributions to medical knowledge. Erasistratus and Herophilus made contributions to anatomy and physiology both empirical and through dissection of the human body. In the area of theory, Erasistratus gave Aristotle's soul theory a physiological basis; that is, the vegetative soul was distilled in the liver and was carried through the veins to the heart, where it was further distilled into the animal soul. Through the arteries the animal soul was carried to the lungs, where it was replenished through respiration. Further distillation took place in the brain to produce the rational soul, which was radiated to all parts of the body by the nervous system. Carrying on from Hippocrates's equilibrium theory of the distribution of humors, the Alexandrian physicians also postulated that disease was caused by an imbalance in the distribution of souls in the body. For example, an excess of blood in the vegetative soul reduced sensitivity (animal soul) and rationality (rational soul), which prohibited the sick human from doing more than vegetating.

[12]Plato, *The Republic,* III, Benjamin Jowett (tr.), *ibid.,* p. 336.
[13]Major, vol. I, *op. cit.,* pp. 140–141.

The remedy, logically, would be to eliminate the excess blood, that is, by bloodletting, a therapeutic practice based on Aristotelian logic, which carried on into the nineteenth century.[14] We can, perhaps, account for the continuation of a therapy long after the rationale for it had disappeared or been discredited by pointing to the tendency for the ancient Greeks to oversimplify theory by looking for a single cause for disease, with consequent oversimplification of therapy. Furthermore, many therapies were practiced on a *traditional* basis which means, among other things, that practices and ideas were accepted uncritically, particularly if justified on religious grounds or espoused by a recognized authority. Moreover, at that time there was no serious competing theory or practice.

As is well known, eventually the locus of culture of the ancient Western world shifted to Rome. The Roman contribution to medicine, however, came not through further innovations, but through codification and organization. The Romans were not particularly original thinkers, but were masters of organization. Over the period 116 B.C. to A.D. 79 three encyclopedists, Varro, Celsus, and Pliny the Elder, compiled and organized the accumulation of medical knowledge up to that time, thus preserving it for posterity. However, they and their colleagues tended to select that knowledge with which they concurred and rejected the rest. Consequently, there developed many medical sects, almost medical faiths, since physicians had to pledge allegiance to the tenets of their chosen sect. The sects included the *Dogmatists,* who accepted Hippocratic humoral theory, but were without the careful empirical approach that Hippocrates had; the *Pneumatists,* who held to the theories and bloodletting practices of Erasistratus; the *Empiricists,* who needed no theoretical framework, but simply used any remedy which seemed to work; and the *Methodists,* who followed the lead of Asclepiades and prescribed fast-acting drugs to relax contracted pores or cause overly relaxed pores to regain their normal tension. For Methodists, disease was caused by an abnormal condition of the body pores rather than by a humoral disequilibrium. Finally, there were the *Eclectics,* who felt none of the other sects was correct and selected parts of each of the others which, when combined, provided the basis of their sect.[15]

In addition to codification, the Romans' other contribution was the organization of medical practice, especially the development of hospitals and public health. As is well known, of course, the Romans were military

[14]Sigerist, vol. II, *op. cit.,* p. 322ff.

[15]This sectarian approach to medicine is important in its ramifications for modern medicine. In the nineteenth century there developed homeopathic medicine, another kind of sect also based on an oversimplification. In this case, drugs were given to produce the symptoms produced by the disease itself. Osteopathy and chiropractic also began as sects and held as an article of faith one therapy for all ailments (see Chap. 8).

people. Part of the military organization included facilities and personnel for treating wounded soldiers on the borders of the Empire. Like many other parts of the military organization, these facilities, that is, the hospital organization, were applied to civilian life. From about A.D. 200 on, nearly every Roman city had a hospital to which the citizen could come for medical and custodial care. The Roman contribution to public health was primarily in public sanitation, e.g., sewers and aqueducts, obligatory street cleaning, and public and private baths. The government of the Roman Empire also initiated free public medical instruction (health education), provided free medical care for the poor by appointing physicians to various regions, and protected the public from malpractice by a series of laws.

To say that the Romans made no original contribution to the field of medicine is not to say that none was made during this period. During this time Greco-Roman medicine reached its furthest point in advancement through the efforts of Galen (ca. A.D. 130 to 200). Through his dissections of apes and pigs (it was then forbidden to use human bodies), Galen located cranial nerves and wrote about the anatomy of the brain. He proposed a theory of heartbeat produced by muscular contraction and relaxation and described the sympathetic nervous system and the relationship between organ functioning and lesions.[16] Galen's dogmatic assertions were sanctioned by the church, and this acceptance by religious authorities had considerable impact on the further development in medicine, as will be indicated in the next section.

At this point we can summarize the development of medicine during the Greco-Roman period by repeating that (1) for the first time medical practice was put on a scientific basis, utilizing observations of patients as data; (2) several theories to account for the presence of diseases were developed, which had impact on medicine in modern times; (3) a system of ethics governing the practice of medicine was established and, with some variations, is still widely used today; and (4) that period also produced codified medical knowledge, organization of the hospital, and certain elementary public health practices.

## MEDIEVAL MEDICINE

With the collapse of the Roman Empire, medicine as well as other sciences was pushed aside in favor of dogmatic religious scholasticism. There was a conflict between the *philosophical* approach to knowledge, in which one could deduce "truth" from accepted (i.e., religious) premises without any reference to the real world, and the *empirical approach,* in which truth could be inferred only from evidence based on careful observation. During

[16]Major, vol. I, *op. cit.,* pp. 190–192.

this time, much of the population was reduced to a subsistence level of economy and an almost nonliterate existence. As a consequence, medical practice was largely that contained in folklore, much like that described in Chapter 5. All this occurred immediately following the final collapse of Rome, but as we shall see, by the sixteenth century medicine had made a comeback. This was due, in part, to the recovery of ancient medical literature saved from destruction by the Arabs; to a broadening base of literature and art; and to certain medical innovations made during the late medieval period.[17]

In the Dark Ages, medicine had lost much of the scientific nature developed by the Greeks. The impact of religious dogmatism hindered further scientific advances by prohibiting dissection of the human body, by denying free inquiry, experimentation, and observation, and by confining acceptable knowledge to ancient texts approved by the church. Public sanitation measures, developed in Rome, were neglected, and seeking secular medical aid was viewed as showing a lack of faith in God. Epidemics were common. According to religious teachings, disease and illness were considered punishment for sin. Thus, for many medieval Christians, disease was not merely a natural phenomenon, but something which had to be interpreted in supernatural terms. Both ecclesiastical and royal powers were considered to have "healing" effects and among the people (where an almost barbaric ignorance prevailed), Saxon, Nordic, Slavic, and other folk beliefs became commingled with Christian philosophies and the remnants of ancient learning. Such physicians as there were (confined mostly to cities, where some semblance of Roman culture remained) were well-versed in Galen and Celsus and other approved doctrines. They catered primarily to the nobility, the clergy, and the upper classes.

The influence of the church had an impact not only on the practice of medicine, but on its organization as well. It will be recalled that in the Greco-Roman era, medical training was obtained by observation and by listening to the instructions of the master. Medieval medicine was taught, for the first time, in the university setting, beginning in Salerno, Italy, around the tenth century. Although it is true that many of the writings of the ancient Greeks were taught in the university setting, after translation from Arabic,[18] the canons of Hippocrates, Aristotle, and Galen were taught as a matter of faith, without their methods of research and observation.

---

[17]Sigerist, vol. II, *op. cit.*

[18]Much of the writings of the ancient Greeks had been rescued by the Arabs from certain destruction at the hands of the barbarians from the North. Through the efforts of scholars such as Avicenna, Albucasis, and Avenzoar, many new improvements were made in surgery, nutrition, and medicine. These writings were then translated from the Arabic for use in European universities. See Major, vol. I, *op. cit.*, pp. 225ff.

Furthermore, medicine was the only science which the church would allow the clergy to practice. Since the clergy could not shed blood, surgery was forbidden to physicians and relegated to a lower class of craftsmen, the barber-surgeons. This occupational group not only treated wounds and performed other surgical treatments, but cut hair as well.[19] Even lower on the prestige scale were the apothecaries, who were trained only through apprenticeship and were otherwise uneducated. This last group practiced mostly folk medicine that characterized this era.

In still a third area the church's influence can be seen. When the Roman Empire collapsed, the hospital system, at that time under government auspices, came under the control of the church. As long as the personnel who tended the sick, the poor, and the homeless were from a religious order, as most of them were, the quality of care was reasonably good despite the lack of medical knowledge. In fact, during this time some of the famous hospitals in London were established, such as St. Bartholomew's and St. Thomas's.[20]

There is, perhaps, one other phenomenon which in its own way made a contribution to medicine: widespread epidemics. It was noted above that not only did medicine not advance during this era, but public health measures, especially sanitation, had declined. These factors, plus overcrowded and generally poor living conditions, presented a favorable environment for the spread of contagious diseases. Probably the worst of these was bubonic plague, or the Black Death, which reduced Europe's population by about one-third between 1340 and 1360. The result of this epidemic was not only widespread death, but also economic depression, labor shortage, and social disorganization. Two practices, still widely used, were begun as a result of observations of the symptoms of plague. First, people began to examine certain past events in the life of the victim; that is, people began to pay renewed attention to case histories. Second, they realized that the disease was contagious and although they had an incorrect belief about how it was carried from person to person, they began to use quarantine as a preventive measure. The church, when dealing with leprosy, also believed to be contagious, used isolation, which prevented further spread of the disease. So the people used isolation for preventing the spread of plague, thus saving some lives.[21]

It is clear that medicine progressed little during the medieval period. Much of what had been learned during the Greco-Roman period had

[19]Vern L. Bullough, "Status in Medieval Medicine," *Journal of Health and Human Behavior,* 2 (Fall, 1961), pp. 204–210.

[20]Major, vol. I, *op. cit.,* p. 453.

[21]Kenneth Walker, *Story of Medicine,* London: Hutchinson, 1954, pp. 90ff.

become lost in religious dogmatism, a system of beliefs controlled by the church, which had an impact on the practice and organization of medicine. Medicine had indeed declined from a high watermark during Galen's time and only slowly worked its way to new heights during the Renaissance.

## RENAISSANCE MEDICINE

Just as the medieval world grew into the modern world with the Renaissance as a period of transition, so medieval medicine grew into modern medicine, again with the Renaissance as a period of transition.[22] During this span of years, roughly 1400 to 1600, two themes emerged which had consequences for the progress of medicine: a basic change in values in the Western world and the recovery of ancient knowledge.

Transitional periods are characterized by change, and certainly one of the historically greatest changes occurred when people revolted against religious scholasticism and began to see that life in this world had some value of its own and was worth trying to make better, rather than waiting for the promised rewards of the hereafter. Attention was turned from the past to the present, in art, music, literature, and science. Important consequences for medicine flowed from this basic change. For example, dissection of human cadavers was again approved, and progress in anatomy, stimulated by the drawings of Leonardo da Vinci, was made by men like Vesalius (1514–1564), a Belgian professor of anatomy at Padua, Italy, one of the leading university centers at the time. As a result of his anatomical explorations, Vesalius challenged the writings of Galen and other ancient masters which, up to this time, had been accepted by the church.

Vesalius' work was followed by discoveries by men like Eustachio (Eustachian tubes), Fallopius (Fallopian tubes), and many others.[23] Another major contributor during this period was Paracelsus (ca. 1493–1541), who advocated cleanliness in surgical techniques (aseptic methods were not discovered until much later), identified certain hereditary maldevelopments such as cretinism, and began studying syphilis. As the Black Death had devastated Europe in the fourteenth century, during the Renaissance the most devastating contagious disease was syphilis, which was correctly attributed to microorganisms (in theory) over 100 years before the invention of the microscope. Finally, new advancements in surgery were made by Paré (ca. 1510–1590), a French military surgeon, who developed new methods of treating war wounds.

[22]See Crane Brinton, *The Shaping of the Modern Mind,* New York: Mentor Books, 1950.
[23]Major, vol. I, *op. cit.,* pp. 408–415.

It can be seen that these developments would not have come about at this time if men had not first challenged the church's authority and dared to perceive life on earth as worth improving. Secondly, the rediscovery of ancient literature stimulated the resumption of the scientific method of observation and recording. At the same time, their observations led Renaissance physicians to rebel against the writings of the ancient masters. It should be kept in mind, however, that although these seem like revolutionary ideas, men did not destroy the scholastic habit of 1,000 years in only 200. Many of these pioneers still believed in alchemy, in potions and drugs. Many of them still adhered to the humoral theory of Hippocrates or the pneumatist theory of Erasistratus, despite their new observations.

## SEVENTEENTH-CENTURY MEDICINE

It was noted that the Renaissance period was important because the scholastic grip of the church was broken—dogma gave way to observation and experiment, faith to logic and reasoning. The seventeenth century might be characterized as the period of contrast in medicine. There was the invention of tools and equipment, but their application was largely overlooked; new data collected and analyzed by scientific methods were added to medical knowledge, but lacked an outlet in medical practice; and, finally, there were advances in clinical medicine, but no organization or classification of these improvements.

Possibly one of the most important physiological discoveries was the circulation of the blood, described by Harvey in 1628. As might be expected, this theory was not widely accepted at first because it diverged from the humoral theory of Hippocrates. It was accepted within Harvey's lifetime, however, and opened the way to further exploration and discovery in physiology: the discovery of capillaries, lymph nodes, and blood cells, to mention only three. Here we find an interesting contrast. Despite his major discovery, made possible by observation and challenging Galen's authority, Harvey continued to be a dogmatic follower of humoral theory and to use drugs without any rational basis.[24]

A major invention which permitted a breakthrough for medical science was the microscope, constructed by Leeuwenhoek, through which he found that blood cells and microorganisms could be observed. This led to further advances in anatomy and physiology, although these new observations were not immediately applied to medical practice. In this same period, advances were taking place in physics (Galileo, Newton) and chemistry

[24]Richard H. Shryock, *The Development of Modern Medicine,* New York: Knopf, 1947, p. 19.

(Boyle, Hooke), but again, few practicing physicians saw any relationship between these developments and the treatment of illnesses in their patients.

Harvey represents the modal type of physician following the Renaissance; Thomas Sydenham is the epitome of the opposite pole. Sydenham, considered by many as the greatest clinician of his time, insisted that the physician's main task was observation of the patient, observation-classification of symptoms, and an approach to therapy based on these observations. Perhaps his major contribution was in distinguishing between the patient and the disease.[25] In other words, he saw in his patients certain objective pathological symptoms which could be expected to reappear in other patients with a similar disease. Unfortunately, identification of various symptoms progressed more rapidly than the organization of these data into a usable classificatory system. As a result, practicing physicians, unable to apply their new knowledge, continued to practice medicine based on the ancient teachings.

Perhaps we might close this section by indicating two other developments which had considerable importance later. One of these was the founding of the Royal College of Physicians in 1660, an organization designed to promote the development of the field of medicine. The second development was the establishment of medical journals as a vehicle for exchanging information about new developments.

## EIGHTEENTH-CENTURY MEDICINE

The contrasts which marked the seventeenth century carried over into the next 100 years, but with a wider separation of the polar types of medical practice; that is, scientific medicine became more distinct from primitive and folk medicines. This was another period of the codification and consolidation of medical knowledge. Many new discoveries of basic importance were made. Yet this also was the era of fragmented theorizing, sectarianism, and unabashed quackery.

By this time the great university centers of medical training had shifted from Padua to Glasgow, Edinburgh, and Leiden. Here the emphasis on scientific medicine was stimulated and fostered resulting in further explorations and additions to the growing fund of medical knowledge. For example, sensitivity of nerves was demonstrated as was the myogenic theory of heart action. Experiments showed the action of gastric juices in digestion. Advances were made in obstetrics, or "male midwifery," and Smellie's treatise described labor and established rational procedures for delivery. Surgery also progressed, especially in the work of John Hunter, Chopart,

---

[25]*Ibid.*, p. 15. See chap. 4.

and Desault. Without the benefit of anesthesia or aseptic techniques, they performed what then were daring feats of surgery.

Similarly, new tools were developed such as the clinical thermometer and forceps. New drugs such as digitalis appeared and were used along with previous discoveries like cinchona. Perhaps the greatest medical discovery of the period was that of smallpox vaccine, by Edward Jenner. Presumably from a dairymaid, Jenner learned a fact of folk medicine, namely, that if one had had cowpox, one did not contract smallpox. Jenner experimented by vaccinating a child (legend makes it his son) with pus from a dairymaid infected with cowpox. Shortly thereafter the child was innoculated with the dread smallpox, but he failed to contract the disease. Jenner finally published his account in 1798, before the advent of the germ theory of disease![26]

Despite these advances, medicine had not become completely scientific. For one thing, theory of disease and illness and, consequently, therapeutic measures, had not yet assimilated the rapidly growing body of facts. More importantly, however, the inability of practicing physicians to apply new knowledge forced them to continue traditional therapeutic practices with generally poor results, consequently lowering their heretofore high prestige and social status. Other, nonmedical, persons began offering "cures" for various ailments. Trips to healing shrines were common. In other words, there was a continuation of spiritual cures, a practice of medieval times. Quackery and charlatanism were prevalent. It was during this period that Mesmer practiced "animal magnetism," the precusor of hypnotism, and Gall introduced phrenology as a "scientific procedure."[27]

In summary, we might suggest that advances in medicine were made *despite* the prevailing climate of opinion. That is, progress in medical research was impeded by the lack of specialization (specialists were considered quacks), by the lack of facilities for clinical research, and by the heavy case loads each physician had, which severely curtailed the amount of time available for private research. It was not until late in the eighteenth century that research became a specialty to which physicians could devote their full time and efforts.[28]

Perhaps it would be well to pause here to point out some additional characteristics of these periods leading up to modern medicine. In this

---

[26]See Iago Galdston, *Progress in Medicine,* New York: Knopf, 1940. Galdston also indicated the scientific tenor of the times by reporting a conversation between Jenner and his teacher John Hunter. When he first heard the dairymaid's tale, Jenner wrote Hunter and asked him what he thought of using cowpox as a preventive of smallpox; "try [it]; be patient; be accurate." *Ibid.,* p. 327.

[27]Eric Jameson, *The Natural History of Quackery,* Springfield, Ill. Charles C Thomas, 1961. See also Stewart H. Holbrook, *The Golden Age of Quackery,* New York: Macmillan, 1959.

[28]Shryock, *op. cit.,* pp. 45ff.

necessarily brief sketch of the development of Western medicine, we have focused primarily on changes which took place within the field itself— innovations in ideas, techniques, and technology. Just as important—and to some writers, more important—are the changes which occurred in the larger society within which medicine was practiced.[29] For example, it was noted above that Hippocrates's contributions were really only part of a much broader intellectual revolution taking place during that period. Similarly, the advances in medical knowledge and technology in later periods (or the lack of them) also took place in the wider context of social change.

In describing the period of medieval medicine, it should be noted that several major changes occurred. Immediately following the end of the Roman Empire was an almost total collapse of civilization. Thus, it is not surprising that much medical knowledge was lost, since nearly all codified knowledge was also temporarily lost. Moreover, although the institution of the church is viewed as inhibiting for a time the development of medicine, it was also the church which contributed much to the gradual recovery of civilization (including the preservation of much ancient knowledge).

Another factor which must be noted is the nonagrarian workers— craftsmen, artisans, and others—and the growth of towns and cities. In addition, the process of urbanization was accompanied by several other characteristics such as the revival of trade and the development of a money economy, a generally rising standard of living, and a hastened pace of life. Thus, during the Renaissance what occurred was not so much rejection of otherworldly values for worldly ones, but the development of new interests in this world in addition to the constituted monastic ideals.

It may usefully be repeated before continuing this discussion, that modern medicine also was greatly affected by developments in the wider society. Holloway has specifically cited how the ideas of "progress" and "individualism" have influenced medical practice and how developments in both medical practice and medical education were linked to the rise of industry and commerce and the emergence of the middle class.[30] These factors are considered in the succeeding pages.

## MODERN MEDICINE

It is difficult to date precisely , but surely it can be argued that modern medicine began in the nineteenth century.[31] This was the era, especially the

---

[29]See, for example, Thomas McKeown, *Medicine in Modern Society,* London: Allen & Unwin, 1965.

[30]S. W. F. Holloway, "Medical Education in England, 1830–1858: A Sociological Analysis," *History,* 49 (October, 1964), 299–324. See especially pp. 311–313.

[31]We have, of course, been arguing that the foundations of Western medicine were laid in the Greco-Roman period and that there has been a historical as well as substantive continuity in the growth and development of medical practice to the present day.

latter half, when a bewildering array of inventions and discoveries was made and used as auxiliary means of getting at the "internal environment." Stern, for example, pointed out that

> . . . clinical diagnostic instruments and techniques were unnecessary as long as the older speculative pathology continued to prevail. Laennec, because he wanted more exact observations in the wards, applied the stethoscope systematically. It has come to be the symbol of the modern doctor, just as the urine glass was that of the medieval physician. Yet it is a sign of the persistence of specialized medicine in the United States that Oliver Wendell Holmes reports that the older physicians smiled at the stethoscope's pretensions, and that the first mention of the instrument in the Harvard Medical School catalogue was in 1868–9.
>
> The stethoscope was followed by other instrumental aids in diagnosis and treatment—the ophthalmoscope in 1851, the laryngoscope in 1855, the stomach tube in 1867, the sphygmomanometer in 1887, the cystoscope in 1898, the respiration calorimeter in 1905 and many others. Skill was required to operate these instruments, to interpret the findings, and to act upon them, and thus the technological basis of medical specialism was laid.[32]

Just as importantly, biology moved from an organismic to a cellular level, and physiological and bacterial processes were being studied at that level. Eventually, the germ theory of disease was formulated, leading to the dominance of a unitary etiology and a search for specific disease agents. Surgery as a therapeutic technique made great strides following the development of anesthesia and asepsis. These, in their wealth of detail and boldness of concept, in their practical results and academic rigor, wrought an ever-accelerating revolution. Furthermore, a significant development in the organization of medical practice, that of specialization, emerged during this time. It was indeed an era of great progress.

It is impossible in this allotted space to recount even a small portion of the major discoveries made during the nineteenth century. A few of the most notable ones are listed in Table 6-1. Nor is there space to do justice to the influence of the French and German schools on the development of medicine. We can but highlight a few discoveries. One of the outstanding researchers was Rudolf Virchow (1821–1902) who utilized the microscope in studies of cellular pathology. He was able to demonstrate that cell growth originated in preceding cells. Earlier, when studying diseases of the blood and vessels, he had described and demonstrated the cause of cerebral vascular accidents and of coronary thrombosis. Perhaps his greatest contribution at that time, however, was in establishing a rigorous scientific method of studying cell structure and pathological processes.[33]

[32]Bernard J. Stern, *Society and Medical Progress,* Princeton, N.J.: Princeton University Press, 1941.
[33]Major, vol. II, *op. cit.,* pp. 806–808.

**Table 6-1 Selected Major Innovations in Medical Science**

| Date | Innovator | Event |
|------|-----------|-------|
| 1628 | William Harvey | Description of circulation of the blood |
| 1670 | Peter Chamberlen | Invention of obstetrical forceps |
| 1673 | Anton Leeuwenhoek | Invention of microscope |
| 1694 | William Cowper | Description of muscular system |
| 1738 | William Smellie | Modification of obstetrical forceps |
| 1761 | Giovanni Morgagni | Description of pneumonia, cancer, gallstones, meningitis |
| 1769 | Percival Pott | Description of fractures |
| 1776 | Matthew Dobson | Description of sugar diabetes |
| 1797 | Edward Jenner | Discovery of smallpox vaccine |
| 1809 | Ephraim McDowell | First ovariotomy performed |
| 1816 | René Laennec | Invention of the stethoscope |
| 1842 | Crawford Long | First surgery with ether anesthetic (U.S.) |
| 1846 | Robert Liston | First surgery with ether anesthetic (Britain) |
| 1846 | William Morton | Perfection of ether as an anesthetic |
| 1849 | Claude Bernard | Discovery of glycogen |
| 1851 | Herman Helmholtz | Invention of ophthalmoscope |
| 1855 | Manuel García | Invention of laryngoscope |
| 1858 | Rudolf Virchow | Description of cellular pathology |
| 1859 | Albrecht von Graefe | Established modern ophthalmology |
| 1866 | Gregor Mendel | Discovery of genetic transmission, mutation |
| 1866 | Joseph Lister | First use of antiseptic methods in surgery |
| 1869 | Gustav Simon | First excision of the kidney |
| 1872 | Jean Charcot | Description of nervous system |
| 1872 | Eduard Pflüger | Description of metabolism |
| 1876 | Robert Koch | Discovery of anthrax bacillus |
| 1877 | Robert Koch | First microphotographs |
| 1882 | Robert Koch | Discovery of tubercle bacillus |
| 1883 | Robert Koch | Discovery of cholera bacillus |
| 1890 | Robert Koch | Discovery of tuberculin |
| 1892 | William Welch | Discovery of staphylococcus |
| 1895 | Wilhelm Roentgen | Discovery of x-ray |
| 1895 | Ronald Ross | Discovery of the cause of malaria |
| 1900 | Walter Reed | Discovery of the cause of yellow fever |
| 1901 | Emil von Behring | Discovery of diphtheria and tetanus antitoxins |
| 1908 | William Osler | Revolutionized system of medical education |
| 1910 | Paul Ehrlich | Discovery of cure for syphilis |
| 1922 | Frederick Banting | Discovery of insulin |
| 1923 | Willem Einthoven | Invention of electrocardiograph |
| 1928 | Alexander Fleming | Discovery of penicillin |
| 1948 | Paul Mueller | Discovery of effects of DDT |
| 1949 | Antonio Moriz | First prefrontal lobotomy |
| 1954 | Jonas Salk | Discovery of polio vaccine |
| 1962 | Francis H. C. Crick James D. Walker Maurice H. F. Wilkin | Description of the molecular structure of dioxyribonucleic acid (DNA) |
| 1965 | Albert B. Sabin | Development of live oral polio vaccine |
| 1967 | Christiaan Barnard | First human heart transplant |
| 1970 | John Charnley | First hip joint socket replacement |

*Source:* Ralph H. Major, *A History of Medicine,* vols. I and II, Springfield, Ill.: Charles C Thomas, 1954 and *Collier's Encyclopedia,* New York: Collier, 1970.

Virchow's French contemporary was Claude Bernard (1813–1878), also a master of experimental procedure. Through his investigations he discovered glycogen and the vasomotor mechanism. His theory of internal secretions led to the founding of endocrinology.[34] Perhaps the two best known researchers were Louis Pasteur (1822–1895) and Robert Koch (1843–1910). Pasteur, of course, is renowned for the development of the process of pasteurization, through the discovery of the effect of heat on bacteria. More importantly, through experimentation Pasteur provided conclusive evidence for the germ theory of disease, which simultaneously sounded a death knell for the humoral theory and opened the way for the discovery of causes of a wide range of diseases.[35]

It was in the latter area that Koch made his contribution. Following the path outlined by Pasteur, Koch and his associates developed techniques in bacteriological research, especially in devising a solid culture medium on which to grow bacilli. His discoveries of specific causes for specific diseases were outstanding. First Koch discovered the anthrax bacillus, which was responsible for the disease anthrax in cattle and sheep. Then came the discovery of the comma bacillus, which was the cause of cholera. Finally, possibly the most significant event of all was the discovery of the tubercle bacillus, which was responsible for over one-seventh of the human deaths of that period.

Concomitantly, great progress was occurring in surgery, the two most significant discoveries being anesthetics and asepsis.[36] Prior to these events, surgery had been a hazardous undertaking despite improved surgical techniques because without anesthesia, surgeons were forced to hurry their work. The lack of aseptic procedure had continually plagued surgery since the time of the barber-surgeons. Joseph Lister (1827–1912) used the work of Pasteur as a basis for introducing carbolic acid for keeping incisions clean during and following surgery. He even sprayed the air in the operating room.[37]

Following Pasteur's lead, many others made startling discoveries in rapid succession. The causes of many infectious and communicable diseases, the most frequent causes of death during the time, were being identified. Also significant was the discovery that inoculation with the disease organisms prevented further catching of the disease, that is, the field of immunology was begun. In retrospect, prevention through immunization was the fruition of medical research begun some 300 years earlier when Renaissance physicians began their anatomical explorations. Their stress on observation and experimentation, however elementary it appears

[34]*Ibid.*, pp. 775–778.
[35]An interesting and detailed account is found in Paul de Kruif, *The Microbe Hunters,* New York: Harcourt, Brace & World, 1926.
[36]Rene Fueloep-Miller, *Triumph over Pain,* New York: Bobbs-Merrill, 1962.
[37]Shryock, *op. cit.,* p. 280.

today, laid the foundation for comparative anatomy and the comparison of normal and pathological structures. This led to the identification of diseases and the consequent search for their causes and finally to the discovery of their cures.[38]

Perhaps in concluding this section, we might say something about twentieth-century medicine. This century is one of consolidation as well as acceleration of the tremendous strides made from about 1875 to 1900. We have already noted the rapid decline in mortality rates from selected diseases since about the turn of of the century. Other crippling, but not always fatal, diseases such as smallpox have since been added to the list.[39] As was pointed out in Chapter 2, there has been a reciprocal rise in the prevalence of chronic diseases, such as heart disease and cancer, which are now the focus of medical research. The advent of two major wars has provided opportunity for improvement of surgical techniques and experimentation with drugs and antibiotics, and the successes have been notable.[40] Finally, along with other sciences, medical science has embarked on exploration in the space age.[41]

## MEDICINE IN THE UNITED STATES

Although it took roughly 2,500 years for medicine to progress from its Hippocratic foundation to its present state, we can see about the same changes occurring in the United States in something under 300 years. Marti-Ibanez has described the situation of early American settlers as having

> . . . in a concentrated and vertiginous form, as in a motion picture, all the stages that had taken centuries in Europe. In medicine, they passed through the equivalent of medieval clerical medicine with Cotton Mather and the cleric-physician; they employed magic, astrology, superstition, and folklore, as was done in the lower Middle Ages; in Virginia, young physicians were apprenticed to their elders who taught them and even boarded them in their own homes, as had been the custom in ancient Greece; they performed empirical heroic surgery during the Indian Wars and the War of Independence, just as the barber-surgeons and the contemporaries of Ambroise Paré had done in the

[38]*Ibid.*, pp. 274ff.

[39]"Smallpox Eradication in 1975," *WHO Chronicle*, 30 (April, 1976), 152–157.

[40]See the dramatic description of the use of modern surgery in N. Amosoff, *The Open Heart*, New York: Simon and Schuster, 1966. In addition, beginning with the work of Christiaan Barnard in South Africa in 1967 (see Table 6-1), modern surgeons have developed a long list of human organs and tissues, as well as plastic and metallic substitutes, that have been successfully transplanted.

[41]See Frank E. Voris, *Medical Aspects of Space Flight*, Washington, D.C.: Government Printing Office, 1964; James P. Henry, *Biomedical Aspects of Space Flight*, New York: Holt, 1966; or Hugh W. Randel (ed.), *Aerospace Medicine*, Baltimore: Williams and Wilkins, 1971.

Renaissance; and in the Middle West they had "factories" that turned out physicians practically overnight, just as "Thessalus and his jackasses had done in Imperial Rome."[42]

That such a rapid transformation was possible is attributed to the fact that American medicine was dominated by men who, although trained in European universities, were imbued with the New World values of exploring and of doing things well, but quickly.[43] In addition, American physicians were less hindered by traditionalism in attempting new therapeutic practices.

Despite these features of American society which permitted, if not encouraged, rapid change in medicine, early American physicians were still profoundly influenced by their European training. No systematic theory of disease had yet appeared to replace the old humoral and pneumatist theories of antiquity. As a result, such leading American physicians as Benjamin Rush (1746–1813) prescribed for fevers "a low diet, heavy purging with calomel and . . . bleeding to the point of fainting."[44] Thus, during a particularly severe epidemic of yellow fever in Philadelphia, Rush and his colleagues

> . . . blamed the disease on "noxious miasma," and evil air caused by rotting matter, stagnant swamps or the breath of infected patients, [and] public minded citizens lighted fires on every street corner to burn the miasma away. A committee of doctors headed by Rush announced that fires were dangerous and probably ineffectual. When they suggested burning gunpowder instead, the citizens got their muskets down from the wall and spent the evening firing at the miasma out of the window. So many people were wounded, that the mayor had to forbid this also. . . . Stopping before the house of a patient, Rush poured vinegar on his handkerchief and pressed it against his nose as he walked up the unswept stairs to the room of death . . . and Rush, although he made his rounds religiously, realized that he could not help. Certainty had deserted him when he needed it most; hesitating in his own mind, he noticed with agony that whatever he prescribed, the sufferers died. . . .
>
> Hearing that a West Indian physician who had often seen the disease was in town, he hurried to his lodgings to beg advice and returned jubilant with a new remedy. The next morning he ordered that buckets of cold water be poured over his patients. To his horror, three out of four who submitted to this remedy died.[45]

[42]Felix Marti-Ibanez, *Centaur: Essays in the History of Medical Ideas,* New York: MD Publications, 1960, p. 335. A recent historical analysis of the development of modern American medicine is John Duffy, *The Healers: The Rise of the Medical Establishment,* New York: McGraw-Hill, 1976.

[43]*Ibid.,* pp. 353–354.

[44]Major, vol. II, *op. cit.,* p. 727. See also Carl Binger, *Revolutionary Doctor: Benjamin Rush (1746–1813),* New York: Norton, 1966.

[45]James T. Flexner, *Doctors on Horseback,* New York: Collier, 1962, pp. 99, 101.

All was not lost, however, for Rush recalled a "scientific" paper which admonished physicians not to be fooled

> . . . by the seeming weakness in a patient since yellow fever was caused by an over-excitement of the body. Even if the pulse were so thin you could hardly find it, you should nontheless prescribe the most violent purges.
>     In the silence of his room, these words struck Rush with the force of divine revelation; he understood everything now. Under all circumstances depletion was necessary. Away then with cowardice; he would purge and bleed to an extent never dared in Philadelphia before![46]

The inability of trained physicians to achieve consistent results in their therapeutic efforts undermined the confidence of the public toward the practice of orthodox medicine, with a consequent rise in soothsayers, charlatans, quacks, and the use of patent medicine.[47]

The occurrence of these events can be traced to the lag between medical science and medical practice. One of the canons of the scientific method is patience, deliberation, and further experimentation until conclusive evidence is produced. Unfortunately, at this time discoveries were slow and their application to medical practice even slower. Shryock illustrates nicely this hiatus between pure and applied science.

> One should go with him [the physician] through the desolate streets of Philadelphia, during the appalling Yellow Fever epidemic of 1793—past the dead-carts with furtive figures walking well to the rear, into houses in which only children remain to greet the doctor silently, and then back to his own home to find both mother and sister desperately ill. Would there be no end to the heat, the dreadful fever, and the dying? Surely something could be done: some remedy must be found! Would it not have seemed sheer frivolity to have spoken then of "suspended judgment" or of "scientific caution?" One grasped at any hint in such emergencies . . . and tried desperately to believe that all recoveries which followed were due to its employment . . . while true medical science waited on progress in other sciences, medical practice could rarely afford to wait.[48]

Other circumstances contributed to the plight of medical practice during these times. First, since specialization was not yet accepted, busy physicians desiring to do research had to schedule time around seeing patients,

---

[46]*Ibid.*, p. 102.

[47]There are several accounts of famous physicians and inventors who vigorously promoted the use of certain techniques which, although ultimately accepted, were resisted by the public and often by the medical organization. See, for example, Benjamin Waterhouse and smallpox vaccination about 1800 and William Morton and ether anesthesia about 1850. See Major, *op. cit.*, pp. 736–737, 754–756.

[48]Shryock, *op. cit.*, pp. 48–49.

and even then there was pressure to get practical results quickly. Second, public morality impeded progress in some areas, notably in obstetrics and the application of anesthesia. Third, but not exhaustively, these conditions prevailed before medical conventions and widespread circulation of medical journals, i.e., communication and transportation facilities were sadly lacking.[49]

It could also be added that at this time, medical education contributed little to improvement in medical practice. Although some medical schools had been founded and were in operation, most medical knowledge was learned by being an apprentice and observing and listening to a frequently self-educated mentor, much as was done during the time of Hippocrates. Licensure was nonexistent, and, as might be expected, the quality of medical care varied considerably.[50] This state of affairs changed quite dramatically after 1825, when European-trained American physicians returned to the United States and began to apply to American hospitals the principles of research as well as the discoveries of the French and German schools. Although these Americans only imitated the European principles of pathology, they gained considerable repute in improving techniques of surgery, especially for the removal of ovarian tumors (1809), in brain surgery (1828), and in the introduction of anesthesia (1842), which as we have noted had far-reaching effects.[51] Slowly, but with increasing momentum, the standards of medical schools and medical practice and cumulation of medical knowledge increased. It became more difficult for one individual to assimilate the growing body of medical knowledge and to gain the whole range of increasingly complex professional skills.[52]

However, the very progress being made was also an impediment to further success. For one thing, not all discoveries were immediately applicable to practice—thus a return of the lag between medical science and medical practice. This was accentuated by great inventions in physical science like the steam engine, which had implications for immediate and practical use. Thus between 1840 and 1870 there was a decline in the public opinion of medical practice.[53] With the discoveries of Pasteur and Koch, not to mention those of Americans such as Walter Reed, there was a rapid return of public confidence.[54]

In the twentieth century, especially the two decades or so following World War II, this public confidence increased in large measure because of

[49] *Ibid.,* pp. 46–47.
[50] See the examples in Richard Dunlop, *Doctors of the American Frontier,* Garden City, N.Y.: Doubleday, 1965.
[51] Major, vol. II, *op. cit.,* pp. 741, 743; Fueloep-Miller, *op. cit.*
[52] Cf., Rosemary Stevens, *American Medicine and the Public Interest,* New Haven: Yale University Press, 1971.
[53] Shryock, *op. cit.,* pp. 248ff.
[54] *Ibid.,* pp. 336ff.

the truly impressive advances in medical science and technology and their application in medical practice. The consequences of some of these innovations, however, have served to raise questions about aspects of contemporary medical ethics and the organization of medical practice, two of the themes of continuity with which we began this chapter.[55] That is, while the Hippocratic oath in modern form is still the ethical guide, technology has contributed to situations which did not exist before and for which the guide is inadequate. For example, we described the dramatic extension of life expectancy in modern nations brought about, at least in part, by application of modern medicine. This change is associated with new ethical situations in population control involving medicine such as the development and use of mechanisms for family planning, genetic engineering, and euthanasia. In dealing with the rising prevalence of chronic, "incurable" diseases, also a consequence of medical technology, ethical questions are raised about the use of life-support equipment. Thus, the "value" of a human life changes with age, degree of incapacity, and ability to preform social roles. Death may be preferred by the patient, but the present code prohibits the physician from giving a lethal drug or "even to suggest it." Yet the code does not provide a clear guide to physicians as to when the use of life-support equipment is no longer in the patient's best interests.[56] Similarly, the implications of medical technology in practice has led to a revised definition of the concept of health and to changes in the relationship among social institutions of medicine, religion, and law.[57] We have noted that in early societies, these functions were often carried out by representatives of the same institution, i.e., the priest-physician. In modern societies, of course, these social institutions are separate, but they still interact at different levels. At one level, law defines some limits of medical practice in terms of medical licensure, mandatory reporting of certain diseases, reporting of treatment of gunshot wounds, prohibition of certain treatments, etc. Law and medicine may have an adversary relationship as in cases of medical malpractice. We have already seen the powerful influence of religious beliefs in primitive medicine, but even in modern societies, religious beliefs

[55]The impact of both administrative and clinical technology is described in a report by Cambridge Research Institute, *Trends Affecting the U.S. Health Care Systems,* Department of Health, Education, and Welfare Publication, no. HRA 76-14503, Washington, D.C.: Government Printing Office, 1976.

[56]One study demonstrated that in practice physicians are sensitive to social as well as medical definitions in deciding whether or not to treat seriously ill patients. See Diana Crane, "Decisions to Treat Critically Ill Patients: A Comparison of Social versus Medical Considerations," *Health and Society,* 53 (Winter, 1975), 1–33. Ethical issues in organ transplants, however, may involve unanticipated social consequences for the relationship between the donor and the recipient. See Renee Fox and J. P. Swazey, *The Courage to Fail: A Social View of Organ Transplants and Dialysis,* Chicago: University of Chicago Press, 1974.

[57]Mervyn Susser, "Ethical Components in the Definition of Health," *International Journal of Health Services,* 4 (Summer, 1975), 539–548.

influence medical practice. Some sects prohibit their members from obtaining certain kinds of treatments—such as blood transfusions or abortions—on religious grounds. Some writers have argued that not only are medicine and religion related in modern societies, but that medicine is *the* state religion in working together to set goals and priorities and in defining which forms of deviance are illness and which are crimes.[58]

A different perspective on the interaction between medicine, law, and religion has been suggested by Zola in terms of the "medicalization of society."[59] Rather than a collaborative relationship between medicine and other institutions, Zola argued that the latter are abdicating their responsibility in favor of medicine because of the past technological achievements in medicine and our continued commitment to science as a rational and objective explanation for all phenomena. Thus, standards of human behavior, definitions of deviance, and treatment of deviants are increasingly being defined in medical terms—in terms of what is "healthy," what is "disease," and what is "treatment." Under these conditions, alcoholism and some other forms of drug addiction are defined as diseases requiring treatment rather than crimes requiring punishment. Until recently, abortion was considered a crime, and a physician who performed one was a criminal. Nowadays—and under certain prescribed conditions—abortions can be performed as treatment. Not only has society shifted the responsibility for these definitions to medicine, but medicine has developed the organizational processes by which it is possible to do so. This issue is addressed in Chapter 7.

## SUMMARY

Some scholars maintain that the foundations for modern Western medicine were laid some 2,500 years ago in an era epitomized by Hippocrates. Archeological evidence shows that medical treatments go back perhaps 20,000 years, but it was during the period when Athens, Alexandria, and Rome were cultural centers of the world that a body of medical ethics was articulated. Many of the prescriptions and prohibitions contained in what is now known as the Hippocratic oath are still a viable part of modern medical ethics. It was also during the period of the classical Greeks that medicine was established as a science, however elementary the ancient methods appear today. Knowledge gained from observation and experimentation

[58]Thomas Szasz, "Medicine and the State: The First Amendment Violated," *The Humanist,* 33 (March–April, 1973), 4–9.

[59]Irving Kenneth Zola, "Medicine as an Institution of Social Control," *Sociological Review,* 20 (November, 1972), 487–504. More recently, see his statement in "In the Name of Health and Illness: On Some Socio-political Consequences of Medical Influence," *Social Science and Medicine,* 9 (February, 1975), 83–87.

was codified and made systematic. The Romans initiated some elementary public health measures, such as purified water and health examinations. They also established the first hospitals.

Much of the progress made in medicine (and other sciences as well) was lost during the medieval period, when nearly every phase of life was dominated by the church. Faith replaced objective evidence; dogma replaced experimentation. Had it not been for the Arabs who salvaged much of the codified medical knowledge and preserved it for posterity, the reemergence of medicine as a science might have taken much longer. As it was, around the beginning of the fifteenth century, medicine as well as other sciences and arts entered the Renaissance period. A shift in basic values seeking "the good life" here as well as in the hereafter promoted further exploration and discovery.

During the seventeenth and eighteenth centuries, many discoveries were made and many medical tools were invented. Instruments such as the microscope were developed, and Harvey published an essay in 1628 correctly describing the circulation of blood in humans. Unfortunately, during this period little of this new-found information was useful to practitioners of medicine, nor were the tools immediately put to use in diagnosis or treatment. It was not until the latter part of the nineteenth century that medicine finally became truly scientific. This event is dated by Pasteur's experimental proof of germ theory. Thereafter followed an amazing outburst of progress, in which the causes of many infectious diseases were discovered, remedies prepared, and finally preventions found. Even today, however, one finds a hiatus between the developments of medical science and their application to medical practice.

## SUGGESTED READINGS

Duffy, John, *The Healers: The Rise of the Medical Establishment,* New York: McGraw-Hill, 1976.

Fueloep-Miller, Rene, *Triumph over Pain,* New York: Bobbs-Merrill, 1962.

de Kruif, Paul, *The Microbe Hunters,* New York: Harcourt, Brace & World, 1926.

Marti-Ibanez, Felix, *Centaur: Essays on the History of Medical Ideas,* New York: MD Publications, 1960.

Ramsey, Paul, *The Patient as a Person,* New Haven: Yale University Press, 1970.

Walker, Kenneth, *Story of Medicine,* London: Hutchinson, 1954.

# Chapter 7

# The Professionalization
# of Medicine

*'Tis no idle challenge which we physicians throw out to the world when we claim that our mission is of the highest and of the noblest kind, not alone in curing disease but in educating the people in the laws of health, and in preventing the spread of plagues and pestilences; nor can it be gainsaid that of late years our record as a body has been more encouraging in its practical results than those of the other learned professions. Not that we all live up to the highest ideals, far from it—we are only men. But we have ideals, which means much, and they are realizable, which means more . . . the rank and file labour earnestly for your good, and self-sacrificing devotion to your interests animates our best work.*

Sir William Osler
*Teaching and Thinking,* 1895

As one reads about the development of medicine, one cannot help but be impressed with the tremendous strides which that field has made in the past and continues to make today. The preceding chapter represents only a brief overview of selected significant events which helped make medicine what it now is. Up to this point, however, we have considered mostly changes within medicine based on new ideas and technological advances but very little about changes in occupational status which accompanied them. Thus, in this chapter, we wish to focus attention on the professional features of medicine and, to a lesser extent, on how medicine became a profession. At the same time, it is important that we examine the process by which recruits to the field become professional persons. In this regard, the process of medical education—selection of candidates, the medical school as a social institution, and postgraduate training—will be examined.

There is, of course, a certain attractiveness inherent in "professional work." In part, this stems from the fact that, in modern societies anyway, professional work receives high social status and monetary rewards, which grow out of public recognition of the unique contribution the professions make to society. Perhaps a part of the attractiveness of professional work may also be attributed to the fact that, generally speaking, professionals work with their heads rather than their hands; that is, professional services are largely intellectual in nature. Moreover, professional work is an explicit manifestation of some values of Western society, particularly achievement and humanitarianism. Recognition—as a professional by the public and as a colleague by the profession—is brought about by achievement, by demonstration of mastery over the knowledge and skills required of a professional activity. In addition, professional work is a service, a scarce service offered to the public—for a price, to be sure—but under such conditions that what is done to or for the consumers is done with their well-being as a primary objective and the personal rewards of the professional as secondary.[1] Finally, it should be noted that professions are characterized by maintaining control over all aspects of their work—what services will be rendered, under what conditions, by whom, for what compensation, and how they will be evaluated.[2]

Although the classical professions—including medicine, law, and the clergy—have developed from the clerical estate, science and technology in modern industrializing societies have contributed greatly to the emergence of a host of occupations which have now obtained recognition as a profession or are yet in the process of achieving recognition. These work activities are the capstone of the social order, evolving out of the relentless push of technological advances.[3] The rapid accumulation of knowledge and development of skills in many fields, however, require that those who would claim some expertise must, perforce, limit their knowledge and skills to specific aspects of their chosen field. In this respect (and some others),

[1]Talcott Parsons, "The Professions and Social Structure," in *Essays in Sociological Theory,* New York: Free Press, 1954, pp. 34–49.

[2]Eliot Freidson, *Profession of Medicine,* New York: Dodd Mead, 1970.

[3]See Anselm L. Strauss and Lee Rainwater, *The Professional Scientist,* Chicago: Aldine, 1962.

the professional in a modern industrial society differs from a member of the "learned professions" of the past. The latter's recognition was based on his broad range of knowledge which was, perhaps, superficial by modern standards but far superior to the poorly educated masses of the time. Today, the scope of knowledge within any given field is too vast for one individual to comprehend, much less utilize, more than a small portion of it.[4]

The influence of science and technology on the subsequent growth of professions in modern society suggests that professions provide a channel for upward social mobility—for both individuals and occupational groups. Since professional work is based largely on the utilization of acquired knowledge and skills, there is no theoretical limit to how much an ambitious person can achieve within his chosen profession. Similarly, occupational groups can and do collectively strive for public recognition of their work as a professional activity. This has recently been the case in nursing and some allied health occupations, several academic disciplines, and some commercial occupations such as accounting. Besides these emerging professions, the continued developments within established professions are also of sociological interest. The study of the impact of increased specialization within a field in terms of altered social relationships between professionals and their clients, their colleagues, and the organizational context within which their services are performed is becoming increasingly important.[5]

Increased specialization is, perhaps, nowhere more evident than in the field of medicine. As the body of medical knowledge continues to expand and as new diagnostic and therapeutic tools come into being, there is a tendency for specialty areas in medicine to become further differentiated into subspecialties and sub-subspecialties. Some are based on particular parts or functions of the body such as cardiology; some on specific diseases like diabetes; some according to a special class of patients like pediatrics; some on especially developed skills such as vascular surgery, etc. Whatever the bases of specialization, it is clear that these developments have greatly improved the quality of technical care but that increased coordinative efforts are needed to provide total care for the patient.[6] What is

[4]Everett C. Hughes, "The Social Significance of Professionalization," in Howard M. Vollmer and Donald L. Mills (eds.), *Professionalization*, Englewood Cliffs, N.J.: Prentice-Hall, 1966, pp. 62–71.

[5]See, for example, Rue Bucher and Anselm L. Strauss, "Professions in Process," *American Journal of Sociology*, 66 (January, 1961), 325–334. Relationships between specialists and others receives extended discussion in Rosemary Stevens, *American Medicine and the Public Interest*, New Haven: Yale University Press, 1971.

[6]See Selig Greenberg, *The Troubled Calling: Crisis in the Medical Establishment*, New York: Macmillan, 1965, especially chap. 3. More recently see Anne Somers, *Health Care in Transition: Directions for the Future*, Chicago: Hospital Research and Educational Trust, 1971, and Eveline M. Burns, *Health Services for Tomorrow: Trends and Issues*, New York: Dunellen, 1973.

relevant for the discussion here is the implication that continued specialization affects the relationships of the specialist with the client. The former is concerned with a smaller and smaller segment of the latter's problem; thus in the field of medicine, it takes more specialists to deal with the whole person. Therefore, patient care is said to become "fractionated." Paradoxically, as medical care becomes technically better, it becomes more impersonal and often less satisfying to the patient.[7]

Concomitantly, specialists' relationships with their colleagues are also altered. In the first place, a network of informal relationships emerges for referring the patient from one specialist to another to provide the services needed. The informal nature of the system permits—if it does not actually promote—referrals on other than strictly objective, rational grounds. Then, too, as specialization increases, members of various subspecialties have less and less in common in interests, objectives, and methods, and a contest for power and influence in the allocation of the resources of the professional group often develops. Furthermore, the performance of some types of specialties such as anesthesiology or radiology is dependent upon the availability of complex and expensive equipment located in institutions; thus the relationship of some specialists to the organization within which their services are performed is also changed.[8]

Finally, it should be noted that two other processes are relevant here for sociological inquiry: (1) how a professional group is organized for presenting itself to and protecting itself from the rest of the community and (2) how professional socialization shapes the attitudes, values, beliefs, and behaviors of recruits to a field in a manner that is desired by and acceptable to the profession. In the paragraphs that follow, these processes will be discussed in the context of the field of medicine—perhaps the prototype of a profession—but the principles evolved from this discussion are, for the most part, applicable to other occupational groups as well.

## CHARACTERISTICS OF A PROFESSION

Medicine has not always been a profession, at least in one modern meaning of the term.[9] It may be recalled that in the early period of its development, it was more like a trade; for many years following the Middle Ages, physi-

[7]Herman M. Somers and Anne R. Somers, *Doctors, Patients and Health Insurance,* Washington, D.C.: Brookings, 1962.

[8]Rodney M. Coe, "Processes in the Development of Established Professions," *Journal of Health and Social Behavior,* 11 (March, 1970), 59–67.

[9]There are, in fact, several definitions of the concept of a profession, including whether one is paid for an activity (professional versus amateur), the degree of education required to perform a task, or the degree of control exercised by members of an occupational group. See Eliot Freidson, "The Futures of Professionalization: An Implicit Essay on Futurology," plenary address at the annual conference of the British Sociological Association, Manchester, Eng., April, 1976.

cians did not hold much status, nor was their work highly respected. Most physicians were only poorly trained; they had little or no control over who could claim to be a physician; and their diagnostic and therapeutic armamentaria were poorly developed and not very effective. However, as was pointed out in the previous chapter, significant progress was made from time to time, slowly and often in widely disparate areas at first. Gradually, as communication and transportation improved and as more and more successful discoveries and inventions were made, knowledge about disease, diagnostic techniques, and therapeutic procedures was greatly increased, and along with it, there was significant improvement in the efficacy of medical practice. As physicians became more effective in dealing with disease and illness, there was also a marked change in attitude of the public toward medicine and medical practice.[10]

As knowledge about diseases increased, scientific medicine became more and more removed from folk medicine and lay people became more dependent upon the practitioner for advice as well as treatment. To protect their newly earned status, physicians gradually gained control over their own colleagues and established standards of practice designed to protect themselves from incompetent claimants to the field and, at the same time, to prevent exploitation of lay people by unscrupulous practitioners. Although a good many responsibilities accompany the role of physician, there are also many prerogatives. One of these is the right to prescribe for the public certain health standards or goals which the public should aspire to. That is, the increasing expertise of the physician makes it almost impossible for anyone outside the field to prescribe the goals of health which are desirable or the conditions under which these goals may be achieved. Gradually, medical practitioners have organized themselves to develop and extend their occupational autonomy. Although never absolute, occupational autonomy is seen as the critical dimension from which flow other characteristics of professionalized occupations and one that ultimately distinguishes those groups which have successfully achieved professional status from those which have not.[11]

Contained in the above overview are most of the characteristics of a profession. First, it may be noted that professionals' expertise is based on an *extensive body of theoretical knowledge,* the development and acquisition of which is sought for its own sake as well as for purposes of being applied in practice. For the most part, this knowledge is highly technical and not generally comprehensible to persons outside the profession. The professions maintain a monopoly of this knowledge, and the expertise of the members of the profession is usually accompanied by increasing social status relative to nonmembers of the profession. Dissemination of profes-

[10]Richard H. Shryock, *Development of Modern Medicine,* New York: Knopf, 1947.
[11]Cf. the discussion in Freidson, *Profession of Medicine,* pp. 71–82.

sional knowledge is guarded in part by the technicality of the language, but more through the establishment of formal organizations designed for that purpose, i.e., professional societies. In this way, professions may exert control over who enters and who completes the program of professional training and who is awarded full privileges of professional status. A further attribute of the body of knowledge is that it is extensive and often difficult—requiring a long period of training if it is to be mastered. Presently in medicine this means, of course, that an extended period of training beyond basic university education is required to master the appropriate amount of the knowledge and achieve admission into the professional brotherhood.

During the training period, more is taught than just technical aspects of professional tasks. In addition, attitudes and values—a particular way of looking at the world—are also inculcated. One of these values which is central to the status of professional is what Parsons calls a "collectivity orientation"—an "other-orientation" involving the offering of a *service* to the public.[12] Because of his expertise in a particular area, the professional is expected to place the needs of clients requiring his help above his personal desires. This kind of orientation is designed to prevent exploitation of the vulnerable lay person by the professional in that any conflicts which may arise would always be settled in favor of the client. The potential for conflict is, of course, very great, since even though professionals offer a technical service to the public, they must also make a living from it. Finding the balance between the needs of the public and the personal needs and desires of the professional depends greatly on the physicians' sense of individual responsibility—to their clients, their profession, and themselves.

Equally important as learning attitudes and values associated with dealing with clients is learning how to collaborate with fellow professionals. For the most part, these relationships among professionals may be characterized as having a *collegial organization* as opposed to a bureaucratic one. This means that professionals band together—in part, to protect themselves from interference by extraprofessional persons or groups and, in part, to protect others from their own members who may behave unprofessionally. In so doing, they, and only they, set the standards of behavior for their profession and enforce compliance with the approved standards. This kind of organization is made possible by the expertise of its members who claim that only members of the profession have sufficient knowledge to judge the quality of performance of a fellow member. This kind of organization is necessary because mechanisms are needed to check the members of a profession from taking advantage of a vulnerable lay person. The collegial organization, then, is at least theoretically impervious to outside intervention, enabling the profession to develop as it sees fit.

[12]Talcott Parsons, *The Social System,* New York: Free Press, 1951, p. 438.

Finally, it should be noted that true professions have both *license and mandate* with respect to engaging in professional behavior.[13] Professions claim license to practice or otherwise impart the special knowledge that they have gained during their extended period of training. This right to practice is often symbolized by diplomas hanging on the office wall as evidence that the practitioner has achieved an approved level of competence and is recognized by fellow members of the profession. Their mandate, however, refers to the right of the profession to declare the standards or goals to which the public should aspire. Thus, the definitions of good health standards or good health practices are determined by the medical profession, and the public is expected to accept and aspire to those standards.

A body of knowledge, a service orientation, a collegial organization, a license, and a mandate are the principal characteristics of a profession. There are, of course, many other attributes or traits, often associated with a profession, which stem from these basic features. Some of these have been noted already, i.e., the power to control who enters the profession, to determine the standards of performance, and to keep the evaluation of the profession in the hands of its own members. In addition, there are other characteristics which are important, such as the increased rewards from professional status in terms of greater income, prestige, and power; these rewards enable a profession to attract high-caliber students.[14] Members identify more strongly with their profession than nonprofessionals identify with their occupations, and, consequently, there is less tendency for members of a profession to leave it for another kind of work than for nonprofessionals to change jobs.[15] Much of the credit for the successful development of a profession lies in the manner in which practitioners in that profession organize themselves to control their membership. Because the organizational factor is an important one, we shall turn now to a brief discussion of organized medicine before returning to the topic of professionalization.

[13]Everett C. Hughes, "Professions," in Kenneth S. Lynn and Editors of *Daedalus* (eds.), *The Professions in America,* Boston: Houghton Mifflin, 1965.

[14]This statements stems from the usual hypothesis that social status and power are associated with occupations that have demonstrated their usefulness to society. However, the validity of the hypothesis depends upon the assumption of a smoothly functioning social system. There is an alternative hypothesis which suggests that prestige is awarded to occupations which encompass both the negative attributes of social stratification and the positive attributes of charisma, i.e., the "ambivalence hypothesis." See Werner Cohn, "Social Status and the Ambivalence Hypothesis: Some Critical Notes and a Suggestion," *American Sociological Review,* 25 (August, 1960), 508–513.

[15]See William J. Goode, "Community within a Community: The Professions," *American Sociological Review,* 22 (April, 1957), 194–200; and William J. Goode, "Encroachment, Charlatanism, and the Emerging Professions: Psychology, Sociology and Medicine," *American Sociological Review,* 25 (December, 1960), 902–914.

## THE ORGANIZATION OF PROFESSIONAL MEDICINE

At this point, it is necessary to distinguish between the organization of medical practice and that of organized medicine. The former refers to the relationships established between medical practitioners and related support groups who, taken together, form the health industry. This topic will be dealt with in some detail in Chapter 12. Our concern here is with organized medicine, the formalized collegial organization from which stems policies concerning all aspects of medical practice and medical education. At the same time, we may get a brief historical overview of the process of the professionalization of medicine.

We have already seen in Chapter 6 how the development of American medicine paralleled that of European medicine but in a much shorter span of time. In the United States, in the latter part of the eighteenth century, young physicians-to-be were still apprenticed to established practitioners as was done in ancient Greece. Although a few doctors graduated from fledgling medical schools of the period, more often a person simply read a few books, purchased a bagful of instruments, and hung out a shingle. Faith healers, charlatans, and outright swindlers posing as doctors were plentiful. A lack of control over their profession—who entered it, how they were trained, and how medical practice was conducted—as well as a sincere desire to raise the standards of practice led to the establishment of early medical societies, especially in the larger population centers. The essential purpose was to gain control over use of the role of "physician" and to raise and maintain standards of practice in order to gain the confidence of the public. With only a few exceptions (the New Jersey Medical Society, for example), these early attempts of practitioners to organize themselves at local and state levels were not very successful, because of the continued inability to cope with epidemics or increased quackery.[16] After 1800, as the need for stronger controls grew acute, more medical societies developed until by midcentury there were over forty medical societies in twenty-two states.[17]

On May 5, 1847, some 250 physician-representatives from medical societies and medical schools met in Philadelphia to establish a national society, the American Medical Association. According to one past president of the AMA, the twofold objectives of the association "were then and are today 'to promote the science and art of medicine and the betterment of public health.'"[18] The efforts of earlier local and state societies had been

[16]Louis Lasagna, *The Doctors' Dilemmas,* New York: Collier Books, Crowell-Collier, 1963.
    [17]Norman A. Welch, "Medical Care, Its Social and Organizational Aspects: The American Medical Association," *New England Journal of Medicine,* 270 (Jan. 23, 1964), 178–182.
    [18]*Ibid.,* p. 179.

directed mostly toward obtaining favorable legislation from their respective state governments to curb the unlicensed and untrained practitioners. The national body added to this a thorough ''cleaning of their own house'' as a first step. In fact, the first elected president of the AMA said in his opening address that ''the medical profession had 'become corrupt and degenerate to the forfeiture of its social position, and with it, of the homage it formerly received spontaneously and universally.'''[19]

But even the establishment of a national organization did not immediately enhance the position of physicians. In fact, matters became worse in the succeeding years. The little progress that had been achieved in upgrading training requirements and licensure was gradually undermined by the reluctance of the various states to establish similar standards and by the general resistance to any kind of interference by governmental bodies in any area of activity. Thus, the argument ran, if it was ''desirable to throw all business and the professions open to unrestricted competition, why not medicine among the rest? If all religious sects were to be tolerated, why not all medical sects as well?''[20] The consequences of this attitude were a further decline in the status of physicians, a deterioration of an already weak system of medical education, and a concomitant rise in quackery. As we have noted before, it was not until the development of germ theory and its subsequent effective application to infectious diseases that medicine, through its national and affiliated organizations, regained control of its own destiny.

Since its inception, the AMA membership has grown until, at the present time, over 190,000 physicians are listed on its rolls, about 50 percent of all physicians in the United States.[21] While much controversy surrounds some positions adopted by the AMA with respect to the provision of medical care, its policies reflect the basic principles established in 1934. Simply stated, they include the following:

**1** All aspects of medical care and medical practice should be controlled by the medical profession.

**2** No third party (such as a governmental body, insurance organization) should be permitted to interfere with the basic relationship between a patient and a physician.

[19]James H. Means, *The Association of American Physicians,* New York: McGraw-Hill, 1961, p. 27.

[20]Shryock, *op. cit.,* p. 262.

[21]This represents a considerable decline in the proportion of physicians who are members of the AMA. In the mid-1960s, almost 90 percent of all physicians were members. Since then, many have dropped out or not joined after completion of training because of disagreement with AMA official policies and because membership is less important now to establishing a successful practice than it used to be.

    3  Patients must be free to engage any qualified physician they choose without any restrictions.

    4  The cost of care should be borne by the patient if at all possible.[22]

In pursuing the goal of better medical care based on these principles, the AMA has encountered conflict in certain areas, such as the issues of compulsory versus voluntary health insurance versus no insurance at all; of whether special provisions are needed to assure medical attention for certain groups, i.e., the poor and aged; and of whether federal monies should be used to expand medical education. In one sense, the AMA "lost" these conflicts since 85 percent of the population is covered by health insurance of some form; Medicare and Medicaid provide for services for the elderly and the poor; and, through capitation, research grants, and other subsidies, the federal government finances a major portion of medical education. In another sense, the medical profession has "won" these conflicts in that it still controls how an insured population will be cared for, how major financial benefits from the federally subsidized health insurance programs for the elderly and the poor will be distributed, and how medical schools will be accredited. Controversy over contemporary issues, however, cannot mask the significant achievements already attained through the efforts of the AMA and its state and local affiliates. For example, firm controls have been established over the quality of medical education. After the Flexner report, an independently supported survey, showed in 1910 how inadequate most medical training was, organized medicine reacted by listing the "diploma mills" as unapproved schools, often over the objection of their physician-owners, and establishing rigorous requirements for certification to practice medicine.[23] Moreover, to improve the practice of medicine, a strict code of ethics has evolved prohibiting disreputable practices, such as fee splitting, and other practices thought to be detrimental to a high quality of care. The AMA has continued its fight against quackery and fraudulent practitioners, including supporting the Pure Food and Drug Act of 1906. Continuing education of practitioners is still another contribution of the AMA. Through the *Journal of the American Medical Association* and specialty journals, physicians have the opportunity to keep abreast of the latest developments. Periodic conferences and training sessions on special topics are also conducted or sponsored by the AMA.[24]

    Although the national association of physicians is often more visible to the public—especially during highly publicized controversies such as Medi-

[22]Lasagna, *op. cit.,* p. 149.
[23]Howard E. Berliner, "A Larger Perspective on the Flexner Report," *International Journal of Health Services,* 5 (Spring, 1975), 573–592.
[24]See Lasagna, *op. cit.,* pp. 149ff. Also Welch, *op. cit.,* pp. 180–181.

care—it is nonetheless true that much of the effectiveness of organized medicine lies in its local organizations. The local (city or county) societies serve many purposes, both professional and political. They are, of course, the backbone of the state and national associations in terms of contributing time and money and implementing national policies. They serve also as a means for exchanging ideas and disseminating new information, as in scientific sessions. But, perhaps most importantly, they serve as a means of ensuring "professional" behavior on the part of their members inasmuch as many of the essential aspects of medical practice depend upon continued collegial support. For example, hospital appointments—vital to a physician's medical practice—or referrals to specialists are often negotiated in the context of the local society. Moreover, these "negotiations" are not always based solely on professional merit, but may also relate to extraneous factors such as race, religion, or ethnicity.[25] Thus, being a member in good standing in the local medical society is vital to practicing physicians' careers, and it behooves them to behave in a manner acceptable to their colleagues.

Since local societies subscribe to a code of medical ethics and support standards of training, the local society provides a means of protection for the patient. That is, patients who seek the services of a member of the society can usually assume that this doctor will treat them in accord with that code. At the same time, the local society provides protection for its members, too, against fraudulent practitioners through cooperation with agencies such as the Better Business Bureau, by establishing a "grievance committee" to listen to complaints from the public, and often by supporting a member involved in a malpractice suit.[26]

Physicians can also act collectively through the local society to achieve political ends, although these ends are often related to the conditions of medical practice. For example, they may force the upgrading of standards of care in a local hospital by demanding the purchase of certain items of equipment or the removal of personnel deemed to be incompetent (and this might include the exclusion of nonmembers of the society from appointment to the hospital voluntary staff). These doctors may act collectively also to resist changes which they believe are detrimental to the

[25]Stanley Lieberson, "Ethnic Groups and the Practice of Medicine," *American Sociological Review,* 23 (October, 1958), 542–549. A more recent study conducted in Canada suggested that influence related more to control of appointments to hospitals and other community health facilities than to social characteristics or ideology. See Donald K. Freeborn and Benjamin J. Darsky, "A Study of the Power Structure of the Medical Community," *Medical Care,* 12 (January, 1974), 1–12.

[26]Richard Carter, *The Doctor Business,* New York: Doubleday, 1958, especially chap. 11.

practice of medicine.[27] In any case, the local medical society is a potent force in organized medicine.

The fact that modern medicine has overcome obstacles and prejudices to become the very model of a professional calling does not free it entirely from problems inherent in professional status. We have already noted briefly the problems which beset an emerging profession in gaining control over its own members, in setting and enforcing high performance standards, and in protecting itself from external influences. Once recognition of professional status is given, efforts must continue to resist external threats of other emerging professions which are viewed as encroaching on areas previously claimed by the established profession.

Professional autonomy, as we have noted, is the crucial feature of a profession and one that organized medicine has worked hard to protect. As long as physicians as a group were seen as meeting the obligations of a profession, there was no serious external threat to that autonomy. Recently, however, some new developments have emerged which have raised questions about the validity of medicine's claim to continued autonomy. One development was the political defeat of organized medicine by Congress over the Medicare and Medicaid programs which became law in 1965. Participation in financing medical care had led to increased participation by the government in planning and regulating services as well. A second development is the continuing reports of fraudulent behavior by a few individual physicians and private clinics who misuse health insurance programs for personal gain. Third, and more important perhaps, is the increased sophistication of consumers about health matters and the advent of organized consumer groups whose demands on the medical care system are more forcefully felt than all individual complaints.[28] A fourth factor is the perception of decreased ability of modern medicine to deal effectively

[27]See, for example, Robin F. Badgley and Samuel Wolfe, *Doctor's Strike: Medical Care and Conflict in Saskatchewan,* New York: Atherton Press, 1967. In the United States, resistance to the proposed Medicare legislation was urged on its members by organized medicine, although later it became apparent that the official view of the AMA was not shared by "rank and file" members in local societies. On forms of resistance, see Richard Harris, "Annals of Legislation: Medicare," *New Yorker,* July 2, 9, 16, and 23, 1966. On physicians' responses see Rodney M. Coe and Jack Sigler, "Physicians' Perspectives on the Impact of Medicare," *Medical Care,* 8 (January–February, 1970), 26–34. More recently, the "malpractice crisis" has stirred organized medicine to action, although responses by individual physicians vary widely. See Reginald W. Rhein, "Malpractice: Grim Outlook for '76," *Medical World News,* 17 (January 12, 1976), 71–77, 83. A general description of problems of and solutions to malpractice is found in Department of Health, Education, and Welfare, *Medical Malpractice: Report of the Secretary's Commission on Medical Malpractice.* Washington, D.C.: DHEW Publication, no. 05-73-88, January, 1973.
[28]Marie R. Haug, "The Erosion of Professional Authority: A Cross-cultural Inquiry in the Case of the Physician," *Health and Society,* 54 (Winter, 1976), 83–106. This report noted a similar process in decline in authority of physicians in the United Kingdom and the U.S.S.R., but for different reasons.

with chronic diseases despite breakthroughs in treatment of some diseases or the capacity to extend some lives by mechanical means.

Despite these developments, some observers believe that not only does medicine still have too much autonomy, but that the deleterious consequences of such power are becoming more obvious. Illich, for example, has described these consequences in terms of three levels of *iatrogenesis*—harm done to the patient by the physician's ministrations.[29] The first level is *clinical* iatrogensis in which patients suffer injury or sickness through errors in judgment, lack of knowledge, or incompetence of the physician. Poor patient management, improper surgical procedures, and over-medication are all examples of this level. A second type Illich called *social* iatrogenesis, which refers to maintaining patients in the sick role and providing legitimation for not participating fully in the labor force. The importance of social iatrogenesis lies in its scope, inasmuch as the tendency in industrialized cultures is to define social problems more and more in terms of disease and illness—what Zola has called the "medicalization of society."[30] The third and most dangerous form is *structural* iatrogenesis in which "so-called health professionals have an even deeper, structurally health-denying effect insofar as they destroy the potential of people to deal with their human weakness, vulnerability and uniqueness in a personal and autonomous way."[31] These consequences, said Illich, stem from the autonomous power of a medical bureaucracy that defines not only what is health, but how that state is to be achieved and maintained.

Illich's argument, which links autonomy of medicine with industrialization, has its critics as well, and not only from representatives of organized medicine. Navarro, for example, argues that Illich's critique falls short because of a conceptual dependence upon industrialization, when the basis of his argument should have been capitalism and its sequelae in terms of corporate control of the health sector.[32] Illich's recommended solutions to the problem—to deregulate medical care altogether to let individuals choose to handle their health any way they wish and to make health care an individual, rather than collective, responsibility—have also been found not

[29]Ivan Illich, *Medical Nemesis: The Expropriation of Health,* London: Calder and Boyars, 1975.

[30]Irving Kenneth Zola, "In the Name of Health and Illness: On Some Socio-political Consequences of Medical Influence," *Social Science and Medicine,* 9 (February, 1975), 83–87.

[31]Illich, *op. cit.,* p. 26.

[32]Vicente Navarro, "The Industrialization of Fetishism or the Fetishism of Industrialization: A Critique of Ivan Illich," *International Journal of Health Services,* 5 (Summer, 1975), 351–371. For an interesting analysis of the power and autonomy of the medical profession in a capitalist, nondemocratic nation, see Jesús M. de Miguel, "The Role of the Medical Profession in Non-democratic Countries: The Case of Spain," Autonomous University of Barcelona, Barcelona, Spain, 1976 (mimeo).

only unworkable, but inappropriate.[33] It is perhaps the case that Illich's thesis, although pointing to a serious problem, is overdrawn and does not have realistic solutions. It also directs attention toward organized medicine itself and away from examining the degree to which its control of the health sector is now shared by corporate organizations. The questions raised about what organizational model will replace organized medicine in controlling the health care industry are not premature—at least in the United States.[34]

In addition, even a relatively secure profession like medicine must continually struggle with internal forces of change. The development of medical specialties has led to a differential sensitivity to events occurring within the profession as well as outside it.[35] Thus, within the framework of organized medicine, private practitioners are concerned with problems which often differ from those of interest to academic or administrative physicians. Moreover, there is further differentiation of interests within the broad categories of private practice, academic and administrative medicine.

The diversity and conflicts of specific interests of various subgroups or segments within a profession lead to internal struggle concerned with jockeying for positions of power and influence to better foster the implementation of special interpretation of policies of control, recruitment, public relations, etc.[36] Resolution of these conflicts is often accompanied by marked changes in the philosophy, goals, or methods of the professional group. For example, it has been noted that the acceptance of germ theory came only after a bitter conflict among members of different approaches to the practices of medicine. The acknowledged scientific validity of germ theory had many repercussions on the medical profession. Similarly, today there is still controversy over the acceptance of psychoanalysis, both as a scientific theory and as an effective practice.[37] It is already clear that establishment of the scientific value of psychoanalysis is having important effects on the practice of medicine.

Some of these conflicts take on the characteristics of a crusade or, more specifically, of a social movement which ultimately affects not only the value system of a profession but its organization as well. For example,

[33]Lawrence G. Miller, "Negative Therapeutics," *Social Science and Medicine,* 9 (November–December, 1975), 673–677.

[34]M. David Ermann, "The Social Control of Organizations in the Health Care Area," *Health and Society,* 54 (Spring, 1976), 167–183.

[35]Harvey L. Smith, "Contingencies of Professional Differentiation," *American Journal of Sociology,* 63 (January, 1958), 410–414.

[36]Bucher and Strauss, *op. cit.* Some evidence to the contrary is presented in Herman Turk, "Social Cohesion through Variant Values: Evidence from Medical Role Relations," *American Sociological Review,* 28 (February, 1963), 28–36.

[37]Joseph Ben-David, "Roles and Innovations in Medicine," *American Journal of Sociology,* 65 (May, 1960), 557–568.

the development of rehabilitation as a medical specialty has been characterized as a social movement.[38] The pressing need for special services and facilities, which was pointed out by the tremendous number of casualties during World War II, led to the expansion of the medical organization to include these features. At the same time, the philosophy of treatment underlying rehabilitation is markedly different from that associated with treatment of acute, infectious diseases. Consequently, there occurred also a change in technical procedures, in attitude toward physically disabled patients, and in rationale for providing the kind of medical care required.

Another problem facing professional societies is to maintain the loyalties of their members. We have noted the tendency for members of a profession to identify with their calling and to be reluctant to leave it. Nonetheless, members of most professional groups work in settings in which organizational values are antithetical to those of a profession. Thus, the professional may also be an employee, thereby possibly dividing the loyalties of the professional.[39] In the case of medicine, the problem is particularly acute because of the strong emphasis on the principle of no third party interference with the one-to-one physician-patient relationship. Field, for example, suggests that in the case of the Russian physician, loyalty to the state is more important and better rewarded than loyalty to the profession. Consequently, however, the Russian physician in industry acts as a means of control over workers and subsequently is given less social recognition than colleagues in other countries.[40] On the other hand, Elinson has shown that in Puerto Rico working for the government is more professionally rewarding, but less so financially, than is private practice. However, lower income is not the only reason why Puerto Rican physicians are reluctant to become government employees. Conflicts between local government officials and professionals in the health department focus attention on the divided loyalties of government workers. Moreover, training in American medical schools stimulates negative attitudes toward full-time, salaried practice and particularly careers in government medical service.[41]

A similar problem of control confronts professional organizations with respect to their members whose major commitment is to nonprofessional

---

[38]Albert F. Wessen, "The Apparatus of Rehabilitation: An Organizational Analysis," in Marvin B. Sussman (ed.), *Sociology and Rehabilitation,* Washington, D.C.: American Sociological Association, 1966, pp. 148–178.

[39]William Kornhauser, *Scientists in Industry: Conflict and Accommodation,* Berkeley: University of California Press, 1962. Also Ronald G. Corwin, "The Professional Employee: A Study of Conflict in Nursing Roles," *American Journal of Sociology,* 66 (May, 1961), 604–615. See also the discussion in Matthew J. Lynch and Stanley S. Raphall, *Medicine and the State,* Springfield, Ill., Charles C Thomas, 1963, especially chap. 8.

[40]Mark G. Field, *Soviet Socialized Medicine,* New York: Free Press, 1967.

[41]Jack Elinson, "Physicians' Dilemma in Puerto Rico," *Journal of Health and Human Behavior,* 3 (Spring, 1962), 14–20.

activities. For example, the physician-administrator or the research physician who works for other organizations, such as hospitals and voluntary agencies, often must espouse values and engage in behaviors contrary to those of their respective professional societies.[42] An even more severe conflict arises when values are widely disparate, such as medical science versus business. In a recent report, Fox described the potentials for conflict in the case of physicians who worked for drug companies as research investigators.[43] The incompatibility between the tenets of scientific methods and the company's desire to be the first to market a new drug often led to ambivalence or anxiety on the part of the research physicians, growing estrangement from their practicing colleagues, and reduced control over the deviant physicians.

In pointing out the kinds of problems facing professional societies, particularly medicine, it must be recognized that the professional organization does not spend all its efforts in keeping its strays in line. As a matter of fact, most members of professional groups do believe in and adhere to the principles for which their profession stands because of their exposure to attitudes and values during the socialization process. Thus, the key to understanding professional behavior, including attitudes and values, lies in examining the process by which such persons become professionalized.

## THE PROCESS OF PROFESSIONAL SOCIALIZATION

As we have pointed out several times, the characteristics by which a professional person can be distinguished from members of other occupations are achieved only by participation in a prolonged and intensive formal educational process. Thus, for medicine the medical school is a crucial element in the process of professional training because it represents the institutional context within which initial socialization takes place. The medical school is important because it is not only the setting in which knowledge and skills, habits, attitudes, and values are transmitted, but it is also the means by which members of the profession control who their colleagues will be and the standards of training they will receive.[44] It is for these reasons that structure and functioning of the medical school are presented here in some detail.

[42]Joseph Ben-David, "The Professional Role of the Physician in Bureaucratized Medicine: A Study in Role Conflict," *Journal of Human Relations,* 11 (1958), 255–274.
[43]Renee C. Fox, "Physicians on the Drug Industry's Side of the Prescription Blank: Their Dual Commitment to Medical Science and Business," *Journal of Health and Human Behavior,* 2 (Spring, 1961), 3–16.
[44]Grace Kleinbach, "Social Structure and the Education of Health Personnel," *International Journal of Health Services,* 4 (Spring, 1974), 297–317.

## The Development of Medical Education

It would not be possible to do justice to a topic so broad as the development of medical education in the little space allocated here, except to highlight a few significant events and trends.[45] In this regard, it would seem appropriate to look first at two converging trends which provide the rationale for contemporary medical education. One trend is the continued expansion and development of medical knowledge and technology which has been described briefly in Chapter 6. The second trend is the emergence of the modern university as the appropriate institutional setting for transmitting and furthering the development of knowledge and technology.[46] For centuries, the development of medical knowledge and technology was largely a product born of necessity in medical practice. Observation and classification of symptoms, invention of instruments, and explorations in anatomy, physiology, and other medically related sciences were accomplished through the efforts of individuals often working alone and driven by a desire to find answers to questions arising in the conduct of their medical practice. As the fund of knowledge grew, the locus of medical education shifted to the university centers. In Europe, this occurred as early as the Middle Ages, more because clerical education in church-dominated institutions was centered there than because the university was a uniquely appropriate setting for the education of physicians. It was not until the last quarter of the nineteenth century that universities developed the capacity to truly foster the development of scientific knowledge. By that time, medical knowledge had accumulated to the point that the apprenticeship method, in vogue since the time of Hippocrates, was no longer adequate by itself; rather formal instruction was necessary to supplement practical training.

In the United States, a similar convergence took place, but somewhat later. To be sure, the biological foundations of medicine laid down in France and Germany in the 1870s and 1880s provided substantial impetus for the development of the American medical practice. But the establishment of the American university as the focus of intellectual and scientific development in medicine did not occur until about 1900. Despite its university affiliation, however, medical education prior to 1910 left much to be desired. In English universities as in the United States, it has been reported that students attended a few lectures, often pursued special interests independently, but learned most of their medical knowledge by accompanying practitioners on their tour of hospital wards to attend patients. Examinations focused mostly on knowledge of basic science subjects but

[45]For a better account, see Richard H. Shryock, *Medicine and Society in America, 1660–1860,* New York: New York University Press, 1960.

[46]Lester J. Evans, *The Crisis in Medical Education,* Ann Arbor: University of Michigan Press, 1964. See also Francis C. Rosecrance, *The American College and Its Teachers,* New York: Macmillan, 1962.

little on their application. Requirements for matriculation were meager. The curriculum was at best flexible and, except for mandatory attendance at a few lectures, pretty much allowed the students to seek out their own education. The fact that lectures were often scheduled in the evening for the convenience of the lecturer is some indication that it was "the student's duty to get his education, not that of his teacher to give it."[47] By and large, examiners were more interested in the students' ability to parrot syllabi than in their ability to practice medicine.

By 1910, in the United States, there had arisen nearly 400 medical "schools," some of which were affiliated with universities, but many of which were proprietary, that is, owned by individuals, often practicing physicians. Despite the type of ownership, however, grave doubts were being expressed about the quality of American medical education in general. It was at this time that the now classic Flexner report, which described the deplorable standards of American medical education, was published.[48] Under the auspices of the Carnegie Foundation, Flexner had visited 155 medical schools in an attempt to determine the standards of instruction and training facilities. He documented the facts that few schools had full-time faculty members, and most were staffed with part-time physicians in private practice; only fourteen or fifteen schools had laboratories specifically set aside for the use of clinical departments, and others were used jointly by other departments or did not exist at all; the quality of instruction was almost uniformly poor and too short in duration, often less than four months of formal instruction; admission standards for students were not uniform, often admitting high school graduates; and proprietary schools seldom turned down students who could pay, regardless of other qualifications.

Flexner's careful documentation of the miserable state of medical education, coupled with the mounting concern of organized medicine and the informed public, represents one of the most important events in the development of American medical education. As a consequence of the report, almost all medical schools obtained a university base (by this time universities had developed to the point where they were the most logical organizational setting for medical education),[49] and the proprietary schools were gradually forced to close their doors. Universities began to allocate larger budgets to their schools of medicine; engage larger, full-time teaching

[47]Charles Newman, *The Evolution of Medical Education in the Nineteenth Century,* New York: Oxford University Press, 1957, p. 26.

[48]Abraham Flexner, *Medical Education in the United States and Canada: A Report to the Carnegie Foundation for the Advancement of Teaching,* New York: Carnegie Foundation, 1910.

[49]H. P. Himsworth, "The University and Medicine," in Brandon Lush (ed.), *Concepts of Medicine,* New York: Pergamon Press, 1961, pp. 29–35.

staffs; and build laboratories and libraries. Concomitantly, universities initiated higher standards for both faculty and students and extended greatly the number of required subjects and the length of time to complete the course of instruction. The increased standards included not only more rigorous selection for admission, but also successful completion of formal education and required postgraduate education. Clearly, the Flexner report so profoundly influenced the direction of medical training in the United States that it deserves to be called the "catalyst of modern medical education."

## THE INSTITUTIONAL CONTEXT OF MEDICAL TRAINING

The processes of acquiring specific knowledge and techniques and acquiring skills, attitudes, and values characteristic of the medical profession take place primarily in specialized institutional settings. Because the most intensive initial contact with aspirants for the profession occurs during the years in medical school, it is the crucial institutional setting within which professional socialization is begun, and, therefore, an appropriate topic for extended discussion.

### Selection

Technically speaking, the initial institutional process is that of selection of school by the student and selection of student by the school. As Hall has pointed out, however, there is a previous step, namely the choice of medicine as a career.[50] While much attention has been given to the general problem of occupational choice,[51] a substantial portion of it has been directed at aspirants for a career in medicine. One of the early studies which focused on the factors leading to a career in medicine was reported by Rogoff.[52] Data were provided by more than 700 medical students in six classes in a medical school. Three were freshman classes, and the other three were sophomore, junior, and senior classes, respectively. The results of this study suggest that most medical students are attracted to the profession at an early age, some as early as age fourteen, but that most career decisions or commitments are made during the college undergraduate career. Of interest also was the finding that 74 percent of the students whose fathers or other relatives were physicians, compared with 40 percent

[50]Oswald Hall, "The Stages of a Medical Career," *American Journal of Sociology*, 53 (March, 1948), 327–336.
[51]Eli Ginzberg et al., *Occupational Choice: An Approach to a General Theory*, New York: Columbia University Press, 1951.
[52]Natalie Rogoff, "The Decision to Study Medicine," in Robert K. Merton, George G. Reader, and Patricia Kendall (eds.), *The Student-Physician*, Cambridge, Mass.: Harvard University Press, 1957, pp. 109–129.

of the students who had no relative who was a physician,[53] first thought about medicine as a career when less than fourteen years old. On the other hand, there was not an appreciable difference in age at time of final decision or commitment between students whose fathers were physicians and students who had no relatives in the medical profession. These and other findings about satisfaction with the decision to study medicine and with the relative amount of support given by parents of the student are consistent with Hall's comment that the decision to study medicine begins with the development of ambitions which are "largely social in character. They had their genesis in social groups . . . one can see why doctors tend to be recruited from the families of professional workers. The latter possess the mechanisms for generating and nurturing the medical ambition."[54] The fact that professional training in medicine requires prolonged delay of rewards means that group support for these ambitions is all the more important.

Studies such as Rogoff's reveal something about how (and when) medicine is chosen as a career and point to the importance of primary group support for sustaining the individual while facing difficult decisions. A second approach to the study of selection of medicine tries to answer why it is chosen, and specifically what are the characteristics of applicants.[55] Essentially, these studies examine social and psychological characteristics of entering students and changes in their attitudes which occur over time.

These studies suggest that students who choose medicine as a career, select science-related undergraduate studies, and finally apply to medical school are not randomly distributed throughout the population, but that they have characteristic traits and follow characteristic patterns leading to medical education. Yet present studies also affirm the fact that there is considerable variation even among the identifiable patterns. In addition, there are always a great many more applicants to study medicine than there are educational facilities to accommodate them. Thus, a second aspect of the selection process is the school's admission of some applicants and not others. For the most part, these studies of the selection of prospective students are aimed at developing criteria to predict success or failure in medical school. Several methods are used to obtain information on appli-

---

[53]*Ibid.*, fig. 2, p. 112.

[54]Hall, *op. cit.*, p. 329. Furthermore, medical ideology as well as medical career commitments are influenced in family settings; cf. John Colombotos, "Social Origins and Ideology of Physicians: A Study of the Effects of Early Socialization," *Journal of Health and Social Behavior*, 10 (March, 1969), 16–29.

[55]See, for example, the articles contained in Helen Hofer Gee and Robert J. Glaser, *The Ecology of the Medical Student*, Evanston, Ill.: Association of American Medical Colleges, 1958. See also the similar findings for dental students in D. M. More and Nathan Kohn, "Some Motives for Entering Dentistry," *American Journal of Sociology*, 66 (July, 1960), 48–54. See also Enrico Quarantelli, "The Career Choice Patterns of Dental Students," *Journal of Health and Human Behavior*, 2 (Summer, 1961), 124–132.

cants including aptitude and psychological tests, letters of recommendation, personal interviews, and even the application form.[56] Admission committees tend to depend most upon grades and the Medical College Admission Test (MCAT), especially the "science" score. The MCAT also tests the applicants' verbal and quantitative skills and their knowledge of general, nonmedical subjects. More often, however, admission committees have come to realize the importance of nonintellectual factors such as personality.[57] Most of these attempts to predict success in medical school on the basis of one or two specific factors have met with only limited success. Rather, it appears that predictability can be improved by combining many of these factors in a single index. Johnson, for example, has reported that in a class of 320 subjects, 98 percent of those with high composite scores on ten factors, including social characteristics and academic and test performance, completed the requirements of medical school, compared with only 37 percent who had low composite scores.[58]

## Social Processes in the Medical School

For the most part, studies in selection of medicine as a career and of students by schools have been characterologic in nature, that is, attempts to identify factors or traits which distinguish the choice of medicine from selection of other careers or to predict success in medical studies. A series of sociological studies has focused on the process of socialization of the medical student for a professional role—the development of and changes in attitudes and values as well as acquisition of knowledge and skills which are characteristic of the profession.[59] Actually, the learning of specific bits of medical knowledge and the development of dexterous skills are more or

[56]J. Ceithaml, "Student Selection in United States Medical Schools," *Journal of Medical Education,* 37 (March, 1962), 171–176.

[57]W. Schofield, "A Study of Medical Students with the MMPI: Personality and Academic Success," *Journal of Applied Psychology,* 37 (January, 1953), 47–52. See also Leonard D. Eron, "The Use of the Rorschach Method in Medical Students' Selection," *Journal of Medical Education,* 29 (January, 1954), 35–39. More recently, see periodic reports like W. F. Dubé, Davis G. Johnson, and Bonnie C. Nelson, "Study of U.S. Medical School Applicants, 1971–1972," *Journal of Medical Education,* 48 (May, 1973), 395–420.

[58]D. G. Johnson, "A Multifactor Method of Evaluating Medical School Applicants," *Journal of Medical Education,* 37 (July, 1962), 656–665. There remains a concern, however, about methodological problems in measuring motivation which has been found to differentiate between students who perform best in the basic science courses from those who perform best in clinical science courses. See John M. Rhoads, Johnnie L. Gallemore, David T. Gianturco, and Suydan Osterhout, "Motivation, Medical School Admissions and Student Performance," *Journal of Medical Education,* 49 (December, 1974), 1119–1127.

[59]Samuel W. Bloom, "The Process of Becoming a Physician," *The Annals of the American Academy of Political and Social Science,* 346 (March, 1963), 77–87. A more complete statement by the same author is in "The Sociology of Medical Education: Some Comments of the State of a Field," *Milbank Memorial Fund Quarterly,* 43 (April, 1965), 143–184.

less taken for granted in sociological studies, except insofar as they affect or are affected by attitudes and values.[60] For example, Fox has noted that early in their academic careers, students are confronted with the enormous amount of medical knowledge available to them, and at the same time, they are made aware of the gaps in current knowledge. Consequently, one of the focuses of sociological studies is the change in attitude from the stereo-typed infallibility of the application of medical knowledge to the coping with varying degrees of "uncertainty," both personal, in the inability to master all medical knowledge, and professional, in the inability of medical science to produce all the answers.[61]

In learning to cope with feelings of uncertainty, students develop attitudes which will stand them in good stead later in practice. The initial uncertainty is largely personal and students tend to blame themselves or question their own intellectual abilities. But they also perceive that these feelings are shared by others. One consequence of this is a heightened motivation to do better.[62] Another consequence is the development of a "student culture," which is discussed below.[63] However, as students begin to acquire more knowledge and develop skills and, more importantly, as they begin to interact with the faculty members while studying actual patients, e.g., during the clinical years, these students perceive the uncer-tainties more in terms of gaps in knowledge than as a personal failing. This attitude, too, receives group support.

A second consequence of the realization that they simply cannot master all the currently available medical knowledge is an orientation toward choosing some medical specialty. The rationale, of course, is that it is better to be very competent in one special area, in which there is some hope of learning almost all of what is presently known and of keeping up with new developments, than to know a little bit about many areas but not enough to be particularly competent in any of them.[64] There is some evidence which suggests that medical students may take this into account when planning their career lines. Kendall and Selvin have reported that about 60 percent of the freshman students in their sample expected to be in general practice compared with about 16 percent of the senior students. On

[60]Howard S. Becker, Blanche Geer, and Stephen J. Miller, "Medical Education," in Howard E. Freeman, Sol Levine, and Leo G. Reeder (eds.), *Handbook of Medical Sociology,* 2d ed., Englewood Cliffs, N.J.: Prentice-Hall, 1972, pp. 191–205.

[61]Renee C. Fox, "Training for Uncertainty," in Merton, Reader, and Kendall, *op. cit.,* pp. 207–241.

[62]T. C. King and J. M. Zimmerman, "Motivation and Learning in Medical School: The Ground Rules," *Journal of Medical Education,* 38 (October, 1963), 865–870.

[63]Howard S. Becker and Blanche Geer, "Student Culture in Medical School," *Harvard Educational Review,* 28 (Winter, 1958), 70–80.

[64]George Rosen, *The Specialization of Medicine,* New York: Froben Press, 1954. See also Stevens, *op. cit.*

the other hand, about 35 percent of the freshmen intended to specialize compared with 74 percent of the seniors.[65] In their explanation, which has not been contradicted by any recent studies, the authors hypothesize that freshmen are more likely to expect to be in general practice and choose rotating internships than are seniors, because the former simply do not know enough about the practice of medicine to have formed any preferences. On the other hand, seniors are more likely than freshmen to expect to go into specialty practice and choose straight internships, in part because that is one way to accommodate themselves to the vast amount of medical knowledge. They may also choose a specialty because it offers greater intellectual challenge and opportunities for learning. Contrary to public opinion, students least often reported choosing a specialty because of shorter hours or higher fees.[66] More recently, an effort has been made to develop a theoretical model of career choice by medical students based on optimizing congruence between personal choice and career opportunities available.[67] Students are thought to make a conscious effort to match their own personal preferences (for specialty, location, type of practice, etc.) with career opportunities available as modified by influences in the medical school environment (faculty pressures, peer advice) and by a cognitive element. A review of the literature supports this conceptualization, in part, but emphasizes the need for more research on the patterns of interaction among students and between faculty and students.[68]

Another attitude which develops in the process of training, considered necessary for professional practice, is a "detached concern" or a perspective of objectivity in dealing with disease, death, and the human body. A physician must avoid emotional entanglements with patients in order to objectively examine the latter's person, make an accurate diagnosis, and prescribe the appropriate treatment. This training begins even with the dissection of a cadaver in freshman anatomy courses and carries on throughout later courses in "clinical" discussions with professors. The training for detached concern, however, has also been interpreted as the development of a cynical perspective with respect to patients. That is, entering students are thought to be full of idealistic notions of healing the sick and giving service to mankind. Under the tremendous pressures of learning great quantities of knowledge, being trained to approach patients

[65]Patricia L. Kendall and Hanan C. Selvin, "Tendencies toward Specialization in Medical Practice," in Merton, Reader, and Kendall, *op. cit.,* pp. 153–174.

[66]Don Calahan, Patricia Collete, and Norman Hilmar, "Career Interest and Expectations of U.S. Medical Students," *Journal of Medical Education,* 32 (August, 1957), 557–563.

[67]Wayne D. Mitchell, "Medical Student Career Choice: A Conceptualization," *Social Science and Medicine,* 9 (November–December, 1975), 641–653.

[68]R. Bruce W. Anderson, "Choosing a Medical Specialty: A Critique of Literature in the Light of 'Curious Findings,'" *Journal of Health and Social Behavior,* 16 (June, 1975), 152–162.

as cases of disease, and acknowledging the limitations of medical knowledge, students are believed to lose their idealism and become cynical. Eron, for example, has shown that medical students scored lower on a "humanitarianism" scale and higher on a "cynicism" scale as they progressed through the four-year curriculum.[69] Another study suggested that students who wavered in their commitment to medicine as a career were mostly those who chose it originally for humanitarian reasons rather than for its scientific attributes.[70]

The transformation of the idealistic freshman medical student to a cynical, hardened physician has appeared too regularly in the literature to be ignored, but it is amenable to different interpretations. Thus far, it has been viewed as an unidimensional, fairly pervasive attitude which develops in students as a result of their interaction with elements of the institutional structure of the medical school. A somewhat different explanation has been given by Becker and Geer.[71] While not denying that cynicism is a prevalent attitude among medical students, the authors point out, first, that it is related to specific educational activities and not to a pervasive attitude toward everything; second, that it is found among freshmen as well as seniors and therefore is not necessarily longitudinal in development; and, third, that the expression of cynicism does not necessarily mean that idealistic perspectives are lost forever. Among freshmen, they report, there is expressed a cynical attitude toward the usefulness of what they are studying for their future needs as practicing physicians, and even this applies more to some courses than to others (anatomy, for example, is viewed as an important course; physiology is not). Senior students, on the other hand, are thought to be cynical because they tend to focus on the physical aspects of illness rather than on the social-psychological aspects. But this is because the students are continually tested on the former by their mentors, who largely ignore the latter also. Thus, the practical matters

[69]Leonard Eron, "Effect of Medical Education on Medical Students' Attitudes," *Journal of Medical Education,* 30 (October, 1955), 559–566.

[70]Leonard Reissman and Ralph V. Platou, "The Motivation and Socialization of Medical Students," *Journal of Health and Human Behavior,* 1 (Fall, 1960), 174–182. On the other hand, there is also some evidence that some students quit a career in medicine because they perceive the physician as an inferior scientist. See Daniel H. Funkenstein, "Failure to Graduate from Medical School," *Journal of Medical Education,* 37 (June, 1962), 588–603. Also by the same author, "A Study of College Seniors Who Abandoned Their Plans for a Medical Career," *Journal of Medical Education,* 36 (August, 1961), 924–933. Although these reasons for withdrawal from medical school are important, the most frequently cited reason is academic failure. See A. E. Swartzman, R. C. A. Hunter, and J. G. Lorenz, "Factors Related to Student Withdrawals from Medical School," *Journal of Medical Education,* 37 (October, 1962), 1114–1120.

[71]Howard S. Becker and Blanche Geer, "The Fate of Idealism in Medical School," *American Sociological Review,* 23 (February, 1958), 50–56. A similar phenomenon seems to obtain in nursing education. See George Psathas, "The Fate of Idealism in Nursing School," *Journal of Health and Social Behavior,* 9 (March, 1968), 52–64.

of obtaining approval from the faculty (and passing the course) inhibit expression of the more humanitarian aspects of medical practice. As the social constraints on idealism are removed, i.e., as one nears the end of the academic training period, cynicism gives way to a more informed idealism in the form of concern for the social as well as medical responsibilities of the practice of medicine.[72] This interpretation has received some support from a later study in which sixty-four graduating seniors responded to scale items on humanitarianism and cynicism at the time of graduation and three years later. At the later time, fifteen were in general practice and the remainder were residents in several specialties. The results showed a statistically significant increase in humanitarianism and an equally signifi-cant decrease in cynicism.[73]

The foregoing interpretation of the development and expression of particular attitudes points to the emergence of a mechanism of accommoda-tion between the students and the institution as represented by the faculty, i.e., the emergence of a student culture, which has been extensively discussed by Becker and Geer and their collaborators.[74] The findings of their research suggest the development of student norms, such as defining how much study is appropriate, minimizing contacts with the faculty, emphasizing the study of some subjects at the expense of others, and giving support (and information) to other students against a mutual "antagonist." Certain academic skills are developed, anticipating what information will be asked for on an examination, becoming "test-wise," etc. These and other elements of the student culture are developed to help the student cope with the pressures of learning incredible amounts of information and to alleviate the frustration of unfulfilled expectations.

The basic difference between the student-culture approach and other studies of the acquisition of professional attitudes and values is that the former rejects the notion that the acquisition occurs only *during* the medical school period. Rather these attitudes and values are seen as latent then and become manifested later during postgraduate training and the early stages of private practice. According to the student-culture thesis, professional attitudes do not develop during medical school training, because the system does not permit it. Thus, the lack of expected contact with patients during the preclinical years, the focus on disease during the

[72]*Ibid.* See also Fox, "Training for Uncertainty," p. 224.

[73]Robert M. Gray, Philip M. Moody, and W. R. Elton Newman, "An Analysis of Physicians' Attitudes of Cynicism and Humanitarianism before and after Entering Medical Practice," *Journal of Medical Education,* 40 (August, 1965), 760–766.

[74]Howard S. Becker, Blanche Geer, Everett C. Hughes, and Anselm Strauss, *Boys in White: Student Culture in Medical School,* Chicago: University of Chicago Press, 1961. A recent report which supports this theme is in Marcel A. Fredericks and Paul Mundy, *The Making of a Physician,* Chicago: Loyola University Press, 1976.

clinical years, and the denial of responsibility for cases throughout all four years obviate the students' adopting professional attitudes toward the work they are doing.

Other studies, however, lend themselves to a different interpretation. Huntington, for example, reported that the tendency for medical students to perceive themselves as doctors increased with their year in school and varied according to the person with whom they were interacting.[75] At the end of their first year, 31 percent of the freshman students reported thinking of themselves primarily as doctors, while 83 percent of the seniors thought the same of themselves. Moreover, students thought of themselves as doctors most often when dealing with patients, less often with nurses, and least with medical school faculty and fellow students.[76] A recent study from Israel, however, suggests that the process of professional identification is more complex than this. Shuval reported that identification with the professional role of doctor was situational in nature and influenced by physician-teachers whose perspectives were, in turn, related to the degree of authoritarianism in the hospital structure. Patients tended to take their cues from physician-teachers, but student-peers regulated the "speed" with which students adopted the professional role.[77]

These results are not necessarily incompatible with the conclusions of the student-culture thesis. The expression of perceiving themselves as doctors as found by Huntington or Shuval may be an element of the submerged but not abandoned idealistic aspirations proposed by Becker and Geer. Most likely, these seemingly contradictory findings may be an artifact of the research questions asked and the methods used to collect data. Huntington reports, for example, that students are least likely to feel like doctors in reference to fellow students or faculty. The student culture necessarily reflects the consensus of beliefs of students, often in opposition to the faculty's beliefs (or desires). As a consequence, in the student-culture context, inquiries concerning perception of being a doctor must necessarily be negative. In any case, considerable further investigation is required to explicate the results of past work.

## Postgraduate Training

Just as the three- or four-year tenure of medical school is crucial to the initiation of professional attitudes and values, so the postgraduate period of

[75]Mary Jean Huntington, "The Development of a Professional Self-image," in Merton, Reader, and Kendall, *op. cit.,* pp. 179–187. Similar evidence has been found for nurses. See Rodney M. Coe, "Self-conception and Professional Training," *Nursing Research,* 14 (Winter, 1965), 49–52.

[76]Huntington, *op. cit.,* pp. 180. 182.

[77]Judith T. Shuval, "From 'Boy' to 'Colleague:' Processes of Role Transformation in Professional Socialization," *Social Science and Medicine,* 9 (August–September, 1975), 413–420.

internship and residency is important to the internalization of the attributes of the physician's role. One writer has stated that there is

> . . . no other year in a doctor's life to compare with internship, no year so crucial to his growth as a doctor, no other single year which so powerfully molds and influences his entire professional life . . . ; it is during his internship year, the so-called "fifth year of medical school," that he is pounded and sweated into the shape and substance of a competent physician. This year is the proving ground: for the first time he takes upon himself the burden of responsibility, and his handling of it determines his success or failure.[78]

Internship and residency, then, may be viewed as an extension of medical school training in that neophyte physicians continue to absorb knowledge and develop technical skills. But it is different from medical school training in that they must learn new organizational and interpersonal skills. Their postgraduate training will most likely take place in a different institutional context, i.e., the medical work setting rather than the medical education setting; and this calls for a realignment of their role vis-à-vis others, both subordinates and superiors, and the development of new interpersonal relationships.[79]

The acquisition of new knowledge and technical skills is, perhaps, the most obvious characteristic of postgraduate training. Although interns assume responsibility for the care of many patients in the hospital, they do so usually under close supervision of the assistant resident, another house officer, or a visiting physician. Gradually, interns are allowed to perform more of the tasks associated with medical care of the patient, and although much of the time the duties are routine (and seemingly endless), there are occasions when a medical crisis calls for immediate action from the fledgling physician. On these occasions the intern often learns from his subordinates as well as from those above him in the medical-staff hierarchy. An anecdote from the diary of an intern illustrates this. The intern had been called to attend an obstetrics patient who was experiencing severe postpartum bleeding. Upon entering the patient's room, he observed that

> . . . this woman was bleeding, I mean she was really gushing. She was just blanched out; her lips looked about the same color as her cheeks. She was

[78]Doctor X, *Intern,* New York: Harper & Row, 1965, pp. 2, 4. It should be noted that some specialties have eliminated a formal internship year, but a first-year residency often serves the same purpose.

[79]For a clear statement of the controversy over who will control graduate medical education in hospital settings see Robert E. Toomey, "Graduate Medical Education: Defining the Hospitals' Role," *Journal of the American Hospital Association,* 48 (August 16, 1974), 43–45 and John A. D. Cooper, "Graduate Medical Education: Whose Responsibility?" *ibid.,* 47–50. Toomey argues that community hospitals and university medical centers ought to share control equally while Cooper supports the view that academic medical centers must assume a greater control to ensure continuity in the medical education process.

conscious, but her pulse was fast and I couldn't even get a blood pressure reading, and she was panting for air and trying to sit up in bed, half-confused and picking at the bed sheets the way I had seen a couple of people do at Johns Hopkins when they were dying and knew it. . . . I stood there and thought, My God, she's just going to exsanguinate with me standing here holding her hand.

Then one of the night nurses, bless her soul, said, "Doctor, I brought the shock blocks [wooden blocks used to elevate the foot of the bed to help combat shock] down here in case you might want them," and suddenly it dawned on me that it wasn't the bleeding I had to worry about right then, that this woman was in *shock,* and I said, "Yes, let's get those blocks under the foot of the bed." So two nurses shoved the shock blocks under the end of the bed while I lifted it up, tipping the woman's feet up at about a 30-degree angle. Then I started massaging her belly, trying to get the uterus to clamp down a little bit, and sent a nurse out to get an IV setup, and started trying to remember what you do for shock instead of what you do for post-partum hemorrhage. By now I was scared silly, and mad at myself as well; for all the dozens of times I had read about shock and what to do about it, I had never actually *seen* or *treated* a patient in shock, and at the moment I couldn't think of a damned thing.

Then in a minute or two the nurse turned up with 1,000 cc's of 5 per cent glucose water in an IV jug and said, "Doctor, if you're going to want to order any blood for this lady, maybe you can draw the blood sample for typing and cross-matching before you start the IV going," and again this gal saved the day—I hadn't even thought of a transfusion. I said, "Yes, I'm going to want three units of blood on an emergency cross-match," and then proceeded to draw the blood sample for the blood bank to use for typing and crossmatch and started the IV going. I knew about plasma expanders like extran, but I was a little scared of them, and the woman was looking a little better now that her feet were tilted up, so I told the nurse to put some Pitocin in the IV, and when she said, "How much do you want in there?" I said, "Well, hell, enough to clamp the uterus down," and went back to the nurses' station with her. She told me they usually put an ampule of Pitocin in 1,000 cc's of glucose, so I said, "Fine, go ahead and do that," even though I didn't have the vaguest idea of how much Pitocin there was in an ampule. An orderly came up to take the blood sample down to the blood bank, and I told him to snap it up, we needed the blood in a hurry.[80]

This excerpt illustrates an important feature of postgraduate training besides the fact that interns acquire technical knowledge and skills from a variety of sources. It suggests also that interns must depend upon others to extricate them from situations in which they have responsibility. This is no doubt more true of the early part of postgraduate training than of the later stages by which time they have presumably acquired not only knowledge, but confidence as well. Even then, however, there must be an exchange of

[80]Doctor X, *op. cit.,* pp. 30–32.

favors as well as knowledge among the members of the medical staff in order that interns may learn and at the same time practicing physicians may be relieved of many details of the care of their patients.

There is, in other words, a series of negotiations which take place in the hospital setting. One study of the process of negotiation suggests that early in their training, interns are dependent upon the clinical clerk (fourth-year medical student) for information about the organization of work on the ward and upon the assistant resident for confirmation of the technical aspects of care rendered by the intern. In return, the clerk has an elevated status because he or she influences a superior, and the assistant resident obtains detailed information about the patient. By the end of their internship period, the interns are familiar with the organizational aspects of the work setting and no longer need the information provided by the clerk. Presumably, then, they assume the formal role relationships of subordinate and superior. At the same time, the interns must continue their relationship with the assistant resident, because the former will succeed the latter at the end of the training period.[81]

It is apparent that the period of postgraduate training involves learning not only technical skills but what might be called "organizational skills" as well. The latter involves learning the location of the procedures for obtaining information and services in the work setting. A part of these, of course, can be obtained through the formal channels, but much of it is available through the informal system (see Chapter 10). In any case, through the time-tested method of exposure to and involvement in the application of their knowledge and skills, physicians not only become more competent, but also come to be fully initiated into the manners of professional life. A study by Bucher has more explicitly identified the various mechanisms of professional socialization, in this case for psychiatric residents, which apply to postgraduate training generally.[82] She points out that in postgraduate training, the "real" nature of the doctor's work is delineated as compared with the essentially intellectual exercises experienced in medical school. It is in the practical training period that what is defined as important by practicing professionals is indicated to those in training. This definition of crucial elements of professional life is made through "coaching and criticism" and by the presentation of role models. Characteristic attitudes

[81]Stephen J. Miller, *Prescription for Leadership: Training for the Medical Elite,* Chicago: Aldine, 1970.

[82]Rue Bucher, "The Psychiatric Residency and Professional Socialization," *Journal of Health and Human Behavior,* 6 (Winter, 1965), 197–206. Similar processes were identified in orthopedic surgery. See Gary Burkett and Kathleen Knafl, "Professional Socialization in a Surgical Specialty: Acquiring Medical Judgment," *Social Science and Medicine,* 9 (July, 1975), 397–404. A full-scale study, comparing interns in two types of settings, further demonstrated the inculcation of specific attitudes and values. See Emily Mumford, *Interns: From Students to Physicians,* Cambridge: Harvard University Press, 1970.

and values may thus be transmitted along with techniques.[83] At the same time, trainees develop special interests in and knowledge of future training possibilities, and this knowledge affects their perception of their professional role and the development of their career plans.[84]

## SOME CURRENT NEEDS IN MEDICAL EDUCATION

A recurring theme of many analysts of contemporary medical education is that its present scope and organization cannot hope to meet the anticipated health needs of the American population.[85] They point out that changes in the age structure of the population, i.e., more very young and more older citizens, will probably mean an increase in the demand for physicians' services. It means also a shift in the kinds of health problems seen by physicians, from infectious diseases, which could be treated by the individual physician, to chronic diseases, which require team performance by a physician and a host of ancillary personnel (see Chapter 3). At the very least, the methods of delivery of health care services will have to be reorganized to care for an expanding, highly mobile, urban population. These trends will all eventually influence medical education both in the expansion of training facilities and capabilities and in the content of medical school curriculum.[86]

In 1972 there were 108 accredited medical schools from which about 9,550 students graduated. These students, plus Canadian and foreign medical school graduates—less deaths and retirements of practicing physicians—brought the total number of all doctors of medicine in the United States to about 370,000 or 174 physicians per 100,000 population. This represents an increase of 18 percent since 1965 in the ratio of physicians to population. By 1990, it is expected that as many as 18,000 students will graduate, bringing the ratio of physicians to 100,000 population to more than 200.[87] These predictions are based on the expansion of medical school facilities, the increased number of applications to medical schools, and the

[83]Melvin Seeman and John W. Evans, "Apprenticeship and Attitude Change," *American Journal of Sociology,* 66 (January, 1962), 365–378.

[84]Bucher, *op. cit.,* p. 204. See also Hall, *op. cit.;* and Miller, *op. cit.* Also David N. Solomon, "Ethnic and Class Differences among Hospitals as Contingencies in Medical Careers," *American Journal of Sociology,* 66 (March, 1961), 464–471.

[85]Frank Bane, "Organizing Medical Education to Meet Health Needs," *Annals of the American Academy of Political and Social Science,* 337 (September, 1961), 29–35. See also John S. Millis, *The Graduate Education of Physicians: Report of Citizens Commission on Graduate Medical Education,* Chicago: American Medical Association, 1966.

[86] Leslie A. Falk, Benjamin Page, and Walter Vesper, "Human Values and Medical Education from the Perspective of Health Care Delivery," *Journal of Medical Education,* 48 (February, 1973), 152–157.

[87]Department of Health, Education, and Welfare, *The Supply of Health Manpower,* Washington, D.C.: Government Printing Office, 1974.

decline in rate of increase of the general population. An increase in the number of physicians available is important, but it is not enough by itself to ensure access to physicians' services by the population. Thus, one continuing need in medical education is to stimulate medical graduates to consider primary care and specialties like family medicine rather than subspecialties and to locate their practices more often in medically underserved areas such as smaller communities and inner cities.

Motivating students to choose career lines that better meet the health needs of the population is complicated by a lack of consensus as to what the medical education process should produce.[88] Several observers have noted the discrepancy between what medical students are taught and what they need to know as practitioners, and point to the urgent need for further research in recruitment, training processes, and preparation for changing demands of medical practice.[89]

A somewhat different, but equally perplexing, problem facing medical educators is how to reorganize the content of what students learn to help them—as future physicians—prepare to meet the changing health needs of the population. As we have noted before (Chapters 2 and 3), the changes in health needs of the population involve principles of organization, social interaction, and methods of research that lie mostly in the fields of the social sciences. Thus, much of the change in medical school curricula and related matters revolves around "fitting" the social sciences into an already crowded course of study. To be sure, the incorporation of social science materials into the curriculum (and social scientists into the faculty) is no longer new to most medical schools.[90] Even so, the addition of social scientists to medical faculties has been relatively slow until the past few years during which the pace appears to be quickening. Moreover, it appears to be a trend which will continue to increase as social scientists demonstrate their usefulness to the processes of medical education.[91]

[88]Robert L. Kane, F. Ross Woolley, and Rosalie Kane, "Toward Defining the End Product of Medical Education," *Journal of Medical Education,* 48 (July, 1973), 615–624.

[89]Ann G. Olmstead and Marianne A. Paget, "Some Theoretical Issues in Professional Socialization," *Journal of Medical Education,* 44 (August, 1969), 663–669; and Ralph B. Freidin, Arthur J. Barsky, David Levine, and Sherman R. Williams, "Medical Education and Physician Behavior: Preparing Physicians for New Roles," *Journal of Medical Education,* 47 (March, 1972), 163–168.

[90]See, for example, a report of a survey of medical schools in Donald S. Kennedy, Evan G. Pattishall, and C. Richard Fletcher, *Teaching Behavioral Sciences in Schools of Medicine,* vol. 1, Summary Report (mimeo), Rockville, Md.: National Center for Health Services Research and Development, July, 1972.

[91]This trend is seen in graduate as well as undergraduate medical education and in medical education systems outside the United States. Cf., for example, Ivan J. Williams, Marian F. Bishop, Brian K. E. Hennen, and Thomas W. Johnson, "The Teaching of Behavioral Sciences in the Family Medicine Residency Programs in Canada and in the United States," *Social Science and Medicine,* 8 (December, 1974), 656–574; Margot Jefferys, "Social Science and Medical Education in Britain: A Sociologic Analysis of Their Relationship,"

Another need in medical education that has been identified is how to accommodate the increased demand for admission to medical schools by female and minority students who have not had an equal opportunity due to biased admission procedures, restrictive institutional policies, and individual prejudice, as well as more ubiquitous socioeconomic factors. Throughout their history in the United States and especially during the last 100 years, medical education and medicine have been elitist occupations dominated by white males, even though a few women and nonwhites have left their mark on American medicine.[92] Nonetheless, admission to medical schools of significant numbers of female and minority students had to wait on the repercussions of the women's liberation and the civil rights movements, increased availability of scholarship money, and other forms of subsidy for medical schools. From 1970 to 1974, the percentage of women admitted to medical schools rose from 11 to 22 percent. During this same period, the proportion of students from minority groups who were admitted rose from 9 to 12 percent. Both proportions declined slightly in 1975[93] as did the amount of money available for student support. These trends raise interesting sociological questions about their effects on changing admission standards, on the socialization process in medical schools, on career plans, and on meeting the health needs of the population through reorganization of medical practice.[94] Answers to these questions will have to wait for further research.

## SUMMARY

In this chapter we have covered a lot of material related to the professionalization of medicine. It was noted that most professions have in common the characteristics of (1) an extensive body of theoretical knowledge, (2) an orientation toward providing a highly specialized service for others, (3) a collegial organization to govern the professional practitioners, and (4) a license and mandate to perform professional activities. The implications and some correlates of each of these characteristics of the profession were discussed.

*International Journal of Health Services,* 4 (Summer, 1974), 549–563; Robert Cohen and Merrijoy Kelner, "Teaching Behavioural Science in Medical Schools: Some Current Issues," *Social Science and Medicine,* 10 (January, 1976), 23–27; and Rodney M. Coe, "Teaching Behavioral Sciences in Schools of Medicine: Observations on Some Latin-American Schools," *Social Science and Medicine,* 9 (April–May, 1975), 221–225.

[92]John Duffy, *The Healers: The Rise of the Medical Establishment,* New York: McGraw-Hill, 1976, especially chap. 18.

[93]"Datagram," *Journal of Medical Education,* 50 (December, 1975), 1134–1136.

[94]James L. Curtis, *Blacks, Medical Schools and Society,* Ann Arbor: University of Michigan Press, 1971.

The acknowledgment of these characteristics of a profession raises the question of how professional people acquire the necessary skills and the attitudes which distinguish them from workers in other occupations. The answer was found in discussion of the process of professional socialization—in this case, the institutional arrangements wherein medical education takes place. A review of current research indicated that there is a two-way selection process initially in which people with certain kinds of traits choose medicine as a likely career (and where they want to pursue it) and faculty members choose their students from the annual list of applicants. The process of selection in both cases involved regularly occurring phenomena which apparently are undergoing some changes.

In the context of medical school training, students not only acquire knowledge and skills but apparently begin to learn certain attitudes and values, such as detached concern, which will have functional significance later in their careers. Although there is some controversy over exactly what attitudes and values are learned in medical school, there seems to be little doubt that during postgraduate training, physicians learn to be competent and polished performers of their professional calling.

**SUGGESTED READINGS**

Becker, Howard S., Blanche Geer, Everett C. Hughes, and Anselm Strauss, *Boys in White,* Chicago: University of Chicago Press, 1961.

Bloom, Samuel W., "The Sociology of Medical Education: Some Comments on the State of a Field," *Milbank Memorial Fund Quarterly,* 43 (April, 1965), 143–184.

Doctor X, *Intern,* New York: Harper & Row, 1965.

Evans, Lester J., *The Crisis in Medical Education,* Ann Arbor: University of Michigan Press, 1964.

Merton, Robert K., George G. Reader, and Patricia Kendall, *The Student Physician,* Cambridge Mass.: Harvard University Press, 1957.

# Chapter 8

# Other Practitioners of the Healing Arts

*You cannot educate a man wholly out of the superstitious fears which were implanted in his imagination, no matter how utterly his reason may reject them.*

Oliver Wendell Holmes

In the previous two chapters, we have noted the development of the role of the medical doctor in the contexts of the growth of the medical profession and the processes of medical education. The present chapter is concerned with other practitioners who also offer therapeutic services to the sick person. Generally speaking, these practitioners may be described as "doctor alternates" or "doctor assistants," depending upon whether the practitioner provides care as an independent substitute for or as an extension and under the supervision of an orthodox physician. Even this simple dichotomy is not completely satisfactory, as some doctor-assistant roles like nursing have moved toward becoming doctor alternate roles and some therapeutic roles like dentistry do not fit well in either category. Some traditional doctor alternates, such as osteopaths, however, can provide essentially the same general care, in both kind and quality. Others, such as chiropractors, also provide treatments, but generally for more limited health problems and not always the same-quality treatment. Moreover, doctor-alternate roles have emerged, in part, as an attempt to claim the prestige and status attributed to the modern orthodox practitioner, although initially they represented competing theories of disease causation at a time when orthodox medicine was unable to deal competently with disease. At the present time, the relatively high cost and maldistribution of the services of medical doctors still contribute to the use of doctor alternates. Since medical services, especially those provided by highly specialized physicians, tend to be concentrated in urban areas, many rural areas and small communities must do without them, and this gap in services may be partially filled by doctor alternates.

Doctor assistants, particularly when viewed in the context of nursing, have been seen as helpers of, but not as alternatives to, the physician. In fact, nurses have been referred to as "handmaidens to the doctors," a term which describes not only their subordinate status but their sex identification as well. Even here, however, several developments have led to marked changes in the occupational status of doctor assistants. In anticipation of a fuller discussion below, we may note first that increased technology has led to increased differentiation of occupational roles in nursing just as it did in medicine. Nurse clinicians, nurse midwives, and nurse anesthetists are examples. Second, as nursing tasks became more specialized, there was a reassignment of new nursing duties. Some tasks, such as taking a patient's temperature, were once the responsibility of the physician, then of the nurse as physicians went on to more complicated duties. Now nursing aides perform this task as nurses go on to more complicated tasks. Third, some tasks were delegated not downward to others lower in the nursing hierarchy, but laterally, which led to development of nonnursing health care specialists or allied health personnel.[1] These might include laboratory technicians, ward clerks, medical record librarians, dietitians, medical social workers, and so on. Finally, the movement for professional recognition of nursing may be seen as movement from the status of doctor assistant to doctor alternate.

To be sure, each of the roles of other practitioners is somewhat unique—in development, in objectives, in practices. They all have in common, however, a movement to claim professional status, to take on more of the characteristics of their role model, the medical doctor. Thus, one way of discussing the roles of other practitioners is by looking at the

[1]Hans O. Mauksch, "Nursing: Churning for Change," in Howard E. Freeman, Sol Levine, and Leo G. Reeder (eds.), *Handbook of Medical Sociology,* 2d ed., Englewood Cliffs, N.J.: Prentice-Hall, 1972, pp. 206–230.

degree to which each has become "professionalized," that is, by evaluating the degree to which doctor alternates meet the sociological criteria of a profession.

In Chapter 7, it was stated that the criteria for professional status are the following. First, it has a body of specialized, theoretical knowledge the acquisition of which requires extended training. This knowledge is developed for its own sake as well as for application to practice. Secondly, a profession has a service orientation; that is, the work of a profession consists of offering highly technical, specialized services for public consumption. Presumably, the motivation behind this service is altruistic rather than economic. Thirdly, a profession has a collegial rather than bureaucratic organization. The members of the profession take responsibility for policing their own behavior and for establishing a code of ethics to protect their clients as well as themselves. Finally, professionals not only have a license to offer their services, but they have a mandate as well.[2] By license is meant that professionals have a legally recognized right to offer their services, and by mandate is meant that they can also set goals for the public with respect to their services and dictate the conditions under which their services can be offered. Although licensing procedures may be controlled or under the supervision of state or federal agencies, even here professionals are usually accountable only to their peers because most of the examining boards for various professions are staffed by members of that profession.

All these characteristics relate to the concept of autonomy—control over all aspects of work—which is the critical dimension that differentiates professionalized occupations from those that have not achieved that status. Professionals thus receive general acceptance by the public, which is seldom able to evaluate their technical competence. Along with this general acceptance come generally high rewards in the form of income, status, and prestige.[3]

## DOCTOR ALTERNATES

### Osteopathy: An Emerging Profession

In some ways, the development of osteopathy has paralleled that of medicine, and at the present time, it is the least different doctor-alternate role. However, in the late nineteenth century, it began as a cult, a pseudoscientific approach to healing. Like other cults, it proposed one cause for all disease and illness—in this case, a dislocation of one or more small bones

[2]Everett C. Hughes, *Men and Their Work,* New York: Free Press, 1958.
[3]Talcott Parsons, "The Professions and Social Structure," in *Essays in Sociological Theory,* New York: Free Press, 1954, pp. 34–49.

in the spinal column—and prescribed only one cure, manipulation or relocation of the disturbed bony structure. In the ensuing years from its founding in 1874 until 1953, osteopathy was viewed by the medical profession as quack medicine and treated accordingly. Since 1953, however, a reassessment of the training and skills of osteopaths has shown that contemporary osteopathy has been placed on a scientific basis to a degree that some state medical societies, California, for example, now recognize osteopaths as scientific healers, include them in a medical school faculty and in their referral system, and otherwise treat them more or less as equals.[4]

Osteopathy had its beginning in Kirksville, Missouri, when its founder, Andrew Taylor Still, had a "divine revelation" from which he developed the theory that disease was caused by a dislocation of one or more vertebrae. However, an essential part of Still's application of manipulation was that "God had placed a remedy for every disease within the house in which the spirit of life dwells," and that there must be a substantial faith in divine power for healing.[5] Like other healing cults, reliance was mostly on *vis medicatrix naturae,* the body's ability to heal itself. The number of cases in which Still effected a "cure" was substantial; some were dramatic, but all "confirmed" the underlying theory. For a time, osteopaths prospered and their numbers grew. After the Flexner report in 1910, however, the sharp contrast between the improved training of physicians and the traditional, although expanded, training of osteopaths revealed more clearly the inadequacies of the latter.

Gradually, the new concepts were introduced into the schools of osteopathy; new forms of treatment, such as hydrotherapy, electrotherapy, and even drugs, were added to manipulation. There was, as New states, a change from "osteopathic manipulation to osteopathic medicine."[6] Course work in medical subjects and in surgery was added to the curriculum along with extended training in internships and residencies. Along with the improved and increased academic and laboratory training, osteopathic students are exposed to a new ideology which holds that they are "as good as anybody" (meaning doctors of medicine) and that "osteopathy is not a deviance from, but a 'specialty of' medicine."[7] A consequence of these changes has been formal recognition by some state medical societies, like California, and finally national recognition by the American Medical Association.[8]

[4]Report of the Committee for the Study of the Relations between Osteopathy and Medicine, *Journal of the American Medical Association,* 152 (June 20, 1953), 734–739.

[5]Morris Fishbein, *The Medical Follies,* New York: Boni and Liveright, 1925, p. 46.

[6]Peter Kong-ming New, "The Osteopathic Student: A Study in Dilemma," in E. Gartly Jaco (ed.), *Patients, Physicians and Illness,* New York: Free Press, 1958, pp. 413–421.

[7]*Ibid.,* p. 414.

[8]See Report of the Committee for the Study of Relations between Osteopathy and Medicine, *Journal of the American Medical Association,* 158 (July 2, 1959), 736–741.

When osteopathy is viewed from a historical perspective, it is at once clear that in the beginning osteopathy was not a profession by the criteria outlined above. In the first place, although osteopathy did have a body of specialized knowledge, neither the theory nor the therapy derived therefrom could be scientifically demonstrated to be true. The amount of training required to obtain a degree was minimal. It is mostly for this reason that organized medicine withheld its recognition from osteopathy as a healing science. However, osteopathy, in theory and practice, now differs little from medicine; i.e., it has been placed on a scientific basis, and training appears to be adequate with the result that osteopaths are beginning to take on the characteristics of professionals. Second, osteopaths have demonstrated a service orientation. Increasingly, the profession has sought to assure that its members develop and maintain a high level of skill and has been instrumental in developing centers, such as osteopathic hospitals, where these services could be made available to all. However, in the early history of osteopathy it is questionable whether service or financial remuneration of the practitioner was the primary motive for engaging in practice. At the present time, the code of ethics is similar to the physicians' and removes that doubt. A third change is the way in which osteopaths have organized themselves. At first they were neither bureaucratically nor collegially organized, but rather each practitioner worked alone. Eventually, under the auspices of the American Osteopathic Association, a collegial organization was devised, although the right to practice remained the prerogative of state and federal licensing agencies. Finally by virtue of its scientific basis, osteopathic medicine is being associated with the mandate of medicine at large.

One consequence of the emergence of an occupational group into professional standing is the dilemma currently facing osteopathy. To obtain public acceptance, a profession must, among other things, be able to legitimize its own existence through performing certain functions which characterize its uniqueness. In some cases, however, this very uniqueness or individuality may prevent the acceptance by the public, which has been conditioned to some other professional groups which perform similar functions. Thus, to obtain public recognition, osteopaths must give up some of their uniqueness, namely, manipulation. In doing so, they risk becoming merged with allopathic medicine, but in a minority status. Under these conditions, a dilemma poses itself. Osteopaths must decide whether they wish to remain associated with somewhat unique practices and thereby maintain their individual identity but run the risk of being seen as "second-class practitioners," or they can relinquish their individual identity and attempt to be fully accepted not only by the public but also by the already established medical profession. This suggests the problem of unqualified acceptance by professional practitioners already in the field. Although osteopathy has enjoyed increased status and recognition from the public, acceptance from the medical profession has not been everywhere whole-hearted.[9] In any case, it appears that osteopathy has become a full-fledged healing profession with all the rights and obligations, but at a cost of its individual uniqueness.

### Chiropractic: A Professional Pretender

A little more than twenty years after Andrew Still began the practice of osteopathy, another cult emerged, namely chiropractic. In 1895 in Daven-port, Iowa, B. J. Palmer, son of the founder, began an intensive campaign to establish the practice of chiropractic. It has never been established whether the basic theory of chiropractic was developed independently of osteopathy as claimed by Palmer or "stolen" from it as claimed by oth-ers.[10] In any case, it is difficult to distinguish between the original theories of osteopathy and chiropractic. Basically, chiropractic theory holds that all diseases result from dislocated bones in the spinal column. The cure, of course, is to manipulate these bones until pressure is removed from the nerves. This theory is of questionable scientific validity, and for this reason, chiropractic has been vigorously attacked by modern medicine.

In the beginning the Palmer School of Chiropractic grew rapidly. There were no entrance requirements, not even a literacy test; no laboratory work; and no clinical training. The only requirement was a series of lectures spread over one year and, of course, payment of tuition. Included in the course of instruction were lessons on salesmanship, since from the incep-tion of chiropractic, chiropractors have had to "sell" their art to the public. With the revolution in medical schools following the Flexner report, chiro-practic practice came under closer scrutiny with the consequence that states began developing licensing laws to regulate this practice and to restrict it to manipulation. In most states, chiropractors are forbidden to engage in major surgery or obstetrics or to prescribe drugs. In four states, they are not allowed to practice at all.[11] At the present time, the status of chiropractors has somewhat improved, but it remains considerably lower than that of organized medicine. Contemporary schools of chiropractic require about three years' training or about 3,600 hours of instruction, although internships are not usually required. Moreover, many states now require that chiropractors pass the Basic Science Examination of the National Board of Medical Examiners. Wardwell has pointed out that although more chiropractors fail the exam than any other medical group, the number of chiropractors who fail the exam is decreasing.[12]

[9]New, op.cit., p. 416.
[10]Fishbein, op. cit.
[11]Walter I. Wardwell, "A Marginal Professional Role: The Chiropractor," in Jaco, op. cit., pp. 421–433.
[12]Ibid., p. 424.

The organization of contemporary chiropractic practice is somewhat tenuous. In part this is due to the ideological differences between the National Chiropractic Association and the International Chiropractic Association. The former advocates expanding practice to include other kinds of therapy, such as heat, light, and water, much as osteopaths did during their drive for professional recognition. The ICA, on the other hand, believes such innovations will dilute the theoretical uniqueness of chiropractic and adheres to a policy of limiting treatment to manipulation.[13] Another source of weakness lies in the fact that most chiropractors engage in solo practice or at best in partnership with another family member. As a consequence, chiropractors compete with each other for clients; there is no established referral system, and their practice is largely under client control. Thus, chiropractors may be vulnerable to patients' demands for services which are not medically indicated or which are beyond the practitioners' level of skills, and they must attempt to supply these services or risk "losing" their patients to other practitioners.[14] In addition, chiropractors have less control over who is admited to practice than do other practitioners. Licensing standards, prohibitions on certain therapies, etc., are more closely controlled by state agencies.

It is apparent from this brief description that chiropractors do not meet the generally accepted criteria for making claims to be a profession. Although in a narrow sense there is a codified body of knowledge, most of it has not been scientifically demonstrated to be accurate. Open to more serious question, however, is the service orientation of many chiropractors (and some of the other practitioners as well). In view of the fact that chiropractic is often seen as a means of upward social mobility, as a way of improving one's status, it seems unlikely that the service motive could be very strong. Similarly, although there is a recognized national association to which most chiropractors belong, it does not exercise the same professional control over its members as does the AMA or AOA. Moreover, the collegial relationships which are crucial to the organization of medicine and osteopathy are absent among chiropractors; rather, they are in competition with each other. Finally, chiropractors can obtain licenses in most states, but in only a few is the licensing decision in the hands of other chiropractors. More importantly, chiropractors do not have a mandate in the sense that we are using it here. That is, they are unable to prescribe the health goals to which the public should aspire or the conditions under which their practice will be conducted. In fact, as was pointed out earlier, chiropractors have to sell the patient on their medical abilities.

[13]New, *op. cit.*
[14]See Eliot Freidson, *Patients' Views of Medical Practice,* New York: Russell Sage, 1961.

Although it can be argued, as we have, that chiropractic does not meet the criteria of a profession, it cannot be concluded that chiropractors serve no useful purpose to the public. Frequently manipulation is the appropriate therapy for ailments such as lower sacroiliac pains. That is, both orthodox physicians and chiropractors might prescribe the same treatment, but they would do so for entirely different theoretical reasons. More importantly, chiropractors have often effectively treated psychosomatic illnesses in patients who were ineffectively handled by a physician. Koos's study of the health patterns of patients in a small New York town showed that about one-third of the illnesses (mostly among lower-class patients) that had first been treated by physicians were then treated by "nonmedical" personnel (mostly chiropractors). The reasons given by respondents who followed this pattern related mostly to dissatisfaction with the physician's treatment because "treatment was unsuccessful," "the physician was uninterested in the case," or "the physician could find nothing wrong with the patient." Also mentioned was the potential cost of treatment, such as recommended surgery, hospitalization, or "too expensive medicine."[15]

The explanation for this pattern probably lies in characteristics of the patient-physician relationship. It should be recalled that affective neutrality, or as Fox put it, "detached concern,"[16] is necessary to enable the therapist to make observations, arrive at a correct diagnosis, prescribe effective treatment, and do so in an objective manner. This reflects the orientation to scientific practice of medicine. Chiropractors, on the other hand, not only do not adhere to scientific explanation of disease, but are in a position necessitating that they sell chiropractic (and themselves) to the patient. In other words, they cannot afford to be affectively neutral toward the patient, but, on the contrary, they must be sympathetic and solicitous. This approach to the patient-therapist relationship would certainly appeal to patients whose problems were psychosomatic and who felt, as did some of Koos's respondents, that the "physician wasn't interested in *their* case" or that the physician "could find nothing wrong."

One consequence of having to sell one's abilities to others is the frequent temptation to exaggerate the potential effectiveness of the product. In this regard, some chiropractors continually flirt with the very ill-defined line separating acceptable chiropractic practice and quackery. For the first time in the history of medical practices in the United States, in 1963 a chiropractor was charged with murder of a young patient who died, not directly from his treatments but because his influence (it is alleged) prohibited the patient from obtaining treatment recommended by a physician

[15]Earl L. Koos, *The Health of Regionville,* New York: Columbia University Press, 1954, especially pp. 104–111.

[16]Renee Fox, *Experiment Perilous,* New York: Free Press, 1959.

which might have saved her life.[17] It is to the discussion of the pseudopractitioner, the medical quack, that we now turn.

### Fraudulent Practitioners: The Medical Quack

It is customary to define a quack, short for quacksalver, as "an ignorant or fraudulent pretender to medical skill, one who pretends professionally or publicly to skill, knowledge, or qualifications he does not possess: a charlatan."[18] In the sense of this definition, there have been fraudulent practitioners as long as there have been orthodox ones, although it is presumably easier to distinguish one from the other now than it was fifty or a hundred years ago. To a certain degree, the progress in medicine makes quacks of legitimate practitioners of an earlier era because increased knowledge alters the basis of medical practice. For example, one of the historically great American physicians, Benjamin Rush (1745–1813), engaged in practices of bloodletting, cupping, and vigorous purgatives in treating his patients. By today's standards, Rush would be defined as a quack and a threat to the lives of his patients. But even while recognized practitioners, such as Rush and those who followed him, were engaging in historically outmoded practices, there were others who then practiced what we have defined as fraudulent medicine.

A French contemporary of Rush was Franz Anton Mesmer. Although today his name is associated with hypnotism (to mesmerize someone), he was better known for his theory and practice of animal magnetism. Mesmer believed that the body contained a gaseous substance which could be manipulated by the human will. His "therapeutic" agents included iron bars in a tub of water around which patients stood while holding on to the bars. While patients were silent, the perfumed room was filled with music played by a hidden orchestra. Mesmer would appear in a costume and pass among the patients touching them with a metal wand and "fixing them with his eyes," thus redistributing the gaseous substance in a more "healthful" manner.[19]

A somewhat more difficult case to judge is that of Elisha Perkins, an American contemporary of Rush. Perkins was an orthodox physician, trained and duly licensed to practice in Connecticut in the last decade of the eighteenth century. At one point in his career, however, he noted that muscles would contract when they came in contact with metal instruments during surgery. From this he developed a theory that diseases could be drawn from the body by metallic "tractors," a pincerlike instrument made of iron and brass. The instrument was placed on or near the ailing part of the body and when removed, "drew" out the disease with it. With his

[17]"Crackdown on Quackery," *Life,* 55 (Nov. 1, 1963), 72–83.
[18]*American College Dictionary,* New York: Harper & Row, 1948.
[19]Louis Lasagna, *The Doctors' Dilemma,* New York: Harper & Row, 1962.

tractors, Perkins had many successful "cures" and received many testi-monials as to their therapeutic efficacy. Eventually, Perkins was expelled from the Connecticut Medical Society and died in 1799 from yellow fever which his tractors could not cure.[20]

One could, perhaps, take the view that Mesmer, Perkins, Andrew Still, B. J. Palmer, and others were not really quacks because medical science was in such a rudimentary state that their efforts were no less innovations than the work of Pasteur and Koch. By the end of the nineteenth century, however, painstaking research and experimentation had placed medicine on a firm scientific basis, and tolerance for acceptance of unorthodox practices was severely curtailed. These practices nonetheless flourished. One of the notables in American quackery was Hercules Sanche, who patented the Oxydonor in 1892. Originally called the Electropoise, the Oxydonor was a hollow metal cylinder from which protruded wires attached to a disc. The cylinder was placed in ordinary water and the disc attached to the wrist or ankle of the user. From this device, the user received "oxygen" to revitalize organs and improve health. A series of improvements (in both complexity and price) resulted in an instrument to "cure all fevers, including Yellow Fever, in a few hours and all other forms of disease."[21] Following the passage of the first Pure Food and Drug Act in 1906, enforcement agencies including the Post Office Department failed to put Sanche out of business permanently. As late as 1952, Sanche was believed to be operating a Hydrotonics, Incorporated, business in Florida.[22]

Perhaps the heights (or depths) to which fraudulent medicine can go are illustrated in the case of Albert Abrams. About 1910, Abrams, who like Perkins was a licensed physician, initiated his departure from orthodox medical practice with what he called spondylotherapy which was very similar to osteopathy and chiropractic in theory and practice. Later he developed E.R.A., Electronic Reactions of Dr. Abrams, a diagnostic sys-tem whereby he would identify disease, sex, race, and even religious preference from a drop of blood (or an autograph) of a patient who did not even need to be present.[23] Until the mid-1920s Abrams and his 3,500 or so disciples took thousands of dollars each week from patients who flocked to their doors seeking quick cures. Abrams' stature as a recognized quack is indicated by his obituary notice in the *Journal of the American Medical Association,* which stated that Abrams was "easily ranked as the dean of all twentieth century charlatans."[24]

[20]Fishbein, *op. cit.,* pp. 16–26.
[21]Stewart H. Holbrook, *The Golden Age of Quackery,* New York: Macmillan, 1959, p. 124.
[22]*Ibid.,* p. 128.
[23]*Ibid.,* p. 130.
[24]*Ibid.,* p. 129.

It is easy, when talking about illustrious quacks in the past, to view fraudulent medicine in terms of the stereotype of the medicine show and the smooth-talking purveyor of bottled elixirs. However, fraudulent medical practices are not a thing of the past but a thing of the present, and if anything, they are today more common and certainly more expensive. For example, it is conservatively estimated that over one billion dollars is spent annually by United States citizens for dubious cures of various sorts. About one-half of this is spent for "health foods," nutritional nostrums, and pills. Another 250 million is spent on worthless cures for arthritis and rheumatism. Cancer victims spend another 50 million each year.[25] Most of this money goes to practitioners who sell these devices and nostrums through the mail (although this method is continually scrutinized by the U.S. Postal Service). A more difficult kind of quackery to control is the house-to-house salesman or, as the AMA calls them, "doorstep diagnosticians." It is difficult to obtain a court conviction against these purveyors unless one has a witness or tape recorder present. Other media for disseminating fake medicines and cures are through "health lectures," which urge people to buy certain products, and "clinics" in which people are fraudulently and quickly separated from their money. Regardless of the means of contact, quacks have several common characteristics. They usually have some secret formula or machine; they will promise quick and complete cures for almost any disease (although some quacks "specialize"); they advertise by means of testimonials from satisfied previous users, some of whom may be nationally known figures; they often claim they are persecuted by organized medicine because of competition and invite impartial investigation; and they claim that their product is superior to widely recognized diagnostic and therapeutic means such as surgery or x-ray. However the selling line is promulgated, the intent is always the same: to bilk the victims of their money.

There are three major areas of quackery: foods and nutrition, mechanical and electrical devices, and drugs and cosmetics. Probably the most widespread, costly form of quackery is in the area of foods and nutrition. For the most part, quacks depend upon lack of knowledge of the consumers to convince them of erroneous conceptions of the relationship of nutrition to health in order to sell their products. In this they are abetted by folklore which remains with us, but cloaked in scientific terminology, and by false or misleading claims. For example, some quacks do a brisk business in selling "tonics" containing ordinary sea water described as containing "mineral nutrients" vital to health. The next step is to claim that these tonics will cure almost any disease.[26] Moreover, statements on the relation-

    [25]George P. Lerrick, "Report on Quackery from the FDA," *Proceedings of the National Congress on Medical Quackery,* Chicago: American Medical Association, 1961.
    [26]Frederick J. Stare, "Nutritional Quackery," *ibid.,* p. 67.

ship between disease and nutrition can be found in many publications on health foods. For example:

> Low calorie, high protein diet lessens the chances of cancer ever attacking you.
> Children are completely free from colds if they don't get the butterfat in whole milk or cream.
> The use of white sugar and white flour products . . . place[s] a strain on the heart, liver and other vital organs and glands.[27]

Much of the use of health foods is harmless or at worst only expensive without any benefit. It is harmful, however, to the extent that persons have nutritional needs that go unmet because medically prescribed regimens are forsaken for health diets. The use of "special" foods to cure diseases often leads to unneccessary and sometimes fatal delays in seeking orthodox medical advice. This point was recently made in testimony before the Senate Special Committee on Aging:

> Nutrition quackery, frauds and faddism without question exist in this country. Americans each year are spending hundreds of millions of dollars on pills, powders, capsules and compounds in search of shortcuts to health. In many instances the result is only economic waste; in others, it can have serious health consequences. People are urged to eat such combinations as cod liver oil and orange juice to cure arthritis, or safflower oil capsules to treat obesity and cardiovascular disease. Belief in such nonsense obviously can delay proper medical attention.[28]

Several classic examples of mechanical and electrical devices such as Perkins's tractors or Sanche's Oxydonor have already been described. At the present time there is a bewildering variety of these devices on the market ranging from a "virilium tube"—a matchstick-sized cylinder supposedly containing a cure for arthritis and selling for 300 dollars—to abandoned uranium mines in which victims pay 10 dollars per day to sit and absorb "healing radiations."[29] In California, Mrs. Ruth Drown was arrested on charges of grand theft. Over several years, she had diagnosed and treated some 35,000 patients and taken in more than 500,000 dollars. Her technique involved having her victims place their feet on the foot pads of her machine which "read" body vibrations. In one case, she told a patient (who had removed his feet from the foot pads when she was not

[27]*Ibid.*, pp. 67–68.
[28]Robert E. Shank, *Hearings before the Special Committee on Aging*, part 1, Washington, D.C.: Government Printing Office, 1963, p. 36.
[29]Public Affairs Committee, *The Arthritis Hoax: $250,000,000 in Frauds and Fallacies*, Public Affairs Pamphlet 297, 1960.

looking) that he had "aluminum poisoning, an infected small intestine and a floating kidney."[30]

The modern equivalent of patent medicine shows and the traveling medicine man is found in drug and cosmetic quackery. People are urged to buy various potions, balms, salves, ointments, and pills which will accomplish anything from removing wrinkles from an aging face, thus restoring youth and beauty, to growing new hair on a bald head, thus restoring sexual potency, to curing cancer and heart disease. Although the public annually spends over one billion dollars for over-the-counter drugs and other patent medicine, most of these are legitimate, tested compounds which will do what the label claims. It is the wide range of untested, privately produced drugs that is of concern here. Enforcement of statutes is difficult because the burden of proof of false claims is on the government; tests of drugs and trials of accused purveyors are time-consuming and costly. Moreover, enforcement agencies such as the Food and Drug Administration, the Federal Trade Commission, the Postal Service, and the Justice Department are chronically shorthanded. For example, it has been reported by Stare that

> One firm which was engaged in promoting a shotgun formula of vitamins combined in a "secret" base of alfalfa, parsley and watercress employed an estimated 15,000 full and part-time canvassers. This army of doorbell ringers is about seven times the size of the entire Food and Drug Administration's current staff of which only eight individuals are assigned to protect the customer from nutritional nonsense.[31]

This brief sketch of the areas of quackery would suggest that the practice of quackery is widespread and very costly to the public, both in terms of cash outlay for worthless cures and in tax money used to investigate and successfully prosecute violators of federal and state statutes. In regard to health, the various nostrums and devices can do no good at best, but may in fact be harmful to the victim's health. In some instances, this is due to harmful or impure substances in the fake medicine itself. More often, the use of such materials serves to delay the victim from obtaining legitimate medical attention. In the case of patients with cancer, this delay could be fatal.[32]

In view of the knowledge already available about quacks, their modes of operation, and their inability to produce medically reliable results, it is legitimate to ask why people continue to purchase their services. To a certain extent, the answer involves the medical profession itself. In the first

[30]"Crackdown on Quackery," p. 79.
[31]Stare, *op. cit.,* pp. 66–67.
[32]For a widely publicized case see "Crackdown on Quackery."

place, there are certain diseases for which orthodox medicine has not discovered the cause, much less a cure. These are notably the chronic diseases such as cancer, some forms of heart disease, arthritis, rheumatism, and some metabolic disorders. Current literature suggests the quacks no longer provide remedies for smallpox, tuberculosis, or other communicable diseases for which cures and means of prevention have been developed. Rather, the bulk of their business lies in selling treatments for the chronic debilitating diseases. Secondly, we have already noted that in the development of orthodox medicine, increased specialization has resulted in "fractionation" of patient care; the practitioner's focus tends to be on the disease rather than on the patient so that the physician does not show a "personal" interest in the patient.[33]

However, the reasons for use of quacks do not lie entirely with changes in the medical profession. On the contrary, the principal reason lies in considerations of response to illness. From a psychiatric frame of reference, the "most basic and generic emotional source of vulnerability to quackery is some form of fear, even when this may be deeply hidden from the individual's own awareness and expressed in disguised and indirect forms. Fears of death and physical and mental incapacitation and weakness . . . are universally powerful motivators of human behavior."[34] The onset of a serious illness becomes a threat to survival; thus victims seek comfort and assistance from others, including the medical profession, in treating the disease. In such a situation, patients naturally want to feel that something is being actively done about their condition, and they are apt to grasp even at "straws" of hope.[35] Now if the situation of this anxious and fearful patient, confronted by a poor prognosis from an orthodox practitioner, is combined with the apparent sympathy and claims of a quick cure of the quack, the appeal of the latter can appear very attractive.[36]

Closely linked with fear are such factors as superstition, ignorance, and gullibility. Lack of education and ignorance of scientific medicine act both to deprive one of a means to assess the "claims" of quacks and to increase the probability of reliance on folk medical beliefs which, as noted above, are played upon and commercialized by these practitioners. When a phenomenon such as disease is not understood either as to cause or to consequences, fear and superstition could be a powerful stimulation to unorthodox health treatments. Moreover, people can be gullible without being superstitious or fearful. It has been pointed out that many people who

---

[33]Koos, *op. cit.*
[34]Viola W. Bernard, "Why People Become the Victims of Quackery," *Proceedings of the Second National Congress on Medical Quackery,* Chicago: American Medical Association, 1963.
[35]Beatrix Cobb, "Why Do People Detour to Quacks?" In Jaco, *op. cit.,* pp. 283–297.
[36]Bernard, *op. cit.*

fall prey to the "vitamin" sales pitch are those who consider themselves to be quite knowledgeable about health matters, even though their "knowledge" comes from Sunday supplements and promotional literature.[37]

These explanations do not account for the patronage of quacks by a third group of patients whom Cobb has called "the straw graspers."[38] Typically, these are relatively intelligent, knowledgeable persons to whom a legitimate physician has said that medical science has done all it can. The patients then "have nothing to lose" (except money) if they try special cures or treatments offered by quacks. A psychiatric interpretation of this situation would be that "the need to believe in a therapeutic miracle when medical science is or seems to be failing can be so strong that it drives one's intelligence into twisting the facts to fit emotional necessity."[39] Finally, frequent customers of quacks are people generally labeled as hypochondriacs and those suffering from psychosomatic disorders. These are patients who typically do not receive any satisfaction from the ministrations of a licensed practioner, who are especially sensitive to the "impersonal" treatment of many modern physicians, and who turn to other kinds of practitioners including quacks for the psychological responsiveness they seek. The full explanation of the successful operation of fraudulent practitioners involves these and perhaps some other factors not mentioned. Basically, the social-psychological factors which seem to be important suggest that quackery is the modern commercialized and hence distorted expression of folk medicine. Its viability depends, in large part, upon lack of knowledge, fear, superstition, and gullibility of its victims. However, the use of unorthodox practitioners seems to occur most often when patients are not only susceptible to these factors but are dissatisfied with the attempts by medical science to deal with their illness, whether real or imaginary.

## DOCTOR ASSISTANTS

The concept of doctor assistants includes personnel that have various names—physician assistant, physician associate, physician extender, and so on—and who are recruited from different occupations such as nursing, military corpsmen, and other health-related jobs. What all of them do, however, is provide a range of services to patients under orders from—if not always under direct supervision of—a physician or group of physicians. The role of doctor assistants has been influenced by many of the same

[37]William H. Gordon, "The Keys to Quackery," *Proceedings of the National Congress on Medical Quackery,* pp. 33–41.
[38]Cobb, *op. cit.,* p. 284.
[39]Bernard, *op. cit.,* p. 54.

factors that have affected the role of doctor alternates. Development of medical technology, growth of the health care industry in scope, increased demand for health services by consumers, and medicine's relative ineffectiveness in dealing with chronic diseases all have contributed to the emergence of occupational groups whose task is to carry out some part of the total health care process. For example, in 1900 there were two or three persons in health occupations for every physician. Today there are fourteen or fifteen health workers for every doctor.[40] In addition, the attractiveness of professional status as enjoyed by the medical profession has contributed to efforts by other occupational groups in the health care industry to achieve that same status. These changes have raised a number of sociologically interesting questions concerning the process of professional socialization, competition and cooperation among health occupations aspiring for professional recognition, role conflict, and evaluation of the effectiveness of non-physician practitioners. To examine these processes more closely, we shall look first at nursing and then at some issues in the development of allied health professions.

### Nursing

One occupational group which has traditionally been recognized as doctor assistants and which has long sought professional status is that of nursing. At the present time, however, it can be seen that the nursing occupation does not fully meet all the criteria of a profession noted above. For example, although nursing does share with medicine a specialized, theoretical body of knowledge which is applied in practice, this body of knowledge is usually given to the nurses in the form of "doctor's orders." Further, nursing does not always require an extended education; often only a few years of training beyond high-school. This contributes to some confusion in the term "nurse," since it has been used to identify nursing aides, practical nurses, and even registered nurses whose occupational status is the same despite the fact that they may be products of a two-year associate nursing program, a three-year diploma program, or a four-year baccalaureate program. Increasingly, however, nursing leaders are pushing for four-year baccalaureate programs and graduate study as a criterion for "professional" nursing.[41] Of all the characteristics of a profession, nursing probably comes closest to fulfilling that of a service orientation. Of course, nurses are compensated, but the nursing ideology underlying the motivation for engaging in this occupation reflects a strong humanitarian belief in

---

[40]Department of Health, Education, and Welfare, *The Supply of Health Manpower,* Washington, D.C.: Government Printing Office, 1974.

[41]George Psathas, *The Student Nurse,* New York: Springer, 1968. See also the panel discussion, "Can We Bring Order out of the Chaos of Nursing Education?" *American Journal of Nursing,* 76 (January, 1976), 98–107.

offering services to patients.[42] Most nurses work in hospitals and have been organized as a part of the administrative hierarchy of the hospital or institution in which they work. Under these circumstances, nurses do not fully have control over their occupational careers nor do they establish a code of ethics independent of that dictated by the medical profession or governmental regulations. Moreover, nurses are not given final responsibility for patients. This rests in the hands of the attending physician, who may delegate certain duties to the nurse, but who retains the final responsibility. Finally, while nurses have a license to practice their occupation, and some state legislatures have passed a nursing practice act that permits a greater degree of independence in practice, nurses have no public mandate for their practice despite the continuing efforts to achieve occupational autonomy by their national associations, the American Nursing Association and the National League of Nurses.

## Problems of Nursing as a Career

Nurses, like everyone else, play certain roles and perform certain tasks within the context of specific social situations. Unlike many occupations, however, the statuses associated with the nursing role involve considerable contradiction, much of which may prove to be intolerable to the role incumbent.[43] This does not deny that contradictions exist in other occupational roles, but the contradictions seem to be more acute at the present time in the field of nursing. The first contradiction of status stems from pressures within the nursing occupation to achieve recognition as a profession. Such pressures are found at practically every level: in the national organization, in the nursing administration of hospitals, and in nursing schools. In industrial societies, professional status is rewarded with high social prestige, substantial monetary rewards, deference, and respect. Nursing is treated by the public in much the same way as social work or elementary school teaching, for example—these rewards are not fully given. In part, the lack of public validation of the status claims of nursing stems from the perception that nursing does not have the same degree of occupational autonomy as medicine. Moreover, being a "female" occupation, nursing encounters a strong antifeminist bias.[44] Furthermore, recog-

[42]Carol A. Brown, "Women Workers in the Health Service Industry," *International Journal of Health Services,* 5 (Winter, 1975), 173–184.

[43]Everett C. Hughes, "Dilemmas and Contradictions in Status," *American Journal of Sociology,* 50 (March, 1945), 353–359. More recently see Barbara Bates, "Doctor and Nurse: Changing Roles and Relations," *New England Journal of Medicine,* 283 (July 16, 1970), 129–134; and by the same author, "Physician and Nurse: Conflict and Reward," *Annals of Internal Medicine,* 82 (May, 1975), 702–706.

[44]Brown, *op. cit.;* Kathleen Cannings and William Lazonick, "The Development of the Nursing Force in the United States: A Basic Analysis," *International Journal of Health Services,* 5 (Winter, 1975), 185–216. See also Leonard I. Stein, "The Doctor-Nurse Game," in Bonnie Bullough and Vern Bullough (eds.), *New Directions for Nurses,* New York: Springer, 1971, pp. 129–137.

nized professions such as medicine view the status claims of nursing as encroaching on their territory and likewise tend to recognize nursing as a full-fledged profession in policy, but not in practice.[45] Even though nursing education has increased the technical competence of nurses, this not only has brought conflict with the doctors with whom the increased competence overlaps, but also has increased communication difficulties by widening the knowledge gap between nurses and the nonprofessional help who work on the nursing units.[46]

A second contradiction in status lies in the conflict between various functions united in one position. This refers especially to pressures put on the hospital nurse to be the administrator for a unit and at the same time to perform nursing services for patients. Both are complicated and time-consuming tasks and frequently are mutually incompatible with respect to the allocation of the nurse's working time. In part, this contradiction arises from increased specialization of the nursing function and the development of the "team" concept. Traditionally, nursing has always been a part of hospital procedure, but only for about one hundred years has there been formalized training for nurses. Like most occupational groups, nursing from the outset has been organized in terms of the concept of "specification of function." All that pertained to care of the patient in the hospital was the concern and responsibility of nursing. Thus the earliest training school curriculum included topics ranging from bed making to ward administration. The goal of nursing education was to train students adequately to care for the "whole patient," and almost any threatened invasion of nurses' responsibilities was met with resistance even when it might offer relief from a heavy work load.

Stimulated by the severe personnel problems of World War II and by rapidly increasing costs, hospitals began to modify this historic, professionally oriented type of organization of nursing education. Since the end of World War II, patient care, like all other aspects of hospital functioning, has increasingly been rationalized in terms of the concept of "specialization of function." Licensed practical nurses, ward clerks, dietitians, attendants, nurse's aides, ward helpers, and others have in various degrees relieved the registered nurse of more traditional responsibilities. The assignment of nonnursing personnel to "nursing" tasks has been institutionalized in the team concept.[47] In this system, the registered nurse becomes captain of a team made up mostly of nonprofessional help. While the new role as

[45]See, for example, the AMA Committee on Nursing, "Medicine and Nursing in the 1970's: A Position Statement," *Journal of the American Medical Association,* 213 (September 14, 1970), 1881–1883, which calls for "constructive collaboration" between medicine and nursing.

[46]Bonnie Bullough, "Barriers to the Nurse Practitioner Movement: Problems of Women in a Woman's Field," *International Journal of Health Services,* 5 (Winter, 1975), 225–233.

[47]Saad Nagi, "Teamwork in Health Care in the U.S.: A Sociological Perspective," *Health and Society,* 53 (Winter, 1975), 75–91.

captain and coordinator brings status, it also effectively removes the nurse from direct participation in patient care. At this point, one can see the potential for frustration and ambivalence which is reinforced by the separation of nursing services and nursing education. In the first place, there is a discrepancy between nursing ideology and nursing practice, at least under the team concept. The traditional ideological orientation of service and loyalty to the patient and to nursing as a profession, much of which is fostered and learned in the nursing school, is expressed in the expectation graduates have of what nursing is like or at least what it "should be like." This diverges sharply from the realities of administrative duties and of coordinating and supervising the efforts of less skilled personnel found in actual practice. Secondly, the discrepancy between ideology and practice may begin very early in the nurse's budding career. It is not unusual for student nurses to be assigned duties on units as part of their educational program. Perhaps at first these duties are only peripherally related to direct patient care, but very quickly students experience the difference between stated philosophy and actual practice.[48]

A third discrepancy between ideology and practice lies in the rewards accruing from the administrative leadership tasks as opposed to basic nursing service to patients. Nursing ideology, anchored securely to the traditional practices when young women were recruited to provide basic nursing skills in hospitals, places high prestige and high value on the provision of these services even in the contemporary setting. In practice, however, the more tangible rewards such as increased salary and promotion to a more responsible position require contemporary nurses more often to supervise these activities performed by others while they attend to administrative duties. Similarly, many nurses move from nursing service to nursing education because tangible rewards are greater and opportunity for advancement is less limited. Surely one would expect nurses as much as anyone else to aspire to culturally approved goals of achievement and success. But as a means to these goals, nursing service offers little opportunity for advancement. On the other hand, a career in nursing education, while offering better opportunities, may also carry the nurse farther and farther away from the patient's bedside.

## Role Conflict

Related to the status contradictions noted above is the role conflict encountered by the nurse in the hospital social structure. We have already indicated that one of the channels of authority is through the bureaucratic line in which the nurse is subordinate to various levels in the hospital administration. As will be indicated in later chapters, there are certain

---

[48]Rozella M. Schlotfeldt, "Planning for Progress," *Nursing Outlook,* 21 (December, 1973), 766–769.

features of the hospital which have consequences for the expectations of incumbents of the nurse's role. For example, the hospital organization has certain goals which they strive to attain through an effective and efficient organization of duties. Other features of the hospital which tend to inhibit role attainment include a rigid stratification system, stereotyped communications, and established authority channels.[49] These structural features of the hospital organization engender certain kinds of expectations of the nurses including that they be efficient administrators, obedient subordinates, effective superordinates, and efficient and competent nurses. At the same time, nurses are subordinate to the physician whose patients are on their ward. The high status of the physician, however, lies outside the bureaucratic structure of the hospital and is based mostly on acknowledged preeminence in clinical judgment. In other words, the nurses are caught up in a role conflict between meeting the administrator's expectations of them as providers of administrative skills and the doctor's expectations of them as providers of nursing skills. Mitigation of this role conflict is often undermined by the fact that while urged on the one hand to be "professional" in their orientation to their duties, nurses are treated as employees, a nonprofessional attribute of an occupation.[50]

On the other hand, certain aspects of the traditional nurse's role, including ideological orientation, are provided by reference to the patient. Many hospital patients tend to see the nurse as a "mother surrogate" or "ministering angel."[51] This expectation derives partly from the public's stereotype of what a nurse is and does.[52] It stems also from the fact that hospital patients are often psychologically disadvantaged because of anxiety over illness and fear of the unknown, perhaps of death. Patients typically are separated from their usual sources of emotional support, mainly their families, and furthermore they tend to become egocentric in their views; that is, the whole world revolves around them and their

[49]Cf., Bullough, *op. cit.;* also Melvin Seeman and John W. Evans, "Stratification in Hospital Care: I. The Performance of the Medical Intern," *American Sociological Review,* 26 (February, 1961), 67–80; and "Stratification in Hospital Care: II. The Objective Criteria of Performance," *American Sociological Review,* 26 (April, 1961), 193-204. See also Albert F. Wessen, "Hospital Ideology and Communication between Ward Personnel," in Jaco, *op. cit.,* 448–468.

[50]Ronald G. Corwin, "The Professional Employee: A Study of Conflict in Nursing Roles," *American Journal of Sociology,* 66 (May, 1961), 604–615.

[51]Sam Schulman, "Basic Functional Roles in Nursing: Mother Surrogate and Healer," in Jaco, *op. cit.,* 528–537. A later analysis by Schulman showed that the mother-surrogate role had been abandoned by nurses. See "Mother Surrogate—After a Decade," in Jaco, *Patients, Physicians and Illness,* 2d ed., New York: Free Press, 1972, pp. 233–239.

[52]Irwin A. Deutscher, *Public Image of the Nurse,* Kansas City, Mo.: Community Studies, 1955. Furthermore, nursing personnel seem to prefer working in institutions where patients' definitions are more influential than the administrations' definitions of the nursing role. See Joseph A. Alutto and Lawrence J. Hrebiniak, "Variation in Hospital Employment and Influence on Perceptions among Nursing Personnel," *Journal of Health and Social Behavior,* 12 (March, 1971), 30–34.

illnesses.[53] Moreover, loss of status through accepting the sick role and loss of property given up when one enters the hospital only serve to intensify a psychological disenfranchisement.[54] When these expectations which the patient has for the nurses are contrasted with conflicting demands placed upon them by attending physicians and by the administration, it is not surprising that some studies have found that nurses become disillusioned and alienated from their chosen calling.

For example, in a sample of head nurses, graduate staff nurses, and students, Corwin and his colleagues found a progressive disillusionment among nurses as a result of the discrepancy between their expectations of their chosen occupation and the realities of working in it.[55] This interpretation was derived from the findings that (1) staff nurses held a significantly less favorable attitude toward nursing as a vocation than did student nurses; (2) job satisfaction was lower for staff nurses than satisfaction with educational experiences by students; (3) the level of success in one's position did not affect the degree of satisfaction for staff nurses, but it did for students; and (4) disillusionment was greater for the most successful personnel. In a similar study, Corwin showed that degree nurses are more frustrated in career aspirations than are diploma nurses.[56] This was in part due to the tendency of diploma nurses to identify with the local hospital connected with their school of nursing, while degree nurses identified more with the more abstract features of the nursing role and went beyond the local situation. In other words, degree nurses more often chose teaching as a career although they were oriented to performing service; hence the frustration was greater.[57]

Finally, the research findings of Pearlin are relevant here even though his investigation was conducted on a slightly different population, namely nursing personnel in a large mental hospital.[58] In this study, over 1,300 questionnaires completed by nursing personnel and over 150 supervisors'

[53]Henry D. Lederer, "How the Sick View Their World," in Jaco, *op. cit.*, 1st ed., 247–256. See also Daisy L. Tagliacozzo and Hans O. Mauksch, "The Patient's View of the Patient's Role," in Jaco, *op. cit.*, 2d ed., pp. 172–185.

[54]Erving Goffman, "Characteristics of Total Institutions," in *Symposium on Preventive and Social Psychiatry,* Washington, D.C.: Walter Reed Army Institute of Research, 1957, pp. 43–84.

[55]Ronald G. Corwin, Marvin J. Taves, and J. Eugene Haas, "Professional Disillusionment," *Nursing Research,* 10 (Summer, 1961), 141–144. See also Marlene Kramer, *Reality Shock: Why Nurses Leave Nursing,* St. Louis: Mosby, 1974.

[56]Ronald G. Corwin, "A Study of Identity in Nursing," *Sociological Quarterly,* 2 (April, 1961), 69–86. Nonetheless, the baccalaureate degree and graduate study are seen as the key to successful career mobility. See Mary A. Dineen, "Career Mobility and Baccalaureate Nursing Education," in Carrie B. Lenburg (ed.), *Open Learning and Career Mobility in Nursing,* St. Louis: Mosby, 1975, pp. 98–104.

[57]Cf. Leonard Reissman and John H. Rohrer, *Changes and Dilemma in the Nursing Profession,* New York: Putnam, 1957.

[58]Leonard I. Pearlin, "Alienation from Work: A Study of Nursing Personnel," *American Sociological Review,* 27 (June, 1962), 314–326.

reports were examined to assess the amount of alienation, defined as powerlessness to control one's own work activities, and the way certain hospital features bear on it. In general, it was found that (1) alienation grows with increasing disparity between hierarchical positions. This means that the farther the superordinate is from the subordinate in the hierarchy, the less often interaction takes place, especially interaction with any degree of spontaneity. Under these conditions, the subordinates' ability to influence the superordinate through interaction is decreased, causing a feeling of greater alienation. Concomitants of this finding include the way in which authority is exercised, e.g., *in absentia* or in a way such that any exchange between the superordinate and subordinate is discouraged. (2) Alienation increases with decreased opportunities for advancement. In this study, alienation was highest among those who were considered "limited achievers" and least among "high achievers" (only nonprofessional nursing personnel were considered). This reflected not only the slow rate at which they were advanced, but also the awareness of the nurses of how far they could go in the hierarchy. (3) Finally, alienation was found to be greater among workers cut off from interaction with peers such as personnel working in isolation wards or on the night shift.

These findings are applicable to nursing personnel in the general hospital also.[59] For example, physicians exercise authority on nursing units in a variety of ways, including leaving orders for the nurses, i.e., *in absentia;* also, orders are frequently communicated in such a way as to discourage any comment. Furthermore, it was noted above that increased technical training of nurses has had the effect of widening the hiatus between them and their subordinates, thus further increasing the potential for alienation among the subordinates. One of the characteristics of nursing service is lack of opportunities for advancement and recognition, which provides potential for alienation. Finally, while it is not likely that isolation from peers, except perhaps on the night shift, is as great in the general hospital as in the mental hospital, the reduced activity and lower number of personnel could have the same consequences.

### Emergence of New Nursing and Allied Health Practitioner Roles

These contradictions in status and related problems of nursing have led nursing leaders to seek ways to improve working conditions specifically and the professional status of the occupation in general. We have already noted the extension of length of training, the improvement in technical competence, and the quest for more responsibility and authority for nurses.

---

[59]The applicability of findings is not uniform, however, but varies by staff orientation and type of clientele. See George A. Miller, "Patient Knowledge and Nurse Role Strain in Three Hospital Settings," *Medical Care,* 14 (August, 1976), 662–673.

These efforts have merged with other trends that have resulted in the emergence of new roles for nurses and the development of other roles for allied health personnel, such as physical therapists, x-ray and laboratory technologists, occupational therapists, etc.[60] One of these trends is the perceived maldistribution, if not shortage, of physicians' services in the United States. A related phenomenon is the continued specialization of physicians. A third is the rising costs of a doctor's care. In other words, at a time when nursing was working hard to achieve full recognition as a professionalized occupation, a perception of a need for more (and better) medical services became most apparent. Thus, after some delay, nursing has taken a more active part in developing the role of the new practitioner.

The new practitioner roles were designed first to increase physician "productivity" through performing routine health care tasks, thus allowing physicians to concentrate more on tasks requiring higher levels of skill for which they were trained. Good examples include the nurse clinicians, whose diagnostic and treatment skills have been used in different settings,[61] for different age groups,[62] and for specific health care needs such as care of the chronically ill[63] and midwifery.[64]

[60]Alfred M. Sadler, "The New Health Practitioner in Primary Care," *Journal of Medical Education,* 49 (September, 1974), 845–848.

[61]The following reports illustrate the applicability of nurse clinicians in settings such as solo practice and general private practice: Jack L. Fairweather and R. N. Kifolo, "Improvement of Patient Care in a Solo Ob-Gyn Practice by Using an R.N. Physicians' Assistant," *American Journal of Public Health,* 62 (March, 1972), 361–363; and Joel H. Merenstein, Harvey Wolfe, and Kathleen M. Barker, "The Use of Nurse Practitioners in a General Practice," *Medical Care,* 12 (May, 1974), 445–452; in neighborhood health centers: Eleanor Brunetto and Peter Birk, "The Primary Care Nurse—The Generalist in a Structured Health Care Team," *American Journal of Public Health,* 62 (June, 1972), 785–794; in formal, group practices: Kay B. Partridge and Carol A. Mahr, "Nursing: A Neglected Dimension of the HMO Challenge," *Medical Care,* 11 (March–April, 1973), 162–167; and Donald M. Steinwachs, Sam Shapiro, Richard Yaffe, David M. Levine, and Henry Seidel, "The Role of New Health Practitioners in a Prepaid Group Practice: Changes in the Distribution of Ambulatory Care between Physician and Nonphysician Providers of Care," *Medical Care,* 14 (February, 1976), 95–120; and in the wider community: Clarence Skrovan, Elizabeth T. Anderson, and Janet Gottschalk, "Community Nurse Practitioner," *American Journal of Public Health,* 64 (September, 1974), 847–853.

[62]For adult medicine see, for example, Stephen L. Taller and Robert Feldman, "The Training and Utilization of Nurse Practitioners in Adult Health Appraisal," *Medical Care,* 12 (January, 1974), 40–48. Significant progress has been made in pediatrics as well. See Henry K. Silver and James A. Hecker, "The Pediatric Nurse Practitioner and the Child Health Associate: New Types of Health Professionals," *Journal of Medical Education,* 45 (March, 1970), 171–176; or Barbara Starfield and Elizabeth Sharp, "Ambulatory Pediatric Care: The Role of the Nurse," *Medical Care,* 6 (November–December, 1968), 507–515.

[63]Cf. Ralph H. Forrester and Charles L. Hill, "Improving Care of the Chronically Ill," *Hospitals,* 49 (January 16, 1975), 57–62, and Gerald H. Stein, "The Use of a Nurse Practitioner in the Management of Patients with Diabetes Mellitus," *Medical Care,* 12 (October, 1974), 885–890. Some problems in this role were identified in Robert Galton, Sidney M. Greenberg, and Sam Shapiro, "Observations on the Participation of Nurses and Physicians in Chronic Care," *Bulletin of the New York Academy of Medicine,* 49 (February, 1973), 112–119.

[64]Schuyler G. Kohl, Gregory Majzlin, Michael Burnhill, James Jones, George Solish,

A second objective of the new practitioner role is to join with the physician to form a health care team to provide comprehensive care.[65] In part, this is an extension of the effort to increase physician productivity, but it is also a response to the increased specialization of function, not only among doctors, but among the new practitioners as well.[66] As all practitioners narrow the scope of their technical activities, it takes more and more specialists to treat the "whole" patient. We have noted how nursing has taken over some of the tasks formerly performed by physicians. Now, as nursing services become more specialized, other roles have been created. Some of these tasks have been delegated downward to lower-ranking nursing personnel. Other tasks have been delegated "laterally" to others who also perform as allied health personnel and who bring unique but important skills to the health care team. Other physician extenders include those called physician assistants, whose training often includes experience as a military corpsman and who took additional training in basic and clinical sciences.[67] They often are found in small towns and rural areas where physicians are in short supply. Other members of the team, who provide special skills, are the clinical pharmacist[68] and the community health worker, usually someone indigenous to a neighborhood who takes special training to work as a health educator, case finder, and health advocate or ombudsman.[69]

It is of sociological interest to ask what have been the outcomes of the development of these new practitioner roles and what impact they have on the professionalization of health occupations. The literature reporting evaluations of the training and performance of nurses and allied health personnel is enormous and growing larger. Even a cursory sampling of studies, however, tends to support the need for and utility of these programs. In

Shirley Okrent, and Elaine Pendleton, "The Nurse-Midwife as a Family Planner," *American Journal of Public Health,* 62 (November, 1972), 1448–1450.

[65]Cf., for example, Jefferson J. Vorzimer and Ronald Winter, "Team Approach Yields Comprehensive Care," *Hospitals,* 46 (August 16, 1972), 61–66.

[66]Richard M. Scheffler and Olivia D. Stinson, "Characteristics of Physician's Assistants: A Focus on Specialty," *Medical Care,* 12 (December, 1974), 1019–1030.

[67]E. Harvey Estes and D. Robert Howard, "Potential for Newer Classes of Personnel: Experiences of the Duke Physician's Assistant Programs," *Journal of Medical Education,* 45 (March, 1970), 149–155.

[68]Lawrence S. Linn and Milton S. Davis, "Occupational Orientation and Overt Behavior—The Pharmacist as Drug Advisor to Patients," *American Journal of Public Health,* 63 (June, 1973), 502–508.

[69]See, for example, Richard T. Smith, "Health and Rehabilitation Manpower Strategy: New Careers and the Role of the Indigenous Paraprofessional," *Social Science and Medicine,* 7 (April, 1973), 281–290; Ralph W. Richter, Barbara Bengen, Peggy Alsup, Bertel Brunn, Margaret M. Kilcoyne, and Bernard D. Challenor, "The Community Health Worker: A Resource for Improved Health Care Delivery," *American Journal of Public Health,* 64 (November, 1974), 1056–1061; and E. J. Watson, "Meeting Community Health Needs: The Role of the Medical Assistant," *WHO Chronicle,* 30 (March, 1976), 91–96.

most areas considered important in health care delivery, new practitioners have performed well. Thus, quality of care by health practitioners is judged equal to that of physicians;[70] physician productivity can be increased;[71] nurse clinicians function better than physicians as health educators (although "organizational efficiency" is lower because they take more time);[72] allied personnel can be trained to perform the triage function (initial classification of patient needs and referral to proper treatment source);[73] and they perform technical functions well in community settings, although other problems of status and recognition do arise.[74] New practitioners, after a period of time, are accepted by patients[75] and by colleagues and physicians.[76]

There remain some unresolved issues in the development of these allied health occupations as they move toward professional recognition. One of these, of course, is the continued resistance of organized medicine to increased autonomy of new professionals, especially nurse practitioners,[77] although even here this resistance can be overcome in some specific situations.[78] On an industry-wide basis, however, none of the new practi-

[70]David M. Levine, Laura Morlock, Alvin I. Mushlin, Sam Shapiro, and Faye E. Malitz, "The Role of New Health Practitioners in a Prepaid Group Practice: Provider Differences in Process and Outcomes of Medical Care," *Medical Care,* 14 (April, 1976), 326–247.

[71]Alfred Yankauer, John P. Connelly, and Jacob J. Feldman, "Physician Productivity in the Delivery of Ambulatory Care: Some Findings from a Survey of Pediatricians," *Medical Care,* 8 (January–February, 1970), 35–46; and Geraldine Holmes, George Livingston, and Elizabeth Mills, "Contribution of a Nurse Clinician to Office Practice Productivity," *Health Services Research,* 11 (Spring, 1976), 21–33.

[72]Beverly C. Flynn, "The Effectiveness of Nurse Clinicians' Service Delivery," *American Journal of Public Health,* 64 (June, 1974), 604–611.

[73]David Paige, Edwardo Leonardo, Eve Roberts, and George F. Graham, "Enhancing the Effectiveness of Allied Health Workers," *American Journal of Public Health,* 62 (March, 1972), 370–373.

[74]E. Fuller Torrey, Deloris Smith, and Harold Wise, "The Family Health Worker Revisited: A Five Year Follow-Up," *American Journal of Public Health,* 63 (January, 1973), 71–74.

[75]See, for example, Lawrence S. Linn, "Patient Acceptance of the Family Nurse Practitioner," *Medical Care,* 14 (April, 1976), 357–364. In the same issue, it was reported that patients seem also to prefer nurse clinicians who take on some of the characteristics of the medical role. See Charles E. Lewis and Therese K. Cheyovich, "Who is a Nurse Practitioner? Processes of Care and Patients' and Physicians' Perceptions," *Medical Care,* 14 (April, 1976), 365–371. Some reservations about acceptance by the general public were expressed by Theodor J. Litman, "Public Perceptions of the Physicians' Assistant: A Survey of the Attitudes and Opinions of Rural Iowa and Minnesota Residents," *American Journal of Public Health,* 62 (March, 1972), 343–346.

[76]Paul D. Lairson, Jane Cassels Record, and Julia C. James, "Physician Assistants at Kaiser: Distinctive Patterns of Practice," *Inquiry,* 11 (September, 1974), 207–219.

[77]Elliott Heiman and Mary K. Dempsey, "Independent Behavior of Nurse Practitioners: A Survey of Physician and Nurse Attitudes," *American Journal of Public Health,* 66 (June, 1976), 587–589.

[78]Charles E. Lewis and Therese K. Cheyovich, "The Clinical Trial as a Means for Organizational Change," *Medical Care,* 14 (February, 1976), 137–145.

tioners groups has gained sufficient autonomy from the medical practitioner to claim fully professional status.

A related issue is the licensure of allied health personnel, which is viewed as a way to insure competence, but also as a competitive threat to practicing physicians.[79] More complex is the issue of physician supervision and responsibility for work done by physician extenders, especially in areas where allied health personnel are acting more as physician alternates, i.e., in rural areas, inner city areas, nursing homes, and so on. Ethical issues also arise in terms of payment for physician services when the work was performed by an assistant.[80] These issues apply generally to all new practitioner roles, but especially to nursing. Not only are nurses the largest single category of health personnel, but one of special interest because they are moving from a traditional subordinate role of doctor assistant to that of doctor alternate in taking on more and more of the tasks formerly reserved for medicine. Autonomy of practice is still an unfulfilled goal in the quest for full professional status, but it remains to be seen if nursing will develop as osteopathy or remain the role of doctor assistants.

## SUMMARY

This chapter has discussed three other practitioners of the healing arts from the perspective of their role vis-á-vis the medical doctor and in terms of their degree of "professionalization." These were the doctor-alternate roles of the osteopath, chiropractor, and the medical quack who more or less compete with the medical doctor and doctor-assistant roles of nurses and allied health professionals. In terms of development toward professional status, osteopathy is recognized in many areas as equivalent to orthodox medicine. Chiropractic practitioners have not yet received such recognition, although their medical group seems to be moving along the same developmental lines as homeopathy and osteopathy had experienced earlier. Fraudulent practitioners, of course, have none of the characteristics of a profession but nonetheless provide a frequently used alternative to orthodox care.

Doctor-assistant roles were analyzed in terms of new developments in nursing as a response to a perceived maldistribution of physician services, increased specialization of physicians, and high costs of their services.

[79]Ruth Roemer, "Licensing and Regulation of Medical and Medically Related Practitioners in Health Service Teams," *Medical Care,* 8 (January–February, 1971), 42–54.

[80]Rodney M. Coe and Leonard J. Fichtenbaum, "Utilization of Physician Assistants: Some Implications for Medical Practice," *Medical Care,* 10 (November–December, 1972), 497–504. See also Barbara H. Kehrer and Michael D. Intriligator, "Malpractice and Employment of Allied Health Personnel," *Medical Care,* 13 (October, 1975), 876–884.

Some new nursing roles have moved from doctor-assistant status to doctor-alternate status, especially those of nurse clinicians, pediatric nurse practitioners, and nurses who become an integral part of comprehensive health care teams. Other practitioner roles emerge from the lateral as well as downward delegation of nursing tasks—hence the development of clinical pharmacists, medical records librarians, laboratory technicians, nursing aides, and indigenous community health workers.

## SUGGESTED READINGS

Bliss, Ann A., and Eva D. Cohen (eds.), *The New Health Professionals: Nurse Practioners and Physician Assistants,* Germantown, Md.: Aspen, 1977.

Bullough, Vern, and Bonnie Bullough, *The Emergence of Modern Nursing,* London: Macmillian, 1965.

Holbrook, Stewart H., *The Golden Age of Quackery,* New York: Macmillan, 1959.

Kramer, Marlene, *Reality Shock: Why Nurses Leave Nursing,* St. Louis: Mosby, 1974.

New, Peter K., "The Osteopathic Students: A Study in Dilemma," in E. Gartly Jaco (ed.), *Patients, Physicians and Illness,* New York: Free Press, 1958, pp. 413–421.

Wardwell, Walter I., "A Marginal Professional Role: The Chiropractor," in E. Gartly Jaco (ed.), *Patients, Physicians and Illness,* New York: Free Press, 1958, pp. 421–433.

Part Three

# Health Institutions: The Hospital

Chapter 9

# Development of the Modern Hospital

*For I haue sene at sondry hospytalles/That many haue lyen dead without the walles/*
*And for lacke of socour have dyed wretchedly/Unto your foundacyon I thynke*
*contrary/Moche people resorte here and have lodgyng/But yet I maruell greatly of*
*one thyng/That in the night so many lodge without.*

Robert Copeland
*The Hyeway to the Spytell House,* 1536

Since adequate hospital facilities are among a community's most important
resources, it is likely that the functions of the contemporary hospital are
well known to nearly everyone. Nonetheless, it may be useful to restate
them briefly here. A hospital is first and foremost a place in which members
of the community can obtain services designed to restore them to good
health. More recently, it has become a place for rehabilitation of the
physically disabled and a setting in which especially older members of the
community can obtain services to restore partially the use of enfeebled
limbs or vital organs worn from age. The modern hospital is also a place of

learning, a center for the practical training of physicians and surgeons-to-be as well as other practitioners. At the same time, advances in scientific knowledge of disease are often made in research conducted in the hospital setting. Yet the modern hospital is also a very large and complex organization in the sociological sense of a recognizable hierarchy of statuses and roles, rights and obligations, attitudes, values, and goals. It is thus an appropriate object for sociological analysis—the essential purpose of this and the following two chapters.

As is typical of most social institutions which have long endured, many of the significant aspects of the modern hospital—the things which mark it sociologically from other institutions—are the consequences of a peculiar set of historical forces. Indeed, much of the social structure of contemporary hospitals cannot be adequately understood unless it is placed in a historical perspective. For example, how does one explain the paradox of the hospital being "big business," yet admitting patients whose ability to pay for the services rendered is doubtful? Why should hospital workers in the past have been notoriously underpaid when their jobs were involved in saving lives? And what have been the social and economic consequences of unionization of some hospital workers that helped raise wages to competitive levels today? Why should doctors be most often associated with hospitals in the capacity of volunteer workers when their services are vital to the continued existence of the hospital? These and other important questions about the current status of the hospital industry are addressed in this chapter concerning the historical development of the hospital. It will be important also to consider the findings of recent research on the effects of the social structure on the people who work within its framework and upon the patients for whom its existence is justified. These matters are taken up in later chapters.

## PAGAN AND CHRISTIAN ROOTS OF THE HOSPITAL: THE MIDDLE AGES AND BEFORE

Hospitals, as they are known today, arise from a nearly unbroken tradition dating back at least 1,500 years. This tradition is a reflection of a larger aspect of culture which is as old as the human race—the ways people have adopted to preserve their health. The basic theories concerning disease, superimposed on societal needs, have provided a major dimension of ideological context within which the hospital has developed. As theories and needs have changed, so has the significance as well as the structure of the hospital been altered. Prior to the development of ancient Greek culture, most ancient civilizations viewed all disease as being supernaturally caused; hence the techniques used to control and cure diseases were usually religious acts. The "physicians" of antiquity were mostly priests or magicians, and the cures they prescribed—even if scientifically sound—were rationalized in religious terms. Medicine was, so to speak, applied religion.[1] Early antecedents of the hospital, therefore, were religious institutions whose purposes were derived from religious dogma and whose activities were religiously definded.[2] (One exception, of course, was the military hospital designed to care for the sick and wounded soldiers, established by the Romans, and later adapted for civilian use.) Evidence of this can be seen in the ancient hospitals for the sick and helpless in India, in the Egyptian temples wherein faith healing was practiced, and certainly in the Greek Temple of Aesculapius where the god of healing was worshipped. Even Hippocrates and other ancient physicians down to the time of Galen, who practiced medicine on a rational basis, could not overcome the cult influence on the healing arts which persisted during pagan times.[3]

Much of this cult influence was changed, however, by the influence of Christianity which was strong and lasting. According to the basic tenets of Christian belief, sickness and suffering, whether or not naturally caused, were ultimately referable to the will of God, and therefore work among the sick was righteous and a manifestation of God's mercy. The motivation for ministering to the sick was not so much to restore health and prolong life as it was to allow people to give service to others, thereby aiding in the salvation of their own souls. Accordingly, early Christian hospitals were primarily structured as institutions for the practice of charity rather than as places primarily devoted to physical healing. With this emphasis, it is not surprising that these early hospitals cared for not only the sick but also anyone in need of shelter. In writing about the earliest known hospital in England, built in A.D. 794, Dainton has stated that "like other early hospitals, [these] were not intended solely for sick people. Their purpose was indicated by their name, which was derived from the Latin adjective *hospitalis*—concerned with *hospites* or guests. These 'guests' were any persons in need of shelter."[4] Typically, medieval hospitals were churchlike in appearance and monastic in their operation. Although the door was open to any and all who sought shelter there—not only the sick and the lame, the poor and needy, but also ordinary travelers seeking comfort for one night—each person admitted was usually required to take an oath to be faithful to

---

[1]Henry E. Sigerist, *A History of Medicine: Ancient and Primitive Medicine,* New York: Oxford University Press, 1951.

[2]Malcomb T. MacEachern, "History of Hospitals," in *Hospital Organization and Management,* Chicago: Physician Record Company, 1957.

[3]George Rosen, "The Hospital: Historical Sociology of a Community Organization," in Eliot Freidson (ed.), *The Hospital in Modern Society,* New York: Free Press, 1963, pp. 1-36. See also the discussion in William A. Glaser, *Social Settings and Medical Organization,* New York: Atherton, 1970, chap. 2.

[4]Courtney Dainton, *The Story of England's Hospitals,* Springfield, Ill.: Charles C Thomas, 1961, p. 17.

God, to be sober and chaste of body, to love fellow inmates, and to be obedient to superiors.[5] Furthermore, Dainton reported that the staff and patients alike

> . . . had to take part in religious services, daily—matins, prime, tierce, mass, sext and none, all had to be observed. At St. James's Hospital, Chichester, the lepers had to rise at 1 A.M. and say the night office. At Sherburn in Durham, those who were too ill to leave their beds had to sit up when they heard the bell and join in prayers; if they were too weak to do this, they had to lie still and pray.[6]

The staff of these hospitals was headed by a chaplain or hospitaller who was responsible not only for ministering to the spiritual needs of patients but for maintaining discipline as well. Supporting the chaplain were "sisters," usually of a religious order, but sometimes laywomen who did the domestic work; a clerk to conduct correspondence and keep books; a porter to guard the gates to prevent alcoholic beverages from being brought into the institution; and, of course, the physician who treated the sick inmates. For the most part, as much if not more attention was paid to the spiritual well-being of the patient as was directed to the physical well-being.

Several basic characteristics of the modern hospital have emerged from this early Christian definition of the hospital. First, the fact that Christian charity motivated the founding of hospitals meant that the purpose of the institution has generally been one of service and welfare in which hospital personnel have been culturally enjoined to work together not for their own advantage but for that of others, i.e., what in modern sociological terminology would be called "collectivity oriented" or "other-oriented."[7] Even today, when modern hospitals are no longer primarily Christian in ethos, they are generally organized on a charitable or nonprofit basis. Second, being guided by the tenets of Christian love meant providing care for any and all who asked for it; thus the early hospital developed a broad or "universalistic" definition of who was eligible for care. With the passage of centuries, the universalistic definition has been narrowed to the sick and injured, but the definition applies more or less equally to all sick and injured persons; thus the image of the hospital is still that of a "community institution." Third, the emphasis on meeting the spiritual needs of patients, as much if not more than the physical needs, led to a definition of the medieval hospital as a custodial institution. When supported by religious beliefs promoting love and charity, such an institutional

---

[5]*Ibid.,* p. 20.
[6]*Ibid.,* p. 27.
[7]Talcott Parsons, *The Social System,* New York: Free Press, 1951, especially chap. 2.

arrangement fares relatively well. However, serious consequences for the hospital developed during the Renaissance period when the supporting religious beliefs were replaced by secular beliefs.

## SECULARIZATION AND SEEDS OF CHANGE: RENAISSANCE HOSPITALS

The orientation toward life, especially the positive valuation of this world, which emerged during the Renaissance, was manifested in two ways with respect to the development of the modern hospital: it altered the motivations underlying providing service in the hospital, and it revolutionized people's attitudes toward the beliefs about disease and therapy. Although the highest ideals of the medieval hospital had not always been realized in the day-to-day operation of the institution, it was the period of the Renaissance and the Reformation which saw the hospital start on a long decline which lasted over 200 years. With the destruction of monasticism in England, many hospitals in the country were temporarily closed, primarily because of the abuse of patrons—financial supporters of the institution who then made inordinate demands for services for their friends and relatives—and gross mismanagement by the wardens who allowed the property to decay and often turned the institution's meager receipts to their own use.[8] The closing of the hospitals created a situation in which the sick and the poor were filling the streets with no place for shelter or no means of obtaining care. Furthermore, "there was now no religious or charitable spirit to lead to the alleviation of the state of affairs, but instead there developed a feeling of citizenship—an idea that the people of London must take action together in order to provide succour for the sick."[9] This "feeling of citizenship" was formally recognized in the form of the English Poor Law passed in 1601. Under the conditions stipulated by this act, local parish officials were empowered to levy taxes for relief of the poor, require able-bodied paupers to work, and establish institutions to care for the poor. Thus, the Poor Law formally reassigned responsibility for care of the poor which during medieval times had largely been undertaken by monastic orders. Petitions to the King from the responsible populace of London finally resulted in reopening some of the hospitals in order that "a greatter nombre of poore nedy sykke and indigent persons shalbe refresshed maynteyned comforted fownde heled and cured of theyre infirmities frankly and frely, by physicions, surgeons and appotycaryes."[10] Thus,

---

[8]Dainton, *op. cit.*, pp. 31ff.
[9]*Ibid.*, p. 32.
[10]*Ibid.*, p. 33.

necessity required their reopening, but the reorganized hospitals were markedly different from their predecessors of the Middle Ages. The service-in-the-name-of-salvation motif which characterized the medieval hospital at its best had become transmuted to a duty of welfare care, grudgingly accepted by the state and community. All the unhappy connotations of the almshouse and the Poor Law came to be applied to the hospital, which had to depend upon the poor tax and the uncertainty of voluntary contributions for its existence. The definition of patient status also underwent a precipitous decline from that of an unfortunate to be cared for and succored to that of a miserable object to be cared for as a public burden.[11]

Some flavor of life in the hospital during the late medieval and early Renaissance period is provided in this excerpt.

> . . . if his case was deemed suitable, the patient was admitted to a ward. He was only admitted if it was thought that he was not suffering from plague or lunacy. Incurables were sent home, to free beds for those the hospital could do more to help. Plague victims were transferred to one of the special Lock Hospitals, usually the one in Kent Street, and Bethlem took any lunatics, unless they needed surgical treatment first, which was given at St. Thomas'.
>
> There were always some who would try to get unsuitable cases admitted. Friends of the sick even contrived to smuggle them in unobserved. Once they were inside no one would take responsibility for them, supply their upkeep or pay for their funeral. . . .
>
> No patients were turned away because they were unable to contribute to their own upkeep, but those who could were expected to pay something. The richer often paid for the poorer, the masters for their apprentices or the prosperous for poor relations. . . .
>
> The diet in the hospital, if plain, was sufficient . . . by the standards of the time the patients were well fed, many better fed then in their own homes . . . [but] . . . the best time to enter hospital was round about Christmas, Shrove Tuesday, Easter or Whitsun, when a double allowance was given and "plum-pottage" as well. . . .
>
> From the patients' point of view, life in hospital had a few drawbacks. Discipline was rather strict and the punishments for infringing the regulations were by modern standards very harsh.
>
> All patients well enough were expected to attend the daily service in the chapel. This was no great hardship in 1574, when it was held between 9 and 10 A.M., but in 1580 the hospitaller, to suit his own convenience, put it at 6 A.M. He was soon made to alter it to 10 A.M. . . .
>
> Besides compulsory attendance in the chapel there was plenty of work to keep the patients busy. It was the avowed policy of the governors to "keep the poor from idleness. . . ."

[11]Bernard J. Stern, *Society and Medical Progress,* Princeton, N.J.: Princeton University Press, 1941.

One of the strictest regulations in the hospital was that made against marriage or engagement. Both were forbidden to patients and staff alike. If two patients became engaged, the stronger one was immediately discharged. . . . For most offences dismissal was the last resort, only used after repeated warnings to the offender. Cases of immorality were punished at the whipping-post or in the stocks, both of which stood on the hospital premises . . . one of the sisters, Joan Thorneton, was punished for licentious behaviour with "twelve strokes well laid on," and a patient, John Marten, was ordered punishment even more severe. On December 8, 1567, he was ordered twenty-five stripes for misconduct and theft. Such treatment was not at all to his taste and a week later he is listed "discharged, having run away."[12]

This excerpt contains elements of both the old and the new, medieval and Renaissance times. Note the admission of any patient regardless of ability to pay; yet some patients were *expected* to pay, surely not an article of Christian charity. Note also the restriction on types of disease, accepting only those whom the hospital could help, others being sent to specialized institutions—a characteristic of the modern hospital industry. This excerpt also illustrates a principle of organizational change, namely that organizational means to an end often become ends in themselves. During the Middle Ages, service to one's neighbor, especially the poor and needy, was viewed as a worthwhile goal because it was a means of sanctifying the doer. The means to this goal were manifested in the establishment and operation of the early hospital. During the Renaissance, however, operation of institutions for the poor became an end in itself, complete with retrenched or limited goals and a consequent shift in ideology. This form of adaptation to change in cultural definitions has been classified by Merton as "ritualism," in which former goals are abandoned in favor of reduced aspirations and the latter are approached by rigid adherence to established institutional rules.[13]

The point at issue here is not so much that during the Renaissance hospitals fell into ignorance and error but that the weakening of the religious context of motivation for service to the sick led to an almost immediate and drastic decline in their effectiveness. Not until science replaced religion as the dominant motivation for service was this situation changed. One effect of the Reformation, as well as of the broader movement, the Renaissance, was to compartmentalize religion. In the Middle Ages, the view of salvation through good works and the ascription of supernatural significance to nearly every action of life compelled the focus of human attention to be upon religion. However, the Lutheran reformation

---

[12]E. M. McInnes, *St. Thomas' Hospital,* London: Allen & Unwin, 1963, pp. 32-36.

[13]See Robert K. Merton, *Social Theory and Social Structure,* New York: Free Press, 1957, especially pp. 139-153.

tended to restrict religion to the content of work and sacrament, and its followers all too frequently used its insight to throw off religious restraints upon life to "sin that Grace may abound." Similarly, Calvinism with its emphasis on sacerdotal austerity stripped religion of the cultural trapping of centuries and made it a morality for the elect in which worldly or secular success had sacred support. In other words, these and other movements freed the energies of man for development along secular rather than religious lines.

One of these lines of secular interest was in the scientific study of the human body, including not only its structure and function but also its pathology. And it was the development of medical science which provided the second set of revolutionary changes in the structure of the hospital. It should be recalled from Chapter 6 that during the Renaissance, the consuming interest in antiquity led to the rediscovery of the medical science of Greek and Roman times or at least those parts of it which had been salvaged by the Turks and Arabs after the fall of the Roman Empire. The rediscovery of disease as a natural phenomenon stimulated interest in the processes of life in this world and renewed efforts toward experimentation and exploration. Disease was less often considered a supernatural phenomenon, but more a visitation upon a person caused by a malfunction of the body. Efforts to cure rather than merely to give care were prosecuted more vigorously. Most importantly, the direction of the therapeutic effort was given to a secular group—the physicians.

However, all knowledge, including medical science, had been more or less marking time for nearly a thousand years. The mere assumption of responsibility for therapy by physicians could hardly be expected to produce an immediate improvement in medical care. For the most part, physicians and surgeons held weekly "grand rounds" except that all the patients came to them for diagnosis and treatment instead of the contemporary procedure of the medical staff going to the patients' bedsides. The major difference, of course, was in the treatment procedures. For example, skin diseases were often treated with ointments made of "mustard, strong vinegar with the addition of verdigris, oil of spikenard, pepper and salt, all boiled together. If that failed and there was a recurrence, another salve was used, a mixture of lard, goose and sheep dung, oil of spikenard, honey, pepper and stavesacre."[14] Another common disease, syphilis, had an equally patent treatment—the victim was segregated from "clean" patients, rubbed with mercurial ointment in front of a fire, and wrapped in flannel to "sweat" it out. Surgeons, who occupied a lesser status than physicians at this time, also were limited in the procedures they could carry out. It took real courage for a patient to willingly undergo surgery during

[14]McInnes, *op. cit.*, p. 40.

this period partly because outcomes were seldom successful, but mostly because the discovery of anesthesia was still 300 years away. Even the surgeons were not so confident that they did not rely on powers other than their own as is revealed in this surgeon's instructions for an amputation:

> . . . let the Surgeon with all his assistances and friends not forget before the beginning of the work heartily to call upon God for a blessing upon their endeavours, and let the patient the day before have notice given him that he may also take time to prepare himself with true resolution of soul and body to undergo the work, as being never performed without danger of death, which done, then let the Surgeon prepare himself also with his helpers, namely at the least five persons besides himself, as for example, one to sit behind the patient to hold him, a second for a holder, who by the surgeon must be instructed to stand fast before him and to bestride the limb to be amputated and to hold the limb; and a third to hold and stay the lower end of the diseased member to be taken off; a fourth to receive and bring back the sharp instruments; a fifth, to attend the Artist and deliver to him his needles and buttons, restrictive rollers, bolsters, bladder and so soon as possibly may be to stay with the palm of his hand the medicines applied to the end of the amputated stump that being the duty of the fifth helper and the sixth is the Artist himself that dismembereth.[15]

The importance of physicians' assuming leadership in therapeutic efforts, however, lies not in their inability to close the gap between medical practice, as illustrated above, and medical science which was beginning to achieve momentum. It lies, rather, in the fact that physicians began to organize themselves as a profession, legitimated in England in 1518 with the chartering of the Royal College of Physicians. The incorporation of people in professional capacities fundamentally influenced the development of the hospital although it took nearly 400 more years to produce the hospital of today. In those early days when the doctor was added to the hospital's personnel as the principal therapeutic agent, the institution still encompassed a far broader kind of service than merely caring for the sick; i.e., it was still a generalized custodial institution. Moreover, the therapeutic services the doctor could render were usually neither time-consuming nor indispensable to the hospital. Since hospital patients, by definition, were the unfortunates of society who needed the aid of charity, physicians had to serve all their paying clientele outside the bounds of the hospital. It is not surprising, then, that doctors were first associated with the hospital on a part-time, charity basis. Even in the present day the physician's status in the institution is typically that of a *volunteer* staff member in the hospital. However, since physicians held a virtual monopoly on medical knowledge which the hospital wanted applied to its patients, the doctor was placed in

---

[15]John Woodall, "The Surgeon's Mate, 1639," quoted in Dainton, *op. cit.,* p. 40.

an unusually advantageous bargaining position. It meant that knowledge vital to hospital operation was in hands other than those which had administrative control over its operation, a structural situation which still exists today.

As a professional person, the doctor was—and is—subject to the prescriptions for behavior held by the medical profession. Thus, the norms for one institution, the medical profession, have been incorporated into those of another, the hospital. By and large, this convergence has come about because certain of the purposes of the medical profession have become part of the purposes of the hospital, such as medical care for patients and the education of students. This, in turn, has allowed the profession to make demands on the hospital to carry out the purpose of education, i.e., setting standards of care; and finally, partly to ensure that their demands are met, physicians have developed a pressure group within the hospital structure, the medical staff.

Since their work is largely practical, it seems only natural that the training of physicians would be carried out in conjunction with the hospital where physicians had access to large numbers of patients on whom they could demonstrate their skills for their apprentices.[16] Rosen has said that

> . . . from the medieval period the hospital was essentially an instrument of society to ameliorate suffering, to diminish poverty, to eradicate mendicity, and to help maintain public order. . . . The same period also saw the beginning of an association with the medical profession, but the physician was not yet a part of the hospital, and remained independent. However, this association did provide the basis for another trend that from the seventeenth century on would lead the medical profession increasingly to use the hospital for the study of disease and for its own practical education. The view that hospitals should be places for the treatment of the sick and at the same time centers for the study and teaching of medicine was to have extraordinarily fruitful consequences in succeeding centuries.[17]

Initially, there was no organized formal course of instruction provided for apprentices until early in the eighteenth century. Rather, there was the traditional academic course: these courses of medicine provided in the universities relied almost entirely on Galen and other classical medical sources. Up to that time, students would "sign on" with a particular physician or surgeon for as many as seven years. For the most part, their instruction came from observing the master at work, much as it had been in the days of the ancient Greeks. Students paid their fees directly to the master and lived with him. Most hospitals, however, limited the surgeons in

---

[16]Richard H. Shryock, *The Development of Modern Medicine,* Philadelphia: University of Pennsylvania Press, 1936.

[17]Rosen, *op. cit.,* p. 18.

the number of apprentices they could have, and eventually the number of applicants far exceeded the number that could be trained. Then too, with the growth of the amount of information in anatomy, chemistry, physics, and physiology which had to be learned, hospitals began employing physicians for the purpose of teaching students and providing care for patients. By 1750, a system of medical education had emerged in Europe which very much resembles the system employed in the emphasis on practical training in the hospital after classroom instruction.

One of the characteristics of professional associations is the ability to enforce rules upon their members. This was true of the budding medical profession also. For example, the Royal College of Physicians could compel its members to render free care under certain circumstances and to examine all medicines sold within a radius of 7 miles from London.[18] The important point is that through their professional association, the physicians have gained control over standards of care given in hospitals. To be sure, during the Renaissance the impact of professional demands was slight and was largely a matter of personal influence of the physician. Renowned physicians could demand and get what they wanted in terms of hospitals' procedures and medical equipment. Although this probably had little effect on the efficacy of therapy during this period, it set an important precedent for contemporary medical practice. Organized medicine has developed to the point where it can demand high standards of services and materials not only from its members on the medical staff, but from the hospital's administration as well. The modern hospital could not exist without the services of practicing physicians and physicians-in-training (house staff), and since these professionals are obliged to comply with the standards set by their profession, so also is the hospital obliged to meet the standards.[19]

Further structural change has been imposed upon the hospital through the custom of physicians in the institutional group entering into consultation with each other on the more difficult cases with which they had to deal. Because of their monopoly on medical knowledge, it became necessary for the doctors to advise managers of the hospitals—the hospitallers—as well. Out of these activities emerged the formally organized medical staff as an independent, but important, facet of the hospital social structure. Not only does the medical staff govern the medical practice of physicians in the hospital—including the determination of who may and may not treat patients there—but it controls many other activities also. In the beginning, of course, the medical staff was concerned largely with the treatment process, but in the contemporary hospital its influence extends to nearly

[18]Alexander Carr-Saunders and P. A. Wilson, *The Professions,* New York: Oxford University Press, 1933.
[19]Cf. Eliot Freidson, *Profession of Medicine,* New York: Dodd Mead, 1970, especially pp. 111–115.

every facet of hospital operations including the educational process, research, standards for nonprofessional employees, and clinical and ancillary services, such as x-ray, outpatient care, and physical therapy. Thus, the extension of influence of the medical profession on the structure and operation of the contemporary hospital has developed from its inception in the Renaissance hospital.

One further impact of doctors on the hospital social structure should be noted and that is the charismatic nature of their authority in the hospital setting. Weber has described charisma, literally "gift of grace," as characteristic of self-appointed leaders whose authority rests on their own abilities to accomplish extraordinary feats.[20] In contrast with a bureaucratic organization in which authority is invested in an office or position filled by an individual who meets certain standard qualifications, charismatic authority is invested in a particular individual because of an intensely personalized ability to move people, especially in times of stress and when other leadership has failed. Such was—and to some extent still is—the position of the physician in the hospital setting. Because doctors had a monopoly on medical knowledge, even when it was based on fallacious theories, it was essential that they control the treatment of patients; thus any cures effected would be to their credit. In the hospital setting, however, the charismatic nature of the doctor's role has greatly exaggerated this control over not only patients but other persons as well, especially nurses and ancillary treatment specialists. Under these circumstances, the atmosphere of the hospital tends to become authoritarian and quasi-military. Discipline and the unquestioned acceptance of authority were (and still are, to a certain extent) necessary to meet situations where life or death hung in the balance. Authority was placed on one leader—the doctor—and among other personnel, lines of responsibility and authority had to be clearly drawn. None of these changes occurred overnight; some did not fully develop until the beginning of the twentieth century. Nonetheless, the seeds of change were planted during the Renaissance.

## MODERN MEDICINE AND THE MODERN HOSPITAL

Despite the growing influence of the medical profession on the social structure of the hospital, little progress was made in therapy itself. As hospitals came to be increasingly restricted in use to the care of the sick, they came to be places

> . . . which the poor must enter for their death agonies. It is little wonder that entrance of a patient to a hospital was like signing a death warrant when one

---

[20]H. H. Gerth and C. Wright Mills (eds. and trs.), *From Max Weber: Essays in Sociology,* New York: Oxford University Press, 1958, especially chap. 9.

considers the offensive sanitary conditions prevailing in the hospital during this period. Windows were always shut tight and the floors sanded. Bedsteads were of wood and since the patients were never washed and seldom had a change of bed linen, the beds often swarmed with vermin.[21]

The degradation which fell upon hospitals was due not only to the changed motivation for service, but also to an indifference to the conditions under which patients had to live. Medicine of the seventeenth, eighteenth, and even part of the nineteenth centuries, with its belief in disturbance of bodily humors as the chief cause of disease, was almost blind to the function of sanitation in preventive medicine. Prior to 1867, when the concept of antisepsis and later, asepsis, was introduced, the conditions of hospital life for the patient were appalling by any modern standards. Not only were hospitals typically dirty and poorly ventilated, but they were also often extremely overcrowded. Each ward was usually filled to capacity with beds lined side by side with barely sufficient space to pass between them. Frequently, more than one patient was placed in a single bed, often without regard to type of disease or condition of the patient. All too often one's bed partner might have died and the body remained for several hours before being removed by the staff. Thus, patients with infectious diseases, patients with gangrenous limbs, and those crazed with fever all could be in the same ward. Before the development of the surgical amphitheater and other segregated facilities, such as maternity wards, all treatments were carried out in the ward including surgery (limited mostly to amputations), physical restraint of the mentally ill, delivery of an infant, and laying out of the dead. To add to the patients' miseries, the attending physicians and surgeons generally ignored even the most rudimentary rules of sanitation when treating patients despite Semmelweis's discovery around 1847 that the medical staff was the cause of infecting newly delivered mothers with puerperal fever. His painstaking search for the cause of death of so many patients led to the conclusion that the staff and students alike caused the infection by not washing their hands or changing clothes after coming from the dissecting room where they had been examining previous victims of the disease and before treating patients who still remained on the wards. That Semmelweis's ideas on the transmission of puerperal fever had still not been wholeheartedly embraced by the medical profession at the time of his death in 1865 is mute testimony to the fact that old ideas and tradition die hard.[22] The generally unspeakable conditions of the hospitals were only part of the problem. Another very important aspect was the therapeutic impotence of the medical profession generally despite its tendency to prosecute therapy with great vigor. Consider, for example, the treatment

    [21]Stern, *op. cit.,* p. 101.
    [22]Frank G. Slaughter, *Semmelweis: Conqueror of Child-bed Fever,* New York: Collier Books, Crowell-Collier, 1961.

given the young Duke of Gloucester in 1700 as reported by one of the physicians who attended him.

> I had inform'd myself of the present circumstances and condition of his distemper—I retird with Dr. Gibbons and Dr. Hanns who were both there before to consult about his recovery before that I came, they had ordered him five blisters which were all put on, wee likewise ordered his Highness a drink to drink of, which was proper to suppress his loosness, which had its effect. . . . Wee ordered him Cordial powders and Cordial Julops to resist the malignity, he tooke a paper of those powders that night which kept him in breathing sweats and brought out the rash in greater quantity, he had but very little rest that night, accompanied with great sighings and dejection of spirits and towards morning complaind very much of his blisters. they were opend in the morning and they were drawn very well and run very well. . . . Wee ordered him in the evening two more blisters which were apply'd and to continue that method he was in, hopeing by the assistance of them and his other medcins he would have a better night, but . . . he was of a suddaine after a little doseing taken with a convulsive sort of breathing, a defect in swallowing and a total deprivation of all sens which lasted about an hour and between twelve and one that night departed this life.[23]

Nearly 100 years later, it would seen that not much progress had been made in developing a more potent therapy. For example, during a particularly severe epidemic of yellow fever in Philadelphia, Benjamin Rush and his colleagues

> . . . blamed the disease on "noxious miasma," and evil air caused by rotting matter, stagnant swamps or the breath of infected patients, [and] public minded citizens lighted fires on every street corner to burn the miasma away. A committee of doctors headed by Rush announced that fires were dangerous and probably ineffectual. When they suggested burning gunpowder instead, the citizens got their muskets down from the wall and spent the evening firing at the miasma out of the window. So many people were wounded, that the mayor had to forbid this also . . . Stopping before the house of a patient, Rush poured vinegar on his handkerchief and pressed it against his nose as he walked up the unswept stairs to the room of death . . . and Rush, although he made his rounds religiously, realized that he could not help. Certainty had deserted him when he needed it most; hesitating in his own mind, he noticed with agony that whatever he prescribed, the sufferers died. . . .
>      Hearing that a West Indian physician who had often seen the disease was in town, he hurried to his lodgings to beg advice and returned jubilant with a new remedy. The next morning he ordered that buckets of cold water be

[23]Lester S. King, *The Medical World of the Eighteenth Century,* Chicago: University of Chicago Press, 1958, pp. 298-299.

poured over his patients. To his horror, three out of four who submitted to this remedy died. . . .[24]

All was not lost, however, for Rush recalled a "scientific" paper which admonished physicians not to be fooled

> . . . by the seeming weakness in a patient since yellow fever was caused by an over-excitement of the body. Even if the pulse were so thin you could hardly find it, you should none the less prescribe the most violent purges.
>
> In the silence of his room, these words struck Rush with the force of divine revelation; he understood everything now. Under all circumstances depletion was necessary. Away then with cowardice; he would purge and bleed to an extent never dared in Philadelphia before.[25]

With medical practice in such a state, it is hardly any wonder that patients thought of the hospital as a place where only the poor go to die, not to mention their general distrust of the physician.

It was, however, a situation destined to undergo drastic change. New developments were being made, slowly at first, but then with increasing rapidity. Perhaps all the new inventions and discoveries could be shown to have had an eventual impact on the hospital, but we shall single out only three: (1) the development of physiology and bacteriology, which finally put medicine on a firm scientific basis, (2) the development of antisepsis and anesthesia, and (3) the establishment of nursing as a basic role in the hospital. As was discussed in Chapter 6, the discoveries of men like Virchow, Bernard, Pasteur, and Koch established medicine on a scientific basis, but more than that, they enabled medical practitioners to deal effectively with a host of infectious diseases with which formerly they had been unable to cope. There resulted a meteoric rise in the status and prestige of physicians in the community. Almost simultaneously, the use of asepsis and antiseptic methods in the hospital dramatically reduced the number of deaths of patients from infections and reduced the amount of time required for recovery. In addition, the introduction of anesthesia meant that surgery could be done relatively painlessly and with a much greater hope for successful recovery. The consequences of these developments for the hospital were significant. In the first place, the image of the hospital as a place where the poor went to die was changed to that of a place where a patient could be cured. As this transition proceeded, the attitudes and expectancies of the public concerning hospitals also changed. People began to consider hospitals as centers of healing.

---

[24]James T. Flexner, *Doctors on Horseback*, New York: Collier Books, Crowell-Collier, 1962, pp. 99, 101.
[25]*Ibid.*, p. 102.

Secondly, since surgeons, who now enjoyed a higher reputation, required special facilities which were often beyond the reach of the private practitioner, the hospital came to be tbe location of choice for the performance of surgical operations. This meant that for the first time, sizable numbers of the well-to-do classes of society began to request hospital accommodations on the advice of their physicians. These advances in medical technology therefore led to a drastic revision of the hospital's purpose. Traditionally, these institutions had been designed for care of the unfortunate poor who were sick or needed shelter, but as a result of the revolution in medical science, they came to be places where medical care could be obtained by anyone who needed it. The shift in basic purpose carries with in an implication for change in the definition of who could be a patient. It was not enough to be in need of charity; a patient also had to need the medical services only a hospital could provide. This redefinition enabled the hospital to charge patients for services, and very soon the major portion of operating revenues came from this source instead of private subscriptions. Because the hospital retained its universalistic orientation, however, provision was made to give free or below-cost care to those patients who needed it. Accordingly, two classes of patients arose, the ward patient to whom charity was extended and the private patient who stood in an essentially commercial, contractual relationship to the hospital.

These shifts in the type of patient and the use of the hospital placed the physician in a new situation in the social structure of the hospital. Although for the most part doctors retained their "volunteer" status, the importance of the hospital to the doctors' practices increased tremendously. As medical techniques came to require more expensive material apparatus, the use of operating rooms, and constant observation and treatment of patients, the hospital became a necessity for the doctors instead of merely an object of their charitable aid. When this situation became established, all of the hitherto latent implications of the doctors' dual role as professionals and hospital staff members rapidly began to gain concrete expression. These implications are discussed more fully in the following chapter.

A status shift also occurred within the medical profession itself. Prior to the mid-nineteenth century, physicians alone had claim to the exalted and scholarly status of "doctor." Surgeons, along with barbers and apothecaries, were a lesser breed of artisans who worked with their hands. The new horizons opened by antisepsis and anesthesia, however, not only made surgeons equally doctors with physicians but rendered their counsel dominant in medical staff organization. Further status shifts have occurred as a result of specialization, a consequence of increased medical knowledge. Moreover, specialization created a need for the hospital to employ a great many more persons and establish several new roles in the hospital setting.

Finally, the third major innovation considered here, the development of nursing, should be given special mention because of its importance to the hospital's social structure. It has already been noted that the quality of medical practice had declined for 200 years following the Renaissance period. So, too, did those who served as nurses sink to a very low estate. Although many of the ward sisters were well intentioned in providing custodial care for the patient, their efforts were often hampered by illiteracy and sometimes drunkenness and not especially desirable moral standards. Most were completely untrained, the hours were long, and the pay was low; thus it is not surprising that the caliber of persons who performed this role was not particularly enviable. This situation resulted in an at best indifferent and often cruel type of patient care and chaotic conditions on the hospital wards. With the advancements in medicine which took place during the nineteenth century, it became untenable to have incompetent nurses care for patients. The emerging science of diagnosis demanded dependable around-the-clock observation, and new forms of therapy were developed which demanded trained hands for their administration. The initiative for raising the standards of nursing care emerged with the first school of nursing, established by Florence Nightingale in 1860 at St. Thomas's Hospital in England.[26] Although some supervision and raising of standards of nursing care had been attempted prior to 1860, almost no formal training was offered. It was this situation that Florence Nightingale wanted to remedy. As a result of her exploits as the "Angel of Mercy" during the Crimean War, she had become a popular heroine and enough money was easily raised to enable her to start the first formalized nurses' training program at St. Thomas's.

It is important to note that the transformation of the role of the nurse was effected largely by "outsiders" possessed of a consuming passion for service and devoted to seeing that the patient received humanitarian service. These women were outsiders in the sense that initially they were not a part of the hospital system which they chose as the proper place for practical training for students and it was only after overcoming the resistance of the medical staff that nurses became part of the hospital social structure. The works of these reformers, however, laid the foundation for a new professional group and, in so doing, instilled a secular spirit of sacrificial service into the ideology of hospital personnel. This ideology has been a most significant factor in "humanizing" the hospital and making it a patient-centered institution.

## DEVELOPMENT OF HOSPITALS IN THE UNITED STATES

The history of the development of hospitals in the United States represents a telescoped description of the development of European hospitals. Just as the stages of growth of American medicine were similar to those of

[26]McInnes, *op. cit.*

European medicine, but occurred in a much shorter period of time (see Chapter 6), so the American hospital has evolved through roughly the same stages as its European counterparts. The period from the founding of the first American hospital in Philadelphia in 1751 to about 1850 corresponds to the Middle Ages in European hospital history in which the basic purpose of Christian charity was established. The next fifty or sixty years constitute the Renaissance period of American hospitals during which time many of the characteristics of modern hospitals had their beginning. Finally, shortly after the turn of the twentieth century, American hospitals began to feel the full impact of the revolutionary changes occurring in medical science. To be sure, this is only a rough comparison inasmuch as there was a great deal of overlap between periods and not all hospitals developed at the same rate. Nonetheless, the pattern of development of American hospitals is strikingly similar to that of European hospitals.

It should be recalled that for nearly a century following the establishment of the first American hospital, medical practice was based largely on the humoral theory of the ancient Greeks or some modification thereof and was, therefore, pretty much ineffective. Physicians, usually trained in England, were helpless in the face of epidemics of cholera, smallpox, dysentery, scarlet fever, and other scourges that threatened the public from time to time. This was the period, too, when most treatment was given in the patient's home. But even in the young country, there were the poor and needy, the infected, and the insane who did not have a suitable place to stay. Thus, many of the early American hospitals were established primarily to give these persons shelter and the little medical care that could be provided.

As might be expected, these precursors of the contemporary hospital were financed by charitable contributions and staffed by a handful of people to provide custodial care of the inmates. Generally, there was a steward or matron, sometimes both, who exercised control over the institution and assumed responsibility for discipline of employees as well as patients. A few women performed the equivalent of the nursing role and sometimes were augmented by "volunteers" who acted as "nurses" for religious or humanitarian reasons. Of course, there were the local doctors who came in from time to time to give their services to the patients. By and large, there was little medical treatment except prescriptions for medicinal compounds, diets, and leechings. Most of the care activities were focused on making the patients as comfortable as possible and preparing them for death, which would likely follow soon after admission.

About the middle of the nineteenth century a few noticeable changes began to occur. Although the underlying rationalization for the establishment and operation of hospitals remained the same—charitable service in the name of Christian spirit—the social structure of the hospital began to take on some of its contemporary features. By the 1870s American hospitals were admitting patients who were "suitable for treatment"; i.e., those with incurable diseases were sent to other community agencies or turned away, and only the curable sick and the poor were admitted. The medical staffs of these institutions began to exert more and more influence on the formulation of policies of the hospital, and this became even more pronounced when hospitals began to affiliate with medical schools.[27] Nonetheless, solicitation for funds was still articulated in terms of Christian duty. Hospital directors pointed out that Christianity had engendered the first desire to care for the sick, and it was their conviction that the "hospital is not only a place to relieve sickness and distress, but . . . a Christian home for the incurable to lie down and die in peace."[28]

It was well that managers of hospitals felt this way, for to be forced to go to a hospital in the 1870s was generally an unpleasant and time-consuming business. The patients, two-thirds of whom were men, could count on an average stay of from eight to ten weeks. At that, their chances of recovery were only two in three, and about 10 percent died. Patients of all ages and conditions were grouped together on open wards. On the women's side might be found, side by side, an old consumptive racked with coughing, a woman agonizing in her travail, a woman crippled with an attack of rheumatism, and the victim of a serious accident. On the men's side, the air was often pierced by the shriek of a drunk horrified by his delirium; fevers, of course, were prevalent, and the therapy of the period did not go far beyond quinine and *spiritus frumenti*. The kind of treatment provided for hospitalized patients at the close of the era preceding the revolution in medical science stands in marked contrast with contemporary care. This is illustrated by excerpts from the records of one American hospital.[29]

> Patrick G_____. Admitted January 31, 1873. Has been sick for years. Was taken with pneumonia and has had a cough ever since, with bloody expectorations two years ago, and has had similar attacks at intervals since. Has a cavity in the left lung, and imperfect respirations in the right. Treatment: Rx 1845 with oil.
>
> July 30—Left on a visit.
> September 5—Admitted. Is failing gradually.
> December 6—Died.

This case not only suggests a long term stay, but an erroneous diagnosis (x-ray had not yet been developed) and inadequate treatment. Another case illustrates the extreme brevity of record keeping in those days.

[27] *Ibid.*
[28] Albert F. Wessen, "The Social Structure of the Modern Hospital," unpublished doctoral dissertation, Yale University, New Haven, Conn., 1951.
[29] *Ibid.*, pp. 76-78.

> Sarah N_____. Admitted April 1873. Has Chronic Rheumatic Arthritis.
>
> December 1—No better. Has a water bed of peculiar kind.
> Died October 4, 1877, of asthenia (weakness).

If physicians were sometimes lacking in therapeutic effectiveness, they did not lack a sense of humor as this case reflects.

> John J_____. Admitted August 21, 1873. Age 68. Physician. Hypochondriasis. Treatment—tonics.
>
> Sepember 4—Had quite a hemorrhage from his bowels today.
> December 1—Cold. Three young wives have taken all the heat out of him. Coughs.

The records also shed some light on the social status of many of the patients of the day. In common with many of the expectant mothers who came to the hospital, Mary G_____ was single—a domestic "in trouble." Although her delivery was uncomplicated and her child healthy, she remained in the hospital for forty-five days, sixteen of them before her delivery. The record of a fifty-year-old laborer typifies another class of patient. His diagnosis upon admission was "lazy, but may prove sick." His record goes on to report:

> December 20—Discharged *cured*—but says he will go to Dr. _____ to get another permit. N.B. the laziness—like a cancer in his system, and is probably not thoroughly eradicated. It may "break out" again.
>
> February 3, 1874—Returned—with some disease.
> March 4—Eloped (left hospital without regular discharge).

Gradually, however, the impact of medical discoveries, both here and abroad, began to be felt. The response to improved care (and rising confidence in the medical profession) was a continuing increase in the number as well as change in type of patients who sought treatment in the hospital. To keep abreast of the rising demand, hospitals were forced to build additions and expand their facilities and services. Interestingly enough, the religious appeal for operating funds tended to be replaced by a secular rationale that the hospital was a necessary community facility for treatment of disease and for protection of the community from epidemics. Concomitantly, the hospital became the training ground for future physicians as well as for nurses and persons in other health occupations. By 1900, hospitals had begun sharply to restrict admissions to patients with acute conditions and to seek other outlets for the aged patient and those whose ailments could not be cured. With ever increasing speed, the hospital began to take on the features which characterize it today.

The events which occurred in medical science following the confirmation of germ theory in the 1870s had an impact on the development of the American hospital that is difficult to describe. In part, this is because there were so many new discoveries and they began to appear with increasing frequency. Mostly, however, the difficulty lies in the fact that these events are all interrelated; that is, each new discovery added to the rapidly accumulating body of medical knowledge, thereby broadening the base from which still more discoveries could be made. In general, however, the effects of these developments on the hospital may be viewed in terms of (1) expansion of the hospital's physical plant and equipment, (2) the enlargement and alteration of the hospital's social structure, and finally (3) a shift in the avowed purpose of the hospital.

Modern developments in medicine have vastly multiplied the amount of material apparatus needed by the hospital. This has been true of both physical plant and equipment. Within only the last generation or so hospitals have required a fivefold increase in the number of operating rooms; four times as much space for nurses' quarters; and a tremendous increase in accommodations for laboratories, x-ray departments, physical therapy, dentistry, medical records, and other special diagnostic, therapeutic, and administrative services. Hospital construction costs, of course, are reflected in this expansion. Whereas in the 1860s a building could be constructed for less than 200 dollars per bed, by 1920 the cost was about 18,000 dollars and by 1976 it had risen to 50,000 dollars.[30] The equipment of a Baltimore hospital in 1851 consisted only of beds, bedding, dishes, other household goods, and five surgical instruments, but the mere listing of items of necessary equipment for the modern hospital covers forty or more pages of fine print.[31] Moreover, it should be recalled that as the medical profession was enabled to treat diseases more effectively and as the hospital death rate declined, private patients began demanding admission to the hospital. Thus, expansion occurred to provide new accommodations for paying patients—private and semiprivate rooms in addition to the open wards for charity patients. Moreover, specialization within the medical profession required that hospitals also provide space and equipment for laboratories and other diagnostic facilities—which became the backbone of clinical practice in the hospital and, later, the community—as well as for therapy and rehabilitation.

[30]See Edward H. Corwin, *The American Hospital,* New York: Commonwealth Fund, 1946. The estimated median cost per bed in 1976 was $46,600 with a low of $10,800 to a high of $91,000. The current average per 1,000 square feet is $60 to $90. See Robert Snow Means Company, Inc., *Building Construction Cost Data, 1976,* Duxbury, Mass.: Construction Consultants and Publishers, 1976.

[31]Henry Sigerist, "An Outline of the Development of the Hospital," *Bulletin of the History of Medicine,* 4 (1936), 573-581.

These same factors—change in type of patient and increase in their numbers, specialization in the medical profession, and increased technology—also had a profound effect on the social structure of the hospital in the enormous proliferation of roles necessary to carry out its purposes. In London hospitals during the late eighteenth century there were, for all practical purposes, only nine role categories: (1) members of the governing board who managed the hospital, (2) steward, (3) matron, (4) ward sisters or nurses, (5) physicians, (6) surgeons, (7) apothecaries, (8) servants, and (9) patients.[32] In a modern hospital the single category of sister or its contemporary counterpart, nurse, has differentiated into as many major role categories.

We have already noted that nursing as a skilled occupation emerged in response to the need for competent care of patients. The change in type of patient also brought about a restructuring of the relationships among hospital personnel. The decrease in the length of time patients remained on the hospital wards resulted in a decline in the significance of the patient culture which ordinarily followed long-term hospitalization of the poor as well as sick. It could not be expected that patients who remained in an institutional environment for an average of only three weeks would be able to establish the complex patterns of social interaction and group behavior as would patients remaining two months or more. Moreover, as the definition of patient shifted to only those who were sick and required the services of the hospital, only acutely ill patients were admitted, and they were confined to their beds during their stay; thus their interaction rapidly fell to a level too low to allow for an informal social organization to be formed. This meant that hospital personnel gave less of their time to disciplinary duties and more to the technical care of the sick, and this was particularly true of nurses. At first, nurses did not only patient care and administrative duties but housekeeping tasks as well. Gradually, they were relieved of these lesser chores by personnel who filled a series of positions of orderlies, attendants, maids, and others. Today, skilled nursing consists mostly of coordinating the activities of many skilled and semiskilled personnel and supervising the execution of physicians' orders for technical care of their patients.

Specialization has had a similar and perhaps more marked effect on the hospital's medical staff. In the first place, there was a functional differentiation of roles within the medical staff. Beginning in the late 1870s the expertise of certain physicians such as pathologists, gynecologists, orthopedic surgeons, radiologists, pediatricians, anesthetists, dental surgeons, psychiatrists, and cardiologists was needed to keep abreast of new developments in medical care, and hence, those physicians were added to

[32]See Dainton, *op. cit.*

the hospital's medical staff. As a consequence, there developed a series of levels of membership on the medical staff such as full-time or house staff including residents and interns, visiting staff with full hospital privileges, and associate or courtesy staff who could treat their patients in the hospital but had little say about the formulation of staff policy.

If specialization among the medical staff increased the number of physician roles in the hospital's social structure, it also increased the number of ancillary services needed for the physicians to carry out their tasks adequately. For the most part, the early improvements were in the art of diagnosis. For example, the discovery of x-ray and the consequent development of radiology required not only a specialist to use the information in diagnosis, but also someone to physically operate the equipment. Similarly, in the laboratory, the development of a host of diagnostic tests required someone to carry out the routine manipulations and report the results for the physician to use. Further, early hospitals hired apothecaries to compound drugs, and this function has been carried on by the hospital pharmacist. Thus, there emerged a new category of technicians to increase the size and scope of the hospital's social structure. This group of workers freed the physicians to treat more patients (previously physicians had done their own testing and compounding prescriptions), and they also substantially increased the physicians' dependence upon the hospital as a base for their medical practice. Another feature of the emergence of technicians is important here. Unlike all the other role categories which emerged during this period, technicians were detached from regular and active contact with patients and therefore represent the culmination of a trend that had begun with Pasteur's discovery. This trend, namely, the decrease of interest in the dependence on *social* contexts in the work of the hospital and an increasing preoccupation with the *scientific* and *technical* aspects of medicine, is very much a consideration in the current controversy of how medical care may best be provided for the greatest number of people.[33]

As both the size of the hospital and the scope of its services increased, it may be expected that the size of the staff required to administer to the institution would also increase. Typically, early hospitals had a board of governors, a small group who made policy and supervised the running of the hospital while carring on their own occupational activities. Very soon it became apparent that one of their number should be detailed to provide more supervision for the increased activity and from this finally emerged the more common structural feature of today's hospital, namely, a board of governors who set institutional policy and a full-time administrative staff

---

[33]See, for example, W. Richard Scott, "Professionals in Hospitals: Technology and the Organization of Work," in Basil S. Georgopoulos (ed.), *Organization Research on Health Institutions,* Ann Arbor: University of Michigan, 1972, pp. 139–158.

who carry out the policies on a day-to-day basis. It should be noted here that the administrative staff, which must operate the hospital as if it were a business, giving consideration to matters of cost and public image, etc., is quite likely to come into conflict with the medical staff, whose main concern is for patient care and whose structural position as *volunteers* in the hospital is vulnerable to control by the nonmedical administration. The nature of this conflict situation and its consequences are noted more fully in the following chapter. What is important at this point is to suggest that it was largely an administrative decision to focus the hospital's services on private (and paying) patients, but at the same time make provision for charity patients who could not be accommodated in public hospitals which had developed for that purpose. Nonetheless, this decision was a fateful one for the future development of the hospital for it meant a redefinition of the essential purpose of the hospital. Prior to 1900, most hospitals had the avowed purpose of serving *all* who sought admittance, especially the poor and the sick. With improved medical care and its attendant rise in costs, this goal was altered to those who applied for aid and care but were not dependent upon public charity, and finally, hospitals were geared to cater to those who desire hospital treatment in preference to home care and who are "abundantly able and willing to pay for such treatment."[34] This shift in policy inevitably engendered a new attitude on the part of the hospital toward its patients. It always had been a service institution whose solicitude was for the sick within its wards, and which did its best to alleviate pain and distress. Now, in addition to this basic work of mercy, it began to cater to the special desires and even the whims of its well-to-do patients. Luxury or "gold coast" suites were provided for the wealthy at costs of up to four times the operating expenses. Patients were no longer looked upon as a group of unfortuantes needing physical care, but as potential sources of donations for care of others. Hospitals began to conceive of themselves less as charity institutions and more as nonprofit associations whose fiscal aim must be to break even each year.

## THE MODERN HOSPITAL AS A COMMUNITY HEALTH CENTER

The contemporary hospital, then, is a product of shifting forces which have functioned for more than fifteen centuries and have acted to shape and reshape its structure. Many of these same forces, in addition to some newer ones, continue to influence change in the hospital. For example, it was pointed out that achievements of medical science had contributed to a significant change in the hospital's public image. Medical science has had

[34]Wessen, *op. cit.,* p. 116.

another effect which has just recently emerged. Because medical science has proved so effective in combating acute, infectious diseases and in discovering causes, cures, and preventives, there has been a dramatic increase in the average length of life of a person born in the United States. As a consequence, there has been a shift in the cause of death and morbidity, as we discussed in Chapter 2. This has had tremendous implications for the hospital, however, in that more people come to the hospital with more kinds of diseases which require a long period of time for treatment.[35] Thus, many general hospitals have established wards or at least special services for the care of the chronically ill. But it also has been demonstrated that patients can recover at least some functioning after a period of intensive therapy; thus some general hospitals now include among their services a rehabilitation unit designed to help patients with almost all kinds of chronic ailments to recover the highest level of functioning possible. In another area of long-term care, the hospital has begun providing psychiatric services, on both outpatient and inpatient basis. Of course, ambulatory outpatient care for general medical problems has long been a service provided by the hospital. More recently the hospital has begun reaching out beyond its own walls to provide care for chronic patients at home. There are several reasons for this. In the first place, the hospital beds have been increasingly filled with chronic cases whose treatment requires a long-term confinement far beyond the ability of these patients to pay for it fully. In addition, many of these cases do not require the level of care received in the hospital but only periodic supervision. Thus, an organized home care program is one method in which the patient may live at home (which is less expensive for the patient and, perhaps, psychologically more beneficial) and yet obtain proper medical supervision as well as having contacts and access to hospital services should they be needed.[36]

Similarly, some hospitals have extended ambulatory and hospital-based support services into the community through affiliation with neighborhood health centers which have emerged in response to the "consumer" movement in health care delivery.[37] In one sense, this may be viewed simply as an extension of the scope of hospital-based services in keeping with the trend. In another sense, the association between the community general hospital and neighborhood health centers may be seen as a countertrend or "decentralization" of health care services in response to inequities in availability of and accessibility to high quality medical

[35]Cf. Daniel M. Harris, "Effect of Population and Health Care Environment on Hospital Utilization," *Health Services Research,* 10 (Fall, 1975), 229–243.

[36]David Littauer, I. Jerome Flance, and Albert F. Wessen, *Home Care,* Hospital Monograph Series, no. 9, Chicago: American Hospital Association, 1961.

[37]Lillian Rubin, "Maximum Feasible Participation: The Origins, Implications and Current Status," *Poverty and Human Resources Abstract,* 2 (1976), 5–18.

care.[38] At issue is the control of the decision-making process and of resources. Unlike hospital-based home care programs in which hospital personnel made the decisions and controlled resources, neighborhood health center representatives have demanded at least a share of control.[39] The degree of control can vary from consumer domination over providers to the opposite extreme of complete powerlessness in which the consumer is "manipulated" by the provider. In between these extremes are varying degrees of delegated authority and advisory status.[40] There are many factors which influence the degree of consumer control such as the formality of their organization,[41] the issues to be decided, particularly financing and personnel,[42] commitment by providers,[43] and programs for training consumers.[44] No uniform approach to resolving these conflicts has yet emerged although some attempts have been partially successful.[45] It is clear, however, that lay community groups have become a more important element in the general hospitals' environment.[46]

The hospital has also become the central training facility for future physicians, nurses, and allied health personnel. Medical education at practically all levels takes place mostly in the hospital setting. With the develop-

---

[38]Melvin A. Glasser, "Consumer Expectations of Health Services," in Lawrence Corey, Steven E. Saltman, and Michael F. Epstein (eds.), *Medicine in a Changing Society,* St. Louis: Mosby, 1972, pp. 29–38.

[39]Godfrey M. Hochbaum, "Consumer Participation in Health Planning: Toward Conceptual Clarification," *American Journal of Public Health,* 59 (September, 1969), 1698–1705. There are other issues, of course, such as level of care given, administrative policies, and funding depending on the stage of development of the health center, described in one analysis as the "formative stage," "charisma testing stage," and "routinization—purposive action stage." See Andrew C. Twaddle and Richard M. Hessler, *A Sociology of Health,* St. Louis: Mosby, 1977,, chap. 12.

[40]Claudia B. Galiher, Jack Needleman, and Anne J. Rolfe, "Consumer Participation," *HSMHA Health Reports,* 86 (February, 1971), 99-106.

[41]Gerald Sparer, George B. Dines, and Daniel Smith, "Consumer Participation in OEO–Assisted Neighborhood Health Centers," *American Journal of Public Health,* 60 (June, 1970), 1091-1102.

[42]Steven Jonas, "A Theoretical Approach to the Question of 'Community Control' of Health Service Facilities," *American Journal of Public Health,* 61 (May, 1971), 916-930.

[43]Chester Douglass, "Effect of Provider Attitudes in Community Health Decision Making," *Medical Care,* 11 (March–April, 1973), 135-144.

[44]Alberta W. Parker, "The Consumer as Policy-maker—Issues of Training," *American Journal of Public Health,* 60 (November, 1970), 2139-2153.

[45]See, for example, Robert J. Bornstein, "Special Board for Public Input," *Hospitals,* 47 (June 16, 1973), 65-67; in the same issue, James J. Potuznick and Mary M. Blanks, "Elected Residents Serve on Board," *Hospitals,* 47 (June 16, 1973), pp. 60-65; Lowell G. Bell, Florence Kavaler, and Al Schwarz, "Phase I of Consumer Participation of 22 Voluntary Hospitals in New York City," *American Journal of Public Health,* 62 (October, 1972), 1370-1378; and Scott S. Parker and James Falick, "How to Make Consumers Real Partners in Planning," *Modern Hospital,* 119 (July, 1972), 103-106.

[46]See the discussion in Edmund D. Pelligrino, "The Changing Matrix of Clinical Decision Making in the Hospital," in Georgopoulos, *op. cit.,* pp. 301-328; and chap. 5 in William R. Rosengren and Mark Leffon, *Hospitals and Patients,* New York: Atherton, 1969.

ment of so many medical and surgical specialties, the cases which present problems for those specialties may not be found anywhere except in the hospital. Then, too, the new and expensive equipment necessary to perform the most advanced diagnostic and therapeutic procedures is most often found in the hospital; thus there also will be found the specialists to use them. The medical staff of hospitals have therefore expanded, creating new pressures and problems for the social structure of the hospital. The point of all this is simply that despite some countertrends, the hospital remains the locus of medical and health care services in the community. Through broadening the scope of its services, by developing new resources, and by maintaining high standards of care, the hospital is now the only community facility with the capability for providing many of these services.[47]

In part, the development of the hospital as the health center of the community depends upon its external image or how it is seen by other health organizations and the community's population. The external image is affected by the kind of information given to the public (i.e., public relations releases), by "word of mouth" testimony by patients (and doctors) who have used the hospital, and by its relationships to other organizations including voluntary support groups.[48] One study of the hospitals in two communities indicated the influence of conditions such as high tax rates for health purposes and professionalized leadership in health agencies as important to hospital growth. More importantly, this study suggested that competition for voluntary contributions and other support is affected by sectarianism and by conflict of hospital leadership groups over the avowed purposes of the hospital, i.e., how broad a service program would be offered.[49] Another study suggested that other factors also were involved. These included elements such as the social-class character of the community power groups, the changing cultural expectations with respect to medical care and medical education, and the degree to which voluntary power groups enlist the aid of political organizations in their drive to expand and improve hospital facilities and services.[50]

More recent analyses of the hospital's role in the community, however, have suggested that public relations, fund-raising, and continued,

[47]Committee on Medical Care Teaching, *Readings in Medical Care,* Chapel Hill: University of North Carolina Press, 1958, especially pp. 225-329.

[48]Basil Georgopoulos and Floyd C. Mann, *The Community General Hospital,* New York: Macmillan, 1962.

[49]Ivan Belknap and John G. Steinle, *The Community and Its Hospitals,* Syracuse N.Y.: Syracuse University Press, 1963.

[50]Ray Elling, "The Hospital-support Game in Urban Center," in Freidson, *op. cit.,* pp. 73-111. See also Ray Elling and Sandor Halebsky, "Organizational Differentiation and Support: A Conceptual Framework," *Administrative Science Quarterly,* 6 (September, 1961), 185-209.

uncoordinated growth will not be enough. Rather, the hospital must adopt a more flexible organizational form to be more responsive to changing community needs.[51] Some of these community needs for services are indicated by trends such as increasing standards of living and personal affluence, rising demand for health care, greater influence of federal and state governments in health care delivery, increasing demand by consumers for a share in making decisions, continued progress in technological development, and so on. These trends will help shape the goals and structure of health institutions of the future so that, as Lippitt suggests, the task " . . . amounts to reorienting hospitals and other social institutions so that, amoeba-like, they are capable of continously and consciously undergoing change and renewal."[52] Some management characteristics needing change have already been identified. These include developing a flexible social structure to meet changing health care needs, moving from autocratic to more democratic decision-making procedures based on confidence rather than obedience, opening the organizational structure to interface with federal and state agencies, establishing mechanisms for dealing with confrontation and organizational conflict, etc. Finally, it has been noted that hospitals of the future will have to take on the responsibility for the consumer health education process as well as being centers for diagnostic and treatment services, research, and medical education if they are to continue to play a central role in a community's health care system.[53] In sum, the hospital is not "an island unto itself," but must depend upon other groups and organizations for its existence and future development.

Despite the problems involved in obtaining support from community resources and maintaining a positive "image," the hospital industry, that is, the number of hospitals and services offered, has grown rapidly. Although statistical information on hospitals is scant for years prior to World War II, reasonably complete data are available from about 1946 to the present.[54] Even in the short span of time since 1946, we can observe considerable change in the types of hospitals, their utilization, and the costs of operating them. Table 9-1, for example, shows the growth in number of hospitals of various types from 1946 to 1975. Overall trends indicate a markedly slowed rate of change in all hospitals after 1963 with only non-federal short-term and psychiatric hospitals showing any increase. When we recall that the early hospital of the Middle Ages and the Renaissance was a custodial institution, later developing into an organization for treatment of acute illnesses, the two important observations from the table are

[51]Gordon L. Lippitt, "Hospital Organization in the Post-industrial Society," *Hospital Progress,* 54 (June, 1973), 55–64.

[52]*Ibid.,* p. 56.

[53]Anne R. Somers, "Adapting Institutions to Changing Needs," *Hospitals,* 48 (May 1, 1974), 41-44.

[54]See Corwin, *op. cit.*

## Table 9-1   Growth of the Hospital Industry, 1946-1975

| Hospital type | Number of Hospitals | | | Percent change | |
|---|---|---|---|---|---|
| | 1946 | 1963 | 1975 | 1946–63 | 1963–75 |
| Nonfederal short-term: | | | | | |
| Voluntary, nonprofit | 2,583 | 3,394 | 3,364 | 31.4 | −0.9 |
| Proprietary | 1,076 | 896 | 775 | −16.7 | −13.5 |
| State and local | 785 | 1,394 | 1,840 | 77.5 | 32.0 |
| Total | 4,444 | 5,684 | 5,979 | 27.9 | 5.2 |
| Nonfederal, long-term: | | | | | |
| Psychiatric | 476 | 499 | 544 | 4.8 | 9.0 |
| Tuberculosis | 412 | 186 | 36 | −54.8 | −80.6 |
| Chronic-disease | 389 | 323 | 215 | −17.0 | −33.4 |
| Total | 1,277 | 1,008 | 795 | −21.1 | −21.1 |
| All federal | 404 | 446 | 382 | 10.4 | −14.3 |
| Total, United States | 6,125 | 7,138 | 7,156 | 16.5 | 0.2 |

Source: American Hospital Association, Hospitals: Guide Issue, 1976, table 1, pp. 7–9.

the increase in government-owned, short-term hospitals and the decrease in special types of institutions, particularly for long-term care. Oddly enough, in terms of number of hospitals of a given type, long-term care hospitals seem to be declining; yet as we have seen in Chapter 2, chronic ailments are the most prevalent kind of health problem. In part, the apparent decrease in long-term hospitals is due to the decrease in tuberculosis sanatoria. It was noted earlier that tuberculosis is one of the chronic diseases for which an effective cure has been found. Thus, there is a declining need for this type of institution. The decrease may also be attributed to the fact that more general hospitals are providing long-term care in units set aside for just that purpose. In other words, many chronically ill patients are cared for in general, short-term hospitals, hence the decline in hospitals classified as long-term only. Perhaps the strongest influence in the decline of long-term chronic hospitals has been the remarkable growth of nursing homes. Although the establishment of nursing homes dates back to 1900, it has only been since the end of World War II that their influence has been felt to strongly. According to one source, many nursing home operators

> . . . were literally backed into the field. Many of them were elderly women who took in another elderly person who needed only personal care and attention. Others began by operating boardinghouses for elderly persons. As the years passed, some of their guests became ill and bedfast and before they knew it, these boardinghouse operators in effect had become nursing home owners for there was no place to send these unfortunate individuals.[55]

[55]U.S. Senate Special Committee on Aging, Nursing Homes and Related Long-term Care Facilities, Part I, Washington, D.C.: Government Printing Office, 1964, p. 22.

The high cost of hospital care and the inability of the medical profession to deal effectively with chronic diseases highlighted the need for other facilities and provided the stimulus for the growth of nursing homes. In 1939 there were about 1,200 homes with 25,000 beds, By 1972 there were more than 23,000 homes with slightly more than one million beds, with most of that growth taking place between 1960 and 1970.[56] This means that there are three nursing homes for every hospital and more beds in nursing homes (1.2 million) than medical and surgical beds in hospitals (1.0 million). Furthermore, expenditures for long-term care have risen from $500 million in 1960 to $7.5 billion in 1974, and more than one-third of the 1974 figure (34 percent) went to nursing homes compared with 31 percent to hospitals.[57] That such phenomenal growth would likely be accompanied by problems of controlling quality, quantity, and cost of services is attested to by the organization of the American Nursing Home Association, which has attempted to raise standards of care and police its membership. Its failure to do so is indicated by many reports citing the continuing social, economic, and medical abuses in the nursing home industry.[58] Although proposals to establish economic incentives for providing good nursing home care have been made,[59] the industry has not yet responded. Since more than half of all payments for nursing home care come from public sources, the Congress will likely continue deliberations on what role the government might play in solving these problems.

As medical science makes progress in discovering causes of chronic disease, it would be expected that more and more patients with those ailments will be cared for in short-term hospitals and nursing homes, thereby further reducing the need for long-term hospitals. It should be noted also that the only type of long-term hospital showing an increase in number is the psychiatric hospital. On the one hand, this reflects the increasing burden of mental illness and on the other hand, an attempt to get away from the old "traditional" state mental institution and to develop many smaller, more accessible mental health facilities with the expectation of a shorter stay for patients.[60]

Since our concern in this chapter has been mostly with the voluntary, nonprofit, short-term hospital, we shall focus the remainder of these remarks on hospitals of this type. It need only be indicated here that this

[56]U.S. Senate Special Committee on Aging, *Nursing Home Care in the United States: Failure in Public Policy, Introductory Report,* Washington, D.C.: Government Printing Office, December, 1974.

[57]*Ibid.,* p. 20.

[58]See, for example, M. A. Mendelson, *Tender Loving Greed,* New York: Random House, 1974.

[59]Robert L. Kane, "Paying Nursing Homes for Better Care," *Journal of Community Health,* 2 (Fall, 1976), 1–4.

[60]Max Pepper, "Reorganization of the Mental Hospital," part 2, *Gerontologist,* 4 (June, 1964), 53-57.

type of hospital represents about 47.0 percent of all hospitals of all types and about 56.5 percent of all nonfederal, short-term hospitals. Thus, we are talking about a substantial portion of the hospital industry. Table 9-2 indicates very clearly the remarkable growth of the number of voluntary, nonprofit short-term hospitals from 1946 to 1963 and a much reduced rate of change from 1963 to 1975. Although during the latter period the number of hospitals has declined, there has continued to be an increase in the number of beds available, in the number of admissions, and in the daily census. Yet the average occupancy rate (the proportion of occupied beds in the hospital on a given day) has remained about the same. This is due to increased efficiency of treatment procedures for many kinds of illnesses and is reflected in the low average length of stay. This is all the more remarkable in view of the increasing number of patients in these hospitals who are chronically ill, with characteristically longer periods of hospitalization. Also noteworthy is the large decrease in number of births which took place in the hospital after 1963 and in the use of hospital outpatient services. Finally, from Table 9-2, it should be noted that the number of personnel needed to operate hospitals continued to grow although the rate of increase had slowed since 1963. From 1946 to 1975 the rate has more than tripled, and the rate per 100 patients has more than doubled, indicating that more special services requiring additional personnel are now provided in the hospital setting.

The increase in the number of personnel required to provide the services offered by a hospital has been a significant factor in the increased expense of hospital operation (thus increased charges to patients). Table 9-3 reveals that the total expense for voluntary, short-term hospitals has continued to increase by a factor of 4, although the rate of increase declined slightly after 1963. The expense per patient-day has also continued to rise

**Table 9-2  Selected Characteristics of Voluntary, Nonprofit Short-Term Hospitals, 1946–1975**

| Characteristic | 1946 | 1963 | 1975 | Percent change 1946–1963 | Percent change 1963–1975 |
|---|---|---|---|---|---|
| Number of hospitals | 2,583 | 3,394 | 3,364 | 31.4 | −0.9 |
| Number of beds (in thousands) | 301 | 486 | 659 | 61.5 | 35.6 |
| Number of admissions (in thousands) | 9,554 | 18,120 | 23,735 | 89.6 | 31.0 |
| Average daily census (in thousands) | 231 | 377 | 510 | 63.2 | 35.3 |
| Bed occupancy (in percent) | 76.7 | 77.7 | 77.4 | 1.3 | −0.4 |
| Average length of stay (in days) | 8.8 | 7.6 | 7.8 | −13.6 | 2.6 |
| Number of bassinets | 59,254 | 72,105 | 57,496 | 21.7 | −20.3 |
| Number of births (in thousands) | 1,596 | 2,653 | 2,131 | 66.2 | −19.7 |
| Number of outpatient visits | — | 55,142 | 132,368 | — | 140.0 |
| Number of personnel (in thousands) | 362 | 921 | 1,714 | 154.4 | 86.1 |
| Number of personnel per 100 patients | 156 | 244 | 336 | 56.4 | 37.7 |

*Source:* American Hospital Association, *Hospitals: Guide Issue,* 1976, table 1, p. 9.

**Table 9-3  Total and Payroll Expenses of Voluntary, Nonprofit Short-Term Hospitals, 1946–1975**

| Type of expense | 1946 | 1963 | 1975 | Percent Change 1946–63 | Percent Change 1963–75 |
|---|---|---|---|---|---|
| Total expenses (in millions of dollars) | $848.00 | $5,491.00 | $27,965.00 | 547.5 | 409.3 |
| Payroll expenses (in millions of dollars) | 431.00 | 3,377.00 | 14,461.00 | 683.5 | 328.2 |
| Total expenses per patient day (in dollars) | 10.40 | 39.87 | 150.24 | 283.4 | 276.8 |
| Payroll expenses per patient day (in dollars) | 5.11 | 24.52 | 80.83 | 379.8 | 229.6 |
| Percent of total expense for payroll | 50.8 | 61.5 | 51.7 | 21.0 | −15.9 |

Source: American Hospital Association, *Hospitals: Guide Issue,* 1976, table 1, p. 9.

rapidly. That cost of personnel is important is shown by the fact that payroll expenses still account for about half of the hospitals' total expenses. Some causes and consequences of cost factors are discussed in Chapter 13.

## SUMMARY

By taking a historical approach to the development of the hospital, we can get a better perspective on the shifts which have taken place as well as obtain some understanding of why the modern hospital has the social structure which now characterizes it. We have seen how the hospital has changed from an institution for charitable care to a public utility, from a refuge for the poor to the doctor's workshop, and from a single purpose organization to one with many goals. We turn now to some contemporary research which attempts to understand the functioning of the modern hospital. In essence, the history of the development of the modern hospital is the story of institutional response to changes in the organization and practice of medicine. During the Middle Ages, when the church dominated the lives of nearly everyone and medical practice was largely in the hands of priest-physicians, the hospital functioned as a shelter for the sick and the poor. The coming of the Renaissance and Reformation, however, marked the beginning of an era in which a secular rationale replaced sacred beliefs. Most importantly, it marked the resumption of scientific investigation. The transition was a difficult one for the hospital, which declined to its lowest ebb because its personnel had neither the benefits of scientific medicine nor the religiously inspired motivation to care for the sick. Hospitals changed, but slowly, from the Renaissance period until the late 1870s, when medical science—soon followed by medical practice—was established on a firm scientific basis. From this time to the present, the hospital fairly exploded with changes—expansion in size of the physical plant to accommodate increasing demand for beds and for space for ancillary services, rapid proliferation of roles within the social structure of the hospital, and particularly, a redefinition of patient status and of the avowed purpose of the hospital.

## SUGGESTED READINGS

Abel-Smith, Brian, and Robert Pinker, *The Hospitals, 1800-1948: A Study in Social Adminsitration in England and Wales,* Cambridge, Mass.: Harvard University Press, 1964.

Dainton, Courtney, *The Story of England's Hospitals,* Springfield, Ill.: Charles C Thomas, 1961.

Freidson, Eliot (ed.), *The Hospital in Modern Society,* New York: Free Press, 1963.

Georgopoulos, Basil, and Floyd C. Mann, *The Community General Hospital,* New York: Macmillan, 1962.

McInnes, E. M., *St. Thomas' Hospital,* London: Allen & Unwin, 1963.

Chapter 10

# Social Structure of the Modern Hospital

*The modern hospital has lost the gloom of its precursor, where every feature reminded one of the proximity of death. Today the hospital remains a place of suffering and disease, but the accent is on life.*

Henry E. Sigerist
*Civilization and Disease,* 1943

The previous chapter has provided an overview of the development of the hospital as a social institution. It sought to demonstrate how changing conditions have transformed the character of hospitals over the centuries. This story is significant, not only as an interesting and important bit of social history, but as a demonstration of the way in which complex organizations evolve. What is particularly important for present purposes, however, is the realization that the nature of the hospital as a *contemporary* organization has been determined in large part by this history.

Although the social structure of every organization is constantly modified as its members and decision makers try to adapt their goals and activities to changing conditions, the very term "structure" implies that organizational activity takes place within a relatively fixed and unchanging context. Organizational behavior, however adaptive, begins within a frame of reference inherited from the past. People tend to relate to one another, to solve problems, to organize their activities as they have come to expect they ought to do from past experience. This tendency is usually buttressed by the memory of past successes and failures, and reinforced by the sentiments and ideologies through which historical memories are expressed. Therefore, even the most "rational" of human organizations, devoted as it may be to organizing the cooperative activities of a group so that their joint efforts can be most effectively coordinated to attain a "joint purpose," will tend to lag in altering its patterns so that they correspond to changed conditions. This lag will tend to be particularly noticeable in areas involving human relations (as opposed to the manipulation of material objects) and intangible goals; it may be least visible in areas in which technology and other applications of scientific knowledge are perceived as useful.[1] In any case, the history of any organization leaves a "precipitate" of values, expectations, and organizational forms which tend to survive even after the conditions in which they were formed have changed.

Organizations differ in the stability of their social structures. Some, perhaps located in a favorable and relatively unchanging environment, can successfully satisfy the aspirations of their members and the demands of their communities in about the same fashion for a very long time. Others are forced constantly to alter their activities and also to modify their goals as a result of changing circumstances. In some social settings, the tendency will be to preserve received social forms as intact as possible, and to adapt to changing environmental demands, if at all, by changing "the way things are done" as little as possible. In other circumstances, it may be felt important to attain an organization's goal if at all possible by doing *whatever* seems rationally appropriate to make an organization's capabilities match the challenge of its environment. In such settings, traditions, however pleasant, are seen as of secondary importance, and change may come to have a positive value in its own right.[2]

We may conclude from the history of hospitals that, within the past century, this type of organization has moved from a relatively static environment in which the place of this kind of institution within the scheme of things was well fixed and the possibilities of what could be accomplished

---

[1]These lines depend heavily on the organizational theories of Chester I. Barnard, *The Functions of the Executive,* Cambridge: Harvard University Press, 1938, and on the classic discussions of social and cultural change in William F. Ogburn, *Cultural Change,* New York: Huebsch, 1922.

[2]Weber touched upon this distinction in his analysis of "traditional" and "rational-bureaucratic" modes of authority. See Max Weber, *The Theory of Social and Economic Organization,* New York: Oxford University Press, 1947.

medically for the sick were quite circumscribed, into a dynamic environment in which the possibilities offered by a growing medical science were constantly expanding and the demands of society changing radically. In more recent years, hospitals have become increasingly subject to principles of rational management: those who have controlled them have increasingly sought to make this kind of organization immediately *responsive* to the changed demands of the environment.[3]

We speak here of the "hospital" as if all hospitals were alike. This, of course, if far from the truth. In reality, the organizations designated by this name show a great range of differences, not only in the kinds of buildings they possess, in their size and available resources, but also in their programs and in the kinds of social environments they present to their patients, to their staff and employees, and to the public at large.[4] These differences are rooted in the particular history and situation of each individual hospital; and, in one sense it is true to say that from the social scientist's point of view, every hospital (like every other organized group) is unique, operating in terms of constraints different from those affecting any other group, and imposing expectations upon its members which are more or less peculiar to each alone.

However, it is equally true that some organizations are more or less alike, so that generalizations can be made about them. The very word "hospital" implies that all organizations so designated will have broadly similar goals, activities, and social structures. But sociological entities (like "hospital," "business firm," "lodge," or "physician") are not merely classificatory devices. They are also, insofar as they are generally recognized, *normative* terms which imply a set of learned and shared *expectations* about what a hospital, a lodge, or a physician—or any other entity— *ought* to be and do. They imply a recognized cultural model that might be called a "type-institution." This cultural model is the outgrowth of a traditional shared by all the specific organizations emerging from it, even though they may scarcely have been a part of it. For example, a new hospital, founded this year, to some degree becomes an heir to all the expectations and traditions associated with the hospital movement, just as contemporary individuals find the full meaning of their citizenship only as they appropriate the traditions of their country. In this sense it is true to say that all hospitals—even those which are newly founded—are in some ways affected by such facts as that hospitals spring from a charitable and

[3]See, for example, Sydney H. Croog and Donna F. Ver Steeg, "The Hospital as a Social System," in Howard E. Freeman, Sol Levine, and Leo G. Reeder (eds.), *Handbook of Medical Sociology*, 2d ed., Englewood Cliffs, N.J.: Prentice-Hall, 1972, pp. 274–314.

[4]See the definitions of different types of hospitals and new institutions that have taken on some hospital-like characteristics in American Hospital Association, *Classification of Health Care Institutions*, Chicago: American Hospital Association, 1972.

altruistic tradition or that they traditionally were custodial institutions whose services to their patients were those of *caring for* rather than *curing* them. In sum, all hospitals are part of a common tradition and are expected to conform to a common (though general) cultural model. And, as we shall see in Chapter 12, there are a number of organizations and groups whose primary concern is to foster such organizational conformity.

For these reasons, the history of an organization—and of the cultural model which it represents—is important for an understanding of what that organization *is*. In fact, the unique characteristics of an organization's social structure may largely be described in terms of its history. Such is the method to be followed by the present chapter. We shall, however, discuss these characteristics first as they affect the overall shape of the social structure of contemporary hospitals, and second, in relation to their implications for the social relations between the hospital, the patient, and those persons who, in their work, serve both. We shall thus analyze both a number of general characteristics of the hospital as an organization and three basic models for patient care which are to be found in various institutions.[5]

One qualification, however, is necessary before we proceed. In analyzing the development of the hospital, it was pointed out that a number of different kinds of hospitals have developed, and that many of these varieties have achieved formal recognition. Thus, in the United States, legal distinctions are drawn between "proprietary" and "voluntary, nonprofit" institutions. Similarly, some hospitals are restricted in their goals to treating only certain kinds of diseases or patients; such "special" hospitals (e.g., psychiatric, lying-in, or children's institutions) are not only commonly distinguished from "general" hospitals and expected to have differing sociological characteristics, but they and their staffs are often organized into special, common interest groupings. And the kind of ownership and control an institution has often has far-reaching implications for the kind of constituency it serves, the type of staff it can attract, and the type of program it can develop. So in the hospital literature, the type of ownership and control of hospitals is always taken as an important differentiating factor. Other factors, such as size or location, are regularly seen as significant sources of difference among hospitals, but not so much as the basis of distinct *types* of institutions.

In one such distinction—that between the university-based medical center and the community general hospital—the medical center can be

---

[5]In choosing to focus on the internal environment, we cannot also include here an extended discussion of the hospital in relation to its external environment. This was briefly noted in the preceding chapter. Other discussions are provided in William Glaser, *Social Settings and Medical Organization,* New York: Atherton, 1970; and in Wolf Heydebrand, *Hospital Bureaucracy,* New York: Dunellen, 1973, pp. 289ff.

described as the kind of hospital (usually large and located in an urban setting) which attempts to offer a comprehensive range of technical services, to draw its patients from a large population base, and to emphasize the training of professional persons (especially physicians) in research as well as the provision of care. Usually associated with a medical school, its staff consists largely of specialists, many of whom are full-time employees.[6] By contrast, the community general hospital[7] emphasizes the provision of medical care to members of its immediate community, sometimes to the exclusion of such other goals as professional education and research. Its medical staff are largely private practitioners, some of whom may be general practitioners. And frequently, the community general hospital is a small institution and in a small community. Sociologists, as well as medical care administrators, are increasingly aware that the medical center may be as different an institution from a community general hospital as is a "special" hospital (e.g., mental hospital) from a general hospital.

In the following pages, our primary model for description and analysis will be the community general hospital.[8] We shall, however, have much to say about the special characteristics of medical center hospitals—which often can be seen as very special examples of certain generic characteristics of hospital social structure. Although we shall, from time to time, mention special hospitals or the effects of such differentiated factors as type of ownership or control, these factors will not be systematically treated here.

## SOME FORMAL PROPERTIES OF THE HOSPITAL AS AN ORGANIZATION

Like every organized enterprise, the hospital has an organizational goal, a raison d'être, so to speak. More precisely, like many large-scale organizations, the hospital has a set of goals. In fact, the hospital has been described as "the prototype of the multi-purpose organization: it is a hotel and a school, a laboratory and a stage for treatment."[9] In general, the multiple

[6]See the description in Amasa B. Ford, *Urban Health in America,* New York: Oxford University Press, 1976, pp. 154–157.

[7]Basil Georgopoulos and Floyd C. Mann, *The Community General Hospital,* New York: Wiley, 1962.

[8]General references would include Chris Argyris, *Diagnosing Human Relations in Organizations: A Case Study of a Hospital,* New Haven: Labor and Management Center, Yale University, 1956; Temple Burling, Edith Lentz, and Robert N. Wilson, *The Give and Take in Hospitals,* New York: Putnam, 1956; George G. Reader and Mary E. W. Goss, "Medical Sociology and Particular Reference to the Study of Hospitals," *Transactions of the Fourth World Congress of Sociology,* 2 (1959), 139–152.

[9]Robert N. Wilson, "The Social Structure of the General Hospital," *Annals,* 346 (March, 1963), 67–76. Quote is on p. 69. See also the discussion in Basil S. Georgopoulos (ed.), *Organization Research on Health Institutions,* Ann Arbor: University of Michigan Press, 1972.

goals of the hospital are subsumed in medical care services, education and training, and research. Thus, most hospitals are designed to provide medical care services to their patients. At the same time, these organizations may be the principal training ground from which valuable experience is gained by fledgling physicians. Still other hospitals may devote considerable resources to research problems. It is by no means clear which of these is the most important goal at any given time (although for humanitarian as well as traditional reasons, patient care is most often stated as the primary goal).

A host of lower-level goals are a part of these more generic purposes. For example, the goal of economic stability, that is, of keeping costs down while providing the best possible care, is emphasized by administrators as a part of the more general objective of providing medical care services. At the same time, to the medical staff the cost factor may not be as important as admitting patients who are suitable as teaching material for medical students, interns, and residents. One may readily see that the attempt to achieve these related but independent goals places a heavy burden on the administration which is charged with the responsibility of coordinating the efforts at goal achievement.[10] On the other hand, it is also apparent that the importance of a goal varies directly with the degree to which a person is involved with it, as in the example of the medical staff being more concerned with providing teaching material than in keeping costs down. Similarly, an expensive piece of diagnostic equipment may be purchased to assist in medical diagnosis even though the equipment is not used to its fullest extent, thereby not returning the money invested in it. In any event, nearly every activity engaged in by an employee or staff member of a hospital can be articulated somehow to be related to patient care and comfort, from the obvious tasks of the medical and allied health personnel to the work of the lowliest janitor. While patient service may have the single highest priority, it is also obvious that it means more to those occupations which deal more directly with it than to those which do not. Thus, there is a proliferation of subgoals related mostly to various occupational groupings found among the hospital's personnel.[11] Yet, as we shall see later, it is precisely this dominant theme of patient care which enables different groups with disparate objectives to work together in the hospital setting.

Achievement of these organizational goals is attempted through the mechanism of *bureaucratic organization*—a hierarchical arrangement of offices and positions for the rational coordination of tasks leading to

[10]Charles Perrow, "Goals and Power Structures: A Historical Case Study," in Eliot Freidson (ed.), *The Hospital in Modern Society,* New York: Free Press, 1963, pp. 112–146.

[11]See Georgopoulos and Mann, *op cit.*

attainment of the group's objectives.[12] Reference to Figure 10-1, which represents the organizational chart of a typical but mythical general hospital, reveals clearly its hierarchical arrangement. However, in several respects the organization chart of a hospital differs from those which typify other formal organizations such as factories or military units. First, it may be noted that the hospital has a more pronounced horizontal development than a vertical emphasis. The hospital organization chart has been described as resembling a "comb" compared to other formal organizations which are said to resemble a "tree." Second, it is suggested that the lines of authority of the hospital director extend only to the heads of departments, particularly those who are not professional or whose activities are less directly related to patient care. This, of course, is in marked contrast to other types of formal organizations in which the lines of authority reach from the administrator or manager, through department heads, down to the level of workers.[13]

In the administrative hierarchy, the board of trustees at the top is the policy-making body of the hospital and is made up of "representatives" of the community to protect the community's interest in the hospital. The levels at which policy decisions must be made vary, of course. They may range from considerations of staff organization or adding new services to deciding on the color of the walls for the washrooms. The translation of these policy decisions into actual practice is the job of the hospital administrator. By delegation of authority from the board, he or she is therefore responsible for the day-to-day operation of the hospital and generally the arbiter of interdepartmental and interpersonal problems which arise in the course of daily interaction. Increasingly, the administrator is also becoming the hospital's representative to the community, the person who interprets hospital functions and services to the people who are potential customers of (as well as potential donors to) the institution.

The hierarchical nature of the hospital organization extends beyond that which is portrayed in Figure 10-1, however. In every department and in every service there is further status differentiation, usually on the basis of the *office* held (although there is also informal status differentiation on the basis of other than technical qualifications). That is, in addition to differential importance of the various departments, there are several posi-

---

[12]Although this form of organization is most frequently found in community general hospitals, it is only one of six ideal-types based on level and mode of coordination. Cf. Heydebrand, *op. cit.*, pp. 280–286. A simpler classification was proposed in Eugene Litwak, "Models of Bureaucracy Which Permit Conflict," *American Journal of Sociology*, 68 (September, 1962), 177–184.

[13]Hans O. Mauksch, "The Organizational Context of Nursing Practice," in Fred Davis (ed.), *The Nursing Profession: Five Sociological Essays*, New York: Wiley, 1966, pp. 109–137.

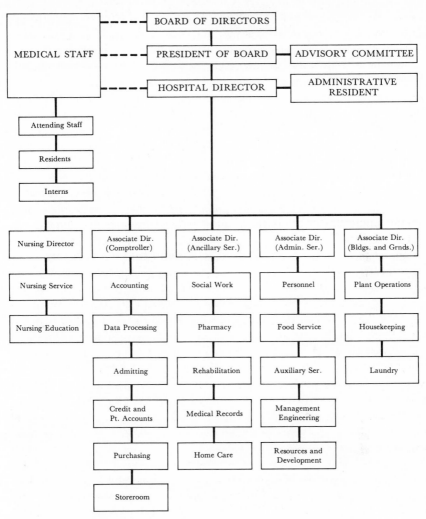

**Figure 10-1**   Administrative organization of a general hospital.

tions within each department filled by incumbents on the basis of skills they
have. Theoretically, the most qualified person occupies the top position
because that person has the requisite skills to carry out the duties of that
office. Thus the office of director of each of the various departments carries
greater prestige and greater rewards than that of other members of the
department. The cognizance of these hierarchical placements is perpetuated through the use of distinctive uniforms and insignia and given social
recognition through deference and respect. Medical personnel habitually
wear white coats (or in the case of visiting physicians, carry a stethoscope

in their coat pocket), nurses of different levels wear different uniforms and insignia, as do personnel occupying other positions, such as white-collar workers, maintenance workers, orderlies, cleaning personnel, etc.

A feature of hospital organization which may not be so obvious from the diagram is the presence of *two lines of authority* (represented by the broken line in Figure 10-1).[14] This, of course, is a direct outgrowth of the historical position of physicians as "visitors" or "guests" in the hospital, and yet because of their virtual monopoly on medical knowledge, no hospital could function without them. Thus, on the one hand, there is the collegial organization of the medical staff (although it, too, is stratified according to specialty and the statuses of practicing physician, resident, intern, student) and on the other hand, there is the bureaucratic arrangement of offices which make up the administration. Because of this peculiar organizational arrangement, the hospital presents a very different kind of line-staff problem. In the customary single authority system found in business, government, or the military, decision-making powers rest in the offices of the managers who direct the activities of line personnel or workers. The staff position in this arrangement is one of a technical specialist who *advises* the management, but does not make decisions or issue orders to workers. In the hospital setting, however, it is the staff (the medical staff) which wields the authority at least with respect to matters concerning patient care (and this is usually interpreted broadly). Thus, the medical staff usually directs the "line" in its activities while the management's authority is often restricted to matters concerning providing the means by which the doctor's orders may be successfully carried out.[15]

The dual authority system has still another consequence, however, for nursing. As the recipient of the doctors' orders for their patients, the nurses are obligated to carry out those orders in a professionally competent manner, but at the same time, they are hired employees of the hospital and consequently, subject to all the rules and regulations of the administrative organization.[16] Often the demands of patient care, especially when they are

[14]Harvey Smith, "Two Lines of Authority Are One Too Many," *Modern Hospital,* 85 (March, 1955), 48–52.

[15]Stanley F. King, *Perception of Illness and Medical Practice,* New York: Russell Sage Foundation, 1962, especially pp. 307–348. Also Amitai Etzioni, "Authority Structures and Organizational Effectiveness," *Administrative Science Quarterly,* 4 (June, 1959), 43–67. It has been suggested, however, that as the ability to store resources and to specify procedures for their use increases, the degree of authority shifts from the professional to the administrator. This would seem to be the case in community hospitals. See Gerald Gordon and Selwyn Becker, "Changes in Medical Practice Bring Shifts in the Patterns of Power," *Modern Hospital,* (February, 1964), 89–91.

[16]See Ronald G. Corwin, "The Professional Employee: A Study of Conflict in Nursing Roles," *American Journal of Sociology,* 66 (May, 1961), 604–615. For a study of conflict between professional and bureaucratic roles of the nurse with respect to dying patients, see Barney Glaser and Anselm Strauss, *Awareness of Dying,* Chicago: Aldine, 1965.

of an emergency nature, cannot be accomplished within the framework of administrative rules; thus the nurses are caught in a conflict between the expectations of the physicians that their orders be carried out and the expectations of the administrator that administrative procedures will be complied with.[17]

Another feature of hospital organization is the *extreme division of labor*. We have already noted this characteristic with respect to the medical profession, but it is no less true of the administrative services and other departments of the hospital. Each of the separate departments and services of the hospital performs a special function presumably all leading to the achievement of the institution's goals. Thus, another of the administrator's major tasks is to coordinate all of the varied services to form some kind of rational whole. The development of these specialties, however, has led to a stratification of hospital personnel along occupational lines roughly divided into professional, administrative, and nonprofessional tasks. This means that while persons in these different categories may occasionally work side by side, their orientation (and loyalty) is normally to their occupational group and not necessarily to the particular situation in the hospital in which they are performing those tasks. For example, one may look at a typical nursing unit and obtain a microscopic view of the division of labor. In general, there is a nursing supervisor (who may have more than one unit to look after) whose major duty is to ensure that all the necessary tasks are accomplished. Under the supervisor is usually a head nurse who is the day-to-day director of activities of the unit. Often one may find an assistant head nurse who replaces the chief at times and otherwise carries out general supervisory duties. There are floor nurses or general duty nurses who provide high-level bedside nursing as well as teach nursing students and nonprofessional personnel. Student nurses are assigned ward duty for varying periods to acquaint them with the realities of nursing in contrast to textbook nursing. Aides, orderlies, and messengers are taught enough to make them useful, and they generally carry out less-dramatic aspects of patient care. Then there are a host of custodial people, cleaning staff, janitors, and so on, who keep the wards clean, remove soiled linen, etc. There may also be a clerk assigned to the unit who assists the head nurse in completing many documents and reports that are necessary for the administration of the unit. This listing does not include others who work on the unit from time to time, but who are assigned elsewhere such as interns, residents, therapists, auxiliary personnel, mechanics, and the like. The point is that while each of the roles involved in the work on the nursing unit contributes directly or indirectly to the ultimate objective of providing

[17]This is a typical incident of "multiple-subordination" described in Jules Henry, "The Formal Structure of a Psychiatric Hospital," *Psychiatry*, 17 (May, 1954), 139–151.

patient care, few participants have more than a cursory understanding of the role of the others. This highly developed division of labor can and does create some problems, not the least of which is establishing effective communication networks so necessary for coordination. In addition, persons with similar roles tend to identify and communicate with each other more easily than they do with others.[18] They have a similar ideology as well as professional aspirations, and, as a consequence, hospital work roles tend to become stratified along occupational lines. As we shall discuss below, this, too, presents some problems.

Finally, but not exhaustively, the *authoritarian nature* of the hospital should be noted. The kind of activities carried out in the hospital, e.g., the saving of life, can only be conducted in a setting in which orders given will be carried out without question and without delay. This is particularly true when the case is an emergency in which action must be taken without hesitation or reference to the prescribed administrative procedure. While most of the activities carried on in the hospital are not emergencies, the hospital staff must be prepared for just such cases. Thus, the purpose of the fairly rigid hierarchy, the clearly demarcated channels of authority (in the administrative structure), and written procedural rules is to assist the staff in handling emergency cases as well as more routine ones. This kind of authority, like that of the military organization, is the rational-legal type, based as it is on the power residing in a particular office and concentrated at the top of the hierarchy. But as we have noted earlier, the authority of the medical staff is charismatic in nature, that is, authority placed in the hands of a person because of certain outstanding attributes of the individual.[19] More importantly, the charisma of physicians has been generalized to many situations in the hospital setting in which the rational authority of the administration is more appropriate, thus making the medical staff a very powerful and influential group in the hospital.[20]

## SOCIAL STRUCTURE AND FUNCTIONING OF THE HOSPITAL

An enumeration of important characteristics of an organization, no matter how elaborate, can only give the outline, the boundaries within which social interaction takes place. Since we wish now to focus directly on the

[18]Albert F. Wessen, "Hospital Ideology and Communication between Ward Personnel," in E. Gartly Jaco (ed.), *Patients, Physicians and Illness,* 2d ed., New York: Free Press, 1972, pp. 325–343.

[19]For a discussion of types of authority and their consequences, see Hans H. Gerth and C. Wright Mills (eds.), *From Max Weber: Essays in Sociology,* New York: Oxford University Press, 1958, especially pp. 245ff.

[20]Georgopoulos and Mann, *op. cit.,* pp. 8–11.

social structure of the hospital, it is necessary to examine the general patterns of social relationships that may be observed within the institutional setting.[21] Insofar as the social structure is derived from institutional patterns, it may be expected that role prescriptions, status, and rules for behavior (norms) would constitute a significant aspect of its form. Thus, the characteristics of the hospital noted above—dual authority system, the division of labor, etc.—have a marked effect on the social structure of, and therefore on interaction in, the hospital. The effect is basically one of channelization; that is, it is the function of social structure to determine the general direction of interaction in specific situations—to dictate, as it were, who speaks to whom. It means that, out of all the potential relationships which could be formed (in a large organization such as the hospital, it could be an infinite number), certain ones become emphasized at the expense of others.

In an analysis of a social structure, one must first determine what groups are a significant part of the structure. We have already noted that generally speaking three main groups can be identified—the medical staff, the administration, and the nonprofessionals. From the point of view of the hospital's goals, it may seem strange to omit patients as a significant group, but this is justified on several grounds. In the first place, the average patients neither have learned the culture patterns distinctive of the institution, nor do they participate actively in the life of the hospital. Their role there is a passive and introverted one centered about their all-engrossing purpose to get well as quickly as possible. Second, modern medicine has greatly reduced the length of time the average patient stays in the general hospital, so that historical precedent of the hospital as a custodial institution has long since disappeared. For this reason, plus the acutely ill patients' "egocentrism," an inmate culture does not usually emerge as a significant factor in the hospital social structure as it does in prisons, mental hospitals, and other long-term care institutions.[22] Thus, while patients are *in* the hospital, they are not *of* it, but rather constitute a reference group for the groups which are a part of the hospital's social structure.

Perhaps one way to examine patterns of social relationships is to focus on organizational problems which emerge from the structural alignment of roles in the institutional setting. To this end, we will examine here some problems arising from the dual authority system and the extreme division of labor. The historical precedent for and some consequences of the dual authority system have already been noted. But there are some larger, more

[21]For a different approach to assessing the social structure of the hospital and its consequences in terms of organizational effectiveness, see Heydebrand, *op. cit.*, especially fig. 1, p. 25.
[22]The emergence of an inmate culture is discussed in Chap. 11.

fundamental issues arising from this peculiar structural feature than staff-line problems or conflict in the nursing role. In the first place, the juxtaposition of two power groups in the same setting almost inevitably leads to conflict over organizational goals. While neither the medical staff nor the administration would likely deny that patient service is their *primary* goal, there are many subsumed goals and ways of achieving them which provide a fertile field for conflict. It should be noted, however, that some areas of authority are clearly demarcated and acknowledged. For example, an administrator would not attempt to advise the medical staff on decisions concerning therapy for patients, just as a physician would be unlikely to influence the way an administrator would organize a system for purchasing supplies. At the same time, it should be recognized that because of the charismatic nature of the doctors' authority and the prestige of their position, their influence has a pervasiveness far out of proportion to their competence. Thus, the doctors may not advise the administrator on how to organize the purchasing office, but they might suggest what to purchase.

There is, however, a large "gray" area in which both the medical staff and the administration have interest and overlapping authority, and it is here that conflict is most likely to arise. For example, such functions as medical records, the pharmacy, and administration of out-patient clinics are important to both groups and come under the purview of each. Essentially, the major goal conflict, whatever the specific arena, is summed up by Smith as "money versus service."[23] On the one hand, there is the administrator with a view to fiscal survival of the institution, who establishes rational procedures for cost accounting, who attempts to minimize the loss of income from service to indigent patients, and who expects formal rules to be followed.[24] On the other hand, the medical staff sees the hospital as the most appropriate setting for performing certain patient care services, services which should be judged on the basis of clinical efficacy and not how much they cost. Furthermore, it is advantageous for the medical staff to have a sizable number of "teaching beds," i.e., beds that are occupied by patients whose cases are used in teaching medical students, interns, and residents. More often than not, however, teaching beds are filled with patients who can ill afford the care of a private physician and the hospital's private facilities. Obviously, the greater the proportion of teaching beds, the more endangered is the financial scurity of the institution.

In the presence of a dual authority system in the hospital, one finds that different groups have a differential perspective of who has authority in what area. One study, for example, asked questions of 282 board members,

[23]Smith, *op. cit.*

[24]For a description of the functioning of a hospital in which the locus of power is in the hands of the business manager as administrator, see Elaine Cumming and John Cumming, "The Locus of Power in a Large Mental Hospital," *Psychiatry,* 19 (November, 1956), 361–371.

hospital administrators, chiefs of medical services, and nursing administrators in thirteen voluntary hospitals in New York State. In addition to background information, the investigators asked questionnaire respondents to judge what role each of the four hospital groups—board members, administrators, doctors, and nurses—should play in making decisions on problems arising in the hospital setting. Respondents also answered questions on some hypothetical situations to judge whether authority was being usurped. The findings indicated that there was some agreement among the respondents as to who should have authority in certain areas. For example, most respondents felt that the medical staff should have the authority to decide on matters of patient treatment. In areas where there was overlapping authority, not only did the groups in conflict reserve more authority for themselves, but also rated their opponents as having the least power. As might be expected, the most differences in perception were between the administrators and doctors with conflicts between administrators and the board members being second. In addition, the investigators also reported that the authority of administrators of large hospitals (over 225 beds) was greater than in small hospitals (225 beds or less). The reverse was true for doctors and board members.[25]

It has often been suggested that if the hospital administrator was also a physician, goal conflict could be reduced. Presumably, a physician-administrator would be able to understand better the medical staff's point of view, and at the same time convince them of the viability of the administration's perspective. Most often, goal conflict has not been resolved in this way.[26] First, most physicians are disinclined to accept full-time administrative responsibilities, although they may agree to a part-time staff position if it does not interfere with their primary career commitment to private practice, teaching, or research. Even if physicians were willing to accept the full-time administrative post, they very quickly are perceived by other physicians as engaging in a "nonprofessional" activity; thus the physician-administrator becomes "one of them, not one of us."[27]

A second problem stemming from the dual authority system and related to goal conflict is the struggle between professional autonomy and bureaucratic control. Because of their expertise in medicine, the physicians maintain that they, and only they, are competent to make decisions regarding patient care. Further, physicians maintain that because they are in a

[25]Frederick L. Bates and Rodney F. White, "Differential Perceptions of Authority in Hospitals," *Journal of Health and Human Behavior,* 2 (Winter, 1961), 262–267.

[26]That such a simplistic notion is bound to fail due to the complexity of the relationships among members of the board of directors, the administration, and the medical staff is described in Robert H. Guest, "The Role of the Doctor in Institutional Management," in Georgopoulos, *op. cit.,* pp. 283–300.

[27]Mary E. W. Goss, "Administration and the Physician," *American Journal of Public Health,* 52 (February, 1962), 183–191.

fully professionalized occupation, only physicians can exercise control over members of their own profession. But as we have already seen, many of the areas related to patient care fall into the gray area of overlapping authority; thus they may also be subject to the authority of the administration. It should be recalled that the authority of the administrator rests with an office near the pinnacle of the organizational hierarchy and emanates down the chain. Thus, as hospitals grow larger, add new services, and make changes in old services, there is a tendency toward increased bureaucratization.[28] This, of course, impinges directly on the functional autonomy of the medical staff and it is resisted vigorously.[29] Engel, however, noted that professional autonomy was affected by degree of bureaucratization only when the latter was extremely high. Under conditions of "moderate" complexity of bureaucratic structure, perceived autonomy by the medical staff was not affected. This suggests that there may be an optimum level of bureaucratization to foster organizational efficiency, but not limit the professional's sense of autonomy.[30] It has been shown, however, that physicians' control over members of their own group is not exercised very strongly. In one study of a large medical group practice, Freidson and Rhea[31] analyzed data from interviews, sociometric ratings, minutes of meetings, and medical records to ascertain how a medical group ensures and maintains an acceptable quality of medical care as practiced by their members. By and large, they reported that members of their group depend heavily on personal endorsements and assume that completion of medical training is sufficient evidence of competence. Once a member is recruited, however, the norms of professional practice are such that one member does not evaluate the work of another nor offer unsolicited advice to a colleague except as these functions are institutionally provided for through committees (of colleagues) established for that purpose. Moreover—and this is central to our discussion of professional autonomy—violations of rules or deviations from what is considered good medical practice are rarely punished except by "talking to," which falls short of even a reprimand. The deficiencies in the behavior of violators are brought to their attention by a colleague, usually a peer or senior person in the same department. Rarely is the matter taken up with the medical director. According to the authors,

[28]Theodore R. Anderson and Seymour Warkov, "Organizational Size and Functional Complexity: A Study of Administration in Hospitals," *American Sociological Review,* 26 (February, 1961), 23–27; also Heydebrand, *op. cit.*

[29]Robert A. Rothman, Allen M. Schwartzbaum, and John H. McGrath, "Physicians and a Hospital Merger: Patterns of Resistance to Organizational Change," *Journal of Health and Social Behavior,* 12 (March, 1971), 46–55.

[30]Gloria V. Engel, "The Effect of Bureaucracy on the Professional Autonomy of the Physician," *Journal of Health and Social Behavior,* 10 (March, 1969), 30–41.

[31]Eliot Freidson and Buford Rhea, "Processes of Control in a Company of Equals," *Social Problems,* 11 (Fall, 1963), 119–131. For a fuller account of autonomy and the process of self-regulation see Eliot Freidson, *Profession of Medicine,* New York: Dodd, Mead, 1970.

this is only one recognized form of punishment short of dismissal, which, as they note, is difficult to achieve.[32] Another study, this one of staff physicians in a clinic setting, showed that even the physician in charge was reluctant to use his legitimate authority, but preferred instead to use personal influence to control the physicians under his supervision.[33] It may very well be that "administrative efforts at control of work [of professionals] are not mere bureaucratic aggrandizement, but conscientious efforts to fill a genuine vacuum engendered by the peculiarities of the professional system of self-regulation."[34]

Among other things, the acknowledged professional status of physicians has contributed to the drive for recognition by other health-related occupations. In Chapter 8, we have already seen how nursing has moved in this direction and the difficulties it has encountered. Similarly, many of the allied health personnel have aspirations in this direction, for example, pharmacists, physical therapists, social workers, etc. Recently a movement has begun to upgrade the status of the hospital administrator through extended education and graduate degrees in addition to practical experience in residency programs. Conflicts arise, however, because most of these occupational groups attempt to adopt professional prerogatives which heretofore had been the property of the medical profession. Physicians, however, are reluctant to abdicate their prerogative and legitimate the professional claims of aspiring occupations. Moreover, recognition for these claims is not given by the general public nor by the hospital industry.

A second major feature of the social structure of the hospital from which certain problems arise is the division of labor. The division of labor, e.g., the development of specialties in the medical profession, has already been discussed in Chapter 7. Some of the same factors, particularly the development of new knowledge and skills, are behind the increasing complexity of the hospital's organization. In addition, one may point to the increased number of services performed in the hospital and to technological advancements, not to mention growth in sheer size of the hospital, as contributing to the finer and finer partitioning of tasks. For example, as medical technology and knowledge grow, there has been a proliferation of new departments which have directed their efforts to a particular aspect of the medical care process. McInnes describes the development in St. Thomas' Hospital between 1870 and 1900: "By 1900 there were eleven special departments for outpatients . . . ophthalmic was the first, started in 1871, the throat department started in 1882 and the skin and ear as a joint department in 1884; the latter was divided in 1885.[35] In addition a depart-

[32]Freidson and Rhea, *op. cit.,* p. 126.
[33]Mary E. W. Goss, "Influence and Authority among Physicians in an Out-patient Clinic," *American Sociological Review,* 26 (February, 1961), 39–51.
[34]Freidson and Rhea, *op. cit.,* p. 131.
[35]E. M. McInnes, *St. Thomas' Hospital,* London: Allen and Unwin, 1963, pp. 147–148.

ment of mental diseases was started in 1893, of gynecology in 1888, and of pediatrics in 1898.[36] While this refers to a particular hospital, a similar process was occurring in many Western hospitals about the same time. This development illustrates the fact that expansion of facilities and services contributed significantly not only to the complexity of the hospital as an organization, but also to the increased stratification through specialization. These trends, of course, gave rise to increased problems of coordination and control on the part of the administration, but they also engendered certain kinds of structural problems.

One of the obvious consequences of the separation of assignments in tasks is the potential for stratification of small groups of people into a status hierarchy based on degree of skills attained, degree to which members deal directly with patients, etc. A rigid stratification leads to "blocked mobility," i.e., places a severe limit on how far one can progress in a given specialty group. Certainly one could, over a long period of time, rise from the worker level to section chief or department head within a given specialty (although that may be only one or two positions up), but rarely does one go from one specialty to another, higher one without additional formal training. Thus, a laboratory technician does not reach the plateau of hospital pathologists, nurses do not become doctors, electricians do not become administrators, etc. Such limited opportunities for achievement are frequently cited as causes of rapid turnover in personnel or low morale among workers.[37] This, in turn, affects the quality of personnel available to the hospital since often the most capable individuals leave first in search of better opportunity, leaving their positions to be filled by default by less capable personnel. One contradictory force in this respect is ideological commitment; i.e., capable persons continue in jobs with limited opportunities because of their commitment to the goals of the organization rather than to personal ambitions.[38]

At the same time, the rigidity of the hospital's stratification may tend to interfere with the development of a functioning team, i.e., may hinder attempts to coordinate the widely disparate activities of hospital personnel. Teamwork in an organizational setting requires recognized channels of authority, but also free-flowing communication. Ordinarily, organizations are designed with formal channels of communications, but as one study

[36]*Ibid.*

[37]Warren G. Bennis, "Authority, Power and the Ability to Influence," *Human Relations,* 11 (May, 1958), 143–155. See also, by the same authors, "Reference Groups and Loyalties in the Out-patient Department," *Administrative Science Quarterly,* 2 (March, 1958), 481–500.

[38]In addition, opportunity for advancement is not always a high-priority item among workers as an element in job satisfaction. See Raymond G. Carey, "Measuring Organizational Climate," *Hospital Progress,* 56 (February, 1975), 53–57.

clearly showed, the more rigid the authority system, i.e., the more stratified, the more likely it is that communications will be disrupted and channelized along occupational lines.[39] Data from interviews and observations in this study revealed that the members of each of three occupational groups—doctors, nurses, and nonprofessionals—interacted with members of their own group far more frequently than with members of the other two groups. Furthermore, the higher the status of a person within a particular group, the lower the likelihood of interaction with members of lower groups. The communication between groups tended to be "businesslike," that is, limited to the job at hand, and did not involve social talk.

The stratification system also has consequences for patient care.[40] Through the use of attitude scales, work evaluations by superiors, and self-reports, Seeman and Evans[41] demonstrated that interns rotating among fourteen nursing units with different degrees of stratification felt that coordinated information concerning a particular patient (a prime requisite for teamwork) was much better in nursing units with the least amount of stratification. Moreover, again according to interns, the best teaching occurred in units with a low degree of stratification. The subjects also reported that they spent less time in highly stratified units giving psychological support to patients. From this evidence, one may conclude that a high degree of stratification in the hospital social structure contributes to a poor quality of patient care through interrupting communication necessary for adequate teamwork and inhibiting the amount of psychological support given the patient.

From the foregoing description, one might be tempted to conclude that the social structure of the hospital severely limits any functioning at all. While the problems that arise should not be minimized, there are some factors which contribute to the achievement of the institutional goals. In the first place, there still remains an ideological commitment to patient care, a historical legacy which at least temporarily resolves conflicts which arise. It has already been noted that commitment to a job enables the hospital to retain some capable personnel. In addition, this commitment, or more

---

[39]Wessen, *op. cit.*

[40]Assessing the quality of medical care, of course, is a very complex undertaking, and the degree of stratification is only one of many influential factors. See the discussion in Mary E. W. Goss, "Organizational Goals and the Quality of Medical Care," *Journal of Health and Social Behavior,* 11 (December, 1970), 255–268, the more general statements in Croog and Ver Steeg, *op. cit.,* pp. 278–282, and Heydebrand, *op cit.,* pp. 58–63.

[41]Melvin Seeman and John W. Evans, "Stratification in Hospital Care: I, The Performance of the Medical Intern," *American Sociological Review,* 26 (February, 1961), 67–80. See also a companion article by the same authors, "Stratification in Hospital Care: II, The Objective Criteria of Performance," *ibid.,* 26 (April, 1961), 193–202. More recent evidence of the influence on quality of care of characteristics of the setting in which care is delivered is found in Rhee Sang-O, "Factors Determining the Quality of Physician Performance in Patient Care," *Medical Care,* 14 (September, 1976), 733–570.

generally, service orientation, is part and parcel of every true profession as well as of many occupations which aspire for professional status. Thus, conflicts arising among personnel who deal directly with patients may be resolved by judgment as to "what's best for the patient." In the same way, conflicts between therapeutic personnel and the administration may be resolved for individual cases and may even lead to new policies which are mutually satisfactory to opposing groups.

A second factor which tends to mitigate the tensions arising from structural features has to do with the development of an *informal* structure and informal communication systems. In any kind of social setting where people interact over an extended period of time, the relationships which emerge may be mostly "primary type relations."[42] That is, there will be a tendency for these persons to take into account more than just the particular organizational roles played by others (e.g., position in the formal social structure), and to see them in terms of their personalities, common extraorganizational interests, etc. In groups characterized by primary relationships, communication tends to be "deeper" and more free-flowing, thus circumventing blocked formal channels and, thereby, some softening of stratification along strictly occupational lines may occur. In other words, conflict over some issues approached by opposing parties from the viewpoint of their respective occupations may be avoided because of kinship or of friendships which extend beyond the walls of the institution. Moreover, informal communication and private understandings may also aid and abet the goal of patient care. For example, a doctor and nurse may share an understanding about the way the doctor wants patients treated which may be idiosyncratic to the doctor's style of practice and not covered in the institutional rules.

These and other factors lead to the conclusion that each conflict arises under some conditions which are peculiar to that specific situation or to groups involved, thereby rendering the resolution of the conflict "negotiable."[43] That is to say, there are some characteristics of the hospital's social structure which make possible conflict resolution by negotiation or bargaining. For example, the generalized organizational goal of providing good patient care does not, of course, cover specifics of individual cases. Thus, the way is opened for negotiation on matters of policy, rights, and obligations, etc., for the parties concerned. One might at first think that in individual cases regarding patient care, the medical staff would prevail, but

[42]Charles H. Cooley, *Social Organization,* New York: Scribner, 1909.
[43]Anselm Strauss, Leonard Schatzman, Danuta Ehrlich, Rue Bucher, and Melvin Sabshin, "The Hospital and Its Negotiated Order," in Freidson, *op. cit.,* pp. 147–169. See also, Burling et al., *op. cit.*

this is not always true. In part, this is because doctors do not always agree among themselves, i.e., there is often an element of uncertainty in medical decision making. More importantly, physicians must depend heavily on others to see that care of their patients is carried out. This is particularly true for the nursing staff, but to a certain extent also with respect to the administration. Thus, physicians are not *always* in a position to force their views on others. Sometimes they must negotiate.[44] This does not imply that conflict is inconsequential, but, more to the point, that because of deep ideological commitment and the development of informal networks of interaction and negotiability, conflicts that do arise can be resolved, thereby enabling the hospital to be a functioning organization.[45]

## SOCIAL STRUCTURE AND MODELS OF PATIENT CARE

In the preceding chapter and the initial parts of the present one, some historical origins and basic features of the social structure of the modern hospital have been provided. Of key importance is the gradual evolution of the hospital from a *charitable* institution—where the social structure was most influenced by values such as the primacy of service to the needy and hospital work as a religious vocation—to a *medical* institution with its multiple goals, proliferation of specialized roles, and professional control. Further, modification in social structure is continuing as trends in medical need and demand change. From this material, it is possible to construct some ideal-type models of hospital-based patient care. That is, a study of institutional social structure is essentially an examination of the organization of roles for the achievement of goals and the normative definition of role behavior derived from the interaction among people playing those roles. In the context of health institutions, focused as they are on the general goal of patient care, the specific objectives as well as role expectations for members of the various subgroups vary from one type of institution to another.[46] Thus, from these characteristics—organizational goals, assumptions about disease, role expectations—different models of patient care may be developed.

Broadly speaking, there are three ideal-type models which are considered here: the custodial care model, the classical (acute) care model, and the rehabilitation model. The basic characteristics of these models are

[44]David Mechanic, "Sources of Power of Lower Participants in Complex Organizations," *Administrative Science Quarterly,* 7 (September, 1976), 349–364.

[45]Hans O. Mauksch, "It Defies All Logic—But a Hospital Does Function," *Modern Hospital,* 95 (October, 1960), 67–70.

[46]Heydebrand, *op. cit.,* pp. 280ff.

**Table 10-1   Models of Patient Care**

| | Dimension | Custodial | Classical | Rehabilitation |
|---|---|---|---|---|
| 1. | Stated goals | Comfort | Cure | Restoration |
| 2. | Assumptions about the disease process | Incurable | Reversible | Mutable |
| | a. Therapy | Sporadic | Central | Supplementary |
| | b. Sick role | Permanent | Temporary | Intermittent |
| 3. | Patient motivation | Obedience to institutional rules | Obedience to "doctor's orders" | Achieve mastery |
| 4. | Resulting institutional model | Total institution | Acute general hospital | Rehabilitation center |

outlined in Table 10-1.[47] One must keep in mind, of course, the fact that these characterizations do not take into account the overlap between the various types of care which are found in the real world. Nor does it really do justice to the fact that the latter two models are the products of modern medicine in contrast to the custodial care model which has persisted for centuries. Nonetheless, the development of ideal conceptualizations provides an analytic lever by which we may initially examine the relationships between patients and hospital personnel. A more detailed analysis is found in the following chapter.

## Custodial Care Model

Simply stated, the underlying goal of custodial care is to provide "decent" care designed to make the patient as comfortable as possible in an enduring situation. As we noted earlier, these hospitals emerged as a means of providing help for the needy poor and for charity patients. The patients' role was linked with expectation associated with philanthropy with the consequent distinction between the patients and their "betters." Thus, patients were expected to be grateful for the services rendered to them and to show the proper amount of deference toward their benefactors. One of

[47]It is tempting to propose a fourth model, called *preventive* patient care. Some basic characteristics can be identified, but as yet no specific institutional model, as we are describing them, has yet emerged (although a prepaid, comprehensive group practice organization has some potential). The stated goal, of course, would be to maintain health. Through the efforts of anticipatory therapy, the disease process is avoidable and the sick role, therefore, is unnecessary. The client (not patient) must be motivated to "live healthfully." At the present time, preventive medicine has little salience in our health delivery system except among certain groups (dentists, pediatricians) and some agencies (public health departments). Consequently these services, when provided, are given in a variety of settings, but not any one with social-structural attributes peculiar to the model.

the ways in which this gratitude and servility could be shown was through sober obedience to rules and regulations laid down for them.

While the stated goal was patients' comfort, the practical objective was to do this as economically and as effectively as possible. Thus, there emerged a rigid, formal hierarchy with a myriad of rules to regulate nearly the whole of the patients' lives, enabling a small number of official personnel to supervise a large number of patients to maintain order and provide what treatment was available. This meant that considerations of individual care were often subordinated to actions for the "common good," especially nonmedical action. Thus, custodial patients became objects of organizational or administrative procedures rather than individuals with particular problems.

In view of the fact that most of the patients were thought to be afflicted with prolonged if not incurable diseases, the treatments utilized were likely to be only sporadically applied (particularly in the era before medical knowledge allowed medical intervention to be effective). Even then, therapy was more likely to be directed at making the patient comfortable rather than as an attack on the patient's disease. It would also be expected that long-term patients would more or less permanently occupy the sick role, thus be dependent upon the institution and its personnel for life. The implication, of course, is that for these patients, motivation to get well and resume normal roles is unrealistic and, perhaps, even psychologically harmful. Rather, patients are encouraged to make their lot less desperate by obeying institutional rules and avoiding clashes with the administration. The nature of these social relationships, both between patients and staff and among patients, results in an institutional model like a "total" institution.[48]

### Classical Care Model

The pertinacious advance in medical sciences has equipped the medical profession with new knowledge and tools for effectively coping with many kinds of diseases. Thus, for the treatment of some known diseases, the goal has become complete cure of the patients. But as we have noted before, there is also an air of emergency associated with treatment in the hospital setting. This imperative, emergency character of medical care has left its mark on expectations concerning social roles in the hospital. Even though most activities concerning medical care are usually routine, the occasional necessity for decisive action to prevent death has been frequently cited as justification for the hospital's quasi-military social structure.[49] The pre-

[48]Erving Goffman, *Asylums,* New York: Doubleday, 1961. The concept of total institution is discussed further in the following chapter.

[49]King, *op. cit.,* p. 319.

sumption that patients are overwhelmingly motivated to be relieved of their suffering is commonly thought to justify expectations of their compliance. For everyone, hospital staff and patients alike, the classical model assumes unquestioning obedience to medical authority in order that the emergencies of disease may be overcome.

In fact, most of the time hospital patients are, by virture of their sickness, dependent and unable actively to make decisions for themselves. Since the nature of most serious physical illness demands that biological intervention occur if cure is to come about quickly, hospital patients are people *"to whom* as well as *for whom* things must be done if recovery is to occur. The result of this is that the patient is expected to be the *passive recipient* of medical care. The 'good' patient does not complain and is cooperative.[50] Hospital personnel, for reasons connected both with the logic of medical practice and with patients' dependence, often tend to see them as *objects.* Both socially and biologically, the patient becomes "a case," which is to be dealt with in a categorical rather than an interactional framework. Patients thus tend to be the objects of medical *procedures,* and these are usually legitimated in terms of the universalistic criteria of medical science. Despite the importance placed upon the ideal of continuity of care, actual interaction between staff and patient tends to be episodic and oriented toward implementation of specific procedures. With specialization and the interchangeable use of many ancillary personnel, these procedures are often carried out by a different person each time. Thus, patients find little opportunity to experience shared meanings and sentiments in the procedures imposed upon them.

The classical care model assumes also that the patient will be treated primarily for *acute* conditions and that once proper diagnosis and treatment have taken place, patients will get well and can presumably then take up their normal roles without benefit of further help. Social work and other supporting services to help patients with their nonmedical roles are ordinarily seen as required only for special problem cases.

Although many persons of several professions, ranks, and specialties are involved in providing hospital care, the classical model assumes that the efforts of these persons will be directed autocratically through a clinical chain of command or organized by a bureaucratic hierarchy. Communications between staff members are therefore to a large extent formal and written and need not involve a full understanding by each worker of the nature of the others' tasks. As long as the hierarchial division of labor is recognized and orders clearly given, little further interchange between staff members is thought to be necessary. The characteristics of this model of

[50]Albert F. Wessen, "The Apparatus of Rehabilitation: An Organizational Analysis," in Marvin B. Sussman (ed.), *Sociology and Rehabilitation,* Washington, D.C.: American Sociological Society, 1966, p. 171.

patient care obviously are represented in the institutional model of the contemporary general hospital.

### Rehabilitation Model

The rehabilitation model may in almost every respect be contrasted to the classical care model. Where the latter model emphasizes acute and emergency situations, usually of short-term duration, the rehabilitation model deals with chronic handicaps, which if they respond to treatment at all, do so only over a relatively long period of time. In place of the classical emphases on cure of disease through diagnostic and therapeutic procedures, the rehabilitation model stresses restoration of normal function, prognosis, adjustment, and retraining. Therefore, patients can no longer be mere passive recipients of care, but rather in the rehabilitation model, they must be encouraged and motivated to collaborate with the staff in achieving the maximum level of functioning. Furthermore, the various types of staff personnel must apply their unique skills in a coordinated fashion; that is, they become members of a treatment team.[51] Therefore, staff members must work to achieve and retain their clients' willingness to cooperate, but at the same time sustain their own motivations to work with patients whose progress is at best limited or agonizingly slow. Thus, unlike the classical care model in which patients' motivations are assumed, and rapid, often dramatic, recoveries are expected, motivation of patients in the rehabilitation model must be deliberately fostered and the staff must learn to be satisfied with only small increments of progress.

It is suggested, then, that the goals as well as assumptions concerning rehabilitation differ from those of both the custodial and classical care models. Moreover, rehabilitation is usually a long-term process, thus interaction between patients and staff will likely lead to the development of group structures which could either facilitate or hinder the rehabilitation of patients. So long as the institutional framework within which the interaction takes place is the rehabilitation center, the influence of group structure is more likely to be positive. However, when rehabilitation is carried on in the general hospital where the goals, assumptions, and expectations of the classical care model are dominant, the influence of group structure is more problematic.[52]

[51]Betty E. Cogswell and Donald D. Weir, "A Role in Process: The Development of Medical Professionals' Roles in Long Term Care of Chronically Diseased Patients," *Journal of Health and Human Behavior,* 5 (Summer–Fall, 1964), 95–103, and Herbert S. Rabinowitz and Spiro B. Mitsos, "Rehabilitation as Planned Social Change: A Conceptual Framework," *Journal of Health and Human Behavior,* 5 (Spring, 1964), 2–14.
[52]See the situation for psychiatric units in the general hospital in Neil H. Cheek, Jr., "Psychiatric In-patient Care in the General Hospital," in Rodney M. Coe (ed.), *Planned Change in the Hospital: Case Studies of Organizational Innovations,* New York: Praeger, 1970, pp. 193–218.

To foster the achievement of treatment in medical settings, several mechanisms have been developed by rehabilitation workers. These include (1) an ideology which stresses that rehabilitation is a special case of application of procedures common to the field of medicine as a whole; (2) the development of specialties both in medicine and in ancillary therapies; (3) the emphasis on teamwork among members of the staff; and (4) the development of out-of-hospital treatment programs such as home care. In other words, the stress is on similarities rather than differences between the prevailing classical care model and the rehabilitation model. The often cited problems of carrying on rehabilitation in the context of the general hospital social structure is indicative that the marriage is not always a happy one.[53]

## SUMMARY

In this chapter, we have tried to describe some salient features of the hospital social structure and develop some understanding of the hospital as a functioning social institution. Among the more outstanding characteristics are: (1) A *dual authority system* prevails in which the administrative organization is based on the principles of a bureaucracy and invested with rational-legal authority while the medical staff is organized along collegial lines and has a charismatic authority. This system of two lines of authority can be traced back to the time when the hospital was primarily a haven for poor people as well as those who were ill. During this period, doctors treated their private patients in the latter's home and treated the sick poor in the hospital mostly out of a Christian spirit of service to the unfortunate. Under these conditions, the doctor was a "guest" in the hospital and not a part of the hospital's organization. A similar status obtains today. The physicans' authority, despite their lack of formal power in the institutional setting, comes from their monopoly on medical knowledge and skills upon which the hospital is dependent for its existence. (2) Extreme *division of labor* is a second characteristic of the hospital, not only among the medical staff members, but in regard to the administrative staff as well. This development may be attributed to new knowledge and skills of paramedical and administrative workers, the increased number of services offered by the hospital requiring special skills, technological advancements, and growth in sheer size of the hospital. (3) A third feature of the modern hospital is its *authoritarian nature*. In part, this stems from the bureaucratic rational-legal type authority in which responsibilities are clearly

[53]See Gary L. Albrecht, "Social Policy and the Management of Human Resources," in Gary L. Albrecht (ed.), *The Sociology of Physical Disability and Rehabilitation,* Pittsburgh: University of Pittsburgh Press, 1976, pp. 257–285.

marked out and rules provided to cover many different situations. In addition, the type of work conducted in the hospital is often of an emergency nature requiring quick action without having to depend upon the slower but more consistent sets of formal rules. Even though most of the activities in the hospital are not of an emergency nature, the organization must be prepared for just such cases. Then, too, charismatic authority, characteristics of physicians, also tends to be dictatorial in nature.

These and other characteristics of the hospital structure often lead to conflict between individuals and groups within the hospital setting. For the most part, the problems which arise are conditioned by occupational loyalties. The extreme division of labor has the tendency to reduce the flow of communication and lead to blocked mobility on the part of some members of the hospital staff. These, in turn, affect the quality of patient care and employee morale as well as influence the hospital's relationships with the community. The split in authority also leads to problems of goal conflict, mostly between the efforts of the medical staff to promote patient care on an individual basis while the administration seeks to promote patient care in the least expensive way. Problems such as this point out the continual conflict between professional autonomy and bureaucratic control of the behaviors of members of the hospital staff.

At the same time, there are forces at work which tend to mitigate the severity of the potential problems stemming from the social structure of the hospital. One of these is the ideology of service, a historical legacy of the middle ages, expressed in modern terms as commitment to a job. A second force is the development of informal groups within the formal organization which permit certain activites to be accomplished regardless of the potential blocks of the social structure. Finally, it was pointed out that no one in the hospital setting has absolute power and that all conflicts are negotiable, that is, through a system of bargaining, of give and take, conflicts can be and are resolved.

An examination of the differing characteristics of the social structure of health institutions provides the basis for development of ideal-type models of patient care. The models discussed were (1) custodial care model associated with "total" institutions; (2) classical (acute) care model common in general hospitals; and (3) the rehabilitation model related to specialized rehabilitation centers.

## SELECTED READINGS

Dainton, Courtney, *The Story of England's Hospitals,* Springfield, Ill.: Charles C Thomas, 1961.

Freidson, Eliot (ed.), *The Hospital in Modern Society,* New York: Free Press, 1963.

Georgopoulos, Basil S. (ed.), *Organizational Research on Health Institutions,* Ann Arbor: University of Michigan Press, 1972.

Georgopoulos, Basil S., and Floyd C. Mann, *The Community General Hospital,* New York: Macmillan, 1962.

Heydebrand, Wolf, *Hospital Bureaucracy,* New York: Dunellen, 1973.

Chapter 11

# The Meaning of Hospitalization

*As sickness is the usual forerunner of death, it should therefore lead you seriously to consider, and reflect on your behaviour in life, and carefully to examine yourselves how far you are prepared for that great change.*

From *Directions and Prayers for the Use of the Patient*
Guy's Hospital, London, ca. 1815

To a certain extent this chapter represents a point of convergence of many of the ideas which have already been presented. Specifically, we wish to examine the situation of the sick person in the general hospital and discuss the important consequences of hospitalization for the patient. To do this, we shall combine some elements of the discussion of the hospital's social structural features (Chapter 10) with some general characteristics of an individual's response to his illness (Chapter 4). There are, of course, many different ways of approaching the examination of the effect on patients of different types of medical care facilities, including hospitals. We could adopt a study of their formal properties,[1] of the societal needs filled by the

[1]Hans H. Gerth and C. Wright Mills (eds. and trs.), *From Max Weber: Essays in Sociology,* New York: Oxford University Press, 1958, especially pp. 196–244.

organization,[2] of the beneficiaries of such establishments,[3] of the relative position of different types of organizations on some selected "dimensions,"[4] or of the nature of the interpersonal relationships found in the setting.[5] For the purposes of this chapter, we shall combine some of these approaches and make use of the ideal-type models of patient care discussed in the preceding chapter. It should be recalled that the three models of care described there—the classical model, the custodial model, and the rehabilitation model—each involved a set of *assumptions* in regard to the disease process, *goals* for caring for patients, and some expectations with respect to the *role* of the patient. By and large, it would be expected that patients' perception of their hospital experience would depend upon the degree of congruence between the model of care they expect to receive and what kind they are given in actual fact.

Before examining the situation of sick people in the hospital, it may be instructive to review briefly some characteristics of sick people, their perception of their illness, and their response to it. It should be recalled that the onset of illness means different things to different people, but that in varying degrees it is eventually disruptive of already established social relationships.[6] At several points in time during the development of an illness, the individual must make certain choices or decisions with respect to his or her behavior. These decisions are influenced by a host of sociocultural and social-psychological factors, such as ethnicity and sensitivity to pain, and certain psychological conditions like apprehension, anxiety, and fear. Moreover, psychological phenomena such as denial, aggression, loss of masculinity, regression to childlike behavior, and egocentrism are described as frequent responses to illness.

Many of these attributes of illness may be carried over to the hospital situation and, perhaps, even exaggerated by some features of the hospital. In the first place, the hospital is a strange environment for most people. It has different sounds and smells than the environments to which most of us are accustomed. There is a sort of "air of emergency" about the place as doctors, nurses, and other uniformed personnel move rapidly from one place to another. Then, too, some people still regard the hospital with

[2]Talcott Parsons, *Structure and Process in Modern Society,* New York: Free Press, 1960.

[3]Peter M. Blau and W. Richard Scott, *Formal Organizations,* San Francisco: Chandler, 1962. See also the entertaining account of the view of the hospital from the perspective of the patient in Michael Crichton, *Five Patients: The Hospital Explained,* New York: Knopf, 1970.

[4]Robert W. Kleemeier (ed.), *Aging and Leisure,* New York: Oxford University Press, 1961.

[5]Sidney Croog, "Interpersonal Relations in Medical Settings," in Howard E. Freeman, Sol Levine, and Leo G. Reeder (eds.), *Handbook of Medical Sociology,* Englewood Cliffs, N.J.: Prentice-Hall, 1963, pp. 241–271.

[6]Talcott Parsons, *The Social System,* New York: Free Press, 1951.

anxiety and misgiving, clinging to the outdated belief that the hospital is where a person goes to die. In more recent times, of course, this belief has been modified so that many believe that to be hospitalized means that an illness is serious, since only the very ill go to the hospital.[7] More important than any of these potential problems, however, is the threatened disruption of normal roles—particularly separation from the family and from the work role.

The onset of illness is, as we have seen, an intensely personal matter calling for personalized or supportive responses from the personal community in the form of expressed concern and succorant behavior. Under ordinary circumstances, this would likely be the type of response elicited from family members and friends. When the sick person is removed from the home setting and admitted to the hospital, he or she is not only deprived of these primary-oriented responses, but also exposed to a series of interactions with others which are characterized as objective and impersonal. They may range from the somewhat bureaucratic, officious behavior of admitting clerks and other administrative personnel to the professional scientific aplomb of nurses and the examining physicians. Moreover, in a work-oriented society such as ours, absence from the occupational role may also generate anxiety over loss of income, inability to resume the job after hospitalization, and perhaps loss of the job altogether. Of course, in these days of liberal fringe benefits (including hospitalization coverage), this may be less of a problem. But the discomfort engendered in having to alter the normal routine of going to work each day remains, and with it any anxiety raised by the unknown aspects of illness. In any case, the process of being hospitalized is one that is fraught with potential for disturbance, both because of separation of the patient from normal roles played in the family and the community and because of anxiety generated by lack of understanding of hospital procedures and apprehension over the prognosis for recovery from the illness and consequent resumption of normal roles.

Hospitalization of a family member may also disturb the delicate balance of social relationships among the remaining family members.[8] This is particularly true if the person hospitalized is one of the adults. According to some writers, the family, like all organizations, has also become highly specialized, focusing on initial socialization of the children and stabilization

---

[7]Minna Field, *Patients Are People,* New York: Columbia University Press, 1958.

[8]Talcott Parsons and Renee Fox, "Illness, Therapy, and the Modern Urban American Family," in E. Gartly Jaco (ed.), *Patients, Physicians and Illness,* New York: Free Press, 1958, pp. 234–245. See also Henry B. Richardson, *Patients Have Families,* New York: Commonwealth Fund, 1945. Hospitalization only accentuates the disturbance in family roles resulting from illness. See Klaus J. Roghmann, Pamela K. Hecht, and Robert J. Haggerty, "Family Coping with Everyday Illness: Self Reports from a Household Survey," *Journal of Comparative Family Studies,* 4 (Spring, 1973), 49–62.

of adult personalities as its major functions.[9] Within the family, each of the members performs certain tasks and plays roles complementary to those of other members. Thus, not only may hospitalization of the adult who is usually the breadwinner deprive the family of its income from the occupational world, but some tasks of that person's role as a family member must be taken on by someone else.

When a child is hospitalized, still other kinds of adjustments must be made in the family. At the very least, one or both of the adults must divide their attention between the remaining children and the one in the hospital. Moreover, illness of a child requires the parents' special attention, and in Western society, it is usually the parent at home who devotes more time to the sick child, shielding the child from the rigors of hospital life, but he or she does this at the expense of the spouse and the other children. There is also potential for conflict here between the family and the hospital since, especially in the case of prolonged hospitalization, the family may have to cede some of its socialization functions to the hospital.[10]

As is often the case nowadays, the modern American family is composed of not only the parents and their children, but also an aged member, usually a parent of one of the adults. The analysis by Parsons and Fox suggests that specialization of family roles now has reached a point that aging parents play no useful role in the family and their presence can disturb the role relationships among the other members.[11] In addition, aged persons are highly susceptible to chronic and disabling diseases, which may require long-term hospitalization and prolonged special care in the home, thus further adding to the family's burden. Other evidence, however, suggests that family loyalty and sense of obligation frequently are stronger than desire for more efficient role arrangements. Nonetheless, hospitalization of an aging member of the family can and often does put an emotional as well as financial strain on the family.[12]

There is one further consideration which should be noted here, namely, hospitalization for mental illness. Up to this point, reference has

[9]Talcott Parsons and Robert F. Bales, *Family, Socialization and Interaction Process,* New York: Free Press, 1960.

[10]Joseph Greenblum, "The Control of Sick Care Functions in the Hospitalization of the Child: Family versus Hospital," *Journal of Health and Human Behavior,* 2 (Spring, 1961), 32–38. See also Robert A. Dentler and Bernard Mackler, "The Socialization of Retarded Children in an Institution," *Journal of Health and Human Behavior,* 2 (Winter, 1961), 243–252. See also David Robinson, "Illness Behaviour and Children's Hospitalization: A Schema of Parents' Attitudes toward Authority," *Social Science and Medicine,* 6 (August, 1972), 447–468.

[11]Parsons and Fox, *op. cit.* More recently, see Donald P. Kent, "Social and Family Contexts of Health Problems of the Aged," in Charles O. Crawford (ed.), *Health and the Family,* New York: Macmillan, 1971, 161–174.

[12]Part of the strain comes from the realization that institutionalization may represent a final separation, especially in nursing homes where death rates soon after admission are extremely high. See Harold J. Wershow, "The Four Percent Fallacy: Some Further Evidence

been made only to the impact on the family of hospitalization for a physical illness, but there is a quantitative and a qualitative difference when the illness is mental. In the first place, hospitalization for mental illnesses ordinarily is for a longer period of time than it is for most physical illnesses. Thus, the disturbance in the role relationships may last for longer periods. Qualitatively, hospitalization for mental illness carries with it a stigma, not only for the patient, but for the rest of the family as well. Not only are the family role arrangements disturbed, but it is often difficult for the remaining members of the family to continue normal relationships with nonfamily members.

It should be noted, however, that hospitalization of a family member may actually *reduce* the strain on family relationships. The disturbance in normal role arrangements will most likely remain, but that disturbance may be preferable to the problems of dealing with a severely disabled member of the family. There is considerable evidence now which suggests that family members tend to adjust their behavior to accommodate the peculiarities of the mentally ill person. It is only when this new adjustment is disturbed that help is sought through professional care and hospitalization.[13] Alternatively, mentally ill persons can be seen as the victims of a power struggle in the family with its attendant interpersonal tensions. This approach would tend to explain the cause of the patient's hospitalization in terms of the interpersonal constellation of the family unit and to view hospitalization of the mental patient as an outcome which secures the positions of the "well" members of the family at the expense of the "extruded" patient.[14]

It also makes a difference which member of the family is ill. For example, among lower-class Puerto Rican families, it was found that if the husband was mentally ill, the wife could successfully take on parts of his

---

and Policy Implications," *Gerontologist,* 16 (February, 1976), 52–55. The inability of families to care for elderly members, combined with the unwanted risks of institutionalization, have given rise to a wide range of new community services. See the review in Eva Kahana and Rodney M. Coe, "Alternatives in Long-term Care," in Sylvia Sherwood (ed.), *Long-term Care: A Handbook for Researchers, Planners and Providers,* New York: Spectrum, 1975, pp. 511–572.

[13]Harold Sampson, Sheldon L. Messinger, and Robert D. Towne, "Family Processes and Becoming a Mental Patient," *American Journal of Sociology,* 68 (July, 1962), 88–96. See also Erving Goffman, "The Moral Career of the Mental Patient," in *Asylums,* New York: Doubleday, 1961; and Nancy E. Waxler and Elliott G. Mishler, "Hospitalization of Psychiatric Patients: Physician-centered and Family-centered Influence Patterns," *Journal of Health and Human Behavior,* 4 (Winter, 1963), 250–257.

[14]Cf. Paul M. Roman and H. Hugh Floyd, "Schizophrenia and the Family of Orientation," in Crawford, *op. cit.,* pp. 129–159. It should be recognized, however, that the family may play a critical role in *helping* the sick member. See, for example, Jerry M. Lewis, W. Robert Beavers, John T. Gossett, and Virginia Austin Phillips, *No Single Thread: Psychological Health in Family Systems,* New York: Brunner-Mazel, 1976; or Lois Pratt, *Family Structure and Effective Health Behavior: The Energized Family,* Boston: Houghton Mifflin, 1976.

role as well as her own and some aspects of the nursing role. Since most of these families were very poor, the loss of the breadwinner did not matter much. Moreover, by keeping her husband at home where she knew what he was doing, the wife did not have to worry about her husband exercising his prerogative of the double sex standard. On the other hand, if the wife was mentally ill, the husband was less able to accept the female role because of the threat to his masculinity, and his frequent absences from home served only to heighten the suspicions and jealousy of his disturbed wife. In these cases, there was tendency for marital strife and eventual hospitalization of the wife, but in the other situation family relationships were more stable and hospitalization less frequent.[15] Other research suggests that severity of disturbance and some social-psychological factors also influence the decision to hospitalize a family member.[16]

Despite the potential hazards of hospitalization, the actual experience is not always bleak, especially for acutely ill patients. There are some characteristics of the classical model of hospital care which tend to mitigate the potential stresses. It should be recalled that the major elements of the classical model included:

**1** The assumption that the disease process is reversible, particularly through accurate diagnosis and technical intervention
**2** The assumption that the patient's condition is acute and self-limiting, and therefore involves only temporary use of the sick role
**3** The perception of patients as cases or objects of procedures, that is, people *to* whom as well as *for* whom things are done
**4** The expectation that patients will comply with doctor's orders as well as with other hospital rules, since this will speed recovery from the disease and enable the patient to resume his or her normal pursuits

In a somewhat oversimplified way, these elements of the classical model may be likened to a two-edged sword—the same characteristic may exagerate anxieties on the one hand, or they may act to alleviate them on the other. To the extent that the patient's conception (or, perhaps, preconception) of an impending hospital experience corresponds to the classical model, the potentials for sociological and psychological disturbance will probably be minimized. For example, concern over separation from family and friends may be reduced by the short length of stay, often less than one week, usually required for treatment of most acute problems. The imper-

    [15]Lloyd H. Rogler and August B. Hollingshead, *Trapped: Families and Schizophrenia,* New York: Wiley, 1965.
    [16]Anthony I. Schuham, Rodney M. Coe, and Naomi I. Rae-Grant, "Some Social-psychological Variables Influencing Parental Acceptance of Residential Treatment of Their Emotionally Disturbed Children," *Journal of Child Psychology and Psychiatry,* 5 (December, 1964), 251–261.

sonality of the medical and nursing staff in this setting may not fill the patient's need for meaningful, personal interaction, but at the same time it is symbolic of the staff's professional competence to deal effectively with the patient's ailment. Similarly, being surrounded with and exposed to strange and complex-appearing equipment may accentuate a lack of understanding of what is happening, but it is also expressive of the application of scientific methods, which may be reassuring to the patient.

There are, of course, some other features of hospital life which tend also to mitigate a patient's anxieties. For example, most modern hospitals have private or semiprivate rooms available to those who can afford them. In addition, such familiar artifacts as television sets, library books, magazines, and newspapers are ordinarily available to a patient. Perhaps most important are the frequent visiting periods during which a patient may interact with family members.

For many people, then, the experience of hospitalization, although not completely free from some anxieties, is one in which potentials for anxiety can be minimized. The greater the degree of congruence between the patients' expectations and their actual experiences, the less traumatic the episode will be. However, a question may be raised about those patients whose expectations are not met by their hospital experiences. This would particularly concern the increasing numbers of chronically ill patients whose ailments are not self-limiting and for which there may be no cure. In other words, what happens to the patients who are oriented to the classical model but whose length of stay is prolonged, who have a residual disability from their disease, and who face living the remainder of their years in a protective environment such as long-term hospital or nursing home? At this point, it may be appropriate to recall some elements of the custodial care model, since this is the most frequently found type of care provided for these patients. This model involves the assumption that invalidism and dependency were on a more or less permanent basis and that the objective of the care was to make the patient as comfortable as possible. In its extreme form, this model approximates what Goffman described as a "total institution."[17]

## TOTAL INSTITUTIONS

One of the basic features of total institutions—indeed, the source of their definition as total—is that they are organized to provide for *all* the basic needs of the "batches" of people who live in them. This is in marked contrast to noninstitutional life in which needs for food, shelter, and

---

[17]Erving Goffman, "On the Characteristics of Total Institutions," in *Asylums,* New York, Doubleday, 1961.

clothing or activities such as work or recreation are supplied or performed in many different settings and with a variety of different people. Thus, in modern society, the workplace is separate from the place where we live; recreational activities often take place in settings outside the home as do the functions of education and religion. By its very nature, however, the total institution supplies all these things in the same setting and for everyone with little regard for their special interests or needs. Specific characteristics as described by Goffman include the following:

> First, all aspects of life are conducted in the same place and under the same single authority. Second, each phase of the member's daily activity is carried on in the immediate company of a large batch of others, all of whom are treated alike and required to do the same thing together. Third, all phases of the day's activities are tightly scheduled, with one activity leading at a prearranged time to the next, the whole sequence of activities being imposed from above by a system of explicit formal rulings and a body of officials. Finally, the various enforced activities are brought together into a single rational plan, purportedly designed to fulfill the official aims of the institution.[18]

Further, there is an almost castelike split between those who administer the institution and those who are administered unto. Generally, the gulf between the two groups is wide with virtually no mobility from group to group and a tendency for communication between staff and patient groupings to be formalized. More important, however, is the existence of two distinct social and cultural worlds, each with its own set of norms, attitudes, and values. Within each of the two groups, there is likely to be hierarchical ordering. In the case of the administrators, it is both formal and informal with all the characteristics of a bureaucracy. Those who are administered to are ranked only informally, since technically all members of this group have equal status. In sum, a total institution provides for all the basic needs of its inhabitants; and to achieve this end, it is organized with centralized authority, regimented activities, lack of social differentiation of those being cared for, and severe restrictions on spatial as well as social mobility.

According to Goffman's analysis, there are at least five different types of total institutions, one of which is designed for care of people who are at once not capable of caring for themselves and who may represent a threat to the rest of the society.[19] In this category, he includes mental hospitals,

[18]*Ibid.*, p. 6.

[19]*Ibid.*, p. 4. The others are (1) institutions for persons both incapable of caring for themselves and harmless (orphanages, old folks' homes); (2) institutions for protection of the community against intentional harm (penitentiaries); (3) institutions developed to achieve a single goal, such as national defense (military organization); and (4) institutions designed as a retreat from the world and providing religious training (monasteries and convents).

tuberculosis sanatoria, and leprosaria. Over the past ten years or so, there has been a rapid accumulation of literature in regard to the general characteristics of mental hospitals, especially concerning the custody-versus-therapy controversy.[20] In different ways and with varying emphases, these studies describe the mental hospital as very closely approximating the typological characteristics of the total institution. For example, most mental hospitals have a centralized authority which provides supervision for all the activities that go on within the walls of the institution. It similarly provides for all the basic needs of the patients in terms of food, shelter, and clothing (although the manner in which these are provided has important ramifications, which will be discussed later). There is also a tendency for manipulation of patients en masse. This involves keeping patients immobilized on locked wards as well as regimenting the movement of patients from one place to another (such as from the ward to the dining room or to various other group activities). This is an administratively efficient way for a small number of staff members to deal with large numbers of patients. In mental hospitals, where there often is little for patients to do, the rigid preset scheduling of activities, each one leading to the next, is less obvious than in the prisons, the military establishment, or even the general hospital. Nonetheless, some features of the mental hospital do coincide with this aspect of the model. For example, therapy sessions, mealtime, administration of medications, and bedtime are usually set a specific time. However, enforced *inactivity* would seem more characteristic of mental hospitals than tightly scheduled activity.

Typical of traditionally organized mental hospitals is the enormous hiatus between the staff and patients. One clue to the separation of these two groups is the provision of segregated facilities such as dining rooms, toilets, and recreation rooms. Status differentiation is noted also in the uniforms of the staff compared with institutional clothing or even personal clothing of patients, in the freedom to go from one place to another in the hospital (symbolized by the attendant's key ring), and in the fact that any staff member at any level has authority over any member of the patient group. There are, of course, some points of communication or contact between the two groups. Some of this is official such as therapy sessions or ward rounds. More frequently contact takes place unofficially, usually

[20]A small sample of these works would include Alfred H. Stanton and Morris S. Schwartz, *The Mental Hospital,* London: Tavistock, 1954; Milton Greenblatt, Richard H. York, and Esther L. Brown, *From Custodial to Therapeutic Patient Care in Mental Hospitals,* New York: Russell Sage, 1955; Ivan Belknap, *Human Problems of a State Mental Hospital,* New York: McGraw-Hill, 1956; Milton Greenblatt, Daniel J. Levinson, and Richard H. Williams, *The Patient and the Mental Hospital,* New York: Free Press, 1957; H. Warren Dunham and S. Kirson Weinberg, *The Culture of the State Mental Hospital,* Detroit: Wayne State University Press, 1960; and, of course, Goffman, *op. cit.*

between patients and the lowest echelon of staff members, the attendants who provide day-to-day supervision. There is a considerable literature on the daily interaction between patients and the staff.[21] From this interaction arise differential status and treatment of patients. The attendant's characterization of "good"-versus-"bad" patients tends to color the thinking of professional staff members, especially insofar as they have little direct contact with patients. It leads also to a further social elaboration of the inmate world; that is, patients form a subculture of their own, distinct from that of the staff.[22]

It would probably be appropriate to pause here to indicate that the foregoing characterization of mental hospitals does not take into account recent developments in the organization of treatment facilities for the mentally ill, such as small, short-term hospitals and community mental health centers for ambulatory care. This trend follows from a shift in ideological position regarding the mental illnesses, namely, that they now are considered treatable and that one can "recover" from them at least enough to function adequately in modern society. Thus, many modern treatment facilities are more like the rehabilitation model inasmuch as they are organized as "therapeutic communities" to provide milieu therapy. According to this treatment philosophy, every experience the patient has in the setting has some therapeutic significance, whether it stems from interaction with the staff or the pleasant environmental surroundings.[23] As one might expect, the characteristics of the therapeutic community are nearly antithetical to those of the total institution. Instead of a centralized authority, there is patient self-government. Instead of batch living, there is encouragement for individuality.[24] Instead of the castelike split between staff and patients, there is a deliberate attempt to reduce status differentiation and the barriers to communication. Staff members do not wear identifying uniforms, wards are often "open," facilities are integrated, etc.

[21]Ivan Belknap, "The Ward Control System in Action: Ward 30," in Dorrian Apple (ed.), *Sociological Studies of Health and Sickness,* New York: McGraw-Hill, 1960, pp. 324–331.

[22]William Caudill, *The Psychiatric Hospital as a Small Society,* Cambridge, Mass.: Harvard University Press, 1956. See also Albert F. Wessen (ed.), *The Psychiatric Hospital as a Social System,* Springfield, Ill.: Charles C Thomas, 1964.

[23]See, for example, Maxwell Jones, *The Therapeutic Community,* New York: Basic Books, 1953. On the importance of the environment, see Robert Sommer and Robert Dewar, "The Physical Environment of the Ward," in Eliot Freidson (ed.), *The Hospital in Modern Society,* New York: Free Press, 1963, pp. 319–342.

[24]One may also wonder if the desire to emphasize individuality has not also become regimented just as the so-called hippies have become more alike in their efforts to be different. The permissiveness which characterizes many psychiatric units organized as a therapeutic milieu for the purpose of allowing the patient to express individuality may not be appropriate for the treatment of patients who continually test the environment in a destructive way, seeking to find what the limits of permissible behavior are.

Although the success of the therapeutic community philosophy has not been adequately demonstrated, the lack of success in the traditionally organized mental hospital has been amply documented.[25]

However, the concern of this chapter is with the general hospital, and we may well ask about the relationship between it and the concept of total institutions. To be sure, the community general hospital is different from a traditional mental hospital; yet they have several features in common. Much of the research on the social structure and formal properties of the general hospital, discussed in the previous chapter, leads to the conclusion that the general hospital, like the ideal-type total institution, does provide all the necessities of life for the patients, although ordinarily for a shorter duration.[26] It could also be said that despite the unique dual authority system in the general hospital, i.e., the medical staff on the one hand and the administration on the other, authority is still centralized as far as the patient is concerned. One exception is that bureaucratic procedures are often temporarily altered by private physician's orders if the patient complains loudly enough. In fact, the idea of individualized therapy in the hands of the private physicians sets sharp limits on how total a general hospital can be despite the fact that this individualization is embedded in the traditional context of custodial care.

Unlike the mental hospital and other total institutions, very few activities are carried on in batches in the general hospital. In part, this is due to the fact that many of the patients are physically too ill to do anything without assistance, much less with a lot of other patients, and to the fact that a wide variety of illnesses are represented on any given nursing unit, each requiring somewhat idiosyncratic treatment procedures. This problem is not so important in traditional mental hospitals, where the source of the patients' mental problems is viewed with an unimaginative homogeneity.[27] Even in the general hospital, however, a number of activities are carried out on a schedule. Feeding, administering medication, bathing, assessing vital signs (blood pressure, temperature, pulse), arising, and retiring are usually controlled by the staff, often on "doctor's orders."[28] There is also a hiatus between the staff and the patient just as in the mental hospital. There is a social stratification within the staff group very much like other medical

[25]Robert A. Cohen, "The Hospital as a Therapeutic Instrument," *Psychiatry,* 21 (February, 1958), 29–37.
[26]Stanley H. King, *Perception of Illness and Medical Practice,* New York: Russell Sage, 1961.
[27]Leo W. Simmons and Harold G. Wolff, *Social Science in Medicine,* New York: Russell Sage, 1954.
[28]See, for example, the dramatic account given in Robert Straus, "Hospital Organization from the Viewpoint of Patient-centered Goals," in Basil S. Georgopoulous (ed.), *Organization Research on Health Institutions,* Ann Arbor: University of Michigan Press, 1972, pp. 203–222.

settings separating physicians from nurses and other treatment personnel and distinguishing all these from members of the administrative hierarchy.[29] Unlike total institutions, however, there is status differentiation among the patients on various critieria—type of illness, type of accommodation, age of the patient, etc.

In summary, it could be stated that compared with the mental hospital—the medical prototype of a total institution—the general hospital has only a few of the same characteristics and usually to a much lower degree. The main points of convergence are the significant distinction between those who give care and those who receive it and the kinds of occupational groups found in the organization and the ways in which these groups are stratified. It must also be recognized that in the general hospital, the average length of stay is much shorter than in the mental hospital and that treatment in the former is much more focused on the physical aspects of disease than it is in the latter.[30] Despite these differences, however, and the judgment that a general hospital is a very mild form of total institution, this conceptualization provides analytic leverage for examination of the impact of hospitalization on the patient. That is to say, the factors which tend to characterize most general hospitals may act either to alleviate feelings of stress and anxiety or they may accentuate them. By viewing the general hospital in the context of its "totalistic" features, we may better examine the potential social-psychological impact of the patient's experience within its walls.

## SOCIAL-PSYCHOLOGICAL ASPECTS OF HOSPITALIZATION

Like all formal organizations, hospitals as well as total institutions are designed to achieve specific although often different goals. Our concern here is with those institutions designed for care of different classes of patients. A peculiar aspect of the status of patients is that the patients tend to be devalued by the managers of the organizations even before they enter the institution; i.e., they are old and infirm, sick or insane. Consequently, justification is provided for manipulation of the lives of large groups of patients, without much concern for their wishes, through exercising control over their behavior; for structuring activities according to the needs of the organization; for impersonal treatment (this is also justified on grounds of scientific approach); and for isolation of patients from the rest of society

[29]S. Kirson Weinberg, "Organization, Personnel and Functions of State and Private Mental Hospitals: A Comparative Analysis," in Jaco, *op. cit.,* pp. 478–491.

[30]Daniel J. Levinson and Eugene B. Gallagher, *Patienthood in the Mental Hospital,* Boston: Houghton Mifflin, 1964.

and from each other. These characteristics are achieved largely through the use of three mechanisms as follows: "stripping," control of resources, and restriction of mobility.

When patients enter the hospital they bring with them a "presenting culture," that is, a set of beliefs, attitudes, values, and social relationships in addition to belongings, such as clothing and other material goods, reputation or status, and deference, which enable them to present their selves to the world.[31] However, in order to make it more convenient to handle large numbers of patients and, indirectly, to reduce differences among patients and to legitimate en masse treatment, these institutions, both knowingly and not, engage in the process of stripping, whereby the individual is systematically separated from these representations of self. In their stead are issued functional equivalents—such as uniforms, bedding, numbers instead of names—which are the same in quality and quantity as those issued to everyone else. In other words, every distinctly personalizing symbol, material or otherwise, is taken away, thus reducing the patient to the status of just one of many. For example, Wade has commented on the induction of the Marine recruit:

> Civilian clothes are gone—either mailed home or given to the Salvation Army. The long hair has been shorn to GI specification. Each man has had a *thorough* shower; been clad in a suit of dungarees . . . been carefully fitted with boots; become burdened with a seabag full of gear to maintain and use in training; and done it all by the numbers. He begins to feel like a Marine, but he isn't one. Not yet. This is only the beginning.[32]

The situation of the patient in the general hospital is often not much different. One study pointed out that "to expedite the hospital procedure, the patient is provided with a type of bed clothes to which he is ill-accustomed and which hardly enhance his self-image."[33] The stripping process is usually justified on grounds other than organizational expediency. For example, in the mental hospital, certain items may represent a danger to patients such as neckties, shoe laces, belts, and pocket knives; thus they may be removed on grounds of patient safety. However it is rationalized, the stripping process is a common mechanism of all institutions—indeed, in milder forms, of all social organizations for initiating new members.

[31]Goffman, *op. cit.,* p. 12.
[32]S. S. Wade, "What Makes a Marine?" *Army Digest,* 16 (July, 1961), 58–67. Quote is on pp. 60–61.
[33]Leon Lewis and Rose L. Coser, "The Hazards of Hospitalization," *Hospital Administration,* 5 (Summer, 1960), 25–45.

Control of resources, like authority, is concentrated in the hands of the staff. This enables them to manipulate the physical environment (including patients, regardless of the desires or expectations of the patients) for the purpose of regulating the patient behavior and continuing the stripping process. For example, the staff can force every patient to wear hospital-issued bedclothes to simplify the job of washing. Bedclothes can be handled en masse and returned without regard for previous "ownership" and often without regard to size, but personal clothing cannot. Ward gives an example from the point of view of the patient in a mental hospital:

> When she [the patient] reached Miss Harte [staff member] she saw that the woman was providing toilet paper. Miss Harte was the dispenser. As you required paper, you asked her for it in advance and she doled it out to you. She was the judge of how much you needed. It was a curious and humiliating procedure. Hadn't they gone deep enough into a woman's privacy when they removed the doors from the booths?[34]

Control of resources includes not only physical items, such as the extreme example above, but also knowledge. It has been noted that these organizations have built-in blocks to communication among the staff, but more often the patients are the ones who are deprived of information about events in the hospital and particularly information concerning themselves, i.e., results of tests, what will be done to them, their prognoses, etc.[35] Titmuss points to lack of information as a major source of patients' complaints about the general hospital:

> What is it that patients complain of more than anything else in relation to the hospital—"No one told me anything"—"I don't know." How often one comes across people who have been disillusioned because the medical magic has not apparently or not yet yielded results, ignorant of what the investigations have shown, what the doctors think, what the treatment has been or is to be, and what the outlook is in terms of life and health.[36]

[34]Mary Jane Ward, *The Snake Pit,* New York: New American Library, 1955, p. 27. On the importance of privacy for self-concept, see Eleanor A. Schuster, "Privacy, the Patient and Hospitalization," *Social Science and Medicine,* 10 (May, 1976), 245–248.

[35]Esther Lucille Brown, "Meeting Patients' Psycho-social Needs in the General Hospital," *Annals of the American Academy of Political and Social Science,* 346 (March, 1963), 117–125. See also Joan S. Dodge, "Nurses' Sense of Adequacy and Attitudes toward Keeping Patients Informed," *Journal of Health and Human Behavior,* 2 (Fall, 1961), 213–216; and James K. Skipper, Jr., Daisy L. Tagliacozzo, and Hans O. Mauksch, "Some Possible Consequences of Limited Communication between Patients and Hospital Functionaries," *Journal of Health and Human Behavior,* 5 (Spring, 1964), 34–39.

[36]Richard M. Titmuss, "The Hospital and Its Patients," in Alfred H. Katz and Jean Spencer Felton (eds.), *Health and the Community,* New York: Free Press, 1965, p. 342.

The third mechanism by which institutions attempt to control the behavior of their patients is through restriction of mobility. Confinement to an area from which the patient is not allowed to leave without explicit permission of the staff ensures immediate access to the patient, may tend to isolate the patient from others, and permits the staff to determine with whom a patient may interact and establish social relationships. The use of segregation cells in the penitentiary and locked wards in mental hospitals serve as examples. In the general hospital, the

> . . . restriction on the mobility of patients, which is therapeutically indicated in many instances, has a secondary advantage for staff—that of assuring accessibility of patients. When asked what he thought were the advantages of hospitals for treatment of the ill, an intern said: " . . . If you had to go to various people's houses to see them, it's inconvenient. . . ." Patients have to be available to medical and nursing staff, and they are impressed with the need for restriction of their movements by being forced to let themselves be wheeled to their beds as soon as they enter the hospital, regardless of their ability to walk.[37]

Restriction of mobility also contributes to intensifying the status of being ill. The mere fact of hospitalization separates the sick from those who are well. Being immobilized in the hospital further segregates the sick from contacts with others, including patients who could perhaps alleviate the situation of the ill persons by introducing them to the strange new culture. Often, however, isolation may initially be desired by the patients as this personal experience described by Hodgins indicates:

> I knew a *no visitors* sign was on the door of 331 by morning: not the printed kind to which no one ever pays attention, but scrawled in Dr. Vancoast's handwriting and affixed by him to the door, slightly askew, with adhesive tape. This way, it carried much more authority. And that morning Dr. Vancoast laid down some additional ground rules: not only no phone calls, incoming or outgoing, but also no messages except as filtered by him; interception of gifts, if any; and finally, with my permission, the opening of any mail addressed to me and, after his scrutiny, its ultimate delivery at what he considered a more appropriate time. In short, a curtain was to come down between me and the world, except the medical world. To all this I readily assented. The world and I were well apart for a while. We had not been getting on at all well and were not really to get back on satisfactory terms for quite some time.[38]

[37]Lewis and Coser, *op. cit.,* p. 28.
[38]Eric Hodgins, *Episode: A Report on the Accident inside My Skull,* New York: Atheneum, 1964, pp. 20–21.

The consequences of these mechanisms—stripping, reduced mobility, enforced dependence, and lack of communication—are a concerted assault on the patient's conception of self. Our feelings about ourselves stem in part from our interpretation of the feelings others show toward us and, in part, from our manipulation of cultural objects and social situations that enable us to present ourselves to others in the most favorable light.[39] When, however, patients are deprived of these objects (clothing, jewelry, and other symbols of identification) and the ability to control or even influence what happens to them in addition to receiving formal, stereotyped responses from others instead of warm, sympathetic ones, the patients' perception of themselves as persons must undergo considerable deterioration—a social process of dehumanization or depersonalization.[40]

Generally speaking, these institutions do not usually initiate the depersonalization process, but rather intensify a process already begun. It should be recalled that the onset of an illness, especially a disabling one, is often accompanied by feelings of being unworthy and being a burden. Disability, pain, and disfigurement all constitute a potential threat to corporeal aspects of a patient's self-image. The conditions of admission to a hospital, especially a mental hospital, are likely to intensify feelings of shame, guilt, fear, and apprehension, which are so often associated with illness.[41] Thus, factors leading to and associated with an illness, coupled with the depersonalizing nature of total institutions, represent a serious threat to the social-psychological (and perhaps physical) integrity of the patient.

As we have pointed out before, however, the conditions found in real-life hospitals vary from the conceptualized potential of the model. There is considerable evidence that the more conditions in the hospital approach those of the model of a total institution and diverge from the normal lifeways of a patient, the more serious their psychological impact will be on the patient.[42] It would therefore be expected that in the general hospital—which we have seen varies considerably from the model—the depersonalizing process would be much less severe than in a mental hospital. Nonetheless, there is evidence that some of the factors are found. One frequently encountered problem in the general hospital is the tendency for hospital personnel to deal with the patients' bodies often without informing the

[39]Erving Goffman, *Presentation of Self in Everyday Life,* New York: Doubleday, 1959. See also Goffman, "On Face-work," *Psychiatry,* 18 (August, 1955), 213–231.
[40]Jules Henry, *Culture against Man,* New York: Random House, 1963 especially pp. 391–440.
[41]Tamara Dembo and Eugenia Hanfmann, "The Patient's Psychological Situation upon Admission to a Mental Hospital," *American Journal of Psychology,* 47 (July, 1935), 381–408.
[42]Rodney M. Coe, "Self-conception and Institutionalization," in Arnold M. Rose and Warren A. Peterson (eds.), *Older People and Their Social World,* Philadelphia: F. A. Davis, 1965, pp. 225–243. See also Rene Spitz, "Hospitalism," *The Psychoanalytic Study of the Child,* vol. I, New York: International Universities Press, 1945.

patients of the reason or perhaps even communicating at all with them. Of course, this is justified on the grounds that doctors and nurses must have access to the patients in order to treat their physical problems. But the body, especially certain parts of it, is culturally defined as "private property," and exposure to and manipulation of parts of the body by strangers, however legitimate their role, may be a degrading experience.[43] Moreover, patients who are teaching cases are exposed, both physically and mentally, to students who are not treating them but learning their profession. Patients have been known to give their life history several times during the same hospitalization, because several students wanted to practice their history-taking techniques. Ward rounds also is a teaching function that may be threatening to the patient.[44] This is the process in which the students follow a faculty member from bed to bed discussing the aspects of interesting cases as if the patient did not exist. This, too, can be depersonalizing.

In the case of the patients in the general hospital, however, it must be remembered that they are often seriously ill, especially at admission; thus the potentially depersonalizing aspects of hospitalization may be lost upon them. In fact, the right to be dependent upon others, to be cared for in every way, may be desired by the patient. It is especially during convalescence that the restrictions or impositions of the hospital routine are perceived by the patient.[45] Moreover, the degree of perception of these problems is influenced by a number of factors. For example, it has been found that middle-class patients can more readily accept the patient role in the hospital than can lower-class patients, partly because they are less skeptical of the abilities of medical personnel, but also because there is less discrepancy between the "culture" of the hospital and the middle-class culture.[46] Other factors such as personality and "secondary gain" from the sick role may also influence the impact of hospitalization.[47]

## MODES OF ADJUSTMENT TO HOSPITALIZATION

The general hospital, then, can be characterized in some degree as having the potential for systematically undermining the self-image of the patients. But maintenance of a conception of self acceptable to the individual is a primary requisite for much human behavior. In fact, the attempt to main-

[43]Lewis and Coser, *op. cit.*

[44]John Romano, "Patients' Attitudes and Behavior in Ward Round Teaching," *Journal of the American Medical Association*, 117 (August, 1941), 664–667.

[45]Walter H. DeLange, "Patient Role Conflict and Reactions to Hospitalization," *Journal of Health and Human Behavior*, 4 (Summer, 1963), 113–118.

[46]Richard J. Ossenberg, "The Experience of Deviance in the Patient Role: A Study of Class Differences," *Journal of Health and Human Behavior*, 3 (Winter, 1962), 277–282.

[47]Talcott Parsons, "Definitions of Health and Illness in the Light of American Values and Social Structure," in Jaco, *op. cit.*, pp. 165–187.

tain a relatively stable and acceptable image of self is a major factor in the observed consistency of human behavior, even when the social situations differ.[48] Similarly, people tend to seek out and join with others to form groups in which the collective standards for behavior are compatible with the maintenance of self-respect. Thus, professional thieves do not associate with petty thieves, because their standards (among other things) are different. In the same way, physicians do not associate with faith healers, because trained physicians could not maintain their self-respect if they engaged in the same behaviors as faith healers. Therefore, it is reasonable to assume that patients whose self-images are being threatened will attempt to resist or at least to reduce the impact of the organization. There are, of course, many ways in which people could adjust to potentially punishing situations. We shall consider here four possible ways in which patients may adjust to hospitalization, namely: withdrawal, aggression, integration, and acquiescence.[49]

**Withdrawal**

An immediately obvious way of coping with a punishing situation is to withdraw from it, much as a person might jump away from a hot stove. Physical withdrawal in the hospital setting is difficult to achieve, however, due to patient immobility (except, of course, those who sign out against medical advice). Thus, withdrawal would more likely be in a psychological sense of not responding to stimuli in the hospital environment. In the extreme, patients may construct a delusional world in which they do not have painful experiences. For example, Shibutani noted that "if a person finds himself immersed in a hostile environment in which he cannot find satisfaction, he may create a substitute world in which his lot is better. Such a scheme may become his only guarantee of security; if so, its preservation becomes a value in itself. . . ."[50]

In a similar vein Cameron has argued that individual differences and an inability to take on certain roles because of inadequate socialization make people unable to communicate their fears and anxieties to others. As a result, such people may well construct a "pseudocommunity," which they organize into a coherent pattern of both real and delusional events. Eventually, however, standards of behavior from the pseudocommunity will conflict with those from the real world. As the painful sanctions of the real

[48]Tamotsu Shibutani, *Society and Personality,* Englewood Cliffs, N.J.: Prentice-Hall, 1961, pp. 260ff.
[49]These modes of adjustment are modified forms of adaptation suggested in "Social Structure and Anomie," in Robert K. Merton, *Social Theory and Social Structure,* New York: Free Press, 1957; also Goffman, "On the Characteristics of Total Institutions," *op. cit.*
[50]Shibutani, *op. cit.,* p. 458.

world are pressed on the patients, they are likely to retreat further and further into this delusional system.[51] In the same vein, but to a much lesser degree, it might be expected that people who resist accepting the sick role, i.e., who do not define themselves as sick, would tend to resist the ministrations of the medical staff and reject the standards of behavior expected of patients. A classical case is the mental hospital patient who claims that he or she is perfectly well and refuses to participate with other patients in ward activities.

It is also obvious that this mode of adjustment is not very efficacious, nor is it actually very common among patients' responses. It is probably most often found among those patients who are only tenuously associated with the real world anyway and for whom very little would be needed to cause them to complete their break with reality. It is also less likely that withdrawal would be found among patients in institutions where the severity of totalistic features is minimal, as in the case of the general hospital. Such a mode of adjustment would be more likely among patients whose condition would require long-term hospitalization and for whom the prognosis of recovery was poor.

## Aggression

Overt resistance to the rules and regulations imposed on patients is another form of adjustment. This may range from disobeying physician's orders, say for bed rest or for medications, to outright physical assault on the members of the staff. Such crude attempts to reshape the organization rather than be shaped by the institution are bound to fail. Every social organization, especially a total institution, has mechanisms by which conformity of group members to standards of behavior is maintained. In total institutions, some of these punishments are usually justified on the grounds of therapy. For example, in regard to the use of seclusion as punishment in a state mental hospital, Belknap reports that the "new attendant learns to give medical, rather than disciplinary or punitive reasons for this seclusion, a procedure made possible by the fact that seclusion under certain rare circumstances is necessary in psychiatric treatment.[52] Often the more effective punishments are unofficial in nature. It is frequently the case that officially sanctioned procedures can be given unofficial interpretation—that is, a perverted rationale for the procedure, which would not be acceptable to responsible officials of the organization, is the one used by low-status

---

[51]Norman Cameron, "The Paranoid Pseudo-community," *American Journal of Sociology*, 49 (July, 1943), 32–38.

[52]Belknap, "The Ward Control System in Action: Ward 30," p. 329.

employees in controlling their charges. Belknap provides an example concerning the use of electroshock therapy in the mental hospital setting.

> The formal purpose of the [shock] treatments was medical and therapeutic, but they depended for their execution on the cooperation of the attendants. They were thus open to uses which were disciplinary rather than therapeutic. In the last analysis, the physician had to take the attendant's word for it that the patient had been acting up, since the physician spent little time on the ward. To an observer who had been on the ward during the week it would be clear that two or three patients were on the list because they had responded with normal resentment to actual ill treatment by an attendant or another patient, or because they had objected to the hospital food by refusing to eat it. The sixth level hallucinatory and delusional "worry warts" were particularly likely to be put on the shock list. One senior attendant said frankly that he put one of these patients on the list to give himself and the ward a rest from a particularly boring story.
>
> The new attendant who kept his eyes on the effects of shock therapy in Ward 30 could see for himself its effectiveness as a threat in maintaining order. Most of the patients who had been on the ward more than a few weeks were afraid of the treatment; those who had not experienced it were, if anything, more afraid of it than those who had. For most patients the threat of being put on the shock list had an instant effect of bringing their conduct into line with the requirements of their position on the ward.[53]

Admittedly, this situation is likely to occur only in institutions very much like the model conceptualization of a total institution. In the general hospital, aggression is more likely to take a verbal form, such as complaining, or a form of resisting therapeutic efforts of the staff. In part, this may also be related to social class position in that the activities of the hospital staff are less comprehensible to the lower-class patient than to middle- or upper-class ones. The latter two classes are also likely to have better accommodations, such as private physicians, relative privacy of room, and bathing and toilet facilities. More important, perhaps, is the ability of the middle-class patients to understand the nature of their sick-role status, that it is likely to be brief and that if they cooperate with the hospital staff, they should return more quickly to their former health status, and so on. Under some circumstamces, however, it has been shown that even middle-class patients have difficulty making the adjustment to patient status. Barker and his associates have pointed out that one of the problems of patients' adjustment to life in a tuberculosis sanatorium is the discrepancy between objective medical condition and the patients' subjective evaluation of how

[53] *Ibid.*, pp. 329–330.

they feel. It is often the case that the painful and debilitating effects of an acute tubercular infection can be medically attenuated, but still require medication and enforced rest. The patients, however, once their symptoms have abated, may feel ready to resume their normal roles and tend to resist enforcement of the required inactivity. Thus occurs the phenomenon of a stricken business executive trying to conduct business from a sick bed and being thwarted by the medical staff. Often patients may even leave the hospital prematurely against medical advice.[54] These, of course, are much milder forms of aggression, but no less likely to fail, since premature discharge will likely result in a relapse and rehospitalization. Like withdrawal, aggression is not a very satisfactory or successful mode of adjustment.

## Integration

In the situation of inmates in total institutions, integration into the inmate culture may be the most efficacious way of blunting the assault on their self-images.[55] It is a way of coming to terms, with not only each other, but other aspects of the environment as well. It enables group members to comply with some institutional rules, yet obtain satisfaction for certain needs from participation in group life. It seems, however, that one necessary condition for such a mode of adjustment to occur is that the group must be together for a relatively long period of time. Thus, in the case of acutely ill hospital patients whose tenure in that status is relatively short and who have an egocentric focus on their illness, integration into the institutional setting is not likely to occur. On the other hand, for hospitalized chronically ill patients who may anticipate a long-term confinement, new patterns of social interaction may emerge and new definitions be given to their situation. Fox has described just such a situation.[56] The patients in her study were all suffering from a metabolic disorder, one for which no cure was known and which was both chronic and frequently fatal. These patients had all volunteered to be subjects for medical research. Thus all the conditions for the emergence of informal patterns of interaction were present. The patients were likely to be together for a long time; they were suffering from a common ailment which was anxiety producing; they occupied a common

[54]Roger G. Barker, Beatrice A. Wright, and Mollie R. Gonick, *Adjustment to Physical Handicap and Illness: A Survey of the Social Psychology of Physique and Disability,* New York: Social Science Research Council Bulletin 55, 1946. A contrary view is presented in Milton S. Davis and Robert P. van der Lippe, "Discharge from the Hospital against Medical Advice: A Study of Reciprocity in the Doctor-Patient Relationship," paper read at meetings of the American Sociological Association, Chicago, 1965.

[55]Gresham Sykes, *The Society of Captives,* Princeton, N.J.: Princeton University Press, 1958. See also Caudill, *op. cit.*

[56]Renee Fox, *Experiment Perilous,* New York: Free Press, 1959.

status vis-à-vis the medical staff; and they were ecologically separated from other patients. Fox goes on to describe how a newly admitted patient is introduced into the system and how his initial problems of adjustment stir memories in the older patients about their first contacts, but most of all, this study illustrates how patients in a painful situation cope with their problems. Illness is a disapproved status in our society; yet on this chronic-disease ward a patient's status was directly related to the gravity of the illness. Certain group values evolved which allowed the patient to act as if he or she were going to recover (thus fulfilling that condition of the sick role) and yet submit to the imposition of the disease including manipulation by the physician-experimenters. Coming to terms with illness in this group was largely a passive process and aided by group evolved definitions and interpretations of patient behavior. Thus, certain events were construed as humorous when such an interpretation may not have been given by an outsider. Integration, then, is a viable mode of adjustment to the rigors of institutional life, although it is less common among short-term patients in the general hospital.

### Acquiescence

By and large, most patients probably adopt acquiescence as a mode of adjustment, at least initially. In the harsh repressive setting of total institutions, compliance with institutional rules may result from the initial shock of entry into the system or to enable the new inmate to establish a new estimate of the situation. In this case, he or she would be doing what Goffman calls "playing it cool."[57] In any case, the resulting observable behavior is compliance with the institutional regimen, that is, acquiescence.

In the general hospital setting, this mode of adjustment is also most likely to occur but for very different reasons. In the first place, as we have noted several times before, patients are usually too ill to do anything but submit to the ministrations of the staff. More than just submit, however, patients (and their relatives) may be relieved to have the responsibility for solution of their problems placed in the hands of appropriate professional groups. Then, too, continued contact with the outside world through personal communication and mass media (not a feature of total institutions) reinforces well persons as a reference group and justifies the temporary acquiescence to hospital routine in order to get well faster. Moreover, patients may identify wholeheartedly with the goals and advice of doctors and nurses, going along willingly with procedures that are difficult, the objectives of which they do not fully understand. In a word, the patient

[57]Goffman, "On the Characterisitcs of Total Institutions," *op. cit.*

may be "converted" into acquiescence. Justification for compliance on these grounds obviates much of the negative ramifications of dependence, such as loss of adult (self-determining) status. Submission to institutional procedures, then, could have the positive effect of enabling the patients to regain their former status as well persons more quickly. This is particularly true for short-term patients whose medical problem is of an acute nature, readily dealt with by the medical profession.

On the other hand, in long-term institutions acquiescence can have a negative effect—that of creating a dependence upon the institution to the degree that the patient cannot readjust to the outside world. This phenomenon has variously been called "hospitalitis" or "institutionalism."[58] The symptoms of becoming adjusted to hospital life beyond the point of effective return to the larger society include losing capacity to make decisions, replacing cultural values with institutional values, developing new patterns of response to stimuli especially suited to institutional life, and becoming apathetic toward changes in the outside world.[59] Under these conditions, the rehabilitation potential of the patients may decline until they are lost forever to the outside world.

The identification of four types of modes of adjustment is, of course, useful for analytic purposes, but it does not imply mutual exclusiveness of the categories nor that these are the only ways in which patients may adjust to the hospital. We have not, for example, discussed the relationship of personality patterns to modes of adjustment.[60] We have, rather, tried to point out some commonly adopted modes of adjustment related to the social characteristics of the institutional setting. The actual mode of adjustment adopted by any group of patients is likely to be some combination of the analytic types described above. These combinations, in turn, will vary according to characteristics of the patient, such as age, sex, race, medical condition, and sociocultural and social-psychological factors, and of the institution—type, size, purpose, and severity of totalistic features. Lederer, for example, suggests that modes of adjustment vary with the stage of illness.[61] Thus, patients acquiesce during the stage of "accepted illness," but become more aggressive or at least resist more during the convalescent stage. In long-term institutions, we may well expect withdrawal or integration to vary also with the state of illness.

[58]J. K. Wing, "Institutionalism in Mental Hospitals," *British Journal of Social and Clinical Psychology,* 1 (February, 1962), 38–51.
[59]J. Marshall Townsend, "Self-concept and the Institutionalization of Mental Patients: An Overview and Critique," *Journal of Health and Social Behavior,* 17 (September, 1976), 263–271.
[60]See Richardson, *op. cit.,* Field, *op. cit.*
[61]Lederer, *op.cit.*

## TWO STUDIES IN PATIENT RESPONSE TO HOSPITALIZATION

### Adjustment to Long-term Hospitalization

To illustrate some of the principles outlined in the preceding sections, we wish to examine here in some detail the results of certain research on response to hospitalization. The first study—actually two related, but independently conducted, projects—focuses on the impact of hospitalization on chronically ill aged patients and the efficacy of skilled nursing care in alleviating the depersonalizing aspects of hospitalization. The first of the two investigations presented here was conducted in three different long-term care settings—a chronic-disease unit in a general hospital, a public institution for intermediate or convalescent care of chronically ill patients, and a large proprietary nursing home.[62] These three organizations had been selected because they represented different points on a continuum of severity of characteristics of total institutions. That is, the chronic-disease unit was least like a total institution, and the nursing home most closely approximated the ideal-type of total institution. The public institution was rated between the two extremes. This judgment was made on the basis of systematic observations of each organization and social interaction that took place on each unit. In addition, a scale which differentiated the staffs of the three organizations on the basis of their attitudes toward chronically ill patients further corroborated this judgment.

The purpose of this study was to demonstrate the relationship between the severity of totalistic features of these organizations and the depersonalization of their patients. If, as we have argued above, there is a direct relationship between these factors, then it would be expected that patients in the chronic-disease unit would be least depersonalized, because that organization was least like the conceptualized model of a total institution. Similarly, it was thought that patients in the nursing home would be most depersonalized, while patients in the public institutions should fall somewhere in between.

Level of self-conception as a measure of depersonalization was evaluated by means of an unstructured instrument called the Twenty Statements Test.[63] The object of this test is to elicit from respondents statements which represent ways in which they identify themselves. These responses can be reliably coded into one of four categories:(1) statements referring to explicitly structured social situations (role responses) such as occupational roles,

[62]Rodney M. Coe, "Institutionalization and Self-conception," unpublished doctoral dissertation, Washington University, St. Louis, 1962.

[63]Manford H. Kuhn and Thomas S. McPartland, "An Empirical Investigation of Self-attitudes," *American Sociological Review,* 19 (February, 1954), 68–76.

sex, and family roles; (2) statements of self-distinguishing habits, moods, or preferences (affect responses) such as likes or dislikes, happy or sad; (3) statements which identify physical attributes (physical responses) such as weight, height, and color of hair; and (4) statements which are so comprehensive that they do not distinguish one person from another (global responses) such as human being, person, and irrelevant responses. Theoretically it would be expected that a patient who is experiencing the process of depersonalization, that is, being symbolically (and physically) detached from the social groups which give meaning to his or her life, would tend, over time, to give responses which show less and less concern for the roles once played in various groups. The TST categories are also ordered according to the degree of attachment to groups, e.g., role, affect, physical and global responses, where role responses represent the highest degree of attachment and global responses the least. The data were collected twice over a four-month period by means of semistructured interviews with a stratified random sample of patients in each of the three institutions. Patients were stratified by length of stay, social class, and sex. The two data collection periods made it possible to assess changes in self-conception over time.

Initially, it was found that patients in the chronic-disease unit did tend to give a higher proportion of role responses than patients in the other two institutions (24 percent compared with 16 percent in the public institution and 7 percent in the nursing home) and, conversely, fewer global responses (27 percent compared with 35 percent and 50 percent, respectively). This would seem to suggest that patients in the nursing home were more depersonalized than patients in either of the other organizations, but especially the chronic-disease unit. Relatively little decline in the level of self-image took place in the intervening time between assessments for patients in the chronic-disease unit and the nursing home. A significant decline was noted for patients in the public institution. Other quantitative analyses show a significant relationship between characteristics of the institution and the level of self-conception.

As might be expected, the characteristic features of the institution were also related to modes of patient adjustment. In the least punitive organization—the chronic-disease unit—the mode of adjustment was usually acquiescence. In part, this was due to the fact that many of these patients were disabled and therefore highly dependent upon others, but it may also reflect the fact that most of the patients were foreign-born Jewish females in whose cultural tradition men were dominant (this was especially true of physicians). These patients were also mostly middle-class in background and tended to see the staff as trying to help them to get well. Some, however, had reached the point where the unit was seen as their home. One patient, for example, commented "I am not happy here. I want to go home, but I got no home to go to. When mine husband died the house we sold. Now I got no place to go. . . . This is my home.[64] In the public institution, two modes of adjustment were in evidence. One, acquiescence to the point of hospitalitis, is revealed in a patient's statement that "I am happy here, where else could I get food and roof for this money?"[65] Many patients, however, tended to be withdrawn and uncommunicative. They tended to sit and stare out the window or at the floor. They were, however, amenable to suggestions from staff members in that if the attendant asked the patient to do something, such as comply with the mandatory toileting rule, the patient would do so without comment or any resistance.

Finally, in the nursing-home setting, the predominant mode of adjustment was withdrawal. Several observations of rebellion were noted, but these outbursts were mostly spontaneous and quickly stifled. Most of these patients were apathetic—they had given up any hope of renewed family relationships as is suggested in this patient's comments: "I wish I was home to see my people more often, but my daughter don't want me. She never comes to see me here; she has forgot me."[66] There were also several patients who had apparently made the break with reality and established their own delusional world. Many of these reported conversations with long-since deceased parents or reported hearing music. An example is shown in this patient's response when asked if he had any relatives or friends.

> Only my wife's kin, you know, not blood kin of mine. (How often did you see them?) Oh, they talk to me all the time—you know, I'm perfect, I never make a mistake. I know you think I'm crazy, but I've got forty people who will vouch for me. They told me last night to go and sin no more. . . . (Who told you that?) Moses spoke to me out of the burning bush and he told me to get my American aircraft ready to go to France or Europe. My mother and father talk to me all the time. Sometimes she says, ———, what are you doing down there? I told you to get up here and I do it. . . . [67]

This study, then, offers some suggestive evidence that the more closely an organization resembles a total institution, the more depersonalized are the patients. It also suggests, more tentatively, that modes of adjustment are also related to the characteristics of the institutions. Perhaps as a closing note, mention should be made of the fact that integration into the patients' subculture was not found as a mode of adjustment precisely because such a subculture had not developed in any of these institutions.

[64]Coe, *op. cit.*, p. 109.
[65]*Ibid.*, p. 113.
[66]*Ibid.*, p. 114.
[67]*Ibid.*, p. 116.

For the most part, subcultures did not develop in the chronic-disease unit because the patients were physically separated from each other in private rooms and because the majority of patients were able to maintain outside contacts through liberal visiting privileges for friends and relatives. In the public institution, a patient subculture did not develop because of physical separation of patients in semiprivate rooms and because so many patients were withdrawn. In the nursing home, where conditions were such that a patient subculture should have emerged, it did not because of the repressive measures of the staff and the few patients in contact with reality.

An interesting question arises at this point. Is it possible within an institutional setting to *reverse* the process of depersonalization? Another study,[68] conducted independently from the one just reported, attempted to reverse the depersonalization process by effective implementation of skilled nursing care. It was felt that by providing continuing verbal and nonverbal stimulation and *personalized* care, an appropriately trained nurse could renew (or at least prevent the deterioration of) the chronically ill patient's attachment with group life. To accomplish this, a variety of behavioral variables were selected as indexing the "personalization" of the individual patient and were studied under controlled conditions for effects produced by skilled nursing care. In general, these variables reflected personalization in (1) readiness to interact, (2) interchange of resources in interaction, and (3) control of resources in interaction. The research design provided for the study of eighteen matched pairs of aged male and female patients selected at random from matched environments. The study was conducted in three different institutional settings, one of which was the nursing home described above and represented different points on the continuum of totalistic features. Six pairs of patients were selected in each of the three institutions. In each of the institutions, one member of each pair received skilled nursing care while the other received only that care which was standard in his or her institutional setting. By virtue of this design, it was possible to study the effects of skilled nursing care upon various selected behavioral manifestations of personalization and at the same time assess the effects peculiar to variations in the settings in which the research was performed.

Statistical analyses of the data collected by the nurse-observers revealed that on most of the indices selected, skilled nursing care produced highly significant enhancement of personalization. At the same time, variation among the settings studied also affected the personalization of the patients and interacted statistically with the effect of skilled nursing care. It

---

[68]Martha M. Brown, "Effects of Skilled Nursing Care upon Personalization of Older Patients," unpublished final progress report, Washington University School of Nursing, St. Louis, 1962.

was concluded that providing institutionalized aged patients with skilled nursing care is likely to enhance their social capabilities. It was also evident, however, that such improvements will be greater in the more deprived institutions than in those which are less like total institutions. One of the important findings of this study with respect to modes of adjustment is that there was a significant difference in the change from what this study called passivity to activity among the experimental patients (i.e., those receiving skilled nursing care) compared with their controls. Similarly, the level of activity was initially higher among all patients in that institution which was least like a total institution, compared with the institution which was most like a total institution (which happened to be the same nursing home as described in the first case report).

**Adjustment to Short-term Hospitalization**

It has been noted earlier that life on the ward of a general hospital involves only a few of the consequences of total institutions and those in relatively mild degree. It was further noted that the most common mode of adjustment to this kind of setting would likely be acquiescence. The second study suggests further that although acquiescence may be the modal form of adjustment, the behaviors observed may stem from different patient orientations.[69] The conclusions of this research are based on data collected by participant observation on medical and surgical wards in a general hospital and by interviews with selected patients at the time of their discharge. On the basis of their expressed attitudes toward physicians and toward the hospital in general, the patients in this study were classified as having an *instrumental orientation* or a *primary orientation*. An instrumental orientation implies an attitude that the physician's only task is to treat illness and that he or she should be highly skilled in doing so, and that hospitals are the appropriate place to have an illness treated, because the necessary resources are there. A primary orientation is one which views the doctor as a person who can make the patient happy—a "dispenser of protection"— and the hospital is seen as a place where physical needs can be gratified and protection obtained.

Although patients in both categories tended to comply, there was a difference in the degree to which they did so and in the reasons why. Responses to key questions indicated that instrumentally oriented patients complied because in this way they would get well sooner and could return to their normal roles. These patients expressed a feeling of unhappiness in that they missed many of their friends and also activities to which they were accustomed. These patients also felt that patients should retain some

[69]Rose L. Coser, "A Home away from Home," in Apple, *op. cit.,* pp. 154–172. See also Ailon Shiloh, "Egalitarian and Hierarchial Patients: An Investigation among Hadassah Hospital Patients," *Medical Care,* 3 (April–June, 1965), 87–95.

semblance of autonomy vis-à-vis the doctor and were quite willing to make suggestions to the medical staff with respect to the operation of the hospital. Patients with a primary orientation, on the other hand, submitted readily to the doctor's orders, "because he will take care of me." These patients were more or less happy to be within the protective environment of the hospital, where everything would be done for them. These patients were reluctant to suggest any changes in hospital procedures, because "everything was fine." In effect, these patients had adopted *in toto* the norms of the hospital and resembled patients showing symptoms of hospitalitis. Thus, adjustment to the hospital was more complete for patients with a primary orientation than for those who were instrumentally oriented.

This leads, finally, to a consideration of the definition of a good and bad patient from the perspective of the organization. In a total institution, the good patient is one who does not cause trouble and appears content with institutional routine. Thus, the withdrawn, easily manipulatable patient is a good one. Those who are aggressive or contrary are bad and are dealt with in a number of ways designed to "bring them back in line." However, the function of a total institution is *custodial care* regardless of what purposes are articulated by its officials. Therefore, the efficient handling of the basic needs of a large group of patients is a primary value and anything which would disturb the routinized procedures for doing so would be avoided or resisted.

In the general hospital, the primary value is restoring the patients to their former status of well persons. The rights attendant upon the sick role are recognized as temporary, and the emphasis is placed on the obligation to want to get well as quickly as possible. At the same time, however, efficient conduct of the care given is also a desired goal. As a consequence, the definitions of good and bad patients in the general hospital become muddied. On the one hand, the compliant, submissive patient—one with a primary orientation—would be seen as a good patient from the institutional perspective. But this mode of adjustment can also lead to hospitalitis or a refusal to get well in contradiction to the primary value placed on restoring the patient to good health. Thus, a compliant patient, if overdependent, can be seen as bad. At the other extreme, a patient who criticizes hospital procedures and questions the judgments of the medical staff would be likely to be seen as uncooperative and a bad patient. But these are precisely the patients who are most likely to recover their former status as a well person most quickly—therefore, a good patient. It is obvious that the good or bad label depends upon whose perspective is being used, in addition to the fact that a patient's status as good or bad may change from day to day. It is also obvious that a patient's status as good or bad is likely to elicit different kinds of responses from the staff; thus it is conceivable that a bad patient is subject to more measures of social control and thus to depersonalizing factors, which may intensify his deviant behavior rather than correct it.

Similarly, a good patient may receive better treatment, thus undermining any desire to get well. It would appear that the shifting definition of good and bad patients may be related to staff expectations in regard to the stages of illness of the patient in the hospital. That is, acutely ill patients are expected to be submissive, but as the crisis passes and the patients begin to convalesce, they are expected to show more interest in regaining their former status and to begin to reassert their independence from the staff. Thus a wider tolerance for deviance in the hospital is accorded convalescing patients because such deviance is indicative of reduced deviance from standards of the outside world; i.e., the patient is getting well.

## SUMMARY

Using the concept of total institutions as a point of departure, this chapter has examined the impact of varying conditions of hospital life on the patient and some characteristic ways in which patients attempt to adjust to institutional life. The central features of total institutions—single authority system, deprivation of resources, restriction of mobility, lack of communication, etc.—act in varying degrees as an attack on the patient's self-image, a social process of depersonalization. Four modes of patient adjustment were discussed: (1) *withdrawal*—nonresponse to environmental stimuli and potential development of delusional systems; (2) *aggression*—overt resistance to institutional rules and regulations; (3) *integration*—absorption of the patient into a patient subculture which provides gratification of certain basic needs; and (4) *acquiescence*—submission to institutional procedures, (*a*) rationally, e.g., because it would speed the patient's return to former status, and (*b*) pathologically, e.g., developing a complete dependence on the institution which would inhibit satisfactory adjustment upon return to the outside world. The modes of adjustment form the basis for an examination of good and bad patients from an organizational perspective.

## SUGGESTED READINGS

Barker, Roger G., Beatrice A. Wright, and Mollie R. Gonick, *Adjustment to Physical Handicap and Illness: A Survey of the Social Psychology of Physique and Disability,* New York: Social Science Research Council, Bulletin 55, 1946.

Fox, Renee, *Experiment Perilous,* New York: Free Press, 1959.

Goffman, Erving, *Asylums,* New York: Doubleday, 1961.

Hodgins, Eric, *Episode: A Report on the Accident inside My Skull,* New York: Atheneum, 1964.

Levinson, Daniel J., and Eugene B. Gallagher, *Patienthood in the Mental Hospital,* Boston: Houghton Mifflin, 1964.

Rosengren, William R., and Mark Lefton, *Hospitals and Patients,* New York: Atherton Press, 1969.

# Part Four

# The Cost and Organization of Health Services

# Chapter 12

# The Web of Medical Organization

*For thousands of years the treatment of the sick was considered the primary task of medicine while today its scope is infinitely broader. . . . The promotion of the people's health is undoubtedly an eminently social task that calls for the coordinated efforts of large groups, of the statesman, labor, industry, of the educator, and of the physician. . . .*

Henry E. Sigerist
"The Place of the Physician in Modern Society," 1960

In the preceding chapters we have noted some significant aspects of the growth and development of the field of medicine. In retrospect, it appears that forms of medical practice and the various medical institutions have arisen largely in response to recognized needs, but without any particular plan. A century ago, the individual practitioner was likely to be responsible for all aspects of the health care of the people in a community. Today, however, the requirements for providing health and medical care services have become so complex that a wide variety of individuals and organizations are now needed to perform and/or support these services.[1] The emergence of what has been called the health industry[2] and the rapidly rising costs of providing care have made it imperative that we examine the ways in which medicine and medical practice are organized for the provision of medical care services. The reasons behind the need for organized services are not hard to find, and in fact, they have been noted in earlier chapters in a somewhat different context. Certainly the expansion of medical knowledge and the attendant trend toward specialization in practice are important factors in the need for organization. The accumulation of new knowledge, new techniques, and new instruments has enabled medical practitioners to provide better care, but at the same time has forced them to limit their practice to a particular specialty. Thus, complete care for the patient requires the coordinated services of several practitioners as well as nursing and allied health personnel. However, not even the combined efforts of the health professions alone can provide all the support needed for total care. As a result, there has been a proliferation of public and private organizations to provide financing for research and training and in some cases health care services for those in need.

The place chosen for this complex and coordinated care has increasingly been the community hospital, the development of which has been considered in some detail in other chapters. Suffice it to say here that today the modern hospital has become the focal point of much of the community's health care. In part, this trend was stimulated by technological discoveries, particularly asepsis and anesthesia, which enabled physicians to treat patients in the hospital more successfully than they could in the patients' homes. More significant for contemporary medical practice is the development of expensive and highly complex diagnostic and therapeutic instruments, which only a large organization such as a hospital could afford to own and operate. The point is, however, that the hospital and other specialized settings have influenced the way in which medical practice is conducted.[3] The fact that physicians must, of necessity, depend upon the hospital in order to treat competently these patients requires them also to enter relationships with others—such as other physicians, technicians, nursing and allied health personnel, administrators. All these trends suggest that the family doctors who not only worked alone, but often even compounded their own prescriptions, are a thing of the past.

[1]See the analysis in Milton Terris, "The Contributions of Henry E. Sigerist to Health Service Organization," *Health and Society,* 53 (Fall, 1975), 489–530.

[2]See, for example, James S. McKenzie-Pollack, "The Health Industry," *American Journal of Public Health,* 54 (October, 1964), 1047–1052; and David Mechanic, "Symposium: Trends in the Delivery of Health Services," *Inquiry,* 8 (March, 1971), 3–8.

[3]Anne R. Somers, *Health Care in Transition: Directions for the Future,* Chicago: Hospital Research and Educational Trust, 1971.

**Table 12-1    Trends in Specialization in Medical Practice, 1963—1972, with Projections to 1980**

| Area of practice | 1963 | | 1972 | | 1980* | | Percentage change 1963–72 | 1972–80* |
|---|---|---|---|---|---|---|---|---|
| General practice† | 66,874 | (26%) | 55,348 | (17%) | 40,310 | (12%) | −17 | −27 |
| Specialties: | | | | | | | | |
| Medicine | 46,518 | (18) | 72,728 | (23) | 83,670 | (26) | 56 | 15 |
| Surgery | 67,005 | (26) | 90,409 | (28) | 103,920 | (32) | 35 | 15 |
| Psychiatry | 15,551 | ( 5) | 22,570 | ( 7) | 32,670 | (10) | 44 | 45 |
| Other | 65,780 | (25) | 79,848 | (25) | 65,250 | (20) | 21 | −18 |
| Total, specialties | 194,854 | (74) | 265,555 | (83) | 285,510 | (88) | 36 | 8 |
| Total, all areas | 261,728 | (100%) | 320,903 | (100%) | 325,820 | (100%) | 23 | 2 |

*Projected.
†Includes family medicine in 1972 and later.
Source: Department of Health, Education, and Welfare, *Supply of Health Manpower,* DHEW Publication no. (HRA) 75–38, Washington, D.C.: Government Printing Office, 1974, tables 30 and 37.

Reference to Table 12-1 provides some idea of the differentiation of tasks within the field of medicine. Note the decline in general practitioners (even when doctors in the growing specialty of family medicine are included), a trend which is expected to continue at an even greater pace. Complementarily, the proportion of specialists is expected to increase to the level of nearly 9 in 10 by 1980. Among specialists there are also differential rates of growth. Rapid growth characterized medical and surgical specialties and psychiatry during the 1960s. Growth is expected to continue except for a few limited specialties, but at a slower pace for the major groups, while psychiatry should continue at its former rate. This represents a phenomenal expansion in specialty practice when we remember that in 1950 only 36 percent of all active physicians claimed a specialty.[4]

Another factor which has influenced the need for organization has been the shift in morbidity from acute infectious diseases to chronic incapacitating illnesses. The need for different levels of care provided over a long period of time has resulted in such developments as the "medical care team" and "comprehensive medicine." Moreover, as the incidence of illness from chronic diseases rises, the demand for more and more health and medical care services also increases along with a rise in costs of care. The combined effects of increased technology, from which has developed a host of paramedical and medical technician roles, and a dramatic change in the kinds of problems facing the medical practitioner, stressing the need to have more things done to more people, have only served to reinforce the necessity of organizing health and medical care services.

[4]U.S. Department of Health, Education, and Welfare, *Health Manpower Sourcebook: Manpower in the 1960's,* Washington, D.C.: Government Printing Office, 1964, p. 29.

A third, related, factor, of course, is the cost of medical care from the perspective of providers as well as consumers. This topic is discussed in detail in Chapter 13. Suffice it to say here only that medical care costs have continued to increase at a rate faster than the rise in costs of other consumer items. As the "value" of services received for the cost is increasingly being questioned, ways to improve the delivery of health services without greater expenditures are being sought through reorganization.

## MEDICAL ORGANIZATION

It may be recalled that during the middle ages the practice of medicine, at least as a recognized special occupation, had virtually disappeared except for isolated academic physicians who followed the teachings of Galen and the church. By and large, medical care for the citizenry was based on folk medical beliefs and practices which were rooted in ignorance and superstition. With the reawakening of the search for truth and the development of scientific methods, medical practice reemerged as an important occupational specialty. But even less than one hundred years ago, practicing physicians carried in their head and their hands about all the knowledge and skills needed to treat their patients.[5]

Stern has illustrated this point in reporting that for the typical late-nineteenth-century physician, the

> . . . regulation fee was twenty-five cents for an office call, and included medicines unless expensive drugs were necessary. A house visit within the township was fifty cents without medicine, seventy-five cents with medicine. The doctor compounded his own prescriptions. In the case of death, there was a three-dollar fee, for which he did most of the work of the present-day mortician. All obstetrical cases, regardless of the length of labor, were five dollars, as were abortions, while miscarriages were billed at one dollar and a half . . . he . . . also functioned as a dentist. A tooth extraction cost twenty-five cents, except when several in a row were removed at the same time, when the fee per tooth was reduced. . . .
>
> As with other doctors of his day, he visited his patients on horseback with saddlebags, by a gig or buggy, carrying a limited supply of fever medicine, sulphur and molasses, obstetric forceps, and a bag of instruments for emergencies. . . . [6]

[5]For some interesting accounts of several American physicians who fit this description, see James T. Flexner, *Doctors on Horseback,* New York: Collier Books, Crowell-Collier, 1962.

[6]Bernard J. Stern, *American Medical Practice in the Perspective of a Century,* New York: Commonwealth Fund, 1945, pp. 19–20.

Thus, working alone and with the equipment they could carry with them, small-town practitioners were able to provide most of the medical care that was available to their patients. In contrast, Stern also describes a more recent case (actually thirty years ago, but still a vivid comparison) in which a patient admitted to the hospital "was observed and described by three visiting physicians, two residents, three interns, ten specialists, and fourteen technicians, a total of thirty-two individuals, and although the record of the case was still incomplete, it already covered twenty-nine pages."[7]

In the ensuing years increased medical knowledge and specialty skills, plus the capital investment required for modern diagnostic and therapeutic equipment, have virtually forced practitioners to band together in various ways, and since nearly two-thirds of all physicians are in private practice, let us look at the various ways in which they organize themselves.

### Private Practice

The simplest kind of organization is the so-called "solo" practitioner. Theoretically, a solo practice is one in which a single physician establishes an office and treats patients who freely choose him or her as their doctor.[8] However, as we have already seen, practicing physicians must depend upon others for recruiting patients and consultation on medical problems outside their sphere of expertise, not to mention the all-important privilege of admitting their patients to local hospitals. In other words, the solo practice is more an ideological type than a reality, although some rural general practitioners may closely approximate this type.

Interestingly enough, although solo practice may be the ideologically preferred form of practice—because of its autonomy and independence—it is also the most unstable form of practice. Freidson has reported that the solo practitioner or one only loosely associated with others is most likely to lose control of his or her practice to either patients or colleagues.[9] For example, because solo practitioners are competing with other physicians for patients, they must give psychologically satisfying as well as technically satisfactory care to their patients. They are, therefore, sensitive to the demands of their patients and may be tempted to yield to their demands even though not medically indicated. At the same time, the solo practitioners are caught on the horns of another dilemma with regard to their colleagues. On the one hand, seeking consultations from others increases the chances that the patients may thereafter go to the consultant as their

[7]*Ibid.,* pp. 20–21.

[8]Eliot Freidson, "The Organization of Medical Practice," in Howard E. Freeman, Sol Levine, and Leo G. Reeder, (eds.), *Handbook of Medical Sociology,* 2d ed. Englewood Cliffs, N.J.: Prentice-Hall, 1972, pp. 343–358.

[9]Eliot Freidson, *Patients' Views of Medical Practice,* New York: Russell Sage, 1961.

doctor. Making referrals to consultants may also lead the patients to suspect the competence of the referring physician or, worse, suspect the physician of unethical practices such as fee splitting. On the other hand, if the solo practitioners do not make referrals or seek consultations, they may be forced to make medical decisions for which they are not qualified, thereby risking a malpractice suit or even losing their license.[10] In the first instance the solo practitioners are subject to "client control," and in the latter case they are subject to "colleague control." This instability in solo practice is a modern version of an earlier and continuing problem. In the days before specialties developed in medical practice—indeed, when specialties were considered unorthodox practice—solo practitioners needed protection of their status from quacks and charlatans. Because the quacks' efforts were more palliative than therapeutically effective, orthodox practitioners were subject to losing their patients to these various individuals selling elixirs and other "sure-cures." Nowadays, however, they are more likely to lose patients to other practitioners whose competence in limited areas exceeds that of the referring practitioner.

One way in which practitioners may offset the potential hazards of solo practice is by banding together in some kind of cooperative practice. The forms which cooperative practice may take vary widely from two physicians with an agreement to "cover" the other's practice when absent to large group practices involving hundreds of physicians.[11] Perhaps the modal arrangement is an *association* of two physicians who have separate clientele, but share overhead expenses such as office rent, bookkeeping service, and receptionist's salary.[12] An arrangement of this type is usually between two physicians in the same specialty, but may also be between different specialties or, on occasion, different disciplines such as medicine and dentistry. The obvious advantage of an association is that one physician can see the other's patients when the associate is ill or on vacation. They can arrange to split night calls or weekend duty, yet each can maintain a separate clientele. Although these advantages are considerable, there is still the danger that patients may like one physician better and switch, even though the more desirable physician makes no effort to attract the associate's patients. Problems may also arise if one physician has a much larger practice than the other and the sharing of expenses is not equivalent to the size of practice or some other agreed-upon criteria.

Many of these problems are eliminated (although some new ones arise) when practitioners become legally bound in joint practice or in what Freidson calls a *partnership*.[13] By some agreed-upon arrangement, profits

[10]*Ibid.*
[11]Freidson, "The Organization of Medical Practice," *op. cit.*
[12]*Ibid.*
[13]*Ibid.*, p. 349.

from fees are shared along with the expenses of the operation. When each partner receives a salary based on contribution to the profits, there is no problem of losing patients to the other partner. If the partners are in different specialties, referrals and consultations can be made more easily. Excess profits can be invested for further gain or, more likely, spent for more equipment such as laboratory facilities to improve the diagnostic capabilities of the partnership but reduce the overhead. Frequently a partnership consists of an arrangement between an older, already estab-lished practitioner and a younger doctor, who may be just beginning a career. Often these arrangements are on a trial basis for a specified period of time with the ultimate goal being that the younger person buy the older doctor's practice, but in easy stages. Assuming that the trial period is mutually satisfactory, there are some advantages to a partnership that do not appear in the association. One is that the younger physician can step into a ready-made, more or less stable practice without going through a lean period during which he or she builds up a separate practice. In other words, the younger partner can begin earning money at a reasonably comfortable level soon after completion of training. At the same time, the older doctor can gradually turn over more and more of the work to the junior partner, but maintain a reasonably high level of income while retiring in stages from active practice. A partnership also offers the advantage of time off for vacation, as does an association. In addition, however, time off can be granted for postgraduate and refresher courses. In a partnership, there is also less chance that time off will disturb the continuity of patient care, since presumably each of the partners deals with all the patients.

Partnerships are not without potential disadvantages, however. Per-haps the most difficult problem is deciding the basis upon which profits are paid to the partners. If the partners are in different specialties, one may have fewer patients, but charge higher fees, and thus feel that he or she should receive more of the income. One partner may attract more new patients than the others. A further potential problem is that each partner's income is likely to be lower during the peak earning period—roughly the middle years of the career—than that of colleagues who practice alone or in association with others. However, both early and late in the career, the partner's income will be somewhat greater than the colleague's not in a partnership. In fact, the lifetime earnings for physicians in a partnership will usually exceed that of physicians in an association or practicing alone, other things being equal.[14] Some of these "other things" which have to be equal include length of time in practice, type of practice (general practice, medical specialty, surgical specialty), size of practice, and region of the

[14]Editorial, "A Financial Profile of the New Practitioner," *Residents, Interns and Senior Students,* 7 (November, 1964), 47–55.

country. Results of one survey of almost 1,800 physicians conducted in 1963 by *Medical Economics* showed that physicians in a partnership generally earned more than solo practitioners, in addition to other benefits of joint practice cited above. Furthermore, according to this report, the peak earning period comes after about ten years of practice and begins to taper off after thirty years in practice. Other data suggested that surgical specialists earn more than medical specialists, who, in turn, earn more than general practitioners, and that larger practices earn more net income for the partners than smaller ones.[15]

Some recent data from a survey of more than 8,000 self-employed physicians published by *Medical Economics* and shown in Table 12-2 indicate that physicians' earnings are higher, but are still influenced by those same factors. Clearly, the net income rises with the number of partners, and this relationship holds for all areas of specialization. Regional differences have shifted slightly, but still persist (despite differences in expenses expressed as a percentage of gross incomes, ranging from 33 percent in the East to 41 percent in the West). Although expenses have risen each year, net incomes seem to have kept pace. Median income for all reporting physicians in 1963 (before Medicare) was $28,960; in 1973 it was $42,140, a rise of 46 percent (for incorporated physicians, it was $56,670).[16]

The next logical step in cooperative practice would be to enlarge the association or partnership to more physicians, i.e., establish a *group practice*. At the present time, there is no concise definition of group practice except that it includes three or more physicians practicing together. Otherwise it varies with number of practitioners involved, whether they are all the same specialty or different ones, whether they share expenses only or profits as well, whether they are based in hospitals, clinics, or private offices, whether they are full time or part time or both, whether they treat anyone or only certain groups, etc.[17] For the purposes of the discussion which follows, group practice is defined here as "three or more physicians (full-time or part-time) formally organized to provide medical services, with income from medical practice distributed according to some prearranged plan."[18]

There is considerable evidence that despite the ideological preference for solo practice with its emphasis on independence and autonomy, the trend is toward group practice. Evidence from an earlier U.S. Public Health

[15]*Ibid.*, pp. 52–54.

[16]U.S. Department of Commerce, *Statistical Abstract of the United States, 1975*, Washington, D.C.: Government Printing Office, 1975, tables 117 and 118, p. 77.

[17]William A. MacColl, *Group Practice and Prepayment of Medical Care*, Washington, D.C.: Public Affairs Press, 1966. See also Edwin P. Jordan, "Group Practice," in Joseph Garland (ed.), *The Physician and His Practice*, Boston: Little, Brown, 1954, pp. 77–88.

[18]U.S. Department of Health, Education, and Welfare, *Medical Groups in the United States*, U.S. Public Health Service Publication 1063, Washington, D.C.: Government Printing Office, 1963, p. 4. Italics omitted.

## Table 12-2   Selected Factors Influencing Physicians' Incomes

| | Net income | | | | | | |
| | | | | 1973* | | | |
| | | | | Private practice | | Academic practice† | |
| Factors | 1963‡ | 1971§ | 1973¶ | Solo | Partner | Assistant professor | Chairperson |
|---|---|---|---|---|---|---|---|
| Type of practice | | | | | | | |
| Solo | $23,312 | $40,450 | | | | | |
| Association | — | 43,250 | | | | | |
| 2 MD partnership | 29,600 | 45,700 | | | | | |
| 3 MD partnership¶ | — | 49,100 | | | | | |
| Location of practice | | | | | | | |
| East | — | | $38,040 | | | | |
| South | — | | 45,760 | | | | |
| Midwest | 27,250 | | 45,420 | | | | |
| West | 26,900 | | 40,860 | | | | |
| Area of specialization | | | | | | | |
| General practice | | | | $35,910 | $45,170 | — | — |
| Family medicine | | | | 38,040 | — | — | — |
| Internal medicine | | | | 38,520 | 51,830 | $25,000 | $45,000 |
| General surgery | | | | 44,220 | 55,470 | 29,100 | 48,600 |
| Obstetrics-gynecology | | | | 45,210 | 57,330 | 27,600 | 44,300 |
| Pediatrics | | | | 36,070 | 42,070 | 23,000 | 43,800 |
| Psychiatry | | | | 36,030 | — | 26,000 | 44,500 |
| Average net income | | | | 39,100 | 52,700 | 30,000 | |

*Data for 1973 are from "After the Freeze: Can Self-employed MD's Break Out?" *Medical Economics*, November 11, 1974, 232–240.
†Data on academic incomes are from "How Ivory-tower Earnings Compare with Yours," *Medical Economics*, May 27, 1974, p. 82.
‡Data for 1963 are from "A Financial Profile of the New Practitioner," *Residents, Interns and Senior Students*, 7 (November, 1964), 46–55.
§Data for 1971 are from "Self-employed Earnings and Expenses," *Medical Economics*, November 20, 1972, 131–147.
¶Group practice.

Service survey showed that the number of groups engaging in active practice increased threefold between 1946 and 1959 and at the latter time included about 9.2 percent of all physicians in private practice.[19] A more recent survey, conducted by the American Medical Association, showed a further threefold increase in medical groups between 1959 and 1969 to a total of 6,371 groups which included about 40,000 physicians or about 17.6 percent of all physicians in private practice.[20] Even with this phenomenal growth, group practice is still not the most common type of medical organization, but because of its increasing importance it seems worthwhile to summarize some characteristics of the more than 6,300 groups that responded to the 1969 survey.

**1   Size**   The average size for all groups was 6.3 physicians. Size of the group tended to be larger for multispecialty groups (10.6) than for single-specialty (4.1) or general practice groups (3.4).

[19]*Ibid.*, p. 9.
[20]C. Todd and M. E. McNamara, *Medical Groups in the U.S., 1969,* Chicago: American Medical Association, 1971.

**2  Location**   About 42 percent of all reporting medical groups were located in the Midwest, roughly bounded by two tiers of states from North Dakota and Minnesota to Texas and Louisiana plus the five states around the Great Lakes. This represents a decline from 54 percent in 1959 with most of the decrease taking place in the West North Central states. The largest percentage growth was in the New England states although this accounted for less than 4 percent of all groups. Other growth areas from 1959 to 1969 were the Pacific Coast states (17 percent of all groups) and the South Atlantic states (14 percent).[21]

**3  Specialization**   About 82 percent of all group physicians in 1969 were specialists, a slight increase over the 79 percent reported in the 1959 survey. Of the total number of group physicians (excluding general practitioners) about one-third were made up of internists (16 percent), general surgeons (9 percent), and radiologists (9 percent). Other specialists mentioned less frequently were obstetricians, anesthesiologists, pediatricians, and orthopedic surgeons.

By specialty type, the largest percentage of private practitioners in group practices were radiologists (48 percent in group practice) and anesthesiologists (35 percent). Other specialties with at least one-fifth of their numbers in group practice were orthopedic surgery, internal medicine, pediatrics, obstetrics and gynecology, thoracic surgery, neurosurgery, and urology.

**4  Form of Organization**   More than two-thirds (68.7 percent) of the survey groups were organized as partnerships with nearly 1,000 groups (15.6 percent) being classified as corporations. Other forms of organization such as an association (9.2 percent), single owner (2.8 percent), or other (3.7 percent) were much less frequently found. Although a substantial majority of each type of group was classified as a partnership, about one-fourth of both single- and multispecialty groups were corporations or associations. As size of group increases, the percentage of partnerships declines in favor of the corporate form of organization.[22]

Proponents claim that among the advantages of group practice organization over a more traditional laissez-faire organization are benefits for providers as well as patients. The positive attributes of a partnership are extended in a group setting providing regular work hours, access to laboratory and diagnostic support services for better patient care, time for continuing education and vacations, and more adequate compensation. A group practice can offer to patients services that are comprehensive in scope, that have continuity in that needed services are coordinated for patients by the group, and that are more accessible and generally less

---

[21]Milton I. Roemer, Jorge A. Mera, and William Shonick, "The Ecology of Group Medical Practice in the United States," *Medical Care,* 12 (August, 1974), 627–637.
[22]Todd and McNamara, *op. cit.,* pp. 4–10, 73–81.

costly.[23] Most of the recent evaluations of group practice organizations tend to support those claims although there are some contradictions and reservations. Graham, for example, reviewed several studies which compared solo with group fee-for-service practice on dimensions of utilization rates, physician productivity, quality of care rendered, and continuity. The studies concluded that group practice was generally superior to solo practice on these dimensions, but methodological inadequacies limited broader generalization of the results of these studies.[24]

Evaluations of prepaid group practice organizations (a form of insurance in which all needed services are provided by the group for a fixed sum paid in advance) also support the benefits of group practice over other forms. In general, utilization of hospital services is less while use of ambulatory services is higher, fewer work days are lost, costs are usually lower, and general health status is correlated positively with broad health plan coverage.[25] Prepaid group practices are often benefit options of business or educational organizations where employees have "dual-choice"; that is, they may choose to obtain care from a prepaid group practice or outside it from other providers in the community. Factors influencing which form is chosen seem to relate more to situational needs than to health characteristics. For example, new residents in a community or people without a regular physician tended to choose a prepaid group practice more often. Convenience of access, short waiting time, ease of obtaining appointments were other reasons given for choosing prepaid group practice.[26] The majority of patients who use services of prepaid groups tend to express satisfaction with those services although some dissatisfaction is expressed in terms of delays in getting appointments and other perceived barriers.[27]

[23]MacColl, *op. cit.*

[24]Fred E. Graham, "Group vs. Solo Practice: Arguments and Evidence," *Inquiry,* 9 (June, 1972), 49–60.

[25]Robert L. Robertson, "Health Services, Health Status and Work Loss," *Journal of Community Health,* 3 (Spring, 1976), 175–187. See also Gerald T. Perkoff, Lawrence Kahn, and Anita Mackie, "Medical Care Utilization in an Experimental Prepaid Group Practice Model in a University Medical Center," *Medical Care,* 12 (June, 1974), 471–485.

[26]Klaus J. Roghmann, William Gavett, Andrew A. Sorenson, Sandra Wells, and Richard Wersinger, "Who Chooses Prepaid Medical Care: Survey Results from Two Marketings of Three New Prepayment Plans," *Public Health Reports,* 90 (November–December, 1975), 516–527; Richard Tessler and David Mechanic, "Factors Affecting the Choice between Prepaid Group Practice and Alternative Insurance Programs," *Health and Society,* 53 (Spring, 1975), 149–172; and Taher A. Moustafa, Carl E. Hopkins, and Bonnie Klein, "Determinants of Choice and Change of Health Insurance Plan," *Medical Care,* 8 (January–February, 1971), 32–41.

[27]Richard Tessler and David Mechanic, "Consumer Satisfaction with Prepaid Group Practice: A Comparative Study," *Journal of Health and Social Behavior,* 16 (March, 1975), 95–113. See also Charles A. Metzner, Rashid L. Bashshur, and Gary W. Shannon, "Differential Public Acceptance of Group Medical Practice," *Medical Care,* 10 (July–August, 1972), 279–287.

Studies of physicians' decisions to choose group practice settings show that early career exposure as well as commitment to continuity of comprehensive care influence that choice.[28] The nature of the setting influences how the physicians practice; this includes less use of ancillary diagnostic services and more referrals[29] and coping with increased demand by decreasing time with patients rather than extending their hours,[30] but no difference in participation in continuing educational activities than non-group physicians.[31] The findings of these and other studies point to the benefits of group practice as an organizational form, but they also indicate some of the potential risks. The equivocal nature of these findings would suggest a continued research effort, especially in view of new legislation promoting prepaid group practices under the concept of Health Maintenance Organizations (HMO's) designed to promote the health of larger population groups rather than provide just episodic care for problems of illness.[32]

It would appear that the forces which have brought about the emergence of group practice in its myriad forms are quite likely to continue. We may expect to see an increasing proportion of physicians in private practice banding together in some form of cooperative practice. Thus, the medical profession is gradually being reorganized to meet the health needs of the population. We shall turn now to other organizations which support the medical profession in this endeavor.

## Public Health Agencies

At this point, it would seem worthwhile to differentiate between "private" health care and "public" health care. It is not a matter of paying versus nonpaying patients, nor is it just that a physician in private practice sees only private patients. (In fact, many private practitioners donate some services to patients in clinics, hospitals, and schools in the community.)

[28]Anne Rankin Mahoney, "Factors Affecting Physicians' Choice of Group or Independent Practice," *Inquiry,* 10 (June, 1973), 9–18; and Marshall H. Becker, Robert H. Drachman, and John P. Kirscht, "A Field Experiment to Evaluate Various Outcomes of Continuity of Physician Care," *American Journal of Public Health,* 64 (November, 1974), 1062–1070.

[29]Raynald Pineault, "The Effect of Prepaid Group Practice on Physicians' Utilization Behavior," *Medical Care,* 14 (February, 1976), 121–136.

[30]David Mechanic, "The Organization of Medical Practice and Practice Orientations among Physicians in Prepaid and Nonprepaid Primary Care Settings," *Medical Care,* 13 (March, 1975), 189–204.

[31]Paul B. Guptill and Fred E. Graham, "Continuing Education Activities of Physicians in Solo and Group Practices: Report on a Pilot Study," *Medical Care,* 14 (February, 1976), 173–180.

[32]William R. Roy, *Health Maintenance Organization Act of 1972,* Washington, D.C.: Science and Health Communications Group, 1972. See also the analyses in Richard McNeil and Robert E. Schlenker, "HMO's, Competition and Government," *Health and Society,* 53 (Spring, 1975), 195–224; and Frederick D. Wolinsky, "Health Service Utilization and Attitudes toward Health Maintenance Organizations: A Theoretical and Methodological Discussion," *Journal of Health and Social Behavior,* 17 (September, 1976), 221–236.

Rather, the distinction may be made in terms of patient responsibility for obtaining services. For health problems experienced *by the patient,* the responsibility for seeking care is largely the patient's and, hence, viewed as part of the private sector. For health problems such as the hazards of air and water pollution or the regulation of potential sources of disease such as imported animals or plants, the individual cannot readily be held responsible; hence these services fall in the public sector. At the same time, it is acknowledged that there will always be some groups which cannot provide for their own health care. Thus services for special populations such as the poor are also usually seen as part of public health responsibility. And, of course, to provide these services there is the need to establish and maintain health facilities in the public sector.

Interest in the health conditions of a population by various government agencies has been a continuous phenomenon dating back to the ancient Greeks. It was noted in Chapter 6 that the Romans had established a pure water supply, medical clinics, and free medical service for indigents. Concomitant with the growth and development of medical knowledge and medical practice has been the growing importance of public health agencies. In the United States, the first public health organization was the Marine Hospital Service established in 1798. Between that time and 1912 when the present U.S. Public Health Service was organized, there had emerged an increasing number of public health organizations at the local and then state levels. In addition, the American Public Health Association, an association of professional and ancillary workers in the field, was formed in 1872.[33] For the most part, the early efforts of public health agencies were directed toward problems of environmental sanitation and control of infectious diseases, especially to prevent epidemics. As more and more effective control was gained over infectious diseases through medical science, public health agencies broadened the scope of their efforts to include prevention of other major health problems.

The goals of public health organizations can generally be described as service, education, and research.[34] Services provided by public health agencies can usually be described as one of three categories: care for special populations, community-wide services, and provision of community health facilities. Public health work has long been associated with direct medical care services to the medically indigent and others for whom the local community would not accept responsibility, such as Indians on the scattered government reservations and, of course, the military services. In 1965, with passage of the amendments to the Social Security Act of 1935

[33]Edward A. Suchman, *Sociology and the Field of Public Health,* New York: Russell Sage, 1963.

[34]U.S. Department of Health, Education, and Welfare, *Final Report of the Study Group on the Mission and Organization of the Public Health Service,* Washington, D.C.: Government Printing Office, 1960.

(Medicare and Medicaid), public responsibility for financing health services was extended to the elderly and the poor. Public involvement in health care organization was further extended to entire community populations with enactment of the Comprehensive Health Planning Act in 1966 (Public Law 89–749) to develop comprehensive health planning agencies throughout the nation. In 1974 this effort was reorganized under the National Health Planning and Resources Development Act (Public Law 93–641), which is described below. Other special populations for whom direct services are provided include children in school health programs, the mentally ill, alcoholics, women in maternal health programs, and victims of specific diseases such as tuberculosis and venereal disease.

Services provided by public health agencies on a community-wide basis are generally preventive in nature. Although this too has been a traditional responsibility, it has only been since the late nineteenth century that these activities have been very effective. In addition to mass immunization and screening programs noted above, public health organizations attempt to control disease-bearing pests through community-wide spraying and vermin control. Establishing and maintaining a pure water supply for the community is still another public health function as is supervising production and processing of food and drugs and establishing safety programs.

Many of a community's health facilities are operated by public health agencies. These may include laboratories for testing diagnoses of communicable diseases, clinics for rendering the kinds of services noted above, research laboratories for testing for air pollution, pollen count, etc. In addition to physical facilities, public health agencies also provide personnel such as nurses, caseworkers, health educators, nutritionists, and field investigators for suspected cases of communicable diseases.

In regard to the second goal, education, the activities of public health agencies are also worthy of note. This includes training of public health workers at all levels and health education for the public as well. In-service training is usually provided for a host of public health workers in various activities. In addition, university-based schools of public health offer advanced degrees for physicians and other health practitioners, social scientists, administrators, engineers, and other scientists. It is worth noting here that the mutual interest of public health officials and social scientists (especially sociologists) has become more intensive in recent years for two important reasons. First, the kinds of problems in medical care which have come to the fore have a pronounced social context with which public health practitioners have largely felt unable to deal adequately. Second, social scientists, and particularly sociologists, are more or less uniquely fitted by training and interest to cope with precisely these kinds of problems. Thus, an increasing number of sociologists are turning their attention to research on public health issues.

The second facet of the educational goal is health education for the public. In part, this is accomplished through talks by public health officials for community groups such as schools, churches, and civic organizations. By far, however, the larger effort is addressed to specific groups on particular topics. For example, public health nurses, nutritionists, and others use their special knowledge to help families achieve a more healthful level of living.

Research is the third goal of public health organizations. It may range from the collection of vital statistics used for simple description to conducting elaborate and long-term studies in epidemiology, disease processes, public health attitudes, evaluation of programs, etc. Much of this research is designed to provide answers to very practical but perplexing problems, such as how to motivate the public to utilize health facilities or participate in health programs. With the advent of chronic diseases, long-term care, comprehensive medicine, and so forth, new research areas have been added to the more traditional ones.

Public health organizations also provide financial support for research done by others in universities, research institutes, and businesses in the private sector. Between 1965 and 1975, the amount provided each year for research and development by the Department of Health, Education, and Welfare rose from $681 million to $2.2 billion. In 1975, 75 percent of that was provided through the National Institutes of Health.[35]

In order to achieve these goals of service, education, and research, public health agencies have been organized at three levels, local, state, and federal. For the most part, local organizations—of which there are over 1,500 in the United States—emphasize the provision of services to the public. These may be rather restricted in scope in small departments or they may be very comprehensive in large departments lócated in major metropolitan areas. In any case, one of the increasingly important functions of local health departments is the coordination of health services and health education of the various health facilities and health-related organizations in the community.[36] Coordination of activities among local health departments is largely a duty of the state organization. Moreover, state departments or commissions encourage, initiate, and often finance research on state health problems. Long-range planning of future health needs of the population and the planning of programs and facilities to meet these needs is another function of the state-level agencies.

At the national level, the largest and most important organization is the U.S. Public Health Service. Primarily, USPHS operates through the state organizations in the form of grants-in-aid, demonstration, and research

[35] *Statistical Abstract of the United States, 1975,* Table 911, p. 549.
[36] Sol Levine and Paul E. White, "The Community of Health Organizations," in Freeman, Levine, and Reeder, *op. cit.,* pp. 359–385.

projects to the various states, although some direct services are provided. Other important federal agencies which provide similar activities, but for special groups, would include the Office of Child Development, the Veterans' Administration, and the Division of Vocational Rehabilitation.

## Voluntary Health Agencies

Another significant group of health organizations is the more than 100,000 voluntary health agencies which, like the public health organizations, are also found at the local, state (or regional), and national levels. There are, however, several different kinds of voluntary agencies with different goals, although there is some overlap among them. First, there is a large number of national associations and their state and local chapters, supported by public donations, whose primary focus is sponsoring research on (1) specific diseases (American Cancer Society, American Heart Association), (2) special groups (National Society for Crippled Children), or (3) special health problems (National Safety Council). Second, there is a large number of agencies whose principal activities are coordination of local services and facilities and fund raising (National Health Association, United Fund, or Community Chest). Finally, but not exhaustively, there are voluntary professional organizations (American Medical Association, American Public Health Association) for disseminating research results and translating them into practical application.[37] In addition to fund-raising and research activities, some of these voluntary organizations provide direct services to the public or act as case finders of certain diseases in the community. Nearly all engage in educational activities through pamphlets, brochures, advertising, and public meetings.

To carry out the many, varied activities, voluntary agencies depend heavily on literally millions of volunteer workers, who donate their time and effort on behalf of the organization. Usually, a coordinator or director is hired to supervise local functioning, and the state director will have a staff to assist in supervising local groups. At the national office level, there is often required a much larger paid staff to supervise and coordinate the activities of all the lower levels.[38] The growth of the bureaucratic organization, together with the increased duplication of effort, has created problems for voluntary associations. In addition to having different goals, these voluntary health associations also have developed from different motivations. Katz[39] has suggested that there is a conventional kind of organization

[37]See Suchman, *op. cit.,* pp. 38–39.

[38]Louis Lasagna, *The Doctors' Dilemmas,* New York: Collier Books, Crowell-Collier, 1963.

[39]Alfred H. Katz, "Conventional and 'Self-organized' Voluntary Agencies: A Comparison," in Alfred H. Katz and Jean Spencer Shelton (eds.), *Health and the Community,* New York: Free Press, 1965, pp. 383–389.

which is formed after the identification of and ability to diagnose, treat, and prevent a specific disease is achieved. The National Tuberculosis Association is clearly of this type. The other kind of organization is the "self-organized" voluntary association which evolves from a realization that there exists a serious *sociomedical* problem, and a society is formed to combat it. The American Heart Association, for example, was begun by a group of public-minded physicians to stimulate research on heart disease. As a result, self-organized associations allow full participation by all members in policy decisions although this function is carried out by the boards of directors of the more conventional type of associations. One consequence of this difference is that when organizational goals are reached (such as successful prevention of a disease) or competition is encountered (such as from the government), self-organized associations tend to die out, but the more conventional ones seem to be able to broaden or change their goals successfully.[40]

Although these voluntary agencies may differ from each other somewhat, they all have a common difference from governmental agencies engaged in similar activities. The development of the voluntary health agencies is an expression of the traditional American value that private citizens (and corporations) must seek out and assume some public responsibility. This has been particularly the case when official agencies, both governmental and private, have failed to discharge their duties to the public. Thus, many of the current organizations got their start as sort of a social reform movement to provide services that were otherwise not available or when new needs arose that lay beyond the jurisdiction of any single group. The National Society for Crippled Children and the American Red Cross are examples. Obviously, voluntary associations differ from governmental agencies in that the latter are tax supported and the former depend upon public donations and membership fees for their operating capital (although voluntary associations are indirectly tax supported in that they pay no taxes, and contributions made to them are tax deductible). That voluntary agencies have become an important element in the provision of health services is illustrated by the fact that from 1960 to 1974, public donations rose from 466 million to 975 million dollars, and these figures do not include gifts of food, clothing, or cash not officially recorded.[41]

It should be noted that voluntary health and welfare agencies of all kinds are receiving increased competition from the federal government, which has expanded its operations and increased its budget for this purpose even more than have voluntary associations. More than that, however, the underlying philosophy of the obligation of private groups to assume public

[40]See David L. Sills, *The Volunteers,* New York: Free Press, 1957.
[41]*Statistical Abstract of the United States, 1975,* table 500, p. 311.

responsibility also seems to be changing. The passage of the government-financed Medicare Act is a case in point. Whereas in 1960, public expenditures for health care were 25 percent of the total 27 billion dollars, in 1973, the public share had risen to 39 percent of the nearly 100-billion-dollar total health bill. During this same period, the amount provided by private philanthropy dropped from 5.3 to 4.9 percent. Other private sources, such as health insurance and direct consumer payment, made up the balance.[42] In view of these trends it may be expected that voluntary associations will face even greater competition from the government, necessitating further adjustments in the role of voluntary agencies in the provision of health and welfare services.[43]

Up to this point, we have been discussing organizations which are more or less directly involved in providing health and medical care services to the public. These range from the various ways in which medical practitioners organize themselves for providing private care, to the large bureaucratic structure of the Public Health Service for public services, to nonprofit, voluntary agencies, which supplement these two. Now we wish to turn to a brief description of organizations which do not give direct medical care services to the public, but rather may be considered as supporting institutions which, nonetheless, influence the provision of these services. These would include, primarily, health insurance carriers and other sponsors of health plans such as trade unions, the hospital and medical equipment industry, and pharmaceutical manufacturers.

### Health Insurance Companies

Although some functions of health insurance and trends in coverage are briefly described in the following chapter, we wish to note here the growth of insurance underwriters as support organizations for financing the provision of medical care. In the United States, the earliest form of health insurance was the compulsory deduction for hospital services from wages of sailors. This was in 1798 after the establishment of the U.S. Marine Hospital Service (the precursor of the Public Health Service). The first *voluntary* health insurance carrier, however, was not begun until 1847 with the organization of the Massachusetts Health Insurance Company of Boston. The first policies for accident insurance followed three years later. During the next sixty years, the number of companies offering these services grew slowly, but at the same time, the benefits provided were enlarged. By 1890, policies offering protection from disability from speci-

---

[42]*Ibid.*, table 101, p. 70.

[43]See, for example, Albert F. Wessen, "The Apparatus of Rehabilitation: An Organizational Analysis," in Marvin B. Sussman (ed.), *Sociology and Rehabilitation,* Washington, D.C.: American Sociological Association, 1966, pp. 148–178.

fied diseases had been introduced. By 1903, limited surgical benefits were included in some policies. In 1907, the first noncancellable and guaranteed renewable plan became available. The year 1910 marked a new milestone with the development of the first group accident and sickness policy. During the 1930s various local communities experimented with prepaid group hospitalization plans and prepayment schedules for physicians' services which led to the establishment of the Health Services Plan Commission (Blue Cross) in 1937 and the Blue Shield Medical Care plan in 1946.

Since World War II, the most notable feature of the health insurance industry has been the rapid expansion in numbers of organizations offering some type of protection against illness and disability. It is, of course, also true that the benefits have become more comprehensive, including such features as protection against loss of income due to illness or disability, specific programs for people over age' sixty-five, plans for various-sized groups of employees and of different organizations, comprehensive major medical plans and other variations of these benefits. The major expansion, however, was in the number of agencies. From 1953 to 1974, the number of commercial insurance companies offering health insurance doubled from 500 to about 1,000. Added to these carriers, which are mostly life insurance companies, are the 74 Blue Cross hospital insurance plans and 70 Blue Shield surgical and medical care plans and about 400 other plans associated with union, employee, and welfare groups.[44]

What seems particularly significant about the rapid growth of insurance carriers is the degree to which they can influence the costs and benefits of the programs as well as policies concerning coverage. In fact, this influence stems from the development of *group* insurance—an outgrowth of labor-management bargaining when wage ceilings were in effect. That is, since wages could not rise appreciably, health care for large groups of employees or union members was sought as a "fringe benefit." The potential for profits from insuring large groups of relatively "low-risk" people (e.g., people in the labor force) attracted the interest of private insurance companies. The influence of insurance carriers on delivery of health services is implemented through control of what services are covered by policies and which are to be excluded.[45] Thus, expensive services, such as long-term care for the chronically ill, psychiatric and dental services, or preventive medical care are seldom included in ordinary policies.

The major contribution of health insurance, of course, is in making medical care available to a large proportion of the population by prepay-

---

[44]*Source Book of Health Insurance Data,* 1975–1976, New York: Health Insurance Institute, 1975.

[45]See, for example, Max D. Bennett, "Influence of Health Insurance on Patterns of Care: Maternity Hospitalization," *Inquiry,* 12 (March, 1975), 59–66.

ment of small, known sums of money against the risk of large, unexpected expenditures for illness and disability. In 1974, 172 million persons or about 80 percent of the United States civilian population were covered by some form of health insurance. Some evidence will be presented in Chapter 13 which shows that people covered by insurance are more likely than noninsured persons to use medical care facilities for preventive or health maintenance reasons or to seek other forms of medical care. In fact, there is some concern about overutilization, or patients obtaining services—especially hospitalization—which may not be medically required, but which they demand because they have "already paid for it."

A second contribution of insurance is in reducing the physicians' uncollected bills. Many major policies now include provision for payment of all or at least part of the physicians' fee for services. Usually this is paid directly to the physician, but some policies provide payment to the subscriber, who then pays the physician. Prepayment of hospital charges and physicians' fees was the forerunner of these kinds of insurance programs designed to provide comprehensive coverage. There are some who would argue that these programs are not comprehensive enough. Others point to policies covering surgery and major medical expenses, such as long-term care, and even insurance against loss of income due to sickness and disability. Although insurance companies are less directly related to the provision of health services than the organizations discussed thus far, their phenomenal growth necessitates their inclusion as part of the web of medical organizations. For example, over 80 percent of the United States population paid $33.3 billion in insurance premiums during 1974, an increase of 200 percent over 1964. Similarly, the benefits paid to subscribers were nearly doubled during this same period to a level of about $28 billion in 1974, representing a substantial profit for the private insurance industry.[46] Thus, health insurance is a large-scale operation and one that cannot be omitted from the network of organizations providing or supporting health care services.

Other organizations also exert an influence on the provision of medical care. These would include, for example, union health plans and the hospital and medical equipment industry. The first union health plan was provided in 1913 by the International Ladies Garment Workers' Union in New York. The second was organized by the United Auto Workers in 1943. During World War II, these and similar plans emerged and grew rapidly primarily as fringe benefits, as we noted above. That union and other industrial health plans are a force that shapes the nature and scope of health services can be seen in the ever increasing provisions contained in contracts arrived at through collective bargaining. The trend nowadays is for more comprehen-

[46]*Sourcebook of Health Insurance Data,* 1975, pp. 40, 45.

sive coverage including long-term disability care, treatment for mental illness, a host of preventive services, and even dental care. To some extent these services are purchased by the union from private practitioners who agree to accept the fee schedule set by the plan. More and more, however, unions have begun providing their own health centers staffed by physicians and members of allied professions who work as salaried employees of the union. The United Mine Workers is an example of this type of plan. Some plans, originally designed to provide health care for workers in a particular union, have grown large enough to offer prepaid, comprehensive services to the general public. The Kaiser-Permanente group in California is a good example of this development. Other organizations, like some universities, have developed prepaid health maintenance plans or HMOS.

### Hospital and Medical Equipment Industry

Still another industry is important for the provision of medical care, namely, the hospital and medical equipment industry. Although the influence of these private suppliers is less noticeable than that of organizations directly involved, the hospital and medical equipment industry is illustrative of the complex relationships which have arisen among organizations which support the medical profession in providing medical care for the public. For example, the federal government plays an active part in regulating this industry through the Department of Commerce, which recommends standards for equipment (through the Division of Simplified Practice). Furthermore, the Public Health Service provides a *Hospital Equipment Planning Guide* for aiding administrators in equipping their hospitals. Professional associations such as the American Hospital Association and the American Medical Association also set standards for equipment, quality as well as use. Finally, private companies, such as the Modern Hospital Publishing Company, exert some influence by providing pricing guides such as the *Hospital Purchasing File*.[47] Even though these organizations have different interests in the medical care field and influence the provision of care in varying degrees, it is important to note that the web of organizational relationships in providing medical care grows more complex as time passes.

### The Pharmaceutical Industry

Another important element in the network of organizations which support the physician in providing medical care is the pharmaceutical industry. A noteworthy aspect of this industry is its rapid emergence as a potent influence on the cost of medical care and the conduct of medical practice.

[47]See Laura G. Jackson, *Hospital and ·Community,* New York: Macmillan, 1964, especially chap. 10.

In the first place, these commercial companies have participated in the discovery of "miracle drugs," especially antibiotics, either in their own laboratories or through grants to research divisions in settings such as medical schools. This support has led to the virtual revolution in both discovery and production of drugs. The rapidly accumulating body of knowledge about drugs and their effects has led to the increased pace of new discoveries. At the same time, pharmaceutical houses have utilized the mass-production techniques of industry to make these discoveries widely available to the medical profession. Secondly, the rising numbers of older citizens and the increased incidence of chronic diseases have created a greater demand for the use of drugs. Because of the nature of many chronic illnesses, chemotherapy is employed to stabilize the progress of the disease or to combat potential infection from reduced resistance. Drugs may often be employed as palliative treatment for demanding patients who insist that something be done for their condition.[48]

As a consequence of these developments, pharmaceutical companies have attained a position which enables them to influence the health status of whole populations as well as the provision of medical care. Profits from the production and sales of drugs have been large enough to result in the development of diversified, multinational corporations that produce items such as chemicals, fertilizers, pesticides, and food additives that strongly influence the nutrition of people in underdeveloped as well as industrialized nations. The capabilities of these corporations also inhibit competition by companies started by nationals from the emerging countries.[49]

The influence on the medical practice of individual physicians can be achieved through sales campaigns utilizing extensive (and expensive) advertising schemes and an army of salespeople, known as "detail men," whose job it is to persuade physicians to prescribe their products. One source, for example, estimates that physicians annually receive some 24,247 *tons* of advertising material.[50] More importantly, drug prices are not subject to the usual competition found in the marketplace because of an increase in the use of "ethical" or prescribed drugs and a concomitant decline in the proportion of over-the-counter preparations sold. Pharma-

---

[48]Ingrid Waldron, "Increased Prescribing of Valium, Librium, and Other Drugs: An Example of the Influence of Economic and Social Factors on the Practice of Medicine," *International Journal of Health Services,* 7 (Winter, 1977), 37–62.

[49]Meredeth Turshen, "An Analysis of the Medical Supply Industries," *International Journal of Health Services,* 6 (Spring, 1976), 271–294. Other industries, such as those producing infant formulas, have also undermined cultural beliefs around breast-feeding in underdeveloped nations and, therefore, affected nutritional status of infants. See Michael B. Bader, "Breast-Feeding: The Role of Multinational Corporations in Latin America," *International Journal of Health Services,* 6 (Fall, 1976), 609–626.

[50]Herman M. Somers and Anne R. Somers, *Doctors, Patients and Health Insurance,* Washington, D.C.: Brookings, 1961, p. 87, note 11.

ceutical houses have played an increasingly important role in the trend toward the use of complex prescription drugs in therapy. Principally, this has been in the preparation and prepackaging of these drugs and in "branding" them. That is, a simple, easily remembered brand name is substituted for the complicated scientific generic name of the drugs. Busy physicians are urged by various media (e.g., detail men, advertising) to prescribe drugs by brand names rather than by generic names (which are usually much cheaper). The patients are the ultimate losers inasmuch as they can purchase only what is prescribed and cannot shop around for a less expensive drug which would produce the same effects. Thus, drug prices are not held down by competition, but may be maintained at inflated levels.

Another way in which drug companies could influence the provision of medical care is through making use of some results of research on adoption of drugs by physicians. About 1954, an investigation of this process was conducted by members of the Columbia University Bureau of Applied Social Research.[51] Over two hundred physicians in four Midwestern communities were interviewed in regard to fellow doctors whom they regarded as their best friends, fellow physicians with whom they frequently consulted on cases, and particularly, physicians to whom they went for advice on drugs. The measure of adoption of a particular antibiotic drug was obtained from an examination of the prescription files of pharmacies in the communities. The comparison of the detailed sociometric data and the rates of adoption suggested that physicians who are oriented to their profession in terms of well-developed colleague relationships more readily adopted the new drug than did practitioners who were more patient-oriented and less well integrated with their colleagues (in terms of number of sociometric choices received).[52] The study also cited the detail man as the single most important source of information about new drugs.

The drug industry has the potential to influence medical practice in other ways as well. For example, it is possible that further financial support may be withheld by a company for a physician's future experiments if the latter's reports are not favorable to the drug company. Publications of unfavorable results can be delayed until the drug is on the market and selling well. On the other hand, reprints of published reports favorable to the drug company product are distributed by the thousands, thus lending

[51]James S. Coleman and Herbert Menzel, *On the Flow of Scientific Information in the Medical Profession: A Study of the Adoption of a New Drug by the Medical Community,* New York: Columbia University Bureau of Applied Social Research, 1955.

[52]See Herbert Menzel, "Innovation, Integration and Marginality: A Survey of Physicians," *American Sociological Review,* 25 (October, 1960), 704–713. More recently, see the discussion in Elina Hemminiki, "Review of Literature on the Factors Affecting Drug Prescribing," *Social Science and Medicine,* 9 (February, 1975), 111–116. See also, John Lilja, "How Physicians Choose Their Drugs," *Social Science and Medicine,* 10 (July–August, 1976), 363–365.

scientific prestige to the product.[53] As the Somerses put it: "Clearly the traditional relationship between the doctor and the drug maker has been radically altered; instead of supplying the products the doctor orders, the manufacturer now tells him what he should order and why."[54] Despite these potential hazards, however, the pharmaceutical industry has become and is likely to remain an integral part of the network of medical organizations.

## COORDINATION OF HEALTH INDUSTRY SERVICES

It should be clear that the provision of medical care services has progressed a long way from the "horse and buggy" doctor of a previous era. It should also be clear that with the proliferation of new direct health care services and supporting services arises a need for coordination and control. For the remainder of this chapter, we shall examine some problems and prospects of coordination both within each of the sectors described above and between them.

Increased specialization within the medical profession, along with geographic maldistribution of physicians' services, continues to cause concern over providing care for the "total" patient. The tendency for some specialists to limit their interest in the patient's problem coupled with a lack of systematic means of referral from one kind of specialist to another has resulted in "fractionated" patient care. The concentration of specialists in middle- and upper-class urban areas at the expense of poor urban and rural areas only exacerbates the problem. In some respects, group practice and larger forms of corporate medical practice have emerged as a response to this concern. Further, greater stress is being placed on training specialists in primary care to use the expertise of specialists to meet the more general health needs of the public. The fact remains, however, that there are few controls over the production of physicians (and other health personnel) or locating them where needs are greatest. Incentive programs designed to increase the likelihood of career choices compatible with national health needs have not succeeded.[55] One solution is a stronger central health authority, such as the federal government, but this move is strongly resisted by the medical profession and some voluntary agencies.

Within the public health agencies, numerous difficulties undermine the ability to achieve the stated goals fully. In the first place, there are many overlapping areas in which different public health organizations offer the same services; thus they compete with each other for clients. This is

[53]Louis Lasagna, "The Drug Industry and American Medicine," *Journal of Chronic Diseases,* 7 (May, 1958), 440–442.
[54]Somers and Somers, *op. cit.,* p. 88.
[55]See the review of several programs in Charles E. Lewis, Rashi Fein, and David Mechanic, *A Right to Health,* New York: Wiley, 1976, especially pp. 47–143.

especially true at the federal level in regard to research grants. The sheer size of the federal organization makes communication and coordination difficult and unwieldy. Perhaps a more serious problem is that public health services—especially direct medical services—still carry the implication of charity despite the many successes already achieved in many different areas. In addition, many useful programs such as mass immunization and mass screening do not reach the goals set, particularly among that segment of the population which needs these services most, i.e., the "hard core" group who make little use of any kind of community health services. Furthermore, public health agencies frequently experience difficulty in attracting high-quality personnel to carry out the health programs because of noncompetitive salary scales. This is more characteristic of local and state public health organizations than those at the federal level.

The problems confronting the various types of voluntary health agencies are somewhat different. The expanding size and scope of the formal aspects of many of these organizations takes a larger and larger share of the contributed dollar. It was reported, for example, that a major portion of the contributions collected by the National Tuberculosis Association was spent for administrative costs, and only 1 percent went to research and a somewhat larger share went for direct services.[56]

Some voluntary organizations are more effective in raising funds than others. In general, associations whose focus is on a disease or category of patients with some emotional appeal are more successful. But this fund-raising principle has little bearing on the importance of the disease with respect to its prevalence. For example, in one year $66.90 were raised for each polio victim (particularly children), but only 16 cents for each victim of arthritis. Yet the prevalence of arthritis was more than 100 times that of polio. Similarly, the National Foundation raised three times the amount of funds as the American Cancer Society, even though cancer kills five times as many children as polio.[57]

The lessening threat of certain diseases has caused some voluntary agencies to expand their efforts to include other diseases, thus competing with other agencies for the public's contributions. The manner in which the dollar is collected has also raised certain other problems. One is the controversy over having each organization solicit its own funds versus having a "united" fund drive. Through separate drives, the larger organizations with efficient fund raisers and which appeal to the public's emotions can usually do very well in raising money, but often at the expense of smaller or new organizations whose goals may be just as important. The public's objection to nearly continuous solicitation has encouraged the use of one larger campaign from which all participating agencies benefit. Larger

[56]Lasagna *The Doctors' Dilemmas, op. cit.,* p. 188.
[57]*Ibid.,* p. 199.

organizations, however, maintain they can do better by themselves. Though this controversy continues, the importance of these organizations cannot be denied, both individually and collectively, for their role in stimulating research, awakening the public to the importance of certain diseases, and rendering direct medical care services to victims of the disease.

We have already pointed out some problems associated with the insurance and pharmaceutical industries. In addition, they are business organizations whose major goal is profit (except Blue Cross-Blue Shield, of course). Thus although their interest in providing the public with a service is genuine, the way in which the service or product is provided must be tempered with considerations for the continual growth and welfare of the organization (an organizational problem shared by Blue Cross-Blue Shield). The contributions of these industries are real, but the costs are high.

Even this brief look at some issues and problems in the delivery of health care in the United States reveals the need for planning and coordination. That is, national health resources in manpower, equipment, and facilities seem adequate to meet identified national health needs, but as noted above, the lack of systematic coordination of these resources leaves gaps in services in some areas and inefficient overlapping of some services in other areas. The larger issue, then, is the development and application of a national health policy and planning to create a health services system. In anticipation of discussion in the final chapter on political aspects of health, some trends in organization of health services are identified.

These trends in health services organization are based on three important assumptions. The first is that every person has a right to adequate health care. A few years ago this statement would have been vigorously challenged on ideological grounds. Nowadays, this belief has become a statement of policy by professional organizations of providers such as the AMA, by governmental agencies, and by various consumer groups.[58] A second assumption, that "adequate health care" should mean comprehensive health services, is more controversial and there is less agreement among providers and consumers. It should be recalled from the discussion in Chapter 3 that comprehensive medicine not only implied the use of teams of health care experts and attention to the patient as a whole person, but included accessibility to a complete range of services and benefits. Today, that concept has been extended to include all preventive, curative, and rehabilitative services that (1) are *available,* are, in fact, present and geographically proximal to users; (2) are *accessible* by being provided at reasonable cost and under conditions such that no one is denied service

[58]Eveline M. Burns, *Health Services for Tomorrow: Trends and Issues,* New York: Dunellen, 1973.

because of inability to pay; (3) have *continuity* with coordination of various specialists' services and continuous recording of a health history; (4) are high in *quality* in terms of technical competence of the providers; and (5) maintain the *dignity* of the patient in assuring his or her rights as a patient and as a person.[59] Finally, it is assumed that any large-scale reorganization of the health industry in the United States will be accomplished by negotiation between public and private elements (providers, consumers, and payers) rather than by legislative fiat. That is, the historical and ideological context of delivery of health services in this country, coupled with the offsetting power and influence of public and private organizations in the health industry would seem to preclude a mandated solution to the organizational problems and to encourage a negotiated solution.[60]

With a national goal of providing comprehensive health care to all the people, at least three trends in organization of health services seem evident.

**1   Decentralization**   Contrary to the post-World War II trend that saw the community hospital emerge as the focus of most community health services, the more recent movement has been for decentralization to relocate services in different parts of the community to improve availability and accessibility. Although hospitals remain the community center for inpatient acute care, much of the long-term care now takes place in specialized institutions. The most dramatic shift, however, has been in the decentralization of ambulatory care, especially in the growth of neighborhood health centers in medically underserved urban and rural areas. Although some freestanding and hospital-based ambulatory care centers have been in existence for years, it was not until the early 1960s that the present movement gained sufficient momentum to become a noticeable trend. Despite the current problems with financing, administrative control, and relationships with supporting hospitals, the concept of improving accessibility to health services through decentralization has been forcefully demonstrated and seems likely to continue.[61]

**2   Public Funding**   As will be demonstrated in the following chapter, the proportion of the total health care costs paid for by public sources has risen each year and in 1975 accounted for about 42 cents of every dollar. A substantial part of this increase may be attributed to the Medicare and Medicaid programs which illustrate the increased use of public funds

[59]Anne R. Somers, "Toward a Rational Community Health System: The Hunterdon Model," *Hospital Progress,* 54 (April, 1973), 46–54.

[60]William L. Kissick, "Health Policy Directions for the 1970s," *New England Journal of Medicine,* 282 (June 11, 1970), 1343–1354.

[61]Roger A. Reynolds, "Improving Access to Health Care among the Poor—The Neighborhood Health Center Experience," *Health and Society,* 54 (Winter, 1976), 47–82. For recommendations on financing see Walter Merten and Sylvia Nothman, "Neighborhood Health Center Experience," *American Journal of Public Health,* 65 (March, 1975), 248–252. The emergence of rural and urban health centers is described in Jerome L. Schwartz, "Early Histories of Selected Neighborhood Health Centers," *Inquiry,* 7 (December, 1970), 3–16.

for services provided in the private sector. At least one proposal for national health insurance would extend the federal government's role as the third-party insurer of a publicly funded program. In part, this trend has emerged in response to (and now has become a source of) increased health costs to individuals. Medicare, for example, had the specific intent to reduce the financial barrier to health care for older people. Increased public funding also has included a movement toward greater public or consumer representation in decision making with regard to the provision of health services. What was described in Chapter 7 as a professional mandate has been partially withdrawn as consumers have increased demands for the health system to be more responsive to needs as perceived by consumers and not just by professionals alone.[62]

**3  Specialization-Coordination**   A third, obvious trend is for continued specialization among providers. The factors underlying the push for specialization—increased knowledge, economic rewards, professional prestige—all will continue and so will specialization, not only among physicians, but among nurses and allied health professionals as well. Less obvious, perhaps, is the complementary trend for increased coordination of the efforts of specialists. The dysfunctional aspects of specialization are well-known and are incompatible with the development of a rational, efficient health delivery system. Thus, since the late 1960s, efforts at planning and coordination have grown rapidly. These efforts have been influenced by the other two trends, namely the need to decentralize health services and the increasing role of public payment for private care. One of the early programs was the Regional Medical Program (RMP) which grew out of the National Program to Conquer Heart Disease, Cancer and Stroke in 1965. RMPs were designed to promote professional and public education and services for these three major killers in their designated geographic regions. In 1966, legislation was passed that created comprehensive health planning agencies (CHPs) for natural geographic regions and for states. This act, managed under DHEW, also funded neighborhood health centers not already covered under the Office of Economic Opportunity, another federal agency. The purpose of the CHPs was to gather evidence of health needs in their regions, plan and coordinate existing public and private resources to meet those needs, and review proposed changes by health service providers in the in the region. A unique facet of the CHP was the requirement that a board of directors of the agency be representative of all interests in the community and that consumers have a majority of seats on the board.

For many reasons which cannot be detailed here, CHPs were not very effective,[63] and further evolution has taken place through the National

[62]Roger M. Battistella, "Rationalization of Health Services: Political and Social Assumptions," *International Journal of Health Services,* 2 (Summer, 1972), 331–348.

[63]See the critique in Jonathan P. West and Michael D. Stevens, "Comparative Analysis of Community Health Planning: Transition from CHPs to HSAs," *Journal of Health Politics, Policy and Law,* 1 (Summer, 1976), 173–211.

Health Planning and Resources Development Act of 1974. This act has created planning and coordinating agencies, now called Health Systems Agencies (HSAs), which have more authority to manage health resources to meet health needs in their regions.[64] Along with this national movement, changes are occurring in local public health systems and in private developments in health maintenance organizations. Although many remain doubtful of the efficacy of this new legislation,[65] the trend toward increased coordination of health services is clear and likely to continue as ways are sought to meet the goal of providing comprehensive care for all.

## SUMMARY

Over the past few decades, the conduct of medical practice has shown a need for increased organization. In part, this need has arisen from the expansion of medical knowledge and its attendant specialization in practice. Further impetus to organization has come from the shift in morbidity from acute, infectious diseases to those of a chronic nature. Increased demand for health and medical care services has also stimulated the need for organization.

The major part of medical care services in this country is provided by private practitioners. Fifty years ago, a physician working alone could just about provide all the medical care required for an entire community. Nowadays, however, physicians have found it necessary to band together in some form of cooperative practice. The ways in which this is done vary considerably, but most often it is an arrangement whereby each of two practitioners treats his or her own patients, but shares "overhead" expenses with the associate, i.e., an *association*. If such an arrangement is formalized and patients are treated by both practitioners, the arrangement becomes a *partnership*. When three or more physicians cooperate under some formal arrangement, it is defined as *group practice*. This kind of organization would also include very large, hospital-based practices such as the Mayo Clinics.

However the medical profession organizes itself to offer medical care services, it is supported by many other agencies and organizations. These would include public health agencies at all levels—federal, state and local; voluntary health organizations some of which are fund-raising units while others are essentially coordinators of community services; insurance com-

---

[64]Leonard S. Rosenfeld and Irene Rosenfeld, "National Health Planning in the United States: Problems and Prospects," *International Journal of Health Services* 5 (Summer, 1975), 441–453.

[65]Elliott A. Krause, "The Political Context of Health Service Regulation," *International Journal of Health Services,* 5 (Fall, 1975), 593–607. In the same issue, see Warren J. Salmon, "The Health Maintenance Organization Strategy: A Corporate Takeover of Health Services Delivery," pp. 609–624.

panies which provide insurance against the high costs of unexpected illnesses and hospitalization; the hospital and medical equipment industry; and pharmaceutical companies which manufacture a variety of drugs for use by the medical practitioner.

As the proliferation of agencies and groups engaged in supporting the medical profession increases, the requirements for coordination and cooperation among them becomes obvious. Many of the current problems of providing health and medical care for the public stem from the present lack of coordination of all these facets of medical practice.

## SUGGESTED READINGS

Burns, Eveline M., *Health Services for Tomorrow: Trends and Issues,* New York: Dunellen, 1973.

Levine, Sol, and Paul E. White, "The Community of Health Organizations," in Howard E. Freeman, Sol Levine, and Leo G. Reader (eds.), *Handbook of Medical Sociology,* 2d ed., Englewood Cliffs, N.J.: Prentice-Hall, 1972, pp. 359–385.

Lewis, Charles E., Rashi Fein, and David Mechanic, *A Right to Health,* New York: Wiley, 1976.

MacColl, William A., *Group Practice and the Prepayment of Medical Care,* Washington, D.C.: Public Affairs Press, 1966.

Suchman, Edward A., *Sociology and the Field of Public Health,* New York: Russell Sage Foundation, 1963.

Chapter 13

# The Cost and Financing of Medical Care

*Man's self-imposed striving for ever-new distant goals makes his fate even more unpredictable than that of other living beings. For this reason, health and happiness cannot be absolute and permanent values, however careful the social medical planning.*

René Dubos
*Mirage of Health,* 1959

Probably no area in the field of medicine has received more attention lately than the cost of health care services. This topic has become the center of public controversy in the United States because it involves the paradox of this country, one of the wealthiest in the world, having the resources to provide high-quality care on an unprecedented scale, yet having a substantial proportion of the population not receiving even minimally adequate care. Although this paradoxical situation has been developing over a long period of time, it is only recently that the consequences have been felt so strongly. In the years since World War II, the costs of medical care have increased tremendously. Year after year, this escalation of cost has far outrun the general increase in cost of living and has been particularly marked with respect to hospital care. Even so, it is not the rise in expenditures per se that has caused concern so much as the lack of evidence that more money has produced a significant improvement in health of the population. Economists have also raised questions about the relationship of increased costs of medical care to the unusual nature of the medical care industry in a free-market economy. As we have already noted, even the private sector of medicine involves nonprofit organizations such as hospitals, restrictions on who can be a health practitioner, and monopolies on some supporting services such as pharmaceuticals. A further concern noted by some analysts is the increasing share of the costs of medical care paid by third-party insurers, especially from public sources.[1] The result is that both the experts and the general public have come to feel uneasy about the economic basis of health care and are examining more closely the value of the services received.

Advances in medical science and changes in the organization of medical practice have enabled contemporary physicians to provide the highest quality of care found almost anywhere in the world. But at the same time the costs of this high-quality care have markedly reduced its availability to certain segments of the population. Low-income families have considerable need for medical attention, in part because of the environment in which they live, yet they have less access to and ability to pay for needed medical services. Young couples just starting in a career and who have little children also require more medical services, but often have less ability to pay for them. Similarly, older people—most of whom also have small and fixed incomes—have health problems that often involve expensive long-term care. It is, of course, true that increased public support, such as Medicaid for the poor, Medicare for the aged, and improved employee health insurance plans in the private sector, have eased this problem somewhat. Yet none of these efforts has been sufficient to provide enough resources to meet the need or to improve significantly the health status of the population.[2] These are some indicators of the paradox noted in the opening paragraph. Within this framework, this chapter will examine the magnitude of health care expenditures and review some sources of increased cost in relation to the adequacy of health care delivery.

[1]Victor R. Fuchs (ed.), *Essays in the Economics of Health and Medical Care,* New York: National Bureau of Economic Research, 1972, especially chap. 2.

[2]Cf., for example, Howard N. Newman, "Medicare and Medicaid," *Annals of the American Academy of Political and Social Sciences,* 399 (January, 1972), 114–124; LuAnn Aday, "Economic and Non-economic Barriers to the Use of Needed Medical Services," *Medical Care,* 13 (June, 1975), 447–456; or the more general statement in Vicente Navarro, "From Public Health to Health of the Public," *American Journal of Public Health,* 64 (June, 1974), 538–542.

## THE MAGNITUDE OF HEALTH CARE COSTS

Trends in the costs of health care services for the United States expressed in terms of total expenditures are shown in Figure 13-1. From 1940 to 1965 (before Medicare and Medicaid), expenditures rose from approximately $4 billion to nearly $40 billion, and by 1975, that amount had reached more than 118 billion dollars (the 1976 estimate was 136 billion dollars). Another way of expressing this trend is in terms of the percentage of the gross national product (GNP) spent for health services. In 1940, the percentage was 4.1, and in 1965, it had risen to 5.9. By 1975, the percentage was 8.3.[3]

[3]Social Security Administration, "National Health Expenditures, Fiscal Year 1975," *Research and Statistics Note,* no. 20, November 21, 1975. The importance of this statistic lies in its relation to morbidity and mortality rates. Except for Sweden, the United States spends a greater share of its total national productivity (GNP) for health care than any other nation, yet it is not among the leaders in key indicators such as rates of infant mortality, mortality at middle age, or life expectancy. See, for example, Ray Elling (ed.), "Comparative Health Systems," a special issue of *Inquiry,* 12 (June, 1975).

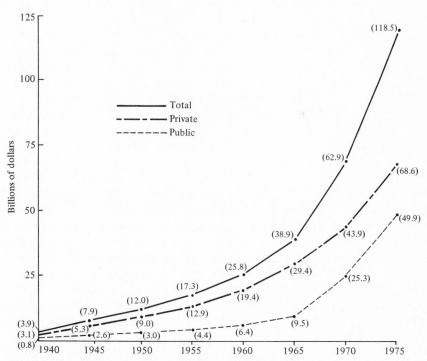

**Figure 13-1** Private and public expenditures for health and medical care, United States, 1940–1975. (*Source: Social Security Administration* "National Health Expenditures, Fiscal Year 1975." *Research and Statistics Note,* No. 20, Nov. 21, 1975.)

**Table 13-1   Magnitude of Costs of Medical Care, 1965 and 1975**

| Type of expenditure | Amount (in millions) | | Percent | | Percent change |
| | 1965 | 1975 | 1965 | 1975 | 1965–1975 |
| --- | --- | --- | --- | --- | --- |
| All expenditures | $40,468 | $118,500 | 100.0 | 100.0 | 192.8 |
| Hospital care | 13,605 | 46,600 | 33.6 | 39.3 | 242.5 |
| Physicians' services | 8,745 | 22,100 | 21.6 | 18.6 | 152.7 |
| Dentists' services | 2,808 | 7,500 | 6.9 | 6.3 | 167.1 |
| Other professional services | 1,038 | 2,100 | 2.6 | 1.8 | 102.3 |
| Drugs and sundries | 4,850 | 10,600 | 12.0 | 8.9 | 118.6 |
| Eyeglasses and appliances | 1,230 | 2,300 | 3.0 | 1.9 | 87.0 |
| Nursing home care | 1,328 | 9,000 | 3.3 | 7.6 | 577.7 |
| Expenses for prepayment | 1,293 | 4,593 | 3.2 | 3.9 | 255.2 |
| Government public health services | 698 | 3,457 | 1.7 | 2.9 | 395.3 |
| Research | 1,469 | 2,750 | 3.6 | 2.4 | 87.2 |
| Construction | 1,912 | 4,500 | 4.7 | 3.8 | 135.4 |
| Other health services | 1,492 | 3,000 | 3.7 | 2.5 | 101.1 |

*Source:* U.S. Bureau of the Census, *Statistical Abstract of the United States, 1975,* Washington, D.C.: Government Printing Office, 1975, table 101, p. 70; and Social Security Administration, "National Health Expenditures, Fiscal Year, 1975," *Research and Statistics Note,* no. 20, November 21, 1975.

Also evident is the trend towards increasing proportion of expenditures from public sources. Prior to 1965, the proportion of expenditures paid from public sources had risen to about 20 to 25 percent. By 1975, that percentage had risen to more than 42 percent. The importance of increased public expenditures on the economics of health is discussed further below.

A clearer picture of where this money goes is given by the data in Table 13-1. In terms of a portion of the health care dollar, hospital care receives the largest share, and this has increased even more between 1965 and 1975. About two-fifths of all expenditures were for hospital care in 1975 compared with one-third in 1965. Physicians' services accounted for the next largest percentage of all expenditures both in 1965 and in 1975, although the size of the share had decreased slightly.[4] A different emphasis emerges from analysis of the percent change from 1965 to 1975. Here it may be seen that nursing home care and government-sponsored public health services far outstripped other elements, although substantial increases were seen also in administrative costs for insurance programs and, of course, for direct hospital care. The contribution of increased spending from public sources should be noted. In 1975, it was reported that the rate of increase in public spending was more than two and one-half times the

[4]This does not mean that physicians' incomes have declined (contrary evidence was shown in Chapter 12), but only that the share of the health care dollar has declined. See Reuben A. Kessel, "Price Discrimination in Medicine," *Journal of Law and Economics,* 1 (October, 1958), 20–53.

rate of increase in private spending in the previous year. Much of that can be attributed to increases in Medicare and Medicaid programs. In 1975, Medicaid alone accounted for more than one-fourth of all public expenditures.[5]

These increases become more meaningful when they are described in terms of the individual consumer. Data in Table 13-2 indicate that the per capita expenditures have risen from about 146 dollars in 1960 to nearly 520 dollars in 1974 or an increase of 254 percent. By far, the largest percentage increase from 1960 to 1974 was for costs of nursing home care (1,234 percent) compared with the percentage increase in hospital care, fourth-ranked at 308 percent. However, increased dollar costs for hospital care are more significant to the consumer than are increased nursing home care costs inasmuch as the former accounts for nearly 40 percent of the total per capita expenditures and the latter only 8 percent. Other data show that over the same period, disposable personal income rose from 350 billion to 980 billion dollars, while the percentage of total disposable personal income used for personal expenditures for health care rose from 5.3 to 6.8.[6]

## SOURCES OF INCREASED COST

At this point, we want to look at some sources of these increased expenditures for health care. Most obvious, perhaps, is the fact that there has been a steady increase in the prices of all goods and services, including medical

[5]"National Health Expenditures," *op. cit.*
[6]*Source Book of Health Insurance Data, 1975–76,* New York: Health Insurance Institute, 1976, p. 50.

**Table 13-2   Per Capita Expenditures for Medical Care, 1960–1974**

| Type of expenditure | 1960 | 1965 | 1970 | 1974 |
|---|---|---|---|---|
| All expenditures | $146.30 | $204.61 | $350.10 | $517.71 |
| Hospital care | 49.46 | 68.79 | 131.69 | 202.00 |
| Physicians' services | 30.92 | 44.21 | 68.65 | 96.09 |
| Dentists' services | 10.75 | 14.20 | 22.79 | 32.99 |
| Other professional services | 4.69 | 5.25 | 7.02 | 9.49 |
| Drugs and sundries | 19.86 | 24.52 | 35.55 | 47.13 |
| Eyeglasses and appliances | 4.22 | 6.22 | 8.57 | 10.46 |
| Nursing home care | 2.86 | 6.71 | 20.79 | 38.16 |
| Expenses for prepayment | 4.68 | 6.54 | 10.13 | 21.25 |
| Government public health services | 2.25 | 3.53 | 7.52 | 14.11 |
| Research | 3.60 | 7.43 | 8.87 | 11.91 |
| Construction | 5.70 | 9.67 | 16.15 | 21.08 |
| Other health services | 7.27 | 7.54 | 12.37 | 13.05 |

*Source:* Social Security Administration, "National Health Expenditures, Calendar Year, 1974," *Research and Statistics Note,* no. 5, April 14, 1976, table 4.

**Table 13-3   Consumer Price Index, 1935–1974 (1967 = 100.0)**

| Year | All items | Medical care | Food | Clothing | Housing | Transportation | Other* |
|---|---|---|---|---|---|---|---|
| 1935 | 41.1 | 36.1 | 36.5 | 40.8 | 49.3 | 42.6 | 41.1 |
| 1940 | 42.0 | 36.8 | 35.2 | 42.8 | 52.4 | 42.7 | 44.8 |
| 1945 | 53.9 | 42.1 | 50.7 | 61.5 | 59.1 | 47.8 | 58.1 |
| 1950 | 72.1 | 53.7 | 74.5 | 79.0 | 72.8 | 68.2 | 67.8 |
| 1955 | 80.2 | 64.8 | 81.6 | 84.1 | 82.3 | 77.4 | 78.1 |
| 1960 | 88.7 | 79.1 | 88.0 | 89.6 | 90.2 | 89.6 | 88.3 |
| 1965 | 94.5 | 89.5 | 94.4 | 93.7 | 94.9 | 95.9 | 95.1 |
| 1970 | 116.3 | 120.6 | 114.9 | 116.1 | 118.9 | 112.7 | 114.2 |
| 1974 | 147.7 | 150.5 | 161.7 | 136.2 | 150.6 | 137.7 | 136.1 |
| Percent change 1967–1974 | 47.7 | 50.5 | 61.7 | 36.2 | 50.6 | 37.7 | 36.1 |

*Includes personal care, recreation, and all other goods and services.
*Source:* U.S. Department of Labor, quoted in *Source Book of Health Insurance Data, 1975–76,* New York: Health Insurance Institute, 1976, p. 53.

care. Data in Table 13-3 clearly illustrate this factor. It should be noted that medical care prices are ranked second in rate of increase, along with housing, while the price of food has emerged as the most rapidly changing item in 1974. Some components of the index of medical care prices are shown in Table 13-4. Here the startling rise in cost of hospital care may be seen again, while increased costs for professional services of physicians and dentists are much less dramatic, although substantial.

A second factor is the growth of the health insurance industry. We shall have more to say about this factor later in this chapter. Suffice it to say here that more than 8 out of every 10 persons in the United States had some

**Table 13-4   Index of Medical Care Prices, 1950–1974 (1967 = 100.0)**

| Year | All medical care | Physicians' fees | Dentists' fees | Optometric examinations and eyeglasses | Hospital room rates | Prescriptions and drugs |
|---|---|---|---|---|---|---|
| 1950 | 53.7 | 55.2 | 63.9 | 73.5 | 30.3 | 88.5 |
| 1955 | 64.8 | 65.4 | 73.0 | 77.0 | 42.3 | 94.7 |
| 1960 | 79.1 | 77.0 | 82.1 | 85.1 | 57.3 | 104.5 |
| 1965 | 89.5 | 88.3 | 92.2 | 92.8 | 75.9 | 100.2 |
| 1970 | 120.6 | 121.4 | 119.4 | 113.5 | 145.4 | 103.6 |
| 1974 | 150.5 | 150.9 | 146.8 | 138.6 | 201.5 | 109.6 |
| Percent change 1967–1974 | 50.5 | 50.9 | 46.8 | 38.6 | 101.5 | 9.6 |

*Source:* U.S. Department of Labor, quoted in *Source Book of Health Insurance Data, 1975–76,* New York: Health Insurance Institute, 1976, p. 54.

**Table 13-5   Percent of Personal Health Expenditures Covered by Insurance, by Age Group, 1966 and 1975**

| Source of payment | All ages | | Under 65 | | 65 and over | |
|---|---|---|---|---|---|---|
| | 1966 | 1975 | 1966 | 1975 | 1966 | 1975 |
| Direct payment | 51.5 | 32.6 | 51.1 | 34.2 | 53.2 | 28.6 |
| Third-party payment | | | | | | |
| Private insurance | 24.7 | 26.4 | 27.3 | 35.3 | 15.9 | 5.4 |
| Government | 21.8 | 39.7 | 19.4 | 28.8 | 29.8 | 65.6 |
| Philanthropy | 2.0 | 1.3 | 2.2 | 1.7 | 1.1 | 0.4 |
| Total | 100.0 | 100.0 | 100.0 | 100.0 | 100.0 | 100.0 |
| Amount* | $32,216 | $103,200 | $27,974 | $72,817 | $8,242 | $30,383 |

*In millions.
Source: Social Security Administration, "Age Differences in Health Care Spending, Fiscal Year 1975," *Research and Statistics Note,* no. 11, May 17, 1976, table 4.

kind of insurance coverage in 1974, and this represents a slight increase over the proportion of persons covered ten years earlier.[7] Not only is a greater percentage of people now covered by some form of insurance, but a greater portion of personal health expenditures is paid by third-party agencies. This pattern of growth is shown in Table 13-5. The percentage of personal health care expenditures paid by insurers rose from less than 50 percent in 1966 to about two-thirds in 1975 with a reciprocal decline in direct payments. Although private insurers provide the largest share of coverage for people under age 65, the rate of change in coverage from 1966 to 1975 was greater for public insurers even for this age group, and, of course, public coverage through the Medicare program is most extensive for beneficiaries aged 65 and over. It should be noted, however, that there is wide variation in insurance coverage in terms of what service is being provided. Hospital care is most extensively covered, while professional services are much less so. Even here, the trend is for increased coverage of all services as illustrated in Figure 13-2.

A third factor, related to increased insurance coverage, is increased demand by consumers as indicated by data on utilization of health care services. For example, the rate of admissions to hospitals has continued to increase. In 1946, fewer than 10 percent of the population were hospitalized, but by 1965, this had risen to almost 14 percent and by 1974 to almost 16 percent.[8] Although the average length of stay has declined, the increased admission rate has resulted in a rise in the number of days of care per 1,000 persons. From 1965 to 1972 the rise was 1,186 to about 1,200, although this varied by age of patient with the largest increase among the elderly. During

[7]*Ibid.,* p. 23.
[8]*Ibid.,* p. 60.

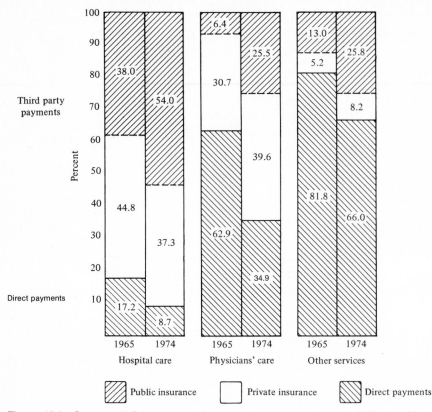

**Figure 13-2** Sources of Payments for Personal Health Expenditures, 1965 and 1974. (*Source: Social Security Administration,* "National Health Expenditures, Calendar Year 1974," *Research and Statistics Note,* No. 5, April 14, 1976, table 5.)

this same period, the hospital care charge per patient-day rose from $25.29 to $73.89 (192 percent).[9] In Chapter 9 we also noted that the number of outpatient visits had increased greatly. Similarly, visits to physician offices have also increased. In 1970, the average number of physician visits per person was 4.6 and in 1973 it was 5.0. Typically, the number of visits per person was higher for women than men, and for the elderly and very young than for youth and adults under age 65.[10]

Other factors may also have a lesser degree of influence on the rise in health care costs. For example, the changing composition of the population

[9] U.S. Bureau of the Census, *Statistical Abstract of the United States, 1975,* Washington, D.C.: Government Printing Office, 1975, table 26, p. 81. Another view is that rising costs are not due to increased demand, but to price increases. See David F. Drake and Kenneth E. Rasker, "The Changing Hospital Economy," *Hospitals,* 48 (November 16, 1974), 34–37.

[10] *Statistical Abstract of the United States, 1975, op. cit.,* table 119, p. 77.

(more than population growth) toward a larger proportion of older people means greater utilization of health services and a larger share paid from public funds. New developments in medical technology are usually costly to use and they may significantly alter patterns of mortality and morbidity. For example, renal dialysis, to purify the blood of patients with malfunctioning kidneys, is an expensive treatment required several times per week for life. Without treatment, these patients would die much earlier than would be expected for their age group and sex.

It is difficult to specify what part of total increase in expenditures is attributable to which source since they are highly interrelated. The factors we have identified, however, suggest that a closer examination of the major components, hospital care and physicians' services, would be warranted. In anticipation of the discussion in Chapter 14, we might note also that these data point out the critical role of physicians in controlling (or not controlling) costs. That is, physicians regulate admissions to hospitals, determine how long their patients remain, and how much is charged for a visit. As we shall see, the reimbursement policies of insurance companies play an important part, too. For now, however, let us look at some factors involved in the costs of hospital care and physicians' services.

It was noted that the largest share of the health dollar was for hospital room rates. There are several possible explanations for this. First, it has been repeatedly noted that the community general hospital has changed its functions markedly in the past two decades. It is now the main center of medical care for the community.[11] Part of the reason for this lies in the expansion of services now provided in the hospital setting, such as long-term care, psychiatric facilities, outpatient clinics, rehabilitation units, home care, and increased laboratory facilities and equipment. Furthermore, the hospitals' labor costs have increased, because of wage increases; more highly trained technicians are required to operate highly technical equipment and more personnel are needed because of strengthened labor regulations.[12] The number of annual admissions has increased, the average length of stay has dropped, thus creating an additional financial burden on the hospitals. That is, in part, the increased cost to the hospital stems from the high turnover in patients; newly admitted patients require the use of nearly the whole range of diagnostic and laboratory facilities. The need for these services declines with length of stay. Thus, per diem costs of care also decline with length of stay. Also, insured patients come to the hospital earlier in the course of their illness when it can usually be more effectively

[11]Ivan Belknap and John G. Steinle, *The Community and Its Hospitals,* Syracuse, N.Y.: Syracuse University Press, 1963.

[12]Herman M. Somers and Anne R. Somers, *Doctors, Patients and Health Insurance,* Washington, D.C.: Brookings, 1961.

and quickly combatted, but uninsured patients tend to delay entering the hospital until their case is more serious and likely to require more services. Of course, the cost of hospital insurance would increase with the cost of the hospital services.

The sources of increases in physicians' fees are difficult to determine with any degree of precision. For one thing, there has been a general rise in the standard of living; thus people have more money to spend for health services and are willing to pay increased fees. Perhaps another factor is the extension in amount of education required for licensing as a physician. Thus, higher fees are charged to compensate for income lost during the prolonged educational process. A third factor relates to the reimbursement of physicians by third-party payers on the basis of "usual, customary, and reasonable charges." That is, physicians may charge whatever they wish within very broad average charges for a geographic regions, and some proportion of that (up to 80 percent, usually) is guaranteed to be paid by coinsurance provisions of policies. Except for a short time between 1971 and 1974 when mandatory economic controls limited the rise in doctors' fees, there have been few limits on what a physician could charge.

Finally, it might be noted that although drug costs have increased less than other medical items, they are rising. Part of this change is due to increased use of drugs generally. But part can be traced to the fact that the drug market is not competitive in the sense that patients can buy only the drug prescribed by their physician even if the same drug is offered by another company at a lower price.[13] Furthermore, since patients buy drugs on the advice of their physician without much regard to cost, the price of drugs can remain high despite increased volume of purchases.

## HEALTH INSURANCE

One attempt to ease the burden of spiraling costs of medical care is prepaid voluntary health insurance. Although some form of health insurance has been known since the guilds during medieval days, it has been only since the mid-1930s that this insurance has become a widely accepted method for payment of medical expenses. The twofold purpose of health insurance has been succinctly described by the Somerses.

> The primary purpose of . . . the traditional "insurance" approach—was to protect people against the risk of large and unusual costs or losses—a financial protection. The second and more recent approach—generally referred to as "prepayment"—was primarily concerned with the actual rendering of medical

---

[13]*Ibid.*, pp. 185–190. See Also Victor R. Fuchs, *Who Shall Live?* New York: Basic Books, 1974, chap. 5.

services. Both undertook to meet their objectives by pooling risks and substituting known small costs for uncertain larger ones. But the insurance emphasis was on large and unusual risks and costs, while "prepayment" aimed for broader coverage to include early preventive services and ambulatory care as well as catastrophic illness.[14]

The adoption of health insurance programs was not an easy process. Shortly after the close of World War I, various companies began experimenting with medical benefits as fringe benefits for the job. At the same time, group health insurance was introduced as a way to provide coverage for large groups of employees at lower rates. It was about this time also that a serious attempt was made to legislate compulsory health insurance, but this was successfully resisted by insurance companies and the American Medical Association. The depression of the 1930s ruined many independent companies, and in conjunction with the passage of the Social Security Act of 1935, compulsory health insurance was again introduced into the legislature and again successfully resisted by commercial companies with the help of local medical organizations. In the late 1930s and early 1940s commercial companies, nonprofit organizations, and others offering voluntary health insurance began to grow at a very rapid rate. Finally, in 1965 with the passage of the amendments to the Social Security Act, compulsory hospital insurance for the aged was established.

Despite this remarkable growth to cover about 80 percent of the population by 1975, about one-third of the costs of care are paid "out of pocket," that is, directly by the consumer. As we noted in Table 13-5, this represents an improvement over the previous decade, in which about half of the cost was borne directly by consumers. In the meantime, insurance companies have profited from income of increased premiums over benefits paid out. In 1966, for example, private insurers collected $12.1 billion in premiums and paid $9.6 billion in benefits, a $2.5 billion difference. In 1974, income was $33.3 billion and benefits paid had risen to $27.8 billion, a difference of $5.5 billion.[15]

In general, there are three broad categories of insurance underwriters: commercial insurance companies selling both group and individual policies, Blue Cross-Blue Shield and other hospitalization and surgical plans sponsored by local medical societies, and so-called "independents" such as the Kaiser-Permanente plan in California and the Health Insurance Plan of New York.[16] Most companies in these categories provide both group and individual plans with the latter being more expensive. Commercial insur-

---

[14]Somers and Somers, *op. cit.*, p. 226.
[15]*Source Book of Health Insurance Data.*
[16]Public supported insurance is provided through commercial companies or the nonprofit Blue Cross–Blue Shield programs as intermediaries.

ance companies, although entering the field later, have increased the number of subscribers to hospitalization insurance to the point that they have surpassed those of Blue Cross plans which had a considerably earlier start. On the other hand, commercial companies have never lost the commanding lead over Blue Shield in the number of subscribers to surgical insurance policies. Meanwhile, the relatively few independent programs have continued to grow, but only very slowly.[17]

Recently, subscribers to many of these companies, including Blue Cross and Blue Shield, have been expressing increasing dissatisfaction with their particular policies. Part of the reason, of course, is increasing cost of premiums without a perceived increase in benefits. Under ordinary circumstances, higher premiums would be expected along with increased costs of other goods and services that are part of medical care. However, one study showed that many subscribers do not feel that health insurance increases quality or quantity of care they receive but is merely a form of economic protection. Physicians, on the other hand, feel that it increases the amount of care the individual is likely to get because the patient is more willing to buy drugs, be hospitalized, and accept expensive laboratory procedures.[18] Other studies indicate that subscribers to various health insurance plans do utilize medical care services and facilities more frequently than nonsubscribers.[19]

The dissatisfaction of many subscribers with increasing premiums is compounded by the fact that the benefits of their health insurance programs have not kept pace with the increased costs of medical care. Unless checked, it is felt that these trends could threaten the future of voluntary

---

[17] *Source Book of Health Insurance Data.*

[18] Milton I. Roemer, Robert W. Hetherington, Carl E. Hopkins, Arthur E. Gerst, Eleanor Parsons, and Donald W. Long, *Health Insurance Effects: Services, Expenditures and Attitudes under Three Types of Plan,* Ann Arbor: University of Michigan School of Public Health, 1972. See also Richard Wersinger, Klaus J. Roghmann, J. William Gavett, and Sandra M. Wells, "Inpatient Utilization in Three Prepaid Comprehensive Health Plans Compared with a Regular Blue Cross Plan," *Medical Care,* 14 (September, 1976), 721–732.

[19] Charles E. Phelps, "Effects of Insurance on Demand for Medical Care," in Ronald Andersen, Joanna Kravits, and Odin W. Anderson (eds.), *Equity in Health Services,* Cambridge, Mass.: Ballinger, 1975, pp. 105–130. See also the earlier studies reported in O. W. Anderson and J. J. Feldman, *Family Medical Costs and Voluntary Insurance,* New York: McGraw-Hill, 1956; Sam Shapiro, L. Weiner, and Paul M. Densen, "Comparison of Prematurity and Perinatal Mortality in a General Population and in a Population of Prepaid Group Practice," *American Journal of Public Health,* 48 (February, 1958), 170–187; Paul M. Densen, Eva Balamuth, and Sam Shapiro, *Prepaid Medical Care and Hospital Utilization,* American Hospital Association, Monograph Series, no. 3, 1958; U.S. Department of Health, Education, and Welfare, *Medical Care Financing and Utilization,* Health Economics Series, no. 1, Washington, D.C.: Government Printing Office, 1962, pp. 104–119; Milton I. Roemer and Max Shain, *Hospital Utilization under Insurance,* American Hospital Association, Monograph Series, no. 6, 1959.

health insurance programs.[20] Other writers, however, point out that voluntary health insurance can be an effective method for meeting health needs of the population if the amount of benefits not only is increased, but is expanded to cover areas important to health which are not now covered. In addition, controls must be exercised, mostly through community action, to ensure a high quality of care, reduce unnecessary utilization of service and construction of facilities, and encourage recognition of the importance of medical organization as a method of promoting quality of care as well as curtailing costs.[21]

At the present time in the United States, there is a growing movement for providing prepaid medical care on a "comprehensive" basis. This movement is partly a response to criticism of inadequate benefits for services rendered by increasing the larger numbers of specialists required for "total" care. It also reflects the growing trend toward group practice.[22] Although many problems have not been entirely solved, the emergence of group practice offers a possible solution to providing comprehensive medical care services under the auspices of insurance programs which can offer comprehensive protection.[23]

At this time, comprehensive prepaid group practice plans are still limited to a few geographic areas of the United States, although their effectiveness in delivery of health care and their acceptability by consumers have been repeatedly demonstrated. One recent study of 600 families in each of three types of insurance plans is representative of these studies.[24] The plan types evaluated included commercial insurance, provi-

[20]Herman M. Somers and Anne R. Somers, "Coverage, Costs and Controls in Voluntary Health Insurance," *Public Health Reports,* 76 (January, 1961), 1–9. More recently, see Thomas Bodenheimer, Steven Cummings, and Elizabeth Harding, "Capitalizing on Illness: The Health Insurance Industry," *International Journal of Health Services* 4 (Fall, 1974), 583–598.

[21]Eleanor M. Parsons and Milton I. Roemer, "Ideological Goals of Different Health Insurance Plans," *Journal of Community Health,* 1 (Summer, 1976), 241–248. See also Marc Renaud, "On the Structural Constraints to State Intervention in Health," *International Journal of Health Services,* 5 (Fall, 1975), 559–571.

[22]C. Todd and M. E. McNamara, *Medical Groups in the U.S., 1969,* Chicago: American Medical Association, 1971.

[23]Cf. Wersinger et al., *op. cit.;* Gerald T. Perkoff, Lawrence Kahn, and Phillip J. Haas, "The Effects of an Experimental Prepaid Group Practice on Medical Care Utilization and Cost," *Medical Care,* 14 (May, 1976), 432–449; Emil Berkanovic, Leo G. Reeder, Alfred C. Marcus, and Susan Schwartz, "The Effects of Prepayment on Access to Medical Care: The PACC Experience," *Health and Society,* 53 (Spring, 1975), 241–254; and Ernest W. Saward, Janet D. Blank, and Merwyn R. Greenlick, "Documentation of Twenty Years of Operation and Growth of a Prepaid Group Practice Plan," *Medical Care,* 6 (May–June, 1968), 231–244. Legislative history regarding the development of prepaid group practice is described in William R. Roy, *Health Maintenance Organization Act of 1972,* Washington, D.C.: Science and Health Communications Group, 1972.

[24]Roemer et al., *op. cit.* See also the discussion of group practice in Chapter 12.

der-sponsored insurance such as Blue Cross, and prepaid group practice plans. The plans were compared on dimensions of utilization of health services, quality of care (in terms of range of services), costs to the family, and attitudes of family members. Data were collected from interviews, self-administered questionnaires, medical records, and a study of the insurance contracts. Most consistent with earlier studies were the findings of markedly reduced hospital use rates and high ambulatory care use rates for families in the group practice plans. Provider plans were highest on both dimensions, while commercial plans were intermediate on hospital use and lowest in ambulatory care visits. Group plans were judged best in quality, especially in terms of preventive services and "rationality of service." Commercial plans rated least with provider plans in between.

More germane to the discussion here is the issue of costs to the family. Consistent with other studies was the finding that group practice families had the lowest out-of-pocket costs (expenses not covered by insurance), but the highest initial insurance premiums, which are associated with a much broader, guaranteed benefit package. A cost-benefit analysis of total costs favored group plans slightly over provider-sponsored plans. Commercial plans were the most expensive of the three types.[25] Often related to cost in terms of perceived benefits received is consumer satisfaction. In this study, families in prepaid group plans showed considerably higher satisfaction with financial coverage (65 percent were very satisfied) than did families in commercial plans (36 percent) or provider plans (28 percent). On the dimension of satisfaction with medical care received, the proportion of families in group plans who were very satisfied (43 percent) was very similar to the proportion of families in commercial plans (46 percent) and provider plans (45 percent). Perhaps a better indicator is expressed dissatisfaction with either financial coverage and care received. On both dimensions, families in group plans were significantly lower than families in either of the two other types of plan.[26] Finally, another measure of dissatisfaction in prepaid plans is the percentage of use of services outside of the program (i.e., the patient pays out of pocket for care that could have been received without further charge under the program). This study reported low rates of outside utilization compared with previous studies.

As we have seen, the problem of how medical care can best be provided has not yet been resolved and it is not likely to be resolved until some previous questions are answered. The previous questions concern the adequacy of health services. How much medical care is enough for our population? Are the *needs* for medical care being met by current resources,

---

[25]*Ibid.;* for poor families in commercial plans, the actual costs were lowest, but this was because of very low utilization of ambulatory care services.

[26]*Ibid.,* pp. 51, 54.

both human and material? Does the *demand* for medical care exceed the capabilities of the resources to provide it? Will more medical care improve the health status of the population? We do not propose to answer these questions here, but rather the intent is to point out salient factors which must affect the answers that are ultimately reached.

At the beginning of World War II, the medical profession became alarmed at the results of draft examinations which revealed a generally high proportion of the American population with unmet medical needs. In some areas, notably in the South, almost one-third of the applicants were rejected from military service because they failed to pass the physical examination. Unmet medical needs were not seen here alone, however, but also in the great amount of medical care required to keep men in the armed forces at a generally accepted level of good health. This kind of study, duplicated in the community for other age groups and for both sexes, has indicated that even in favored areas of the United States, medical needs go unmet.[27]

There is some evidence that demand for medical care is increasing.[28] Besides hospital use rates and average number of physician visits, which are increasing, other indicators suggest greater demand. For example, in 1940 the total expenditure for health care, expressed as a percent of the gross national product, was 4.1. In 1975, this figure was 8.3 percent.[29] In other words, the proportional demand had doubled. In addition, while there seems to be no general awareness on the part of the population that medical care is not available when it is wanted,[30] studies of conditions under which services are or are not used suggest that there may be a serious problem of access to services.[31] A more difficult issue is whether more medical services will significantly improve the health of the population. In economic terms, the issue is one of marginal gain or the increment of gain in "output" (health status) per unit of increased "input" (medical services). Most efforts, exploratory at this point, suggest that increased services will not significantly alter the health status of the population.[32]

It appears that to resolve the question of adequacy, we need first to distinguish between the *demand* for medical care and the *need* for medical

[27]Amasa B. Ford, *Urban Health in America,* New York: Oxford University Press, 1976.

[28]Fuchs, *Essays in the Economics of Health and Medical Care,* pp. 62–68.

[29]"National Health Expenditures, Fiscal Year 1975," *op. cit.*

[30]Stephen P. Strickland, *U.S. Health Care: What's Wrong and What's Right,* Washington, D.C.: Potomac Associates, 1972.

[31]LuAnn Aday and Ronald Andersen, *Access to Medical Care,* Ann Arbor: Health Administration Press, 1975.

[32]Fuchs, *op. cit.* Lee Benham and Alexandra Benham, "The Impact of Incremental Medical Services on Health Status, 1963–1970," in Andersen et al. (eds.), *op. cit.,* pp. 217–228. Some writers take an opposite view and suggest that increased medical services would be iatrogenic, that is, harmful to the health status of people. See Ivan Illich, *Medical Nemesis: The Expropriation of Health,* London: Calder and Boyars, 1975.

care. Demand for medical care is an economic concept based on the perceptions of individuals, what they think their needs are and their willingness to pay for health care services. Need, however, is an analytical concept which is based on the estimates of physicians and public health officials as to what they think the public *ought* to have if good health care standards are to be met. It is mostly on the basis of the latter that current arguments about comprehensive care exist. (The fact that the public is not consulted about their needs with respect to the adequacy of care may help account for public complacency in public health programs.)

However, even for professionals, the determination of the need of a large heterogeneous population is difficult. We can read certain reports on vital statistics and conclude that the health standards in the United States are continually improving. For example, it can be shown that mortality rates for the population, or better still, infant mortality rates, have declined from 47.0 deaths per 1,000 in 1940 to 17.7 deaths per 1,000 for that age group in 1973. Similarly, the expectation of length of life at birth has risen from 54.1 years in 1920 to 71.3 years in 1973, although this varies slightly by sex and race.[33] Furthermore, as was pointed out in Chapter 2, deaths due to infectious diseases have been drastically reduced so that chronic diseases are now the primary causes of death. In addition, there are numerous reports of new medical and surgical procedures being carried out every day.

Critics of this position point out that although the above is generally true, there are still certain segments of our population, especially the poor and aged, who have severe health problems that are not being met.[34] The very fact that chronic diseases are now the number-one killers indicates that a shift in emphasis is required and that chronic ailments should receive the attention once given to acute conditions.[35] Unfortunately, even if every individual could afford to see a physician when the need arose, we would still not be able to set up precise standards of good medical care.

At this point, it should be clear that although our general health standards are demonstrably better than many other countries, there is a "climate of opinion" that they are not good enough. For one thing, the technical abilities of the medical profession are not evenly distributed throughout the population. For example, in 1973 the number of physicians per 100,000 population in the Northeastern states varied from 121 in Maine to 240 in New York. In the South, comparable figures were 94 in Mississippi to 245 in Maryland (the District of Columbia was highest anywhere

[33]*Statistical Abstract of the United States, 1975,* tables 82, 88, pp. 59, 63.
[34]Aday, *op. cit.*
[35]Cf., for example, the discussion in Rodney M. Coe and Henry P. Brehm, *Preventive Health Care for Adults: A Study of Medical Practice,* New Haven: College and University Press, 1972.

**Table 13-6    Distribution of Selected Health Personnel, by Size of Community, 1967**

| Size of community | Health personnel per 100,000 population | | | |
| --- | --- | --- | --- | --- |
| | Physicians* | Dentists | Nurses | Pharmacists |
| Metropolitan | | | | |
| 5,000,000 or more | 233 | 79 | 313 | 66 |
| 1,000,000–5,000,000 | 195 | 65 | 329 | 61 |
| 500,000–1,000,000 | 163 | 58 | 354 | 55 |
| Nonmetropolitan | | | | |
| 10,000–25,000 | 58 | 32 | 178 | 43 |
| Under 10,000 | 48 | 28 | 152 | 48 |

*M.D.'s only.
*Source:* Bureau of Public Health Economics, *Medical Care Chart Book*, 5th ed., Ann Arbor: University of Michigan School of Public Health, 1972, p. 128.

with 534). Midwestern states had a low of 87 in South Dakota and a high of 162 in Minnesota. In the Far West, California was highest with 205 and Idaho was lowest with 99.[36]

Similarly, it can be shown that there are important rural-urban differences in provision and use of health services. The data shown in Table 13-6 indicate that the ratio of physicians per 100,000 population declines with size of community. This is especially true for the number of specialists. The same trend holds for dentists and, to a lesser extent, for nurses and pharmacists, too. These figures suggest that small towns and rural communities are constantly faced with the problem of providing health services for the people. The shortage of health care personnel in these areas reflects the inadequacy of hospital facilities, the small population, the isolation from colleagues, the longer work hours, and so on.[37]

Other data indicate that rural dwellers receive less health service than urban residents. For example, in 1970 the average number of visits per person to physicians for urban dwellers was 4.7 and 4.2 for rural nonfarm persons. For rural farm people it was only 3.1. In 1969, urbanites spent an average of 9.5 days in the hospital per admission, while ruralites spent 9.8, but there were 121 discharges per 1,000 persons for urban patients and only 109 discharges per 1,000 persons for rural patients.[38] Finally, we have seen that there still is differential use of medical facilities by social class although the patterns have changed somewhat.[39]

[36] *Statistical Abstract of the United States, 1975,* table 111, p. 74.

[37] U.S. Department of Agriculture, *Health Services in Rural America,* Information Bulletin no. 362, Washington, D.C.: Government Printing Office, 1974.

[38] Quoted in Ford, *op. cit.*

[39] Aday, *op. cit.;* see also Lois Montiero, "Expense Is No Object . . . Income and Physician Visits Reconsidered," *Journal of Health and Social Behavior,* 14 (June, 1973), 99–115.

## THE PRICE OF ILL HEALTH

The adequacy of medical care is related to the cost of care, not only in terms of the total expenditures for services, but also in terms of the savings to the national economy as a result of promoting good health and of reducing the amount of incapacitating illness and disability in the labor force.[40] It can be argued that in those areas of the world where medical science and public health practices have combined to reduce the death rates from communicable and acute diseases, hence increasing life expectancy, a substantial contribution has been made to the economy of those areas. For example, in most industrialized nations, it is said that an investment is made in each child up to the age of about sixteen to eighteen without any return. Beyond that point, the individual begins making a return on that investment by contributing to the labor force and by purchasing in the market. The longer the individual continues these activities, the more return is realized on the original investment. It seems reasonable, then, that if the child should die before entering the labor force, the investment would be a total loss—greater if the child was near age sixteen and less if he or she died at birth. As was noted in Chapter 2, one characteristic of industrialized areas is a low death rate, a slightly higher but stable birth rate, and an increasing life expectancy. Therefore, these countries should realize the largest return on the investment in each child. In the case of underdeveloped countries, however, the situation is just the reverse. That is, infant mortality and maternal death rates are high and life expectancy is low. Thus the investment made in each of these children, although considerably less than in industrialized areas, is still likely to bring a disproportionately smaller return.[41]

It would be difficult, of course, to place an actual value on the life of each individual and his or her potential contribution to the economy. Winslow, for example, reported that as long ago as 1948 the price of ill health for the United States in terms of depriving the economy of its returns was about thirty-eight billion dollars, or about 10 percent of the national income that year.[42] A more recent study, conducted in Great Britain, estimated the cost of ill health in terms of benefits paid for work absences. The costs rose from £ 66 million (about $185 million) in 1951 to £ 515 million (about $1.4 billion) in 1972.[43] The author pointed out that these are

---

[40]See, for example, Fuchs, *Essays in the Economics of Health and Medical Care,* pp. 5–12.

[41]See the discussion in Abdel R. Omran (ed.), *Community Medicine in Developing Countries,* New York: Springer, 1974, especially pp. 81–98.

[42]C. E. A. Winslow, *The Cost of Sickness and the Price of Health,* Geneva: World Health Organization, Monograph Series, no. 7, 1951, p. 14.

[43]George Teeling-Smith, "The Cost of Ill Health," *Journal of the Royal Society of Health,* 96 (April, 1976), 62–66.

conservative estimates since they do not take into account losses from premature mortality or decline in productivity due to social and psychological distress associated with illness. It should also be remembered that these data are for developed countries. We can only speculate what the burden of these costs would be for developing nations.

## IMPROVING THE DELIVERY OF HEALTH SERVICES

At this point it is clear that if the adequacy of care, that is, the distribution of health services, could be improved, there should result a savings to the economy of the nation, not only in strict economic terms, but also in a general social and psychological sense of well-being of the society. Improvement in the health status of the population, then, may be less dependent upon increasing the amount of health services than it is on reorganizing them to improve their availability and accessibility. In this respect, a comparison can be made between the traditional fee-for-service medicine in the United States and the service-on-demand medicine practiced in Great Britain. Although there are many recognized differences in the two countries, there are also many similarities such as the heritage of language and economic and political systems. More to the point, the contrast between the two health care systems illustrates the issues in the paradox mentioned in the beginning of this chapter. The United States has greater resources and investment in the health industry than does Great Britain, yet on most dimensions of "outcome," Great Britain surpasses the United States. Some simple comparisons which illustrate this may be seen in Table 13-7. The United States spends more money on health services, has more personnel and higher utilization rates for hospitals, but lower utilization rates of personnel. On typical outcome measures, however, people in Great Britain enjoy an advantage over Americans. Although it is recognized that mortality rates are influenced more by the standard of living and quality of life (nutrition, environment, personal habits) than by medical care, it is increasingly felt that some share of the differences in outcomes can be attributed to differences in the way health services are organized and delivered.[44] Let us look briefly at some elements of the British National Health System and, where appropriate, compare it with the practice of medicine in the United States.

### National Health Service Act of 1948 (Great Britain)

In 1948 the Parliament adopted what is officially called the Health Service Act as a capstone to more than thirty years of discussion. As early as 1919 and until 1942, Parliament was urged to increase the coverage on national health insurance. In 1942, for the first time officially, it was suggested that

[44]D. Stark Murray, *Blueprint for Health,* New York: Schocken Books, 1974.

**Table 13-7   Comparison of the United States and Great Britain on Selected Health Industry Dimensions**

| Dimension | United States | Great Britain* |
|---|---|---|
| Financing | | |
|    Total expenditures (1968) | $54 billion | $5 billion |
|    Per capita expenditures (1968) | $269 | $95 |
|    Percent of national income (1968) | 7.5 | 5.2 |
| Personnel and facilities | | |
|    Physicians per 100,000 population (1967) | 158 | 119 |
|    Nurses per 100,000 population (1968) | 331 | 218 |
|    Dentists per 100,000 population (1968) | 57 | 24 |
|    Hospital beds per 1,000 population (1968) | 8.3 | 9.6 |
|    Physicians in general practice (percent) (1967) | 23 | 48 |
|    Hospital-based physicians (percent) (1967) | 24 | 51 |
| Utilization | | |
|    Hospital admissions per 1,000 population (1968) | 149 | 106 |
|    Days of hospital care per 1,000 population (1968) | 1,154 | 1,132 |
|    Number of physician visits per year per person (1968) | 4.3 | 5.9 |
|    Percent population using prescription drug (1968) | 43 | 62 |
|    Percent population seeing a dentist (1968) | 38 | 43 |
| Outcome | | |
|    Infant deaths per 1,000 live births (1966) | 23.3 | 19.2 |
|    Age-adjusted total mortality per 1,000 (1965) | 9.4 | 8.9 |
|    Expected years of life at birth (1965) | 70.2 | 71.1 |
|    Percent of premature births (1968) | 8.1 | 6.6 |

*England and Wales only.
*Source:* Odin W. Anderson, *Health Care: Can There Be Equity?* New York: Wiley, 1972, Appendix.

comprehensive medical care be offered to the entire population and not just to the workers, with the cost of this care to be borne by the government. The survey reports of 1944 and 1945 indicated that some kind of drastic action was required to provide better medical care to all, but especially to segments of the population who were excluded from health insurance coverage.[45]

The avowed purpose of the NHS was primarily to eliminate the financial barrier between the patient and the doctor and permit *all* those in need of medical care to obtain it without consideration of cost. At the same time, the NHS was organized to provide comprehensive care, that is, to meet all the health needs of each individual. A third goal was to adjust the distribution of medical care services, especially doctors and hospitals, to the distribution of population in need of those services.[46]

[45] Almont Lindsey, *Socialized Medicine in England and Wales,* Chapel Hill: University of North Carolina Press, 1962.

[46] Harry Eckstein, *The English Health Service,* Cambridge, Mass.: Harvard University Press, 1958, pp. 167–172.

Achievement of these goals required a large reorganization not only of the administrative offices of the Ministry of Health, but also of the operation of the hospitals and clinics. And this had to be accomplished without destroying the benefits accruing from the doctor-patient relationship. The most sensitive area was, of course, the effect of these changes on the practice of the individual physician, especially the general practitioner. At first, a general practitioner was paid on a capitation basis according to the number of patients he or she enrolled with a maximum limit of 3,500 patient per year. These capitation fees were scaled to favor medium-sized practices and to encourage group practice. At the same time, the physician was permitted to have as many private (fee-for-service) patients as he or she wished.[47]

Hospitals now are nationalized and are the locus of activities of specialists and consultants. Construction of new facilities has somewhat eased the problem of available bed space, but the physical condition and inadequacies of very old hospitals remain a problem to NHS. Under NHS, because hospital care is free, general practitioners were to have had much greater resources at their command, especially the hospital with its staff of part-time salaried specialists and consultants and centralized services such as x-ray and laboratory facilities. This was to have placed general practitioners in a position so that they could again become family physicians. Although patients are free to choose or change their doctors, they must consult a general practitioner who is the referral agent to the specialist.

The changeover from fee-for-service medicine to socialized medicine was not free of disagreement, anxiety, and apprehension. At the time the health act was proposed, the British Medical Association was deeply disturbed and voiced its opinion in various media. Chief among their objections was the prediction of a decline in the quality of care. It was felt that physicians would not be able to cope with the predicted rush for free medical service and that without the economic stimulus, the quality of care would decline. Furthermore, it was felt that if physicians became salaried, they would also become bureaucratic in the ministration of care, thus further reducing the quality. More serious, they felt, was the potential role conflict between the physicians' loyalty to their oath and their loyalty to their "employer," the government.[48] There was anxiety, too, that young physicians would leave the country to practice medicine in areas where the traditional fee-for-service system was employed. They feared also for the

[47]According to one report in 1960, the average case load was 2,300 patients, with 3 percent of the population as private patients. Richard M. Titmuss, "What British Doctors Really Think about Socialized Medicine," *Harper's Magazine* (February, 1963), pp. 16ff.

[48]See, for example, the consequences of role conflict in the case of the Russian doctors. Mark G. Field, *Doctor and Patient in Soviet Russia,* Cambridge, Mass.: Harvard University Press, 1957.

status and prestige (and income) of the general practitioner. Finally, but not exhaustively, it was felt that the cost of the program would bankrupt the country because of the increased demand for services.

The most serious charge was the decline in quality of care. Here we are faced with an old problem, how to measure quality of care beyond typical mortality and morbidity statistics. For example, one report concluded that apparently money does not affect the doctor-patient relationship as much as is often presumed. For example, dentists spent more time for certain operations on the state patients than they did for these same operations on private patients. Furthermore, there were only twenty-two revocations of licenses for physicians out of over 40,000 and only a small number of disciplinary actions for violations of the Hippocratic oath. In addition, it was found that the interference in the doctor-patient relationship by ministry officials was "ridiculously small."[49] Moreover, the vast majority of the population claimed they were satisfied, even grateful, for the medical care services they received under NHS.[50]

In regard to young physicians emigrating to other countries, it has been pointed out that this generalization refers mostly to specialists who are unable to obtain hospital appointments or who wish further specialist training that could not be obtained in Great Britain.[51] The belief is also based on statistics that include foreign-born physicians who are trained in England and return home after completion of their training. These statistics are further distorted by including British doctors who are working temporarily in the World Health Organization in underdeveloped countries, or who are working and studying overseas before returning to England to practice, and by including many female British doctors who marry foreign doctors and go to live in the countries of their spouses.

We have already noted above how the new system was to have increased the prestige of the general practitioners and make them more important to the family. The more or less continuous battle between the physicians and the government, the charges and countercharges, buttressed by various statistics, make it difficult for interested observers to arrive at an accurate judgment regarding the efficacy of the National Health Service program. It is clear, however, that some problems still persist. In 1965, a significant proportion of the British general practitioners threatened to resign en masse if some steps were not taken by the Ministry of Health and the representatives of organized medicine.[52] Specifically, the demands of the general practitioners had to do with increased payments for their

---

[49]Eckstein, *op. cit.*, pp. 225, 228.

[50]Lindsey, *op. cit.*, p. 77.

[51]David Mechanic, *Public Expectations and Health Care,* New York: Wiley, 1972, p. 192.

[52]David Mechanic and Ronald Faich, "Doctors in Revolt: The Crisis in the English National Health Service," *Medical Care,* 8 (May–June, 1970), 442–445. For a study of a

services to patients. But the financial aspects apparently masked some other more serious problems related to the analysis presented above.

To be sure, the financial aspect was a real problem for the general practitioners, not in absolute terms, but relative to the hospital-based doctors and consultants. That is, a committee of the Royal Commission on Doctors' and Dentists' Remuneration had recommended an increase in salaries for all physicians, general practitioners as well as consultants. Such a recommendation, however, differentially benefited the consultants whose expenses for their practice were much less than for general practitioners.[53] This seemingly benevolent move only accentuated the relative deprivation of status felt by the general practitioners vis-à-vis their hospital-based colleagues. In a very real sense, the latter viewed the former as second-class practitioners.[54]

Not only had there not been the increase in the perceived status of general practitioners, but their role as "family" physicians apparently never came to full flower either. In the first place, the average general practitioner had experienced an increase in patient load, and without extending the number of hours of the work week beyond endurable limits, he or she faced the prospect of providing "assembly-line" care for the patients, a prospect that was not very appealing.[55] Second, the referral system did not function smoothly. Physicians who referred patients to the hospital were told there would be some delay—often a long delay—before the patient could be accommodated. Further, reports back to the general practitioner about the patient were not always regularly made. These and other problems served only to heighten the physician's frustration with the discrepancy between what "could be" and "what is."[56]

Finally, in regard to the cost of care under NHS, it was found that the predicated cost before the act was adopted was unrealistically low. After one year of operation (1949) the cost, twice the predicted amount, was over one billion dollars. By 1968 the cost had risen to over five billion dollars. However, the latter expenditures amounted to only 5.2 percent of the national income of Britain (compared with 3.8 percent in 1950). In the United States, the expenditure for medical care in 1968 was 7.5 percent of the national income.[57] More important, however, is that increased services accompanied the increased expenditures in Britain. The number of hospital

similar problem in Saskatchewan, Canada, where physicians did temporarily boycott the reorganized health services system, see Robin F. Badgley and Samuel Wolfe, *Doctors' Strike: Medical Care and Conflict in Saskatchewan.* New York: Atherton, 1967.

[53]Rosemary Stevens, *Medical Practice in Modern England,* New Haven, Conn.: Yale University Press, 1966.

[54]Ann Cartwright, *Patients and Their Doctors: A Study of General Practice,* London: Routledge & Kegan Paul, 1967.

[55]Mechanic, *op. cit.,* pp. 143–171.

[56]Thomas McKeown, *Medicine and Modern Society,* Allen & Unwin, 1967.

[57]See Table 13-7.

beds increased faster than the population, the number of doctors per 1,000 patients increased, child care services increased, and mental health programs improved greatly.[58]

In view of the fact that the United States is in relatively the same position as England in terms of national growth and population trends (e.g., increase in aged and young),[59] it may very well be that a reorganization of our traditional fee-for-service medicine is in order. There are some who argue that the benefits of a plan similar to that of the NHS in Great Britain could be very large indeed. It would enable the United States to come closer to a goal of providing truly comprehensive care to all its citizens. It will be recalled from the discussion in Chapter 9 that comprehensive care referred to the provision of a complete range of preventive, curative, and rehabilitative services that were available and readily accessible to the population without financial or other impediments. These services could be organized so that continuity of high-quality care could be provided. There are others who share the goal of providing better health care to the population, but oppose reorganization as a method of achieving it. The arguments and counterarguments are not very different from those expressed during the reorganization of the British health system. Needless to say, the controversy in the United States is still alive and will not easily be resolved. For example, although several proposals for a national health insurance program are being discussed, no one has seriously proposed a national health *system*. And, while recognizing that some unique characteristics of American medicine preclude adoption *in toto* of a model of the British NHS or that of any other nation, the time has come to " . . . examine real challenges and risks in any medical program."[60]

### Amendments to the 1935 Social Security Act

What emerged in the United States in 1965, in response to such a challenge, was Public Law 89-97, amendments to the Social Security Act of 1935, popularly known as "Medicare." Perhaps the most innovative change in social legislation since enactment of the Social Security Act itself, the Medicare Act provides payment for certain health services for nearly everyone over age sixty-five.

Although former President Truman is often given credit for having stirred legislative interest in what finally became Public Law 89-97 (he was the first president to publicly state support for a federally subsidized

---

[58] Agnes W. Brewster and Estelle Seldowitz, "Trends in the National Health Service in England and Wales," *Public Health Reports,* 77 (September, 1962), 735–744. More recently, see Murray, *op. cit.*

[59] W. W. Rostow, *Stages of Economic Growth,* New York: Cambridge University Press, 1960.

[60] Lord Taylor, "America's Medical Future," *The Nation,* September 28, 1963, p. 179.

program), Medicare has had a history of on-again, off-again legislation dating back more than fifty years. Earlier in this chapter, a brief sketch of the developments of voluntary-versus-compulsory health insurance programs was presented. The phenomenal growth of voluntary health insurance, particularly from the late 1940s to the late 1950s, did much to quiet any concerted interest in compulsory federally subsidized health insurance program. Even during this period, however, some proposals—such as the Murray-Wagner-Dingle bill—were periodically resurrected, debated, and then dropped. Just before President Truman left office, two events occurred which provided considerable stimulation for the passage of Medicare nearly fifteen years later. The first was the introduction of a bill to provide subsidized health insurance, but only to the elderly, namely, those on social security. Many previous proposals had been designed to cover nearly everyone—thus they were deemed far too expensive or they provided too few needed benefits. Limiting eligibility to the aged meant, theoretically, at least, that provision of a wide range of services for this group was financially feasible. The second factor, although related to the first, was more important inasmuch as it meant a radical change in the nation's perspective on all health and medical care. This was noted in one of the conclusions of the final report of the Commission on Health Needs of the Nation. The belief that health services were a purchasable commodity, available more in quantity and quality to those who could afford them, was no longer a viable perspective. Rather, the commission's report said, "access to the means for attainment and preservation of health is a *basic human right*."[61] This recommendation implies that, along with other basic human rights, the government not only can but *ought* to provide the means whereby every citizen can obtain needed and necessary services to achieve and maintain a status of good health.[62] Thus, the way was paved for some form of federally subsidized plan for health insurance.

During the eight years of the Eisenhower administration repeated attempts to produce a workable program failed for a variety of reasons: the administration did not officially favor such legislation, powerful lobbies worked against passage of such a bill, the political importance of the growing number of older citizens was dissipated through lack of organization, the number of people covered by voluntary insurance policies rose, etc. In the presidential campaign of 1960, however, the mounting evidence

[61]Quoted in Richard Harris, "Annals of Legislation—Medicare, Part II, More Than a Lot of Statistics," *New Yorker*, July 9, 1966, p. 31. Emphasis added. Acceptance of this principle was not immediate, however. After considerable debate and delay, the AMA finally adopted this position officially in 1969.

[62]Robert H. Felix, "A Look at the Future of Health Care," in *Closing the Gaps in the Availability and Accessibility of Health Services, Bulletin of the New York Academy of Medicine*, 41 (December, 1965), 1338–1342.

of inadequate health care for the aged established the basis for an issue of major proportions, and in February, 1961, the new administration's bill—called Medicare—was introduced in the Congress.

Between the time of introduction in 1961 and final passage into law in July, 1965, the Medicare bill was the focus of lengthy legislative hearings, heated debate, enormous pressures, both pro and con, from outside groups, and finally, a good deal of political "horse trading." Even so it was largely due to the lopsided victory for the Democratic party in the 1964 presidential election that sufficient votes in various committees could be mustered to bring the bill to a vote at all. Once this was accomplished, it was inevitable that the much discussed, much revised, bill was finally passed in both houses of Congress and signed into law.[63]

There are two parts to the insurance program. Part A is compulsory hospitalization insurance; Part B is voluntary health insurance for out-of-hospital care and requires payment of a small monthly premium. Initially, persons covered by the act received

**1   Inpatient hospital services:** payment (less deductibles and coinsurance) toward room and board, regular nursing services, operating room charges, drugs administered in the hospital, laboratory tests, x-ray and other radiologic services, other medical supplies or appliances furnished by the hospital.

**2   Post-hospital care** in an extended care facility (now called Skilled Nursing Facility): board and room, special modalities of rehabilitation therapy, and other supporting services similar to a hospital stay. There were limits on the length of stay covered by the insurance.

**3   Home health services:** available under both Parts A and B, they included part-time nursing care, modalities of rehabilitation therapy, services of home health aides, social services, and medical appliances furnished by the agency.

**4   Physicians' services:** under Part B, covered part of the payment for "usual, customary, and reasonable" charges for office visits or hospital outpatient services, medical and surgical care, dental surgery, diagnostic procedures, medical supplies, and some drugs. Omitted from coverage were routine physical examinations, dental care, immunizations, eye glasses, hearing aids, and prescription drugs.

### The Impact of Medicare

For more than a decade now, this innovative program has been evaluated in terms of meeting explicit and implicit legislative intent and as an indicator of larger programs of health care that would include all residents in the

[63]For an interesting history of this legislation, see Harris, *op. cit.;* and Eugene Feingold, *Medicare: Policy and Politics,* San Francisco: Chandler, 1966.

country and provide even more comprehensive care.[64] The explicit intent of the legislation, of course, was to reduce the financial barrier to needed health services by the elderly. Funds were allocated to make it possible for the elderly to pay for health services at the time they were needed. The implicit intent of the program was to foster voluntary collaboration among a community's providers, physicians, hospitals, extended care facilities, home health, etc. That is, Medicare was expected to stimulate utilization of health resources by the elderly (although the extent of the increase was greatly overestimated). Since a community's resources are not limitless, it was anticipated that for their own benefit as well as for the patients', health care providers in the community would voluntarily organize themselves to provide more comprehensive care with continuity and economy.[65] The outcomes would have obvious implications for developing a universal health insurance program.

The evaluation thus far is not encouraging for prospects of a universal program. We noted earlier in this chapter that a large share of the rapid escalation in health care costs can be attributed to Medicare. About 10 percent of the population is age 65 or over, yet they account for more than one-quarter of public expenditures for medical care. To be sure, utilization by the elderly of physicians' services and hospital care has increased, but without demonstrable benefit in health status of the elderly. There has been an enormous increase in costs, however, in part aided by a policy of cost reimbursement to hospitals and physicians and no incentive for cutting or even controlling costs. Thus, the explicit goal was achieved, but with deleterious consequences that were not anticipated.

A five-year follow-up of the impact of Medicare in several Midwestern communities concluded that the implicit intent of the legislation was not accomplished at all.[66] The study, conducted from 1966 to 1971, interviewed panels of physicians, hospital administrators, home health agency directors and other providers in five communities three times during that period. The hypothesis of voluntary, collaborative organization of providers could not

[64]Some evaluations of Medicare may be found in ongoing publications such as the *Social Security Bulletin* and *Research and Statistics Notes*. A focus on finances is found in Robert J. Myers, *Medicare*, Bryn Mawr, Pa.: McCahan Foundation, 1970; program evaluations are reviewed in Charles E. Lewis, Rashi Fein, and David Mechanic, *A Right to Health*, New York: Wiley, 1976, especially pp. 144–164; and operations are discussed in Ervin Witkin, *Impact of Medicare*, Springfield, Ill.: Charles C Thomas, 1971.

[65]Rodney M. Coe and associates, *Medicare Report: Evaluation of the Provision and Utilization of Community Health Resources*, Kansas City: Institute for Community Studies, 1970.

[66]Rodney M. Coe, Henry P. Brehm, and Warren A. Peterson, "Impact of Medicare on the Organization of Community Health Resources," *Health and Society*, 52 (Summer, 1974), 231–264.

be demonstrated. In fact, the findings indicated that (1) physicians had not altered their methods of practice although they acknowledged the need for other levels of out-of-hospital care, (2) Medicare was used to justify expansion of acute care facilities in hospitals, (3) home health care remained largely outside the orbit of physicians and hospitals, and (4) comprehensive health planning agencies (whose mandate was to aid cooperation) were judged ineffective. The study concluded that " . . . what is required is some change in the Medicare legislation and in reimbursement practices—combined with other efforts to encourage and reward the development of comprehensive, coordinated delivery systems."[67]

As we noted earlier, several legislative proposals to provide universal health insurance coverage are being debated. The experience with Medicare provides some lessons that will be ignored at our peril. That is, what course should not be followed is rather clear. What path should be followed is not so obvious. Some factors in this decision are discussed in the next chapter.

## SUMMARY

One of the more interesting paradoxes in the area of medical care in the United States is that despite the increasing technical quality of care available, there is also an increase in the public dissatisfaction with the care received. In part, this paradox is related to the ever-rising costs of care in that it has become economically out of reach of a substantial proportion of the population. The total expenditures for all medical care soared from $3.9 billion in 1940 to $118.5 billion in 1975. At the present time, nearly two-fifths of the total expenditures goes for hospital care (39 percent), 19 percent is paid for physicians' services, and another 9 percent is spent on drugs. The fastest increasing component is the cost of nursing-home care which now accounts for 8 percent of all expenditures. The principal sources of increasing costs were identified as rising prices for all commodities, including medical care, the growth of insurance programs, and increased demand for service by the public as reflected in rising rates of utilization of community health resources. Other factors included the changing composition of this population and the fee-for-service payment structure.

The problem of medical care in the United States is not so much one of *quality* of care available, but rather one of *adequacy* of care, where adequacy is defined in terms of comprehensiveness and continuity. There are parts of the country such as rural and inner-city areas where services are not available because of maldistribution of physicians' services and health facilities. Even where resources are present they are not always

[67]*Ibid.* p. 264.

accessible to people in need because of financial and other barriers to appropriate utilization. Most of all, there is no coordinated system of care providing preventive, curative, and rehabilitative care to all the people. It is evident that past attempts to correct this problem have not succeeded. A major innovation in the United States in this regard is Medicare. The act provides for certain kinds of subsidized health services for people age 65 and over. After ten years of operation, Medicare has lowered (not eliminated) the financial barriers to care for older people, but it has not had any impact on the organization of community health resources. Close examination of other systems of providing health services and financing them reveals some solutions, but also some new problems. It is apparent that everyone—health professionals, government agencies and the general public—will have to work together to solve these problems.

## SUGGESTED READINGS

Elling, Ray H. (ed.), *National Health Care: Issues and Problems in Socialized Medicine,* New York: Atherton, 1971.

Fuchs, Victor R. (ed.), *Essays in the Economics of Health and Medical Care,* New York: National Bureau of Economic Research, 1972.

Fuchs, Victor R., *Who Shall Live?* New York: Basic Books, 1974.

Harris, Seymour E., *The Economics of Health Care,* Berkeley, Calif.: McCutchan, 1976.

Murray, D. Stark., *Blueprint for Health,* New York: Schocken Brooks, 1974.

Somers, Herman R., and Anne R. Somers, *Doctors Patients and Health Insurance,* Washington, D.C.: Brookings, 1961.

# Chapter 14

# Notes on the Politics of Health Care Delivery

*As to the honor and conscience of doctors, they have as much as any other class of men, no more and no less.*

George Bernard Shaw

The many changes in the field of medicine that have occurred since this book was first written have prompted the preparation of this final chapter, new to this revised edition. Throughout this second edition, the aim has been to provide additional documentation for established sociological concepts, to identify new theoretical developments, and to assess their application to practice. While some change has been noted for nearly every aspect of the field of medicine, it is obvious that the most dramatic and potentially far-reaching changes have taken place in the context of the delivery of health services. As we have seen, good health and good health care are all-encompassing concepts. They involve health providers and consumers both individually and collectively, health institutions and supporting services and, indeed, other social institutions as well. For this reason, health care delivery provides a convenient focus for pulling together various themes discussed in the text—a "summing up" of the issues and potential solutions to problems in the delivery system. The objective of this chapter is more than just providing a summary, however. Our intent also includes reviewing some dimensions of a national health policy, discussing some major barriers to implementation of policy, and mentioning a few potential solutions.

As we have also seen, however, there is not complete consensus as to what the problems are (or to what degree there are problems) in health care delivery; there is even less agreement on what the causes are; and very little concurrence on the most effective, realistic remedies for those problems. Thus, the process of providing health services takes on a "political" dimension in the sense of identification of problems, negotiation and compromise; hence the title, "Notes on the Politics of Health Care Delivery."

It is worth a brief digression here to define more clearly what is meant by the "politics" of health. Swanson, for example, has said, "Politics, in its broadest sense, is that activity wherein some people attempt to maintain or shift the pattern of action of government and its public officials. The politics of health then is the effort to have the commonwealth and public officials assume certain responsibilities for the health care of the people."[1] This definition is illustrated by analysis of decision making in four communities and the subsequent development of a paradigm of the politics of health. The paradigm is a system analysis of inputs and outputs in the context of differing types of power structures and degrees of political ideology. Of most interest are the system processes—politicization, reform, mediation, management—emerging from various combinations of inputs and outputs. Politicization is a process associated with a radical political ideology and mass (public) participation in decision making in response to severe "system stress." At the other extreme, management processes are associated with a conservative political ideology with "elitist" decision makers responding to less than severe systems stress. The application of the paradigm to the issue of government participation in health care identified those who advocated expansion and those who advocated reduction or contraction in the role of government. Expansionists advocated decision making by direct participation of the public in open meetings, development of a comprehensive coverage as policy, major funding from public sources, and administration by the public. Contractionists supported decision making by representatives in closed meetings, tailoring coverage to individual

[1]Bert E. Swanson, "The Politics of Health," in Howard E. Freeman, Sol Levine, and Leo G. Reeder (eds.), *Handbook of Medical Sociology,* 2d ed., Englewood Cliffs, N.J.: Prentice-Hall, 1972, pp. 435–455. Quote is on p. 435.

needs, limited funding from government sources, and control by health professionals.[2]

This model neatly summarizes the polar types of views, and in a superficial way, the types resemble the positions taken by the Democratic and Republican political parties. However, as Silver has noted, the positions taken by the two national parties, that is, their platforms, do not necessarily reflect performance. Indeed, he concludes that the performance in health delivery under either party has been very similar (and inadequate), even though the avowed principles are different.[3] In part, the failure of either party to match performance to promise lies in the similarity of philosophy of providing health or any other kind of social services. The philosophy operant in the United States is derived from the culture of individualism, a private entreprenurial perspective that emphasizes self-achievement where opportunities are plentiful. To a substantial degree, both major parties subscribe to this philosophy. Thus, definition of the problem is made difficult and agreement on solutions even more so. The philosophical perspective that characterizes our society stands in sharp contrast with that of other nations. For example, the Soviet system views health of the people (workers) as a major contribution to its natural resources; thus the government gives strong central direction to the planning, development, allocation, and use of its resources. Soviet health professionals have a different status and political, as well as professional, roles to play, but only as instruments, not formulators, of health policy.[4]

In the United States, similarity in political philosophy does not by itself explain the lack of substantial change in the health delivery system in response to perceived deficiencies. Rather, power and influence of providers, especially physicians, have been pinpointed as key elements, along with an emphasis on scientific achievement and a generalized distrust of bureaucracies and planning organizations.[5] The strength of resistance to change is dramatized by its success in the face of forces promoting change. Some of these we have identified as increased technology, medical specialization, higher costs, changing population composition, and the movement toward consumer representation.

The politics of health, then, involve a process of negotiation between unequal power blocs, providers and consumers (and their constituencies),

[2]*Ibid.*, p. 451.

[3]George A. Silver, "Medical Politics, Party Health Platforms, Promise and Performance," *International Journal of Health Services,* 6 (Spring, 1976), 331–343.

[4]Cf. the discussion in David Mechanic, *Politics, Medicine and Social Sciences,* New York: Wiley, 1974, especially pp. 1–5.

[5]Duane F. Stroman, *The Medical Establishment and Social Responsibility,* Port Washington, N.Y.: Kennikat Press, 1976. A fuller statement is in Eliot Freidson, *Profession of Medicine,* New York: Dodd, Mead, 1970, and by the same author, *Professional Dominance,* New York: Atherton Press, 1970. See also Mechanic, *op. cit.*

to establish a national health policy that defines realistic health goals, assigns a priority to health relative to other national needs, and provides guidelines for development of a program for implementation. A sociological analysis of this process should allow us to identify (1) public expectations of the health delivery system, (2) what issues or problems arise from unmet expectations, (3) why public expectations have not been met, and (4) potential solutions to the problems.

## PUBLIC EXPECTATIONS AND ISSUES IN HEALTH CARE DELIVERY

There have been many analyses of the health delivery system from the consumer's perspective ranging from simple descriptions of opinion surveys to thoughtful interpretations of data from various sources.[6] While the emphasis varies in these reports, there does seem to be a consensus about what consumers want in terms of health care which can most simply be described in terms of

**Availability:**  the factual presence of the full range of health services—preventive, curative, and rehabilitative.
**Accessibility:**  providers of services are distributed geographically so that time, distance, and lack of transportation are not bars to utilization.
**Affordability:**  costs of services are reasonable for care received and no one is denied services because of inability to pay for them.
**Accountability:**  providers are responsible for assuring the quality of services rendered, both technically and organizationally, to monitor continually the scientific competence and the continuity of services provided.
**Acceptability:**  services must be provided in a way that will maintain the dignity of the patient as a person and provide understanding for the patient of his or her situation.[7]

This alliterative list of what consumers want in a health care system may also be viewed as what many of them do not yet have, that is, as a list of problems or issues in health care delivery.[8] Thus, the issue of availability

[6]An example of the first type would be Stephen P. Strickland, *U.S. Health Care: What's Wrong and What's Right,* New York: Potomac Associates, 1972. An example of the latter type would be David Mechanic, *Public Expectations and Health Care,* New York: Wiley, 1972.
[7]Cf. the discussion in Anne R. Somers, "Toward a Rational Community Health Care System: The Hunterdon Model," *Hospital Progress,* 54 (April, 1973), 46–54.
[8]There is a huge literature discussing the issues in health care delivery. See the bibliography in Ozzie G. Simmons and Emil Berkanovic, "Social Research in Health and Medicine: A Bibliography," in Freeman et al., *op. cit.,* pp. 523–584. Specific references might focus on the economy, such as Dorothy P. Rice and Douglas Wilson, "The American Medical Economy: Problems and Perspectives," *Journal of Health Politics, Policy and Law,* 1 (Summer, 1976), 151–172; or organization, such as Stroman, *op. cit.;* or politics, such as Silver, *op. cit.*

of services is related to the trend in increased specialization of medical and allied health professionals. It is also concerned with how allied health professionals are to be used—as doctor alternates or doctor assistants. Accessibility touches on rural-urban differentials in amount and types of personnel and facilities located there. It involves also the problem of medically underserved, inner-city areas and poor transportation modes. From the provider's perspective, accessibility is linked with freedom to choose where to locate one's practice or to establish a hospital or clinic.

Affordability, often the most sensitive area, reflects a variety of issues. It is certain that health services must be paid for, but there is still controversy about how health services are to be paid for, when payment should be made, and from what sources. Thus, while most groups favor a program of health insurance, questions remain about how much coverage is necessary, whether to favor public or private sponsorship, what should be the role of third-party insurers in cost control, and so on. As we noted in Chapter 13, fee-for-service payment is the most common way payment is made in the United States, but prepaid programs of care are increasing in popularity. We noted also the trend for increasing use of public funds to pay for health care, and that this is a source of controversy. Some want less government participation, while others would increase the federal government's share (and role in delivery) even more.

The term accountability also describes a range of important concerns. Not the least of these is ensuring the technical quality of care rendered by providers. That the consumers' faith in the efficacy of medical treatments has declined may be seen in the dramatic rise in the number of malpractice suits where patients claim that damages were done through medical negligence.[9] Consumer consciousness has also been raised concerning the rights of human subjects in medical research and experimentation. The procedures to protect those rights and to assure "informed" consent by patients volunteering for studies have been made more explicit. Quality of care, however, extends to the organization of services to provide continuity of care. Providers ought to organize themselves so that the discrete services the patient receives through various modalities are " . . . continuously and competently monitored not only for technical quality, but for relevance to his individual problems and for continuity of records and communications between the various professionals and facilities involved in his case."[10] Finally, acceptability may be seen as patient satisfaction, not only with the medical outcomes of treatment, but with the social interaction in the process of treatment. A substantial part of the satisfaction will depend upon

[9]See the appendix in Stroman, *op. cit.* See also Department of Health, Education, and Welfare, *Secretary's Report on Medical Malpractice*, Washington, D.C.: 1973.
[10]Somers, *op. cit.*, p. 47.

the communication skills employed by providers to help the patient understand his or her health condition.

Throughout this volume, we have discussed the sources of, and some proposed solutions to, these problems, and reviewed research, where available, bearing on these issues. It is obvious that the problems still exist and that the various attempts to solve them have been largely unsuccessful. There are many explanations for why this is so. One reason why programmatic solutions fail is due to the piecemeal attack on symptoms of the problem rather than on the "root" causes. Thus, infusion of money alone to pay for care is not enough. Increasing the number of health personnel or facilities alone is not enough. Creating health facilities in neighborhoods alone is not enough. Another reason is that health is not always a high priority among citizens and providers, or even as a national policy. Health becomes a priority more in its absence; that is, sick care is more important than (preventive) health care. There are many other elements that "explain" the problems of health care delivery.[11]

From a sociological perspective, however, a principal source both of problems and of failure to resolve them is the issue of *professional autonomy*—in this case, the autonomy of the medical profession. The conceptualization and practical implications of autonomy in medicine have already been well described by others,[12] and this same orientation has been noted in several preceding chapters. Still, it is worth noting again the key elements in professional autonomy before addressing their relationship to health care delivery. One element, of course, is the ideology promoted by organized medicine that has changed little since the founding of the organization in 1847. Basically this views the practice of medicine as a free enterprise activity completely controlled by the medical profession. The argument is that only where the physician can use his or her best professional judgment in providing care will the quality and appropriateness of care be guaranteed. A second element is what areas are controlled. Over time, the profession has gained control over who (and how many) can enter the field of medicine, what training standards are required, who makes judgments about all matters related to diagnosis and treatment of disease, how services are to be organized, where they will be located, and how they will be financed.

A third element, the power to maintain this extensive monopoly, is based on several factors. In the first instance, a public mandate to leave health care to the health professionals is based on past performance.

---

[11] An example of such an explanation is Sidney Shindell, Jeffrey C. Salloway, and Colette M. Oberembt, *A Coursebook in Health Care Delivery,* New York: Appleton-Century-Crofts, 1976.

[12] Freidson, *op. cit.;* Stroman, *op. cit.*

Organized medicine did contribute much to raising the standards of entrance and training of physicians, to promoting research and technology, and to conquering communicable diseases. On the basis of these achievements, the profession was given a mandate to promote the health interest of the public. Secondly, the power inherent in the mandate is supported by a well-organized and well-financed political organization within the profession that works to influence legislation to favor the profession and to promote its interests over other groups. The effectiveness of the mandate is maintained by the organization because there is no competition and too little advocacy for the consumer.[13]

As we have seen, however, the ideology of organized medicine and its subsequent expression in medical education and the organization of medical practice have not kept pace with the changes in health needs in the population. A more detailed look at some elements of professional autonomy and their relationship to specific issues in health care delivery may provide some clues to more effective solutions. Three major issues in this regard include the fee-for-service payment philosophy, control of diagnosis and treatment resources, and self-regulation as ideological elements that are dysfunctional to health care delivery.

1  **Fee-for-service** or payment at the time service is received is based on the belief that medical care will have value only when the patient has personal responsibility for paying for some part of it. Payment at the time of service is to deter "unnecessary" utilization; i.e., care will be sought only when it is needed. The application of this philosophy in practice, however, has led to serious problems. From the patients' perspective, fee-for-service has resulted in two levels of care, one for those who can pay and another for those who cannot. Fee-for-service has contributed to the rapid growth of specialization, to limitations on the use of allied health professionals (except when salaried by hospitals), to the maldistribution of physicians and hospitals, and to the growth of the health insurance industry. The health insurance industry has, itself, contributed to escalating costs of care and misuse of hospitals.[14] From a policy perspective, a fee-for-service

---

[13]Some recent trends seem to be weakening the degree of autonomy and monopolistic control of the health delivery system by the medical profession. These trends include the increasing effectiveness of organized consumer groups; greater participation in regulatory activities by governmental agencies; and providing services. See G. R. Weller, "From 'Pressure-group Politics' to 'Medical-industrial-complex': The Development of Approaches to the Politics of Health," *Journal of Health Politics, Policy and Law,* 1 (Winter, 1977), 444–47; and Judith S. Warner, "Trends in the Federal Regulation of Physicians' Fees," *Inquiry,* 13 (December, 1976), 364–370.

[14]Stroman, *op. cit.* See also Thomas Bodenheimer, Steven Cummings, and Elizabeth Harding, "Capitalizing on Illness: The Health Insurance Industry," *International Journal of Health Services,* 4 (Fall, 1974), 583–598; Eleanor M. Parsons and Milton I. Roemer, "Ideological Goals of Different Health Insurance Plans," *Journal of Community Health,* 1 (Summer, 1976), 241–248; and Vicente Navarro, "The Political and Economic Determinants of Health and Health Care in Rural America," *Inquiry,* 13 (June, 1976), 111–121.

orientation has promoted treatment of the sick and not care for the healthy. That is, the resources are devoted to treating health problems and not maintenance of health and prevention of problems.[15]

**2  Control over diagnosis and treatment resources** stems from the claim that advances in scientific knowledge and technology have made medicine so complicated that only physicians are competent to understand the issues in decisions about diagnosis and treatment. In a limited way, this may be the case especially as it concerns biological processes in the body. As we have seen, most lay persons possess only the most rudimentary understanding of these processes. Two trends have served to complicate this issue. One is what Zola called the "medicalization of society," a trend toward defining social problems in terms of health and illness, thereby placing responsibility for solving the problems in the hands of the medical profession although physicians have no special competence or training in these areas.[16] An obvious example is defining narcotic addiction as a disease requiring treatment rather than as a crime requiring punishment. Less obvious, but no less important, is the influence of plastic surgery on defining esthetic qualities of appearance or defining aging as primarily a health problem and extending health care of the elderly to housing, social interaction, transportation, etc.

A second trend, related to the first, is medicine's control over ancillary sources of treatment. Most notably, medicine has maintained legal control over the prescription of drugs as part of the treatment process although we have seen how technical knowledge of drugs varies widely among physicians.[17] Similarly, insurance programs are tied to physicians' services both in and out of the hospital. It should be remembered that only physicians can admit patients to the hospital, and this often holds for reimbursement from insurance for other community agency services as well.[18]

**3  Self-regulation** is a key element in a sociological definition of a professionalized occupation. It is also a principle vigorously defended by organized medicine. It relates to the profession's responsibility to protect the public by ensuring the competence of new members, monitoring the quality of services rendered by all members, and promoting effective delivery and financing mechanisms. On every count, the profession has been criticized for incomplete, if not ineffective, performance. Peer review—that is, the review of performance of doctors by other doctors—

[15]John Gordon Freymann, "Medicine's Great Schism: Prevention vs. Cure: An Historical Interpretation," *Medical Care,* 13 (July, 1975), 525–536.

[16]Irving Kenneth Zola, "In the Name of Health and Illness: On Some Socio-political Consequences of Medical Influence," *Social Science and Medicine,* 9 (February, 1975), 83–87. See also an earlier statement by Zola in "Medicine as an Institution of Social Control," *The Sociological Review,* 20 (November, 1972), 487–504.

[17]Samuel Proger (ed.), *The Medicated Society,* New York: Macmillan, 1968. There is also widespread use of nonprescription drugs. See Bruce C. Busching and David C. Bromley, "Sources of Non-medicinal Drug Use: A Test of the Drug Oriented Society Explanation," *Journal of Health and Social Behavior,* 16 (March, 1975), 50–62.

[18]Sylvia Law, *Blue Cross: What Went Wrong?* New Haven: Yale University Press, 1974.

and the sanctions for poor performance have been shown to be ineffective.[19] The peer review mechanism established through Medicare to exercise cost control through limiting hospital utilization has not been effective nor has the extension of this philosophy through legislation on Professional Standards Review Organizations (PSROs) to all medical care settings.[20]

## ATTEMPTED SOLUTIONS TO PROBLEMS OF HEALTH DELIVERY

The analysis of the role of organized medicine in problems of health care delivery, outlined in the foregoing paragraphs, is not new, of course. In fact, there have been several programmatic attempts to correct the uncoordinated organization of services and to control the ever-increasing costs and uneven quality of care related to the autonomy of the medical profession. These include programs of comprehensive health planning, Medicare and Medicaid, hospital utilization review committees, and so on. The success of most of these efforts has been minimal at best because none of the programs directly altered the autonomy of the medical profession; rather they represented efforts to "treat symptoms" of the problem rather than the "cause." Let us review briefly evaluations of some of these programs.

### Comprehensive Health Planning

We noted in Chapter 12 the trend toward coordination of community health resources as part of an effort to improve health care delivery. The current attempt is based on the National Health Planning and Resources Development Act of 1974 (Public Law 93-641) which created Health Systems Agencies (HSAs) in every state to plan, allocate resources, and monitor health services in their areas. The HSAs replace a similar type of organization authorized by previous health planning legislation enacted in 1966. These were designated Comprehensive Health Planning agencies (CHPs) and designed to foster cooperation between providers and consumers in establishing priorities for health programs, identifying needs, and planning for their solution. There were some notable achievements made by a few CHPs in reaching their stated goals, but as West and Stevens have reported:

> The CHP experience was, to some extent, one of frustration coupled with
> intermittent successes. Inadequate guidelines in the old CHP law and in the

[19]Eliot Freidson and Buford Rhea, "Processes of Control in a Company of Equals," *Social Problems,* 11 (Fall, 1963), 119–131. A more recent general evaluation is Elliott A. Krause, "The Political Context of Health Service Regulation," *International Journal of Health Services,* 5 (Summer, 1975), 593–607.

[20]Odin W. Anderson, "PSROs, the Medical Profession and the Public Interest," *Health and Society,* 54 (Summer, 1976), 379–388.

accompanying federal regulations, opposition from health providers, unwieldly jurisdictions, lack of accountability, inadequate technical assistance for planners, slow development of health plans, and the absence of adequate legal authority and enforceable sanctions, restricted the ability of areawide CHP agencies to effect significant change.[21]

Their analysis cites several organizational problems which served to limit the effectiveness of CHPs, including responsibility for areas that were too large, competition between state and local CHPs, and the fact that local agencies "became captives of local hospital and medical associations"[22] despite the legal requirement of 51 percent consumer representation on boards of directors.

Many of the problems that plagued CHPs have been addressed in the new law creating HSAs. HSAs have more legal authority, strengthened criteria for staff skill requirements and membership on boards, limits on scope of jurisdiction, and better financial support from the federal government. Nevertheless, West and Stevens predict that HSAs will still encounter some problems similar to those which frustrated CHPs, and chief among these is the continued domination of decision making on planning and resource allocation by health providers including, but not limited to, the medical profession.[23]

## Controlling Costs of Health Care

In Chapter 13, considerable attention was directed toward identifying the sources of rising costs of health care in the United States. We also discussed the concept of health insurance and its relationship to the increase in expenditures while providing better access to health services. In the case of Medicare as a specific illustration, it was found that while financial barriers to care have been reduced, the program has had no effect on the reorganization of community health resources and costs of the program have reached such extremes that deterrents to effective use have been reestablished and the scope of services has been reduced.[24] One major contributor to this failure was the specific prohibition in the legislation

[21]Jonathan P. West and Michael D. Stevens, "Comparative Analysis of Community Health Planning: Transition from CHPs to HSAs," *Journal of Health Politics, Policy and Law,* 1 (Summer, 1976), 173–211. Quote is on pp. 174–175.

[22]*Ibid.,* p. 177.

[23]*Ibid.,* p. 194. Other analysts of health planning legislation have come to the same conclusion about CHPs, but cite different strengths and weaknesses in the HSA legislation, especially the failure to promote a national health policy. See Leonard S. Rosenfeld and Irene Rosenfeld, "National Health Planning in the United States: Prospects and Portents," *International Journal of Health Services,* 5 (Summer, 1975), 441–453 and Bruce C. Vladeck, "Interest-group Representation and the HSAs: Health Planning and Political Theory," *American Journal of Public Health,* 67 January, 1977), 23–29.

[24]Rice and Wilson, *op. cit.* See also the special issue of *Health and Society* 52 (Summer, 1974) devoted to evaluations of the Medicare program.

against interfering with the practice of medicine. In other words, part of the compromise between Congress and organized medicine in getting the legislation enacted at all was the preservation of professional autonomy.[25]

The problems of costs of health care delivery have persisted, and discussion in Congress has turned to programs of larger scope: national health insurance. At present there are many different legislative proposals to be considered which vary widely in scope of benefits, sources of financing, implementation, and administration.[26] Some critics suggest that none of the current proposals is adequate because they represent nothing more than increased public subsidies for a financially troubled health power structure.[27] Other observers, however, see possibilities for improving health care delivery while controlling costs and maintaining an acceptable level of quality of care. For example, there is considerable evidence both from the United States and other countries that universal health insurance does not result in immediate and massive increases in utilization demands (even for unmet need),[28] that those most in need can benefit the most from universal insurance plans,[29] and that most physicians favor such a plan although preferably under conditions that place no constraints on the financing mechanism.[30] Even so, most present proposals have not resolved inequities induced by provisions such as cost sharing, means testing, employee contributions, etc., that remain as reminders of the autonomy of the medical profession.[31]

These problems are illustrated in Table 14-1 in the contrasts between two widely different proposals that have been considered by Congress. The Medicredit Act represented the least change from the *status quo,* while the Health Security Act was the most innovative proposal. The Medicredit

[25]Cf. Eugene Feingold, *Medicare: Policy and Politics,* San Francisco: Chandler, 1966.

[26]Eveline M. Burns, "A Critical Review of National Health Insurance Proposals," *HSMHA Health Reports,* 86 (February, 1971), 111–120.

[27]Thomas S. Bodenheimer, "The Hoax of National Health Insurance," *American Journal of Public Health,* 62 (October, 1972), 1325–1327. See also Richard E. Cairl and Allen W. Imershein, "National Health Insurance Policy in the United States: A Case of Non-decision-making," *International Journal of Health Services,* 7 (Spring, 1977), 167–178.

[28]Louis Munan, Josef Vobecky, and Anthea Kelly, "Population Health Care Practices: An Epidemiologic Study of the Immediate Effects of a Universal Health Insurance Plan," *International Journal of Health Services,* 4 (Spring, 1974), 285–295; Mike Gorman, "The Impact of National Health Insurance on Delivery of Health Care," *American Journal of Public Health,* 61 (May, 1971), 962–971; and Gordon H. DeFriese, "On Paying the Fiddler to Change the Tune: Further Evidence from Ontario Regarding the Impact of Universal Health Insurance on the Organization and Pattern of Medical Practice," *Health and Society,* 53 (Spring, 1975), 117–148.

[29]Cf., for example, Bruce C. Stuart, "National Health Insurance and the Poor," *American Journal of Public Health,* 62 (September, 1972), 1252–1259.

[30]John Colombotos, Corinne Kirschner, and Michael Millman, "Physicians' View of National Health Insurance: A National Study," *Medical Care,* 13 (May, 1975), 369–396.

[31]Rachael Floersheim Boaz, "Equity in Paying for Health Care Services under a National Insurance System," *Health and Society,* 53 (Summer, 1975), 337–352.

**Table 14-1 Comparison of Two Major Proposals for National Health Insurance**

| Item | Health security | Medicredit |
|---|---|---|
| Concept | Universal comprehensive health insurance for all U.S. residents | Voluntary income tax plan; tax credits to partially offset cost of qualified private health insurance; amount of credit graduated; Medicare retained, Medicaid eliminated |
| Sponsors | Sen. Edward Kennedy (D-Mass.), Rep. Martha Griffiths (D-Mich.) | Sen. Clifford Hansen (R-Wyo.), Rep. Joe Broyhill (R-Va.), Rep. Richard Fulton (D-Tenn.) |
| Supporters | Committee of 100, AFL-CIO Teamsters, UAW, church and consumer groups | American Medical Association |
| Benefit pattern | Benefits cover the entire range of personal health care services including prevention and early detection of disease, care and treatment, and medical rehabilitation | A "qualified" policy would offer insurance against the expenses of illness, subject to deductibles, co-pay, and limitations |
| Financing | Health Security Trust Fund derived from general tax revenue; tax on employer payroll | The government would pay all premiums for the destitute—individuals and dependents with no income tax liability. For others, the government would pay between 10 and 99%, based on family or individual income |
| Administration | Publicly administered program in HEW. Policy-making, five-member, full-time Health Security Board appointed by the President. Field administration through ten HEW regions and approximately 100 health subregions. Advisory councils at all levels with the majority of members representing consumers | Establishes an 11-person Health Insurance Advisory Board, including the HEW Secretary and the IRS Commissioner. The remaining members, not otherwise in the employ of the U.S., would be appointed by or under the direction of an M.D. or D.O. |
| Effect on health system | Provides legal and financial means to restructure health delivery system | NA |
| Quality | Establishes quality control commission and national standards for participating professional and institutional providers. Regulation of major surgery and certain other specialist services; national licensure standards and requirements for continuing education | NA |

*Source:* Sidney Shindell, Jeffrey C. Salloway, and Collette M. Oberembt, *A Coursebook in Health Care Delivery,* New York: Appleton-Century-Crofts, 1976, pp. 349–350.

program, sponsored by the American Medical Association, could be national in scope, but was a voluntary plan in which families purchase insurance through private companies. The key here is that Medicare would have been retained for the elderly and Medicaid would have been replaced by federal subsidies (through tax reduction) for the poor so that they could also purchase insurance in the same manner as families that received no tax relief. The benefits were for sick care, not promotion of health, and were limited by deductible and coinsurance provisions that are typical of most current insurance programs. Current provisions for setting fees and quality assurance would have been employed. Administration and control would have been in the hands of an advisory council controlled by representatives of the medical profession.

An alternative was the Health Security Act, sponsored by unions and consumer groups, that would provide universal insurance coverage for the entire population. Care would have been prepaid through payroll taxes and from general tax revenues; i.e., the federal government would have been the largest, if not the only, "insurance company." Out-of-pocket costs for consumers would have been minimal. Benefits were to be "comprehensive" in scope (but did not include dental care and had limited psychiatric care) and emphasized preventive services. A major change was proposed in the organization and administration of services in that they would have been publicly controlled (with professional advisories) in health service regions. Part of the control was in the budgeting process, which would have limited the amount of expenditure for health services, but not limit the amount of care provided on demand. Such an obvious source of potential conflict would be minimized by joint consumer and provider collaboration in committees to set standards of care, regulate service utilization, monitor quality of services, and set requirements for licensure. In these respects, the Health Security Act did attempt to temper the power of professional autonomy. Debate on these issues continues now in Congress, and an agreed-upon program does not yet seem near at hand.

## Self-regulation and Quality Assurance

We have noted several times that self-regulation has been a cardinal tenet in measuring professionalization and a fundamental element in professional autonomy. Until recently, it also has been the only mechanism which served to monitor and assure the quality of health services. It is worth noting that, in fact, there are several points where quality control can be exercised, such as admission to medical school, licensure, continuing education, and medical practice. The point is that all are controlled by the medical profession.[32] To be sure, other groups such as insurance companies, hospital associations, and other groups of health professionals partici-

[32]Stroman, *op. cit.*, p. 122.

pate in efforts at quality control. State governments exercise some influence in that licensing boards are authorized by state laws. It should also be said that most programs to assure quality of care even though dominated by the medical profession are done in good faith, but it apparently has not been enough. Interestingly, it was not the increase in malpractice suits or unchanging rates of morbidity and mortality that attracted attention to mechanisms of quality control as much as it was the runaway costs of care. Third-party payers were especially interested since, as we have seen, the most dramatic rise in costs has been for hospital care. Then, in 1965, with the establishment of Medicare, the federal government became a major buyer of health care services, and, therefore, interest in promoting regulations to control costs emerged rapidly.[33] At first, these regulations were confined to hospital utilization review activities to determine, on a case-by-case basis for Medicare beneficiaries, if the services were medically necessary, if the quality met local standards, and if the level of care (ambulatory, inpatient, etc.) was consistent with medical need. These are difficult judgments to make, and criteria and capabilities would vary widely from one community to another. Finally, amendments to the Social Security Act were passed to authorize development of Professional Standards Review Organizations (PSROs), which are organizations that will develop standards for medical practices in a given geographic region, establish limits on acceptable practices, review the performance of providers in the area, and take appropriate action for noncompliance. A PSRO is "a governmental plea for medical involvement in the effective and efficient distribution of medical services. . . . PSRO is organized medicine's opportunity for self-regulation. Given the pressures which now exist for national health insurance, failure of PSRO may well initiate other, less workable forms of bureaucratic control over the practice of medicine."[34]

The portent for success of PSROs is not encouraging. Peer review, the principal mechanism for arriving at judgments about quality, meeting needs, appropriateness of level of care, etc., has not been effective in hospitals, in clinics, or, where data are available, in private offices.[35] It seems clear that responsibility for assuring quality of care can not be left solely in the hands of one group. Rather, decisions on setting standards, monitoring performance, and enforcing compliance ought to be shared with other providers and consumers.

A central sociological issue, to repeat, lies in the degree of professional autonomy enjoyed by the medical profession. The consequences of this autonomy have contributed directly to what has been described as the

[33]Shindell et al., *op. cit.*

[34]B. Decker and P. Bonner, *Professional Standards Review Organizations*, Cambridge, Mass.: Arthur D. Little, 1973, p. 6, quoted in Shindell et al., *op. cit.*, pp. 358–359.

[35]Stroman, *op. cit.*, pp. 132–139. Also see Robert C. Derbyshire, "Medical Ethics and Discipline," *Journal of the American Medical Association*, 228 (April 1, 1974), 59–62.

health care crisis in terms of deficits in availability and accessibility of services, their high cost relative to the value received, the lack of accountability for technical and organizational dimensions of quality, and the lack of concern for human dignity in delivery of care. Solutions to these problems that do not alter the degree of professional autonomy have not been successful. Given the lack of justification for maintaining the present degree of autonomy by the medical profession,[36] other solutions must be sought.

## TOWARD A NATIONAL HEALTH POLICY

It is relatively easy to find fault with the health care delivery system in the United States. It is quite another matter to suggest alternatives that are both workable and acceptable to all interest groups involved in the provision and receipt of that care. We have labeled as the "politics of health" that continuous process by which interest groups with varying objectives, resources, and degrees of power and influence negotiate with one another over issues in health care delivery. These negotiations take place at all levels—national, state, local community, and in agencies or institutions. The contribution of the social sciences to this political process, at least in the United States,[37] would seem to be limited to providing information from research and providing a social science perspective on issues. The value of this contribution is compromised somewhat by unresolved methodological inadequacies in social science research and by lack of definitive conclusions from which policy decisions could be made. Moreover, policy decisions often involve long-range plans where few social science data are available.

Despite these difficulties, the social sciences have an obligation to contribute toward the formulation of a national health policy which identifies goals and assigns their priorities among other national goals; defines the responsibilities of individuals, physicians and other health providers, and institutions for maintaining the health of the population; and provides definitive guidelines for implementing health care delivery. From the analysis presented in this chapter, it could be assumed that one tenet of the policy is that all residents have a right to adequate health care on demand.

[36]Freidson, *Professional Dominance, op. cit.*

[37]Social scientists apparently play a larger role in other countries. See, for example, Magdalena Sokolowska, "Social Science and Health Policy in Eastern Europe: Poland as a Case Study," *International Journal of Health Services,* 4 (Summer, 1974), 441–452; and in the same issue, Joyce Leeson, "Social Science and Health Policy in Pre-industrial Society," *International Journal of Health Services,* 4 (Summer, 1974), 429–440. The role of social sciences in U.S. health policy is addressed in Mechanic, *op. cit.,* chap. 4; David Falcone and Jon Jaeger, "The Policy Effectiveness of Health Services Research: A Reconsideration," *Journal of Community Health,* 2 (Fall, 1976), 36–51 and David H. Banta and Patricia Bauman, "Health Services Research and Health Policy," *Journal of Community Health,* 2 (Winter, 1976), 121–132.

A second tenet is that the power to make decisions about goals and implementation must be shared among all interest groups.

Earlier in this chapter, some desirable attributes of a comprehensive health care delivery system were described in terms of availability, accessibility, affordability, accountability, and acceptability. These descriptors may also be seen as objectives of a delivery system to which specific programs should be directed. However, given the interrelatedness of the objectives as part of a health system, not to mention the present lack of consensus among providers and consumers on goals and methods and the ambiguities in findings of social science research, it would seem more appropriate to indicate here a set of general principles underlying health delivery rather than detailed program specifics.

The issues of *availability* and *accessibility* of health services and how they are to be financed (*affordability*) are addressed by the following elements of a health policy.

## Universal Health Insurance

The right to health can best be protected by an insurance program that provides comprehensive care for the entire population with equal benefits for all. Such a program should be prepaid and provide for differential rates of premium payments. Consumers ought to have a choice of providers under such a plan. Similarly, providers ought to have a choice of type of setting in which they wish to work, but payment for services ought to be linked to capitation or to salaries adjusted for experience and special training. Incentives for location of practices (and facilities) of providers ought to be part of the payment scheme also (even though financial incentives for influencing practice locations have not been successful under a fee-for-service system). Finally, but not least, the insurance program ought to give as much emphasis to preventive medicine and health maintenance as to curative medicine and rehabilitation.

## Health Personnel Management

Judgments on how many and what types of health personnel are necessary will always be difficult to make. Such decisions, however, ought to be made jointly by providers and consumers in a national-level planning council rather than by any vested interest group alone. The range of consumer choice could be expanded by altering the licensure laws to increase competition among providers by allowing more doctor assistants to be doctor alternates. Here, research evidence is indefinite as to what kinds of people would choose a doctor alternate over a physician, or what the consequences of competition would actually be, given that medical care does not operate like a commodity in a free market. Maldistribution of health personnel could be affected by adoption of policies found in many Latin

American countries. That is, medical education (and allied health training) is free or heavily subsidized. New graduates are obliged (without exception) to work for one or two years in assigned stations usually in remote and medically underserved areas. Supervision is provided by physicians in government service. At the end of the assigned tour, graduates are permitted to continue their education (specialization) or to establish themselves in practice wherever they choose. While not perfect, the system does provide adequate medical coverage for all the people.

## Resource Allocation

Most major urban areas have sufficient health resources (personnel and facilities), but lack a means to coordinate them in the best interests of the public. Other communities need to develop resources. The present HSAs were developed to respond to these needs. There needs to be further development of a central coordinating body, with authority at national, state, and local levels. These coordinating bodies ought to address issues of institutional resources as a first priority. In general, it has been found that communities are "overbedded" in hospital resources; i.e., there are too many hospital beds available. Empty beds tend to be filled, often unnecessarily, because a low bed-occupancy rate is financially hazardous to the institution's health. Concomitantly, the emphasis on hospital development has drawn attention from the development of institutional services at other levels of care and of agency-based home health services. Decentralization of health services under a strong central authority is an important element of policy.

Accountability and acceptability of health care involve some additional policy elements, as follows.

## Regulation

Peer review has not been a very effective way to regulate the quality of care or to assure the appropriateness of the services provided. In the area of protection of human rights in research, peer review has not been effective either, not only in medical research, but in behavioral science research as well.[38] Current developments in providing oversight in research involving humans and as illustrated in PSRO concept are relevant here. The principle is to extend the responsibility for surveillance, reporting, and corrective action to several disciplines. For example, new guidelines for protecting the rights of human subjects in university-based, federally financed research require review and approval by representatives from medicine, behavioral

[38]Bradford H. Gray, *Human Subjects in Medical Experimentation*, New York: Wiley, 1975.

sciences, law, administration, clergy, and others. Similarly, PSRO committees ought to be broadened even more than they already have been to include nonmedical professionals and consumers. In addition, social criteria ought to be included along with medical criteria for judging the quality of care. Perhaps greater choice for consumers may induce more competition among providers and act as a stimulus to better quality on social as well as technical dimensions.

### Health Education

Much of the foregoing is predicated on the assumption of an informed public. Given the discussions in Chapters 4 and 5, it is a risky assumption at best. There are many, many factors that influence how individuals define health and illness, how they respond to indicators of illness, how they perceive providers, how much they know about sources of care, and so on. Moreover, good health is not always a most salient goal for individuals: witness poor nutrition and increased use of cigarettes and alcohol despite knowledge to the contrary. The objective of developing a public informed enough to make rational choices of health plans, to know what care is needed, to know from whom it is available, and to judge its quality would call for a radical change in the priority of and procedures for health education. While the kind of lifelong indoctrination procedures on health (and other matters) used by the Chinese seem inappropriate for our culture, they have been successful in many ways in raising the level of sophistication of the people. Similarly, health education in the United States ought to have much higher priority in service and research, and it should be provided often and at all levels, in formal education, community settings, and homes. The important role of health professionals in educating the public needs also to be remembered. Training of health professionals does not often teach students how to reach the client best as well as what to tell the client. Changes in the health delivery system will not be effective unless the consumer is prepared to make intelligent choices among the options offered.

### Research Program Development

It is obvious that support for continued research in biomedical and behavioral sciences, although not related specifically to the five $a$'s, must be a part of a national health policy. Successes in past research are part of the reason why health needs have changed, and we are discussing a new system to meet those needs. There is every reason to believe that new research discoveries will alter again the patterns of morbidity and mortality and raise demands for yet further research. We have noted, too, that social science research has contributed to the fund of information about health care delivery. Much more remains to be done in this area. A policy of support for research (and its application) is necessary if we are ever to achieve our objectives for providing high-quality health care for each citizen.

## SUMMARY

Based on analysis of research studies and their implications presented in previous chapters, this has been a summary of alternative positions taken regarding the delivery of health care services in the United States. The nature of the decision-making process in developing a national health policy regarding goals, priorities, methods of implementation and control was described as the "politics of health." A means for discussing the politics of health was to describe both current problems and desired objectives in health care delivery in terms of availability, accessibility, affordability, accountability, and acceptability. The central sociological concept employed to "explain" the problems was the power of professional autonomy—in this case, the autonomy of the medical profession. Specifically, we focused on fee-for-service payment, control of treatment resources, and self-regulation as elements contributing to problems in health care delivery. Attempts to solve these problems without influencing professional autonomy have not had much success. Those noted here included comprehensive health planning legislation, efforts to control costs of care, and peer review. In working toward a national health policy, some elements were identified as (1) universal health insurance, (2) health personnel management, (3) resource allocation, (4) regulation, (5) health education, and (6) research program development.

## SUGGESTED READINGS

Anderson, Odin W., *Health Care: Can There Be Equity?* New York: Wiley, 1972.

Freidson, Eliot, *Professional Dominance,* New York: Atherton, 1970.

Illich, Ivan, *Medical Nemesis: The Expropriation of Health,* London: Calder and Boyars, 1975.

Mechanic, David, *Politics, Medicine and Social Science,* New York: Wiley, 1974.

Stroman, Duane F., *The Medical Establishment and Social Responsibility,* Port Washington, N.Y.: Kennikat Press, 1976.

# Index

**429**